MODERN AUDITING
Second Edition

MODERN AUDITING

Second Edition

Graham W. Cosserat

John Wiley & Sons, Ltd

Other Wiley Editorial Offices

John Wiley & Sons Inc., 111 River Street, Hoboken, NJ 07030, USA

Jossey-Bass, 989 Market Street, San Francisco, CA 94103-1741, USA

Wiley-VCH Verlag GmbH, Boschstr. 12, D-69469 Weinheim, Germany

John Wiley & Sons Australia Ltd, 33 Park Road, Milton, Queensland 4064, Australia

John Wiley & Sons (Asia) Pte Ltd, 2 Clementi Loop #02-01, Jin Xing Distripark, Singapore 129809

John Wiley & Sons Canada Ltd, 22 Worcester Road, Etobicoke, Ontario, Canada M9W 1L1

Wiley also publishes its books in a variety of electronic formats. Some content that appears
in print may not be available in electronic books.

Library of Congress Cataloging-in-Publication Data

Cosserat, Graham W.
    Modern auditing / Graham Cosserat. – 2nd ed.
        p.   cm.
    Includes bibliographical references and index.
    ISBN 0-470-86322-6 (pbk. : alk. paper)
  1. Auditing I. Title.
    HF5667.C655 2004
    657'.45 – dc22   2003027636

British Library Cataloguing in Publication Data

A catalogue record for this book is available from the British Library

ISBN 0-470-86322-6

Typeset in 10/12pt Sabon by Laserwords Private Limited, Chennai, India
Printed and bound in Great Britain by Antony Rowe Ltd, Chippenham, Wiltshire
This book is printed on acid-free paper responsibly manufactured from sustainable forestry
in which at least two trees are planted for each one used for paper production.

CONTENTS

CONTENTS

PREFACE

BACKGROUND TO FIRST EDITION

The text is based on an original US text by Walter G. Kell and Richard E. Ziegler adapted for use in Australia by Gudarshan Gill and Graham Cosserat. (The latest edition of the US text is authored by William C. Boynton and Walter G. Kell.) Gill and Cosserat developed the Australian text through six editions between 1985 and 2001 during the course of which it has become a leading text adopted by many Australian universities and colleges. For the fifth and sixth editions Gill and Cosserat were joined by Philomena Leung, Associate Professor at the RMIT University, Melbourne and Paul Coram of the University of Western Australia. During the course of its Australian development the text has benefited immensely from feedback from lecturers and students. It is, in every respect, a fully tried and tested text.

With the harmonisation of auditing standards the decision was taken to produce a text of universal application to auditing worldwide. The text is now available in both an Australian and this, a UK, version, each of which is written to be fully compliant with both domestic and international accounting and auditing standards. This reflects the development of auditing as a wholly universal profession and develops students capable of practising auditing in a truly global marketplace.

OVERVIEW TO SECOND EDITION

This text is written for introductory courses in auditing at undergraduate, graduate and professional levels. The objective of the text is to provide a comprehensive and integrated coverage of the latest developments in the environment and methodology of auditing. At the time of writing, the Auditing Practices Board of the UK and Ireland had announced its intention of adopting International Standards on Auditing issued by the International Auditing and Assurance Standards Board with effect from 2005 in accordance with European Commission proposals for harmonising financial reporting within the European Union. This text, therefore, is wholly based on International Standards in order to prepare auditing students for the real world of audit practice.

At the beginning of the text are four chapters setting out the audit environment dealing with the role and organisation of the accounting profession in the context of auditing, the nature and purpose of financial statement audits, an explanation of the nature and significance of ethical responsibilities in meeting professional expectations and a discussion as to the legal responsibility of auditors to those relying on their services.

The basic techniques of planning and performing the audit are explained in Chapters 5 to 9. Their application to major transaction classes and account balances and the issue of the auditors' report is then described in Chapters 10 to 15. This aspect of the audit process is developed in a logical and consistent fashion explaining the implications of risk assessment in developing the audit strategy and the relevance of assertions in identifying the applicable audit objectives.

The final two chapters, 16 and 17, look to the future and identify issues likely to be of concern to the next generation of auditors.

At the time of writing the practice and regulation of auditing was undergoing substantial revision. Among ongoing changes were:

- transfer of responsibility for the regulation of auditing practice from the professional bodies to the Financial Reporting Council;
- revision of corporate governance and, in particular, the role of the audit committee and its responsibility for relations with the independent auditors;
- revision of Auditing Standards with respect to risk assessment procedures and quality control;
- revision of standards relating to assurance and review engagements and the overall structure of statements relating to auditing and assurance;
- consideration of auditor independence with particular reference to the provision of non-audit services and auditor rotation; and
- proposed revision of the Companies Act in the UK with possible developments in the extent of auditors' responsibilities, to auditors' liability and to the responsibility of directors and officers in their dealings with auditors.

This text reflects these developments so far as their outcome can be reasonably anticipated in order to ensure that it reflects the current state of auditing at the time of publication. However, readers are expected to be aware of these developments and to amend their understanding of auditing by reference to developments after the date of publication. In particular, it should be noted that the IAASB project on revision of the reporting standard had only just commenced. The text, therefore, assumes that the UK standard will continue to apply as at the date of publication. Readers should be aware that this is likely to be replaced by a revised International Standard during the currency of this text.

Particular features of this text

- a glossary introducing technical terms used in auditing standards and throughout the text, as a ready means of reference by students;
- at the start of each chapter:
  - an overview of the chapter contents;
  - learning objectives applicable to that chapter;
  - international professional statements on auditing and accounting relevant to the chapter;
- within each chapter:
  - learning checks at the end of each section to identify and reinforce the key issues, ideal for reviewing chapter content and for revision;

- at the end of each chapter:
  - a comprehensive bibliography of further reading;
  - multiple-choice questions to test the understanding of material presented in the chapter;
  - discussion questions to stimulate thinking and to promote discussion in class use;
  - professional application questions drawn mainly from the examinations of professional bodies in the UK and overseas which both encourage students in developing professional skills and prepare those intending to sit the examinations of such professional bodies;
- answers to multiple-choice and professional application questions are provided at the end of the text to enable readers to test their comprehension and to provide a guide as to how to answer examination questions.

Supplementary material available to colleges adopting the text

- an instructors' manual containing extensive further questions and answers; and
- PowerPoint presentation disks which may either be used for on-screen presentations or printed out for use on overhead projectors.

AUDITING AND THE PUBLIC ACCOUNTING PROFESSION

OVERVIEW

THE EVOLUTION OF AUDITING PRACTICES
The traditional conformance role of auditing
The development of an enhancing role
Auditing – a shifting paradigm

THE ACCOUNTING PROFESSION AND ITS ASSOCIATED ORGANISATIONS
Private sector organisations
Standard setting bodies
Audit regulation

SERVICES PROVIDED BY PUBLIC ACCOUNTANTS
Assurance services
Non-assurance services

TYPES OF AUDIT ACTIVITY AND AUDITOR
Types of audit activity
Types of auditor

REGULATORY FRAMEWORK FOR ENSURING QUALITY SERVICES
Standard setting
Firm regulation
Self-regulation
Independent regulation

SUMMARY

NOTES

FURTHER READING

MULTIPLE-CHOICE QUESTIONS

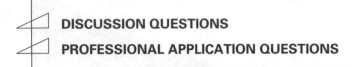

DISCUSSION QUESTIONS

PROFESSIONAL APPLICATION QUESTIONS

 LEARNING **OBJECTIVES**

After studying this chapter, you should be able to:

1   appreciate how auditing developed

2   discuss the historical and other factors which influence the role of auditors, and the resulting complexities of meeting public expectations

3   explain the scope of auditing within the assurance framework and its relationship with other non-audit services

4   describe the accounting profession in the UK and the constituencies which influence the profession and audit practices

5   explain the nature of and scope of assurance services performed by public accountants

6   explain the nature of non-audit services, and describe several types performed by public accountants

7   distinguish different types of audit activity and auditor

8   explain the regulatory framework for ensuring quality services

9   state the elements of quality control applicable for audits.

PROFESSIONAL STATEMENTS

IAASB	(Proposed) International Framework for Assurance Engagements
ISA 200	Objective and General Principles Governing an Audit of Financial Statements (October 2003)
ISA 240	Fraud and Error
ISA 250	Consideration of Laws and Regulations in an Audit of Financial Statements
ISA 220	Quality Control for Audit Engagements (Draft)
IAPS 1010	The Consideration of Environmental Matters in the Audit of Financial Statements
ISQC 1	Quality Control for Audit, Assurance and Related Services Practices (Draft)

Auditing plays a vital role in business, government and our economy. The nature of this role will be explained in Chapter 2. Evidence of its importance is provided by the fact that all of the following bodies are required to have an annual audit:

- all public and larger private companies;

- government departments, local authorities, NHS Health Trusts and local authorities; and
- registered charities and other 'not-for-profit' organisations, including educational institutions.

It is estimated that over a million audits annually are conducted in accordance with statutory requirements in the member states of the European Union.

Auditing services have been changing rapidly over the last decade. Audit practices have been evolving in response to growing public expectations of accountability, and to the complexities in economic and technological advances being made in business organisations. An important recent development has been the challenge of globalisation and the need for harmonisation of financial reporting in facilitating the most efficient allocation of investment funds globally. Harmonisation applies not only to the financial reporting standards applied in preparing financial statements but to the credibility attached by the audit process. As a vocation, therefore, auditing offers the opportunity for challenging and rewarding careers in a dynamic business environment, and the chance to develop a thorough understanding of professional services, primarily serving the interests of users of financial information.

This chapter traces the conceptual development of auditing over the years. It also provides a broad framework of the accounting and auditing profession and its related associations, a description of the general types of audit activity, and a review of the system of quality procedures prescribed for the profession.

THE EVOLUTION OF AUDITING PRACTICES

Auditing has developed from what, in the twelfth century, was primarily a check of the accounting for stocks and revenues by authorised officers of the Exchequer of England into a sophisticated professional assurance service performed by independent accountants for the interests of their clients and other users of financial information. This section describes the development of the role of auditing over the years, with particular reference to the nature and objectives of auditing, the responsibilities of auditors, and the evolution of the accounting and auditing profession. This historical perspective is particularly relevant given the current shift away from traditional accounting and auditing services to a broad variety of assurance services more relevant to the emerging information revolution.

The traditional conformance role of auditing

The traditional conformance role of auditing first appeared in the UK during the 1800s. The nature of this role was articulated in major legal case decisions at the end of that century. In fact, the development of the auditing role is very much an outcome of court cases, as is seen in the following sections.

AUDITING IN THE UK

The word 'auditing' comes from the Latin word *audire*, meaning 'to hear'. In the late Middle Ages in Britain, both accounts of revenue (tax receipts) and expenditure for manors and estates were 'heard' by an auditor, whose task was to examine such accounts. With the spread of double-entry book-keeping, first described by Luca Pacioli in 1494, associations of accountants were formed, and auditing gradually established an important role.

Auditing as we know it today can be traced back to the development of joint-stock corporations in the UK during the Industrial Revolution from the early 1800s. The increasing use of the company form of business organisation led to growth of a professional class of managers who handled large sums of capital on behalf of shareholders. Recognising the need for periodic reporting by managers to shareholders, the *Joint Stock Companies Registration and Regulation (Joint Stock Companies Act) 1844* stipulated that 'Directors shall cause the Books of the Company to be balanced, and a full and fair Balance Sheet to be made up'. The Act provided for the appointment of auditors who were empowered to examine the accounts of the company.

Regulation 94 of the *UK Companies Act 1862* required the auditors to state in their report

> ... whether, in their Opinion, the Balance-Sheet is a full and fair Balance-Sheet, containing the particulars required by these Regulations, and properly drawn up so as to exhibit a true and correct view of the State of the Company's Affairs ... such Report shall be read, together with the Report of the Directors, at the Ordinary Meeting.

Table 1.1 shows the development of the audit function through successive Companies Acts. In particular it shows how the audit first became compulsory for all companies in 1900, how the auditors were required to have appropriate professional qualifications from 1948 and how the accounts to be reported on and the wording of the report gradually evolved over time. Sometimes the legislation was revolutionary and designed to curb abuses, such as the introduction of compulsory audits for specific classes of business during the latter part of the nineteenth century. On other occasions the legislation merely confirmed and regularised practices that had become commonplace. By 1900 most companies with significant numbers of outside shareholders were audited and, by 1948, most auditors were professionally qualified.

It is sometimes suggested that the emphasis of the Companies Act auditing requirements has changed over the years from fraud and error detection to attesting the credibility of financial statements for investment purposes. For example, in Lawrence R. Dicksee's book *Auditing: A Practical Manual for Auditors*,[1] published in 1892, the objective of an audit was said to be three-fold:

1. the detection of fraud;
2. the detection of technical errors; and
3. the detection of errors of principle.

The *Companies Act 1985* recital of auditors' responsibilities still reflects the unsophisticated methods employed by Victorian directors to mislead their shareholders, notably the requirement to ensure that the accounts are in agreement with the books. With the increasing sophistication of creative accounting and the development of the securities

Table 1.1 Development of audit requirements in companies legislation

	ACT	AUDIT REQUIREMENTS	INFORMATION TO BE AUDITED	REPORT WORDING
1844	*Joint Stock Companies Act*	Required but neither independent nor professional	Balance sheet	Full and fair
1856	*Companies Act*	Not compulsory. Model set of articles, published as a Table to the Act, and whose adoption was optional, incorporated the audit requirements of the 1844 Act	Balance sheet	Full and fair
1868	*Regulation of Railways Act*	Compulsory audit	Uniform balance sheet	
1871 1879 1882	Gas Banks Electricity	Similar requirements as for railways		
1900	*Companies Act*	Compulsory audit. Not by a director or officer. Auditor given right of access to books, records, information and explanations	Balance sheet	True and correct
1948	*Companies Act*	Professional audit	Balance sheet	True and fair
1976 1980 1981	*Companies Act*	Auditors' powers progressively strengthened especially against arbitrary dismissal and given right of access to subsidiaries' records	Increasing disclosure requirements in P&L and notes to be covered by auditors' report. True and fair override introduced	True and fair
1989	*Companies Act*	Statutory regulation of auditors	Recognition of accounting standards	True and fair

markets, directors are more likely to defraud investors by producing accounts intended to mislead the securities markets rather than by the simple device of paying dividends out of capital. In recent additions to companies legislation we see an increasing concern with full disclosure and with increasing responsibility being imposed on auditors to determine whether the accounts are indeed fair.

THE INFLUENCE OF CASE LAW ON AUDITING

While 'hearing' the accounts and checking records were then the predominant functions of auditors, two major audit cases in the late 1800s helped to establish the fundamental principles of auditing. These cases, London and General Bank (1895)[2] and Kingston Cotton Mill Co. (1896),[3] are described in Chapter 4. They make clear that auditing is a professional activity with auditors required to exercise reasonable care and skill, but that what is proper conduct in any set of circumstances is inevitably a subjective question which the court determines with hindsight.

The complexity of accounting and the business environment makes it impossible for auditors to detect all aspects of fraudulent activity in an organisation. Hence, the auditors' responsibility for detecting fraud and errors continues to be a much debated issue. Nonetheless, following these two landmark cases, efforts continued to be made to define the responsibilities of the auditors, with the primary duties being subsequently confirmed in legislation.

AUDITING IN THE USA – FURTHER DEVELOPMENTS

Auditing in the USA has developed along similar lines to its development in the UK and developments in the USA are closely watched by both the profession and the courts in the UK.

In 1931 the Ultramares case in America prompted the accounting profession to clarify that the auditors were expressing an opinion and not giving a guarantee, and that the 'balance sheet and the related statement of income and surplus present fairly . . .'.

In responding to severe criticism of the financial community and corporate management, the Congress of the United States passed the *Securities Act 1933* and the *Securities Exchange Act 1934*. These Acts contained the requirements for the audit of financial statements of corporations seeking to issue securities, or corporations wanting to register with the Commission for the public trading of securities. The Acts placed a significant responsibility on professional accountants and increased their authority.

The hearings held by the Securities Exchange Commission into the McKesson & Robbins fraud case in 1939 and the findings released the following year had an impact not only on audit procedures, but also on the development of Auditing Standards and the content of the auditors' report. The confirmation of debtors and the observation of stock-taking procedures were made mandatory.

The development of an enhancing role

Apart from a change in the audit approach, auditors face an increasing demand for more accountability and for more perceived benefits for users. One development has been the issue of formal standards to improve the quality and consistency of auditing. There is also an expectation that auditing, as a professional service, should not only provide assurance for the credibility of financial statements, but also enhance the integrity of financial information and its usefulness in decision-making by management and other users.

DEFINING REASONABLE CARE AND SKILL

A number of cases such as that of Thomas Gerrard & Son Ltd 1967[4] have indicated that what constitutes reasonable skill and care evolves with time. These cases made it clear that auditors should pay due regard to the possibility of fraud and actively investigate that probability should suspicious circumstances arise. The courts also continued to exercise their prerogative to assess the reasonableness of professional standards in specific circumstances, and therefore what constitutes reasonable care and skill.

ENHANCING THE CREDIBILITY OF FINANCIAL INFORMATION

In the 1970s, auditors described their role as one of enhancing the credibility of financial information and furthering the operations of an effective capital market.[5] In the *New York Times* of 6 April 1975, audits were said to affirm the truthfulness of financial statements and ensure that financial statements were 'fairly presented'. This function was loosely linked to various audit practices, including:

- the review and testing of company records and the procedures and controls used to assemble financial information;
- the approval to use various accounting principles; and
- the examination of financial statements to ensure they contained no material misstatements, omissions or misleading presentations of data.[6]

AUDITING AS A SERVICE TO PROVIDE REASONABLE ASSURANCE TO USERS

The International Auditing and Assurance Standards Board (IAASB) of the International Federation of Accountants (IFAC) defines an assurance engagement as one:

in which a practitioner expresses a conclusion designed to enhance the degree of confidence that intended users can have about the evaluation or measurement of a subject matter that is the responsibility of a party, other than the intended users or the practitioner, against criteria.[7]

The IAASB's (Proposed) International Framework for Assurance Engagements states that an assurance engagement involves the following elements:

- *a three party relationship* involving the practitioner, such as the independent auditor, the responsible party, such as the board of directors of a company, and the intended users, such as the company's shareholders;
- *a subject matter*, such as the financial statements, whereby the directors demonstrate their accountability to the shareholders;
- *suitable criteria*, such as truth and fairness in accordance with international financial reporting standards;
- *evidence*, such as the company's books and records; and
- *an assurance report*, such as the auditors' report.

An engagement may be at an audit level or a review level. In an audit-level engagement the practitioner:

- identifies the risks that the subject matter may be materially misstated;
- performs procedures to gather and evaluate evidence in response to those risks to reduce the overall level of risk that the subject matter is materially misstated to an acceptably low level; and

- expresses a positive opinion with respect to the agreed criteria, such as 'in our opinion *the subject matter* conforms in all material respects with *the criteria*'.

In a review-level engagement the practitioner obtains assurance through inquiry and analytical procedures. Further procedures are carried out only if there is reason to suspect the subject matter may be misstated. The resultant assurance is limited and expressed in a negative form, such as 'nothing has come to our attention that causes us to believe that *the subject matter* does not conform, in all material respects, with *the criteria*'.

For practical purposes the IAASB also distinguishes between engagements to provide assurance on historic financial statements and other assurance engagements, since the former constitute the major focus of assurance services provided by professional accountants. In these engagements the subject matter of the engagement are the financial statements and the criteria being their agreement with International Financial Reporting Standards (or some other appropriate financial reporting framework). International Standards on Auditing issued by the IAASB constitute the major source of regulation covering the performance of such engagements.

However, recognising the growing importance of providing assurance on other subject matter, the IAASB has commenced providing guidance in the form of International Standards on Assurance Engagements. The importance of other forms of financial disclosures is discussed below.

Professional accountants may provide other services that provide some but not all of the elements of assurance services, such as:

- *agreed-upon procedures* which result in a report as to findings after performance of specified procedures; and
- *a compilation* that provides no specific assurance but users derive benefit from the fact that the accountant has applied an appropriate level of skill and care in performing the service.

Guidance in the provision of such services is provided by International Standards on Related Services. It is important that, in providing non-assurance services, users are not misled into believing that any level of assurance is being provided.

ASSURANCE SERVICES – SATISFYING THE INFORMATION NEEDS OF USERS

For many years, independent auditors have provided assurance on an entity's financial statements. However, traditional financial reporting is being criticised for failing to meet developing users' needs. In 1991, the American Institute of Certified Public Accountants (AICPA) formed a special committee, the Jenkins Committee, to assess the needs of the users of financial information and recommend improvements to the financial reporting framework. One recommendation of the Committee was that business reporting should provide more forward-looking information. However, such recommendations were a conundrum for the world of financial reporting, and the accounting profession in particular.[8] On the one hand, there was justifiable demand for improvement in financial reporting. On the other hand, any change in the direction of providing more forward-looking information would, where auditors give assurance as to the presentation of financial data, potentially increase auditors' risk of exposure to liability/litigation. It is in this context that the AICPA formed another special committee on assurance services – the Elliott Committee. The charge of the Elliott Committee was to:

> . . . analyse and report on the current state and future of the audit/assurance function and the trends shaping the audit/assurance environment, focusing on the current and changing needs of users of decision-making information and other stakeholders in the audit/assurance process, and how best to improve the related services.

The Elliott Committee recognised the need for the profession to diversify its product potential away from the traditional financial statement audit in the light of declining demand for that service. It recommended that this be achieved by embracing and significantly expanding the assurance services provided by the profession in order to consolidate its existing markets, and to capitalise on its competitive advantages in the emerging information markets.[9] Furthermore, it recommended that the audit/attestation function should evolve into the assurance function, with a significant movement towards broader-based assurance services.[10]

The collapse of the giant US corporation Enron at the end of 2001 provided an increased impetus in the development of improvements in financial reporting and auditing. Among proposals currently being considered are requirements for auditors to report on the effectiveness of entities' risk frameworks and on the Operating and Financial Review which is to become a mandatory disclosure by listed companies.

While the professional, regulatory and standard setting bodies reassess their position regarding audit and assurance services, the professional firms continue to address the complexity of the changing needs of users and the rapid growth of information technology. In a 1997 publication by KPMG Peat Marwick LLP, William Kinney Jr, its Director of Assurance Services, announced that business viability and profitability assessments are essential elements of financial statement auditing today.[11] He refers to the need to establish, as key audit steps, the audit procedures of strategy analyses, business processes, key indicators necessary to monitor business performance and risk assessment. The viability of the business strategy, the reasonableness of business plans, and the effectiveness of internal controls are all essential matters about which decisions need to be made in determining audit procedures.

The following paragraph provides some indication of how auditing practices are evolving to yet another level – an enhancing role that adds value to business reporting.

> As the global economy, the business organisations operating within it, and organisations' business strategies become increasingly complex and interdependent, we believe more attention should be paid to the development of audit methods and procedures that focus on assertions at the entity level – methods and procedures that promise greater power to detect material misstatements as they allow the auditors to ground key judgements in a more critical and holistic understanding of the client's systems dynamics. We further believe that today's complex economic world requires a break from the auditing traditions that have evolved from the early balance sheet audit – traditions under which the auditors' attention is focused primarily at the sub-unit level, and his views about what is evidence are heavily skewed toward tangibility (i.e. the physical existence of assets, the existence of tangible documentation supporting transactions, etc.). Today's auditors should place more weight on knowledge

about the client's business and industry, and its interactions with its environment, when forming an opinion about the validity of financial statement assertions ...[12]

Auditing – a shifting paradigm

From the previous sections, it is clear that the role of auditing has evolved through a number of stages. The relevance of auditing was established through its historical value in ensuring the correctness of the accounts, detecting fraud and errors, and providing an independent opinion on the truth and fairness of financial statements for users. Nowadays, to address the complexity of the information needs of users, auditors are expected not only to enhance the credibility of financial statements, but also to provide value-added services, such as reporting on irregularities, identifying business risks and advising management on internal control weaknesses. Alongside the changes in audit expectations is the increasingly competitive audit environment, where traditional audit services are blurred with non-audit services. The paradigm of independent auditing can be argued to be shifting, and the auditors' role is being redefined. Changes in three major aspects of auditing:

1. its scope with respect of the detection of fraud and error;
2. the essential characteristics of audit independence; and
3. the sustaining factor of auditors' liability;

are discussed below.

DETECTION OF FRAUD AND ERRORS

Prior to the collapse of Enron in 2001, auditing had been moving away from the fraud detection emphasis as described by Dicksee, quoted on page 4. Greater emphasis had been placed on the truth and fairness of the financial statements as such, regardless of whether the misstatement was fraudulent or accidental. Enron showed that such an approach lulled auditors into disregarding deliberate management intent in producing fraudulent financial statements. However, two recent changes in auditing standards have strengthened the auditors' responsibility to detect fraud, whether leading to the misappropriation of assets or the misstatement of financial statements.

First, auditors are now required to evaluate the effectiveness of an entities' risk management framework in preventing misstatements whether through fraud or otherwise, in all audits. Previously they had been required to undertake such an evaluation only where they chose to place reliance on that framework and reduce the extent of their own investigation. Moreover, all staff members engaged on an audit are required to communicate their findings to prevent situations where staff members, working independently on their own section of the audit, fail to appreciate the significance of apparently minor irregularities that, if combined, take on a more sinister aspect.[13]

Second, auditors are now required to be more proactive in their search for fraud. They are required to identify the likelihood of fraud occurring. This includes considering incentives, opportunities and rationalisation, among potential fraudsters, that the fraudulent act may be justified. They are also expected to inquire more closely into the reasons behind such matters as errors in accounting estimates, unusual transactions that appear to lack business rationale and a reluctance to correct immaterial errors discovered by the audit. Again, the need for collaboration among audit team members is emphasised.[14]

AUDITOR INDEPENDENCE

As auditors provide assurances on the credibility of the financial statements, the concept and practice of audit independence – the cornerstone of auditing – is also subject to much debate. The codes of ethics laid down by the professional bodies of accountants refer to a range of risks concerning actual and perceived independence. Independence is the essence that underlies the success and credibility of the accounting profession and its service to the public. It helps to provide the objectivity that permits the profession to perform its attestation and monitoring functions effectively. The current paradigm for addressing independence issues is based on the underlying belief that allowing auditors to perform non-audit functions for audit clients, or to engage in management activities, presents the greatest potential for conflict. Those espousing this viewpoint would argue that auditors should do little non-audit work for audit clients. After the collapse of Enron, the USA passed legislation banning auditors from providing a wide range of non-audit services for their audit clients.[15] However, as pointed out by Wallman,[16] while this approach to audit independence may seem reasonable, it fails in a number of respects and may well be contrary to the public interest. It is perceived to have failed to recognise the complexity of audit practices, the sophisticated business environment and the acute competition in which accounting firms operate. The UK and other countries have failed to follow the US lead, but have imposed rules for tighter control over and transparency of the provision, by auditors, of non-audit services to audit clients. Moreover, responsibility for setting and enforcing ethical codes of conduct has been transferred from the professional bodies to independent regulators. This is further discussed in Chapter 3.

AUDITOR LIABILITY

Another example of changes in the auditing environment is in relation to auditors' liability. In an audit conducted in accordance with the *Companies Act 1985*, the auditors are liable under statute and common law to the shareholders, who made the appointment and to whom auditors report, for any negligent performance of statutory duties. These duties cannot be restricted or reduced. The auditors' liability to the organisation being audited is contractual and stems from having undertaken to perform, with due care, for the purpose of expressing an opinion on the financial statements. A considerable body of case law has built up over the years with respect to the duty of care auditors owe to the auditee and the owners of the entity.

The common law concerning the auditors' liability to third parties is complex and has been subject to broad interpretation. The landmark case of *Caparo Industries PLC v. Dickman and Others* (1990) 1 All ER 568 saw the concept of proximity redefined. This case reversed the judgement in *Hedley Byrne & Co. Ltd v. Heller & Partners* (1963) 2 All ER 575 and restricted the auditors' duty of care. As auditors they are responsible only to members of the company relying on audited financial statements for collective decisions as to the management of the company. The auditors hold no duty of care for economic loss suffered by potential investors and individual shareholders unless the auditors have held out, to such parties, that they could place reliance on the financial statements.

The development of auditing practices over the years suggests a possible shift of the auditors' conformity role into a far more dynamic role of enhancing the value of financial reporting. Although the fundamental principle of audit assurance services has not changed explicitly, one can envisage the development of an expansion of assurance services within the audit function. On the other hand, there have been fundamental changes in the business environment within which auditors' professional services are required. The increasing expectations of business entities, and the high level of accountability required of the auditors, give rise to a change in the audit framework. It might be too early to predict the auditing practice of the future; however, it is apparent that there is a possible shift in the audit paradigm from a conformative attestation to the enhancing role of a value-added service.

A wide ranging review of company law has recently been undertaken by the Department of Trade and Industry with a view to modernising the Companies Act. The question of auditor liability was raised by the review along the lines considered in Chapter 4. However, no firm proposals have yet been made. The European Commission has also considered the issue of auditor liability from the perspective that variations in liability within member states may affect the internal market within the European Union. Again the matter remains under review.

LEARNING **CHECK**

1.1 Auditing, in the last century, was confined to the conformance role of ascertaining the correctness of accounts and the detection of fraud and errors.

1.2 The development of case law and other economic factors have impacted on the expectations of auditing.

1.3 An audit is now defined as a service to provide a reasonable level of assurance in which a positive opinion is rendered about an accountability matter.

1.4 Although primarily concerned with financial statements, the auditor needs to examine analyses of strategy and business processes (as well as many other factors) as part of a complex process of providing audit assurance.

1.5 The auditing environment is changing to facilitate the expanded role of auditing.

THE ACCOUNTING PROFESSION AND ITS ASSOCIATED ORGANISATIONS

Accounting bodies have influenced the development of the profession and audit practice through:

- maintaining standards of qualifications achieved through accredited courses, examinations and practical experience for accountants seeking to become members;
- furthering standards of practice achieved through research and the issuance of standards, the provision of continuing professional education and the establishment of rules of professional conduct to be observed by the members; and
- ensuring professional conduct, and effective regulation on quality of service.

In recent years the second function and elements of the third relating to matters that are described as being in the public interest have been devolved to independent regulatory bodies.

Private sector organisations

The accounting profession traces its origins back to eighteenth century Scotland and the management of estates confiscated after the 1745 rebellion. From this beginning, legislation dealing with the management of bankrupt and deceased estates developed more rapidly in Scotland than in England. It was a natural progression from such work to take on other employment requiring the preparation and maintenance of accounting records, such as for growing industrial firms. In order to protect their image from the risk of adverse publicity brought about by the incompetent and even dishonest administration of estates, a group of accountants in Edinburgh set themselves up as a society committed to upholding sound ethical principles in the conduct of their professional practices. Soon, similar societies were springing up elsewhere in Scotland and then in England and Ireland. Membership of the newly formed professional bodies expanded rapidly with auditing becoming their major source of revenue in the closing decades of the nineteenth century. Local bodies joined forces with each other to create national bodies until, in 1880, the Institute of Chartered Accountants in England and Wales was formed and, in 1891, the Association of Chartered Certified Accountants.

The public accounting profession continues to be represented directly by these two prominent accountancy bodies and also by the Institute of Chartered Accountants of Scotland and the Institute of Chartered Accountants in Ireland. The three Institutes of Chartered Accountants co-operate closely in matters such as setting ethical standards and investigating complaints against members and will be referred to collectively as the Institutes. Membership of these bodies is voluntary, but is nevertheless important. For example, membership is necessary to satisfy the registration qualification for company auditors. Membership provides for self-regulation within the profession in setting competency standards. This is in the public interest.

The Association and the Institutes provide a broad range of services to their respective members to assure that they serve the public interest in providing quality professional services. The accountancy profession is also active internationally. All of the bodies are represented on the International Accounting Standards Committee (IASC), the International Federation of Accountants (IFAC), and on the three IFAC committees – the International Auditing and Assurance Standards Board (IAASB), the international Public Sector Committee (PSC) and the international Financial and Management Accounting Committee (FMAC). The work carried out by the international technical committees forms a valuable part of the process in developing accounting and auditing standards within the UK and Ireland.

ASSOCIATION OF CHARTERED CERTIFIED ACCOUNTANTS

The Association has about 90,000 members and 200,000 registered student members. The Association is expanding rapidly internationally. Over 65% of students come from outside the UK and Ireland; its examinations are sat in about 130 countries. Approximately 29% of its members are engaged in public practice and 44% in commerce and industry. The remaining members are employed in the public sector or in education. The Association issues professional and technical statements, has a code of ethics, conducts education programmes aimed at continuing professional development, funds research and holds annual congresses. It maintains libraries and publishes a monthly journal (*Accounting & Business*) and a separate journal for student members (*Student Accountant*).

THE INSTITUTE OF CHARTERED ACCOUNTANTS IN ENGLAND & WALES

The Institute of Chartered Accountants in England & Wales was established by Royal Charter in 1880. Until recently, it recruited educated and trained members in public practice. However, it is now encouraging commerce and industry to participate in the training of chartered accountants. It has 125,000 members a third of whom work in public practice. The services it provides to its members are similar to those of the Association and, additionally, includes a highly successful advisory service to members on professional ethics. In addition to its monthly journal *Accountancy*, the Institute publishes a quarterly research journal, *Accounting and Business Research*. Members who hold public practice certificates are subject to the Institute's practice monitoring programme.

PRACTICE ENTITIES

Since the 1970s the accounting profession has been dominated by giant multinational firms. There were eight such firms in 1990 but, as a result of mergers, the number is now reduced to four, who between them audit the majority of companies quoted on stock exchanges around the world. The Big Four firms are continually engaged in innovative strategies in order to deliver the range of professional services demanded by clients. The growth of electronic commerce and technology is pushing the profession to develop continuous or 'live' audits, and engage in a wider range of information-based management services. It is argued that accountants and auditors will need to be 'reskilled' in order to meet the dynamic growth in business advisory and consulting services.

Below the Big Four is a second tier of 10 to 15 national firms. These firms have offices in the major towns and cities in the UK and serve mainly medium sized and small clients. Their main strength is in the private and family company sector. Many of these firms have some form of association with smaller firms in other countries to handle the international needs of their clients.

Regional firms have offices within a limited geographical area and usually serve smaller clients relative to the size of those served by international and national firms. Local firms may consist of a sole practitioner or a relatively small partnership. These are by far the most common form of practice unit. Such firms serve small entities and individual clients providing mainly tax and write-up services. Some of the smaller regional and suburban firms have flourished by developing their own specialities such as specific aspects of tax practice, pension consulting, provision of litigation support and business advisory services. In summary, the expertise and experience of the practitioner and the size and resources of the practice entity dictate the range of services a firm is able to offer.

Vigorous competition has encouraged the growth of multi-service practice entities. The Big Four accountancy firms are able to provide a broad range of services to their clients, although, in response to growing concern over the provision of non-audit services to audit clients, the management consultancy arms have been demerged into separate business entities. Medium to smaller sized firms tend to be more localised and specialised in the nature of the services they offer.

Two of the leading UK firms of accountants, Price Waterhouse (now Pricewaterhouse-Coopers) and Peat Marwick Mitchell (now KPMG) established branch offices in New

York at the end of the nineteenth century to oversee the interests of British investors into American companies. British accountants also opened up branch offices throughout the Commonwealth. An accounting profession modelled on the UK profession thus developed in the USA and most countries of the British Commonwealth. As a result accounting and auditing practices have also developed along similar lines in these countries, which has facilitated the development of international harmonisation in recent years. This harmonisation has been encouraged by UK and US firms who had developed links with each other and with firms elsewhere in the world. These links have proved particularly useful with the development of multinational industrial corporations after the Second World War. Audit reliability could be strengthened if the parent company auditors knew that subsidiaries were being audited by associated auditing firms whose reputation they could rely upon.

LONDON STOCK EXCHANGE

The London Stock Exchange (LSE) is a private sector entity that organises a national market for company securities. The listed companies enter into a contract with the LSE to comply with their rules and regulations. Responsibility for setting listing rules has now been transferred to a statutory body, the UK Listing Authority under the oversight of the Financial Services Authority. However, prior to this the LSE played a useful role in directing the attention of the accounting profession to important financial reporting issues. In particular it was the LSE, together with the accountancy profession, that set up the Committee on Financial Aspects of Corporate Governance under the chairmanship of Sir Adrian Cadbury in 1992. The work of this committee set international precedents in developing improved financial reporting. Responsibility for development of the resultant Combined Code on Corporate Governance, incorporated within the Listing Rules, now lies with the Financial Reporting Council.

Standard setting bodies

The principal standard setting body within the UK and Ireland is the Financial Reporting Council (FRC). In the interests of European and global harmonisation, the FRC and its subsidiary bodies are adopting, with effect from 2005, International Financial Reporting Standards (IFRS) set by the International Accounting Standards Board (IASB) and International Standards on Auditing (ISA) set by the International Auditing and Assurance Standards Board (IAASB).

FINANCIAL REPORTING COUNCIL (FRC)

The chairperson of the FRC is appointed jointly by the government and the Bank of England and its members are required to be broadly representative of users and preparers of financial statements. The FRC appoints members to its subsidiaries bodies, which are:

- Accounting Standards Board (ASB)
- Auditing Practices Board (APB)
- Financial Reporting Review Panel
- Professional Oversight Board for Accountancy
- Accountancy Investigation and Discipline Board.

All of these bodies are important to the audit function and the reader is advised to take careful note of their names as they will be referred to frequently in this and the next two chapters.

In appointing members the FRC is required to consider the respective requirements of expertise and independence. Technical expertise predominates in the case of the ASB but independence and a majority of lay members (i.e. not members of the accounting profession) predominate in the case of the Professional Oversight and Investigation and Discipline Boards. Expertise is necessary among members of the APB but a majority should not be practising auditors.

The APB is also responsible for establishing ethical standards on independence, objectivity and integrity applicable to independent auditing and assurance services. The professional bodies are responsible for setting ethical codes of conduct in other matters.

The constitution of the FRC and its subsidiary bodies is so drawn up as to maximise their independence and freedom from any accusation that the standard setting process is captured by any group in its own self-interest.

INTERNATIONAL ACCOUNTING STANDARDS BOARD (IASB)

Financial statements prepared in accordance with International Financial Reporting Standards (IFRS) issued by the IASB are acceptable on any stock exchange except in the USA. The ASB has adopted IFRS as the basis for its own standards. Many other countries also use IFRS as the basis for financial reporting. In the European Union IFRS must form the basis for group financial statements prepared by listed companies.

The International Accounting Standards Committee is an independent entity governed by a body of Trustees. The Trustees represent both geographic and sectional interests, such as the accounting profession, preparers and users, and are required to fill vacancies in their ranks to maintain a similar representation. They appoint the members of the IASB having backgrounds as auditors, preparers and users who have the authority to set IFRS in consultation with national standard setters. As with the FRC, the intention is to maintain the independence of the standard setting mechanism from any attempt to manipulate that process.

INTERNATIONAL AUDITING AND ASSURANCE BOARD (IAASB)

The IAASB is a technical committee of the International Federation of Accountants (IFAC) whose membership comprises professional bodies of accountants worldwide and whose aims are the improvement and harmonisation of professional services. As well as auditing and assurance, it also provides recommendations on ethics, education and public sector accounting. Until recently the aims of the IFAC (and the IAASB) have been purely advisory. The decision to endorse or adapt recommendations has been made by authoritative bodies in each country and it is these bodies that take on responsibility for ensuring an absence of bias in those recommendations. With the decision by the European Commission to require the application of IAASB standards on all statutory audits performed within member states, the status of the IAASB has been raised from advisory to authoritative. Its constitution is likely to be revised along the lines of the IASB to ensure the independence of its standard setting process.

Audit regulation

The *Companies Act 1989* lays down provisions

> for the purposes of securing that only persons who are properly supervised and appropriately qualified are appointed company auditors, and that audits by persons so appointed are carried out properly and with integrity and with a proper degree of independence.

To be eligible for appointment as a company auditor a person must be a member of a recognised supervisory body and eligible for appointment under the rules of that body.

PROPERLY SUPERVISED

A supervisory body is one which maintains and enforces rules as to persons eligible to seek appointment as company auditors and the conduct of company audit work which is binding on its members. Supervisory bodies must maintain registers of their members open to public inspection. Members must describe themselves, after their signature on the auditors' report, as 'registered auditor'. It is an offence for a person who is not eligible to act as a company auditor. A second audit may be required for any company audited by an ineligible auditor.

For recognition as a supervisory body the *Companies Act 1989* requires that there must be rules and practices to ensure that:

- persons eligible for appointment as company auditor are:
    - appropriately qualified; and
    - fit and proper persons;
- audit work is conducted with integrity by persons with no conflicts of interest;
- technical standards are established and applied;
- there are procedures for maintaining competence (such as post-qualifying education);
- there are adequate arrangements and resources for effective monitoring and enforcement of compliance with its rules;
- rules relating to membership, eligibility and discipline are fair and reasonable and provide for appeals;
- there are effective arrangements for investigating complaints both against eligible persons and the body itself;
- persons eligible under its rules are able to meet claims against them by means of adequate indemnity insurance or otherwise; and
- high standards of integrity in the conduct of audit work are promoted and maintained by co-operation with other bodies.

APPROPRIATELY QUALIFIED

For the most part an appropriate qualification will be membership of a qualifying body being a UK body offering a professional qualification in accountancy. A qualifying body must have rules, which it has power to enforce, with respect to:

- requirements for admission to a course of study leading to the qualification; and
- those approved for the purposes of giving practical training.

EUROPEAN UNION

The *Companies Act 1989* incorporated into UK law the requirements of the 8th *EU Company Law Directive* applicable to statutory audits. This Directive is currently under review.[17]

FINANCIAL SERVICES AUTHORITY (FSA)

The FSA is an independent non-governmental body, given statutory powers by the *Financial Services and Markets Act 2000*. One of its subsidiary bodies, the UK Listing Authority, lays down requirements for the admission of securities for listing on the stock exchange. This includes both the financial reporting and auditing requirements listed companies are to meet. It is also proposed to expand its role to a more proactive investigation of listed company financial statements, in conjunction with the Financial Reporting Review Panel (of the FRC). This may lead to the reporting of auditors to the Accountancy Investigation and Disciplinary Board for association with improperly prepared financial statements.

 LEARNING **CHECK**

1.6 The practice of auditing is influenced by three main types of constituency: private sector organisations, standard setters and regulatory bodies.

1.7 The private organisations operate under the broad guidelines of the standard setters, while the regulatory organisations monitor the process.

SERVICES PROVIDED BY PUBLIC ACCOUNTANTS

Accountants in public practice provide a variety of services. Each service may be classified as an assurance service or a non-assurance service.

Assurance services

An assurance service is one in which a public accountant issues a written communication that expresses a conclusion about the reliability of a written assertion that is the responsibility of another party. In recent years, there has been a growing demand for a variety of assurance services. These services (as already described in previous sections) include the audit or review of historic financial statements and the audit or review of other financial information.

Non-assurance services

The principal types of non-assurance services rendered by public accountants are those of traditional accounting, taxation, management consulting or advice, and insolvency and business recovery. The common characteristic of these services is that they do not result in the expression of an opinion, negative assurance or other form of assurance, by the public accountant.

TRADITIONAL ACCOUNTING AND TAXATION SERVICES

A public accountant may be engaged by a client to perform a variety of accounting services, such as manual or automated book-keeping, journalising and posting adjusting entries, and preparing financial statements. Accountants who specialise in taxation are thoroughly knowledgeable about the intricacies of the tax laws. Most accountancy firms have tax specialists and many have separate tax departments. Tax services include assistance in filing tax returns, tax planning, estate planning and representation of clients before government agencies in relation to tax matters. Tax services constitute a significant part of the practice of most accountancy firms. The preparation of financial statements and the filing of tax returns are two examples of compilation services. In performing any of these services, the public accounting firm serves as a substitute for, or a supplement to, the accounting personnel of the client. The accounting firms do not assume the decision-making role of management, which remains responsible for the preparation of financial statements and the filing of tax returns.

MANAGEMENT CONSULTING OR ADVISORY SERVICES

Management consulting or advisory services entail providing advice and technical assistance to clients to help them better use their capabilities and resources to achieve their objectives. Examples of such services include advising on staff recruitment, the use and acquisition of information technology and the provision of internal audit services.

When providing management consulting services, the practitioner is acting as an outside expert business consultant and, in this capacity, should not be making management decisions. Many of the larger accounting firms have separate management advisory services departments. Today, management advisory services revenues represent a significant proportion of the total billings of many accounting firms.

INSOLVENCY AND BUSINESS RECOVERY

Many accounting firms provide a professional service in the area of insolvency and business recovery. These services are provided pursuant to the *Insolvency Acts,* the *Companies Act 1985* and other statutes. When businesses are in difficulty, secured creditors might intervene in a variety of ways in order to protect their interests. Accounting firms might take on the assignment to review and perhaps reconstruct companies which are still solvent but have underlying difficulties. Also, much of the work required in the area of insolvencies and liquidations is quasi-legal administrative work. It relates generally to establishing and documenting competing claims and obtaining information required for alternative courses of action.

Accounting firms nowadays are at the forefront of information technology. Each of the Big Four now has its own web site. Students should consult these web sites for up-to-date information on the accounting profession.

◁ LEARNING **CHECK**

1.8 Auditors are engaged to carry out a variety of tasks: assurance services are those which involve providing an opinion on written assertions (audit, review and agreed-upon procedures), while non-assurance services are all other types of professional advisory service which require the expertise and competence of the auditor or accountant.

TYPES OF AUDIT ACTIVITY AND AUDITOR

Audit and audit-related service engagements can involve different types of activity and be performed by different types of auditor.

Types of audit activity

As well as financial statements, audit and other assurance engagements may involve other financial and non-financial information such as:

- the adequacy of internal control systems;
- compliance with statutory, regulatory or contractual requirements;
- economy, effectiveness and efficiency in the use of resources (value-for-money auditing); and
- environmental practices.

FINANCIAL STATEMENT AUDIT

International Standard on Auditing ISA 200, Objective and General Principles Governing an Audit of Financial Statements, states that:

> The objective of an audit of financial statements is to enable the auditor to express an opinion whether the financial statements are prepared, in all material respects, in accordance with an applicable financial reporting framework.

The financial statement audit involves obtaining and evaluating evidence about an entity's financial affairs in order to establish the degree of correspondence between the management's assertions and the established criteria, such as Financial Reporting Standards and legal requirements. This type of audit is performed by independent auditors appointed by the shareholders of the company, or by equivalent proprietors of non-incorporated entities, whose financial statements are being audited. The auditors must be qualified and able to exercise their skills in an independent and objective manner. The nature and extent of the audit examination are functions of the requirements of these entities in terms of the audit mandate. Sections 235 and 237 of the *Companies Act 1985* provide guidelines for an audit stipulated by that Act. This is further explained in Chapter 2.

INTERNAL CONTROL EFFECTIVENESS

At present, auditors may review certain of the controls laid down by management to ensure the reliability of their financial accounting information in the course of undertaking a financial statement audit. If they discover weaknesses in those controls they will advise management as will be explained in Chapter 14. However, assessing internal control is not the purpose of a financial statement audit and reports to management refer only to weaknesses discovered incidentally to the examination of the financial statements. The

Turnbull Report in the UK[18] and the *Sarbanes-Oxley Act* in the USA require directors to evaluate and to report on the effectiveness of their entity's internal controls. It is expected that the directors would be assisted in this matter by their independent auditors or other public accountants. Guidelines for the provision of such services are discussed in Chapter 3.

COMPLIANCE AUDIT

A compliance audit involves obtaining and evaluating evidence to determine whether certain financial or operating activities of an entity conform to specified conditions, rules or regulations. The established criteria in this type of audit may come from a variety of sources. Management, for example, may prescribe policies (or rules) pertaining to overtime work, participation in a pension scheme, and conflict of interests. Compliance audits based on criteria established by management may be undertaken frequently during the year. This type of audit is usually carried out by company employees who perform an internal audit function.

Business enterprises, not-for-profit organisations, government units, and individuals are required to prove compliance with a myriad of regulations. In many instances, the audit opinion issued under the requirements of the *Companies Act 1985* has elements of a compliance audit, where the audit is required to express an opinion on the company's compliance with the provision of the Act.

In the public sector, the term audit is used to denote an examination which reports on the legality and control of operations and the probity of those dealing with public funds, including the expression of an opinion on an entity's compliance with statutory requirements, rules, ordinances or directives that govern its activities.

Findings related to a compliance audit are generally reported to the authority that established the criteria and may include:

- a summary of findings; or
- an expression of assurance as to the degree of compliance with those criteria.

VALUE-FOR-MONEY AUDIT

A value-for-money (VFM) audit involves obtaining and evaluating evidence about the efficiency, economy and effectiveness of an entity's operating activities in relation to specified objectives. This type of audit activity may also be referred to as a performance, operational or management audit. The term 'value-for-money audit' is usually applied in the public sector. The other terms are common to both private and public sectors. Auditing literature provides strong support for equating the conceptual definitions of a VFM audit, performance auditing, operational auditing and management auditing.

In a business enterprise, the scope of a value-for-money audit (management audit) may encompass all the activities of a division, or a function which applies across a number of business units. In the public sector, a value-for-money audit is an independent, expert and systematic examination of the management of an organisation or function for the purposes of:

- forming an opinion about the extent of the economy, efficiency and effectiveness; and
- the adequacy of internal procedures for promoting and monitoring the economy, efficiency and effectiveness;

of such organisation or function. In this context 'economy' can be defined as the acquisition of financial, human, physical and information resources of appropriate quality and quantity at the lowest reasonable cost, and 'efficiency' is the use of a given set of resource inputs to maximise outputs and focuses on the achievement of an intended outcome. The auditors in a value-for-money audit task provide a report on the extent to which predetermined goals have been achieved economically and efficiently.

ENVIRONMENTAL AUDIT

Environmental matters may have an impact on the financial statements. Some examples of environmental matters affecting financial statement accruals, impairment of assets, disclosures, or the basis of preparation include, for example:

- pollution prevention system, the cost of which may be accrued for remediation costs;
- liability relating to transportation of or contamination by hazardous waste; or
- obsolescence of stock due to environmental laws and regulations.

Auditors are required to carry out their audit with an attitude of professional scepticism, recognising that the audit may reveal conditions and events that would lead to questioning whether the entity is complying with relevant environmental laws and regulations. International Standard on Auditing ISA 250, Consideration of Laws and Regulations in an Audit of Financial Statements, requires auditors to obtain a general understanding of the legal and regulatory framework applicable to the entity. In addition, International Audit Practice Statement IAPS 1010, The Consideration of Environmental Matters in the Audit of Financial Statements, lists a number of factors which the auditors should take into consideration when obtaining knowledge of the business, and when identifying risk and internal controls in respect to environmental matters.

The environmental audit is a recent trend, and normally involves a review or an agreed-upon procedures engagement. Such an audit is the subject of a discussion paper issued in 1995 by the International Auditing Practices Committee.[19]

INTERNAL AUDIT

While the previous audit activities are classified according to the outcome of the activity, an internal audit merely refers to any of the above audit activities carried out by audit professionals who are employees of the entity being audited. Internal audit is a management tool used by the organisation to enhance internal control. The role of internal auditors varies. It may involve straightforward internal checking, complex systems review, intensive forensic investigations, internal appraisals of operations and financial planning, or, in some cases, a financial statement audit. It is possible that the independent auditors may be able to work with the internal auditors in some aspects of the work where objectives are similar.

Internal audit professionals are sometimes qualified accountants. The Institute of Internal Auditors, which was formed in the USA in 1941, operates in chapters worldwide. The UK chapter offers a number of professional development services to its members.

With the growth of consultancy and audit-related services demanded by clients, public accounting firms are seen to engage themselves in internal audit tasks. The outsourcing of internal audit, whereby the expertise of an accounting firm is employed to carry out an audit-related assurance service of an internal audit nature, is a recent trend.

Types of auditor

Individuals who are engaged to audit economic actions and events for individuals and legal entities are generally classified into three groups: independent auditors, internal auditors, and government auditors.

INDEPENDENT AUDITORS

Independent auditors, sometimes referred to as external auditors, are either individual practitioners or public accounting firms who render professional auditing services to clients. By virtue of their education, training and experience, independent auditors are qualified to perform each of the types of audit previously described. The clients of independent auditors may include profit-making business enterprises, not-for-profit organisations, government agencies, and individuals. Like members of the medical and legal professions, independent auditors work on a fee basis. There are similarities between the role of an independent auditor in a public accounting firm and a solicitor who is a member of a law firm. However, there is also a major difference: the auditor is expected to be independent of the client in making an audit and in reporting the results, whereas the solicitor is expected to be an advocate for the client in rendering legal services. Audit independence involves both conceptual and technical considerations. It is enough to say at this point that to be independent, an auditor should be both without bias with respect to the client under audit and appear to be objective to those relying on the results of the audit. More attention will be given to independence in later chapters.

The audit of companies in the UK can be performed only by auditors registered with a supervisory body. The purpose of registration is to ensure that audits are performed by persons who are properly supervised and appropriately qualified. The criteria for registration of auditors are described on page 17.

INTERNAL AUDITORS

Internal auditors are involved in providing an independent appraisal activity, called internal auditing, within an organisation as a service to the organisation. The objective of internal auditing is to assist the management of the organisation in the effective discharge of its responsibilities. The importance of the internal audit function in minimising risk is such that the Combined Code on Corporate Governance requires listed companies without an internal audit function to explain why they do not regard an internal audit function as necessary.

Traditionally internal auditors have been employed directly by the entity. However, this tends to impair their ability to deter wrongdoing by the more senior executives since it might threaten their continued employment. In recent years it has become common for public accounting firms to provide an internal audit service which improves the independence of those undertaking internal audit activities as well ensuring the quality of the service provided. Moreover, a good internal audit may reduce the cost of the independent audit. The potential cost savings are maximised where the internal audit function is provided by the same firm that acts as independent auditor. This practice, however, has recently come in for criticism in that it potentially impairs the independence of the independent auditor as will be explained in Chapter 3.

GOVERNMENT AUDITORS

Audits of government departments are the responsibility of the National Audit Office headed by the Comptroller and Auditor General. The Comptroller and Auditor General is appointed directly by Parliament, not by the government, and reports to the Public Accounts Committee of Parliament. The Public Accounts Committee has the power to require the Comptroller and Auditor General to undertake specific audits and investigations of government departments in addition to the required reporting on departmental accounts. Most of the audit work on government departments is undertaken by staff of the National Audit Office, although outside experts, including firms of public accountants, may be called in to undertake special investigations.

The audits of local authorities are regulated by the Audit Commission under the Controller of Audit who is appointed by the Secretary of State for the Environment. The Audit Commission may appoint one of its own officers or a firm of public accountants as the auditors of the local authority. The auditors then report to the Commission, not to the local authority, and have the power to initiate legal proceedings against the authority and its officers for unlawful expenditure or losses.

For most other public sector bodies, the sponsoring government department is responsible for appointing the auditors, determining the auditors' terms of reference to the extent that they are not specified by statute, and taking appropriate action on receipt of the auditors' report.

As noted previously, this text deals primarily with financial statement audits performed by independent auditors practising as members of the public accounting profession. We will learn more about financial statement audits in the next chapter. For now, we turn our attention to some important background information about the public accounting profession.

◁ LEARNING **CHECK**

1.9 The different types of audit include the financial statement audit, the compliance audit, the value-for-money audit and the environmental audit. Internal audit refers to all types of audit activity carried out by internal employees of the organisation.

1.10 Independent auditors are those auditors who provide audit and other services for the public, and are independent of the auditees.

1.11 Internal auditors are employees of the organisations who are appointed to carry out certain types of audit or review functions within the organisation.

1.12 Government auditors are employees of the government who are employed to carry out different types of public sector audits.

REGULATORY FRAMEWORK FOR ENSURING QUALITY SERVICES

Every profession is concerned about the quality of its services, and the public accounting profession is no exception. Quality audits are essential to ensure that the profession meets its responsibilities to clients, to the general public, and to regulators who rely on independent auditors to maintain the credibility of financial information. To help assure quality audits, the profession and the regulators have developed a multi-level regulatory framework. This framework encompasses many of the activities of the organisations associated with the profession that were described in previous sections of this chapter. For the purposes of describing the multi-level framework, these activities may be organised into the following components:

- *Standard setting*. The Financial Reporting Council (FRC), International Accounting Standards Board (IASB) and International Audit and Assurance Board (IAASB) establish standards for financial reporting, auditing, quality control and codes of ethics to govern the conduct of accountants and practice entities.
- *Firm regulation*. Each public practice entity adopts policies and procedures to ensure that practising accountants adhere to professional standards.
- *Self-regulation*. The accounting profession has implemented a comprehensive programme of self-regulation including mandatory continuing professional education, and a programme of quality control and practice monitoring.
- *Independent regulation*. The government has the power to recognise professional accountancy bodies as meeting the statutory criteria as supervisory and qualifying bodies. Company audits may only be undertaken by auditors who are properly supervised and appropriately qualified.

Each component is discussed further in the following sections.

Standard setting

The roles of the FRC, IASB and IAASB in setting standards for the various types of assurance services have been noted in previous sections. The accounting bodies also establish rules of professional conduct for accountants as discussed more fully in Chapter 3. All these professional pronouncements provide guidance to individual practitioners who aspire to do high-quality work.

QUALITY CONTROL STANDARDS

The pursuit of quality practice must occur at the firm level as well as the individual level. The quality of auditing services rendered by a firm is dependent upon Auditing Standards and upon quality control policies for the firm's auditing practice as a whole and procedures for each engagement. The statement relevant to audit practice as a whole is (Draft) International Standard on Quality Control ISQC 1, Quality Control for Audit, Assurance and Related Services Practices. This statement describes general quality controls applicable to the audit practice as a whole. (Draft) International Standard on Auditing ISA 220, Quality Control for Audit Engagements, requires the engagement partner to ensure that the firm's quality control procedures are appropriately applied in each audit engagement.

The firm is required to establish a system of quality control designed to provide it with reasonable assurance that the firm and its personnel comply with professional standards and applicable regulatory and legal requirements, and that reports issued by the firm or engagement partners are appropriate in the circumstances. The system of quality control is required to include documented policies and procedures addressing:

- leadership and responsibilities within the firm;
- ethical requirements;
- acceptance and continuance of client relationships and specific engagements;
- human resources;
- engagement performance;
- engagement quality control review; and
- monitoring.

Firm leadership and responsibilities

These are basic principles and essential procedures regarding leadership and responsibilities within the firm to promote an internal culture that recognises that quality is essential in performing engagements. There is a requirement that the firm's policies and procedures acknowledge that the senior partner (or equivalent) of the firm has ultimate responsibility for the firm's system of quality control.

Ethics

The firm is required to establish policies and procedures designed to provide it with reasonable assurance that the firm and its personnel comply with relevant ethical requirements. In this way, ethical requirements are given due weight and recognition. With regard to independence specifically, the firm is required to establish policies and procedures to provide it with reasonable assurance that the firm and its personnel maintain independence. It is also required to establish policies and procedures designed to provide it with reasonable assurance that it is notified of matters that may pose a threat to independence so that appropriate action can be taken to resolve such situations. The firm is also required to obtain, at least annually, confirmation of compliance with its policies and procedures on independence from all firm personnel required to be independent.

The firm is required to establish policies and procedures that require the rotation of the engagement partner after a specified period of time for all audits of financial statements of listed entities. The firm is also required to set out criteria against which audits of non-listed entities as well as assurance and related services engagements should be evaluated for the purpose of determining whether the engagement partner should be rotated.

Acceptance and continuance of client relationships and specific engagements

The firm should have basic principles and essential procedures regarding acceptance and continuance of client relationships and specific engagements. These involve the integrity of the client, the competence of the firm to provide the engagement service and ability to comply with ethical requirements.

Human resources

The firm is required to establish policies and procedures to provide it with reasonable assurance that it has sufficient personnel with the competencies and commitment to ethical principles necessary to perform its engagements in accordance with professional standards. It is also required that the firm assigns an engagement partner and appropriate staff with the necessary competencies to undertake each engagement.

5 Engagement performance

The firm must establish principles and procedures to ensure that each engagement is properly performed in accordance with professional standards and applicable regulatory and legal requirements including an appropriate level of supervision and review. These policies and procedures must require consultation on contentious matters and provide for the resolution of differences of opinion.

6 Engagement quality control review

Such reviews are required for all financial statement audits of listed entities. The firm is also required to set out criteria against which other audit, assurance and related services engagements should be evaluated to determine whether they should be subject to engagement quality control reviews. An engagement quality control review includes an objective evaluation of the significant judgements made by the engagement team, conclusions reached in formulating the report and other matters that have come to the attention of the reviewer. The review involves discussion with the engagement partner, a review of the financial statements or other subject matter and the report, and, in particular, determining whether the report is appropriate. The actual extent and depth of review depend on the complexity and risk of the engagement as well as the experience of the engagement team.

7 Monitoring

The firm is required to establish policies and procedures to provide them with reasonable assurance that their quality control policies and procedures are relevant, adequate and complied with in practice. The monitoring process includes both ongoing consideration and evaluation of the elements of the system of quality control, and the periodic inspection of a selection of completed engagements, with the inspection cycle ordinarily spanning no more than three years.

The firm is also required to establish policies and procedures for dealing with formal complaints and allegations about whether the work performed fails to comply with applicable professional standards.

Firm regulation

Firm regulation occurs within the public accounting firm. A prime example is implementing a system of quality control as mandated by quality control standards discussed in the preceding section. This means that the firm's day-to-day actions will comply with the policies and procedures pertaining to quality control elements. For example, to assist staff in meeting professional standards, firms generally provide on-the-job training and require their professionals to participate in continuing professional education courses. Personnel who adhere to standards for professional services will receive pay raises and promotions. Personnel whose work is substandard should be counselled and, if improvement is not forthcoming, their employment terminated. Motivation also results from the desire to avoid the expense and damage to a firm's reputation that accompanies litigation and other actions brought against the firm for alleged non-compliance with professional standards. Auditors' exposure to litigation is discussed in Chapter 4.

Self-regulation

The Institutes and the Association independently undertake quality assurance practice reviews as part of their responsibilities as supervisory bodies. In order to continue to hold an auditing certificate, members have to demonstrate compliance with quality control standards. Members are obliged to give assurance that the established quality control requirements are being met. Practice inspectors appointed by the Institutes and the Association visit all practices on a cyclical basis. Findings from the reviews are confidential. The reviewed practice is given an assessment made by the reviewer. If there are unsatisfactory findings, the practitioner is required to take remedial action and will be subject to re-review within an agreed time frame. Serious deficiencies are dealt with through disciplinary procedures. The primary focus of practice reviews, or self-regulation, is educational.

Independent regulation

Regulatory activities of the professional accountancy bodies are monitored by the Professional Oversight Board for Accountancy in respect of training, professional development, ethical matters, professional conduct and discipline, registration and monitoring. This review also includes ensuring that the professional bodies take appropriate action with respect to decisions by the Accountancy Investigation and Discipline Board, such as removal of a member's practising certificate where recommended by that Board. In addition, firms auditing listed and other public interest entities are subject to direct monitoring by the Audit Inspection Unit of the Professional Oversight Board for Accountancy.

A further source of regulation is through the monitoring of published financial statements by the FSA and FRRP described on page 18. If the Panel finds auditors failing to encourage adherence to financial reporting standards where appropriate, they may raise the matter with the auditors' supervisory body or the Accountancy Investigation and Discipline Board with a view to possible disciplinary action being taken.

A significant, additional regulatory mechanism occurs through the courts where an accountant may face a lawsuit for negligence and incur costs and damages for failure to comply with the profession's standards of practice. This aspect is considered in Chapter 4.

All these forms of regulation are important. They are interrelated and aspire to the overall objective of improving the quality of audit practice. However, each uses a different means to achieve the desired objective. Each acts as a sieve in detecting substandard practice and preventing audit failure.

◁ LEARNING CHECK

1.13 The regulatory framework to ensure quality service includes the system of standard setting and regulations.

1.14 The standard setting process provides quality control standards with which auditors should comply.

1.15 Regulatory controls exist within firms, in the profession's own regulatory procedures in terms of memberships, standards, behaviour and quality, and through independent bodies such as the Professional Oversight Board for Accountancy.

SUMMARY

This chapter has provided an overview of the auditing environment. Auditing practice has evolved over the last century from a relatively straightforward activity of checking books and accounts, to a dynamic role of enhancing the credibility of financial information. The development of audit practice has demonstrated a shift in public expectations, especially in terms of the auditors' role. The chapter also briefly describes the impact of such changes on auditor independence and audit liabilities. With a number of complex factors influencing the scope and responsibilities of auditors, a trend towards having to satisfy the information needs of users has become the key topical issue.

As the market becomes more sophisticated, so, too, appear to be the information needs of users. The expertise and competence of auditors are sought for a variety of financial services, requiring the auditors to give different levels of assurance. The traditional conformance role of auditing is no longer seen to be relevant, and auditors are now expected to be able to add value to their clients' functions.

The collapse of Enron has also focused attention on the regulation of the audit function. In restoring public confidence the former regulatory role of professional accountancy bodies with respect to standard setting and monitoring has been transferred to independent bodies such as the Financial Reporting Council. Moreover, in the interests of facilitating European and global investment, standards on financial reporting and auditing set by international standard setting bodies are replacing standards set nationally so as to reassure investors as to the consistency of financial reporting and auditing worldwide.

NOTES

[1] Dicksee, L. R. *Auditing: A Practical Manual for Auditors.* Gee and Co., London, 1892.

[2] *London and General Bank* (1895) 2 Ch. 673.

[3] *Kingston Cotton Mill Co.* (1896) 2 Ch. D279.

[4] *Thomas Gerrard & Son Ltd* (1967) 2 AER 525.

[5] Carmichael, D. R. 'The Assurance Function – Auditing at the Crossroads', *Journal of Accountancy* (September 1974), pp. 64–72.

[6] Silverman, E. J. 'Practitioner's Forum: Why have an audit?' *Journal of Accountancy* (April 1971), pp. 80–81.

[7] IAASB Proposed International Framework for Assurance Engagements, March 2003.

[8] Miller, R. I. & Young, M. R. *Financial Reporting and Risk Management in the 21st Century.* Fordham Law Review, April 1997.

[9] Schelluch, P. & Gay, G. 'Assurance Services and the Profession', *Communique* (October 1997).

[10] Uzumeri, M. W. & Tabor, R. H. 'Emerging Management Metastandards: Opportunities for Expanded Attest Services', *Accounting Horizons* (Vol. 11, No. 1, March 1997), pp. 54–66.

[11] Bell, T., Marrs, F., Solomon, I. & Thomas, H. *Auditing Organisations Through a Strategic-Systems Lens: The KPMG Business Measurement Process*. KPMG Peat Marwick LLP, Illinois, 1997.

[12] Taken from the Foreword to the research monograph cited in Note 11. It was made by William R. Kinney, Jr (Charles and Elizabeth Prothro Regents Chair in Business, and Price Waterhouse Auditing Fellow, Graduate School of Business, University of Texas, Austin) in commenting on the new scope of work involved in financial statement audits as a result of changes in information technology and the extensive acceptance of non-financial dimensions of business reporting.

[13] ISA 315 'Understanding the Entity and Its Environment and Assessing the Risks of Material Misstatement'.

[14] (Proposed revised) ISA 240 'The Auditor's Responsibility to Consider Fraud in an Audit of Financial Statements'.

[15] *Sarbanes-Oxley Act 2002*.

[16] Wallman, S. M. H. 'The Future of Accounting, Part III: Reliability and Auditor Independence', *Accounting Horizons* (Vol. 10, No. 4, 1996), pp. 76–97.

[17] Commission of the European Communities, '*Reinforcing the Statutory Audit in the EU*', Brussels, 21 May 2003.

[18] ICAEW *Internal Control; Guidance for Directors on the Combined Code*, 1999.

[19] IAPC '*The Audit Profession and the Environment*', 1995.

FURTHER READING

Bell, T. B., Bedard, J. C., Johnstone, K. M. & Smith, E. F. 'Krisk: A Computerized Decision Aid for Client Acceptance and Continuance Risk Assessments', *Auditing: A Journal of Practice and Theory* (Vol. 21, No. 2, 2002), pp. 97–103.

Brierley, J. A. & Gwilliam, D. R. 'Human Resource Management Issues in Audit Firms: A Research Agenda', *Managerial Auditing Journal* (Vol. 18, No. 5, 2003), pp. 431–438.

Chandler, R. & Edwards, J. R. 'Recurring Issues in Auditing: Back to the Future?', *Accounting, Auditing and Accountability Journal* (Vol. 9, No. 2, 1996) pp. 4–29.

Fearnley, S. & Hines, T. 'The Regulatory Framework for Financial Reporting and Auditing in the United Kingdom: The Present Position and Impending Changes', *International Journal of Accounting* (Vol. 38, Issue 2, 2003), pp. 215–234.

Grant, J. 'A Principled Approach to Providing Assurance', *Accountancy* (April 1998), p. 90.

Holstrum, G. & Hunton, J. E. 'New Forms of Assurances Services for New Forms of Information; The Global Challenge for Accounting Educators', *The International Journal of Accounting* (Vol. 33, No. 3, 1998), pp. 347–358.

Mancino, J. M. & Landes, C. E. 'A New Look at the Attestation Standards', *Journal of Accountancy* (July 2001).

Manson, S., McCartney, S. & Sherer, M. 'Audit Automation as Control within Audit Firms', *Accounting, Auditing & Accountability Journal* (Vol. 14, No. 1, 2001), pp. 109–130.

Saul, R. S. 'What Ails the Accounting Profession', *Accounting Horizons* (June 1996), pp. 131–337.

Street, D. L. 'Large Firms Envision Worldwide Convergence of Standards', *Accounting Horizons* (Vol. 16, Issue 3, 2002), pp. 215–219.

Shields, G. 'Non-stop Auditing', *Camagazine* (September 1998), pp. 39–40.

Willett, C. & Page, M. 'A Survey of Time Budget Pressure and Irregular Auditing Practices Among Newly Qualified UK Chartered Accountants', *British Accounting Review* (June 1996), pp. 101–120.

MULTIPLE-CHOICE QUESTIONS

Choose the best answer for each of the following:
(Answers are on page 597)

1.1 What was the predominant objective of an 'audit' before 1900?
  (a) To ensure that the financial statements were free from all material errors.
  (b) To detect fraud.
  (c) To ensure that all internal controls were operating effectively.
  (d) To check all transactions of the company.

1.2 What would *not* be described as part of the conformance role of auditing?
  (a) Evaluate reasonableness of business plans.
  (b) Check that the organisation complies with statutory matters.
  (c) Ensure the organisation conforms with policies and procedures correctly.
  (d) Ensure that all material errors have been detected.

1.3 What is the main concern of the accounting profession in relation to an increase in the level of assurance required for audits?
  (a) Their time budgets will become tighter.
  (b) It will increase their exposure to liability.
  (c) It is not what an audit is designed to achieve.
  (d) It will not sufficiently satisfy users' needs.

1.4 What provides the highest level of assurance?
  (a) Audit.
  (b) Agreed-upon procedures.
  (c) Review.
  (d) It depends on the nature of the engagement.

1.5 What has been the primary growth area in recent years for the public accounting profession?
  (a) Auditing services.
  (b) Consulting services.
  (c) Taxation services.
  (d) Insolvency services.

1.6 The primary objective of a financial statement audit is to:
  (a) ensure that the company is free from all fraud.
  (b) provide assurance about the future viability of the entity.
  (c) express an opinion on the truth and fairness of the accounts.
  (d) ensure the company complies with all aspects of the Companies Act.

1.7 When hiring a new staff member, what should the firm consider to comply with quality control standards?
  (a) The person should have a broad range of interests to ensure that they become 'well-rounded employees'.

(b) The person should have adequate qualifications.

(c) The person should have proven skills in working within a team environment.

(d) The person should have high morals to ensure that they will comply with all ethical standards.

DISCUSSION QUESTIONS

1.1 Compare and contrast the conformance and enhancing roles of auditing.

1.2 Discuss reasons why responsibility for setting standards for financial reporting and auditing is being transferred from the profession to independent non-governmental bodies.

1.3 Explain the concept of assurance and locate audits within an assurance framework.

1.4 Compare and contrast the functions of internal and independent auditors.

1.5 Describe assurance services offered by public accountants other than financial statement audits.

PROFESSIONAL APPLICATION QUESTIONS

(Suggested answers are on pages 607–608)

1.1 Audit objectives

You have obtained employment in the accounting firm of Dickens and Partners as an Audit Assistant. You have heard that the firm is not very modern in its approach. On the first day at work, Mr Dickens calls you into his office and hands you a copy of *Auditing: A Practical Manual for Auditors* by Lawrence Dicksee, published by Gee and Co. of London in 1900. The Partner proudly claims 'This is the Bible of auditing.' You open the book (after blowing the dust off the cover) and read the following statement on page 7:

> ... The detection of fraud is a most important portion of the auditor's duties. Auditors, therefore, should assiduously cultivate this branch of their activities.

From your limited audit knowledge, this does not appear to be 'current practice'.

Required

Write a brief memo to the Audit Partner, Mr Dickens, discussing major changes that have occurred in the objectives of auditing since the publication of Dicksee's book in 1900.

1.2 Types of audit and auditors

After performing an audit, the auditor determines that:

1. The Department of Transport is in violation of an established government employment practice.

2. The supervisor is not carrying out the responsibilities that have been assigned.

3. The accounts clerk has not been stealing from the company.

4. A company's receiving department is inefficient.

5. The company's financial statement presents a true and fair view.

6. The company has an adequate provision to fill the mine pit at the expiration of the lease term.
7. Controls over the sales invoicing system are operating effectively.
8. A department is not meeting the company's prescribed policies concerning overtime work.
9. The tax office is complying with government regulations, and its financial statements are stated fairly.

Required

1. Indicate, for each of the above, the type of audit that is involved: (1) financial, (2) compliance, (3) value-for-money, (4) environmental, or (5) internal.
2. Identify the type of auditor most likely to be involved: (1) independent, (2) internal, or (3) government.

FINANCIAL STATEMENT AUDITS

OVERVIEW

FUNDAMENTALS UNDERLYING FINANCIAL STATEMENT AUDITS
Relationship between accounting and auditing
Verifiability of financial statement data
Need for financial statement audits
Explanatory theories of auditing
Economic benefits of an audit
Limitations of a financial statement audit

THE APPOINTMENT OF THE INDEPENDENT AUDITORS
Principles of appointment of auditors
Registration of auditors
Removal and resignation of auditors

DUTIES OF COMPANY AUDITORS
Statutory duties of auditors
Duty to carry out the audit
Duty to be independent

INDEPENDENT AUDITOR RELATIONSHIPS
Management
Governing body
Internal auditors
Shareholders

**MANAGEMENT'S AND AUDITORS' RESPONSIBILITIES
UNDER THE COMPANIES ACT**
Division of responsibility

AUDITING STANDARDS
Importance of Auditing Standards

AUDITORS' REPORT
Unqualified auditors' report

Qualified auditors' report
Management responsibility statement

SUMMARY

NOTES

FURTHER READING

MULTIPLE-CHOICE QUESTIONS

DISCUSSION QUESTIONS

PROFESSIONAL APPLICATION QUESTIONS

LEARNING **OBJECTIVES**

After studying this chapter, you should be able to:

1   explain the relationship between accounting and auditing

2   describe the conditions that create a demand for, and the benefits and limitations of, financial statement audits

3   discuss the legal and professional issues in appointing independent auditors

4   describe the auditors' relationship with the board of directors, audit committee and other important groups

5   state the statutory and other duties of the independent auditors

6   state the statutory and other duties of directors pertaining to financial statements

7   indicate the current Auditing Standards and their major concepts

8   explain the impact of Auditing Standards on the profession

9   prepare an auditors' report and explain its basic elements

10 indicate the types of qualified auditors' reports and where each is appropriate.

PROFESSIONAL STATEMENTS

ISA 200 Objective and General Principles Governing an Audit of Financial Statements (October 2003)
ISA 210 Terms of Audit Engagements
ISA 610 Considering the Work of Internal Auditing
ISA 700 (Revised) The Independent Auditor's Reports on a Complete Set of General Purpose Financial Statements (Draft)
SAS 600 Auditors' Reports on Financial Statements

As noted in Chapter 1, financial statement audits play an important role in our free market economy. This chapter begins by examining several fundamentals underlying financial statement audits. The chapter then looks at issues surrounding the appointment of independent auditors, important auditor relationships, and the auditors' responsibilities and rights – issues which, collectively, underpin the conduct of financial statement audits. It also identifies the sources and form of the Auditing Standards that guide the performance of audits. The auditors' report on financial statements is then introduced in order to provide an understanding of the end-product of the financial statement audit, with several alternative types of report being presented and the circumstances in which each is appropriate.

FUNDAMENTALS UNDERLYING FINANCIAL STATEMENT AUDITS

This section begins by examining the relationship between accounting and auditing. It then identifies an important assumption on which auditing is based, and considers the conditions that have created a demand for auditing, as well as the economic benefits and limitations of a financial statement audit.

Relationship between accounting and auditing

There are significant differences between the accounting process by which financial statements are prepared and the process of auditing these statements. Each process has different objectives and methods, and the parties responsible for each are not the same. Accounting methods involve identifying the events and transactions that affect the entity. Once identified, these items are measured, recorded, classified and summarised in the accounting records. The outcome of this process is the preparation and distribution of financial statements in accordance with Financial Reporting Standards and regulatory requirements. The ultimate objective of accounting is the communication of relevant and reliable financial information that will be useful for stewardship and decision-making. An entity's employees are involved in the accounting process, and ultimate responsibility for the financial statements lies with the entity's directors.

The audit of financial statements involves obtaining and evaluating evidence on management's financial statement assertions. Auditing culminates in the issue of an auditors' report that contains the auditors' opinion on whether the financial information gives a true and fair view. The auditors are responsible for adhering to Auditing Standards both in gathering and evaluating evidence, and in issuing an auditors' report that contains the auditors' conclusion. This conclusion is expressed in the form of an opinion on the financial information. Rather than creating new information, auditing adds credibility to the financial statements prepared by management. The relationship between accounting and auditing in the financial reporting process is illustrated in Figure 2.1.

Verifiability of financial statement data

Auditing is based on the assumption that financial data are verifiable. Data are verifiable when two or more qualified individuals, working independently of one another, reach essentially similar conclusions from an examination of the data. Verifiability is primarily

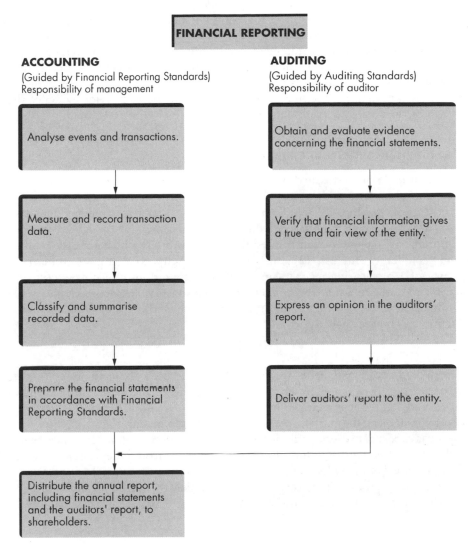

Figure 2.1 *Relationship between accounting and auditing*

concerned with the availability of evidence attesting to the validity of the data being considered. In some disciplines, data are considered verifiable only if the examiners can prove beyond all doubt that the data are either true or false, or right or wrong; however, this is not the case in accounting and auditing. Auditors seek only a reasonable basis for the expression of an opinion on the truth and fairness of the financial statements.

In making the examination, auditors obtain evidence to ascertain the validity and propriety of the accounting treatment of transactions and balances. In this context, validity means sound or well grounded, and propriety means conforming to established accounting rules and customs. Financial statements contain many specific assertions about individual items. With respect to stock, for example, management asserts that the stock is in existence, owned by the reporting entity, and properly stated at cost (or net realisable value). In auditing the financial statements, the auditors believe the individual assertions are verifiable (or auditable) and that it is possible to reach a conclusion about the truth and fairness of the report taken as a whole by verifying the accounts that comprise the report. The use and importance of audited financial statements provide evidence that the assumption of verifiability is well founded.

Need for financial statement audits

The Statement of Principles issued by the Accounting Standards Board (ASB) states that relevance and reliability are the two primary qualities that make accounting information useful for decision-making. Users of financial statements look to the independent auditors' report for assurance that these two qualities have been met. The need for independent audits of financial statements is attributed to four conditions, which are discussed further below: (1) conflict of interest, (2) consequence, (3) complexity, and (4) remoteness. In the absence of a monitoring mechanism, these four conditions collectively contribute to information risk; the risk that the financial information may be incorrect, incomplete or biased. Thus, it can be said that an audit enhances the credibility of financial statements by reducing information risk.

CONFLICT OF INTEREST
Many users of financial statements are particularly concerned about an actual or potential conflict of interest between themselves and the management of the entity. This apprehension extends to the fear that the financial statements and accompanying data, being provided by management, may be intentionally biased in management's favour. Conflicts of interest may exist also among the different classes of users of financial statements such as shareholders and creditors. Thus, users seek assurance from independent auditors that the information is both (1) free from management bias and (2) neutral with respect to the various user groups; that is, they seek an assurance that the information is not presented in a way that favours one user group over another.

CONSEQUENCE
Published financial statements represent an important and, in some cases, the only source of information used in making significant investment, lending and other decisions. Thus, users want the financial statements to contain as much relevant data as possible. This need is recognised by the extensive disclosure requirements imposed by the *Companies Act 1985*. Because of the significant economic, social and other consequences of their decisions, users look to the independent auditors for assurance that the financial statements are prepared in accordance with accepted Financial Reporting Standards and that the statements contains all the appropriate disclosures.

COMPLEXITY
Both the subject matter of accounting and the process of preparing financial statements are becoming more and more complex. The debates and problems that occur in respect to

accounting methods for leases, pensions, taxes and earnings per share are some examples of the complexities faced in financial reporting. As the subject matter becomes more complicated, there is a greater risk of misinterpretation and unintentional error. Users, therefore, are finding it more difficult or even impossible to evaluate the quality of financial statements. Accordingly, they look for the opinion of independent auditors to assess the quality of the information contained therein.

REMOTENESS

Few users have direct access to the accounting records from which financial statements are prepared. Furthermore, in instances when records are available for scrutiny, time and cost constraints normally prevent users from making a meaningful examination. Remoteness prevents users from directly assessing the quality of the statements. Under such circumstances, users have two alternatives: (1) to accept the quality of the financial data in good faith, or (2) to rely on the attestation of a third party. In terms of financial data included in financial statements, users clearly prefer the second alternative.

Explanatory theories of auditing

The separation of ownership from control is the necessary feature of the corporate form which creates a demand for auditing. On this basis, some explanatory theories are discussed here,[1] namely:

- agency theory (stewardship/monitoring hypothesis);
- information hypothesis; and
- insurance hypothesis.

AGENCY THEORY

In an agency relationship, investors, as principals, entrust their resources to managers (the company's directors), as agents. There is a behavioural assumption that all parties involved in the relationship will act rationally and will attempt to maximise their benefits. Company promoters seek to raise capital for a venture in which they, as directors, will act as agents for the principals. The promoters anticipate that investors will suspect that they, the principals, will misuse the investors' capital. This is known as agency risk; the expectation that the agent's self-interest will diverge from the principals' interest. To compensate themselves for this risk, investors will require a higher rate of return, i.e. they will pay less for the shares than their intrinsic value. To minimise the size of this risk premium, which effectively adds to the cost of acquiring capital, the promoters will offer a monitoring mechanism, in the form of regular reports providing an account of the agent's performance. Furthermore, the directors will recognise the value of an audit in further reducing agency risk. Directors will incur additional costs for an audit if these costs are less than the related increase in the cost of the company's share capital if no audit were offered.

INFORMATION HYPOTHESIS

Investors require information to make an assessment of the expected returns and risks associated with their investment decision-making. They demand audited financial information because it is a means of improving the quality of the financial information on which their decisions are based. An audit is also valued as a means of improving financial data for internal decision-making. Audits can detect errors and motivate employees to exercise more care in preparing records in anticipation of an audit. There is some degree of overlap of the information hypothesis with the stewardship monitoring hypothesis (or agency theory). Information that is useful in monitoring an agent's performance is also useful for making investment decisions. In the stewardship/monitoring hypothesis, the agent is the source of demand for audits; the information hypothesis stresses the increase in the reliability of information as an input to decision-making.

INSURANCE HYPOTHESIS

This is a more recent explanation of the demand for auditing. Insurance is an important factor in the litigation crisis (discussed in Chapter 4). Wallace describes the insurance hypothesis as follows:

> The ability to shift financial responsibility for reported data to auditors lowers the expected loss from litigation or related settlements to managers, creditors, and other professionals involved in the securities market. As potential litigation awards increase, this insurance demand for an audit from managers and professional participants in financial activities can be expected to grow.[2]

Wallace identifies four reasons why managers and professionals look to auditors for insurance:

- An audit function is well accepted by society. Professionals and managers can substantiate that they exercised reasonable care by using auditing services.
- Auditors have developed in-house legal expertise, and may provide more efficient insurance coverage as a co-defendant than an insurance company could provide as a third party.
- While an insurance company will make a cost–benefit choice of legal defence versus settlement out of court based on monetary loss, the common interests of the auditors and management will ensure the proper consideration of the effects of litigation on the reputation of the parties.
- The courts view auditors as a means of socialising risk; that is, because auditors are held responsible for business failures, they, in turn, shift this cost, first to clients through higher fees, and then to society through higher prices and lower returns on investment. Risks otherwise faced by investors are borne by society.

Another dimension of the insurance hypothesis is the incentive of politicians to require audits. Whenever there are notable corporate failures – for example, the financial failure of Enron – it is often convenient for the politicians/legislators to make auditors the scapegoats. The usual question in these situations is 'why didn't the auditor discover and disclose the problem?' As Wallace goes on to say:

> Political benefits are derived from mandating audits, increasing liability exposure of auditors to provide greater remedies to individual investors who lose money in

the market, and focusing attention on audit failure which places auditors in the defendant's chair.[3]

Government regulators and politicians can insure themselves against blame by requiring that corporate entities be audited by public accounting firms. In fact, this provides support for the legislative demand theory.

The demand for auditing services is an induced demand from government agencies. As explained in Chapter 1, statutory audits have been required in the UK since 1844 with the introduction of the *Joint Stock Companies Act* and in the USA since 1934, when the 'certification' of financial statements was stipulated under the *Securities Act*.

A quasi-judicial model of the auditors' role is articulated through the actions of the legislature and the judiciary. Auditors are conferred rights and duties under the *Companies Acts of 1985 and 1989* to make a quasi-judicial inquiry as to the truth and fairness of the accounts. The judiciary examines the role of the auditors in adjudicating conflicts between the auditors and members of society. Reference to case law determines the extent of due care auditors may be expected to bring to bear in the performance of their professional responsibilities, and those parties to whom the duty of care is owed. This is discussed in Chapter 4. Some argue that the role of the auditors is not adequately defined in terms of the auditors' strict legal responsibility. Society's expectations impose other responsibilities. The public perception of auditors' responsibilities has been a matter that has been debated and considerably researched since the mid-1970s. It is discussed in the latter part of Chapter 3.

Economic benefits of an audit

Irrespective of the view held or the dominance of any particular explanatory theory, auditing provides several benefits. These are described in the following sections.

ACCESS TO CAPITAL MARKETS
Public companies must satisfy statutory audit requirements in accordance with the *Companies Act 1985*. The UK Listing Authority imposes its own requirements for listing securities. Without audits, companies may be denied access to the capital markets.

LOWER COST OF CAPITAL
Small companies often have financial statement audits to obtain bank loans on more favourable borrowing terms. Because of reduced information risk resulting from audited financial statements, potential creditors may offer low-interest rates and potential investors may be willing to accept a lower rate of return on their investment. In short, audited financial statements improve an entity's credibility.

DETERRENT TO INEFFICIENCY AND FRAUD
Financial statement audits can be expected to have a favourable effect on employee efficiency and honesty. Knowledge that an independent audit is to be made is likely to result in fewer errors in the accounting process and reduce the likelihood of misappropriation of assets by employees. Similarly, the auditors' involvement in an entity's financial reporting

process is a restraining influence on management. The fact that its financial statement assertions are to be verified reduces the likelihood that management will engage in fraudulent financial reporting.

CONTROL AND OPERATIONAL IMPROVEMENTS

Based on observations made during a financial statement audit, the independent auditors can suggest how controls could be improved and how greater operating efficiencies within the entity's organisation might be achieved. This economic benefit is especially valuable to small and medium-sized entities.

It has been observed that the release of audited financial information generally has little or no direct effect on the market price of a company's securities. This is because financial results and audit findings are often made available by management to the financial press before the formal issuance of the audited financial statements. However, such financial statements help to assure the efficiency of the financial markets by deterring the prior dissemination of inaccurate information or by limiting its life.

Limitations of a financial statement audit

Under s.363(1) of the *Companies Act 1985*, the annual return of a company must be lodged with the Companies Registrar. While all public and larger private companies are required to annex a certified copy of all financial statements and reports, small private companies may submit an abbreviated statement.

Traditionally, the financial statements have been regarded as primarily for the benefit of the members of a company. By receiving full and accurate information on the financial affairs of their company, members are able to assess the performance of its management. A financial statement audit performed in accordance with Auditing Standards provides an objective assurance of the credibility of the assertions by management. However, as there are constraints (such as the timing of the annual general meeting, the cost-effectiveness of the independent audit, and the broad range of interpretation and judgement required in applying Financial Reporting Standards), the financial statement audit is subject to a number of inherent limitations. Some of these limitations are described below.

TIME LAPSE

There is a lapse of time between the balance sheet date and the presentation of the auditors' report which may result in the auditors assessing 'dated' information, which may be of a more dynamic nature. On the other hand, the shorter the lapse, the less time is available for the auditors to evaluate the financial information fully. Following a suggestion by the ASB,[4] the proposed new Companies Act is likely to require listed and other public interest companies to publish a short form financial statement, similar to the existing *Preliminary Announcement* required by the UK Listing Authority, within six weeks of the financial year-end. However, unlike the *Preliminary Announcement*, this statement would constitute the main financial report and would be reported on by the auditors.

AUDIT TESTING ON SAMPLES AND OTHER SELECTED DATA

Audit testing may involve either using sampling methods to obtain representative data, or selecting individual items for testing, exercising an element of judgement based on the auditors' understanding of the business. Audit testing based on less than 100% has limitations. The auditors look for persuasive evidence, which is not conclusive.

OVER-RELIANCE ON EXPERT SYSTEMS
It is common practice within audit firms to conduct audits using either general or specialised computer audit packages and other expert systems. Auditors may tend to rely heavily on such expert systems to evaluate audit risk areas (such as the possibility of management fraud), especially when the audit is conducted under time and cost constraints.

FORMING PROFESSIONAL JUDGEMENTS IN HIGHLY SPECIALISED AREAS
Auditors are required to form a professional judgement on areas which may be highly specialised, or which are not dealt with in Financial Reporting or Auditing Standards (for example, in industries that are highly technologically developed, or in respect of accounting items concerning the environment). Audit judgement, in such situations, can be influenced by a number of factors. Also, professional judgement is required in determining an adequate materiality level for misstatements in the financial statements, or for determining whether the going concern assumption is appropriate for the financial statements of a business, which faces financial difficulties.

REPORT FORMAT LIMITATIONS
Finally, the auditors are required to report within a standard format of auditors' reports, as prescribed by Auditing Standard SAS 600, Auditors' Reports on Financial Statements (International Standard on Auditing ISA 700 (Revised), The Independent Auditors' Reports on a Complete Set of General Purpose Financial Statements (Draft)). The auditors' report and, indeed, the body of the financial statements are subject to interpretation. The standard format of the auditors' report may not necessarily reflect fully the complexities involved in the audit process, and the decision of the audit opinion.

Estimates are an inherent part of the accounting process, and no-one, including auditors, can foresee the outcome of uncertainties. An audit cannot add exactness and certainty to the financial statements when these factors do not exist. Despite these limitations, a financial statement audit adds credibility to the financial information. As a result, this type of audit has become an indispensable part of our society.

◁ LEARNING **CHECK**

2.1 Accounting is the process of identifying, measuring and reporting economic transactions, while auditing is a function to verify the correctness and adequacy of such a process, and to review and report on its outcome.

2.2 Financial statement audits are required by the Companies Act on larger companies. They are necessary because of such factors as:

- the potential conflict of interest of management;

- the likely consequences of financial statements in influencing economic decisions made by the public;

- the complexity of the financial information; and

- accessibility problems for users of companies' financial information.

2.3 Auditing is generally required to satisfy the need of users based on a stewardship arrangement, demand for information and as an insurance factor.

2.4 The economic benefits of an audit are numerous. They provide, for example, an informed access to capital markets, a potentially lowered cost of capital, a deterrent to inefficiency and fraud, and a means of improving control and operations.

2.5 Financial statement audits can be limited by such factors as the lapse of time before the audited financial statements are published, the inherent limitations in the audit tests themselves, the need to rely on expert systems, technical uncertainties, and the prescribed format of audit reports.

THE APPOINTMENT OF THE INDEPENDENT AUDITORS

The appointment of the independent auditor is governed by the *Companies Act 1985*. This section outlines the basic principles of auditor appointment, the applicable statutory provisions, and the procedures for resignation and removal of auditors.

Principles of appointment of auditors

As a general rule, auditors are appointed by the members of a company (i.e. shareholders with voting rights). In the case of a newly formed company, the first auditors must be appointed by the directors within one month after incorporation. The duration of the first appointment is only until the first annual general meeting (AGM), at which auditors are appointed by the members. Any vacancy in the office of auditor is to be filled at subsequent AGMs. Once auditors are appointed, the company is liable to pay the auditors' reasonable fees and expenses in carrying out the audit. Auditors hold office until their death, removal or resignation. The removal or resignation of auditors is governed by the *Companies Act 1985*. Auditors also cease to hold office after a company goes into liquidation.

Where a vacancy occurs in the office of auditor, other than a vacancy caused by their removal, the directors may fill the vacancy. In this event, the auditors appointed hold office until the next AGM.

A person may be appointed to act as the auditor of a company, only if he or she has so consented in writing before the appointment. Appointment without such consent is of no effect, and constitutes an offence by the company and any officer in default.

STATUTORY PROVISIONS

Private companies may adopt an 'elective resolution' dispensing with the holding of an annual general meeting unless specifically required by any shareholder or the auditors (*Companies Act 1985*, s.379A). Where such a resolution applies, the auditors are deemed to be reappointed (s.386).

Private companies with a turnover not exceeding £1 million are generally not required to appoint an auditor unless shareholders holding at least 10% of the voting shares request the company to prepare audited financial statements for a particular year (ss.249A and 249B). The audit exemption limit has been progressively raised from £90,000 when first introduced in 1993 with no adverse consequences. About 68% of eligible companies take advantage of the exemption. Others continue to submit their financial statements voluntarily to audit for reasons such as access to capital. In view of the absence of any problems associated with audit exemption, the limit is to be further raised to the maximum allowed under European Union law of £5,600,000.

Registration of auditors

The *Companies Act 1989* requires that audits be conducted by persons who are properly supervised and appropriately qualified. Regulations pertaining to this requirement are described in Chapter 1 on page 17. An auditing firm cannot act as auditor of a company unless at least one member of the firm is registered as a company auditor.

There are benefits for a registration procedure for company auditors. A list of registered company auditors is maintained for public reference. Registration provides an assurance of the qualification, level of competence and experience of the auditor concerned. Moreover, formal registration and post-registration procedures allow a regular quality control of the auditor in practice. Alongside the registration requirements are conditions which require the accounting bodies to maintain and monitor a comprehensive and mandatory code of ethics and other rules, and to continue the professional development of members.

Removal and resignation of auditors

Auditors may be removed from office only by resolution of the company at a general meeting for which special notice of 28 days is required. When a company receives special notice of a resolution to remove the auditors, it must send a copy of the notice to the auditors. The auditors are then given the opportunity to make representation in writing, with copies of the representation being sent to all members entitled to attend the meeting. The auditors have the right to be heard at the meeting. Where auditors are removed from office at a general meeting, the company may appoint other auditors at that meeting. These provisions regarding removal of auditors have the effect of strengthening the auditors' independence. Auditors who qualify their opinion on the financial statements cannot be removed by the directors without due process. This issue is considered more fully in Chapter 3.

In order for auditors of a company to resign, the company must be notified in writing. The notice must be accompanied by a statement of any circumstances to be brought to the attention of members or creditors or a statement that there are no such circumstances. The purpose of such a statement is explained in Chapter 3.

◁ LEARNING **CHECK**

2.6 Companies (except for small private companies) are required to appoint an independent auditor.

2.7 Appointment is by the members at the AGM except that directors appoint the first auditor and fill casual vacancies.

2.8 Company auditors must be members of a recognised supervisory body and eligible for appointment as a company auditor under its regulations.

2.9 The removal of auditors must be by resolution of the company, and resignation must be accompanied by a statement as to circumstances.

DUTIES OF COMPANY AUDITORS

When auditors accept an appointment, they enter into a contractual relationship with the company. The audit engagement letter, agreed and signed by the auditors and the client, details some of the duties of auditors for a company (ISA 210, Terms of Audit Engagements). There are express or implied terms in such contracts that the auditors will:

- carry out an audit;
- report to members their opinion, based on the audit, as to whether the financial statements are properly drawn up so as to give a true and fair view of the company's financial position, in accordance with Financial Reporting Standards and other applicable regulations;
- be independent of the company; and
- exercise a reasonable degree of skill and care.

In addition, there are specific duties imposed by the *Companies Act 1985*. In the following paragraphs, references are to sections of that Act.

Statutory duties of auditors

The auditors are required to provide an auditors' report to the members (i.e. shareholders with voting rights) of the company concerning the financial statement audit. The format of the auditors' report is governed by Auditing Standards (SAS 600; ISA 700), while the matters on which the auditors must express their opinions are specified by statute. There are also other regulatory matters which, under certain circumstances, are required to be disclosed and reported upon by auditors.

DUTY TO REPORT
Auditors are under a statutory duty to report on the company's financial statements for an accounting period and on the accounting records relating to those financial statements (s.235). A copy of the auditors' report must be sent to members, with the financial statements and directors' report, not less than 21 days before the date of the AGM at which they are to be laid.

CONTENTS OF AUDITORS' REPORT
Sections 235–237 set out the matters which must be contained in an auditors' report. The report must state whether or not, in the auditors' opinion, the financial statements

are properly prepared in accordance with the Act so as to give a true and fair view of the state of the company's affairs as at the end of the financial year and its profit or loss for the financial year. The report must state the names of the auditors and be signed by them.

The following conditions must be reported upon if there is any deficiency, or failure to comply:

- whether the auditor has obtained all the information and explanations required;
- whether proper accounting records have been maintained;
- whether returns from branch offices are adequate;
- whether the financial statements are in agreement with the records and returns; and
- particulars of directors' emoluments if not properly disclosed in the financial statements.

THE AUDIT OPINION

The opinions expressed in an auditors' report must be in accordance with SAS 600 (ISA 700). The audit opinion can be either unqualified or qualified. A qualified opinion should be expressed as:

- a qualified 'except for' opinion;
- an adverse opinion; or
- a disclaimer of opinion.

An auditors' report that contains either an unqualified or a qualified opinion may, in certain cases, include additional information as to fundamental uncertainties. The format and contents of the auditors' report are discussed below.

Duty to carry out the audit

Before auditors can form an opinion on whether or not the company's financial statements are properly drawn up, an audit must be carried out, with due consideration given to proper procedures in relation to the possibility of fraud, errors and other irregularities. Chapter 3 considers the nature of these procedures and Chapter 4 reviews case law in relation to such duty.

Duty to be independent

The *Companies Act 1985* reinforces the requirement that the auditors for a company must be independent by disqualifying certain categories of person connected with the company. Supervisory bodies are required to have rules and practices relating to independence. These rules will be explained in Chapter 3.

Auditors are entitled to seek assistance from the company's directors, officers and accountants in carrying out their function. However, they should not rely on information obtained in this manner without exercising reasonable care and diligence, and applying their own tests and independent judgement as required.

◁ LEARNING **CHECK**

> **2.10** The statutory duties of auditors are stipulated in the *Companies Act 1985*. This includes the duty to report to members in accordance with legislative requirements.

INDEPENDENT AUDITOR RELATIONSHIPS

In a financial statement audit, the auditors maintain professional relationships with four important groups. These are: (1) management; (2) the governing body; (3) internal auditors; (4) shareholders.

Management

The term 'management' refers collectively to individuals who actively plan, co-ordinate and control the operations and transactions of the entity. In an auditing context, management refers to the entity officers including executive directors, chief accountant and key supervisory personnel. During the course of an audit, there is extensive interaction between the auditors and management. To obtain the evidence needed, the auditors often require confidential data about the entity. It is imperative, therefore, to have a relationship based on mutual trust and respect. An adversarial relationship will not work. The approach the auditors should take towards management's assertions may be characterised as one of professional scepticism. This means the auditors should neither disbelieve management's assertions nor glibly accept them without concern for their truthfulness. Rather, the auditors should recognise the need to evaluate objectively the conditions observed and evidence obtained during the audit.

Governing body

The board of directors of an entity is responsible for seeing that the entity operates in the best interests of the members. The auditors' relationship with the directors depends largely on the composition of the board. When the board consists primarily of executive officers of the entity, the auditors' relationship with the board is the same as with management. However, when the board has a number of outside or non-executive directors, a different relationship is possible. Outside members are not officers or employees of the entity. In such cases, the board, or a designated audit committee composed exclusively or primarily of outside members of the board, can serve as an intermediary between the auditors and management, and have oversight responsibilities for the financial reporting and auditing process.

Authoritative guidance on corporate governance including the role of the audit committee is the Combined Code on Corporate Governance (the Code) issued by the Financial Reporting Council.[5] Compliance with the Code is not mandatory but the UK Listing Authority requires listed companies to disclose, in their annual report, the extent of compliance with the Code and to explain reasons for significant departures. A principal feature of the Code's requirements is the establishment of an audit committee composed of non-executive directors. The role of the audit committee has been enhanced in the wake of inquiries into the implications of the Enron collapse in the UK. The Higgs Report[6] looked into the appointment and role of non-executive directors and the Smith Report[7] made recommendations on the role and duties of the audit committee.

As recommended by the Higgs Report, the Code lays down criteria for the appointment of non-executive directors laying considerable stress on their independence. It further recommends that at least half of the members of the board of directors be independent non-executive directors.

The principal function of the audit committee is the oversight of financial reporting and auditing. The Code includes the following statement:

The main role and responsibilities of the audit committee should be set out in written terms of reference and should include:

- to monitor the integrity of the financial statements of the company, and any formal announcements relating to the company's financial performance, reviewing significant financial reporting judgements contained in them;
- to review the company's internal financial controls and, unless expressly addressed by a separate board risk committee composed of independent directors, or by the board itself, to review the company's internal control and risk management systems;
- to monitor and review the effectiveness of the company's internal audit function;
- to make recommendations to the board, for it to put to the shareholders for their approval in general meeting, in relation to the appointment, re-appointment and removal of the independent auditor and to approve the remuneration and terms of engagement of the independent auditor;
- to review and monitor the independent auditor's independence and objectivity and the effectiveness of the audit process, taking into consideration relevant UK professional and regulatory requirements;
- to develop and implement policy on the engagement of the independent auditor to supply non-audit services, taking into account relevant ethical guidance regarding the provision of non-audit services by the independent audit firm; and to report to the board, identifying any matters in respect of which it considers that action or improvement is needed and making recommendations as to the steps to be taken.

Note that appointment of the independent auditor is the responsibility of the audit committee. If the board does not accept the audit committee's recommendation, the reasons should be set out in the annual report. If there is no internal audit function, the audit committee must reconsider the need for such a function annually and explain the reasons for the absence of such a function in the annual report.

Internal auditors

Independent auditors ordinarily have a close working relationship with the entity's internal auditors. The independent auditors also have a direct interest in the work of internal auditors that pertains to the entity's internal control structure. From the perspective of the independent auditors, internal auditing is a component of the entity's control environment. As an independent unit within the entity, internal auditing examines, evaluates and monitors the adequacy and effectiveness of the internal control structure.

The work of the internal auditors in conducting tests of controls is likely to influence the nature, timing and extent of independent auditors' audit procedures. International Standard on Auditing ISA 610, Considering the Work of Internal Auditing, requires the independent auditors to assess the work of the internal auditors for the purpose of planning the audit and developing an effective audit approach. The internal auditors' work cannot be used as a substitute for the independent auditors' work. However, it can be an important complement. ISA 610 requires that, in determining the effect of such work on the audit, the independent auditors should consider: (1) the organisational status, (2) the scope of work, (3) technical training and proficiency of internal auditors, and (4) due professional care observed in the work of internal auditors.

Shareholders

Shareholders rely on the audited financial statements for assurance that management has properly discharged its stewardship responsibility. The auditors, therefore, have an important responsibility to shareholders as the primary users of the auditors' report. During the course of an audit engagement, the auditors are not likely to have direct personal contact with shareholders who are not officers, key employees, or directors of the entity. On the other hand, the auditors' appointment, removal or resignation is ultimately determined by (or influenced by) the shareholders. In theory, the directors' powers to appoint the auditors are limited. In practice, the recommendations of the directors are generally accepted by the members of the company. It is for this reason that the Combined Code on Corporate Governance requires the audit committee to recommend the independent auditors and not the full board.

△ LEARNING **CHECK**

2.11 The independent auditors must retain a degree of professional scepticism when dealing with the management of the organisation, while maintaining objectivity and mutual respect. The auditors must be independent and must be seen to be independent in the conduct of the audit, in exercising professional judgement and in giving advice.

2.12 Governance of companies is being increasingly devolved to an audit committee consisting of independent non-executive directors. It is the audit committee that should recommend appointment of the independent auditor, oversee their performance and consider the desirability of employing the same firm of accountants for the provision of non-audit services.

2.13 The independent auditors should review the work and the position of the internal auditors (i.e. effectively review the internal audit function within the organisation) in order to be satisfied, if necessary, that it can be relied upon for the purposes of the financial statement audit.

2.14 Auditors do not have direct contact with shareholders. However, the shareholders normally rely on the auditors to add credibility to the financial statements.

MANAGEMENT'S AND AUDITORS' RESPONSIBILITIES UNDER THE COMPANIES ACT

Previous sections of this chapter have dealt with the relationship between accounting and auditing, and the relationship between the independent auditors and management. This section further describes the division of responsibility between management and the auditors in the financial reporting process.

Division of responsibility

Fundamental to a financial statement audit is the division of responsibility between management and the independent auditors. This difference in responsibility is well established. Paragraph 24 of Auditing Standard ISA 200, Objective and General Principles Governing an Audit of Financial Statements, states:

> While the auditor is responsible for forming and expressing an opinion on the financial statements, the responsibility for preparing and presenting the financial statements . . . is that of the management of the entity . . . . The audit of the financial statements does not relieve management . . . of [its] responsibilities.

The *Companies Act 1985* stipulates that directors are to:

- ensure that the company keeps proper accounting records. The accounting records must enable balance sheets and profit and loss accounts to be prepared that are in accordance with the Act (s.221).
- prepare the profit and loss and balance sheet of the company for each financial year giving a true and fair view (s.226); and
- state whether applicable Financial Reporting Standards have been complied with and, if not, to give particulars and reasons (Sch.4 (36A));

◁ LEARNING **CHECK**

2.15 Management is primarily responsible for the preparation and presentation of financial statements.

2.16 Detailed responsibilities of the directors are included in the Companies Act. These include keeping proper accounting records and preparing and presenting the financial statements in accordance with the Act and with Financial Reporting Standards.

AUDITING STANDARDS

In discharging their responsibilities, auditors rely on a codified set of Statements of Auditing Standards. Until 2004 Auditing Standards applicable to audits conducted in the UK and Ireland were set by the Auditing Practices Board (APB), established by the Consultative Committee of Accountancy Bodies (CCAB) in 1991. The APB became a subsidiary body of the Accountancy Foundation in 2002 which, in turn, was absorbed by the Financial Reporting Council (FRC) in 2003.

As part of its drive towards harmonisation of markets within Europe, the European Union recommended that, from 2005, all statutory audits within the European Union be conducted in accordance with International Standards on Auditing (ISAs) set by the International Audit and Assurance Board (IAASB) of the International Federation of Accountants (IFAC). These bodies are described in Chapter 1.

The development of Auditing Standards is not unlike that of Financial Reporting Standards. Once a project is identified, IAASB staff develop an issues paper which is considered by the IAASB. The next stage is the publication of an exposure draft, usually accompanied by an explanatory memorandum. Responses to the exposure draft are considered and a definitive standard is then issued. The APB plays an active role in determining a UK response to exposure drafts and negotiating appropriate modifications with the IAASB.

In addition to International Standards on Auditing (ISAs), the IAASB also issues International Standards on Assurance Engagements (ISAEs) and International Standards on Related Services (ISRSs), as explained in Chapter 1. ISAs, ISAEs and ISRSs contain:

- the basic principles and essential procedures with which auditors are required to comply in the planning, conduct and reporting of an audit; and
- explanatory and other material to assist the auditors in interpreting and applying the basic principles and essential procedures.

The basic principles and essential procedures are identified separately in bold type (black lettering) in each of the standards and must be complied with whenever a financial statement audit or assurance engagement is conducted. A departure from the basic principles and procedures must be explained in the auditors' report as a limitation on the scope of the audit.

In addition to the engagement standards, the IAASB also issues International Standards on Quality Control to be applied by those providing engagement services. Practical assistance in implementing engagement standards is provided by International Auditing Practice Statements and International Assurance Engagements Practice Statements.

The structure of the ISAs is reproduced in Table 2.1. They are arranged in a logical order based on subject matter.

It can be argued that auditing pronouncements tend to codify what is generally accepted practice. There is no conceptual basis to support a particular practice. Various matters are dealt with in isolation. Unlike the Statement of Principles that provides a framework in support of Financial Reporting Standards, there is no comparable project by the IAASB to counter misconceptions about the role and practice of auditing.

Importance of Auditing Standards

Auditing Standards set a minimum standard of technical proficiency in auditing, codifying current best practice. They are applicable in each financial statement audit undertaken by

Table 2.1 Auditing Standards

Terms of Reference
Preface to International Standards on Quality Control, Auditing, Assurance and Related Services
Glossary of Terms

Introductory Matters

ISAE 100   Assurance Engagements
ISA 120   Framework of International Standards on Auditing

Responsibilities

ISA 210   Terms of Audit Engagements
ISA 220   Quality Control for Audit Engagements
ISA 230   Documentation
ISA 240   The Auditor's Responsibility to Consider Fraud in an Audit of Financial Statements
ISA 250   Consideration of Law and Regulations in an Audit of Financial Statements
ISA 260   Communication of Audit Matters with those Charged with Governance

Planning

ISA 300   Planning the Audit
ISA 315   Understanding the Entity and its Environment and Assessing the Risks of Material Misstatement
ISA 320   Audit Materiality
ISA 330   The Auditor's Procedures in Response to Assessed Risks

Internal Control

ISA 402   Audit Considerations Relating to Entities Using Service Organisations

Audit Evidence

ISA 500   Audit Evidence
ISA 501   Audit Evidence – Additional Considerations for Specific Items
ISA 505   External Confirmations
ISA 510   Initial Engagements – Opening Balances
ISA 520   Analytical Procedures
ISA 530   Audit Sampling and Other Selective Testing Procedures
ISA 540   Audit of Accounting Estimates
ISA 545   Auditing Fair Value Measurements and Disclosures
ISA 550   Related Parties
ISA 560   Subsequent Events
ISA 570   Going Concern
ISA 580   Management Representations

Using Work of Others

ISA 600   (Revised) The Work of Related Auditors and Other Auditors in the Audit of Group Financial Statements (Draft)
ISA 610   Considering the Work of Internal Auditing
ISA 620   Using the Work of an Expert

Audit Conclusions and Reporting

ISA 700   (Revised) The Independent Auditors' Reports on a Complete Set of General Purpose Financial Statements (Draft)
ISA 701   Modifications to the Independent Auditors' Report (Draft)
ISA 710   Comparatives
ISA 720   Other Information in Documents Containing Audited Financial Statements

---

independent auditors regardless of the size of the entity, the form of business organisation, the type of industry, or whether the entity is for profit or not for profit. Shareholders and other users are informed in the scope section of the auditors' report that the audit has been conducted in accordance with Auditing Standards.

The professional accounting bodies, as recognised supervisory bodies, are required to have rules and practices as to technical standards to be applied. Auditing Standards constitute an appropriate set of technical standards for this purpose. Furthermore, the professional bodies must have arrangements for monitoring and enforcing compliance with those standards. Failure to comply with Auditing Standards may result in enquiry by the professional body with the possibility of disciplinary action being taken. In law, they provide guidance to a minimum level of care required in performing an audit. Ultimately, though, the courts determine whether the requirements of a standard have been met during a particular engagement.

 ## LEARNING **CHECK**

2.17 Auditing Standards followed in member states of the European Union are those set by the IAASB. They address key issues concerning auditing, such as responsibilities of auditors, the detailed audit process of audit planning, evaluating internal control, ascertaining audit evidence, soliciting the work of other experts, and other areas of audit judgement and reporting.

2.18 Auditing Standards are important to maintain quality service and to safeguard the auditors when called upon to justify their opinion. Shareholders and other users of auditors' reports can also be assured of the minimum standards employed by the auditors in arriving at the audit opinion.

AUDITORS' REPORT

The auditors' report is the auditors' formal means of communicating to interested parties a conclusion about the audited financial information. In issuing an audit opinion on financial statements, the auditors must comply with SAS 600 (ISA 700).

Unqualified auditors' report

An unqualified auditors' report is the most common type of report issued. It contains an unqualified opinion stating that the financial statements give a true and fair view of the state of the entity's affairs and of its profit in accordance with applicable statutory and other requirements. This conclusion may be expressed only when the auditors have formed such an opinion on the basis of an audit performed in accordance with Auditing Standards.

Because of its importance in a financial statement audit, a basic understanding of the form and content of the auditors' report is essential. The prime objective of the standard report format is to communicate the work done by the auditors to users of audited financial statements, and the character and limitations of an audit. A second objective is to clearly differentiate between the responsibilities of management and of the independent auditors in the financial statement audit. The third objective is to state clearly the level of assurance provided by the auditors' opinion. An example of an auditors' report on financial statements is presented in Table 2.2. To the right of the sample report is a listing of the basic elements of the report. Each of these elements is prescribed in SAS 600 (ISA 700). The report consists of basic elements, each of which is explained below.

Table 2.2 Recommended form of auditors' report containing an unqualified opinion[8]

INDEPENDENT AUDITORS' REPORT	BASIC ELEMENTS
Auditors' report to [addressee]	Title identifying the report and the person or persons to whom the report is addressed.
We have audited the financial statements of . . . . . . on pages . . . to . . . . These financial statements have been prepared under the historical cost convention and the accounting policies set out therein.	Introductory paragraph identifying the financial statements audited.
Respective responsibilities of directors and auditors The directors' responsibilities for preparing the Annual Report and the financial statements in accordance with applicable law and (United Kingdom) accounting standards are set out in the Statement of Directors' Responsibilities. Our responsibility is to audit the financial statements in accordance with relevant legal and regulatory requirements, (United Kingdom) Auditing Standards and the Listing Rules of the Financial Services Authority. We report to you our opinion as to whether the financial statements give a true and fair view and are properly prepared in accordance with the Companies Act 1985. We also report to you if, in our opinion, the Directors' Report is not consistent with the financial statements, if the company has not kept proper accounting records, if we have not received all the information and explanations we require for our audit, or if information specified by the law or the Listing Rules regarding directors' remuneration and transactions with the company is not disclosed. We review whether the Corporate Governance Statement reflects the company's compliance with the seven provisions of the Combined Code specified for our review by the Listing Rules, and we report if it does not. We are not required to consider whether the board's statements on internal control cover all risks and controls, or form an opinion on the effectiveness of the company's corporate governance procedures or its risk and control procedures.	Respective responsibilities of directors (or equivalent persons) and auditors: • responsibility of members of governing body; • auditors' responsibility including matters on which the auditors are required to provide negative assurance only.

(continued overleaf)

Table 2.2 (*continued*)

INDEPENDENT AUDITORS' REPORT	BASIC ELEMENTS

We read other information contained in the Annual Report and consider whether it is consistent with the audited financial statements. This other information comprises only (the Director's Report, the Chairman's Statement, the Operating and Financial Review and the Corporate Governance Statement).

Basis of audit opinion

We conducted our audit in accordance with (United Kingdom) Auditing Standards issued by the Auditing Practices Board. An audit includes an examination, on a test basis, of evidence relevant to the amounts and disclosures in the financial statements. It also includes an assessment of the significant estimates and judgements made by the directors in the preparation of the financial statements, and of whether the accounting policies are appropriate to the company's circumstances, consistently applied and adequately disclosed.

We planned and performed our audit so as to obtain all the information and explanations which we considered necessary in order to provide us with sufficient evidence to give reasonable assurance that the financial statements are free from material misstatement, whether caused by fraud or other irregularity or error. In forming our opinion we also evaluated the overall adequacy of the presentation of information in the financial statements.

The basis of the auditors' opinion (scope):

- audit conducted in accordance with Auditing Standards;
- assessing accounting policies used and significant accounting estimates made by management;
- planning and performing audit to obtain reasonable assurance that financial statements are free of material misstatement;
- examining evidence on a test basis;
- evaluating overall financial statements.

Opinion

In our opinion, the financial statements give a true and fair view of the state of the company's affairs as at . . . and of its profit [loss] for the year then ended and have been properly prepared in accordance with [the Companies Act 1985].

Auditors' opinion on the financial statements:

- gives a true and fair view of financial position, performance and cash flows;
- in accordance with financial reporting framework, relevant statutory and other requirements.

Registered Auditors
Address

Manuscript or printed signature of the auditor:

- being the audit firm.

Date

Date of the auditors' report:

- actual date signed and delivered.

(Adapted from APB Bulletin 2001/2 Revisions to the wording of Auditors' Reports on Financial Statements and the Interim Review Report, Appendix 1)

INTRODUCTORY SECTION

The introductory section identifies the financial statements and the accounting convention. Where the report is included in a bound document with the financial statements, it is usually sufficient to identify the page numbers. Where the auditors' report is a separate document or the financial statements are to be made available on the Internet, the name of the entity and accounting period need to be specified.

RESPONSIBILITY SECTION

The objective of this paragraph is to distinguish clearly between the responsibility of the governing body and the auditors. The responsibilities of the governing body are usually given in a separate statement. If they are not, they should be stated within the auditors' report. This section acknowledges that responsibility for the financial statements rests with the members of the governing body and is intended to refute the notion that the auditors develop the representations underlying the financial statements.

SCOPE OF THE AUDIT

This section identifies the Auditing Standards followed, such as ISAs, and describes the nature and scope of the audit. In so doing, it identifies several limitations of an audit. These include:

- the notion of reasonable (but not absolute) assurance;
- the limitation of the extent of the audit to the discovery of material misstatements, not all misstatements;
- reliance on a test basis such that there is a risk that evidence not examined may be important in assessing the overall truth and fairness of the financial statements; and
- reliance on judgement in assessing estimates and judgements made by management, making it clear that financial statements are not based entirely on facts.

Further disclosures are needed where:

- the scope of audit is restricted relative to Auditing Standards; and
- the financial statements are subject to fundamental uncertainties.

OPINION SECTION

This is intended to make clear that the report relates to an opinion being expressed by professional, experienced and expert persons. It is incorrect to use phrases such as 'We certify', 'We guarantee', or 'We are certain (or positive)'.

The opinion refers to the entity's financial position, results of operations and cash flows. The meaning of the phrase 'true and fair' has caused much debate. In some jurisdictions, notably the USA, the phrase 'presents fairly' is preferred. Either phrase, *inter alia*, means that:

- the financial statements have been prepared using appropriate accounting policies consistently applied;

- the financial statements have been prepared in accordance with relevant legislation and an identified financial reporting framework with departures adequately explained and justified; and
- there is adequate disclosure relevant to a proper understanding.

Qualified auditors' report

A qualified audit opinion is issued when either of the following circumstances occurs:

- a disagreement with management regarding the financial statements; or
- a limitation on the scope of the audit.

Auditors may disagree with management when, in the auditors' opinion, (1) an inappropriate accounting policy is selected, (2) an accounting policy is misapplied, (3) the appropriateness of an accounting estimate is questioned, or (4) if there is failure to make adequate or appropriate disclosures required by Financial Reporting Standards and relevant statutory and other requirements.

In a scope limitation, the auditors are unable to obtain sufficient appropriate evidence regarding one or more of management's material assertions in the financial statements. This may be due to factors outside the control of auditors or directors, such as destruction of accounting records by fire. Alternatively it may be a restriction imposed by the directors, such as a refusal to allow access to certain books and records.

Whenever the auditors' opinion is qualified, the opinion section of the auditors' report should be headed 'Qualified Audit Opinion'.

On occasions, financial statements are materially affected by a fundamental uncertainty, such as the outcome of a major court case. The position given by the financial statements can only be understood in the context of that uncertainty. An unqualified opinion may be given if the uncertainty is adequately disclosed, but the readers' attention must be drawn to that uncertainty by a paragraph within the basis of opinion section of the auditors' report.

Additional consideration is given to auditors' reports on audited financial statements in Chapter 15.

Management responsibility statement

In the first section of this chapter, it was noted that management is responsible for preparing the financial statements and the auditors are responsible for auditing the information and expressing an opinion on it. The auditors emphasise this division of responsibility in the auditors' report. Auditors may, nonetheless, assist in the preparation of the financial statements. For example, they may counsel management as to the applicability of a new Financial Reporting Standard, or propose adjustments to the entity's financial statements based on audit findings. However, management's acceptance of this advice and the inclusion of the suggested adjustments in the financial statements do not alter the basic separation of responsibilities. Ultimately, management is responsible for all decisions concerning the form and content of the financial statements.

It is common practice for such a statement of management's or directors' responsibility to be made separately from the auditors' report but adjacent to it. The statement should refer to the following directors' responsibilities:

- for preparing financial statements giving a true and fair view, including:
    - selection and consistent application of appropriate accounting policies,
    - making reasonable and prudent judgements and estimates;
    - stating whether applicable Financial Reporting Standards have been followed;
    - preparing financial statements on a going concern basis where appropriate;
- for keeping proper accounting records, including:
    - responsibility for safeguarding the assets;
    - detection of fraud and other irregularities.

 LEARNING **CHECK**

2.19 There are two types of auditors' reports: unqualified and qualified. Unqualified auditors' reports signify a 'clean' opinion. Qualified auditors' reports can be further divided into those qualified because of a disagreement with management and those qualified because of a lack of sufficient evidence.

SUMMARY

This chapter distinguishes auditing from accounting, and highlights the nature and scope of financial statement audits. Financial statement audits are governed primarily by the *Companies Act 1985*, and this chapter discusses details of the regulations relating to the requirements of the audit, auditor appointment, and responsibilities of the auditor.

The relationship between accounting and auditing in the financial reporting process involves a basic division of responsibilities between the management of an entity and its independent auditors. Management is responsible for preparing the financial statements in accordance with Financial Reporting Standards and regulatory requirements, and the auditors are responsible for expressing an opinion on the financial statements on an audit performed in accordance with Auditing Standards. Auditing Standards followed are normally those issued by the IAASB.

Users of financial statements look to the auditors for assurance that the financial information meets the qualitative characteristics of relevance and reliability, and that the financial statements, taken as a whole, give a true and fair view. The auditors' report on financial statements clearly distinguishes the responsibilities of management and the auditors, explains the character and limitations of an audit, and expresses the auditors' opinion as to whether the financial statements give a true and fair view. Qualified auditors' reports are used when there are circumstances requiring the need to issue a qualified opinion. It has been suggested that a management responsibility statement be included in the financial statements to highlight the division of responsibilities between management and the independent auditors.

NOTES

[1] Wallace, W. A. *The Economic Role of the Audit in Free and Regulated Markets*, Touche Ross & Co., New York, 1980.

[2] Wallace, p. 21.

[3] Wallace, p. 23.

[4] Accounting Standards Board, *Year-end Financial Reporting: Improving Communication*, ASB 2000.

[5] Financial Reporting Council, *Combined Code on Corporate Governance*, FRC July 2003.

[6] Department of Trade and Industry, *Review of the Role and Effectiveness of Non-executive Directors* (Higgs Report), January 2003.

[7] Financial Reporting Council, *Audit Committees – Combined Code Guidance* (Smith Report), January 2003.

[8] References to the Directors' Remuneration Report have not been included but are explained in Chapter 15.

FURTHER READING

Dewing, I. P. & Russell, P. O. 'Models for the Regulation of UK Company Audit', *Managerial Auditing Journal* (Vol. 12, No. 6, 1997), pp. 271–280.

Fargher, N., Taylor, M. H. & Simon, D. T. 'The Demand for Auditor Reputation Across International Markets for Audit Services', *International Journal of Accounting* (Vol. 36, Issue 4, 2001), pp. 407–422.

Gómez-Guillamón, A. D. 'The Usefulness of the Audit Report in Investment and Financing Decisions', *Managerial Auditing Journal* (Vol. 18, No. 6, 2003), pp. 549–559.

Schilder, A. 'Research Opportunities in Auditing in the European Union', *Accounting Horizons* (December 1996), pp. 98–108.

Welle, J. T. 'Occupational Fraud: The Audit as Deterrent', *Journal of Accountancy* (April 2000).

MULTIPLE-CHOICE QUESTIONS

Choose the best answer for each of the following.
(Answers are on pages 597–598)

2.1 Which of the following relates to the auditing function in the financial reporting process?
   (a) Analyse events and transactions.
   (b) Distribute auditors' report to shareholders in the annual report.
   (c) Obtain and evaluate evidence concerning the financial statements.
   (d) Prepare financial statements in accordance with the identified financial reporting framework.

2.2 Even if there were no statutory requirement for an audit, some people suggest that self-interest would still impel management to engage auditors to audit the financial statements. What theory of auditing is this predominantly based on?
   (a) Information hypothesis.
   (b) Agency theory.
   (c) Insurance hypothesis.

(d) None of the above – if there were no statutory requirement, there would be no audits.

2.3 An independent audit provides a number of benefits to the company because it:
    (a) assures the readers of financial statements that all fraud has been detected.
    (b) confirms the accuracy of management's financial representations.
    (c) guarantees that financial information is true and fair.
    (d) lends credibility to the financial statements.

2.4 Who is responsible for the appointment of the auditors to a company?
    (a) The managing director of the company.
    (b) The members of the company.
    (c) The audit committee of the company.
    (d) The Registrar of Companies.

2.5 What would be a valid reason for the company to remove its auditors?
    (a) Evidence that the auditors did not perform a proper review of the company's fixed assets.
    (b) A disagreement between the auditors and management – resulting in a very poor working relationship.
    (c) An increase in the audit fee charged for the year.
    (d) A difference of opinion between management and the auditors over the appropriate accounting treatment of goodwill.

2.6 What is the meaning of the principle that requires the auditors to be independent?
    (a) The auditors must be without bias with respect to the client under audit.
    (b) The auditors must adopt a critical attitude during the audit.
    (c) The auditors' sole responsibility is to third parties.
    (d) The auditors may have a direct ownership interest in their client's business if it is not material.

2.7 Which of the below is a prime objective of Auditing Standards?
    (a) To provide guidance on all procedural matters to be followed during an audit.
    (b) To give assurance to auditors that they are performing the audit appropriately so they will not be subject to litigation.
    (c) To ensure that the auditors are fulfilling all their duties as required by law.
    (d) To detail mandatory procedures and principles with which the auditors must comply.

2.8 Independent auditors' primary reporting responsibility is to the:
    (a) members of the board of directors.
    (b) Companies House.
    (c) creditors of the entity.
    (d) members of the entity.

DISCUSSION QUESTIONS

2.1 Relevance and reliability are the primary qualitative characteristics of financial reports. Consider the argument that the auditors' need for verifiability results in financial reporting standards that emphasise reliability at the expense of relevance.

2.2 To what extent are the explanatory theories of auditing conflicting or complementary?

2.3 It is sometimes argued that the corporate form of entity and the capital markets on which it depends could not exist without an effective audit function. Consider the implications if society lost faith in the integrity of the audit function.

2.4 Under the Companies Act the auditors are appointed by the members at the AGM. Why is it often suggested that the directors appoint the auditors to the extent that the Combined Code specifically requires the audit committee to recommend the independent audit firm to be appointed?

2.5 Discuss the reasoning behind requiring auditors to make a statement on ceasing to hold office.

2.6 Discuss the relative merits of Auditing Standards being set nationally reflecting the circumstances prevailing in each country, and of adopting an international set of Auditing Standards.

2.7 The auditors' report dwells excessively on what the auditors are not responsible for instead of what they are responsible for. Do you agree?

PROFESSIONAL APPLICATION QUESTIONS
(Suggested answers are on pages 608–610)

2.1 Relationship between accounting and auditing
Listed below in alphabetical order are the steps that are included in preparing, auditing and distributing financial statements.

1. Analyse events and transactions.
2. Classify and summarise recorded data.
3. Deliver auditors' report to entity.
4. Distribute financial statements and auditors' report to shareholders in annual report.
5. Express opinion in auditors' report.
6. Measure and record transaction data.
7. Obtain and evaluate evidence concerning the financial statements.
8. Prepare financial statements per identified financial reporting framework.
9. Verify that financial information gives a true and fair view.

Required
(a) Prepare a diagram of the relationship between accounting and auditing in the preparation and audit of financial statements. Show each of the steps in the proper sequence.
(b) 'Management and the independent auditors share the responsibility for the assertions contained in financial statements.' Evaluate and discuss the accuracy of this statement.

2.2 Management and auditor responsibilities
Footnotes are important in determining whether the financial statements give a true and fair view. Following are two sets of statements concerning footnotes.

1. Auditor A says that the primary responsibility for the adequacy of disclosure in the financial statements and footnotes rests with the auditor staff member in charge of

the audit. Auditor B says that the partner in charge of the engagement has the primary responsibility. Auditor C says that the staff person who drafts the statements and footnotes has the primary responsibility. Auditor D contends that it is the client's responsibility.

2. It is important to read the footnotes to financial statements, even though they often are presented in technical language and are incomprehensible. The auditors may reduce their exposure to third party liability by stating something in the footnotes that contradicts completely what they have presented in the balance sheet or profit and loss statement.

Required
Evaluate the above statements and indicate:

(a) those (or, in the case of the first statement, which auditor) you agree with, if any;
(b) those whose reasoning is misconceived, incomplete or misleading, if any.

(Adapted with permission. © The American Institute of Certified Public Accountants)

CHAPTER 3

PROFESSIONAL ETHICS

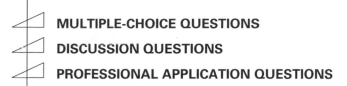

MULTIPLE-CHOICE QUESTIONS

DISCUSSION QUESTIONS

PROFESSIONAL APPLICATION QUESTIONS

 LEARNING **OBJECTIVES**

After studying this chapter, you should be able to:

1   explain the role of a professional accountant

2   state the objectives and implications of professional ethics

3   explain the key principles of Codes of Professional Conduct

4   identify the key principles and rules of professional independence

5   state the importance of audit quality and standards for technical competence

6   discuss the responsibilities of fraud, irregularities and illegal acts

7   explain the current audit environment affecting the auditors' ethical behaviour

8   discuss recommendations for bridging the audit expectation gap

9   explain the concept of corporate governance as it relates to auditors.

PROFESSIONAL STATEMENTS

ISA 240   (Revised) The Auditors' Responsibility to Consider Fraud in an Audit of Financial Statements (Draft)

ISA 570   Going Concern

ISQC 1   Quality Control for Audit, Assurance and Related Services Practices (Proposed)

One of the distinguishing characteristics of any profession is the existence of a code of professional conduct or ethics for its members. In Chapter 1, we noted that one of the original roles of professional bodies of accountants was the establishment of codes of professional conduct. Concern over the adequacy of auditor independence that may have led to Enron's collapse has led to responsibility for ethical guidance relating to independence, objectivity and integrity applicable to independent auditing and assurance services being transferred to the Auditing Practices Board (APB) in 2003.

However, ethical behaviour requires consideration of more than just rules of conduct. No professional code of ethics can anticipate all the situations for which a personal judgement on ethical behaviour is required. Accordingly, we begin this chapter with a discussion of the role of professional accountants. We then examine the codes of ethics governing professional conduct with an emphasis on the organisation of the public accounting practice and, in a separate section, audit independence. The chapter then considers the extent of auditors' professional responsibilities, particularly for the detection of fraud, and considers the current debate as to whether this meets users' reasonable expectations.

THE ROLE OF A PROFESSIONAL ACCOUNTANT

This section describes the role of an accountant in society as a professional and an individual. The concept of a profession is first discussed to identify some characteristics and skills that differentiate professionals from non-professionals, and to provide a context for understanding the role of a professional accountant. The role of the professional accountant can be defined as one in which the fiduciary relationships involved in the performance of accounting services are examined for interested parties, with the altruistic purpose of benefiting society as a whole. This section then goes on to discuss accountants' duties – specifically, the services they offer – and to examine the significance of the ethical values raised.

The concept of a profession

To distinguish professional occupations from those that are not, Greenwood outlines five attributes of a profession.[1] These are:

- a systematic body of theory;
- authority;
- community sanction;
- ethical codes; and
- a culture.

Greenwood stresses, however, that the true difference between a professional and a non-professional is quantitative not qualitative as these five attributes are also possessed by non-professionals to a lesser degree. Well-organised and undisputed professions display these identified attributes to the maximum extent.

The skills that characterise a profession flow from and are supported by a body of knowledge which has been organised into systematic theories or propositions that underpin and rationalise complex operations. Preparation for a profession requires not only intellectual cultivation, but also practical experience. For example, the *Companies Act 1989* specifies that, to be eligible to audit companies in the UK, auditors must be members of a recognised qualifying body (which are those professional bodies meeting the Act's requirements). These bodies must require a minimum educational attainment of university entrance level or seven years' relevant professional experience. Candidates must also undertake a course of theoretical instruction, receive three years' approved practical training and pass examinations testing theoretical knowledge and the ability to apply that knowledge before being admitted to membership.

PROFESSIONAL CULTURE

Every profession operates through a network of groups such as professional firms, universities and research centres, and the professional bodies which act as a focus of common interests and aims. The interactions of social roles required by these groups generate a social configuration unique to the profession, namely a professional culture. A professional culture distinguishes itself from a non-professional culture through its values, norms and symbols of practice. The professional value is the belief that the profession provides a service to society as a social good which benefits the community. The norms of a professional group form, for its members, both guides to behaviour in social situations and role definitions. The controlling values, behavioural norms and symbols of practice distinguish professional from non-professional occupations. The concept of a profession thus evolves around the five elements referred to above. In relation to this concept, Brooks[2] identifies the duties of a profession as including the maintenance of:

- competence in the field of expertise and knowledge;
- integrity in client dealings;
- objectivity in the offering of services;
- confidentiality in client matters; and
- discipline over members who do not discharge these duties according to public expectations.

These duties are vital to the quality of service provided by the professional in maintaining a proper fiduciary relationship with clients. The client, in turn, trusts or relies upon the professional's judgement and expertise. The maintenance of such trust or credibility inherent in the fiduciary relationship is fundamental to the role of a professional person.

REGULATION

Because of the complexity of a professional's role, clients must rely on their expertise. This reliance provides the professional with a monopoly of judgement and authority in specific spheres. A professional's benefit to society is demonstrated by his or her superior performance in fulfilling a highly competent and sophisticated role in that society. Clients are not in a position to evaluate independently the quality of the service provided. This makes the professional subject only to peer scrutiny. However, the profession must continue to assure society of its benefits in order to maintain its authority and monopoly. The powers and privileges sanctioned by the community include the profession's control over its accrediting process and the privilege of both confidentiality and a relative immunity from community judgement on technical matters.

The monopoly enjoyed by a profession vis-à-vis its clients and the community is fraught with hazards. For example, a monopoly may be abused due to self-interests. To counter this, a profession normally has a built-in regulatory code to compel ethical behaviour on the part of its members. A profession's ethical code is partly formal and partly informal. The formal part is the written code to which the individual usually swears to abide by admission to the profession. Through its ethical code, the profession's commitment to social welfare becomes a matter of public interest, thereby helping to ensure the continued confidence of society. A professional code possesses altruistic overtones and is public service oriented. The specifics of ethical codes are generally described in terms of client–professional and colleague–colleague relations. Also, a profession generally enforces observation of its ethical code through controlling measures designed to engender self-discipline.

Increasingly society is challenging the traditional powers of professional bodies and subjecting them to scrutiny by outsiders and independent regulation. Whether this arises from an increasing tendency among professionals to bow to commercial pressure and to relax their ethical standards, or a growing awareness among society that self-regulatory codes have often been a device for disguising self-interest in protecting the profession's monopoly, is a matter for debate. Nevertheless now, more than ever before, professional organisations are required to be increasingly transparent in the exercise of their self-regulatory powers. In 2003 the APB assumed responsibility for setting ethical standards on independence, objectivity and integrity applicable to independent auditing and assurance services. At the same time, responsibility for investigating breaches of ethical rules affecting the public interest will be made by the Accountancy Investigation and Discipline Board. Both of these bodies are controlled by the Financial Reporting Council which appoints their members, including an appropriate proportion of lay members.

The duties of an accountant

The credibility of an accountant's services is founded on the values, norms and symbols displayed by accountants in the performance of their duties. Such duties involve not only the exercise of competence in the technical aspects of financial services, but also, more importantly, integrity and objectivity in discharging these services.

THE DUTIES OF A PROFESSIONAL ACCOUNTANT

Consistent with Greenwood's proposition, the accounting profession has features that accord with four of the five attributes he identified:

- it has an established body of knowledge;
- it has organised bodies to exercise its authority in the discharge of services to the public;
- it maintains community sanction concerning its control over memberships and accreditation; and
- it attains a high image in society through its professional culture.

As explained above, the profession has surrendered aspects of its control over technical and ethical standards to independent bodies.

A professional accountant, whether engaged in auditing or management, or as an employee or a consultant, is expected to be both an accountant and a professional. That means professional accountants are expected to have special technical expertise associated with accounting and an understanding of related fields (such as law, management, economics, taxation, and information technology) that exceeds that of the lay person. In addition, they are expected to adhere to the general professional duties and values described above, as well as to those specific standards established by the professional body to which they belong.

Brooks considers that the accounting profession has the duties, rights and values detailed below – each of which is also attributable to a professional accountant.

- duties that must be carried out to sustain a fiduciary relationship:
    - displaying behaviour that espouses responsible values;
    - paying continual attention to the requirements of clients and other stakeholders;
    - acquiring and maintaining the skills and required knowledge;
    - maintaining a credible reputation for the profession;
    - maintaining an acceptable personal reputation;
- rights allowed:
    - right to represent oneself as a designated professional who is able to provide importance fiduciary services;
    - right to be involved in the development of accounting and audit practice;
    - right to establish entrance standards and to examine candidates;
    - right to require self-regulation and discipline of members of the profession based on specified codes of conduct;
    - right to have access to certain or all areas of accounting and auditing activity;
- values required to carry out duties and maintain rights:
    - honesty;
    - integrity;
    - wish to exercise due care;
    - objectivity;
    - confidentiality;
    - competence;
        a commitment to put the needs of the public, the client, the profession, and the employer ahead of any self-interest.

Deviation from these expected norms can result in a lack of credibility for, or confidence in, the entire profession. In recent years, the spate of corporate collapses and the considerable number of allegations made against accountants (and auditors) have resulted in a credibility crisis for the profession, triggering public inquiries into the affairs of the profession in general. Such was the case with the Treadway Commission[3] in the USA and the passage, in 2002, of the *Sarbanes-Oxley Act* in that country following the collapse of Enron. In the UK the profession collaborated with the London Stock Exchange in setting up the Cadbury Committee[4] enquiring into Financial Aspects of Corporate Governance, recognising the need to involve the directors of companies as well as the accounting profession in seeking a solution. More recently, the Department of Trade and Industry (DTI) set up the Co-ordinating Group on Audit and Accounting Issues to review the UK's regulatory practices for statutory audit and financial reporting. Simultaneously, the DTI undertook a *Review of the Regulatory Regime of the Accountancy Profession*. It was this review that led to the transfer of ethical standards and professional oversight to bodies under the control of the Financial Reporting Council.[5] The recommendations of the Co-ordinating Group on Audit and Accounting Issues led to developments in the role of audit committees described in Chapter 2. The Group also made recommendations relating to auditor independence which will be considered later in this chapter.

LEARNING **CHECK**

3.1 Professional persons possess five characteristics:

- education within a specialised body of knowledge;

- the authority of an organised constitution with an ability to practise for the public interest;

- the community's sanction for such a constitution to operate independently and with minimal interference;

- an enforceable code of conduct; and

- a self-defined culture.

3.2 Accountants' performance of professional services is safeguarded by a set of demonstrated values, acceptable norms of behaviour and by the fact that their work is governed by codes of ethical conduct.

3.3 The values necessary to discharge their duties are honesty, integrity, competence and due professional care.

PROFESSIONAL ETHICS AND THE ACCOUNTANT

Ethics is concerned with the evaluation of choices where the options are not clear, or where there is no absolute right or wrong answer. The study and practice of ethics is important in order to enable an accountant to examine critically a situation where there is a conflict of loyalties and interests, involving issues that relate to the role and responsibilities of an accountant (both as an individual and a professional). Minz[6] goes one step further in his perception of what ethics means. He sees it as a system or code of conduct based on moral duties and obligations that include how one should behave; this code deals with the ability to distinguish right from wrong, and the commitment to do what is right. He also defines professionalism as the conduct, aims or qualities which characterise a professional person. The fundamental ethical characteristics required of professional accountants are competence, objectivity and integrity. While professional ethics may, as Minz argues, largely refer to the written code of ethics put forward by a professional body, the practice of ethical behaviour requires:

- an understanding of ethical issues;
- a framework within which a responsible decision can be made; and
- an awareness of the consequences of such decisions.

The nature of ethics

The word 'ethics' is derived from the Greek word *ethos*, meaning 'character'. While morality focuses on the 'right' and 'wrong' of human behaviour, ethics focuses on how and why people act in a certain manner. It concerns itself more with a study of morality.

(Notwithstanding this difference, the two terms are sometimes used interchangeably.) Ethics provides a framework of beliefs and a reasoned and systematic analysis of decisions, in order to help individuals acquire the skills and insights necessary for ethical decision-making.

The skills required for ethical decision-making and moral competency are an ability to:

- make competent decisions by learning, practice, trial and error, and life experience;
- determine whose interests are at stake in a given situation, and to identify one's obligations;
- identify problems clearly;
- identify and prioritise the ethical principles relevant to a specific problem;
- take account of experience, and to consider a variety of possible options for decision and action;
- conduct an informed and intelligent option appraisal based on relevant facts, practical experience and the knowledge of one's rights and duties; and
- act with resolve and in pursuit of clear, achievable objectives, and to carry out the action objectively and responsibly through to its conclusion.

The decision-making models are systematic procedures designed to help individuals to arrive at a well-informed and ethical decision under different circumstances. Where individuals face an ethical problem or dilemma, such models will assist them to address issues such as duties, consequences and priorities, and to assess alternative actions. Different decision-making models or tools have been introduced. A commonly used model is that by Rockness and Langenderfer,[7] also known as the AAA (American Accounting Association) model.

Professional ethics for accountants

Professional ethics extend beyond moral principles. They include standards of behaviour for a professional person that are designed for both practical and idealistic purposes. Professional ethics for accountants refer to the objectives of the accountancy profession to work to the highest standards of professionalism, to attain the highest levels of performance and, generally, to meet the public interest requirement. A professional accountant acts both as a responsible individual, and as a professional person who is duty bound to operate within a set of professional norms and values.

A professional code of ethics may be designed, in part, to encourage ideal behaviour, and must be both realistic and enforceable. The two principal codes governing professional accountants in the UK are those issued by the Joint Ethics Committee of the Institutes of Chartered Accountants of England and Wales, Scotland and Ireland (the Institutes) and by the Association of Chartered Certified Accountants (the Association). The IFAC has also issued a code.[8] All three codes stress that members of the profession should not be guided merely by the terms of the code but also by its spirit. Compliance with its provisions is mandatory for all accountants who are members of the relevant professional body. Non-compliance can lead to disciplinary proceedings.

More specific guidance is included within the codes for professional accountants in public practice and, in particular, for accountants engaged in providing independent audit and assurance services. In the UK, ethical guidance relating to independence, objectivity and integrity in the provision of auditing services is now entrusted to the APB. The APB has not yet established its own code of ethics but it is likely to adapt the relevant elements' codes already developed by the UK professional bodies and by the IFAC, incorporating recommendations of the Co-ordinating Group on Audit and Accounting Issues (see page 69).

FUNDAMENTAL PRINCIPLES

The codes are introduced by a statement of Fundamental Principles. Table 3.1 shows the principles laid down by the IFAC Code of Ethics.

Table 3.1 Fundamental principles

Integrity	A professional accountant should be straightforward and honest in performing professional services.
Objectivity	A professional accountant should be fair and should not allow prejudice or bias, conflict of interest or influence of others to override objectivity.
Professional Competence and Due Care	A professional accountant should perform professional services with due care, competence and diligence and has a continuing duty to maintain professional knowledge and skill at a level required to ensure that a client or employer receives the advantage of competent professional service based on up-to-date developments in practice, legislation and techniques.
Confidentiality	A professional accountant should respect the confidentiality of information acquired during the course of performing professional services and should not use or disclose any such information without proper and specific authority or unless there is a legal or professional right or duty to disclose.
Professional Behaviour	A professional accountant should act in a manner consistent with the good reputation of the profession and refrain from any conduct which might bring discredit to the profession. The obligation to refrain from any conduct which might bring discredit to the profession requires IFAC member bodies to consider, when developing ethical requirements, the responsibilities of a professional accountant to clients, third parties, other members of the accountancy profession, staff, employers, and the general public.
Technical Standards	A professional accountant should carry out professional services in accordance with the relevant technical and professional standards. Professional accountants have a duty to carry out with care and skill the instructions of the client or employer insofar as they are compatible with the requirements of integrity, objectivity and, in the case of professional accountants in public practice, independence. In addition, they should conform with the technical and professional standards promulgated by: • IFAC (*e.g.,* International Standards on Auditing); • International Accounting Standards Board; • The member's professional body or other regulatory body; and • Relevant legislation.

(Adapted from the IFAC Code of Ethics for Professional Accountants. Copyright © International Federation of Accountants)

THE PUBLIC ACCOUNTING PRACTICE

Many of the matters dealt with by the codes are applicable to members in public accounting practice in such a way that clients can be assured of the quality, objectivity and integrity of the service provided by members and member firms of the professional accountancy bodies. The matters dealt with in this section include those described below.

Professional fees

Fees must reflect fairly and equitably the value of work performed, taking into account the skill and knowledge required for the type of work, the level of training and experience of the personnel necessarily engaged, the degree of responsibility applicable, and the time required by all persons engaged on the work. Before undertaking an assignment, the accountant must advise the client of the basis on which fees are charged and clearly define the billing arrangement. Where a fee is quoted in advance the client must not be misled as to the services that fee is intended to cover. In investigations into allegations of unsatisfactory work, the fact that work may have been obtained by quoting an unrealistically low fee will be taken into consideration. The client should also be informed in writing if the accountant is provided with an agency fee or a commission earned from a third party. A contingency fee arrangement for professional services requiring independence and objectivity must not normally be entered into. However, members may charge a client a fee for advisory services and/or may receive commissions from third parties in respect of advisory services provided to a client. Full disclosure should be made to the client regarding the form of arrangement, the identity of the third party, the method of calculation of the agency fee or commission, and any other benefit directly or indirectly provided to the member.

Professional appointments

Professional appointments are governed by professional etiquette such as communicating with the outgoing accountant before accepting an appointment, and accepting referrals without impairing the position of others. Also, members of the profession may advertise or seek publicity for their services provided that the content or nature of such advertising is not false, misleading or deceptive. Soliciting of professional work is allowed; however, accountants in public practice must ensure that communications are terminated if so requested by the recipient. There are also other matters that require members to comply with certain prescriptive procedures so as to ensure quality and objectivity. These include keeping records for clients' monies held in trust by the accountant, and not engaging in incompatible businesses while providing professional services.

Maintaining standards

Discharging responsibilities with due professional care and adequate competence in the public interest is a characteristic of a professional person. When auditors face pressures (from management or time constraints), the audit quality may be compromised. In this section we look at a number of proposals intended to maintain both the quality of audit services and the public's perception of that quality.

TECHNICAL STANDARDS

Non-compliance with accounting standards, auditing standards and professional standards for related areas of work such as insolvency represents unacceptable professional conduct.

Financial Reporting Standards

Financial Reporting Standards are applicable to financial statements intended to give a true and fair view. Members of the accounting profession are expected to use their best endeavours to ensure that accounting standards are observed and departed from only where necessary, with such departure disclosed and justified in the financial statements. Auditors should be in a position to justify departures from accounting standards where they have issued an unqualified opinion as to truth and fairness. Financial statements are subject to review by the Financial Reporting Review Panel. Apparent failures by auditors to ensure appropriate compliance with accounting standards are likely to be referred to the auditors' professional body for investigation.

Auditing Standards

As stated in Chapter 2, compliance with Auditing Standards is required of members of the professional bodies when performing an audit.

Standards for other services

The professional bodies also provide standards to be followed by members offering other services such as insolvency and corporate finance which are also mandatory for members. Although not directly relevant to the provision of auditing services, they assist in maintaining the reputation and standing of the profession.

Quality assurance

Chapter 1 explained the current provision for ensuring the quality of audit work performed, notably the requirements of the proposed ISQC 1, Quality Control for Audit, Assurance and Related Services Practices. Compliance with this standard is monitored by the practice inspections carried out by the professional bodies and by the Audit Inspection Unit of the Professional Oversight Board for Accountancy.

Professional discipline

The value of the work of a professional accountant is significantly enhanced by the public's recognition of the high standards of practice and professional conduct of the accountant. This is of critical significance in the context of expression of an opinion, as auditors, as to the truth and fairness of financial statements. This recognition is derived largely through the auditors' membership of a professional body and the public acceptance of the high standards demanded by that body of its members. This recognition comes in three ways:

- high entry standards;
- high standards of performance and conduct required of members; and
- the power to discipline, and, in extreme cases, to dismiss from membership those whose performance falls short of required standards.

The Institutes and the Association have powers to investigate complaints against their members and to impose appropriate penalties, the most extreme of which is exclusion from the profession. Disciplinary action is likely to be taken against any member (or firm) who:

- has been guilty of any breach of the professional bodies' rules;
- has been guilty of dishonourable practices or conduct likely to bring discredit on the profession of an accountant;
- has failed to observe a proper standard of professional care, skill or competence; or
- has become insolvent.

Where a breach is considered to be of such magnitude that its investigation is deemed to be in the public interest, it will be investigated by the Accountancy Investigation and Discipline Board and not by the member's or firm's own professional body. In such cases appropriate publicity will be given to the Board's investigation in order that the public may be satisfied as to its thoroughness. The Professional Oversight Board for Accountancy monitors disciplinary actions taken by the professional bodies in relation to audit matters other than those referred to the Accountancy Investigation and Discipline Board.

 ## LEARNING **CHECK**

3.4 Ethics involves a study of choices. Such choices involve the rights and wrongs of human behaviour, and relate to choices between values such as a realisation of utility or the common good for society.

3.5 Accountants face ethical dilemmas in their relationships with various parties. Professional ethics normally refers to the application of ethics in a professional environment, and is generally governed by certain guidelines specified in the professional code.

3.6 The codes of professional conduct deal with fundamental principles of professional behaviour, such as serving the public interest, integrity, objectivity, technical and professional standards, competence and due care.

3.7 Auditors need to comply with not only all technical standards (Financial Reporting Standards and Auditing Standards) but also all quality control standards and mechanisms to ensure that audits are discharged in a professional manner.

3.8 A characteristic of a profession is the ability to self-regulate. One feature of self-regulation is the establishment and monitoring of disciplinary procedures in order to ensure that members of a professional body comply with a minimum set standard of behaviour.

PROFESSIONAL INDEPENDENCE

Independence is the cornerstone of the auditing profession. Ethical situations exist when accountants are faced with situations where there are no 'correct' courses of action. The nature of their work requires accountants to make professional judgements, many of which depend on the circumstances of the particular case. Faced with no clearly correct course of action, accountants may compromise their professional integrity because of outside pressures. For example, auditors may be pressured by management to compromise their objectivity in deciding on an accounting policy, or an accountant may be instructed by a superior to amend the financial statements so as to show a profitable return. Many of the ethical situations faced by accountants and auditors involve professional objectivity and integrity. Without independence, the auditors' opinion is suspect. It is important to note that independence has two facets – the fact of independence, and the appearance of independence. These may also be referred to as actual independence and perceived independence. The fact of independence is significantly dependent on the auditors' integrity and objectivity (see Table 3.1). A related quality is that of strength of character; the ability to withstand pressure and maintain one's integrity and objectivity.

The greatest potential threat to the independence of auditors is the auditors' relationship with the directors. Directors' remuneration, the value of the shares they hold, and even their position within the company may all depend on the reported financial performance of the company. Recognising this, directors may seek to influence the auditors. Without the strength of character to withstand such pressure, the auditors may not be able to express an independent opinion.

The fact of auditor independence is not always readily visible to those relying on the auditors' opinion. Situations where a reasonable person might consider the auditors' independence to be impaired have been criticised in the past. So that the *fact* of independence be more visible, the codes stipulate rules and guidelines which emphasise the need for the *appearance* of independence.

Integrity, objectivity and independence

The key principle of professional independence applicable to all professional accountants is the duty to be objective in carrying out professional work, whether or not the appearance of professional independence is attainable. Accountants performing professional work in commerce, industry and in public service must recognise the problems created by personal relationships or financial involvements that might threaten their objectivity.

PUBLIC PRACTICE

Accountants in public practice must be, and be seen to be, free of any interest that is incompatible with objectivity. The criterion is whether a reasonable person, having knowledge of the relevant facts and taking into account the conduct of an accountant and his or her behaviour under the circumstances, could conclude that the accountant had placed himself or herself in a position where objectivity could be impaired.

The threats to independence are those of:

- *self interest* such as financial interest in a client;
- *self-review* such as evaluating controls previously recommended to a client;
- *advocacy*, where the auditors have acted on the client's behalf such as in negotiating a reduction in tax liability, which may appear to be incompatible with the special objectivity required as auditors;
- *familiarity or trust* which arises out of a long association with the directors or management; and
- *intimidation* such as by a director with a dominant personality.

In particular, there is concern that auditor independence may be undermined by:

- concern about losing clients at the level of the audit firm, the individual office and the individual partner;
- the value and the nature of non-audit service provision to the audit client;
- too close an identification by the auditors with the objectives and interests of management, even where these may not coincide with the interests of shareholders; and
- the effective control of auditor appointment and remuneration in many companies by the executive directors.[9]

Auditors need to recognise the risks and take steps to guard against loss of objectivity. The major risks are those of:

- undue dependence on audit clients;
- beneficial interests in shares and investments;
- loans and overdue fees;
- provision of other services; and
- incompatible duties.

Undue dependence on audit clients

Since public accountants depend on fees for their livelihood, a practice could conceivably be reluctant to displease an audit client – for instance, by qualifying the audit report – for fear of losing income. This argument is especially pertinent if the audit practice depends on the client for a significant proportion of its fee revenue. Current guidelines suggest that no more than 15% (10% in the case of listed or other public interest clients) of the practice's gross revenue should be obtained from the one client or group of connected clients. They also warn against situations where one client may be significant to a partner's position within a firm.

Proposals include giving greater prominence to the threat at the level of the individual office or partner, requiring firms to publish the names of clients contributing more than 5% of fee revenue and ensuring that the audit committee communicates such a level of dependency to the shareholders.

Beneficial interests in shares and other investments

Partners and persons closely connected with them[10] should not hold shares in clients and staff should not be engaged on the audit of clients in which they hold shares. As a matter of convenience many firms prohibit the holding of shares by audit staff in any client company. Special provisions apply where the shares are held within unit trusts, pension funds etc. or as trustee or are acquired other than by purchase, such as on inheritance.

Loans and overdue fees

Loans to clients and overdue fees from previous audits may discourage auditors from issuing an opinion that could threaten the client's survival as a going concern. A review must be made by a partner not involved in the audit that objectivity will not be impaired before commencing an audit. (Loans exclude normal commercial loans to or from clients in the business of making or receiving loans.)

Provision of other services

The provision of non-audit services to audit clients is a hotly debated issue on the grounds that it potentially introduces all five of the threats to independence. In the wake of the Enron collapse in 2002 the US Senate passed the *Sarbanes-Oxley Act* that forbids the provision, to audit clients, of:

- book-keeping and financial statement preparation services;
- financial information systems design and implementation;
- appraisal and valuation services;
- internal audit services;
- management functions and executive recruitment services;
- investment advisory services;
- legal services.

Current practice in the UK is much less restrictive. The rules of independence require that a practice must avoid becoming involved in executive decision-making on behalf of an audit client when it is providing management consultancy and other non-audit services. The Combined Code on Corporate Governance[11] requires the audit committee to approve the use of the audit firm for the provision of other services and, in the annual report, to justify such appointments. It is not sufficient that the non-audit services are simply provided by a different department or different members of the firm or practice. However, the rules are under review and the debate will be considered on pages 89–90.

It is common practice for audit firms to provide a compilation service; that is, to keep the books and prepare the financial statements for smaller audit clients. In such cases, clients must be required to accept full responsibility for the books, and care must be taken to ensure that the write-up work does not require that anyone in the practice make executive decisions on behalf of the client. Audit firms may adopt the practice of not involving personnel in the audit function if they have kept books and prepared the financial statements of an audit client. Except in exceptional circumstances, as permitted by the rules, write-up services should not be provided for public company audit clients.

Incompatible duties

The following stipulations apply in respect to incompatible duties:

- No partner or staff member of an audit practice shall be an officer of an audit client (for example, the company secretary).
- No partner or staff member shall be a director of a company, which exerts a significant influence over an audit client.
- Any partner or staff member who used to be employed by an audit client shall not personally be involved in the audit of that client for a financial period commencing within two years of the severance of the association.

Other

Other risks threatening independence that need to be avoided or kept under review include:

- Accepting goods, services or hospitality from audit clients on a scale not commensurate with normal social courtesies.

- Partners or audit staff having family, personal or business relationships with officers or senior employees of audit clients.
- Voting on audit appointments by audit staff holding shares in audit clients.
- Actual or threatened litigation between an auditor and audit client.

Review procedures

No list of risks can identify all of the threats to independence. Audit firms need to develop procedures to review independence as part of their quality control arrangements as described in Chapter 1. These include:

- Instructing staff to communicate concerns over objectivity to a separate partner.
- Appointment of review partners, especially on sensitive engagements such as those close to the fee threshold.
- Annual reviews on client continuance.
- Appropriate procedures on new client acceptance.

A particular problem is that of personal relationships with audit clients. By its very nature, an audit brings members of the accounting practice into close contact with management and employees of clients over a period of years. Cordial relationships are usually desirable and facilitate the effective conduct of the audit. However, in the context of independence, the existence of a cordial relationship could adversely influence auditors' judgements when confronted with evidence of a fraud. To minimise this risk, the engagement partner should be rotated every seven years. The issue of audit firm rotation is more contentious and will be considered on page 89.

It is common for audit partners and other staff members to receive offers of employment from audit clients. This, it is claimed, introduces an unwholesome relationship between newly employed senior financial officers and the audit engagement team. It is suggested that there should be a 'cooling-off' period between being a member of an engagement team and taking up employment with the client entity. The Institutes of Chartered Accountants recommend that two years should elapse in the case of engagement partners of listed company clients taking up such appointments.

Statutory provisions enhancing auditors' independence

The *Companies Acts* of 1985 and 1989 include provisions relating to the appointment and dismissal of auditors, auditors' rights and ineligible persons. There are also special provisions that apply when auditors cease to hold office.

STATUTORY PROVISIONS

The law recognises the need for audit independence. As with the codes of professional ethics, these provisions establish an appearance of auditor independence. The *Companies Act 1985* requires that, in general, members have the power to appoint (s.385) or remove (s.391) auditors. The appointment of the first auditors and the filling of casual vacancies may be performed by the directors, but such appointments are in force only until the conclusion of the next annual general meeting of members. This is intended to protect the auditors from intimidation by the directors. Section 390A of the *Companies Act 1985* entitles the auditors to reasonable fees. Disclosure of these is required in the published accounts. Theoretically, it is the shareholders who have the power to set fees, but, in practice, negotiations are usually delegated to the directors. Low fees could be an indication of 'low-balling' to gain market share (see page 90). Conversely, high fees could be an extraction of quasi-rent as a result of incumbency.

The statutory rights and responsibilities of the auditors, embodied in several provisions of the *Companies Act 1985*, are intended also to allow the auditors' independence of action in the conduct of the audit. These provisions relate to:

- access to accounting records (s.389A)(1));
- right to information and explanations from the company and its subsidiaries (s.389A(1)(3)); and
- right to receive notice of, and to attend and be heard at, meetings of members, on any part of the business of the meeting that concerns the auditors (s.390(1)).

Section 389A(2) states that it is an offence to deliberately mislead the auditors. There are also statutory provisions, which make certain categories of people ineligible for appointment as auditors on the grounds that they lack independence. In accordance with the *Companies Act 1989*, s.27(1), a person is ineligible for appointment as auditor of the company, if he or she is:

- an officer or employee of the company; or
- a partner or employee of an officer or employee of the company.

CEASING TO HOLD OFFICE

Fear of losing an audit client in the event of a disagreement with management stems largely from an awareness that it *is* management (and not those to whom the audit report is addressed and by whom the auditor appointment is ostensibly made) that exerts the strongest influence on the choice of auditors. In companies, this situation arises because few members actually attend general meetings of the company. Furthermore, most of the votes cast at such meetings are proxy votes held by directors. Naturally, the directors must approve all resolutions that the board has put on the agenda, including resolutions as to a change of auditors.

Shareholders need to be apprised of any serious matters affecting their interests vis-à-vis those of management in the event of a proposed change of auditors before abrogating their voting rights on such a proposal. To this end, the *Companies Act 1985* affords some protection. Special notice (28 days instead of the normal 21 days) is required of a resolution to be put before a general meeting for the replacement of the auditors (s.391A(1)). The company is required, if the auditors so request, to circularise to all shareholders a statement, by the auditors, as to why they should not be replaced (s.391A(3,4)).

There are situations where auditors may believe that their position is made untenable, such as the directors' refusal to take appropriate action in the event of fraud or other illegal act. Whenever auditors resign they may issue a statement of circumstances which the company must send to the registrar of companies as a public document (s.392). They may also require the directors to call an extraordinary general meeting at which they may bring the matter to the attention of members and creditors (s.392A).

Reasons for resignation or removal from office are often sensitive and auditors, especially if they feel intimidated by the directors, such as through a threat of legal action for defamation if they make public their concern, may prefer not to advise shareholders of the circumstances. To avoid this, auditors are required, when ceasing to hold office for whatever reason, to issue a statement of circumstances which should be brought to the attention of members or creditors, or a statement that there are no such circumstances (s.394(1)). The company must send this to all the members unless they obtain the court's consent that the auditors are using the statement to secure needless publicity for defamatory matter (s.394(6)).

 LEARNING **CHECK**

3.9 Independence is the cornerstone of the auditing profession. The auditors must not only be independent, but be seen to be independent. Independence is related to the auditors' integrity, objectivity, and strength of character.

3.10 Rules of independence are specified in ethical codes. They include prohibition of financial interests in client business affairs, and avoiding incompatible duties and other conflicts.

3.11 Statutory requirements, which enhance the auditors' independence, include the procedures for appointment and resignation and the auditors' rights of access to the books and records of auditee organisations.

3.12 There are special statutory provisions requiring auditors to make public reasons applicable to shareholders on ceasing to hold office as auditors.

FRAUD AND ILLEGAL ACTS

In its early days, the primary objective of the independent audit was the detection of fraud and error. Nowadays, the primary objective is to determine whether the financial statements give a true and fair view. Nevertheless, surveys of users find that many still believe fraud detection to be the primary objective of the audit. This belief even extends to fraud that is not material to the financial statements as a whole. A research report of the Institute of Chartered Accountants of Scotland[12] on the audit expectation gap identified several users' expectations regarding audit assurance. Essentially, it found that the general public tends to regard an unqualified opinion as a clean bill of health for a company. In particular, the public regards the audit as providing assurance that:

- there has been no fraud; and
- the company has acted within the law.

Moreover the public regards auditors as responsible for reporting to a third party if they suspect that the directors are involved in fraud or other illegal acts.

This section explains the current responsibilities of auditors for the detection and reporting of fraud and illegal acts as laid down by Auditing Standards. It will consider the argument that the profession is not doing enough to meet user expectations, and will discuss suggestions for reducing the incidence of fraud and enhancing the profession's responsibility for detecting and reporting fraud.

Responsibilities for detecting fraud and error

Auditors examine the financial statements and may only reasonably be expected to discover fraud where it causes a material misstatement of those financial statements. (Draft) ISA 240, The Auditors' Responsibility to Consider Fraud in an Audit of Financial Statements, classifies fraud into two basic categories:

- misstatements resulting from fraudulent financial reporting; and
- misstatements resulting from fraudulent misappropriation of assets.

Fraudulent financial reporting involves:

- falsification or alteration of records or other documents;
- wilful misrepresentation or omission of transactions or of the entity's state of affairs; and
- intentional misapplication of accounting policies.

Fraudulent misappropriation of assets may involve false or misleading documents or records in order to conceal the fact that the assets are missing.

An error is accidental, and the individual responsible for the error neither expects nor realises any personal gain. In contrast, a fraudulent act is premeditated and the perpetrator usually hopes to achieve personal gain or some other specific objective. The distinction between errors and other irregularities is one of intent. Errors, however, may have the same effect as fraud and the auditors will need to enquire into the circumstances to determine whether fraud may be involved. This is not always easy to determine, especially in matters involving judgement. Whether an irregularity is fraudulent is a matter for the courts to determine. The auditors' concern, therefore, is with suspected rather than proven fraud.

PREVENTION AND DETECTION OF FRAUD AND ERROR

The prevention and detection of fraud and error is primarily the responsibility of management. Auditors have a professional duty under ISA 240, The Auditors' Responsibility to Consider Fraud, to plan and conduct an audit in such a way that there is a reasonable expectation of detecting material misstatements arising from fraud. This assurance will be obtained through the use of audit procedures as required by Auditing Standards. This duty is not the same as a duty to discover all material fraud. It means that, in the planning and execution of an audit programme, auditors should be aware of the possibility of fraud. When auditors believe that material misstatements exist, they should extend the scope of their examination to either dispel their beliefs or determine that the irregularity has been corrected or properly reflected in the financial statements. Consequently, an unqualified opinion on financial statements implicitly means that, in the auditors' opinion, the financial statements are not materially misstated because of fraud.

However, an examination in accordance with Auditing Standards cannot guarantee the detection of all material irregularities as an audit involves only the selective testing of transactions and balances. It is possible, therefore, that any fraud may not have been a part of the evidence examined. In particular, the perpetrators of fraudulent acts are likely to have taken steps (such as management override of controls, forgery or collusion) to conceal the evidence of their acts from auditors and others. Whether it should have been detected will depend on the auditors' adherence to Auditing Standards and the adequacy of the auditing procedures undertaken in the circumstances.

PLANNING TO DETECT FRAUD

In planning the audit, auditors must be alert to the possibility of fraud and assess the risk that fraud might occur. In this process it is important that the auditors not be unduly swayed by past experience with the entity. In particular auditors need to consider incentives, opportunities and rationalisations as explained in Table 3.2.

Where there is an assessed risk of materially misstated financial statements due to fraud auditors would pay particular attention to matters such as:

- revenue recognition such as by inquiring into accounting policies used and investigating cut-off;
- stock quantities by physical observation, test counting and considering reasonableness;
- management estimates by considering the possibility of consistent bias even if individually immaterial; and
- unusual transactions that do not appear to make good business sense.

An important procedure is a brainstorming session among audit team members pooling their knowledge of the entity in attempting to identify how a determined management or individual could perpetrate a fraud. The results of the fraud risk assessment including the brainstorming session must be fully documented. It is also important to communicate any suspicions to an appropriate level of management, whether or not potentially material.

Surveys of fraud typically identify poor internal controls, collusion between employees and third parties, and management override of controls to be the main reasons for fraud. Frauds perpetuated by management included those involving purchase for personal use, conflict of interest, the expense account, kickbacks, unnecessary purchases, false financial statements, credit card fraud, and diversion of sales and information.

If there are suspicions that any members of management are associated with fraudulent activities, further investigation should be made in order to find out more about the circumstances. If the auditors are unable to confirm the absence of fraud, they should advise senior management. In such circumstances, the auditors may find that it is not possible to complete the audit and they should seek legal advice about their responsibilities and their future course of action. Notwithstanding this, an auditor is not an insurer of good faith and reliability on the part of management.

Table 3.2 Examples of risk factors alerting auditors to the risks of fraudulent financial reporting

---

Incentives

Management or other employees may have an incentive or be under pressure, which provides a motivation to commit fraud

• Threat to profits or financial stability	– Increased competition
	– Changes in technology
	– Declining demand
	– Negative cash flows
	– Changes in regulations
• Pressure to meet third party expectations	– Expectations of investment analysts
	– Need to raise additional funds
• Threat to personal finances of individuals in management	– Performance related pay
	– Significant financial interests

Opportunities

Circumstances exist that provide an opportunity for fraud to be perpetrated

• Nature of industry or its operations	– Related party transactions
	– Accounting estimates significant in financial reporting
	– Significant foreign operations in countries with different business cultures
• Ineffective monitoring	– Management dominated by an individual or small group
• Complex organisational structure	– Ultimate ownership unclear
	– Unduly complex structure
	– High turnover of senior management or directors
• Deficient control	– Poor interim reporting structure
	– Ineffective accounting, IT or internal audit staff
	– Poor internal control

Rationalisation

Those involved in a fraud are able to rationalise a fraudulent act as being consistent with their personal code of ethics. Some people possess an attitude, character or set of ethical values that allows them to knowingly and intentionally commit a dishonest act

- Poor communication of entity's ethical values
- Known history of violation of laws and regulations
- Excessive interest in maintaining share price or meeting analysts' expectations
- Failure to correct known control weaknesses
- Strained relationship between management and auditor

Non-compliance with law and regulations

Many lay people believe that an audit must surely detect all illegal acts committed by an entity. However, this is not necessarily the case. An audit may result in the detection of illegal acts, but it cannot be relied on to do so. There are two reasons for this:

- The determination of whether an act is illegal or not involves matters of law that may be beyond the auditors' competence.

- Illegal acts may pertain to aspects of the entity's operations that are generally unrelated to the financial statements.

It should also be recognised that management may be able to conceal the occurrence of illegal acts. Moreover, there are limitations in the auditing process that may permit illegal acts to remain undiscovered. For audit purposes, there are three principal categories of illegal act:

- those pertaining to the form, content and preparation of the financial statements;
- those having a fundamental effect on operations, a breach of which would jeopardise the viability of the entity or a major part of it; and
- others such as equal employment opportunity, occupational health and safety, and environmental protection legislation.

Auditors should plan the audit so that they have a reasonable expectation of detecting illegal acts in the first category. In planning the audit, they should also identify any other illegal acts that could have a fundamental effect on an entity's operations and assess the risk of material misstatements arising from these. They are not, however, responsible for searching for other illegal acts that are not expected to result in material misstatements.

Reporting of irregularities

All irregularities (whether discovered or suspected) should be reported to an appropriate level of management, regardless of materiality, and the future course of action agreed upon. Care must be exercised to ensure that the manager to whom the matter is reported is unlikely to be implicated in the irregularity. Where there is suspicion that top management is involved in fraudulent or other illegal acts, the findings should be reported to a level of authority high enough for appropriate action to be taken. This may be the audit committee or, in some cases, the board of directors. If appropriate action is not forthcoming, the auditors should seek legal advice and consider severing any further business relationship with the entity. In extreme cases where the entity's governing body is believed to be implicated, it may be necessary to seek direct legal advice, so as not to provide the governing body with the opportunity to destroy or conceal the evidence. Where the irregularity is clearly immaterial, no further action need be taken. However, it must be noted that failure to report a fraud, no matter how immaterial, and failure to ensure that appropriate action is taken by management may lead the auditors to being sued for damages by the client (as in the case of *WA Chip & Pulp Co. Pty Ltd v. Arthur Young* (1987) 12 ACLR 25).

Where the irregularity is possibly material, further investigation is necessary to confirm or dispel suspicions and to determine materiality. In evaluating the materiality of an irregularity, particularly an illegal act, the auditors should consider related fines, penalties, damages, and possible loss contingencies such as expropriation of property and forced discontinuance of operations. Where the presence of a material irregularity is confirmed, the auditors will need to consider such matters as:

- effect on the financial statements or audit report;
- evaluation of internal control, the possibility of the occurrence of similar irregularities and the need for further audit procedures;

- management's proposed actions to prevent the recurrence of the irregularity; and
- public interest implications of the irregularity.

REPORTING OF ILLEGAL ACTS TO REGULATORY AUTHORITIES

The auditors' contractual obligation to observe client confidentiality prevents the reporting of any aspect of the client's affairs to a third party. Notifying other parties of the occurrence of irregularities is the responsibility of management. The auditors have no obligation or right to notify other parties except:

- statutorily required reports to regulators such as under the *Building Societies Act 1986* and the *Financial Services and Markets Act 2000*;
- in the public interest.

The 'public interest' represents a common law duty which overrides the auditors' duty of confidentiality to the client. It arises where the illegal act or intended illegal act could result in great social harm. In such cases, the auditors should consult legal advisers as to whether the matter should be reported to the authorities.

Meeting public expectations for detecting and reporting irregularities

The profession believes users' expectation that the principal objective of an audit is the detection of fraud is unreasonable. The cost of performing the extensive audit procedures that would be needed to detect all material fraud, and the resultant delay in completing the audit, would be disproportionate to the benefits received by users.

The legal responsibility is uncertain. There have been few recent cases involving fraud that have been decided in court with most claims involving the failure of auditors to detect fraud having been settled out of court. Critics argue that auditors have a legal duty to detect fraud, and that ISA 240 represents an improper attempt by the profession to persuade courts and the public to accept a lower standard of responsibility for fraud. Notwithstanding that ISA 240 represents a substantial advance in directing the auditors in making a robust examination for fraud, it is conceivable that user expectations will be difficult to shift in this regard. Every time a fraud is perpetrated and not discovered by the auditors – no matter how skillfully it might have been concealed or how senior the level of management responsible – the competence of the whole audit will be called into question.

Reducing the incidence of undetected irregularities

Despite the difficulty auditors face in accepting greater responsibility for detecting and reporting fraud, there are a number of initiatives that could reduce the extent of losses through fraud. Not least among these are proposals to improve the effectiveness of internal control structures and to emphasise management's responsibility for doing so. These proposals are further discussed in the section on corporate governance (see page 93). The establishment of an audit committee also helps communication between the auditors and the entity, where top management fraud is suspected. In the absence of an audit committee, the auditors cannot be sure which executive members of the board are not a party to the fraud. There may not be anyone to whom the auditor can address their suspicions.

The APB's Discussion Paper *The Audit Agenda*[13] discusses a number of ways of reducing undetected fraud. Many auditing firms have developed expertise in forensic audits, entailing an in-depth assessment of an entity's arrangements to minimise fraud and investigations into any apparent areas of weakness. Such exercises are costly, especially if conducted as part of the independent audit, with the auditors accepting full responsibility for any fraud that evades detection. However, if performed separately, or even if undertaken by internal audit (without the same degree of risk being carried by the consultant or auditors), they would be less costly, and management could be persuaded to commission such investigations in fulfilling its responsibility for internal control.

The training and education of auditors could also be extended to incorporate aspects of behavioural and forensic audits. Top management fraud often involves powerful, plausible individuals, and many frauds (undetected by experienced auditors for years) have continued because the auditors have been the subjects of clever persuasion and manipulation. Recognising behavioural patterns and knowing some of the methods used in previously investigated frauds could help to reduce the extent to which perpetrators of fraud are able to deceive auditors.

There are other regulatory bodies and individuals who investigate aspects of an entity's affairs and who can, therefore, become aware of irregularities. However, there is no requirement for those bodies and individuals to communicate any suspicions of irregularities to the independent auditors. In the reporting of fraud, auditors often complain they are in an impossible situation. They do not have the investigative powers of law enforcement agencies and, at best, have suspicions and not proof of the occurrence of fraud. If their suspicions prove to be unfounded, premature revelation of their suspicions could result in an action for defamation. Moreover, they have a duty of confidentiality to the entity. Where top management is believed to be implicated in a fraud, auditors have no right to inform the appropriate authorities unless required to do so in the 'public interest'. This is an ill-defined concept. Timeliness of reporting is vital in such matters and rarely allows the auditors time to seek legal advice. Auditors of companies within the financial sector generally have protected privilege (against claims for breach of confidentiality or defamation) when alerting an appropriate regulatory body in good faith of suspicions of irregularity. The expansion of such safe harbour provisions to all statutory audits has often been advocated but not yet implemented. It is argued that such a measure would ensure that all suspicions of irregularities are properly reported and investigated.

LEARNING CHECK

3.13 Irregularities comprise fraud, errors, unintentional misstatements and non-compliance with laws and regulations. Fraud is an act involving the use of deception, while errors are unintentional mistakes.

3.14 The prevention and detection of fraud is primarily the responsibility of management, while auditors have a professional duty to plan and conduct their audits so that there is a reasonable expectation that any material misstatements arising from irregularities can be detected.

3.15 Where the presence of irregularity is confirmed, the auditors will need to consider the effect on the financial statements and auditors' report, the possibility of the occurrence or recurrence as a result of poor internal control, management's actions to prevent such recurrence, and the implications for the public interest.

3.16 The extent of auditor responsibility for detecting and reporting fraud and other irregularities is controversial. Proposals include offering fraud detection as a service additional to the audit and assisting entities reduce the incidence of such irregularities.

THE SIGNIFICANCE OF ETHICAL VALUES FOR AUDITING

Threats to independence are frequently encountered by auditors and accountants in public practice and are complex issues. Some of the threats are a direct consequence of the auditor–client relationship, such as management pressure, and the phenomenon of non-audit services being provided by accountants in public practice which may have an impact on the appearance of auditor independence. The accountants' and auditors' decisions are dependent on their ability to identify and prioritise various conflicting interests and duties, while maintaining professional competence and independence. How independent these decisions are in reality often depends on how successfully the auditors deal with issues such as those discussed below.

The environment affecting professional conduct

Auditors often face pressure situations that present them with an ethical dilemma – one in which they have to choose between unclear alternatives, some of which may compromise their integrity. Not all of these situations are easily defined, and there may be occasions when the auditors need to look beyond the requirements of the professional codes for guidance. Some of these situations are described below.

MANAGEMENT PRESSURE ON AUDIT APPOINTMENT

As explained above, shareholders generally do not intervene in the appointment of auditors and usually assign their voting rights to the directors. This gives rise to the practice known as 'opinion shopping' whereby directors of an audit client invite another firm of accountants to offer a second opinion on a proposed accounting treatment with which the incumbent auditors disagree. This puts pressure on the auditors to issue an unqualified audit report in order not to lose the audit to the second firm. Suggested solutions include restricting fees from individual clients, audit rotation and banning the provision of non-audit services.

Fee income limits

Existing solutions to such problems include restricting the total fee income that an audit firm may derive from one reporting entity from both audit and non-audit services. The loss of an audit, therefore, would not cause the audit firm to lose substantial revenue, thus encouraging the auditors to adopt a firmer attitude in disagreements with management. The Combined Code on Corporate Governance has recently been amended to require the audit committee to recommend auditor appointment (see page 49). The audit committee is additionally required to advise on the appointment of the audit firm for the provision of non-audit services and to justify such appointments. This is part of a package of recent amendments to the Combined Code on Corporate Governance that includes measures to ensure the independence and competence of non-executive directors forming the audit committee. How effective these measures will be is yet to be determined. One problem is the fact that, in the UK, the audit committee is merely a subcommittee of the board of directors and has no special status in law.

Audit rotation

A more radical proposal is that of audit rotation. Under this arrangement, auditors are appointed for a fixed term of five or seven years during which they cannot be removed from office. At the end of this term, they must be replaced by another firm. Such a move limits the opportunities for the development of personal relationships between the engagement team and client management and reduces incentives to secure audit appointments primarily for the benefit of fees from the provision of non-audit services the audit firm would hope to secure. This proposal is rejected by the profession on the following grounds:

- the loss of cumulative knowledge and experience on audits leading to potential audit failure in the initial years;
- the cost of building up knowledge and experience in the initial year/s of an audit;
- diminution of audit rigour in the final years of an audit appointment; and
- the limited choice of auditors for major corporations; others of the Big Four may be ineligible for various reasons such as working for a competitor or carrying out consulting work.

The Co-ordinating Group on Audit and Accounting Issues[14] does not recommend mandatory audit firm rotation. However, in the US, the *Sarbanes-Oxley Act 2002* requires the proposal to be given further consideration.

An alternative to rotation is compulsory retendering at the end of a set period. The Office of Fair Trading sees this as an opportunity to open up the market for listed company audits to mid-tier accounting firms. However, the Co-ordinating Group on Audit and Accounting Issues rejects the suggestion on the grounds that, if not properly controlled:

- the process could be flawed with the entity having no intention of replacing the incumbent firm of auditors; and
- it could encourage 'low-balling' whose potential dangers are explained below.

Even more extreme proposals have been suggested more recently, for example where auditors are directly appointed by a government body such as the Audit Commission which already has experience of appointing auditing firms to the audits of local authorities.[15]

Non-audit services

As explained in Chapter 1, firms of public accountants provide a range of services in addition to audits. The auditors of an entity have a competitive advantage over other accounting firms in providing non-audit services to that entity. First, knowledge gained during the audit reduces the cost of providing other services (e.g. preparing tax returns). Second, the audit provides the firm with a chance to identify opportunities for selling other services to the entity. As the revenue from non-audit services often exceeds that from audit services it is alleged that firms of accountants offer to supply audits at low cost in order to secure appointment as auditors. This practice is referred to as 'low-balling' and raises a number of issues that potentially affect audit quality. If, after appointment, the firm does not secure contracts for the supply of non-audit services, it will lose money on the audit and may be tempted to reduce the loss by lowering audit quality. The firm will also be reluctant to enter into disputes with management over audit and financial reporting matters lest it prejudice their access to contracts for non-audit services. Even without low-balling, the fact that auditors provide non-audit services to management may be seen as conflicting with audit independence and their duty of care to shareholders.

There is a vigorous debate as to whether auditors should provide non-audit services at all. Professional bodies see nothing wrong with the practice, subject to ethical safeguards to ensure that independence is not prejudiced. These parties argue that entities should be free to choose their professional advisers and may prefer to use an auditing firm in which they have confidence, and which may be able to provide a service at a lower cost than another. Disclosure of fees from non-audit services in the financial statements is already required by the *Companies Act 1985*[16] and the Combined Code on Corporate Governance[17] provides a market control over the extent of provision of such services. Such disclosure enables the securities market to form a view on whether the extent of non-audit services could threaten the auditors' independence and thus the reliability of the audited financial statements. In such a case, the share price would fall, thus signalling to management that it should reduce the number of other services which the audit firm provides.

It is further argued that the provision of non-audit services by audit firms both spreads good management practices and improves the quality of the audit. With their privileged access to audit clients, audit firms operate a legitimised industrial espionage service. Good practices observed while auditing one client can be sold to another as part of a management consultancy service, subject only to the requirement to observe confidentiality.

The modern audit approach stresses the importance of assessing the risks of financial report misstatement and concentrating audit effort on identified risks. A major contributor to the risk of financial report misstatement is the risk associated with the uncertainties of the business process and the ability of management to deal with such risks. The provision of non-audit services provides auditors with greater knowledge and understanding of the business and this enhances their ability to conduct a more effective audit.[18]

The alternative viewpoint is that auditors of public companies and similar entities should be banned from providing other services to the entity if public confidence in the auditors' independence from the influence of management is to be assured. It has been found, for example, that companies which face potentially high agency costs in management tend to require a smaller amount of non-audit services from the auditors, as the provision of non-audit services by the auditors is perceived to jeopardise the desired appearance of independence of the auditors.[19]

Professional judgement in accounting and auditing

Although accounting and auditing are based on relatively systematic techniques, few financial allegations result from methodological errors. Rather, many are cases of judgements about the appropriate use of a technique or standard. Some may be errors of judgement; others may result from either a misinterpretation of the problem, a lack of awareness due to complexity, or a failure to observe the ethical values of honesty, integrity, objectivity, due care, confidentiality and a commitment to the public interest. For example, an accounting treatment in accordance with a Financial Reporting Standard may be biased if it is based on inadequate or incomplete information wrongly judged to be sufficient to support it. A non-disclosure of an accounting item may not be a question of competence, but of misplaced loyalty to management, to a client, or to one's own self-interest, rather than to the public who rely on the information.

Auditing and Financial Reporting Standards, though a sound basis for professional practice, will not cover every contingency. In complex situations where the course of action is not clearly prescribed, accountants must be able to maintain integrity and objectivity in making a judgement. When a professional accountant finds a problem that exceeds his or her expertise, it is the professional's ethical values that will compel him or her to recognise such limitations, seek advice, remain objective and disclose the relevant facts. This is necessary to maintain the trust within a fiduciary relationship. There are cases, however (due to the complexity of business transactions), where Financial Reporting Standards and technical guidelines are insufficient to provide an objective basis for accounting treatment. Consequently, even though technical feasibility may govern the short-term solutions, in the longer term, ethical considerations such as the potential consequences of such accounting problems should dominate.

Priority of duty and loyalty

As the role of professional accountants is to provide fiduciary services to society as a whole, the performance of such services involves choices between the interests of various parties – the client or the employer of such services, the management of the client or employing organisation, the current and prospective investors of the business being examined, other stakeholders, employees, the government, etc. For example, auditors are appointed by the shareholders or members of the client to examine the financial affairs of the organisation. The underlying principle in this engagement is to protect the interest of the resource providers against possible pursuit of self-interests by management. To the extent that the stakeholders mentioned above are considered the 'public', the auditors have a fiduciary relationship with the public that requires the exercise of the same duties and values as would apply with a more direct contractual relationship. The choice of accounting and auditing methods and treatments that maximise certain current benefit at the expense of future income would therefore breach the trust required for the fiduciary arrangement with the public. Accordingly, the loyalty to the public should not be less than the loyalty owed to existing shareholders or owners. It is pertinent to note that defining the legal liability of auditors in this respect has been complex. The establishment of auditors' relationships with various parties has broadened the strict privity of contract in terms of liability. This is further discussed in Chapter 4.

For accountants employed within an organisation, there is no contractual relationship to shareholders or the public. However, in performing their duties to their employers, accountants are required to adhere to the values expected of a professional person by considering their responsibility to others who might be disadvantaged by an act at the request of their superior. Accountants employed in this capacity, therefore, need also to consider the accuracy and reliability of their work for the benefit of the end-user (that is, the public as the stakeholders). This situation is a complex one, entailing consideration of such debatable issues as confidentiality to one's employer, and the ethical premises for 'whistleblowing' (that is, where one discloses unethical deeds outside of an organisation). Although the code of a profession endeavours to provide guidelines to follow in difficult ethical situations, accountants often have to rely on personal integrity and values to make the 'right' decision. One viewpoint is that a professional accountant facing a difficult choice should consider that loyalty is owed to affected stakeholders in the following order: the public, the profession, the client/employer, and, finally, the individual.[20]

In recognition of the public significance of the work of accountants, particularly as auditors, and concerns that the professional bodies may be unduly influenced by the commercial considerations of their members, most of the standard setting activities of the profession have been transferred to an independent body, the Financial Reporting Council. While still harnessing the skills of the profession, the inclusion of lay members on many of the bodies supervised by the FRC, reassures society that their deliberations are not unduly influenced by purely professional concerns.

Professional competence

While the ethical provisions in the Code deal principally with business matters relating to public accounting, ethical responsibility also extends to technical competence. Competence is the product of education and experience. Education begins with preparation for entry into the profession and extends to continuing professional education (CPE) throughout the member's career. Experience involves on-the-job training and acceptance of increased responsibilities during a member's professional life. The professional bodies require members to maintain their level of competence throughout their professional career, and to undertake only work in which they are competent. Minimum annual CPE hours are prescribed for all members, holding a certificate of public practice. Compliance with these rules is monitored by requiring members to keep a personal record of time spent on CPE.

The audit expectation gap

Users of financial reports, such as investors, expect auditors to provide assurance concerning material fraud, irregularities, and the viability of the business and its management. When entities fail through fraud or mismanagement, there is a tendency to blame the auditors for not having given adequate warning of the problems. Until recently, the profession argued that the problem lay with users' failure to understand the role of the auditors, and the limitations of financial reporting. The profession has undertaken various measures, such as the introduction of expanded auditors' reports, to ensure that users are better informed and do not hold unrealistic expectations of the assurance provided by audited financial statements.

In recent years, however, the profession has come to recognise the need to undertake active measures to improve the quality of financial reporting so as to reduce any part of the gap caused by inadequate performance. Some of these measures relate directly to the audit function; for example, by improving the quality of audit work performed or by enhancing the independence of the auditors. As has been explained in this chapter, development of the audit function has been accelerated by initiatives undertaken in the wake of the collapse of Enron at the end of 2001.

Alongside the developments in auditing have been developments in corporate governance and this chapter has already made reference to the Combined Code on Corporate Governance. Improvements in financial reporting tend to be based on parallel developments in auditing and corporate governance.

CORPORATE GOVERNANCE IN REDUCING THE EXPECTATION GAP

Corporate governance refers to the role of directors in discharging their duties and has emerged as one of the best vehicles for reducing the expectation gap. Corporate best practice is demonstrated by various studies, such as the Treadway Report and the Cadbury Report. The Cadbury Committee issued a Code of Best Practice endorsed by the London Stock Exchange and included within its Listing Rules (now administered by the UK Listing Authority of the Financial Services Authority). Responsibility for the Code now rests with the Financial Reporting Council and its recommendations expanded by the Hampel Report of 1998, the Turnbull Report of 1999 and the Higgs and Smith Reports of 2003. Requirements of the Code of particular relevance to the audit include.

- separation of the functions of chairman and chief executive officer;
- maintenance of a balance of executive and independent non-executive directors on the board;
- accompanying financial statements with:
  - statements as to the separate responsibilities of directors and auditors; and
  - statement by directors that the business is a going concern;
- maintenance of a sound system of internal control whose effectiveness is reviewed annually with a report to shareholders that such a review has been performed;
- keeping under review the need for an internal audit function if it does not already exist; and
- establishing an audit committee of at least three non-executive directors to:
  - review the application of the financial reporting and internal control principles of the code;
  - consider the scope and effectiveness of the independent audit and the independence of the auditors; and
  - review the extent of provision of non-audit services by the auditors.

The function of the audit committee was explained in Chapter 2 and its responsibility for overseeing the independent auditor appointment in ensuring auditor independence has been explained earlier in this chapter.

The duty of the audit committee to review and report on the use of controls in managing the entity's risks will be explained in Chapter 7.

Going concern

A major cause of concern has been the unexpected failure of apparently healthy companies. Criticism is levelled at auditors under the belief that the most recent audited financial statements should have provided some warning of the impending failure. This problem has been addressed in two ways. The Combined Code on Corporate Governance requires directors to report whether their company is a going concern with supporting assumptions or qualifications as necessary. Auditors' responsibility for evaluating going concern is covered by ISA 570, Going Concern. This standard requires auditors to review evidence on which directors have based their presumption that the entity is a going concern. If the directors have failed to undertake a sufficient evaluation, the auditors may qualify their opinion on the financial statements on the grounds that there is insufficient evidence to determine the applicability of the going concern assumption. This requires auditors to put pressure on directors to consider risks threatening the future, which the directors might, otherwise, not have done. Threats are more likely to be identified and addressed and unexpected failure is less likely.

LEARNING **CHECK**

3.17 Auditors need to appreciate the current audit environment, which might present threats to the auditors in securing independence, quality of work, and objectivity. Features of the audit environment include competition, potential management pressure, the provision of non-audit services, and the discharge of professional judgement in interpreting and applying standards.

3.18 It is important that auditors be aware of duty and loyalty priorities when making difficult decisions. The auditors' decision may affect a number of stakeholders and it is important that the responsibility to serve the public interest is not diminished by competing interests.

3.19 Latest developments in the audit expectation gap investigations demonstrate the professional bodies' support for strengthening audit independence, while recognising the scope of the auditors' work in the interest of the public.

SUMMARY

Ethics deals with how people act towards one another and underpins the foundations of a profession. Accountants, like other professionals, are expected to demonstrate adherence to ethical values and professional conduct, in accordance with the norms established by their profession. This framework provides a basis for exercising their professional judgements and decisions.

The willingness of accountants to subscribe, voluntarily, to a written code of ethics has contributed significantly to the stature and reputation of the profession. The professional body's codes of conduct provide mechanisms for investigating complaints of unethical conduct, and imposing sanctions on members. These codes address the issue of professionalism through a set of fundamental principles, and prescribe practical and enforceable standards, which evolve over time to reflect changes in the profession and expectations by society.

However, the ethical environment in which accountants and auditors operate has been subject to a gap between the expectations of users and what the profession believes is required of auditors. In response, the profession has recently taken it upon itself to investigate improvements in financial reporting, thus reducing the number of instances where users are dissatisfied. In the process, auditors have involved other parties, including the governing bodies of the entities being audited, the government, and accounting and auditing standard setters. As a consequence, the role of the audit is undergoing intense scrutiny at the moment, and is evolving as one of the parties within the corporate governance structure. A recent change has been the recognition of the desirability to transfer responsibility for setting ethical codes relating to the audit function to an independent body in recognition of the significance of public interest in that function. Other developments arising out of this scrutiny are a greater emphasis on monitoring audit quality, clarification of the auditors' role in detecting and reporting fraud and illegal acts, and a re-emphasis of the importance of independence.

NOTES

[1] Greenwood, E. 'Attributes of a Profession', *Social Work* (July 1957), pp. 45–55.

[2] Brooks, L. J. *Professional Ethics for Accountants*, West Publishing 1995.

[3] *Report of the National Commission on Fraudulent Financial Reporting.* A report by Sir James Treadway, Chairperson, National Commission on Fraudulent Financial Reporting, Washington USA 1987.

[4] *Report of the Committee on the Financial Aspects of Corporate Governance*, chaired by Sir Adrian Cadbury, London 1992.

[5] Proposals for regulating the accountancy profession were first discussed in the Department of Trade and Industry's 1998 Consultative Document 'A Framework for Independent Regulation for the Profession' and the Consultative Committee of Accountancy Bodies' 1998 paper 'Modernising Regulation – The Proposals of the Leading Accountancy Bodies'. The proposals led to the creation of the Accountancy Foundation in 2002. However, following the more recent review, the bodies making up the Accountancy Foundation were reorganised and transferred to the Financial Reporting Council in 2003.

[6] Minz, S. M. *Cases in Accounting Ethics and Professionalism*, 2nd edn, McGraw-Hill Inc., 1992.

[7] The American Accounting Association (AAA) model originates from Rockness, J. W. & Langenderfer, H. Q. (1989) who introduced a seven-step decision-making model. These steps are to (1) determine the facts, (2) define the ethical issue, (3) identify the major principles, rules and values involved, (4) specify alternatives, (5) compare the values and alternatives and see if a clear decision emerges, (6) assess the consequences, and (7) make a decision.

[8] Joint Ethics Committee of the Institutes of Chartered Accountants of England & Wales, Scotland and Ireland (the Institutes), *Guide to Professional Ethics,* the Association of Chartered Certified Accountants, *The Rules of Professional Conduct*, and the IFAC's *Code of Ethics for Professional Accountants.*

[9] Beattie, V., Fearnley, S. & Brandt, R. 'Perceptions of Auditor Independence: UK Evidence', *Journal of International Accounting, Auditing and Taxation*, 1999.

[10] Closely connected persons are spouses, cohabitees, minor children and companies in which an interest of 20% or more is held.

[11] Financial Reporting Council, Combined Code on Corporate Governance, paras C3.2 and C3.7, FRC 2003.

[12] Institute of Chartered Accountants of Scotland, *Auditing into the Twenty First Century*, 1993.

[13] Auditing Practices Board, *The Audit Agenda*, 1994.

[14] Co-ordinating Group on Audit and Accounting Issues, *Final Report*, Department of Trade and Industry URN 03/567, 2003.

[15] Chartered Institute of Public Finance and Accountancy, an Assessment of the Possible Application of the Public Sector Audit Model to the UK Private Sector, CIPFA, 2002.

[16] Following a recommendation by the Cadbury Committee.

[17] Financial Reporting Council, Combined Code on Corporate Governance, paras C3.2 and C3.7, FRC 2003.

[18] Gwilliam, D. *Audit Methodology, Risk Management and Non-audit Services; What Can We Learn from the Recent Past and What Lies Ahead*, P. D. Leake Lecture, Institute of Chartered Accountants in England & Wales, May 2003.

Jeppeson, K. 'Reinventing Auditing, Redefining Consulting and Independence', *European Accounting Review*, September 1998.

Power, M. *The Audit Implosion: Regulating Risk from the Inside*, Centre for Business Performance, ICAEW, 2000.

[19] Firth, M. 'The Provision of Non-audit Services by Accounting Firms to their Audit Clients', *Contemporary Accounting Research* (Vol. 14, No. 2, Summer 1997), pp. 1–21.

[20] Brooks, L. J. *Professional Ethics for Accountants*, West Publishing, 1995.

FURTHER READING

Abbott, L. J., Parker, S., Peters, G. F. & Raghunandan, K. 'An Empirical Investigation of Audit Fees, Nonaudit Fees, and Audit Committees', *Contemporary Accounting Research* (Vol. 20, Issue 2, 2003), pp. 215–235.

Auditing Practices Board. 'Fraud and Audit: Choices for Society', 1998.

Beattie, V. & Brandt, R. 'Perceptions of Auditor Independence: U.K. Evidence', *Journal of International Accounting Auditing & Taxation* (Vol. 8, Issue 1, 1999), pp. 67–108.

Beattie, V. & Fearnley, S. 'Audit Market Competition: Auditor Changes and the Impact of Tendering', *British Accounting Review* (September 1998), pp. 261–290.

Beattie, V, Brandt, R. & Fearnley, S. 'Look to Your Laurels', *Accountancy* (July 1997), pp. 140–141.

Bell, T. B. & Carcello, J. V. 'A Decision Aid for Assessing the Likelihood of Fraudulent Financial Reporting', *Auditing: A Journal of Practice and Theory* (Vol. 19, No. 1, 2000), pp. 169–184.

Catanach, Jr., Walker, A. H. & Source, P. L. 'The International Debate Over Mandatory Auditor Rotation: A Conceptual Research Framework', *Journal of International Accounting Auditing & Taxation* (Vol. 8, Issue 1, 1999), pp. 43–67.

Citron, D. B. 'The UK's Framework Approach to Auditor Independence and the Commercialization of the Accounting Profession', *Accounting, Auditing & Accountability Journal* (Vol. 16, No. 2, 2003), pp. 244–274.

Cohen, J. M., Ganesh, K. & Wright, A. M. 'Corporate Governance and the Audit Process', *Contemporary Accounting Research* (Vol. 19, Issue 4, 2002), pp. 573–595.

Colbert, J. L. 'Corporate Governance: Communications from Internal and External Auditors', *Managerial Auditing Journal* (Vol. 17, No. 3, 2002), pp. 147–152.

Dewing, I. P. & Russell, P. O. 'UK Fund Managers, Audit Regulation and the New Accountancy Foundation: Towards a Narrowing of the Audit Expectations Gap?', *Managerial Auditing Journal* (Vol. 17, No. 9, 2002), pp. 537–545.

Ezzamel, M., Gwilliam, D. R. & Holland, K. M. 'Some Empirical Evidence from Publicly Quoted UK Companies on the Relationship Between the Pricing of Audit and Non-Audit Services', *Accounting and Business Research* (Winter 1996), pp. 3–16.

Institute of Chartered Accountants of Scotland. *Auditing into the Twenty-First Century*, 1993.

International Federation of Accountants. 'Code of Ethics for Professional Accountants'.

Jeppesen, K. K. 'Reinventing Auditing, Redefining Consulting and Independence', *The European Accounting Review* (Vol. 7, No. 3, 1998), pp. 517–539.

Kinney, W. R. Jr. 'Auditor Independence: A Burdensome Constraint or Core Value?', *Accounting Horizons* (March 1999), pp. 69–75.

McEnroe, J. E. & Martens, S. C. 'Auditors' and Investors' Perceptions of the "Expectation Gap"', *Accounting Horizons* (Vol. 15, Issue 4, 2001), pp. 345–359.

Makkawi, B. & Schick, A. 'Are Auditors Sensitive Enough to Fraud?', *Managerial Auditing Journal* (Vol. 18, No. 6, 2003), pp. 591–598.

Mautz, R. K. & Sharaf, H. A. *The Philosophy of Auditing*. American Accounting Association, Sarasota, Florida, 1961.

Owusu-Ansah, S., Moyes, G. D., Oyelere, P. B & Hay, D. 'An Empirical Analysis of the Likelihood of Detecting Fraud in New Zealand', *Managerial Auditing Journal* (Vol. 17, No. 4, 2002), pp. 192–204.

Percy, J. P. 'Auditing and Corporate Governance – A Look Forward into the 21st Century', *International Journal of Auditing* (Vol. 1, No. 1, 1997), pp. 3–12.

Shafer, W. E., Morris, R. E. & Ketchand, A. A. 'Effects of Personal Values on Auditors' Ethical Decisions', *Accounting, Auditing & Accountability Journal* (Vol. 14, No. 3, 2001), pp. 254–277.

Shelton, S. W., Whittington, O. R. & Landsittel, D. 'Auditing Firms' Fraud Risk Assessment Practices', *Accounting Horizons* (Vol. 15, Issue 1, 2001), pp. 19–34.

Thomas, A. R. & Gibson, K. M. 'Management is Responsible Too', *Journal of Accountancy* (April 2003).

Wallman, S. M. H. 'The Future of Accounting, Part III: Reliability and Auditor Independence', *Accounting Horizons* (December 1997), pp. 76–97.

Wolnizer, P. W. 'Are Audit Committees Red Herrings?', *Abacus* (Vol. 31, No. 1, 1995), pp. 45–66.

MULTIPLE-CHOICE QUESTIONS

Choose the best answer for each of the following
(Answers are on page 598)

3.1   What *should* differentiate a 'professional' from a 'non-professional' culture?
   (a)   Professionals generally earn higher salaries.
   (b)   Non-professionals do not have community sanction or ethical codes.
   (c)   A professional provides a service to society as a social good to benefit the community.

    (d)   Because professionals have a monopoly over a body of knowledge, they are required to be monitored by the government.

3.2   Which of the following best describes why the accounting profession issued a Code of Professional Conduct and established means for ensuring its observance?
    (a)   A requirement for a profession is the establishment of ethical standards that stress primarily a responsibility to clients and colleagues.
    (b)   A distinguishing mark of a profession is its acceptance of responsibility to the public.
    (c)   An essential means of self-protection for a profession is the establishment of ethical standards.
    (d)   The government requires that all professions establish a code of ethics.

3.3   Which of the following is most likely to be ethically unacceptable?
    (a)   Sending a brochure to all managing directors of the top 50 firms in your local region advertising your services.
    (b)   Earning a large commission for recommending life insurance services to a client.
    (c)   Receiving a bonus for performing the annual audit of a client within a prescribed time period.
    (d)   Holding client's monies in trust for extended periods of time.

3.4   Which of the following would be deemed acceptable by the accounting profession in evaluating whether a firm was maintaining independence?
    (a)   Ownership of shares by auditors of a firm in their audit clients.
    (b)   The son of a partner within the firm having a material beneficial interest in the audit client.
    (c)   A recently retired partner of an audit firm taking a position as a non-executive director of one of the firm's audit clients.
    (d)   The audit firm having a number of clients within the same industry.

3.5   An audit independence issue might be raised by auditors' participation in management advisory services engagements. Which of the following statements is most consistent with the profession's attitude towards this issue?
    (a)   Information obtained as a result of a management advisory services engagement is confidential to that specific engagement and should not influence performance of the audit function.
    (b)   The decision as to loss of independence must be made by the client based on the facts of the particular case.
    (c)   The auditor should not make management decisions for an audit client.
    (d)   The auditor who is asked to review management decisions is also competent to make these decisions, and can do so without loss of independence.

3.6   How are auditors normally appointed to audit a public company?
    (a)   By directors on behalf of the shareholders.
    (b)   By committee of shareholders.
    (c)   By being selected by the Financial Controller from a number of tenders submitted.
    (d)   By being selected by the largest shareholder.

3.7   What does a signed audit report mean with respect to the 'possibility' of fraud within a company?

(a) There is a reasonable expectation that material irregularities due to fraud have been detected.

(b) It is unlikely that immaterial irregularities have been detected; however, all material irregularities should have been detected.

(c) An audit is not designed to detect fraud; therefore, an audit report gives no assurance as to whether fraud did or did not occur during the year.

(d) All fraud should have been detected.

DISCUSSION QUESTIONS

3.1 Responsibility for statutory audits makes the accounting profession different from any other in terms of its duty to society. Discuss.

3.2 Critics argue that the professional accountancy bodies are no more than trade associations for the benefit of their members. Do you agree?

3.3 It is suggested that the holders of senior financial positions in public companies should be members of the accounting profession. Why might this be so?

3.4 Is there an ethical conflict within the practice of public accountancy between running the practice as a business with a view to profit maximisation and providing a professional service?

3.5 Distinguish between the fact and the appearance of independence. Why might the latter be regarded as more important?

3.6 The provision of non-audit services by auditors may expose the auditor to each of the five threats to independence. Explain.

3.7 Fraud risk is advanced as being a combination of incentive, opportunity and rationalisation. Explain this in the case of fiddling travel expense claims.

3.8 Discuss the extent of an auditor's responsibilities for breaches of health and safety regulations.

3.9 Consider the arguments for and against audit rotation.

3.10 Consider the arguments for and against allowing the provision of non-audit services by the audit firm.

PROFESSIONAL APPLICATION QUESTIONS

(Suggested answers are on pages 610–611)

3.1 Professionalism

You are the auditor for a company. In discussion with one of the company's accounts department employees, you are advised as follows:

'You accountants think you are something special calling yourself "professionals". I do not think it is appropriate. There have been so many cases recently where accountants have been found to have acted dishonestly or unethically. I don't think that your organisation acts any differently to my trade union. Both our groups act in the best interests of their members. To claim that your organisation upholds higher virtues or values than mine is rubbish! Even if it did, your members would still act in their own best interests anyway – people always try to maximise their own personal interest.'

Required

Explain how you would try to convince the cynical accounts department employee that the accounting profession can make a valid claim to being professional.

3.2 Ethical issues

The following situations involve Sarah Scruples, an audit senior with the accounting firm of Fobel & Hirst. She is involved with the audit of Freelance Ferries Ltd (Freelance).

1. The accounts clerk of Freelance resigned two months ago and has not been replaced. As a result, Freelance's transactions have not been recorded and the books are not up to date. To comply with the terms of a loan agreement, Freelance needs to prepare interim financial statements but cannot do so until the books are posted. The managing director of Freelance wants Sarah to help them out because she performed the audit last year. The audit partner of Fobel & Hirst allows them to use her for one month before the start of the annual audit.
2. During the annual audit of Freelance, Sarah discovered Freelance had materially understated net income on last year's tax return. The client is unwilling to take corrective action. Sarah decides to inform the taxation office.
3. On completion of the fieldwork of the audit of Freelance, Sarah is offered six free cinema tickets by the managing director. He tells her this gesture is meant to show his appreciation of a job well done. Sarah accepts the tickets.
4. The partner of Fobel & Hirst is not very pleased with the time Freelance is taking to pay its audit fee for the year. He decides to take £5000 out of a trust fund that Fobel & Hirst holds for Freelance. He intends to replace it as soon as Freelance sends payment of its audit fee.

Required

For each of the above four situations (a) identify the ethical issues involved, and (b) discuss whether there has or has not been any violation of ethical conduct. Support your answers by reference to the relevant professional statements.

AUDITORS' LEGAL LIABILITY

LEARNING **OBJECTIVES**

After studying this chapter, you should be able to:

1   comprehend the impact of the changing legal environment on the profession

2   explain auditors' liabilities to shareholders and auditees

3   describe the concept of due care owed by auditors to those entitled to rely on their services

4   explain the circumstances giving rise to negligence in the conduct of audit

5   identify the issues and rulings of legal cases with respect to the auditors' liability to third parties

6   enumerate the precautions the auditor should take to avoid litigation

7   describe the types and rationale of legal reforms concerning auditor liability.

Auditors are accountable in law for their professional conduct. This responsibility may arise under common law or under statute law. Responsibility under common law may be under contract to clients or, in certain circumstances, to third parties to whom a legal duty of care is owed. Also of interest is the extent of liability in terms of the determination of damages awarded by the courts where negligence is proved; and defences that may be offered by the auditors in full or part mitigation of their responsibility.

These issues are illustrated by reference to decided cases. The extent of auditors' statutory responsibilities is also described. The vulnerability of the auditing profession to negligence lawsuits has been brought to notice in recent years by two sets of events. The first is the litigation crisis and the second is the debate over the limitation of company auditors' exposure to liability.

THE LEGAL ENVIRONMENT

Throughout its history, the public accounting profession has had an extremely low percentage of alleged audit failures to the total number of audits conducted. In recent years, both the volume and cost of litigation related to alleged audit deficiencies have caused some concern to the profession. This can be attributed, in part, to several widely reported business failures that resulted in significant losses to investors. However, not all business failures can be equated to audit failures. There is a growing concern that too often following a business failure and alleged fraudulent financial reporting, the plaintiffs and their legal representatives prey on the auditors regardless of degree of fault, simply because the auditors may be the only party left with sufficient financial resources to indemnify the plaintiffs' losses (the so-called 'deep pockets' theory).

The requirement to hold a practising certificate imposes an obligation on auditors to carry professional indemnity insurance for possible liability to their clients and members of the public. This source of compensation creates a perception that auditors have 'deep pockets' and, arguably, it contributes significantly to the extent of claims filed against them. There is a presumption that the courts, finding this source of compensation a means of loss spreading, are easily influenced by the arguments of the plaintiffs' solicitors.

On the other hand, accountants should be aware of the trap generally known as the 'no transaction' claim. A typical example of this is where a client enters into a risky venture, supported by funding from a financier. For a minimal fee, the accountant provides advice with respect to a certain aspect of the venture. If the venture fails the client, the financier, or both, may sue the accountant. The basis for their case is that were it not for the accountant's negligent advice, the venture would not have proceeded, and consequently the accountant should compensate the client or the financier for all losses following the failed venture. This argument ignores the fact that the negligent advice in question may have caused only a small part of the total loss. The loss may actually be due to a combination of factors, including bad business decisions on the client's part, the financier's breaching of its own prudential standards, or external influences such as economic downturn.

Assuming that the 'no transaction' claims are accepted by the courts, the test for adequacy of an accountancy practice's limit of indemnity ought not to be the level of fees earned. Rather, it should be a value based on the transactions undertaken by the clients, which is difficult to estimate. Therefore, how much professional indemnity is enough is impossible to estimate.

The settlement of claims by insurance companies leads to increases in future premiums. Consequently, professional indemnity insurance is becoming increasingly and almost unacceptably expensive. Insurance premiums can vary substantially, depending on the firm's claims, experience and risk profile. A benchmark of around 1 to 2% of turnover has been quoted. Furthermore, the cover that can be obtained often falls well short of meeting the claims that are being made. This coverage gap between the potential liability and available insurance cover exposes auditors to the risk of significant personal liability. Many argue that this represents a real threat to the viability of the profession. Another factor that can further influence litigation against auditors is the increasing internationalisation of the profession. International firms may well be caught up directly in lawsuits originating overseas. UK firms auditing controlled entities or branches of multi-national companies with overseas creditors and ownership interest could well find themselves being sued in overseas courts.

The litigation crisis

Litigation against auditors is argued to be having an adverse effect. Firms are retreating from serving high-risk clients, and some smaller firms are shying away from audits – a trend that is counter to the public interest. The litigation crisis is also causing professional staff to question their continued association with audit firms, and deterring new graduates from entering into public practice. How can a profession with a multi-level regulatory framework, including technical, ethical and quality control standards, and a system of quality or practice reviews, find itself in such a predicament? Certainly, there have been some audits that did not measure up to existing standards. Some litigation can also be attributed to the audit expectation gap discussed in Chapter 3. This chapter examines the issues of auditors' liability to client companies and to third parties and discusses the latest developments in limiting professional liability.

◿ LEARNING **CHECK**

4.1 Allegations against accountants have arisen from many factors, including what is known as the 'deep pocket' theory and the audit expectation gap.

4.2 The cost of maintaining sufficient indemnity to meet the cost of claims adds significantly to total audit costs. Moreover, the threat of the firm being involved in major lawsuits, even if successfully defended, discourages potential new entrants to the profession.

LIABILITY TO SHAREHOLDERS AND AUDITEES

For audits conducted in accordance with the *Companies Act 1985*, the auditors are liable under statute and common law to the shareholders for any negligent performance of statutory duties. These duties cannot be restricted or reduced.

Auditors are also liable in the same manner as any other citizen for cases of fraud or defamation. One of the major problems in accepting greater responsibility for reporting suspected fraud to a regulatory body is that, if the auditors are mistaken, they may be liable to an action for defamation by the party identified by the auditors as perpetrating the fraud. Also, negligence, if proven to be wilful, may constitute a conspiracy with management to defraud the company or other parties. Auditors in the UK and the USA have found themselves in court on the criminal charge of fraud after issuing unqualified reports on financial statements subsequently found to be misleading.

In respect of the provision of auditing services, auditors are liable to compensate a plaintiff if:

- a duty of care is owed to the plaintiff;
- the audit is negligently performed or the opinion negligently given;
- the plaintiff has suffered a loss as a result of the auditors' negligence (causal relationship as reasonably foreseeable); and
- the loss is quantifiable.

Due care

The development of the concept of due care as applied to the performance of auditors' duties is examined by means of cases decided in the courts. Consideration is then given to the relevance of professional standards; namely of:

- Auditing Standards in determining the adequate performance of audit work; and
- Financial Reporting Standards in determining the basis for expressing an opinion as to truth and fairness.

The classic statement of the extent of auditor responsibility in performing an examination of the accounts to be reported on is contained in the Kingston Cotton Mill Co. case of 1896. The key facts and judgement of this case are featured below.

KINGSTON COTTON MILL CO. (No. 2) (1896) 2 Ch. 279

Facts of the case: For several years the manager of Kingston Cotton Mill had been exaggerating the quantities and values of the company's stocks so as to fraudulently overstate the company's profits. This came to light when the company was unable to pay its debts and its true financial position was revealed. The auditor had relied on a certificate signed by the manager and ensured that the amount appearing in the accounts was consistent with that certificate. The valuation of stocks was described in the accounts as being as 'per manager's certificate'. In line with contemporary practice, the auditor did not physically observe stocks or attempt to verify the valuation of individual items. Neither did the auditor reconcile stocks with the opening balance and purchases and sales during the year, all of which would have alerted the auditor that something was amiss.

Judgement: As regards stocks, Justice Lindley had the following to say:

> I confess that I cannot see that their omission to check his [the manager's] returns was a breach of their duty to the company. It is no part of the auditor's duty to take stock. No-one contends that it is. He must rely on other people for details of the stock-in-trade in hand. In the case of a cotton mill he must rely on some skilled person for the materials necessary to enable him to enter the stock-in-trade at its proper value in the balance sheet.

In relation to the auditor's responsibilities in general, particularly the detection of fraud, the following points from the judgement of Justice Lopes are important:

> It is the duty of an auditor to bring to bear on the work he has to perform that skill, care and caution which a reasonably competent, careful and cautious auditor would use. What is reasonable skill, care and caution must depend on the particular circumstances of each case. An auditor is not bound to be a detective, or, as was said, to approach his work with suspicion or with a foregone conclusion that there is something wrong. He is a watchdog, but not a bloodhound. He is justified in believing tried servants of the company in whom confidence is placed by the company. He is entitled to assume that they are honest, and to rely upon their representations, provided he takes reasonable care. If there is anything calculated to excite suspicion, he should probe it to the bottom but, in the absence of anything of that kind, he is only bound to be reasonably cautious and careful.
>
> The duties of auditors must not be rendered too onerous. Their work is responsible and laborious, and the remuneration moderate.
>
> Auditors must not be made responsible for not tracking out ingenious and carefully laid schemes of fraud, when there is nothing to arouse their suspicion and when those frauds are perpetrated by tried servants of the company and are undetected for years by the directors. So to hold would make the position of an auditor intolerable.

> The Kingston Cotton Mill case laid down some fundamental auditing principles such as the 'watchdog' rule and the notion of reasonable skill and care.

An equally famous case dealing with the auditors' responsibility for reporting on the accounts is the 1895 London and General Bank case.

LONDON AND GENERAL BANK (No. 2) (1895) 2 Ch. 673

Facts of the case: The bank made loans to customers for which it held inadequate security. Interest due on the loans was accrued but not received, yet dividends were paid out of profits arising from such interest. The auditor made a full report to the directors as to the valuation of these loans and the need for a provision for bad debts against both the loan and the accrued interest. However, in his report to the shareholders, the auditor merely qualified his opinion with the sentence, 'The value of the assets as shown on the balance sheet is dependent upon realisation'.

Judgement: As regards the auditor's responsibility for reporting, Justice Lindley observed:

> It is no part of an auditor's duty to give advice either to directors or shareholders as to what they ought to do.
> It is nothing to him whether the business of the company is being conducted prudently or imprudently, profitably or unprofitably; it is nothing to him whether dividends are properly or improperly declared, provided he discharges his own duty to shareholders. His business is to ascertain and state the true financial position of the company at the time of the audit and his duty is confined to that.
> He is not an insurer; he does not guarantee that the books do correctly show the true position of the company's affairs; he does not guarantee that the balance sheet is accurate according to the books of the company. If he did, he would be responsible for an error on his part, even if he were himself deceived, without any want of reasonable care on his part – say, by the fraudulent concealment of a book from him. His obligation is not so onerous as this.
> Such I take to be the duty of the auditor: he must be honest – that is, he must not certify what he does not believe to be true, and he must take reasonable care and skill before he believes that what he certifies is true.

As to the specific issues of the case, however, Justice Lindley had the following to say:

> It is a mere truism to say that the value of loans and securities depends upon their realisation. We are told that a statement to that effect is so unusual that the mere presence of those words is enough to excite suspicion. But, as already

stated, the duty of an auditor is to convey information, not to arouse enquiry, and although an auditor might infer from an unusual statement that something was seriously wrong, it by no means follows that ordinary people would have their suspicions aroused by a similar statement if, as in this case, its language expresses no more than an ordinary person would infer without it.

The judgement also discussed at length the extent of inquiry necessary to enable an auditor to express an opinion on the accounts. This part of the judgement was relied on by Justice Lopes in arriving at his judgement as to the auditor's responsibilities in the Kingston Cotton Mill Co. case.

IMPLICATIONS OF THE KINGSTON COTTON MILL CO. AND LONDON AND GENERAL BANK CASES

These two cases have formed the basis for all subsequent decisions as to the determination of auditor's negligence. Of crucial importance in both instances is the recognition of auditing as a profession. The auditors do not guarantee that the financial statements give a true and fair view any more than solicitors guarantee to win a case, or doctors to effect a cure. Neither do auditors warrant to bring to bear the highest degree of skill in the performance of their duties, since there may well be more skilful auditors within the profession. Neither are the auditors necessarily answerable for an error of judgement provided they exercise the skill and care of reasonably competent and well informed members of the profession.

Nevertheless, a too literal interpretation of the Kingston Cotton Mill Co. case has been criticised as retarding the development of improved auditing practices. For 60 years after the case, auditors continued to rely heavily on management representations (such as stock certificates), notwithstanding developments in auditing techniques that enabled the auditors to acquire a significantly higher degree of assurance with relatively little increase in audit effort.

In fraud detection, experience led auditors to anticipate common frauds and to design audit procedures so as to have a reasonable chance of detecting such frauds; nonetheless they continued to rely on the Kingston Cotton Mill Co. case in denying any legal responsibility for the detection of fraud where their suspicions were not aroused.

The developments in the USA arose out of criticisms of auditors contained in the Securities and Exchange Commission's report of 1941 into the McKesson and Robbins fraud. From that date, the evaluation of internal control, attendance at stocktaking and the circularisation of debtors became required procedure in that country.

A comparable advance in the UK came about with Lord Denning's observation in *Fomento (Stirling Area) Ltd v. Selsdon Fountain Pen Co. Ltd* (1958) 1 WLR 45 at 61 as to an auditor's approach:

... he must come to it with an enquiring mind – not suspicious of dishonesty, I agree – but suspecting that someone may have made a mistake somewhere and that a check must be made to ensure that there has been none.

Auditors hold themselves out as possessing special skills. As a result, the courts will require a higher standard of care. Justice Pennyquick's observation in Thomas Gerrard & Son Ltd (1967) 2 All ER 525 at 536 was another advance:

> The real ground on which re Kingston Cotton Mill Co. (No. 2) is, I think, capable of being distinguished is that standards of reasonable care and skill are, on the expert evidence, more exacting today than those which prevailed in 1896. I see considerable force in this contention.

Negligence

Negligence has been defined as any conduct which is careless or unintentional in nature and entails a breach of any contractual duty or duty of care in tort owed to another person or persons. The auditors' duty of care to a client arises either in contract or in the tort of negligence. If the auditors have been negligent, the client may sue them for breach of an implicit term of the contract to exercise reasonable care and skill in order to recover any consequential loss suffered. The client may sue the auditors in the tort of negligence to obtain damages sufficient to restore the client to its original position. The case of negligence is, however, very much dependent on the court's judgement under the circumstances of the case. Compliance with Financial Reporting Standards, Auditing Standards and other guidelines provides a certain degree of assurance that the auditors have exercised reasonable care and skill.

In making a report, the auditors express an opinion as to whether the financial statements give a true and fair view of the affairs of the entity and its profit for the period. In most of the cases so far described, the plaintiff has alleged that the auditors' investigation was flawed, thus preventing the auditors from being in a position to express an opinion. There have been very few cases against the auditors solely on the grounds that the financial statements did not give a true and fair view of the entity's financial position or that, as in the London and General Bank case, any qualification in the auditors' report was not sufficiently informative as to the extent of the financial statement's failure to give a true and fair view. In the 1970s, a period of high inflation, it was argued that financial statements based on the historical cost convention were misleading, yet financial statements based on this convention continued to be prepared and to be reported on by auditors as presenting a true and fair view.

Although the *Companies Act 1985* requires financial statements to be prepared in accordance with applicable Accounting Standards unless there are exceptional circumstances, the auditors must still exercise judgement as to the application of standards to the specific circumstances of the entity being reported on. Judgement must also be exercised in those rare circumstances where compliance with Accounting Standards would not give a true and fair view and the true and fair override is invoked.

In the USA, the right of the auditors to rely on Generally Accepted Accounting Principles (GAAPs) is also subject to an overriding requirement for fair presentation. GAAPs are those principles laid down by authoritative pronouncements of the Financial Accounting Standards Board and its predecessor bodies, and other accounting practices for which there is substantial authoritative support. In *Continental Vending (United States) v. Simon*

(1969), 425 F 2d 796, it was held that the requirement to report on fairness is separate from the requirement to report on compliance with GAAPs. The US profession has challenged this finding by issuing an Auditing Standard requiring fairness to be determined within the framework of GAAPs.

The collapse of Enron in 2001 arose in part from an understatement of its liabilities in prior years through the use of special purpose entities. These entities were so constituted as not to fall into the category of controlled entities required to be included in the consolidated financial statements. By transferring liabilities to these special purpose entities Enron was able to avoid having to recognise them on its consolidated balance sheet. The entities were constructed, with the advice of the accounting firm Arthur Andersen (which was also Enron's auditor), to exploit a loophole in the rules incorporated in US Financial Reporting Standards. As auditors, Andersen claimed that Enron's financial statements were fairly presented in accordance with generally accepted accounting practices. As a result the US is currently reviewing its financial reporting standards setting process with a view to reducing their appearance as 'rules' and to re-emphasise the professional need for judgement as to fairness in the light of more general principles. The subsequent outcry has reinforced the importance of the concept of fairness and warns auditors against undue reliance on the narrow interpretation of Financial Reporting Standards in condoning an accounting treatment that is manifestly inconsistent with economic reality.

In determining whether an audit has been negligently performed, compliance with Auditing Standards is a necessary first consideration. This has become particularly true in recent years. Prior to 1995 there was only a single Auditing Standard in the UK supplemented by non mandatory guidelines. Since 1995 a more rigorous set of standards has been in force derived from International Standards on Auditing which, themselves, become the authoritative standards in 2005. Moreover, the foreword to International Standards on Auditing has recently been amended to give authority to the entire wording of each standard. Previously only key requirements were mandatory, the so-called black-letter standards, with the grey lettering merely constituting guidance. A further development has been the transfer of responsibility for setting Auditing Standards from the direct control of professional bodies to a body wholly independent of the profession. Whereas it used to be said that Auditing Standards would guide the courts but not constrain them if they felt that performance consistent with the standards still fell short of reasonable expectations, compliance with the standards is now more likely to constitute a good defence against negligence. However, the acceptability of the current Auditing Standards has not yet been effectively tested by the courts.

Privity of contract

The term 'privity of contract' refers to the contractual relationship that exists between two or more contracting parties. In a typical auditing relationship, it is assumed that an audit (or audit-related service) is to be performed in accordance with professional standards unless the contract (engagement letter) contains specific wording to the contrary. Remember, also, that where auditors are appointed under the *Companies Act 1985* then, under s.310 of that Act, any contractual reduction of the auditors' liability is void.

There is sometimes misunderstanding as to the parties to the contract in an audit under the Companies Act where the auditors' report is addressed to the members. The term 'members' is used collectively and does not indicate responsibility to individual shareholders or to others entitled to receive copies of the accounts. The auditors may be sued, under contract, only by the directors or, more commonly, by the liquidator or receiver, in respect of losses incurred by the company arising out of the auditors' negligence. Monies recovered by way of damages from the auditors are applied first to meet the prior claims of creditors, with only the residue, if any, being available for the shareholders. Individual shareholders, creditors, employees, directors and others have no claim against the auditors under contract.

Causal relationship

A causal relationship exists between the breach of duty by the defendant and the loss or harm suffered by the plaintiff. This relationship must have been reasonably foreseeable, and it must be proven that the loss suffered is attributable to the negligent conduct of the auditors in a negligent case. In *Caparo Industries PLC v. Dickman & Others* (1990) 1 All ER 568, Lord Bridge stated:

> In advising the client who employs him, the professional man owes a duty to exercise that standard of skill and care appropriate to his professional status and will be liable both in contract and in tort for all losses which his client may suffer by reason of any breach of that duty.

The application of the principal of causal relationship is illustrated by the case below.

GALOO LTD V. BRIGHT GRAHAM MURRAY (1994) BCC 319

Facts of the case: For the purposes of appreciating the development of audit liability, a recent decision of the English Court of Appeal in the *Galoo Ltd v. Bright Graham Murray* case has reaffirmed the causation relationship requirement in order to establish the liability of the auditor. Galoo Ltd had incurred losses of £25 million between 1986 and 1990, and had paid a dividend of £500,000 in 1988. It sued the auditor for breach of its contractual duty to exercise reasonable care and skill, maintaining that the trading losses were attributable to the continued existence of the company, which, in turn, was due to reliance on the allegedly negligent audit opinions.

Judgement: The court of appeal held that there was no causal connection between the alleged negligence and the losses incurred. The financial reports may have allowed the company to continue trading, but the company's existence was not the cause of its losses. The claim against the auditor was struck out.

Contributory negligence

Contributory negligence relates to the failure of the plaintiff to meet certain required standards of care. It contributes to bringing about the loss in question, together with the defendant's negligence. The judgement in the Australian AWA case is the landmark decision on contributory negligence in an auditor–client relationship.

AWA LTD V. DANIELS T/A DELOITTE HASKINS & SELLS & ORS (1992) 10 ACLC 933

Facts of the case: This case provides a landmark for the principle of contributory negligence. Under the established principle that the auditor's duty has to be evaluated in the light of the standards of today, the auditor was held to have been negligent in failing to warn management of internal control weaknesses discovered during the course of the audit, even though that was not the principal purpose of the audit. An important development, however, was that the company was held to be guilty of contributory negligence through not establishing adequate controls in the first place. This reverses findings of earlier cases in which it was held that the extent of an auditor's responsibility was not diminished by failings of management that contributed to the losses.

Judgement: In the AWA case, the court accepted that the directors have a duty to establish a sound system of internal control to safeguard the company's assets. Their failure to do so was held to be contributory negligence. In the words of the judgement:

> ... the primary complaints of the plaintiff are failure on the part of the auditors to report on the insufficiency and inappropriateness of the plaintiff's internal controls. Now that was not the principal purpose of the audit. It was something that the auditors discovered in the course of preparing to do their audit. I am of the view that AWA should be held to have been guilty of contributory negligence ... Contributory negligence is a plaintiff's failure to meet the standard of care to which it is required to conform for its own protection and which is a legally contributing cause, together with the defendants' default, in bringing about the loss.

In May 1995, Australia's New South Wales Court of Appeal reduced the auditor's share of the damages, placing further responsibility on AWA management. The court upheld the notion of proportionate liability. As a result, AWA management shared from 20% to 33.3% of the loss, the auditors' liability was reduced from 72% to 66.6%, and the Chief Executive Officer's responsibility was reduced from 8% to zero.

Damages

Where auditors fail in their duty to act with reasonable care and skill, whether under contract or in tort, a plaintiff is entitled to recover any economic loss arising out of such breach of duty. Two issues need to be considered here. First, what is the purpose of financial reporting that may give rise to reliance reasonably being placed on them? Second, to what extent may responsibility for any loss be assigned on the one hand to the auditors' negligence, and on the other, to other causes and other parties?

The Australian Cambridge Credit case (1985 and 1987) provides a suitable basis for examining some of these issues. Cambridge Credit Corporation failed in 1974 and it was determined that the audit of the 1971 accounts had been negligently performed. Had the auditors' report been appropriately qualified, the amended view of the company's financial position would have required the trustee for the debenture holders to appoint a receiver. It was alleged that, through the auditors' negligence, the company was allowed to remain in business for a further three years, incurring further losses before a receiver was finally appointed in 1974. Damages were claimed in the amount of losses incurred by virtue of the company being liquidated in 1974 instead of 1971.

As regards the purpose of accounts, the law is much clearer on this than is most accounting theory. Accounts form the basis for the determination of legal relationships between the company and other parties. For instance, where dividends are paid out of capital (contrary to the provisions of the Companies Act) because of an overstatement of profits, the auditors are liable to the extent of such dividends. In the Cambridge Credit case, the debenture trust deed provided that if the company's gearing ratio as per the audited accounts exceeded a given amount, the debenture trustee would be entitled to appoint a receiver. Due to an overstatement of profits undetected by the auditors, the gearing ratio appeared sufficient to support the level of borrowing. In this case, the receiver sued the auditors for losses arising out of the failure to appoint a receiver in 1971.

It is at this point that the issue of the extent of loss caused by the auditors' negligence must be considered. The original verdict in the Cambridge Credit case 1985 determined damages in an amount based on the losses of the company incurred through its continued trade over a further three years. However, the auditors appealed on the grounds that they could not have foreseen the economic downturn that caused the losses to reach the level they did, nor did they have any control over the actions of management (notably decisions to expand borrowings and real estate investments at a time when the real estate market was being particularly affected by the economic decline) that may have further contributed to the extent of the actual losses. The Court of Appeal agreed that there was no causal connection between the auditors' negligence and the losses eventually sustained by the company, and upheld the principle that the auditors are not liable for all the consequences of their negligence, only those which they directly cause.

The level of damages was also an issue in the 1995 UK High Court judgement against BDO Binder Hamlyn. The plaintiffs, ADT, claimed that they relied on recent audited financial statements of the Britannia Security Group in making a takeover bid of £105 million. Subsequently to acquiring Britannia Security it was discovered the company was worth only £40 million. The auditors, BDO Binder Hamlyn, were sued for the difference. The amount claimed exceeded the auditors' professional indemnity insurance by a substantial margin leaving partners liable to make up the shortfall. The legal defence hinged on duty of care rather than quantum of damages which was unresolved as the parties settled out of court before going to appeal. The lack of a definitive judgement is unfortunate but it renewed concerns that auditors are still being seen as responsible for the full losses of failed business ventures.

△ LEARNING CHECK

4.3 The auditors are liable under statute and common law to the shareholders for any negligent performance of statutory duties. These statutory duties cannot be restricted or reduced.

4.4 To establish auditors' liabilities, there must be proven factors. These factors are (1) that the auditors owe a duty of care towards the plaintiff (due care), (2) that the duty has been breached (negligence), (3) that the plaintiff suffers losses as a result of the auditors' negligence (causal relationship), and (4) that losses were incurred (quantifiable losses).

4.5 The concept of contributory negligence was confirmed to be applicable in the AWA case, where management was found to be liable for a failure of internal control, thus sharing part of the damages.

LIABILITY TO THIRD PARTIES

Action for damages may also be brought against auditors, outside of any contractual relationship, under tort – committing a wrongful act which is injurious to another person. In *Donoghue v. Stevenson* (1932) AC 562 it was held that a duty of care is owed to third parties in the absence of contract where the plaintiff has suffered physical injury. The case related to a woman who drank a bottle of ginger ale purchased by her sister. She found a revolting mess at the bottom of the bottle which looked like the remains of a snail. She was taken ill and subsequently sued Stevenson, the soft drink manufacturer. Justice Atkins in defining the limits as to when a duty of care is owed, stated:

> You must take reasonable care to avoid acts or omissions which you can reasonably foresee would be likely to injure your neighbour. Who, then, in law is my neighbour? The answer seems to be – persons who are so closely and directly affected by my act that I ought reasonably to have them in contemplation as being so affected when I am directing my mind to the acts or omissions which are called in question.

From this case, it became evident that a duty of care can be owed to third parties through negligent acts. A third party is one who is not privity with the parties to the contract, but may, nevertheless, be a primary beneficiary or other beneficiary to the contract. Liability to third parties for financial injury is still confused. Prior to the Hedley Byrne case of 1963, the precedent was derived from such cases as those of *Ultramares Corporation v. Touche Niven & Co.* (1931) 255 NY, an American case, and *Candler v. Crane Christmas & Co.* (1951) 1 All ER 426 in the UK. In the Ultramares case, Justice Cardozo found for the defendant accountants on the grounds that:

> If liability for negligence exists, a thoughtless slip or blunder, the failure to detect a theft or forgery beneath the cover of deceptive entries, may expose accountants to a liability in an indeterminate amount for an indeterminate time to an indeterminate class.

In the Candler case, it was found that the defendants owed no duty to the plaintiffs in the absence of any contractual relationship and the negligence claim could not be sustained. Of interest in this case, however, was the dissenting judgement by Lord Denning:

> [Accountants] owe a duty, of course, to their employer or client, and also, I think, to any third person to whom they themselves show the accounts, or to whom they know their employer is going to show the accounts so as to induce him to invest money or take some other action on them. I do not think, however, the duty can be extended still further to include strangers of whom they have heard nothing and to whom their employer without their knowledge may choose to show their accounts. Once the accountants have handed their accounts to their employer, they are not, as a rule, responsible for what he does with them without their knowledge or consent. . . . [This duty] extends, I think, only to those transactions for which the accountants knew their accounts were required.

This view was upheld by the House of Lords in reaching its decision in the Hedley Byrne case. The majority decision in the Candler case was expressly overruled, and Lord Denning's dissenting judgement upheld as correctly stating the law.

HEDLEY BYRNE & CO. LTD V. HELLER & PARTNERS (1963) 2 All ER 575

Facts of the case: The Hedley Byrne case involved not an auditor but a bank. The bank (Heller & Partners) was approached by Hedley Byrne, an advertising agency, for a credit reference on a potential client, Easipower Ltd, which was a customer of the bank. The reference was supplied by the bank without making a careful check of its records. The negligence of the bank in supplying the reference was not disputed. On the strength of the reference, the advertising agency incurred costs on behalf of its client, which went into liquidation before the costs were recovered. The bank's first defence was that it owed no duty of care to the plaintiff in the absence of any contractual or fiduciary relationship with the advertising agency. The bank's duty of care was owed to its client. The second defence was the presence of a disclaimer at the foot of the reference supplied.

Judgement: In reaching a decision, the House of Lords upheld Denning's minority judgement in the Candler case. Lord Reid, in his judgement, said in relation to the limits of duty:

> I can see no logical stopping place short of all those relationships where it is plain that the party seeking information or advice was trusting the other to exercise such a degree of care as the circumstances required, where it was reasonable for him to do that, and where the other gave the information or advice when he knew or ought to have known that the inquirer was relying on him. I say 'ought to have known' because in questions of negligence we now apply the objective standard of what the reasonable man would have done.

> The verdict, however, was in favour of the defendant on the grounds that the disclaimer of liability was a good defence, notwithstanding that a duty of care existed.

Under the Hedley Byrne principle, auditors' liability to third parties to whom they owe a duty of care is no different from their liability to clients in that (1) they must have been negligent in the performance of their duties, (2) the plaintiff must have suffered an economic loss arising directly from that negligence, and (3) the loss must be quantifiable. The problem lies in determining to whom that duty of care is owed. The Hedley Byrne case identified a number of relevant factors, and emphasised that different factors would have different weights in different types of cases. The issue has come to be known as that of proximity. The Pandora's box envisaged by Justice Cardozo in the Ultramares case has not, in fact, been opened.

Proximity

As a result of the reluctance of professional indemnity insurers to allow cases to come to court for reasons explained earlier in this chapter, there have been very few decided cases of any significance involving claims by third parties against auditors. Examination of these cases demonstrates the law's confusion about the matter. Most of these cases involve action being brought by companies relying on audited accounts in making a takeover bid for another company. Proximity is held to arise through the fact that where a company's financial condition is such that it is a likely takeover target, auditors should be aware that the accounts will be relied upon by potential suitors and that a duty of care thus arises.

In the New Zealand case of *Scott Group Ltd v. McFarlane* (1978) 1 NZLR 553, two out of three appeal court judges held that the auditors owed a duty of care to the plaintiff, but only one judge thought that any loss had been suffered as a result of reliance on the negligently audited accounts, and the quantum of loss (if any) could not be determined. In the JEB Fasteners case (described below) Justice Woolf held that the auditors owed a duty of care, but that the plaintiff's loss had not arisen out of reliance on the audited accounts. In the Twomax case, a third party was successful in recovering losses suffered through reliance on negligently audited accounts. The essential elements in a negligence action that must be proven to the satisfaction of the courts are demonstrated in Figure 4.1.

JEB FASTENERS V. MARKS, BLOOM & CO. (1981) 2 AER 289

Facts of the case: Marks, Bloom & Co. was the auditor of BG Fasteners Ltd. Marks, Bloom was aware that BG Fasteners was in financial difficulty. A company, JEB Fasteners Ltd, previously unknown to the auditor, took over BG Fasteners. Subsequently, JEB Fasteners sued the auditor for negligence on the grounds that stocks of the company were overstated. It was alleged that JEB Fasteners paid more for the acquisition than it would have, had it known the true facts.

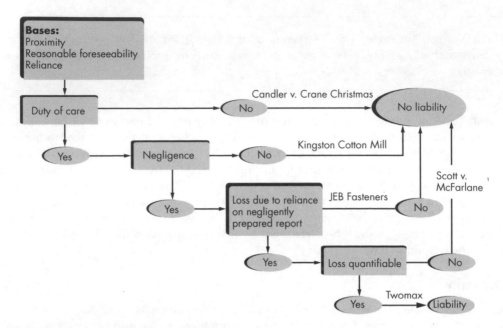

Figure 4.1 *The essential elements in negligence actions*

> *Judgement:* The test applied was one of reasonable foreseeability that the company would use the audited financial statements to obtain financial support, or be a subject of a takeover. It was held that there was a sufficient degree of 'proximity or neighbourhood' hence a duty of care was owed to the plaintiff. No damages were awarded because the plaintiff's purpose for taking over the company was to obtain the services of two directors of BG Fasteners. The causal relationship between the auditor's negligence and economic loss was not established.

In a majority verdict in the UK Court of Appeal hearing of the Caparo case (which was subsequently reversed in the House of Lords), two of the judges held that a duty of care was owed only to third parties who were existing shareholders to whom the auditors knew their report would be sent and relied upon. This reversed the findings in the previous cases which all held that a duty of care was owed to those relying on the accounts for the purposes of making a takeover bid, regardless of whether they were already shareholders.

On appeal, the UK House of Lords retreated further from the Hedley Byrne principle on the grounds that the purpose of audited financial statements is to serve a stewardship function. Reliance on those financial statements for investment purposes is ancillary to their intended purpose. The verdict in *Caparo Industries Pty Ltd v. Dickman* (1990) 1 All ER 568 makes it doubtful that any third party·claim against auditors in respect of the auditors' report under the *Companies Act 1985* would succeed.

CAPARO INDUSTRIES PTY LTD V. DICKMAN (1990) 1 All ER 568

Facts of the case: Caparo Industries Pty Ltd relied on the audited accounts of Fidelity plc in making a successful takeover bid for that company. The audited accounts for Fidelity showed a profit for the year ended 31 March 1984 of £1.2 million. After taking Fidelity over, Caparo discovered that the result should have been a loss of over £400,000 and alleged that the auditors had been negligent in auditing the accounts. The trial was of a preliminary issue as to whether the auditors owed a duty of care to the plaintiff. The issue of negligence has not been determined. The High Court judge found that no duty of care was owed to the plaintiff. This verdict was overturned by a majority verdict in the Court of Appeal but, as explained above, on different grounds from that of previous cases. Because of the importance of the matter, leave was given for a final appeal to the House of Lords, the highest court in the UK.

Judgement: Their Lordships reached their verdict by identifying the statutory purpose for the audit:

> The structure of the corporate trading entity, at least in the case of public companies whose shares are dealt with on an authorised stock exchange, involves the concept of more or less widely distributed holdings of shares rendering the personal involvement of each individual shareholder in the day-to-day management of the enterprise impracticable, with the result that management is necessarily separated from ownership. The management is confined to a board of directors which operates in a fiduciary capacity and is answerable to and removable by the shareholders who can act, if they act at all, only collectively and only through the medium of a general meeting, hence the legislative provisions requiring the board annually to give an account of its stewardship to a general meeting of the shareholders. This is the only occasion in each year on which the general body of shareholders is given the opportunity to consider, to criticise and to comment on the conduct of the board of the company's affairs, to vote on the directors' recommendation as to dividends, to approve or disapprove the directors' remuneration and, if thought desirable, to remove and replace any or all of the directors. It is the auditors' function to ensure, so far as possible, that all the financial information as to the company's affairs prepared by the directors accurately reflects the company's position in order, first to protect the company itself from the consequences of undetected errors or, possibly, wrongdoing (by, for instance, declaring dividends out of capital) and, second, to provide shareholders with reliable intelligence for the purpose of enabling them to scrutinise the conduct of the company's affairs and to exercise their collective powers to reward or control or remove those to whom that conduct has been confided.
> (Lord Oliver)

> On this basis it was argued that it would be unreasonable:
>
> > to widen the area of responsibility ... and to find a relationship of proximity between the advisor and third parties to whose attention the advice may come in circumstances in which the reliance said to have given rise to the loss is strictly unrelated either to the intended recipient or to the purpose for which the advice was required. (Lord Oliver)
>
> And neither was it the intention of the Act:
>
> > For my part, however, I can see nothing in the statutory duties of a company's auditors to suggest that they were intended by Parliament to protect the interests of investors in the market. (Lord Oliver)
>
> In summary, therefore, the House of Lords argued that the purpose of the financial statement on which auditors express an opinion is to assist the shareholders in their collective function of scrutinising the company's affairs. It would be unreasonable, therefore, to hold the auditors responsible for their use, by shareholders or others, for any other purpose.

It is interesting to note that in the cases preceding the Caparo case, in which the courts held that the auditors owed a duty of care to those relying on the accounts in making a takeover bid, in only the Twomax case did the court find that any loss arose from that reliance. In the Scott Group and JEB Fasteners cases the courts found no direct link between reliance on the accounts and any loss suffered. In so doing, they recognised the limitations of financial statements as a basis not only for investment decision-making but also for the reliance, by investors, on many other sources of information.

REACTION TO THE CAPARO CASE VERDICT

Reaction to the House of Lords verdict in the Caparo case has generally been unfavourable. The general view of the legal profession is that the verdict appears to be treating auditors more favourably than other experts on whom third parties place reliance. There is also concern that it appears to be turning the clock back on what is seen as a socially desirable development in law of holding experts liable for the consequences of negligent advice.

Even auditors are divided in their reaction. Many accept that audited financial statements do provide investors with a reliable source of information. The value of auditors' services is, therefore, seen to be diminished. One response by third party users of financial statements (such as investors, lenders and suppliers of goods and services) has been to request a letter from the auditors in which they acknowledge the user's reliance on the audited financial statements, thereby establishing a relationship with the required foreseeability and proximity. Such letters are known as privity or comfort letters. In the case of *ADT v. BDO Binder Hamlyn* the required proximity was alleged to have arisen from a verbal assurance by a BDO Binder Hamlyn partner to an ADT director, that the firm stood behind their audit opinion on Britannia Securities.

In reaching its verdict on Caparo, the House of Lords implied that it is up to the UK Parliament to introduce legislation whereby auditors' statutory responsibilities could be extended directly to meet the interests of investors.

POST-CAPARO CASE DEVELOPMENTS
In a number of subsequent cases the courts have established a duty of care to takeover bidders to whom the auditors have indicated, directly or indirectly, that the audited financial statements could be relied upon, as in the ADT case referred to. In general a duty of care to a third party arises if that party acted on information, such as an auditors' report on financial statements, where:

- the report was prepared on the basis that it would be conveyed to a third party;
- the report would be conveyed for a purpose which was likely to be relied upon by that third party; or
- the third party would be likely to act in reliance on that report, thus running the risk of suffering the loss if the statement was negligently prepared.

Avoidance of litigation

The following precautions may be taken by auditors wishing to avoid or minimise the consequences of litigation.

- *Use engagement letters for all professional services.* Engagement letters (as described in Chapter 6) are of particular importance on non-audit engagements where misunderstanding might arise as to the nature of the public accountant's association with the financial statements. They are also important on audit engagements where there may be some misunderstanding as to the extent of auditors' responsibilities, particularly as to the detection of fraud.
- *Investigate prospective clients thoroughly.* Establishing of a policy on client acceptance is seen as a means of reducing exposure to litigation. Litigation tends to follow corporate collapse. It can be limited by avoiding clients which are in poor financial health or which are managed by directors whose business ethics or competence is suspect as a result of past association with failed corporations.
- *Comply fully with professional pronouncements.* Strict adherence to Statements of Auditing Standards is essential. Auditors must be able to justify any material departures from established guidelines.
- *Recognise the limitations of professional pronouncements.* Professional guidelines are not all-encompassing. In addition, it should be recognised that subjective tests of reasonableness and fairness will be used by the courts and regulatory agencies in judging the auditors' work. The auditors must use sound professional judgement during the audit and in the issuance of the auditors' report.
- *Establish and maintain high standards of quality control.* The dominant objective of quality control is the assurance that all of the firm's work complies with required professional standards. Recent cases have emphasised the particular importance of:
  - the assignment of appropriately competent staff to engagements and their proper supervision;

- adequate documentation of all audit procedures; and
- compliance with independence guidelines, especially as regards personal relationships with clients.

- *Maintain adequate professional indemnity cover.* Professional indemnity insurance has been the cause of misunderstanding. Some argue that it protects auditors against their legal responsibilities, encouraging a less than desirable standard of care, since any losses can be claimed against insurance. A contradictory view is that the possession of indemnity insurance encourages lawsuits on the grounds that the insurance company will have to pay. It is generally held, however, that responsible public accountants need to carry such insurance for the protection of their clients. Professional indemnity insurance is required in order to obtain a certificate of public practice.

- *Be prepared to issue a privity letter, on request.* Following the Caparo decision, auditors may be asked to acknowledge the third party's reliance on audited financial statements (the privity letter). The purpose of the privity letter is to establish a relationship with required foreseeability and proximity, and thereby a duty of care by the auditors to the third party.

 ## LEARNING **CHECK**

4.6 Under the Hedley Byrne principle, auditors' liability to third parties to whom they owe a duty of care is no different from their liability to clients, in that (1) they must have been negligent in the performance of their duties, (2) the plaintiff must have suffered an economic loss arising directly from that negligence, and (3) the loss must be quantifiable. The problem lies in determining to whom that duty of care is owed.

4.7 The common law judgements relating to auditors' liability to third parties have been inconclusive. Criteria of proximity, reliance and reasonable foreseeability have been used in various cases, but the courts' rulings have been inconsistent.

4.8 The most recent development in case law concerning auditors' liability to third parties comes from the Caparo case. Essentially, auditors' liability can be established only if:

- the report was prepared on the basis that it would be conveyed to a third party;

- the report would be conveyed for a purpose which was likely to be relied upon by that third party; or

- the third party would be likely to act in reliance on that report, thus running the risk of suffering the loss if the statement was negligently prepared.

4.9 Auditors should avoid litigation by complying with standards, ensuring a clear letter of engagement to be agreed between the parties, and by good quality control procedures.

THE NEED FOR LEGAL REFORM

The potential claims against auditors reporting on entities responsible for many millions of pounds of assets and liabilities are astronomical. The damages awarded against the auditors can be far in excess of their ability to pay, either from their own resources, or through their professional indemnity cover. The award is likely to be totally unrelated to the audit fee received for the work performed, as is exemplified by the initial award of £105 million in the case of *ADT v. BDO Binder Hamlyn* (1995). The collapse of Arthur Andersen worldwide in the wake of the collapse of Enron, of which it was the auditor, indicates the risk. Only one office was directly implicated and yet the potential size of lawsuits destroyed the entire firm. Previously two mid-sized US firms had failed in the wake of lawsuits, Levanthal & Horwarth and Spicer & Oppenheim. The current concern is that if another of the remaining Big Four firms fails as a result of actual or potential exposure to liability, the remaining three firms will be too few for a viable competitive audit market to exist. The liability system is regarded as a risk transfer mechanism and the auditors are the prime transferees.

The International Federation of Accountants (IFAC) Auditors' Legal Liability Task Force produced a paper in June 1995 analysing the worldwide situation regarding auditors' legal liability.[1] In the UK the government requested the Law Commission to look into certain aspects of the law relating to professional liability. In their response to the Department of Trade and Industry's consultation on the Law Commission's report, the Institute of Chartered Accountants in England and Wales claimed that the current imbalance in the risk/reward relationship threatens the public interest in the following ways:

- audit firms will refuse to take on clients in high risk industries such as financial institutions and those involving high technology:
    - companies in these industries are those most in need of competent and rigorous audit;
    - withdrawal of audit from such companies will handicap the development of vital market sectors;
- the audit profession will be unwilling to accept new responsibilities such as in connection with the electronic exchange of information;
- audit cost will rise to cover the growing risks; and
- the audit profession will lose its appeal to the brightest graduates.

Methods of reducing professional liability addressed by the DTI's[2] consultation are as follows:

- eliminate joint and several liability in favour of a system of proportionate liability;
- allow auditing firms to limit their liability by contract;
- adopt a statutory limitation or 'cap' on professional liability for negligence;
- adopt a statutory requirement for professional advisers and directors of companies to have adequate insurance cover; and
- amend the organisational structure of auditing firms.

/ Proportionate liability

Professional negligence claims are dealt with under a principle known as joint and several liability. Under this principle each defendant is wholly liable for the loss suffered by the plaintiff. If shareholders lost money through an illegal act by a manager in the company perpetrated through a lack of adequate controls, the company can sue three parties. These are the manager who perpetrated the act, the directors who failed to provide adequate controls and the auditors for failing to discover it. Given the choice the plaintiffs will invariably sue the auditors because of the deep pockets of their professional indemnity insurers. Neither the managers nor the directors are usually worth pursuing. Thus auditors tend to end up paying damages in situations where they were only partly to blame.

One suggestion is that some form of proportionate liability should be introduced whereby the plaintiff's loss is divided among the defendants according to their share of responsibility. Under proportionate liability, defendants are required to compensate the plaintiff only in proportion to their involvement in any wrongdoing. This essentially enables courts to assess awards that reflect the degree of responsibility of each defendant. In the US, Congress has accepted the injustices of joint and several liability in certain situations and has passed the *Private Securities Litigation Reform Act 1995*. This legislation only relates to fraud in connection with the purchase and sale of securities. Claims covered by this legislation represent nearly one-third of US accounting firms' exposure to litigation. Under the Act, a defendant's liability is limited to its proportionate share of the damages subject to a 50% increase in the event of an insolvent co-defendant. Proportionate liability rules also apply in Denmark and France.

In their report in 1996 the Law Commission[3] argued against abandoning joint and several liability on the grounds of inequity. If one of the defendants were insolvent the plaintiff would fail to recover their full loss. This appears iniquitous when there are partly guilty parties capable of compensating the wholly blameless.

In its response to the Law Commission paper the Institute of Chartered Accountants in England and Wales[4] rebutted the presumption that the plaintiff was always blameless.

> Investors in and lenders to a company, and suppliers who do business with that company, do so willingly. They enter into a relationship with the company recognising and accepting some risk of loss – including that from fraud and similar causes – and accepting that some advisors or other persons with whom they are dealing will be unable to compensate them if any loss occurs for which these other parties may be responsible. They weigh all this against the reward of potential profit. It is a basic premise, in an economy which operates through limited liability companies, that investors accept that the extent to which they will be able to recover their losses from others is limited. To refer, therefore, to the totally blameless plaintiff, who should expect full compensation for loss, is to deny the realities of modern commercial life.
>
> Auditors, on the other hand, bear the risks of client's activities – in terms of the scope of potential litigation exposure – but do not enjoy any added reward from their client's success. Auditors stand in sharp contrast to plaintiffs in this respect, but the law does not recognise this distinction.

The Company Law Review Steering Group (CLRSG), set up by the Department of Trade and Industry to advise on the future of company law in the UK, acknowledged the ICAEW's concerns in advising against any statutory removal of the Caparo limitation on liability to third parties. However, they endorsed the Law Commission's rejection of proportionate liability.

2. Contractual limitation

At present s.310 of the *Companies Act 1985* prohibits auditors from obtaining exemption from any liability which would otherwise arise in respect of a breach of duty towards the company. On the face of it this seems wholly reasonable. The directors could persuade the members to accept a contractual arrangement with the auditors that restricted the auditors' liability to a fixed sum. The auditors would be less vigilant knowing that if the directors did defraud the company their liability, as auditors, would be limited.

The ICAE&W[5] argues for the total repeal of s.310 of the *Companies Act 1985*. It is sufficient, they argue, that any contractual restriction on auditors' liability is made known by members when voting on auditor appointments and is further disclosed in the financial statements for the benefit of other users placing reliance on the auditors' opinion.

The ICAE&W is further concerned that the distinction between audit work, to which s.310 or any amendment thereof applies, and non-audit work needs to be made clear. It is unclear, for example, whether advising directors on the effectiveness of internal controls would be deemed to be provided in their capacity as auditors or as a non-audit service provided by professional accountants. The ICAE&W is also concerned that the *Unfair Contract Terms Act 1977* may nevertheless be held to render contractual limitations of liability ineffective even in the case of non-audit work. The ICAE&W calls for guidelines to be issued such that the effectiveness of contractual limitations clauses may be relied upon without the risk of their being retrospectively challenged in the courts.

The CLRSG endorsed the ICAEW's proposed repeal of s.310 as the most appropriate method of overcoming the current liability dilemma. They recommended introducing statutory guidelines to be followed in passing a resolution reducing auditors' liability to avoid problems associated with the *Unfair Contract Terms Act*. However, the government has chosen to defer introducing any variation to auditors' liability into prospective legislation for the time being.

3. Statutory cap

A widely debated proposal is the introduction of a statutory cap on auditors' liability, being a multiple of the audit fee. The statutory cap (as a multiple of the audit fee) introduces a direct correlation between the nature and size of the audit engagement (as reflected by the fees) and the potential liability. It is argued that such a scheme, together with a requirement for compulsory indemnity insurance and risk management strategies, can provide appropriate protection to users and some guarantee of payments to claimants. The counter-argument is that it would represent an unwarranted intrusion by the state in private relationships between auditors and those to whom they owe a duty of care, and might lead other professions to seek similar concessions.

Such a cap exists in certain states in Australia. For example, the *New South Wales Professional Standards Act 1994* limits the liability for members of approved professional and other occupational associations to a capped amount, referred to as a 'limitation amount'. The maximum amount is determined by either a multiple of the fee charged or by a specific amount backed by professional indemnity insurance and/or business assets. The maximum liability of accountants is $A50 million. Compulsory insurance, risk management schemes and a complaints system are also stipulated in the Act.

4 Mandatory insurance for directors

Auditors, it is claimed, are targeted by plaintiffs because of the deep pockets of insurance companies providing their indemnity insurance cover. If other parties potentially responsible for corporate losses were similarly required to carry insurance, plaintiffs would sue all parties, thus removing the iniquities of joint and several liability. Indemnity insurance, however, is provided with respect to professional services. The ICAE&W is concerned that its extension to services of directors might not be feasible. As directors are not members of a professional body with recognised codes of professional conduct, the anticipated incidence of claims may result in unrealistically high premiums. There is also the problem that such insurance would merely transfer the auditors' problem to directors with a rising incidence of claims against directors by plaintiffs seeking to tap the insurers' deep pockets.

5 Organisation of auditing firms

Traditionally, limited liability has been seen as incompatible with the provision of professional services. For many years, however, professional bodies have required the maintenance of adequate indemnity insurance as a necessary condition for holding a practising certificate. It is now common practice for plaintiffs to sue for the full amount of loss on a corporate collapse. Such a claim may exceed a firm's indemnity cover. Although plaintiffs are invariably content to settle for a much lower sum, the personal assets of partners, most of whom, in a large practice, are remote from the actual event giving rise to the claim, are frozen during the lengthy period taken to resolve the claim.

All larger and many smaller auditing firms have incorporated their practices under the *Limited Liability Partnerships Act 2000*. In the event of a claim rendering the firm insolvent partners are only liable to repay drawings within the previous two years. Otherwise their personal assets are not at risk. For the protection of the public such firms must make appropriate arrangements for meeting claims that may be made against them and must publish annual financial statements in order that their financial liquidity may be established.

◁ LEARNING **CHECK**

4.10 There have been various types of legal reform suggested to limit auditors' liability for negligence. These are, in the main, statutory limitation or capping, changing joint and several liability into proportionate liability, permitting contractual limitation of auditors' liability and providing flexibility for more organisational options for accounting firms such as limited liability partnerships.

4.11 The USA allows proportionate liability in certain claims affecting auditors. Certain Australian states permit the statutory capping of liabilities.

4.12 In the UK the government allows audit firms to incorporate as limited liability partnerships.

SUMMARY

Litigation has had a significant impact on the public accounting profession and it seems reasonable to expect that it will continue to do so in the foreseeable future. To avoid litigation, it is vital that the auditors comply fully with professional pronouncements in completing each audit engagement and use sound professional judgement during the audit and at the time of issuing the auditors' report.

This chapter has described the current legal environment faced by audit firms, and introduced the detailed development of court decisions on auditors' liability. The issue of auditors' liability is very much an unresolved matter. Auditors are liable under statute to their clients for breach of duty under the *Companies Act 1985*. However, interpretation of the law has been largely dependent on court cases. The concept of due professional care has been used in the Kingston Cotton Mill and London and General Bank cases, and was further defined in the Thomas Gerrard case.

The chapter has also examined the concepts of negligence, privity of contract, causal relationship, and contributory negligence. These concepts provide a framework for understanding how and when a duty of care arises, and to what extent liability is incurred. The AWA case was the first to establish the application of contributory negligence, and helps to define in more exact terms the extent of liability or damages attributable to the auditors' negligence. Case law concerning auditors' liability to third parties is inconsistent, however. The key case of Caparo refers to auditors' liability to third parties being based on the premise that the auditors indicate their understanding that their report will be relied upon by a third party for a financial decision and that the third party subsequently suffers a loss because of the auditors' negligence in preparing the report. The application of the tests for proximity and reasonable foreseeability have been inconclusive.

Finally, this chapter looked at the development of legal reforms in the UK and internationally. So far, reforms affecting auditors' liability have been slow, and to some extent ineffective.

NOTES

1 The report *Auditors' Legal Liability in the Global Marketplace: A Case for Limitation* was published in June 1995 by the International Federation of Accountants. It analyses some of the causes and developments in auditors' liability issues, and makes some recommendations for legislative reforms.
2 The methods of reducing auditors' liability raised in the DTI consultation paper are similar to those suggested in the IFAC's above report.
3 Law Commission, *Feasibility Investigation of Joint and Several Liability*, 1996.
4 ICAE&W, *Joint and Several Liability: Finding a Fair Solution*, 1996.
5 ICAE&W, op. cit.
6 Company Law Review Steering Group, *Modern Company Law for a Competitive Economy: Final Report*, URN 01/942 Ch. 5, Department of Trade and Industry, 2001.
7 Company Law Review Steering Group, op. cit. Ch. 8.

FURTHER READING

Grout, P. J., Ian Pong, C. & Whittington, G. 'Auditors', *Economic Policy* (October 1994), pp. 307–51.

Keenan, D. 'The AWA Case – What's New?', *Accountancy* (October 1996), p. 132.

Maldoom, D. & Laslett, R. 'Auditor Liability – An Economic Case for Reform', *Accountancy* (August 1998), p. 75.

Perkins, A. 'Desperately Seeking Limited Liability', *Accountancy (International edition)* (July 1996), p. 66.

Vanasco, R. R., Skousen, C. R. & Jenson, R. L. 'Audit Evidence: The US Standards and Landmark Cases', *Managerial Auditing Journal* (Vol. 16, No. 4, 2001), pp. 207–214.

MULTIPLE-CHOICE QUESTIONS

Choose the best answer for each of the following
(Answers are on pages 598–599)

4.1 What most appropriately describes the implications of the Kingston Cotton Mill (1896) and London and General Bank (1895) cases?
   (a) The auditor has a responsibility to the shareholders and all interested users of the financial statements.
   (b) The auditor has a responsibility to exercise the skill and care of a reasonably competent and well informed member of the profession.
   (c) The auditor is to act like a watchdog and ensure that no fraud goes undetected.
   (d) The auditor should not trust management in relation to any issues affecting the audit of the financial statements.

4.2 In which of the following situations is it least likely that the auditors would have been negligent in failing to detect a material misstatement of stock?
   (a) The auditors relied on a certificate provided by an independent expert.
   (b) The audit programme is drawn up by an experienced auditor and was fully signed off by the junior staff member assigned to the audit of stocks.
   (c) The senior partner called off further investigation of discrepancies after receiving personal assurance from the chairman of the company that stocks were properly valued.
   (d) As in previous years, the auditor relied on the investigations of internal audit rather than increase audit costs by duplicating the auditing work.

4.3 In which of the following situations would failure to detect a fraud constitute grounds for a claim of negligence?
   (a) The fraud was perpetrated by a senior management override of internal controls which had been relied upon in reducing the extent of detailed testing.
   (b) The auditors reported discrepancies to local management but did not investigate further as the likely impact on the accounts was not material.
   (c) The auditors accepted local management representations as to discrepancies as the potential impact of the fraud was not material to the accounts as a whole.
   (d) The auditors relied on sample evidence and thus failed to detect the fraudulent transactions.

4.4 In which of the following situations might a claim arise under privity of contract?
(a) A bank makes a loan to a company on the strength of a report commissioned by the bank.
(b) A bank makes a loan to a company on the strength of a report commissioned by the company for that specific purpose.
(c) The holder of 100% of the shares increases investment in the company on the strength of the audited accounts.
(d) The engagement letter calls for the preparation of accounts of a partnership without an audit, but one of the partners tells the public accountant that another partner is suspected of fiddling expenses.

4.5 The decision in the Caparo case (1990) restricted the duty of care of auditors to:
(a) all users known to the auditors.
(b) all users that ought reasonably to have been known to the auditors.
(c) the shareholders as a group.
(d) all users of the financial statements, except for investors.

4.6 Would an investor who requests a copy of the audited financial statements of the company from company management before the audit is completed be able to rely on the work of the auditors?
(a) Yes.
(b) Yes, provided the auditors knew.
(c) No.
(d) No, unless this information induced the investor to behave in a different way to how he or she would have behaved without receiving the financial statements.

4.7 What type of reform is being implemented by the UK government to alleviate audit liability?
(a) Limiting audit liability (liability cap).
(b) Proportionate liability.
(c) Allowing accounting firms to incorporate.
(d) None of the above.

DISCUSSION QUESTIONS

4.1 Under what circumstances might auditors be liable for negligence for failing to discover a material misstatement in a financial statement on which they issued an unqualified opinion?

4.2 If a company goes bankrupt and the auditors are found to have been negligent, who can sue the auditors and who is likely to benefit from damages recovered from the auditors?

4.3 Investment decision-making is often said to be the major objective of information provided by general purpose financial reports. In the Caparo case, the court argued for a much narrower objective of financial reporting under the Companies Act. Discuss the implications for auditor liability.

4.4 Discuss problems in determining the amount of damages a plaintiff may be awarded on successfully suing an auditor for negligence.

4.5 Auditors are continually demanding a reduction in their exposure to liability. To what extent are such demands justified?

4.6 Consider the separate proposals for reducing the auditors' exposure to liability and consider their respective merits and drawbacks.

PROFESSIONAL APPLICATION QUESTIONS

(Suggested answers are on pages 611–612)

4.1 Due care

You are an audit senior and you have just finished the audit of Speedy Spares Ltd – a used car parts company. One month later . . .

Your audit partner calls you into his office – he is not happy! Speedy Spares has just gone into liquidation. It seems the financial controller was diverting company funds into a Swiss bank account and has left the country to live in Majorca. The lawyers for the creditors of Speedy Spares are taking action against the partner for not performing an appropriate audit. They believe that in the course of a properly conducted audit, such a fraud should have been detected. The fraud was substantial; however, it was not material from the company's point of view. You explain to the partner that the audit was performed in accordance with all Auditing Standards and nothing was found to arouse suspicion during the audit. The audit took the same amount of time as last year and all appropriate work steps were performed. Your work was reviewed by a manager and the entire file was reviewed by the audit partner.

The audit partner is still concerned. He rings an audit partner in an associated office of your accounting firm and asks her to review the audit file. She agrees and spends a day reviewing the file. After completing her review, she is satisfied that the audit was performed properly.

Required

(a) Has your accounting firm acted with 'due care'? What do you think will be the court's decision if the case goes to trial?

(b) Even if the partner is convinced he acted with 'due care', why would he possibly offer Speedy Spares a substantial settlement amount?

4.2 Negligence, liability to third parties

Western Ltd purchased the assets of Green Ltd. The financial report of Green Ltd was audited by Donaghue Partners, registered company auditors. While performing the audit, Donaghue Partners discovered that Green's accounts clerk had embezzled £500. Donaghue Partners also had some evidence of other embezzlements by the book-keeper. However, the auditor decided that the £500 was not material, and that the other suspected embezzlements did not require further investigation.

Donaghue Partners did not discuss the matter with Green's management. Unknown to the auditor, the accounts clerk had, in fact, embezzled large sums of cash from Green Ltd. In addition, the debtors were significantly overstated. Donaghue Partners did not detect the overstatement because of its inadvertent failure to follow its audit programme.

Despite the foregoing, Donaghue Partners issued an unqualified opinion on Green's financial statements and furnished a copy of the audited financial statements to Western Ltd. Unknown to the auditor, Western Ltd required financing to purchase Green's assets and gave a copy of Green's audited financial statements to City Bank to obtain approval of the loan.

Based on Green's audited financial statements, City Bank loaned £600,000. Western Ltd paid Green Ltd £750,000 to purchase its assets. Within six months, Western Ltd began experiencing financial difficulties and later defaulted on the City Bank loan. City Bank commenced legal action against Donaghue Partners citing negligence on the part of the auditor for its failure to discover the fraud, and the overstatement of debtors.

Required
Will City Bank succeed in its action against Donaghue Partners? Explain.

AUDIT RISK AND AUDIT EVIDENCE

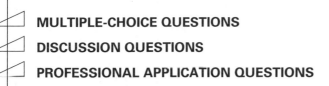

- **MULTIPLE-CHOICE QUESTIONS**
- **DISCUSSION QUESTIONS**
- **PROFESSIONAL APPLICATION QUESTIONS**

 LEARNING **OBJECTIVES**

After studying this chapter, you should be able to:

1   explain the importance of the concept of audit risk and its three components

2   describe the relationship between audit risk and audit evidence

3   define the concept of materiality used in auditing

4   state how the auditor arrives at judgements about materiality at the financial statement level and in relation to individual account balances

5   describe the relationship between materiality and audit evidence

6   state the categories of management's financial statement assertions

7   derive specific audit objectives from the categories of assertions

8   indicate the factors that affect the sufficiency and appropriateness of audit evidence

9   identify the types of corroborating information available to the auditor

10 enumerate and describe the types of auditing procedure that may be used in an audit

11 describe the three classifications of auditing procedure and the purpose of each.

PROFESSIONAL STATEMENTS

ISA 200	Objective and General Principles Governing an Audit of Financial Statements
ISA 315	Understanding the Entity and its Environment and Assessing the Risks of Material Misstatement
ISA 320	Audit Materiality
ISA 500	Audit Evidence
ISA 505	External Confirmations
ISA 580	Management Representations
ISA 620	Using the Work of an Expert

Having considered the environmental factors pertaining to auditing, this chapter begins to explain the nature of the investigation that auditors undertake to arrive at an opinion as to the truth and fairness of the financial statements. This chapter will look at the fundamental issues relating to the audit process, namely:

- the risks that the financial statements may not be fairly presented;
- the threshold of materiality that auditors use in identifying misstatements that could materially affect the decisions and judgements of users placing reliance on the financial statements;
- the different types of assertion that combine to ensure the financial statements give a true and fair view and that underpin the objectives of the audit process;
- the types of evidence available to auditors; and
- the procedures used by auditors in obtaining the different types of evidence.

The next chapter will examine the application of these issues in planning and performing specific audit engagements.

To begin, it is necessary to consider the nature of the financial statements being subject to audit examination. The statements are made up of the elements of assets, liabilities, revenues and expenses – or, in accounting terminology, account balances. Account balances are built up from entries in the accounting records, which arise mostly from transactions such as purchases and cash receipts. Thus, the account balance, trade creditors, is the difference between purchase transactions creating the liability and cash payment transactions decreasing the liability. In verifying the balance, auditors may investigate the balance directly, such as by examining suppliers' statements. Alternatively, auditors can verify the transactions that make up the balance, such as by examining purchase transactions and cash payment transactions. By the use of such tests auditors can substantiate the correctness of the amounts recorded as account balances. Also of importance is the examination of the presentation and disclosure of account balances. This includes their description on the face of the financial statements and supplementary disclosures in the notes. Procedures verifying transactions and account balances and their presentation and disclosure are referred to as substantive procedures. As will be explained in this and subsequent chapters, auditors also use other types of procedure.

Entities are aware of the importance of maintaining reliable accounting records and design information systems intended to reduce the likelihood of errors. The use of double-entry book-keeping is itself a means of self-checking the accuracy of the records by its use of the balancing process. The sum of the procedures that entities use to ensure the reliability of their accounting records is known as internal control. The components of internal control will be described in detail in Chapter 7.

AUDIT RISK

Audit risk is the risk that the financial statements are misstated and that the auditors fail to detect such misstatement resulting in the expression of an inappropriate opinion on the financial statements (ISA 200). This arises when the auditors express the opinion that the financial statements are fairly presented when they are misstated.[1]

The more certain the auditors want to be of expressing the correct opinion, the lower will be the audit risk that they are willing to accept. In setting the desired audit risk auditors seek an appropriate balance between the costs of an incorrect audit opinion and the costs of performing the additional audit procedures necessary to reduce audit risk.

The default presumption is that all transactions in a transaction class and all items in an account balance are potentially misstated and that substantive procedures must be sufficient to minimise the risk that misstatements remain undetected. However, experience teaches auditors that most transactions and account balance items are correctly stated, but that the actual level of misstatements varies from one entity to another. Experience also suggests that the principal causes of variation lie in the nature of the entity and the effectiveness of its risk management framework including its internal controls. In many cases, therefore, auditors can reduce audit risk by investigating and assessing the likelihood that the financial statements are misstated.

The first step involves obtaining an understanding of the entity's business and industry, its management, the intended users of its financial information, its legal and financial stability, and its operations. This includes considering the business risks that may cause an entity to suffer unexpected losses or some other catastrophe that may affect its ability to survive as a going concern, as well as risks directly associated with financial reporting. The auditors then consider the effect these factors could have on the risk that its financial statements might be misstated. They then look at the entity's risk management procedures for identifying and managing such risks. Not only does this direct the auditors' attention to matters that could affect the risk of financial report misstatements, it also enables auditors to use their risk management skills to alert management of the entity to shortcomings in their approach to risk. For this reason, the approach is sometimes referred to as an 'added value audit'. If the auditors assess the entity as being well managed and financially sound they may reduce their overall assessment of audit risk.

Auditors also obtain an understanding of the internal control framework that the entity adopts to guard against the likelihood of errors occurring or remaining undetected in its accounting records and causing misstatements in its financial statements. If the auditors assess these procedures as being effective, then they may reduce the overall assessment of audit risk. Conversely, if the auditors consider the entity to be in financial difficulty or to have an inadequate internal control framework, then they may assess audit risk as being higher, requiring a more extensive audit investigation.

Audit risk components

Audit risk is commonly assessed within three components: inherent risk, control risk and detection risk. Each component will be discussed in the following sections.

INHERENT RISK

Inherent risk is the possibility that a misstatement could occur. At this level the auditor does not consider the presence of control procedures that may detect the misstatement (ISA 200).

The assessment of inherent risk requires consideration of both matters that may have a pervasive effect on the entity as a whole and matters that may affect only specific accounts.

The inherent risk of misstatement is greater for some industries than for others. Entities operating in the gas and oil exploration or insurance industries, for example, have unique accounting problems compared with merchandising or manufacturing entities. The existence of related parties, foreign exchange dealings and other complicated contracts also presents opportunities for misstatements to occur.

Further, inherent risk may be greater for some accounts, transactions or disclosures than for others. Cash, for example, is more susceptible to misstatement through misappropriation than are tangible fixed assets. Similarly, the valuation of assets held under a finance lease is more susceptible to misstatement (as a result of the complex nature of finance lease calculations) than is the valuation of similar assets owned outright. (Matters that may have a pervasive effect on the entity and matters that may pertain to specific accounts only are shown in Table 5.1.)

Table 5.1 Illustration of the audit risk concept

	EXAMPLES OF ATTRIBUTES CONSIDERED BY THE AUDITORS		RESPONSE BY AUDITORS
	INHERENT RISK	CONTROL RISK	DETECTION RISK

Matters pervasive to many account balances or transaction classes	• Profitability relative to the industry
	• Sensitivity of operating results to economic factors
	• Going-concern problems
	• Nature, cause and amount of known and likely misstatements detected in prior audits
	• Management turnover
	• Management reputation
	• Management accounting skills
		• Business planning, budgeting and monitoring of performance
		• Management attitude and actions regarding financial reporting
		• Management consultation with auditors
		• Management concern about external influences
		• Audit committee
		• Internal audit function
		• Personnel policies and procedures
		• Effectiveness of the accounting system
			• Overall audit strategy
			  – Number of locations visited
			  – Significant balances or transaction classes
			• Degree of professional scepticism
			• Staffing – levels of supervision and review

Matters pertaining to specific account balances or transaction classes	• Accounts or transactions that are difficult to audit
	• Contentious or difficult accounting issues
	• Susceptibility to misappropriation
	• Complexity of calculations
	• Extent of judgement related to assertions
	• Sensitivity of valuations to economic factors
	• Nature, cause and amount of known and likely misstatements detected in prior audits
		• Effectiveness of the accounting system, personnel policies and procedures
		• Adequacy of accounting records
		• Segregation of duties
		• Adequacy of safeguards over assets and records (including software)
		• Independent checks on performance
			• Substantive analytical procedures and tests of details
			  – Nature of tests
			  – Timing of tests
			  – Extent of tests

Source: AICPA Control Risk Audit Guide Task Force. Audit Guide: *Consideration of the Internal Control Structure in a Financial Statement Audit*, 1990, p. 210.

Inherent risk exists independently of the audit of financial statements. Thus, auditors cannot change the actual level of inherent risk. They are required to assess the inherent risk of particular misstatements in order to plan an approach to the audit that reflects their expectation of the likelihood of such misstatements occurring.

CONTROL RISK

Control risk is the risk that a misstatement that could occur will not be prevented or detected and corrected on a timely basis by the entity's internal control (ISA 200).

Control risk is a function of the effectiveness of the design and operation of internal control relevant to financial reporting. Effective internal controls reduce control risk. Control risk can never be zero, because internal controls cannot provide complete assurance that all misstatements will be prevented or detected. Controls may be ineffective, for example, as a result of human failure due to carelessness or fatigue. Factors that influence the auditors' considerations of control risk are depicted in Table 5.1.

Auditors cannot change the level of control risk. They can 'influence' control risk by recommending improvements in internal controls, but this influence is more likely to affect future periods and then only to the extent that the entity's management implements the suggestions. As with inherent risk, the auditors must consider the risk of particular misstatements in order to plan an approach to the audit that reflects their expectation of the likelihood of such misstatements occurring. Since the assessment of the risk of misstatement is a combination of the inherent risk of a misstatement occurring and the control risk of its not being prevented or detected, auditors may arrive at a joint assessment of the risk of misstatement.

The initial assessment of internal control is restricted to an assessment of their design effectiveness and, if effective, whether the controls have been implemented. As will be explained in Chapter 6, testing whether controls are actually operating effectively depends on the audit strategy adopted for each transaction class, account balance or disclosure.

For smaller entities auditors usually undertake a combined assessment of inherent and control risk since they are unlikely to place reliance on controls in planning their audit strategy. The purpose of the assessment is to ensure that substantive procedures are designed with an awareness of the likely risks of misstatement. This will also be the case for specific transaction classes, account balances or disclosures in the audit of larger entities where most evidence is likely to be derived from substantive procedures.

Auditors, while being unable to control inherent and control risk, can assess these risks and design substantive procedures to produce an acceptable level of detection risk, thus reducing audit risk to an acceptable level.

DETECTION RISK

Detection risk is the risk that the auditors' substantive procedures will not detect any misstatements that occur and are not prevented or detected by internal control (ISA 200).

Detection risk is a function of the effectiveness of substantive procedures and their application by auditors. Unlike inherent and control risk, the actual level of detection risk is controllable by auditors through:

- appropriate planning, direction, supervision and review;
- proper determination of the nature, timing and extent of audit procedures; and
- effective performance of the audit procedures and evaluation of their results.

The audit risk model is illustrated by way of a rain cloud analogy in Figure 5.1.

Once the auditors have assessed inherent and control risk and determined the risk of misstatement they proceed to develop an audit strategy along with the procedures for

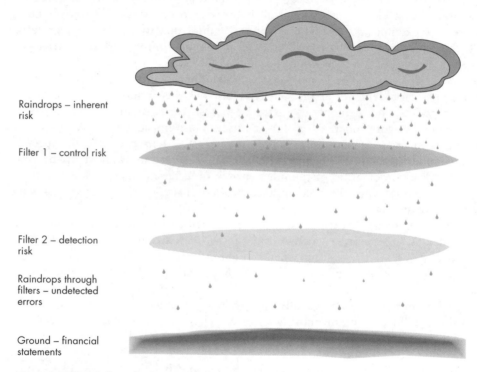

The raindrops falling from the cloud represent errors that occur as a result of the nature of the entity's business – this is known as the inherent risk of the entity. Filter 1 represents the entity's internal control system. The assessment of how effectively this filter stops the raindrops (errors) is the auditors' assessment of the level of control risk. If this assessment of control risk is less than 100%, then the auditors must perform some tests of control. Filter 2 represents the substantive audit procedures performed by the auditors. The assessment of how effectively this filter stops the raindrops (errors) that have passed through Filter 1 (the internal control system) is the level of detection risk. Audit risk is, therefore, the chance that raindrops (errors) will pass through both filters and reach the ground (undetected errors).

Figure 5.1 *Rain cloud analogy*

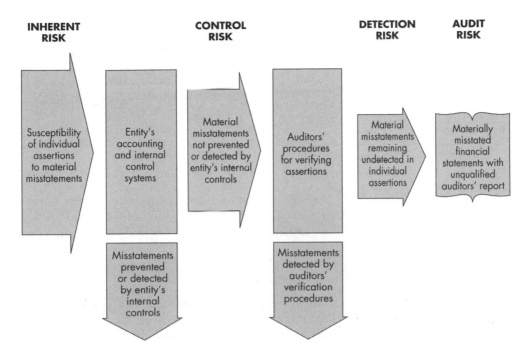

Figure 5.2 *Summary of risk components*

properly planning and controlling the audit process. This will be explained in Chapter 6. A summary of the components of audit risk is presented in Figure 5.2.

The relationship among risk components

Given that the auditors' objective is to achieve as low a level of audit risk as is practicable, and recognising the cost of performing audit procedures, there is an inverse relationship between the assessed levels of inherent and control risks and the level of detection risk that they can accept. Thus, if inherent and control risks are assessed as being low, auditors can tolerate a higher level of detection risk, enabling a reduction in the extent of substantive procedures they must undertake. Table 5.2 provides guidance as to the acceptable level of detection risk. (The light shaded area represents detection risk.)

In relating the components of audit risk, auditors may express each component in quantitative terms (such as percentages) or non-quantitative terms (such as low, medium and high). In either case, the auditors must understand the relationships expressed in the audit risk model in determining the planned acceptable level of detection risk.

QUANTIFIED AUDIT RISK MODEL

The audit risk model expresses the relationship among the audit risk components as follows:

$$AR = IR \times CR \times DR$$

The acronyms represent audit risk (AR), inherent risk (IR), control risk (CR) and detection risk (DR). To illustrate the use of the model, assume the auditors have made the

Table 5.2 Acceptable detection risk matrix

	AUDITORS' ASSESSMENT OF CONTROL RISK IS		
	HIGH	MEDIUM	LOW
AUDITORS' ASSESSMENT OF INHERENT RISK High Medium Low	Lowest Lower Medium	Lower Medium Higher	Medium Higher Highest

Source: IAS 400. Copyright © International Federation of Accountants.

following risk assessments for a particular transaction class or account balance – that IR and CR both equal 50%. Now, assume the auditors have specified an overall AR of 5%. Detection risk can be determined by solving the model for DR as follows:

$$DR = \frac{AR}{IR \times CR} = \frac{0.05}{0.5 \times 0.5} = 0.20 (\text{or } 20\%)$$

If the auditors decide that IR cannot be assessed, or that the effort to do so will exceed the benefits of a lower assessment, then they can take the conservative approach of assessing IR at 100%. In this case, the model yields a DR of 10% – that is, $0.05 \div (1.0 \times 0.5)$. If the auditors also assess CR at 100%, then DR becomes 5% – that is, $0.05 \div (1.0 \times 1.0)$.

The model assumes that inherent and control risks are independent of each other. However, management responds to inherent risk by designing an internal control framework to prevent or detect misstatements (see Figure 5.2). As a result, in many instances inherent and control risks may be interrelated. In these circumstances a separate assessment of inherent and control risks would be inappropriate and the auditors will arrive at a joint assessment.

It is important to be aware that the numerical values attached to risks do not have any real meaning but are used to facilitate consistency in the application of judgement. An assessment of control risk at 50%, for example, does not mean that the control system will not detect 50% of errors. Similarly, when auditors assign a value of 5% to overall audit risk, it does not mean that an incorrect audit opinion is given on one audit in every 20.

Few auditors attempt to quantify each of the risk components. However, even when the risk assessment is not solved mathematically, familiarity with the model makes the following relationship clear: given that the aim is to hold audit risk to a specified level, the higher the assessed levels of inherent and control risks, the lower will be the acceptable level of detection risk.

RISK COMPONENTS MATRIX

Auditors may use non-quantitative expressions for risk, such as the risk components matrix shown in Table 5.2. The matrix is consistent with the quantified audit risk model in that the acceptable levels of detection risk are inversely related to the assessments of inherent and control risks.

If the auditors' assessment of control and inherent risks is at a maximum, then the acceptable level of detection risk will have to be very low – that is, the risk that the auditors' substantive procedure will not detect misstatement will need to be low.

Audit risk at the financial statement and account balance levels

The auditors specify an overall audit risk level to be achieved for the financial statements as a whole. In contrast, the assessed levels of inherent and control risk and the acceptable level of detection risk can vary for each account balance and transaction class.

 LEARNING **CHECK**

5.1 The auditors' objective in planning and performing the audit is to reduce audit risk to an appropriately low level to support an opinion as to whether the financial statements give a true and fair view.

5.2 Audit risk is the risk that the auditors may give an inappropriate audit opinion when the financial statements are materially misstated.

5.3 The three components of audit risk are inherent risk, control risk and detection risk.

5.4 The components of audit risk may be expressed in quantitative terms or non-quantitative terms.

5.5 For a specified level of audit risk, there is an inverse relationship between the assessed levels of inherent risk and control risk and the level of detection risk the auditors can accept.

5.6 There is an inverse relationship between audit risk and the amount of evidence needed to support the auditors' opinion on the financial statements.

MATERIALITY

So far audit risk has been described in terms of the risk that the financial statements might be misstated. It should be evident that some misstatements are more serious than others. An error of a few pounds in determining the value of stock worth a million or more pounds is unlikely to warrant further investigation, whereas the omission of a building from the total of the entity's property is likely to be serious. The term 'material' is used to distinguish misstatements of audit significance from those that are not. The full definition of audit risk thus refers to the risk of 'material' misstatements. Materiality thus underpins the application of Auditing Standards and it has a pervasive effect in a financial statement audit. Auditors should consider materiality in planning the audit and evaluating the truth and fairness of the financial statements.

The concept of materiality

In relation to financial statements, materiality is defined as follows:

Information is material if its omission or misstatement could influence the economic decisions of users taken on the basis of the financial statements. Materiality depends on the size of the item or error judged in the particular circumstances of its omission or misstatement. Thus, materiality provides a threshold or cut-off point rather than being a primary qualitative characteristic which information must have if it is to be useful.[2]

Material information means information that matters, is important or is essential. In the measuring or disclosing of accounting information, the emphasis is on the needs of users.

In auditing, materiality pertains to the extent of misstatements (uncorrected errors, erroneous disclosures or omissions) that exist in the financial statements. Auditors plan and execute an audit with a reasonable expectation of detecting material misstatements. The assessment of what is material is a matter of the auditors' professional judgement of the needs of the reasonable person relying on the information.

Auditors consider materiality when:

- determining the nature, timing and extent of audit procedures; and
- evaluating the effect of misstatements on the truth and fairness of the financial statements (ISA 320).

Materiality at the financial statement level

Financial statements are materially misstated when they contain errors or irregularities that act, individually or in aggregate, to prevent the statements from being presented fairly in accordance with Financial Reporting Standards. In this context, misstatements may result from misapplication of applicable standards, departures from fact, or omissions of necessary information.

More than one level of materiality may relate to the financial statements. For the profit and loss statement, materiality could be related to revenue or profit. For the balance sheet, materiality could be based on shareholders' equity, assets or liability class totals.

In making a judgement about materiality, the auditors should use the smallest aggregate level of misstatement considered to be material to any one of the financial statements. This decision rule is appropriate because the financial statements are interrelated and many audit procedures pertain to more than one statement. The audit procedure to determine whether year-end credit sales are recorded in the proper period, for example, provides evidence about both debtors (balance sheet) and sales (profit and loss statement).

Materiality judgements involve an assessment of both the amount (quantity) and the nature (quality) of the misstatements. Materiality considerations may be influenced by legal and statutory requirements; for example, disclosures pertaining to audit fees and directors' remuneration must be made irrespective of the amounts involved.

QUANTITATIVE GUIDELINES

In assessing the quantitative importance of a misstatement, the auditors need to relate the amount of the error to the financial statements under examination. In determining whether an amount or aggregate of an item is material, the auditors should compare the item with the more appropriate of the base amounts described below:

- for items relating to the balance sheet:
  - equity or the appropriate asset or liability class total;

- for items relating to the profit and loss account:
  - operating profit or loss for the current financial year; or
  - average operating profit or loss for a number of years (including the current financial year); and
- for items relating to cash flows:
  - net cash provided or used in the operating, investing, financing or other activities, as appropriate for the current financial year; or
  - average net cash flows provided by or used in the operating, investing, financing or other activities, as appropriate for a number of years (including the current financial year).

Average profit or cash flow is preferred where the current year's profit or cash flow is substantially different from previous years.

There is no agreed guideline for determining this relationship but, in the absence of evidence or a convincing argument to the contrary:

- an amount that is equal to or greater than 10% of profit is presumed to be material;
- an amount that is equal to or less than 5% of profit may be presumed not to be material; and
- whether an amount between 5% and 10% is material is a matter of judgement.

Materiality judgements relating to profit and loss should ordinarily exclude the effect of unusual items or abnormal fluctuations, exceptional events or transactions, and discontinued operations.

Other commonly used bases and materiality thresholds (expressed as a percentage of that base) are as follows:

BASE	MATERIALITY THRESHOLD (%)
Turnover	0.5
Gross profit	2.0
Total assets	0.5
Equity	1.0

Sometimes auditors use the blended method – that is, combining the four thresholds listed above with equal weights, and computing an average of the sum.

QUALITATIVE CONSIDERATIONS

In planning the examination, auditors generally are concerned only with misstatements that are quantitatively material. The errors are not yet known, so their qualitative effect can be considered only as evidence becomes available.

Qualitative considerations relate to the causes of misstatements or to misstatements that do not have a quantifiable effect. A misstatement that is quantitatively immaterial may be qualitatively material. This may occur, for instance, when the misstatement is attributable to a control weakness, an irregularity or an illegal act by the entity.

Discovery of such an occurrence could lead the auditors to conclude there is a significant risk of additional similar misstatements. Other examples of qualitative misstatements include:

- an inadequate or improper description of an accounting policy;
- a failure to disclose the breach of regulatory requirements;
- a change in accounting method which is likely to affect materially the results of subsequent financial years;
- a related party transaction or event requiring disclosure; and
- a probability of a breach of a financial covenant; for example, a loan agreement may require the entity to maintain a specified minimum current ratio as at the balance sheet date. The company may be tempted to overstate current assets or understate current liabilities. For this reason auditors might choose to use a lower materiality threshold for current assets and current liabilities.

Although it is suggested that auditors should be alert for misstatements that could be qualitatively material, ordinarily it is not practical to design procedures to detect them.

Materiality at the account balance level

Account balance materiality is the minimum misstatement that can exist in an account balance for it to be considered materially misstated. Misstatement up to that level is known as tolerable error. The recorded balance of an account generally represents the upper limit on the amount by which an account can be overstated. Thus, accounts with balances smaller than materiality are sometimes said to be immaterial in terms of the risk of overstatement. However, there is no limit on the amount by which an account balance could be understated. Thus, accounts with immaterial balances could still be materially understated.

In making judgements about materiality at the account balance level, auditors must plan the audit to detect misstatements that, although immaterial individually, may be material to the financial statements taken as a whole when aggregated with misstatements in other account balances.

Allocating financial statement materiality to accounts

When the auditors' preliminary judgements about financial statement materiality are quantified, a preliminary estimate of materiality for each account may be obtained by allocating financial statement materiality to the individual accounts. The allocation may be made to both balance sheet and profit and loss statement accounts. However, because most profit and loss statement misstatements also affect the balance sheet, and because there are fewer balance sheet accounts, many auditors make the allocation on the basis of the balance sheet accounts.

To illustrate the allocation, assume that the total assets of Hart Company consist of the following:

	BALANCE	%
Cash	£500,000	5
Debtors	1,500,000	15
Stocks	3,000,000	30
Plant and machinery	5,000,000	50
Total	£10,000,000	100

Assuming the preliminary estimate of financial statement materiality is 1% of total assets, or £100,000, consider the following alternative allocation plans:

	MATERIALITY ALLOCATION			
ACCOUNT	PLAN A	PER CENT	PLAN B	%
Cash	£5,000	5	£2,000	2
Debtors	15,000	15	18,000	18
Stocks	30,000	30	50,000	50
Plant and machinery	50,000	50	30,000	30
Total	£100,000	100	£100,000	100

In Plan A, materiality has been allocated proportionately to each account. It is a conservative approach and inefficient in terms of audit effort. In Plan B, the allocation is based on the auditors' subjective judgement of the inherent risk relative to size and of the probability of misstatements. The largest materiality allocation is made to plant and machinery where few misstatements are expected and, particularly with regard to the depreciation provision, users do not expect the recorded amounts to be precise. The lowest allocation is to cash where users expect the amount to be correct and where a slight misstatement could affect assessment of liquidity.

Although the foregoing example suggests a certain degree of precision in allocating overall materiality to accounts, in the final analysis the process heavily depends on the subjective judgement of the auditors.

Preliminary judgements about materiality

The auditors' preliminary judgements about materiality may be made several months before the balance sheet date. Thus, the judgements may be based on interim financial statement data.

Alternatively, they may be based on prior years' financial results adjusted for current changes, such as the general condition of the economy and industry trends. This assessment, often referred to as planning materiality, may ultimately differ from the materiality levels used at the conclusion of the audit in the evaluation of the audit findings because the surrounding circumstances may change and additional information about the entity will have been obtained during the course of the audit. As a result of errors discovered during the audit, for example, the auditors may know that the entity's financial position is worse than they presumed when planning the audit. In such cases, the materiality level used in evaluating the audit findings may be lower than the planning level of materiality.

In planning an audit, the auditors should assess materiality at the following two levels:

- the financial statement level (overall materiality), because the auditors' opinion on truth and fairness extends to the financial statements taken as a whole; and
- the account balances class of transactions and disclosures level (testing materiality), because the auditors verify account balances in reaching an overall conclusion on the truth and fairness of the financial statements.

The overall level of materiality and the nature of account balances enable the auditors to determine which account balances to audit and how to evaluate the effects of misstatements in financial information as a whole. Materiality at the account balance and class of transactions level assists the auditors in determining which items in a balance or transaction class to audit and which audit procedures to undertake (for example, whether to use sampling or analytical procedures).

The relationship between materiality and audit evidence

Materiality, like risk, is a key factor that affects the auditors' judgement about the sufficiency of audit evidence. It is generally correct to say, for example, that the lower the materiality level, the greater the amount of evidence that is needed (an inverse relationship). This is the same as saying that it takes more evidence to obtain reasonable assurance that any misstatement in the recorded balance of stocks does not exceed £100,000 than it does to be assured the misstatement does not exceed £200,000. It is also generally correct to say that the larger or more significant an account balance is, the greater the amount of evidence that is needed (a direct relationship). This is the same as saying that more evidence is needed for stocks when it represents 30% of total assets than when it represents 10%.

USING MATERIALITY TO EVALUATE AUDIT EVIDENCE
If there are misstatements in the accounts, then the auditors may perform additional audit procedures or request that management correct the errors. If uncorrected errors exceed materiality and management refuses to make adjustments, then the auditors may consider issuing a qualified audit opinion. The uncorrected aggregated misstatements that the auditors need to examine when considering whether they misstate the financial statements include:

- uncorrected errors specifically identified during the audit (known misstatements);
- projected errors where audit components have been tested by sampling techniques (likely misstatements); and
- the net effect of uncorrected likely misstatements from a prior period that affect the current period's financial statements. (ISA 320)

Auditors review the aggregate of the total misstatements and consider the need to approach management about having these corrected. The auditors may issue a qualified audit report if aggregated uncorrected misstatements exceed materiality (ISA 320).

In this chapter our focus is planning materiality. Making a final assessment of materiality will be explained in Chapter 14.

 LEARNING **CHECK**

5.7 The auditors plan and execute an audit with a reasonable expectation of detecting material misstatements.

5.8 Materiality pertains to the amount of misstatements that could affect the user's decisions.

5.9 Materiality is a matter of professional judgement.

5.10 In the planning phase auditors assess materiality at the financial statement level and then assign a level appropriate to each account balance or individual audit component.

5.11 Planning materiality may differ from materiality levels used in evaluating the audit findings.

5.12 For planning purposes the auditors use the smallest aggregate level of misstatements considered to be material to any one of the financial statements.

5.13 Materiality judgements are both quantitative and qualitative.

5.14 Materiality and audit evidence are inversely related.

5.15 In evaluating the truth and fairness of financial statements, the auditors assess whether the aggregate of uncorrected misstatements is material.

AUDIT OBJECTIVES

The overall objective of a financial statement audit is 'to enable the auditors to express an opinion whether the financial statements are prepared, in all material respects, in accordance with an identified financial reporting framework' (ISA 200). To meet this objective, it is necessary to identify specific audit objectives for each transaction class, account balance and disclosure. In preparing the financial statements the management of the entity can be said to be making a set of assertions about each transaction class, account balance or disclosure – referred to as financial statement assertions.

The auditors formulate an opinion on the financial statements as a whole on the basis of evidence obtained through the verification of assertions related to individual account balances, transaction classes or disclosures. The objective is to restrict audit risk at the account balance level so, at the conclusion of the audit, the audit risk in expressing an opinion on the financial statements as a whole will be at an appropriately low level. Thus, the overall audit risk is disaggregated to each account balance, transaction class or disclosure.

Management's financial statement assertions

Management's financial statement assertions are both explicit and implicit. ISA 500, Audit Evidence, presents a classification of these financial statement assertions. These are defined in Table 5.3.

Although the assertions are subdivided into transactions, balances and disclosures, they are interrelated such that auditors do not need to obtain evidence separately for transactions, balances or disclosures. For example, if the auditors verify the completeness of recorded transactions, it follows that the related account balance and disclosure is also likely to be complete. It is further possible to group the assertions of occurrence and existence, and the assertions of accuracy, classification and valuation. The existence of an asset or liability can only be the consequence of the occurrence of a transaction. On initial recognition the appropriate carrying value of an account balance item is determined by a transaction that is accurately recorded at the proper amount and to the correct account (i.e. classification). However, in reaching their conclusion, auditors must reflect whether they have sufficient evidence pertaining to each separate assertion.

Although cut-off is related to both occurrence and completeness in that it refers to the recognition of all transactions and events that occurred within the accounting period, it

Table 5.3 Definitions of financial statement assertions (ISA 500, Audit Evidence)

ASSERTION	DEFINITION
Transactions	
Occurrence	Recorded transactions or other events have occurred and pertain to the entity.
Completeness	All transactions and events that should have been recorded have been recorded.
Accuracy	Amounts and other data relating to recorded transactions and events have been recorded appropriately.
Cut-off	Transactions and events have been recorded in the correct accounting period.
Classification	Transactions and events have been recorded in the proper accounts.
Account balances at period end	
Existence	Assets, liabilities and equity interests exist.
Rights and obligations	The entity holds or controls the rights to assets and liabilities are the obligations of the entity.
Completeness	All assets, liabilities and equity interests that should have been recorded have been recorded.
Valuation	Assets, liabilities and equity interests are included in the financial statements at appropriate amounts.
Presentation and disclosure	
Occurrence and rights and obligations	Disclosed matters have occurred and pertain to the entity.
Completeness	All disclosures that should have been included in the financial statements have been included.
Transparency	Financial information is appropriately classified and disclosures are understandable.

Source: IAS 400. Copyright © International Federation of Accountants.

is treated as a separate assertion for audit purposes since it is the timing of the recording that is critical, not the occurrence or completeness of recorded transactions or events.

For a snapshot understanding of some of these assertions, consider the following balance sheet component:

Current assets:
Cash £252,900

In reporting this item in the balance sheet, management makes the following explicit assertions:

- Cash exists (existence).
- The correct amount of cash is £252,900 (valuation).
- There are no restrictions on the use of cash (transparency).

Management also makes the following implicit assertions:

- All cash that should be reported has been included (completeness).
- All cash transactions have been properly recorded (accuracy).
- All cash transactions have been recorded in the correct accounts (classification).
- All cash transactions have been recorded in the correct accounting period (cut-off).
- All the reported cash is owned by the entity (rights).

The last assertion follows from the presentation of cash in current assets and the absence of any reference to footnote disclosures. If any of these assertions is a misrepresentation, then the financial statements could be misstated.

The following sections will describe each category of assertion and provide examples. Specific audit objectives for cash, derived from each category of assertion, will then be illustrated.

EXISTENCE OR OCCURRENCE

Existence applies to accounts with physical substance, such as cash and stocks, as well as to accounts without physical substance, such as debtors and accounts payable. In the above example, this assertion refers to the existence of items included in cash, such as petty cash funds, undeposited receipts and bank accounts. It does not extend to whether £252,900 is the correct amount for these items. The latter relates to the valuation assertion, as will be explained.

The auditors' principal concern about this assertion relates to the possible overstatement of financial statement balances through the inclusion of items that do not exist, the effects of transactions that did not occur or the improper inclusion of transactions that do not pertain to the entity.

Management also asserts that the revenues and expenses shown in the profit and loss statement are the results of transactions and events that occurred and pertain to the entity. Again, this occurrence assertion extends only to whether transactions and events occurred, not to whether the amounts reported are correct. This assertion would be misrepresented if reported sales transactions were fictitious or if reported expenses include personal expenses improperly charged to the entity.

COMPLETENESS

For each account balance presented in the financial statements, management implicitly asserts that all related transactions and events have been included. Management asserts, for example, that the cash balance of £252,900 includes the effects of all cash transactions and all the cash funds mentioned above. The completeness assertion for cash would be misrepresented if a bank balance was omitted or cash receipts transactions that occurred were not recorded.

The auditors' concern about completeness assertions relates primarily to the possible understatement of financial statement balances through the omission of items that exist or of the effects of transactions that occurred. If omissions are identified, then the issue of the correct amounts at which they should be included relates to the accuracy or valuation assertion.

This assertion is the most difficult for auditors to verify because the starting point of the inquiry is what ought to be recorded, not what is recorded. It is also the audit objective that causes the greatest difficulty for students.

CUT-OFF

Cut-off is a special case of occurrence and completeness in that it refers to the erroneous inclusion of transactions or events that occurred after the end of the period or deferring the recording of transactions or events occurring in the period until after the end of the period. For example, an entity might include as cash, monies that were not received until a day or two after the period end or might fail to record payments made prior to the period end in the cash book until after the period end.

RIGHTS AND OBLIGATIONS

The rights and obligations assertion deals with assets and liabilities, unlike the other assertions, which relate to revenue and expenditure accounts as well. This assertion refers to rights constituting a degree of control over future economic benefits sufficient for recognition as an asset, and to obligations (legal or constructive) sufficient to require recognition as a liability. Management implicitly asserts, for example, that it controls the cash and other assets reported in the balance sheet and that creditors and other liabilities are the obligations of the entity.

ACCURACY, CLASSIFICATION AND VALUATION

The reporting of an account balance at an appropriate amount means that the amount has been determined in accordance with applicable Financial Reporting Standards and is free of mathematical or clerical errors. The determination of amounts in accordance with applicable Financial Reporting Standards includes the proper valuation of assets, liabilities, revenues and expenses through:

- proper measurement at cost on initial recognition and proper valuation at fair value (such as net realisable value, market value or present value) on subsequent remeasurement;
- the reasonableness of management's accounting estimates; and
- consistency in the application of accounting policies.

Thus, for example, debtors are reported at net realisable value; stocks are reported at lower of cost or net realisable value; and investments, depending on their characteristics, are reported at cost or market value. Accounting estimates, such as bad debt provisions and net realisable values of stock, should be reasonable. Where applicable the valuation requirements of Financial Reporting Standards should be consistently applied across periods except when a change is justified.

Accuracy refers to the accurate depiction of transactions and events and to the clerical accuracy of journal entries, postings to ledger accounts and the determination of account balances. It also applies to the correctness of computations for such items as accruals and depreciation. Continuing our cash illustration from page 147, mathematical errors in adding the cash receipts or payment journals, or clerical errors made in recording the nature or amount of a transaction or in posting the journal totals to the general ledger account for cash, would cause a misstatement in the valuation assertion for cash.

TRANSPARENCY
In the financial statements, management implicitly asserts that the financial information is properly presented and that accompanying disclosure is adequate. In the cash example, it would be a misrepresentation of this assertion if the use of cash was restricted and the notes included in the financial statements did not indicate this fact.

Specific audit objectives

Auditors develop specific audit objectives for each account balance using the financial statement assertions. Table 5.4 illustrates the derivation of specific audit objectives for cash. Specific audit objectives are tailored to fit the circumstances of each audit entity, such as the nature of its economic activity and its accounting policies and practices. From the evidence accumulated, the auditors reach a conclusion as to whether any of management's assertions are misrepresentations. Subsequently, the auditors combine conclusions about the individual assertions to reach an opinion on the truth and fairness of the financial statements as a whole.

◁ LEARNING **CHECK**

5.16 Management's financial statement assertions are a useful starting point in developing specific audit objectives for each account balance, class of transaction or disclosure.

5.17 If any of these assertions is a misrepresentation, the financial statements could be materially misstated.

5.18 A misstatement of the existence or occurrence assertion will result in the overstatement of financial statement components.

5.19 A misstatement of the completeness assertion will result in the understatement of financial statement components.

5.20 A misstatement in the accuracy, classification or valuation assertion will occur if an applicable Financial Reporting Standard is incorrectly applied, items are incorrectly

Table 5.4 Specific audit objectives for cash

ASSERTION CATEGORY	SPECIFIC AUDIT OBJECTIVE
Existence or occurrence	The petty cash funds, undeposited receipts, cash at bank and any other items reported as cash exist at the balance sheet date.
Completeness	Reported cash includes all petty cash funds, undeposited receipts, and other cash on hand.
	Reported cash includes all bank account balances.
Cut-off	Transactions and events either side of the end of the period have been properly recorded in the correct accounting period.
Rights and obligations	All items included in cash are owned by the entity at the balance sheet date.
Accuracy, classification and valuation	The items comprising cash have been correctly totalled.
	Cash receipts and payments journals are mathematically correct and have been properly posted to the correct accounts in the general ledger.
	Cash on hand has been correctly counted.
	Bank account balances have been properly reconciled.
Transparency	All items included in cash are unrestricted and the cash is available for operations.
	Required disclosures such as compensating balance agreements have been made.

computed or added, revenues or expenses are recorded in the wrong accounting period or estimates are unreasonable.

5.21 A misstatement in the transparency assertion will occur if financial information is not presented in accordance with applicable Financial Reporting Standards and regulatory requirements, and if accompanying disclosures are inadequate.

AUDIT EVIDENCE

Audit evidence is a fundamental concept in auditing by which the auditors achieve the objective of reasonable assurance that none of management's assertions is materially misstated. Audit evidence consists of:

- underlying accounting data; and
- all corroborating information available to the auditors.

Examples of each type of evidence in each category and the relationship of the categories to the Auditing Standard are shown in Table 5.5. In a computer information system (CIS) environment, the underlying accounting data may be in electronic format and may or may not be printed out.

Both categories of evidence are required in making an audit in accordance with Auditing Standards. Underlying accounting data are indispensable, for they provide the basis for the

Table 5.5 Categories and types of audit evidence

NATURE OF AUDIT EVIDENCE	RELATIONSHIP TO AUDITING STANDARDS
Underlying accounting data • Books of original entry • General and subsidiary ledgers • Related accounting manuals • Informal and memorandum records, such as worksheets, computations and reconciliations **Corroborating information** • Documents such as cheques, invoices, contracts etc. • Confirmations and other written representations • Information from inquiry, observations, inspection and physical examination • Other information obtained or developed by the auditors	SUFFICIENT AND APPROPRIATE AUDIT EVIDENCE

entity's financial statements. However, it is imperative that the auditors obtain supportive or corroborative evidence of the reliability of the financial records. Much of this evidence is available within the entity, but recourse to sources outside the entity (such as customers and independent experts) is also necessary.

The process of identifying specific sources of evidence to meet specific audit objectives for individual account balances is covered extensively in later chapters of this book. This chapter will establish a general framework for identifying the types of evidence and the financial statement assertions to which they relate.

The Auditing Standard pertaining to evidence

ISA 500 states that:

> The auditor should obtain sufficient appropriate audit evidence to be able to draw reasonable conclusions on which to base the audit opinion.

The standard specifies that 'sufficient' (enough) 'appropriate' (relevant and reliable) audit evidence should be obtained to provide a 'reasonable' (rational) basis for an opinion. If sufficient appropriate evidence is not available, then the scope of the audit is restricted, which may prevent the auditors from giving an unqualified opinion. The audit evidence required to support an opinion is a matter for the auditors to determine in the exercise of professional judgement after a careful study of the circumstances of the specific audit engagement. Considerations that may influence the auditors' judgement are discussed in the following sections.

SUFFICIENCY OF AUDIT EVIDENCE

Sufficiency relates to the quantity of audit evidence. Factors that may affect the auditors' judgement of sufficiency include:

- materiality and risk;
- economic factors; and
- the size and characteristics of the population.

Materiality and risk

In general, more evidence is needed for accounts that are material to the financial statements. Thus, in the audit of a manufacturing company, the quantity of evidence needed in support of the audit objectives for stocks will be greater than the quantity needed for the audit objectives for prepaid expenses.

Similarly, more evidence is normally required for accounts that are likely to be misstated than for accounts that are likely to be correct. Normally, for example, there is a higher risk of error in the valuation of stock than in the valuation of land used as a factory site. The required degree of assurance (conversely, audit risk) has an impact on the sufficiency of evidence. The auditors will obtain evidence to reduce the level of audit risk to an acceptably low level.

Economic factors

Auditors work within economic limits that dictate that sufficient evidence must be obtained within a reasonable time and at a reasonable cost. Thus, auditors are frequently faced with a decision as to whether the additional time and cost will produce commensurate benefits in terms of both the quantity and quality of the evidence obtained. To verify the existence of stock at each of an entity's 25 branches, for example, the auditors can visit each branch. A less costly alternative is to visit five of the branches and rely on the reports of the entity's internal auditors for the other 20.

Population size and characteristics

The size of a population refers to the number of items that comprise the total – for example, the number of credit sales transactions or the number of customer accounts in the sales ledger. The size of the accounting populations underlying many financial statement items makes sampling a practical necessity in gathering evidence. The nature of audit sampling will be explained in Chapter 8.

APPROPRIATENESS OF AUDIT EVIDENCE

Appropriateness refers to the quality of audit evidence. For evidence to be appropriate, it must be relevant and reliable.

Relevance

Relevance means that evidence must be sufficient with respect to each of the auditors' objectives. Auditors may determine, for example, the existence of stock through inspection, but must also perform tests of pricing of stock to provide evidence for valuation.

Reliability

The reliability of evidence is influenced by factors such as the source and nature of the information, and its timeliness and objectivity. The importance of these factors is illustrated by the following examples.

SOURCE AND NATURE OF THE INFORMATION

Evidence may be oral or written and may be created by the auditors, obtained from sources outside of the entity or obtained from sources within the entity. ISA 500 recognises the following presumptions about the effects of the source of the information on the reliability of audit evidence:

- Audit evidence from external sources is more reliable than that obtained from the entity's records.
- Audit evidence obtained from the entity's records is more reliable when the related internal control structure operates effectively.
- Evidence obtained directly by the auditors is more reliable than evidence obtained by or from the entity.
- Evidence in the form of documents and written representations is more reliable than oral representations.
- Original documents are more reliable than photocopies or facsimiles.

Suppose that you, as an auditor, seek evidence concerning the amount of cash on hand and the amount owed by customer X. You conclude that the cash should be counted, but by whom – you or the entity? If you count it, you have direct personal knowledge of the amount on hand; if the entity makes the count and gives you a report, you have indirect knowledge. Clearly, the former provides more appropriate evidence. For the customer's balance, you can examine evidence within the entity (such as the duplicate sales invoice) or ask the customer to confirm the balance owed. In this case, the latter is considered to be the more reliable evidence because the customer is a third party who is independent of the entity.

TIMELINESS

Timeliness relates to the date to which the evidence is applicable. The timeliness of the evidence is especially important in verifying current asset, current liability and related profit and loss balances. For these accounts, the auditors seek evidence that the entity has made a proper cut-off of cash, sales and purchase transactions at the balance sheet date. This task is facilitated when appropriate auditing procedures are applied at or near that date. Similarly, evidence obtained from physical counts at the balance sheet date provides better evidence of quantities on hand at that date than counts made at other times.

OBJECTIVITY

Evidence that is objective in nature is generally considered more reliable than evidence that is subjective. Evidence of the existence of tangible assets, for example, can be ascertained with a substantial degree of conclusiveness through physical inspection.

In contrast, evidence in support of management's estimates of stock obsolescence and of provisions for product warranties may be largely subjective. In such cases the auditors should:

- consider the expertise and integrity of the individual making the estimate; and
- assess the appropriateness of the processes followed by the entity in arriving at the estimate.

REASONABLE BASIS

The auditors are not expected or required to have an absolute, certain or guaranteed basis for an opinion. In arriving at their professional judgement of reasonable assurance, they are guided by the persuasiveness of the evidence.

Professional judgement

Given that professional judgement is involved, different auditors will not always reach identical conclusions about the quantity and quality of evidence needed to reach an opinion on financial statements. However, several factors contribute to achieving a uniform application of the reasonable basis requirement.

Auditing Standards contain many specific requirements about audit evidence and provide guidance about ways in which to meet these requirements. Auditors are required to justify any departure from the requirements and must consider carefully the desirability of not complying with the guidance.

The practice of auditing involves two counterbalancing forces. On the one hand, the auditing firm is well aware that an inadequate basis for an opinion may result in lawsuits by those harmed by reliance on an incorrect auditors' report. On the other hand, competition tends to make each firm cost and fee conscious. Accordingly, the firm is restrained from obtaining an inordinately high degree of assurance in a specific engagement because other firms may be able to perform the audit at less cost.

Professional scepticism

Management is responsible for the financial statements and is also in a position to control much of the corroborating evidence and underlying accounting data that support those statements. Professional scepticism is about achieving an appropriate balance between distrusting management and placing complete trust in the integrity of management. In conducting the audit the auditors must be alert to any suspicious circumstances that may require a greater degree of scepticism than would otherwise be appropriate.

Types of corroborating information

The auditing student should already be familiar with the basic components of underlying accounting data identified in Table 5.5 (i.e. journals, ledgers, worksheets, reconciliations, etc.). This section will identify and elaborate on each of the principal types of corroborating information and consider its nature, reliability and the categories of assertion to which it is most relevant.

ANALYTICAL EVIDENCE

Analytical evidence involves comparisons of current period entity data, such as total revenues or return on assets, with expected values. The normal expectation is that the values will be similar to prior period values. Alternatively, the auditors may expect current values to be related to budgeted amounts, industry data or specially developed values based on known changes in the period. The comparisons are then used to draw inferences about the truth and fairness of specific financial statement balances in terms of existence, completeness and valuation.

When several related financial variables all conform to expectations, the reliability of this type of evidence is enhanced. When recorded sales, cost of sales, gross profit margin and debtors and stock turnover rates all conform to expectations, for example, the analytical evidence may be viewed as supporting the existence, completeness and valuation assertions for sales and cost of sales balances. The existence and effectiveness of controls influence the reliability of analytical evidence. When controls are effective, the auditors have greater confidence in the reliability of the information and therefore the results of analytical procedures.

CONFIRMATIONS

Confirmations are direct written responses made by knowledgeable third parties to specific requests for factual information. Table 5.6 shows the items that are frequently confirmed.

ISA 505, External Confirmations, provides guidance on the use of confirmations that are generally considered to have a high degree of reliability. It is normal practice for the auditors to obtain confirmation evidence for debtors whenever it is practical and reasonable to do so, and it is standard practice to obtain confirmations for bank balances. The use of confirmations in other applications depends on the relative cost and reliability of alternative forms of evidence that may be available to the auditors. However, the effort involved in preparing and sending confirmation requests and in analysing the responses can be quite time consuming, often making this a costly form of evidence.

This type of evidence may support any of the assertions, but it is primarily related to the existence or occurrence and cut-off assertions.

DOCUMENTARY EVIDENCE

Documentary evidence includes documents relating to transactions such as invoices and requisitions, as well as such items as minutes of the board of directors, lease agreements and bank statements. Documents, which may be generated externally or internally, are usually contained in entity files and are available for the auditors' inspection on request.

Examples of externally generated documents include customer order forms, suppliers' invoices, tax assessments and bank statements. Externally generated documents are considered to be reliable because they originate from independent third parties. However, they may be altered by an employee at the entity before being shown to the auditors. This risk is particularly high if the auditors are offered a photocopy or facsimile. The

Table 5.6 Frequently confirmed items and their sources

ITEM	KNOWLEDGEABLE RESPONDENT
Cash in bank	Bank
Debtors	Individual customers
Stock stored in public warehouse	Warehouse custodian
Accounts payable	Creditors
Debentures payable	Trustee
Lease terms	Lessor
Ordinary shares issued	Registrar
Insurance coverage	Insurance company

reliability of externally generated documents can be enhanced when the auditors obtain copies directly from the external party. Thus, while the auditors normally examine the copy of the bank statements held by the entity, they may request the entity to have the bank send a statement as of a particular date directly to the auditors for use in verifying cash balances.

Examples of internally generated documents include sales order forms, sales invoices, purchase orders and goods received notes. Given that it is possible for entity employees to create internal documents to support fictitious transactions, the reliability of internally generated documents is enhanced when they bear evidence of having been circulated to external parties before being placed in the entity's files. A delivery note prepared by the entity but signed by the customer to acknowledge receipt of the goods, for example, provides strong evidence that the transaction occurred. Similarly, a deposit slip receipted by the bank provides strong evidence that a deposit was actually made. In contrast, duplicate file copies of sales invoices and purchase requisitions that bear no evidence of external circulation may be less reliable. Figure 5.3 summarises the effects of circulation on the reliability of documentary evidence.

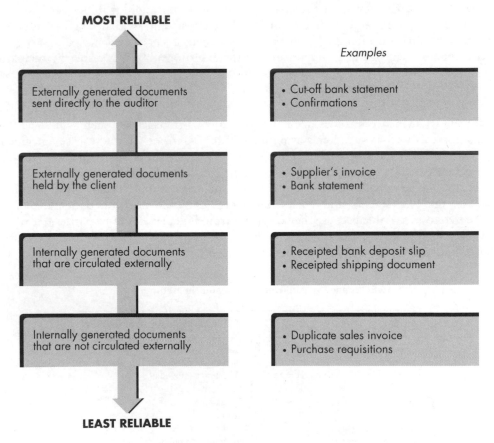

Figure 5.3 *Effects of circulation on reliability of documentary evidence*

The physical characteristics of documents may also affect their reliability. Special papers, pre-numbered documents and machine-imprinted data, for example, make it more difficult to alter documents or to create phony documentation.

Documentary evidence is used extensively in auditing and may pertain to any of the categories of management assertion. There are two special classes of documentary evidence: (1) confirmations, which have already been discussed, and (2) written representations, which will be discussed in the next section.

WRITTEN REPRESENTATIONS

Written representations are responses to inquiries by auditors by responsible and knowledgeable individuals. They may be differentiated from confirmations in two ways: (1) they may originate either from within the entity's organisation or from external sources, and (2) they may contain subjective information or an individual's opinion about a matter, rather than factual information.

ISA 580, Management Representations, requires auditors to obtain certain written representations from management. Commonly presented in the form of a letter, such representations are designed to document management's replies to inquiries made by the auditors during the audit. These representations may reveal information that is not shown in the accounting records, such as the existence of contingencies that may require investigation. The use of a management representation letter will be explained in Chapter 14.

During the course of an audit, the auditors may also request written representations from outside experts. The independent auditors are not expected to possess the expertise of a geologist in estimating the quantity of ore in a mine or of a lawyer in evaluating litigation pending against the entity. When such evidence is needed, ISA 620, Using the Work of an Expert, states that auditors may use the work of a specialist. A relatively high degree of reliance may be placed on this type of evidence, especially when the response validates other information that has come to the auditors' attention. Written representations may pertain to any of the assertions.

MATHEMATICAL EVIDENCE

Mathematical evidence results from recomputations by the auditors and a comparison of those results with entity computations. This may involve the results of: (1) routine tasks such as checking the additions of journals, ledgers and supporting schedules, and (2) complicated recalculations such as reconciliations. Mathematical evidence generated by the auditors is reliable, has a relatively low cost and contributes to the basis for the auditors' conclusions about valuation and accuracy assertions.

ORAL EVIDENCE

During an audit, auditors will make frequent oral inquiries of officers and key employees of the entity. Oral evidence is rarely reliable by itself. Its primary value lies in directing the auditors to other sources of evidence, corroborating other types of evidence and disclosing matters that may merit further investigation and documentation.

When oral evidence plays a key role in an audit decision, the source, nature and date of the evidence should be documented in the working papers. When obtained from management, the auditors may request that such evidence be reaffirmed in writing in management's representation letter. Oral evidence may pertain to any of the categories of financial statement assertions.

PHYSICAL EVIDENCE

Physical evidence is obtained from physical inspection of tangible assets. For example, the auditors will acquire direct personal knowledge of the existence of undeposited cash receipts or stocks by inspecting them.

Physical evidence is also helpful in determining the quality (or condition) of an asset that may relate to the valuation assertion. In some cases, the auditors may not be qualified to determine quality, condition or value based on the physical evidence, so may engage an expert to examine the physical evidence. The auditors would then rely on the expert's written representation, together with the physical evidence.

ELECTRONIC EVIDENCE

Electronic evidence is any information produced or maintained by electronic means that is used by auditors. 'Electronic' means the use of computers, scanners, sensors, magnetic media and other electronic devices associated with the creation, manipulation, transmission and reception of electronic data.

When transactions are conducted over computer networks, many traditional accounting documents are eliminated. An entity's computer may be used, for example, to: (1) determine when a stock item needs to be reordered, (2) generate and electronically transmit the order to a supplier's computer, (3) receive shipping and invoicing information directly from the supplier's computer, and (4) initiate the electronic transfer of funds from the entity's bank account to the supplier's bank account to pay for the order.

In such cases, the auditors must use the electronic evidence of the transactions. The reliability of such evidence is a function of the controls over the creation, alteration and completeness of such data, and the competence of the tools (audit software) that the auditors use to access the electronic evidence.

The impact of technology on other traditional forms of evidence also poses new opportunities and challenges, such as the faxing of confirmations. Again, the auditors must consider controls related to the origin, transmission and receipt of faxed information in assessing the reliability of the evidence.

Electronic evidence may substitute for several of the traditional types of evidence discussed previously and may pertain to any of the categories of assertions.

◁ LEARNING **CHECK**

5.22 Audit evidence comprises underlying accounting data and corroborating information.

5.23 Audit evidence needs to be sufficient and appropriate to afford a reasonable basis to form an opinion.

5.24 Factors that affect the sufficiency of audit evidence are materiality and risk, economic factors and size and characteristics of the population.

5.25 For evidence to be appropriate it must be relevant and reliable.

5.26 The principal types of corroborating information consist of analytical evidence, confirmations, documentary evidence, written representations, and mathematical, oral, physical and electronic evidence.

AUDITING PROCEDURES

Auditing procedures are methods and techniques used by the auditors to gather and evaluate audit evidence. Each procedure has a particular advantage for obtaining evidence for an assertion. In selecting a procedure, auditors must take care to balance the potential effectiveness of the procedure in meeting specific objectives against the cost of performing the procedure. Some of these procedures are discussed below.

Types of auditing procedure

Auditing procedures include analytical procedures, inspecting (documents and assets), confirming, inquiring, counting, observing, reperforming and computer-assisted audit techniques.

ANALYTICAL PROCEDURES

Analytical procedures involve comparing recorded accounting data with historical information, budget expectations or external benchmarks. These procedures enable the auditors to assess the overall reasonableness of account balances and they produce analytical evidence. These procedures will be discussed in detail in Chapter 6.

INSPECTING DOCUMENTS

Inspecting documents involves careful scrutiny or detailed examination of documents and records. This procedure is used extensively in auditing.

Inspecting documents provides a means for evaluating documentary evidence. Inspection of documents permits the auditors to determine the precise terms of invoices, contracts and agreements. This enables auditors to ensure that transactions have been accurately recorded in the accounting records and, where appropriate, confirms rights or obligations arising as a result of the transactions. When performing this procedure it is important that auditors assess the authenticity of the documents as audit evidence and take care to detect the existence of alterations or questionable items. Inspecting documents is an important procedure in obtaining evidence pertaining to the accuracy and rights and obligations assertions.

Inspection may involve tracing (see below), vouching (see below) or scanning. The term 'scanning' is used to refer to a less careful scrutiny of documents and records.

Tracing

Tracing involves inspecting documents created when transactions were executed and determines that information from the documents was properly recorded in the accounting records. The direction of the testing is from the documents to the accounting records, thus retracing the original flow of the data through the accounting system. This procedure provides assurance that data from source documents were ultimately included in the accounts, so it is especially useful for detecting understatements in the accounting records. Thus, it is an important procedure in obtaining evidence pertaining to completeness assertions.

The effectiveness of tracing is enhanced when the entity uses serially pre-numbered documents and the auditors combine this procedure with counting to verify the completeness of the numerical sequence.

Vouching

Vouching involves selecting entries in the accounting records and inspecting the documentation that served as the basis for the entries, so as to determine the propriety and validity of the recorded transactions. In vouching, the direction of the testing is opposite to that used in tracing.

Vouching is used extensively to detect overstatements in the accounting records. Thus, it is an important procedure in obtaining evidence pertaining to existence or occurrence assertions. Figure 5.4 shows the principal differences between vouching and tracing.

INSPECTING TANGIBLE RESOURCES

Inspecting tangible resources provides auditors with direct personal knowledge of the existence of tangible resources such as stocks and plant and machinery. This procedure primarily provides evidence as to existence but it also contributes to the valuation assertion where the physical condition of the assets suggests possible impairment.

CONFIRMING

Confirming is a form of inquiry that enables auditors to obtain information directly from an independent source outside the entity. Normally, the entity makes the request of the outside party in writing, but the auditors control the mailing of the inquiry. The request should ask the recipient to send the response directly to the auditors. This auditing procedure produces confirmation evidence.

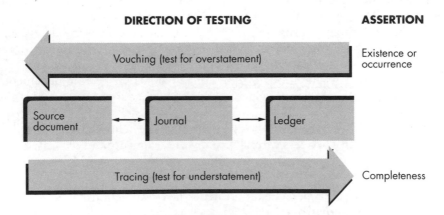

Figure 5.4 *Differences between vouching and tracing*

INQUIRING

Inquiring involves either oral or written inquiry by the auditors. Such inquiries may be made internally to management or employees, as in the case of questions pertaining to the obsolescence of stock items and the collectibility of debtors, or externally, as in inquiries to lawyers concerning the probable outcome of litigation. In performing this procedure the auditors must pay due regard to the competence of the person being questioned and to the manner in which the inquiries are put and the responses evaluated. Inquiry produces either oral evidence or evidence in the form of written representations.

COUNTING

The two most common applications of the counting procedure are the physical counting of tangible resources (such as the amount of cash or stock on hand) and accounting for all pre-numbered documents. The first provides physical evidence of the quantity on hand. The second may be used by the auditors to obtain documentary evidence of the completeness of the accounting records.

OBSERVING

Observing pertains to watching or witnessing the performance of some activity or process. The activity may be the manner in which cash is safeguarded or the care taken by the entity in counting stock. The subject matter of such observation is personnel, procedures and processes. From these observations, the auditors obtain direct personal knowledge of the activities in the form of physical evidence. Observation of procedures provides highly reliable evidence as to their performance at a given time but not necessarily as to their performance at other times. For this reason auditors often perform observation procedures on a surprise basis.

REPERFORMING

A major application of reperforming is to check the accuracy of the accounting process from totalling journals to posting the ledgers and extracting trial balances. It also involves checking calculations and reconciliations made by the entity on schedules and working papers supporting the financial statements such as the bank reconciliation and amounts computed for depreciation and accrued interest. Mathematical evidence is produced by this procedure. Auditors may also reperform selected aspects of the processing of selected transactions to determine that the original processing conformed to prescribed control policies and procedures. The auditors may reperform, for example, the customer credit check for a sales transaction to determine that the customer did indeed have sufficient credit available when the transaction was processed.

COMPUTER-ASSISTED AUDIT TECHNIQUES

When the entity's accounting records are maintained on electronic media, the auditors may use computer-assisted audit techniques in performing several of the procedures described in the preceding sections. The following are examples of how the auditors can use computer audit software:

- to perform the calculations and comparisons used in analytical procedures;
- to select a sample of debtors for confirmation;

- to scan a file to determine that all documents in a series have been accounted for;
- to compare data elements in different files for agreement (such as the prices on sales invoices with a master file containing authorised prices); and
- to reperform a variety of calculations, such as totalling the sales subsidiary ledger or stock file.

The relationships among auditing procedures, types of evidence and assertions

During the course of an audit, in meeting the numerous specific audit objectives derived from management's financial statement assertions, the auditors will use all the auditing procedures and all the types of evidence described in this chapter. Some examples of the relationships among auditing procedures, types of evidence and assertions are depicted in Figure 5.5. This figure shows that tracing, vouching and inspecting involve the use of documentary evidence. The procedure of inspecting may involve the use of physical evidence, as do the procedures of counting and observing. Also, the procedure of inquiring may produce either written representations or oral evidence, depending on the nature of the inquiry and the response.

Classification of auditing procedures

Auditing procedures are usually classified by purpose into the following three categories (ISA 500):

1. risk assessment procedures;
2. tests of controls; and
3. substantive procedures.

RISK ASSESSMENT PROCEDURES

Auditing Standards require auditors to obtain an understanding of the entity and its environment, including its internal control, sufficient to assess the risks of material misstatement at both the financial statement and assertion levels as a basis for planning the audit. These procedures will be explained in Chapter 6.

TESTS OF CONTROLS

Tests of controls are made to provide evidence about the effectiveness of the operation of internal controls. Assume, for example, that a control activity requires cash receipts to be deposited in the bank daily. The auditors can test the effectiveness of the control by observing actual deposits being made or by inspecting duplicate deposit slips. Tests of controls also include inquiry of employees as to their performance of control activities and reperformance of control activities by the auditors. The extent to which auditors perform of tests of controls in a financial statement audit depends largely on the audit strategy adopted, which will be explained in Chapter 6. However, Auditing Standards require tests of controls in situations where substantive procedures, on their own, do not provide sufficient appropriate audit evidence.

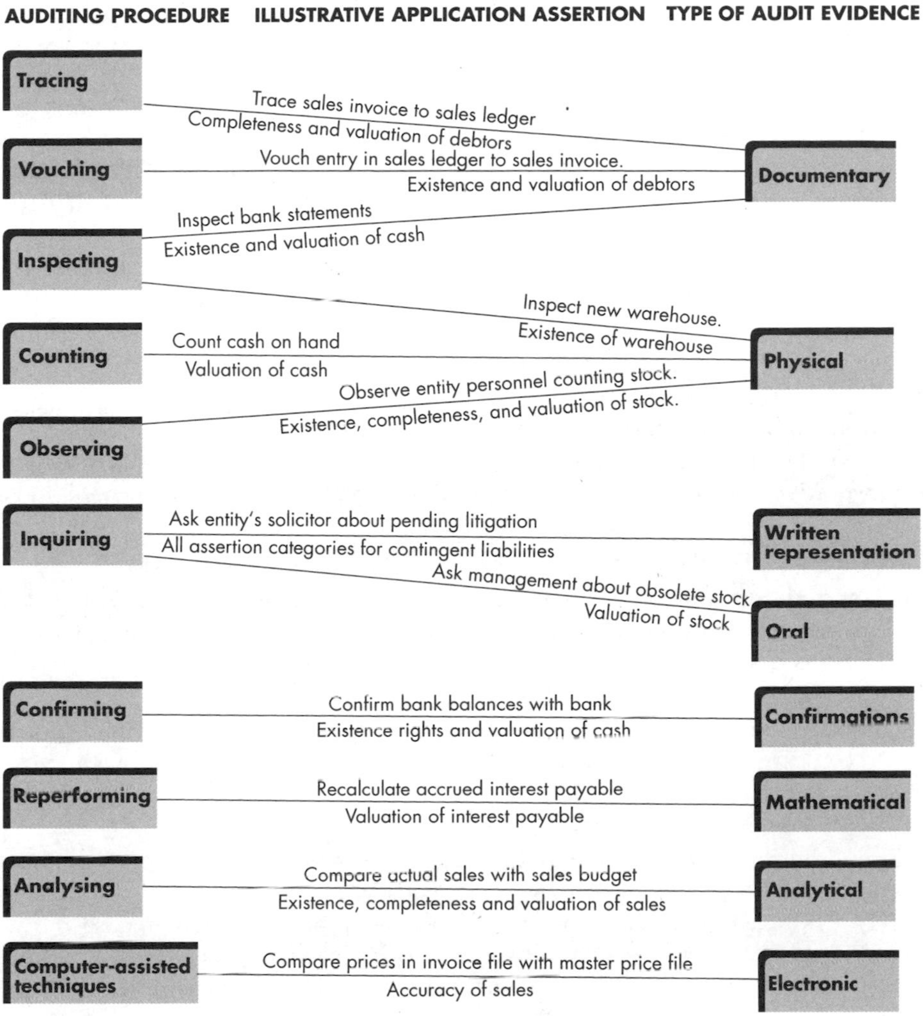

AUDITING PROCEDURE   ILLUSTRATIVE APPLICATION ASSERTION   TYPE OF AUDIT EVIDENCE

Figure 5.5 *Relationships among auditing procedures, types of evidence and specific auditing objectives*

SUBSTANTIVE PROCEDURES

Substantive procedures provide direct evidence as to the absence of material misstatement. Their design reflects the auditors' assessment of the risk of misstatement at the assertion level after taking into consideration the results of tests of controls. This category of auditing procedure consists of:

- analytical procedures;
- tests of details of transactions;
- tests of details of balances; and
- tests of details of disclosures.

Analytical procedures involve the use of comparisons to assess reasonableness – for example, a comparison of an account balance with the prior year's balance or a budgeted amount.

Tests of details of transactions involve examining support for the individual debits and credits posted to an account (for example, vouching the debits in debtors to entries in the sales journal and supporting sales invoices). Similarly, tracing the details from source documents to journals and the affected ledger accounts constitutes a test of details of transactions.

Tests of details of balances involve examining support for the closing balance directly (for example, confirming debtors directly with the customer).

These three types of substantive procedures are complementary. The extent to which each type is used on a given account can vary based on such factors as the relative effectiveness for that account and the cost.

Tests of details of disclosure are usually performed at the final review stage.

Because of the inherent limitations in internal controls, Auditing Standards require that some substantive evidence be obtained for each material account balance.

DUAL-PURPOSE TESTS

An efficient audit often involves situations where a single audit process provides evidence as to both details of transactions and the effective operation of control activities. For example, inspection of purchase invoices may provide evidence:

- as to the accurate recording of a purchase transaction; and
- that the control activity, requiring purchase invoices to be approved by an authorised officer, has been complied with.

Auditors must ensure that the nature and extent of such dual-purpose tests are applicable for both purposes. Auditors must also recognise that the results must be separately evaluated. For example, an invoice may be accurately recorded but not approved. In this case it provides substantive evidence that purchase transactions are accurately recorded but represents a control deviation in that control activities are not properly performed.

Evaluation of evidence obtained

To have a reasonable basis for an opinion on the financial statements, the auditors need a preponderance (i.e. a consensus or majority) of persuasive evidence for each financial statement assertion that is material. When the auditors lack a reasonable basis for an opinion, they express an inability to issue an opinion. When a reasonable basis for an opinion has been obtained, the auditors should issue either an unqualified, 'except for' or adverse opinion, depending on the degree of correspondence of the assertions established by the evidence obtained with the concept of truth and fairness.

The process of obtaining and evaluating audit evidence and determining the effects on the auditors' report is summarised in Figure 5.6.

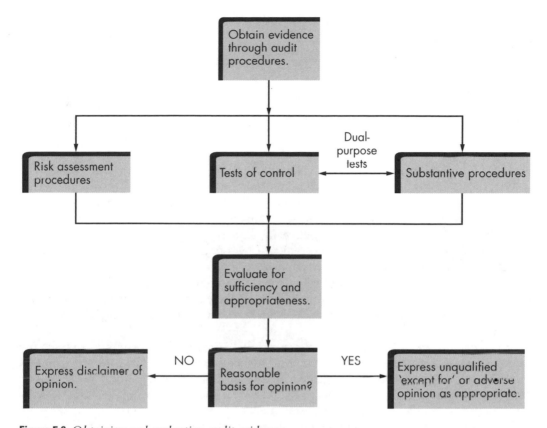

Figure 5.6 *Obtaining and evaluating audit evidence*

◁ LEARNING **CHECK**

5.27 Audit procedures are the techniques used to obtain evidence.

5.28 The common types of auditing procedure are as follows: analytical, inspecting, confirming, inquiring, counting, tracing, vouching, observing, reperforming and computer-assisted audit techniques.

5.29 Auditing procedures can be classified by purpose into three categories: (1) risk assessment procedures; (2) tests of control; and (3) substantive procedures.

5.30 Risk assessment procedures are required in every financial statement audit.

5.31 Tests of control are made to provide evidence about the effectiveness of the operation of internal control.

5.32 Substantive procedures consist of analytical procedures, tests of details of transactions, tests of details of balances and tests of details of disclosures.

5.33 Substantive procedures provide evidence as to the truth and fairness of management's financial statement assertions.

SUMMARY

Audit risk consists of three components. The inherent and control risk components are beyond the auditors' control, and the auditors merely assess these risks. Detection risk is inversely related to the other components. The auditors keep audit risk to an appropriately low level by controlling detection risk. Audit risk may be expressed in either quantitative or non-quantitative terms and has an inverse effect on the amount of evidence needed.

Materiality is considered at both the financial statement and account balance levels, and may be expressed in either quantitative or non-quantitative financial statement terms. There is an inverse relationship between materiality levels and the level of evidence needed.

Auditors achieve their overall objective of rendering an opinion on financial statements by collecting and evaluating evidence pertaining to numerous specific audit objectives. These objectives are derived from the management assertions relating to transactions, account balances and disclosures that combine to make up the financial statements. The major categories of management assertions are: (1) existence or occurrence, (2) completeness, (3) accuracy, classification and valuation, (4) cut-off, (5) rights or obligations, and (6) transparency.

In performing the audit, auditors exercise professional judgement in selecting from a variety of auditing procedures and types of evidence to meet the numerous specific audit objectives. They also exercise judgement at the conclusion of the audit in evaluating whether sufficient appropriate evidence has been obtained to provide a reasonable basis for the opinion on the overall financial statements.

The application of considerations of risk, materiality and types of audit evidence in planning an audit engagement will be explained in Chapter 6. In Chapter 7 the process of assessing control risk will be described, while in Chapter 9 the use of audit evidence and procedures for obtaining evidence in the development of specific audit programmes will be explained.

NOTES

[1] The risk that auditors could incorrectly express an opinion that the financial statements are materially misstated does not apply since, where the auditors suspect misstatement, more extensive procedures are applied which would lead to the correct conclusion being reached.

[2] IASC Framework for the Preparation and Presentation of Financial Statements.

FURTHER READING

Alderman, C. W. & Tabor, R. H. 'The Case for Risk-Driven Audits', *Journal of Accountancy* (March 1989), pp. 55–61.

Arnold Sr., Bernardi, D. F., Neidermeyer, R. A. & Source, P. E. 'The Association between European Materiality Estimates and Client Integrity, National Culture, and Litigation', *International Journal of Accounting* (Vol. 36, Issue 4, 2001), pp. 459–484.

American Institute of Certified Public Accountants (AICPA). Control Risk Audit Guide Task Force. Audit Guide: *Consideration of the Internal Control Structure in a Financial Statement Audit.* AICPA, New York, 1990.

Beasley, M., Carcello, J. & Hermanson, D. 'Top 10 Audit Deficiencies', *Journal of Accountancy* (April 2001), pp. 63–66.

Dusenbury, R., Reimers, J. & Wheeler, S. 'The Audit Risk Model', *Journal of Accountancy* (September 2000), p. 103.

Eilifsen, A., Knechel, W. R., Wallage, P. & Source, P. E. 'Application of the Business Risk Audit Model: A Field Study', *Accounting Horizons* (Vol. 15, Issue 3, 2001), pp. 193–208.

Dutta, S. K. & Graham, L. E. 'Considering Multiple Materialities for Account Combinations in Audit Planning and Evaluation: A Cost Efficient Approach', *Journal of Accounting, Auditing and Finance* (Vol. 13, No. 2, Spring 1998), pp. 151–71.

Grant, C. T., Depree, C. & Grant, G. 'Earnings Management and the Abuse of Materiality', *Journal of Accountancy* (September 2000), pp. 41–44.

Hatherley, D. 'Is the Risk Driven Audit too Risky', *Accountancy* (August 1998), p. 86.

Hellier, C., Lyon, R., Monroe, G. S., Ng, J. & Woodliffe, D. R. 'UK Auditors' Perceptions of Inherent Risk', *British Accounting Review* (March 1996), pp. 45–72.

Holstrum, G. L. & Mock, T. J. 'Audit Judgment and Evidence Evaluation', *Auditing: A Journal of Practice and Theory* (Fall 1985), pp. 101–108.

Iselin, E. R. & Iskandar, T. M. 'Auditors' Recognition and Disclosure Materiality Thresholds: Their Magnitude and the Effects of Industry', *British Accounting Review* (September 2000), pp. 289–309.

Jennings, M., Kneer, D. C. & Reckers, P. M. J. 'A Re-Examination of the Concept of Materiality: Views of Auditors, Users and Officers of the Court', *Auditing: A Journal of Practice and Theory* (Spring 1987), pp. 104–115.

Leslie, D. A. *Materiality, the Concept and its Application to Auditing.* Canadian Institute of Chartered Accountants, Toronto, 1985.

McKee, T. E. & Eilifsen, A. 'Current Materiality Guidance for Auditors', *The CPA Journal* (July 2000), pp. 75–79.

Marchant, G. 'Analogical Reasoning and Hypothesis Generation in Auditing', *Accounting Review* (July 1989), pp. 500–513.

Mautz, R. K. & Sharaff, H. A. *The Philosophy of Auditing*, Monograph No. 6. American Accounting Association, Sarasota, FL, 1961, Chapter 5, pp. 68–110.

Messier, W. F. & Austen, L. A. 'Inherent Risk and Control Risk Assessments', *Journal of Accountancy* (September 2000), p. 104.

Moeckel, C. L. & Plumlee, R. D. 'Auditors' Confidence in Recognition of Audit Evidence', *Accounting Review* (October 1989), pp. 653–666.

Pany, K. & Wheeler, S. 'A Comparison of Various Materiality Rules of Thumb', *The CPA Journal* (June 1989), pp. 62–63.

Perrin, S. 'Spot the Difference', *Accountancy* (June 1998), pp. 84–85.

Seidler, L. J. 'The Old Ways Don't Hold Water. Materiality Decisions in the Computer Age', *The CPA Journal* (May 1999), pp. 22–24.

Whittington, R., Zulinski, M. & Ledwith, J. W. 'Completeness – The Elusive Assertion', *Journal of Accountancy* (August 1983), pp. 89–92.

Winograd, B. N., Gerson, J. S. & Berlin, B. L. 'Audit Practices of PricewaterhouseCoopers', *Auditing: A Journal of Practice and Theory* (Vol. 19, No. 2, 2000), pp. 175–182.

Yardley, J. 'Explaining the Conditional Nature of the Audit Risk Model', *Journal of Accounting Education* (Vol. 7, 1989), pp. 107–114.

MULTIPLE-CHOICE QUESTIONS

Choose the best answer for each of the following.
(Answers are on page 599)

5.1 Which of the following can be controlled by the auditor?
   (a) Inherent risk.
   (b) Detection risk.
   (c) Control risk.
   (d) Both detection and control risk.

5.2 If the auditor assesses control and inherent risks as low, what would you expect the auditor to do?
   (a) Perform no substantive procedures.
   (b) Perform no tests of control because of the low level of control risk.
   (c) Perform a relatively small number of substantive procedures.
   (d) Re-evaluate his or her acceptable level of audit risk.

5.3 Inherent risk would be considered to be high where:
   (a) the company's profit for the year is the same as last year.
   (b) the chief accountant has been with the company for 15 years.
   (c) the newly appointed finance director was previously the marketing manager.
   (d) the company has decided to set up an internal audit department.

5.4 Which of the following statements best describes the audit approach to materiality?
   (a) Materiality is a matter for professional judgement.
   (b) Materiality is only relevant when planning the audit.
   (c) Materiality relates to the relative size of items within the financial statements.
   (d) Materiality is determined by reference to the professional standards.

5.5 In determining the level of planning materiality for an audit, what should not be considered?
   (a) Prior years' errors.
   (b) Trends in the industry within which the company operates.
   (c) The cost of the audit.
   (d) The users of the financial statements.

5.6 Which of the following audit procedures is primarily intended to provide evidence as to completeness?
   (a) Adding the debtors' aged trial balance.
   (b) Searching for unmatched goods received notes.
   (c) Confirming debtors' balances with customers.
   (d) Reviewing the outstanding cheque listing.

5.7 The auditor will check balances from suppliers' statements to the bought ledger in order to:
   (a) verify the existence of creditors.
   (b) confirm that the recorded balances are obligations of the entity.
   (c) determine that the purchases were properly authorised.
   (d) ascertain the completeness of recorded creditors.

5.8 Which of the following audit procedures is primarily intended to provide evidence as to existence?

    (a) Comparing shipping documents to related sales invoices.

    (b) Recalculating depreciation expense.

    (c) Confirming recorded debtors with the customers.

    (d) Comparing sales invoices with sales orders.

5.9 What does 'sufficient appropriate' audit evidence mean?

    (a) The amount of audit evidence that can be obtained given the time budget on the task.

    (b) Adequate evidence has been obtained in the auditor's professional judgement.

    (c) All material errors have been detected.

    (d) A qualified audit report does not need to be issued.

5.10 In verifying the valuation of work completed, by a construction company, on a long-term building contract, which source of evidence would you consider as most reliable?

    (a) An independent architect called in to supply a valuation but who has not otherwise been involved with the contract.

    (b) An architect employed by the other party to the contract who has been involved throughout in liaising with the company.

    (c) An architect employed by the company who has direct responsibility for building work on the contract.

    (d) An independent but unqualified building surveyor.

DISCUSSION QUESTIONS

5.1 Because management usually addresses the inherent risks at the account balance and class of transactions level by implementing appropriate control activities, is it practicable for auditors to assess inherent risk at this level separately from control risk?

5.2 Most guidance provided to auditors on materiality addresses its quantitative aspect. Is there a risk that auditors could fail to detect misstatements that are small but qualitatively material?

5.3 One of the major weaknesses in audit practice is said to be the absence of any logical basis for determining the extent of testing materiality at the level of each account balance or transaction class. Explain why this is a problem.

5.4 The occurrence assertion has two aspects. First, there is the issue of whether the recorded transaction actually occurred. Second, there is the issue of whether it is a transaction that may legitimately be recorded as a transaction of the entity. Discuss this distinction.

5.5 Professional scepticism is an important quality to be possessed by auditors in interpreting evidence. Explain what is meant by professional scepticism and suggest problems that might arise in achieving an appropriate level of scepticism.

5.6 In their theoretical examination of auditing, 'The Philosophy of Auditing', the authors, Mautz and Sharaf, distinguished within audit evidence between those assertions for which compelling evidence is available and those for which compelling evidence is not available. (They were using the term assertion in the context of types of corroborating information.) Discuss the validity of this distinction.

PROFESSIONAL APPLICATION QUESTIONS

(Suggested answers are on pages 612–616)

5.1 Audit evidence

ISA 500 *Audit Evidence* requires that 'Auditors should obtain sufficient appropriate audit evidence to be able to draw reasonable conclusions on which to base the audit opinion.' The explanatory material contained within ISA 500 identifies procedures for obtaining audit evidence. ISA 500 also offers guidance as to assessing the reliability of audit evidence.

Required
(a) Identify and describe the procedures for obtaining audit evidence.
(b) For each of the procedures, describe an audit test using that procedure to obtain evidence as to the balance of plant and machinery including the related balances of accumulated depreciation and charges to profit and loss.
(c) For each of the procedures, discuss considerations affecting your judgement as to the reliability of the evidence with particular reference to the test described in your answer to (b).

(Adapted from Question 3, Audit Framework, June 1999. Reproduced by permission of ACCA)

5.2 Audit objectives and evidence reliability

ISA 500 *Audit Evidence* provides a framework for evaluating the role of evidence in forming an opinion. Among other matters it:

(a) describes the **objectives** of audit evidence as being either to test controls or provide substantive evidence. Tests of controls are further analysed into tests of design and tests of operations. Substantive procedures are classified as tests of details of transactions, tests of details of balances and analytical procedure;
(b) identifies **financial statement assertions** to which evidence relates; and
(c) discusses the **reliability** of different kinds of evidence.

The following procedures appear in the creditors' audit programme for Gordon plc.

(1) Select a sample of purchase transactions recorded in the purchase journal during the year and vouch them to suppliers' invoices.
(2) Observe the goods received clerk accepting delivery of goods.
(3) Check the numerical continuity of a sequence of goods received notes and trace them to suppliers' invoices and to the entry in the purchase journal.
(4) Select a sample of purchase invoices and see that they have been initialled as being agreed to the goods received note and to the purchase order.

(5) Consider the reasonableness of the relationship between the year-end creditors' balance and the total of credit purchases during the year.

(6) Add the list of creditors' balances and agree the total to the control account in the general ledger.

(7) Enquire into the procedures used to ensure the reliability of cut-off.

Required

For each procedure (2) to (7) inclusive:

(a) identify its principal objective;

(b) explain its objective in terms of the account balance or transaction class involved and the financial statement assertion to which the evidence principally relates;

(c) discuss the reliability of the evidence obtained.

For your guidance an answer to the first procedure would be:

TEST	(A) OBJECTIVE	(B) ASSERTION(S)	(C) RELIABILITY
1	Substantive test of details of purchase transactions.	To verify the occurrence of purchase transactions by ensuring that each recorded purchase is supported by evidence of being invoiced by the supplier.	Suppliers' invoices are reasonably reliable being third party documents providing the copy examined is the original and has not been altered.

(Adapted from Question 2, Audit Framework, June 2001. Reproduced by permission of ACCA)

CHAPTER 6

ACCEPTING THE ENGAGEMENT AND PLANNING THE AUDIT

DISCUSSION QUESTIONS

PROFESSIONAL APPLICATION QUESTIONS

LEARNING **OBJECTIVES**
After studying this chapter, you should be able to:

1   identify the phases of a financial statement audit

2   state the steps involved in accepting an audit engagement

3   state the purpose and content of an engagement letter

4   explain the components of an audit plan

5   describe the procedures used in obtaining an understanding of the entity and assessing the risks of material misstatements

6   explain the role of analytical procedures in audit planning

7   differentiate between alternative audit strategies

8   explain the purpose and function of audit working papers

9   apply the essential techniques of good working paper preparation.

PROFESSIONAL **STATEMENTS**
ISA 210   Terms of Audit Engagements
ISA 220   Quality Control for Audit Work (Exposure draft)
ISA 230   Documentation
ISA 315   Understanding the Entity and Its Environment and Assessing the Risks of Material Misstatement
ISA 520   Analytical Procedures
ISA 550   Related Parties

Chapter 5 described the factors determining the general approach to an audit, the assessment of the risks, the concept of materiality, the identification of the objectives of the audit, and the types of evidence available. This chapter will explain the application of these matters to a specific audit engagement. First, the steps involved in completing the initial phase of an audit will be discussed – that is, accepting the engagement. Second, the first two steps involved in the planning phase of the audit will be identified – namely, obtaining an understanding of the entity's business and industry and assessing the risks of material misstatement. Third, the types of audit strategy will be described and their application under specific circumstances explained. Finally, the importance of documenting all phases of the audit will be explained, giving guidance as to how to set about preparing working papers and accumulating them into audit files.

It is common practice to refer to the business, which is the subject of the audit, as the 'entity'. This reflects the fact that the auditors' duty of care, in a financial statement audit, is to the shareholders or other owners of the business, not to the business or its management. This chapter will also use the term 'client' in connection with the engagement, because it reflects the contractual relationship between the auditors and the entity subject to audit. The distinction may appear sometimes confusing, especially given that the term 'client' is still widely used to refer to the management and directors. The current view, however, is that use of the term 'client' to refer to management and directors may lead auditors to overlook the fact that their ultimate responsibility is to the shareholders. For other assurance engagements it is also important that the auditors or reporting accountants are clear as to which party or parties a duty of care is owed. To avoid confusion you should also be aware that the term 'firm', in auditing, refers to the audit firm and should not be confused with the entity that is the subject of the audit.

The procedures that will be described in this chapter apply principally to the acceptance and planning of a financial statement audit engagement that results in the issue of an auditors' report meeting the requirements of the Companies Act. Similar requirements apply to the acceptance and planning of other assurance engagements, subject to the specific nature of the proposed service.

ACCEPTING THE AUDIT ENGAGEMENT

The following four phases of an audit can be identified:

- accepting the audit engagement;
- planning the audit;
- performing audit procedures; and
- reporting the findings.

In each phase, the auditors should be mindful of the environment in which audits are performed, as described in the preceding chapters. Environmental factors include the impact of regulation, the public's expectations, exposure to litigation, and the need to comply with professional standards.

The initial phase of a financial statement audit involves a decision to accept (or decline) the opportunity to become the auditors for a new client or to continue as auditors for an existing client. In most cases, the decision to accept (or decline) is made several months before the client's financial year-end.

Auditors are not obliged to perform a financial statement audit for any entity that requests it. In accepting an engagement auditors take on professional responsibilities to the public, the client and other members of the public accounting profession. The client's best interests must be served with competence and professional concern. In relation to other members of the profession, auditors have a responsibility to enhance the stature of the profession and its ability to serve the public. Auditors wishing to avoid legal liability would not associate with clients that pose a high risk of litigation. Thus, a decision to accept a new client or continue a relationship with an existing client should not be taken lightly.

The decision to accept or continue an audit engagement depends on the client evaluation and ethical considerations. Client evaluation involves:

- assessing the integrity of the principal owners, management and those charged with governance of the entity;
- communicating with the existing or previous auditor; and
- identifying significant risks associated with accepting the client or the engagement.

Ethical considerations involve determining:

- the independence of both the firm and the engagement team;
- the competence of the engagement team to undertake the engagement;
- the firm's ability to meet the reporting deadline;
- conflicts, if any, with existing clients; and
- any proposed use of other auditors' work. (ISA 220)

If the audit firm is of the opinion that the audit can be completed in accordance with professional standards, then the firm prepares an engagement letter to confirm the auditors' responsibility.

The series of steps involved in the evaluation process is shown diagrammatically in Figure 6.1.

Client evaluation

Client evaluation is an important element of quality control. ISA 220, Quality Control for Audit Engagements, requires that prospective clients are evaluated and existing clients

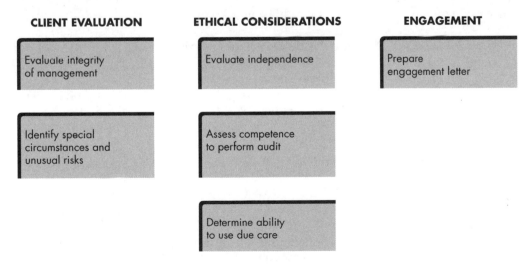

Figure 6.1 *Considerations in accepting an audit engagement*

are reviewed on an ongoing basis. In making a decision to accept or retain a client, the integrity of the client's management and the audit firm's independence and ability to serve the client properly are considered.

EVALUATING THE INTEGRITY OF MANAGEMENT

In undertaking a client evaluation, auditors seek reasonable assurance that an entity's management can be trusted. When management lacks integrity, there is a greater likelihood that material errors and irregularities may occur in the accounting process from which the financial statements are prepared. For a new client, prospective auditors should make inquiries of the predecessor auditors and of third parties. For an existing client, the auditors should consider previous experience with the client's management.

Making inquiries of third parties

Auditors may obtain information about a client management's integrity from knowledgeable persons in the community such as the prospective client's bankers, legal advisers, investment banker, and others in the financial or business community who may have such knowledge. Other potential sources of information include news items in the financial press on changes in senior management.

Reviewing previous experience with existing clients

Before making a decision to continue an engagement with an existing audit client, the auditors should carefully consider prior experiences with the entity's management such as the discovery of any material errors or irregularities and illegal acts in prior audits. During an audit, the auditors make inquiries of management about such matters as the existence of contingencies, the completeness of all minutes of board of directors' meetings, and compliance with regulatory requirements. The truthfulness of management's responses to such inquiries in prior audits should be carefully considered in the evaluation of the integrity of management.

The evaluation of existing clients should be undertaken:

- after the expiration of a period of time, such as every three years;
- on the occurrence of a significant change since the first evaluation (for example, a change in management or the nature of the client's business); and
- on becoming aware of the existence of conditions that would lead the auditors to reject a client had they existed at the time of the initial acceptance of audit engagement.

COMMUNICATING WITH EXISTING AUDITORS

Knowledge acquired by the existing auditors of a client's management is essential information. The statements on *Changes in Professional Appointments* in both the ACCA's *Rules of Professional Conduct* and the ICAEW's *Guide to Professional Ethics* require the prospective auditors to communicate with the existing auditors. The communication should be made with the client's permission and the client should be requested to authorise the existing auditors to respond fully to the inquiries. Authorisation is required because the profession's code of ethics prohibits auditors from disclosing confidential information obtained in an audit without the client's permission. If the client refuses to permit the existing auditors to disclose information the prospective auditors should not accept appointment.

In the communication, the prospective auditors should make specific and reasonable inquiries regarding matters that may affect the decision to accept an engagement. Inquiries should address questions such as the integrity of management, disagreements with management about accounting policies and audit procedures, and the existing auditors' understanding of the reasons for the change of auditors.

The existing auditors are expected to respond promptly and fully, assuming the client gives consent. If the existing auditors do not respond it may be assumed there are no matters to be communicated. On occasions the existing auditors may prefer to communicate orally such as where they have unconfirmed suspicions of unlawful acts by the client. Whatever the reply, it is for the prospective auditors to decide whether to accept the appointment.

The previous auditors' working paper files are a valuable source of information about a new client. The new auditors may, therefore, ask to review these files. The previous auditors are under no obligation to consent to such a review, but many firms will consent to a supervised review, given the client's permission.

IDENTIFYING SPECIAL CIRCUMSTANCES AND UNUSUAL RISKS

This step in accepting an engagement includes identifying the intended users of the audited financial statements, making a preliminary assessment of the prospective client's legal and financial stability, and evaluating the entity's auditability.

Identifying intended users of the audited financial statements

In Chapter 3 it was noted that the auditors' legal responsibilities in an audit may vary based on the intended users of the financial statements. Thus, the auditors should consider (1) the prospective client's status as a private or public company, (2) any named beneficiaries or foreseen or foreseeable third parties to whom the potential for liability exists under common law, and (3) what, if any, statutes apply in the circumstances. The auditors should also consider whether general purpose financial statements will meet the needs of all intended users or whether any special reports will be required. Added reporting requirements may mean additional competency requirements, add to audit costs and broaden the auditors' legal liability exposure.

For assurance engagements, other than a financial statement audit, it may be necessary to restrict the report to specific identified users.

Assessing a prospective client's legal and financial stability

If an entity experiences legal difficulties, and if plaintiffs can find any pretext for claiming reliance on the financial statements, then such litigation will probably also involve the auditors, who are often thought to have 'deep pockets'. Thus, auditors may incur the financial and other costs of defending themselves, no matter how professionally they performed their services.

For this reason, auditors should attempt to identify and reject prospective clients that pose a high risk of litigation. These may include entities whose operations or principal products are the subjects of either material lawsuits or investigations by authorities, the outcome of which could adversely affect the viability of the business. Clients to reject may also include entities already known to be experiencing financial instability, such as an inability to meet debt payments or to raise needed capital. Auditors can identify such matters by inquiring of management; reviewing credit agency reports; and analysing previously issued audited or unaudited financial statements, and, if applicable, previous annual returns with regulatory agencies.

Evaluating the entity's auditability

Before accepting an engagement, the auditors should evaluate whether other conditions exist that raise questions as to the prospective client's auditability. Such conditions may include the absence or poor condition of important accounting records; management's disregard of its responsibility to maintain other elements of adequate internal control; or restrictions imposed by the prospective client on the conduct of the audit. In such cases, the auditors should decline the engagement or make clear to the client the possible effects of such conditions on the auditors' report.

Ethical considerations

In conducting an audit, the auditors should comply with professional ethical requirements and with Auditing Standards, legislation and regulation and, where appropriate, the terms of the audit engagement.

EVALUATING INDEPENDENCE

Statements on Integrity, Objectivity and Independence in both the ACCA's *Rules of Professional Conduct* and the ICAEW's *Guide to Professional Ethics* require that members in public practice must both be and be seen to be free of any interest which is incompatible with objectivity. Auditing Standards and the *Companies Act 1985* require the observance of this rule.

Thus, before accepting a new audit client, an audit firm must evaluate whether there are any circumstances that would compromise its independence with respect to the client. One procedure is to circulate the name of a prospective client to all professional staff to identify any prohibited financial or business relationships. If it is concluded that the independence requirements are not met, steps should be taken to eliminate the cause; for example, to sell the shares. If such steps are not taken the engagement should be declined. Consideration must also be given to whether the expected level of fees might affect actual or perceived independence. In addition, the firm should determine that acceptance of the client engagement would not result in any conflict of interest with other clients.

For a continuing audit, a professional independence questionnaire may be completed annually for all audit clients to ensure that the firm's quality control policies and procedures on independence continue to be complied with. Some firms require the engagement partner to provide a written representation to this effect. If the firm is unable to meet the independence criteria or perform the audit properly, the engagement partner may propose some action that would enable the firm to meet the ethical criteria. Consultation with a second partner is then necessary.

ASSESSING COMPETENCE TO PERFORM THE AUDIT

The audit firm should ensure that it has sufficient personnel with the competencies and commitment to ethical principles necessary to perform the engagement in accordance with professional standards. The firm will rely on its human resources policies (such as on hiring, continuing professional development and advancement) to ensure compliance with the above policy.

For a prospective client, the firm will have to identify an engagement team that will match the staffing needs of the engagement. The typical engagement team consists of:

- an engagement partner, who has both overall and final responsibility for the engagement;
- an audit manager, who co-ordinates and supervises the execution of the audit programme;
- one or more seniors, who may oversee the conduct of the audit with specific responsibility for work in complex areas; and
- staff assistants, who perform many of the required procedures under the supervision of the seniors.

The engagement team must possess the following competencies:

- understanding and practical experience of similar engagements through appropriate training and participation;
- understanding of professional standards and applicable regulatory and legal requirements;
- knowledge of auditing, accounting, tax and information technology at the appropriate level;
- knowledge of specific industries;
- ability to apply professional judgement; and
- understanding of the firm's quality control policies and procedures. (ISA 220)

The team may also need the assistance and guidance of experts, such as computer audit specialists. If the audit firm does not have the required skills, it may engage external consultants to provide the necessary expertise. Auditors are not expected to have the expertise of a person trained for, or qualified to engage in, the practice of another profession or occupation. ISA 620, Using the Work of an Expert, recognises that the auditors may use the work of experts to obtain sufficient appropriate audit evidence. Examples are the use of:

- appraisers to provide evidence about the valuation of assets such as property, works of art and precious stones;
- geologists and engineers to determine the quantities of mineral and petroleum reserves and remaining useful life of plant and equipment;
- actuaries to determine amounts used in accounting for a pension plan;
- lawyers to assess the probable outcome of pending litigation, interpretations of agreements, statutes and regulations; and
- computer specialists to assist in evaluating database management systems.

Before using an expert, the auditors are expected to become satisfied as to the professional qualifications, reputation and objectivity of the expert. The auditors should consider, for example, whether the expert has appropriate professional qualifications, relevant experience in the matters in question, adequate standing within the profession, and any relationship with the client that may impair his or her objectivity.

DETERMINING ABILITY TO MEET THE REPORTING DEADLINE

The audit team and consultants must be available to perform the proposed engagement during the relevant period. Consequently, audit work is scheduled. The detailed schedule for completing an engagement may not be finalised until several steps in the audit planning phase have been completed. Nonetheless, the probable impact of accepting a new client on the firm's overall work schedule must be considered prior to accepting the engagement. A limiting factor for many audit firms is the requirement to be present at many clients at, or close to, their financial year-end to observe stock-taking, count cash, etc.

Preliminary work on a time budget for the audit is often done as part of the scheduling considerations. The development of a time budget involves estimating the hours expected to be required at each staff level (partner, manager, senior and so on) for each part of the audit. These time estimates may then be multiplied by the charge-out rates for each staff level to arrive at an estimate of total costs for the engagement. The audit firm may use these estimates as the basis for discussions with the prospective client about fee arrangements. Although some audits are carried out on a fixed-fee basis, the use of daily charge-out rates plus expenses is the more typical arrangement.

If the engagement is accepted and the appointment is properly confirmed, then details of the time budget and scheduling of the audit will be further developed as additional steps in the planning phase are performed. Then, as work on each area of the audit progresses, the audit firm can monitor actual hours and compare them with the budget to help to control overall audit costs.

The use of client personnel can also have an impact on staffing and scheduling and, thus, on audit cost. The work of internal auditors in obtaining an understanding of the internal control structure and in performing tests of control and substantive procedures may (subject to evaluation of the effectiveness of internal audit) reduce the extent of independent audit work in certain areas. Other client personnel can be used to perform tasks such as preparing schedules of insurance policies in force, notes receivable, and fixed asset additions and disposals. To demonstrate that the audit was undertaken with due care, the auditors must plan to review and test all such work.

Preparing an engagement letter

As a final step in the acceptance phase, in compliance with Auditing Standards and good professional practice, it is important to confirm the terms of each engagement in an engagement letter, as in Figure 6.2.

The form and content of the letter may vary for different clients, but should generally include the following:

To [the governing body (e.g. the board of directors) or the appropriate representative of senior management]:

Scope
You have requested that we audit the balance sheet of [entity] as of [date], and the related statements of profit and loss and cash flows for the year then ending. We are pleased to confirm our acceptance and our understanding of this engagement by means of this letter. Our audit will be conducted pursuant to the [relevant statutory and other requirements] with the objective of expressing an opinion on the financial statements.

We will conduct our audit in accordance with Auditing Standards. Those standards require that we plan and perform the audit to obtain reasonable assurance about whether the financial statements are free of material misstatements. An audit includes examining, on a test basis, evidence supporting the amounts and disclosures in the financial statements. An audit also includes assessing the accounting principles used and significant estimates made by management, as well as evaluating the overall financial statement presentation.

Because of the test nature and other inherent limitations of an audit, together with the inherent limitations of any accounting and internal control system, there is an unavoidable risk that even some material misstatements may remain undiscovered.

In addition to our report on the financial statements, we expect to provide you with a separate letter concerning any material weaknesses in accounting and internal control systems which come to our notice.

We remind you that the responsibility for the preparation of financial statements including adequate disclosure is that of the management of the company. This includes the maintenance of adequate accounting records and internal controls, the selection and application of accounting policies, and the safeguarding of the assets of the company. As part of our audit process, we will request from management written confirmation concerning representations made to us in connection with the audit.

We look forward to full co-operation with your staff and we trust that they will make available to us whatever records, documentation and other information are requested in connection with our audit. Our fees, which will be billed as work progresses, are based on the time required by the individuals assigned to the engagement plus out-of-pocket expenses. Individual hourly rates vary according to the degree of responsibility involved and the experience and skill required.

This letter will be effective for future years unless it is terminated, amended or superseded.

Please sign and return the attached copy of this letter to indicate that it is in accordance with your understanding of the arrangements for our audit of the financial statements.

Yours faithfully   Acknowledged on behalf of [entity] by (signed)

(signed)

Name and Title, Date   Name and Title, Date

Figure 6.2 *Auditors' engagement letter as per IAS 210 (Reproduced by permission of IAASB. Copyright © International Federation of Accountants)*

- a reminder to management that it is responsible for preparing the financial statements and providing the auditors with access to the accounting records and other related information;
- the objective or purpose of the audit;
- reference to professional standards (e.g. Auditing Standards) to which the auditors will adhere (and, if applicable, to statutes such as the Companies Act or any other governing legislation or regulations);
- an explanation of the nature and scope of the audit and the auditors' responsibilities;
- a statement to the effect that weaknesses in the entity's accounting system identified in the course of the audit will be brought to management's attention but may not be provided to third parties;
- an indication that management will be asked to provide certain written representations to the auditors;
- a requirement to sight all other disclosures to be issued with the financial statements;
- a statement that management are responsible for safeguarding the entity's assets and that the audit should not be relied on for detecting all material misstatements;
- a description of any other services provided by the auditors;
- the basis on which fees will be computed and any billing arrangements; and
- a request for the client to confirm the terms of the engagement by signing and returning a copy of the letter to the auditors.

To eliminate the need to prepare a new letter each year, the letter normally includes a statement that it continues in force until replaced. A new letter may be appropriate on the occurrence of events such as a change in management, ownership, nature and/or size of the entity's business or legal requirements.

Auditors appointed in accordance with the provisions of the Companies Act must fulfil their statutory responsibilities. However, they may assume additional responsibilities if that is the desire of both parties. When auditors are appointed by an entity not incorporated under the Companies Act – for example, a partnership or a tertiary education institution – it is even more important to confirm the nature of duties and responsibilities through an engagement letter.

An engagement letter constitutes a legal contract between the auditors and the client. By clearly stating the nature of services to be performed and the responsibilities of the auditors such letters may help the auditors to avoid becoming involved in litigation. The letter in Figure 6.2 is for use as a guide, in conjunction with the considerations outlined in ISA 210, Terms of Audit Engagements, and will need to be varied according to individual requirements and circumstances.

◿ LEARNING **CHECK**

6.1 The four phases of an audit are: (1) accepting the audit engagement, (2) planning the audit, (3) performing audit procedures, and (4) reporting the findings.

6.2 The decision to accept an audit engagement is dependent upon client evaluation and ethical considerations.

6.3 Client evaluation involves a consideration of the integrity of management and identi-fication of any special circumstances and unusual risks associated with the entity.

6.4 In evaluating the integrity of management, information is usually sought from the existing auditors and inquiries are made of third parties. For continuing clients, the auditors consider prior experience with the entity's management.

6.5 An assessment of special circumstances and unusual risks of a prospective client is made by identifying intended users of the audited financial statements, making a preliminary assessment of the client's legal and financial stability, and evaluating the entity's auditability.

6.6 Ethical considerations relate to the firm's ability to meet the independence criteria and to complete the audit competently within the available time period.

6.7 Determining competency generally involves identifying key members of the audit team and considering the need to seek assistance from consultants.

6.8 The engagement letter specifies the separate responsibilities of management and auditors for the issue of audited financial statements.

PLANNING THE AUDIT

The second phase of the audit requires the development of a plan for the conduct and scope of the audit. Planning is crucial to a successful audit engagement because it enables auditors to meet their professional responsibilities at a reasonable cost. Some pre-planning would have been accomplished when the auditors decided to accept the engagement. However, more detailed planning is required for an effective and efficient audit. Audit planning is usually carried out three to six months prior to the entity's fiscal year-end. The components involved in audit planning will be explained in this and the next two chapters.

Adequate planning helps to ensure that the risks of material misstatement are appro-priately identified, that the nature, timing and extent of audit procedures are linked to the assessed risks and that work is completed expeditiously. It is also necessary in co-ordinating the work done by other auditors and experts. The audit should be planned with a degree of professional scepticism in relation to matters such as the integrity of management, errors and irregularities, and illegal acts. The amount of planning required in an engagement will vary with the size and the complexity of the entity, and the auditors' knowledge of the business and experience with the entity. Considerably more effort is needed to plan an initial audit than a recurring audit. It should be recognised, too, that planning is continual throughout the engagement.

Steps in planning the audit

Planning starts with obtaining an understanding of the entity's business and industry and its internal control. ISA 315, Understanding the Entity and Its Environment and Assessing the Risks of Material Misstatement, requires auditors to obtain an understanding sufficient to:

- assess the risks of material misstatement of the financial statements; and
- design and perform further audit procedures.

This chapter explains how auditors obtain an understanding of the entity's business and industry and use that understanding in assessing inherent risk. Obtaining the understanding of internal control and assessing control risk will be explained in Chapter 7.

In all but the smallest engagements, the auditors will make a preliminary visit to the entity, usually before its financial year-end. This visit is referred to as the interim audit. During the interim audit, the auditors obtain an understanding of the entity and its internal control. An audit programme is then developed on the basis of a final determination of detection risk for each assertion, consistent with the overall level of audit risk and materiality levels (see Chapter 9).

Obtaining an understanding of the entity's business and industry

To plan an audit, the auditors should obtain sufficient knowledge of the entity's business to understand events, transactions and practices that may have a significant effect on the financial statements. This understanding provides a framework for planning an overall audit approach that responds to the unique characteristics of the entity. In recurring engagements, the auditors' emphasis is on evaluating new developments in the entity's business and industry. Changes may be gradual or sudden, and may increase or reduce the likelihood of material misstatements.

The auditors need knowledge of the economy and industry within which the entity operates. More detailed knowledge is required of the operations of the entity. Specifically, the auditors need knowledge about:

- the type of industry and its vulnerability to changing economic conditions, and major industry policies and practices;
- the type of business, types of product and service, entity locations and operating characteristics of the entity, such as its production and marketing methods;
- government regulations that affect the entity and its industry and reports to be filed with regulatory agencies;
- accounting policies adopted by the entity;
- recent financial performance of the entity; and
- the entity's internal control.

The auditors are interested not only in assessing the direct risks of material misstatements but in appreciating the nature of business risks facing the entity whose financial consequences may indicate a risk of material misstatement.

Sources for obtaining knowledge of the industry and the entity include:

- inquiries of management, entity personnel, connected parties such as legal counsel and business contacts, and any other relevant external sources;
- observation and inspection; and
- analytical procedures.

INQUIRIES

For both new and recurring engagements, discussions with management may reveal current business developments affecting the entity that may have audit significance. In addition, management should be knowledgeable about new industry and government regulations that affect the entity. In some cases, areas of particular audit interest to management – such as a new division or a controlled entity – may be discussed.

Inquiries of management may also concern the extent and timing of entity personnel's involvement in preparing schedules and analyses for the auditors. In addition, the auditors can inquire about the internal audit function and matters pertaining to corporate accountability, such as codes of conduct, potential conflicts of interest and possible illegal payments.

The audit committee of the board of directors may provide the auditors with special insights into the entity's business and industry. The committee may have information about, for example, the strengths and weaknesses of the company's internal controls in a specific division or in a newly implemented computer information system. The committee may also be able to inform the auditors of significant changes in the entity's management and organisational structure. In some cases, the audit committee may request additions or modifications to the auditors' planned audit.

Knowledge of general economic factors and of the industry can be obtained from trade journals, industry statistics compiled by government or private agencies, data accumulated by the audit firm, and professional guidance statements where available.

Although all auditors are knowledgeable about Financial Reporting Standards and Auditing Standards, special accounting principles and audit procedures may apply in certain industries or to certain types of business activity. The auditors may refer to audit and accounting guides, if available, that describe distinctive characteristics of the industry or activity covered, alert the auditors to unusual problems, and explain regulations and other special factors to take into account. These guides may illustrate financial statement treatment and the form and wording of audit reports whenever applicable.

The auditors should also consider the impact of applicable pronouncements of regulatory agencies such as the Financial Services Authority and the stock exchanges. Finally, consideration should be given during the planning phase of the audit to the impact of any newly effective Financial Reporting Standards and Auditing Standards.

OBSERVATION AND INSPECTION

Procedures include reviewing prior year audit working papers, inspection of important legal documents relating to the entity and visiting the entity's premises.

Audit working papers

In a recurring audit engagement, the auditors can review the prior year's audit working papers for knowledge about the entity. In addition, the working papers may indicate problem areas in prior audits that may be expected to continue in the future; for example, they may reveal that the entity has ongoing internal control weaknesses or complicated profit-sharing bonus plans. However, the auditors must undertake sufficient inquiry to ensure that no changes have affected the continuing relevance of information recorded in the prior year's audit working papers.

185

For a new client, the previous auditors' working papers may be helpful. The client must consent to the successor's review of these papers and the previous auditors must be willing to co-operate. The review is normally limited to matters of continuing audit significance, such as analyses of balance sheet accounts and contingencies. During the review, the previous auditors may be available for consultation.

Inspection of documents

To obtain knowledge of the entity's business, the auditors may inspect the entity's legal documents, minutes of directors' and shareholders' meetings, and significant contracts. The principal legal documents of the company are the memorandum of association and the articles of association. The memorandum of association is the constitution of the company. It contains information on the name, objectives and powers of the company; the types and amount of share capital authorised; the liability of members; and the subscribers to the company's capital. The articles regulate the internal management of the company, particularly in relation to the allotment of shares; the calling of general meetings; the powers, duties and appointment of directors; and how dividends are declared and reserves are provided.

Auditors must have a knowledge of pertinent legal documents to determine that the financial statements are properly presented. The disclosures pertaining to shareholders' funds and the declaration of dividends must be in accordance with these documents.

Minutes of meetings of directors are important to the audit. Information contained in minutes provides corroborative evidence for the company's significant transactions and for practices such as:

- authorisations for capital expenditures;
- new business undertakings;
- long-term loans;
- officers' remuneration;
- important contracts;
- approval for pledging assets; and
- the opening and closing of bank accounts (and the specification of persons authorised to operate those accounts).

Important continuing contracts may relate to such matters as loan agreements, leases and pension plans. Auditors need an understanding of the contracts to determine the correctness of the terms of the transactions and to ensure that disclosures in the financial statements are appropriate.

Other sources of information on the entity are internal documents. These documents include annual and interim financial statements, tax returns, reports to regulatory agencies and special reports prepared by management, internal auditors or consultants for internal decision-making.

Visiting the entity's premises

A tour of the operating facilities and offices is a significant help to auditors in obtaining knowledge about a new client's operating characteristics. During a tour of the factory, the auditors should become familiar with the factory layout, the manufacturing process, storage facilities and potential trouble spots such as unlocked storerooms, obsolete materials and excessive scrap.

During a tour of the office, auditors should become knowledgeable about the work habits of personnel and the types and locations of accounting records and computer-processing facilities. An important by-product of both tours is the opportunity to meet personnel who occupy key positions within the organisation. The auditors should document the information obtained from the factory and office tours.

In a recurring engagement, audit personnel new to the engagement should be expected to tour the operating facilities.

ANALYTICAL PROCEDURES

Analytical procedures involve a study and comparison of relationships among data to identify expected or unexpected fluctuations and other unusual items. The common types of analytical procedure involve a comparison of the entity's financial information with:

- comparable information for a prior period or periods;
- anticipated results such as budgets and forecasts; and
- industry averages.

Analytical procedures also include the study of relationships:

- among elements within the financial statements, such as a study of gross margin percentages; and
- between financial information and relevant non-financial information, such as a study of payroll costs for a number of employees.

ISA 520, Analytical Procedures, requires auditors to apply analytical procedures at the planning stage to:

- assist in understanding the entity's business; and
- identify areas of potential risk.

Generally, analytical procedures performed during the planning phase use highly aggregate entity-wide data which are based on year-to-date or expected annual data. However, for entities with diverse operations, some disaggregation by product line or division may be necessary. In other cases, such as a company with seasonal business, it may be desirable to perform the analysis on monthly or quarterly data rather than on year-to-date or annual data.

Determining effects on audit planning

Unexplained fluctuations and unusual relationships indicate an increased risk of misstatement in the accounts involved. In such cases, the auditors will usually plan to perform more substantive tests of details of those accounts. By directing the auditors' attention to areas of greater risk, analytical procedures may contribute to performing a more effective and efficient audit.

Analytical procedures are also used as a substantive procedure. Their use for this purpose will be explained in Chapter 9. They are also used in the overall review of the financial statements immediately prior to the issue of the auditors' report. This use will be explained in Chapter 14.

Discussion and documentation

Having obtained an understanding of the entity, members of the audit team should consider the implications for the risks of material misstatements. In the case of control risk the assessment is relatively structured as will be explained in Chapter 7. In the case of business risk, however, it is important for team members to exchange views as to how and where the financial statements might be susceptible to material misstatement. The discussion serves both to enable more senior team members to pool their knowledge and ensures that more junior team members are made adequately aware of the risks and approach the audit with an appropriate degree of professional scepticism.

The understanding of the entity should be documented together with the outcome of the discussion as to assessed risks at both the financial statement and assertion levels.

Determining the existence of related parties

In the process of obtaining information about the entity it is usually convenient to undertake a search to identify related parties which are the subject of special auditing and financial reporting procedures. Management is responsible for identifying and disclosing related parties and related party transactions. Auditing Standards require that the auditors obtain sufficient appropriate evidence to ensure adequate disclosure of related parties.

The concern about related party transactions results from the realisation that 'arm's length' bargaining of terms and conditions of transactions between such parties may not apply. Alternatively, related parties may conspire to enter into transactions intended to obscure financial or other business problems that would otherwise be reflected in the financial statements. Thus, the auditors will ordinarily require more appropriate evidence for related party transactions than for transactions between unrelated parties. To ensure that such evidence is obtained, the auditors must take steps in the planning phase to determine the existence of related parties.

Certain related party transactions may be clearly evident, such as those between a controlling and a controlled entity, between or among entities under common control, or between an entity and its executive officers. ISA 550, Related Parties, indicates that specific audit procedures, including the following, should be used to determine the existence of other related parties:

- Inquire of management.
- Review the prior year's working papers for names of known related parties.
- Inquire as to the names of all pension and other trusts established for the benefit of employees and the names of their management and trustees.
- Inquire as to the affiliation of management with other entities.
- Review shareholder records to determine the names of principal shareholders.

- Inquire of other auditors involved in the audit or predecessor auditors as to their knowledge of additional related parties.
- Review the entity's tax returns and other information supplied to regulatory agencies.
- Review the entity's procedures for identifying related parties.
- Review minutes of the meetings of shareholders, the board of directors and other important committees, as well as other relevant statutory records such as the register of directors' interests.

A list of identified related parties is usually maintained in the permanent audit file. These parties should be made known to all members of the audit team so they can be alert to evidence of transactions with these parties.

 ## LEARNING **CHECK**

6.9 The primary objective of planning the audit is to obtain a sufficient understanding of the entity and its internal control to assess the risks of material misstatement of the financial statements and to design and perform the necessary further audit procedures.

6.10 The understanding of the business should extend to the identification of business risks that may affect financial reporting as well as the identification of direct risks of material misstatement of the financial statements.

6.11 The understanding is obtained through inquiry, inspection and observation and analytical procedures.

6.12 The audit team should discuss the implications of the understanding of the entity obtained with respect to the risk of material misstatement in order to pool their knowledge and to ensure a consistent application of professional scepticism.

6.13 The process of obtaining the understanding can also be used to identify related parties.

AUDIT STRATEGIES

Given the interrelationships among evidence, materiality and the components of audit risk, the auditors may choose from among alternative audit strategies in planning the audit of individual assertions or groups of assertions. This section identifies the components of audit strategies, describes two alternative strategies and explains their application to transaction classes and account balances.

Developing the audit strategy

The process of developing the audit strategy commences with obtaining an understanding of the internal control structure. This is a requirement of all audits, whatever strategy is to be adopted.

The default presumption is that all of the evidence will come from the performance of substantive procedures – sometimes referred to as the predominantly substantive approach. Substantive procedures are those that substantiate the amounts recorded in the financial statements. They are normally costly to perform. A more efficient audit can be performed if controls are judged to be sufficiently effective to enable a reduction in the level of substantive procedures undertaken. This is illustrated in Figure 6.3.

Furthermore, in certain situations, substantive procedures may be unable to provide sufficient evidence and a more effective audit could be performed if the auditors could rely on certain controls. The completeness of cash receipts is an obvious example; unless controls over the receipt of cash are effective, it may be impossible to determine, through the use of substantive procedures, that all cash to which the entity is entitled has been properly recorded.

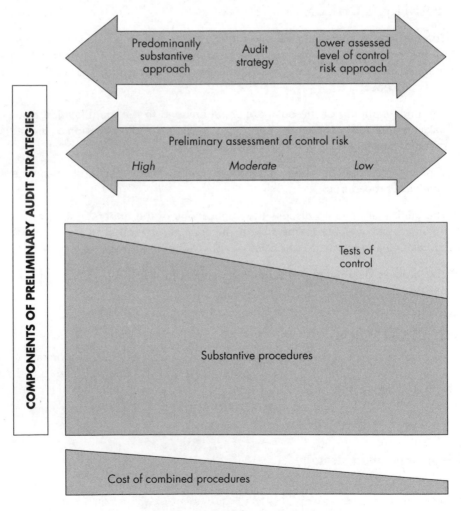

Figure 6.3 *Preliminary audit strategies for material financial statement assertions*

An audit strategy that relies on internal controls to support using a reduced level of substantive procedures is sometimes referred to as a lower assessed level of control risk approach. This is not a single strategy, but a range of strategies determined by the relative effectiveness of applicable control procedures (combined with assessments of inherent risk and materiality). The auditors must make four separate decisions before adopting such a strategy, and each decision (except the first) must be supported by relevant evidence.

1. Is it cost-effective to adopt a lower assessed level of control risk strategy?
2. Are control procedures effectively designed?
3. Are control procedures effectively operated?
4. Do the results of substantive procedures confirm the assessment of control risk?

It may not be cost-effective to adopt a lower assessed level of control risk strategy where there are few transactions in a transaction class or items making up an account balance, such that substantive procedures are unlikely to be costly. This is commonly the case with smaller entities and, in larger entities, with transactions and balances relating to share capital and investments.

Where a lower assessed level of control risk strategy is likely to be cost-effective, the sequence of events is as follows. In the planning phase the auditors obtain an understanding of the design of control procedures and identify the presence of procedures that are likely to reduce control risk for a particular assertion. Based on this preliminary assessment, the auditors will plan the audit, incorporating both tests of control and substantive procedures appropriate to the preliminary assessed level of control risk. The tests of control are designed to verify that control procedures are actually operating as laid down. The level of planned tests of control depends on the assessed level of control risk to be confirmed: that is, the lower the assessed level of control risk, the more extensive the tests of control required to confirm that assessment and, conversely, the lower the planned level of substantive procedures.

In some respects it may be better if the auditors wait until completing tests of control before planning substantive procedures. However, experience has shown that the results of tests of control usually confirm the assessed level of control risk and, thus, the planned audit strategy. By designing substantive procedures at this stage, the auditors can commence detailed planning of the final audit. Moreover, tests of control are typically performed during the interim audit, simultaneously with substantive tests of details of transactions, sometimes as dual-purpose tests. Given that both tests are applied to the same records, it is more efficient to draft the audit programme so as to incorporate all tests to be conducted on the same records simultaneously.

If the tests do not confirm the operation of the control as planned, then the auditors will need to reconsider the audit strategy and increase the level of use of substantive procedures as appropriate.

Procedures employed in assessing control risk will be explained in Chapter 7. These procedures include methods of obtaining the understanding of the internal control structure and of assessing the design effectiveness of controls, the design of tests of control and the interpretation of the results of tests of control in making the final assessment of control risk.

EFFECT OF THE ASSESSMENT OF CONTROL RISK
ON SUBSTANTIVE PROCEDURES

In considering the effect of the assessment of control risk on the level of substantive procedures necessary to achieve the desired level of detection risk, the auditors may vary the nature, timing or extent of such procedures.

The nature of substantive procedures may vary between tests of details and analytical procedures. Because they examine individual transactions and items making up an account balance, tests of details are far more persuasive than analytical procedures, which consider only the reasonableness of recorded totals. However, where a relatively high level of detection risk may be tolerated, analytical procedures may be sufficient. In such cases the use of analytical procedures would be the preferred option because they are less costly than tests of details to perform.

The timing of substantive procedures refers to the distinction between those performed at the balance sheet date and those performed prior to that date. Performance of procedures prior to the year-end reduces pressure on the auditors and enables the audit to be completed earlier. Where controls over stock records are effective, for example, reliance may be placed on a stock-take prior to the year-end updated by transactions in the intervening period. Where controls are particularly effective, reliance on perpetual stock records supplemented by attendance at a cyclical stock-take alone may be sufficient (see Chapter 12).

It should be recognised, however, that it is inappropriate under Auditing Standards for the auditors to conclude that inherent and control risks are so low that it is unnecessary to perform any substantive procedures for all assertions pertaining to an account. Some evidence must always be obtained from substantive procedures for each significant account balance, although not necessarily for each financial statement assertion. The design of substantive procedures is explained in more detail in Chapter 9.

The relationship between strategies and assertions

The strategies are not intended to characterise the approach to an entire audit. Rather, they represent alternative approaches to auditing individual assertions. Frequently, however, a common strategy is applied to groups of account balance assertions affected by the same transaction class. The rationale is that many internal controls focus on the processing of a single type of transaction. Double entry means that each transaction class affects two or more account balances. Sales transactions relate to debtors in the balance sheet and to sales in the profit and loss statement. Thus, the assessed control risk for the occurrence assertion for sales transactions will apply to the existence assertion in the audit of both sales and debtors' balances. Because the debtors' balance is affected by cash receipts and sales adjustment transactions as well as sales transactions, the auditors also consider the assessment of control risks for all three transaction classes in developing the audit strategies for debtors' assertions.

◢ LEARNING **CHECK**

6.14 Two alternative audit strategies are: (1) the predominantly substantive approach and (2) the lower assessed level of control risk approach.

6.15 Components of audit strategies are:

- the preliminary assessment of control risk;

- tests of control to be performed in assessing control risk; and

- the planned level of substantive procedures to be performed to reduce audit risk to an appropriately low level.

WORKING PAPERS

Evidence collected in support of an audit opinion (for example, worksheets and checklists) is recorded in the working papers. The term 'audit working papers' is used to include all documentation stored in paper, film or electronic media.

Types of working paper

Types of working paper prepared during an audit include:

- a working trial balance;
- schedules and analyses;
- audit memoranda and documentation of corroborating information;
- adjusting and reclassifying entries; and
- audit programmes.

Working papers may be prepared manually or by using software developed for micro-computers. Figure 6.4 is an example of a computer-generated working paper. The use of electronic working papers provides several advantages: auditors can obtain more information on their own from the entity's system; data can be instantaneously retrieved; the audit team can share information with members who are not on site; and review can take place at any time and anywhere.

The purpose and function of working papers

Working papers are the subject of ISA 230, Documentation. Properly prepared working papers demonstrate that the audit was performed in accordance with Auditing Standards. They show that the audit was properly planned and carried out, that adequate supervision was exercised, that an appropriate review was made of the audit work undertaken and, most importantly, that the evidence is sufficient and appropriate to support the audit opinion.

Working papers also serve to monitor the progress of the audit, especially where responsibility for separate tasks is allocated to different staff members. When completed, the working papers also provide a guide to the planning and performance of audits in subsequent periods.

The auditors' working papers should record the audit plan; the nature, timing and extent of the audit procedures performed; and the conclusions drawn from the audit evidence obtained.

Omni Co. Ltd   W/P Ref. AA-1
Working trial balance – Balance sheet   Prepared by: _G.B.C._ Date: _10/2/X2_
31 December 20X1   Reviewed by: _A.R.E._ Date: _15/2/X2_

W/P Acc. Ref. No.	Description	Final balance 31.12.X0	Ledger balance 31.12.X1	Adjustments		Adjusted balance 31.12.X1	Reclassifications		Final balance 31.12.X1
				AJE Ref.	Debit (Credit)		RJE Ref.	Debit (Credit)	
	Assets								
	Current								
A	Cash	392 000	427 000	(1)	50 000	477 000			477 000
B 150	Marketable securities	52 000	62 200			62 200			62 200
C	Debtors (net)	1 601 400	1 715 000	(1)	(50 000)	1 665 000	(A)	10 000	1 675 000
D 170	Stocks	2 542 500	2 810 200	(2)	133 000	2 943 200			2 943 200
E	Prepaid expenses	24 900	19 500			19 500			19 500
	Total current	4 613 000	5 033 900		133 000	5 166 900		10 000	5 176 900
F 240	Fixed asset investments	3 146 500	190 000			190 000			190 000
G	Tangible fixed assets (net)		3 310 900			3 310 900			3 310 900
	Total	7 759 500	8 534 800		133 000	8 667 800		10 000	8 677 800
	Liabilities and shareholders' equity								
	Current liabilities								
M 400	Notes payable	750 000	825 000			825 000			825 000
N 410	Creditors	2 150 400	2 340 300	(2)	(133 000)	2 473 300	(A)	(10 000)	2 483 300
O 420	Accruals	210 600	189 000			189 000			189 000
P 430	Taxes payable	150 000	170 000			170 000			170 000
	Total current	3 261 000	3 524 300		(133 000)	3 657 300		(10 000)	3 667 300
R 500	Debentures payable	1 000 000	1 200 000			1 200 000			1 200 000
S 600	Ordinary shares	2 400 000	2 400 000			2 400 000			2 400 000
T 700	Profit and loss appropriation	1 098 500	1 410 500			1 410 500			1 410 500
	Total	7 759 500	8 534 800		(133 000)	8 667 800		(10 000)	8 677 800

Figure 6.4 _Partial working trial balance working paper_

Working papers should be tailored to meet the needs of the specific audit engagement. ISA 230 states that the form and content of the working papers is influenced by the:

- nature of the engagement;
- form of the auditors' report;
- nature and complexity of the business;
- nature and condition of the entity's accounting and internal control systems;

- needs in the particular circumstances for direction, supervision and review of work performed by assistants; and
- specific audit methodology and technology used in the course of the audit.

Working paper files

Working papers are generally filed under one of two categories: (1) a permanent file and (2) a current file.

PERMANENT FILE

A permanent file contains data that are expected to be useful to the auditors on many future engagements with the entity. Items typically found in a permanent file are:

- extracts or copies of the memorandum and articles of association. These describe, among other matters, the objectives of the company, the number and types of shares authorised for issue, their par value, the rights of shareholders and the duties of directors;
- copies of important long-term operating agreements or contracts such as leases, pension plans, profit-sharing and bonus agreements, and labour contracts;
- analysis of accounts that are important to the audit each year (such as shareholder fund accounts and long-term debt);
- analytical review schedules from prior years, including ratios and percentage analysis or trend statements for various items. A review of these schedules enables the auditors to focus on unusual changes in the current year's account balances compared with those for previous periods;
- a description of the entity's accounting and internal control systems. This may consist of the description of the control environment, control policies and procedures, internal control questionnaires, flow charts, decision tables, and a chart of accounts and sample forms to aid in obtaining an understanding of the company's procedures; and
- information relevant to audit planning, such as the master copy of the audit programme, information on accounts (bank accounts or cost centres) or locations (controlled entities or branches) tested on a rotation basis.

CURRENT FILE

The current file contains evidence gathered in the performance of the current year's audit programme.

Working trial balance

A partial working trial balance is illustrated in Figure 6.4. Note that columns are provided for the current year's ledger balances (before audit adjustments and reclassifications), adjustments, adjusted balances, reclassifications and final (audited) balances. Including the final (audited) balances for the prior year facilitates the performance of certain analytical procedures.

The working trial balance may be prepared by the entity or the auditors. When the former occurs, the auditors verify the trial balance by adding the columns and tracing the account balances to the general ledger. A working trial balance is of paramount importance during the conduct of the audit because it:

- provides a basis for controlling all the individual working papers;
- serves as a connecting link between the entity's general ledger and the financial statements; and
- identifies the specific working papers containing the audit evidence for each financial statement item.

Figure 6.4, for example, indicates that the amount reported in the financial statements for marketable securities is based on general ledger account 150 and that the evidence used by the auditors to evaluate management's assertions about marketable securities can be found in a section of the working papers with a reference or index of B. The absence of an account number for cash in Figure 6.4 indicates that this financial statement item is the aggregate of several general ledger cash accounts. In such cases, the initial working paper of the section referenced on the working trial balance (A in this case) should contain a schedule showing which general ledger accounts have been combined for this financial statement item. The link between the cash line item in the working trial balance for Omni Co. Limited (working paper AA-1) and Omni's balance sheet presentation of cash is illustrated in the bottom portion of Figure 6.5.

Schedules and analyses

The terms 'working paper schedule' and 'working paper analysis' are used interchangeably to describe the individual working papers that contain the evidence supporting the items in the working trial balance. Working papers are normally filed by balance sheet item, with a further section for the profit and loss account. The first schedule for each item is referred to as a lead schedule. This schedule groups the general ledger accounts that are combined for reporting purposes and identifies the individual working paper schedules or analyses that contain the audit evidence obtained for each account comprising the group. The middle portion of Figure 6.5 illustrates the use of a cash lead schedule for Omni Co. Limited (working paper A) and how it is linked both to the cash line of the working trial balance (working paper AA-1) and the supporting working papers for the two general ledger cash accounts listed on the lead schedule (i.e. working paper A-1 for A/C 100 Petty cash and working paper A-2 for A/C 101 Cash in bank).

Individual schedules or analyses often show the composition of an account balance at a particular date, as in working paper A-1 of Figure 6.5. Other examples would include a list of customer balances comprising the sales ledger control account balance and a list of investments comprising the marketable securities account balance. A working paper schedule may also show the changes in one or more related account balances during the period covered by the financial statements, as illustrated in Figure 6.6. In some cases, the auditors use schedules prepared by the entity, which are indicated by the letters 'PBC' for 'prepared by client'. Such schedules need to be checked against the accounting records to ensure their accuracy. Audit work performed is indicated by the tick marks and related explanations on the working paper, as illustrated in Figure 6.6.

Schedules are of particular importance where evidence is obtained from the examination of a sample. The schedule should indicate the basis of selection and the specific items

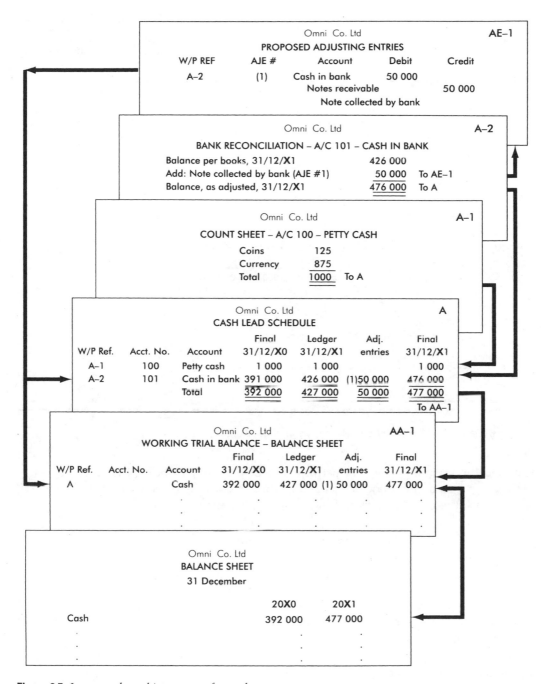

Figure 6.5 *Integrated working papers for cash*

Omni Co. Ltd
Notes receivable and interest
31 December 20X1

W/P Ref. C-4
Prepared by: __A.C.E.__ Date: _20.01.X2_
Reviewed by: __G.A.R.__ Date: _04.02.X2_

Accts 160, 161, 450

					Notes receivable				Interest			
Maker	Made	Date due	Interest rate (%)	Face amount	Balance 31/12/X0	Debits	Credits	Balance 31.12.X1	Accrued 31.12.X0	Earned 20X1	Collected 20X1	Accrued 31.12.X1
Coffman Ltd	1/7/X0	30/6/X1	10	25 000	25 000 ✗		25 000 C	—	1250 ✗	1250 ∅	2500 C	—
Morrison Bros.	1/11/X0	31/10/X1	10	30 000	30 000 ✗		30 000 C	—	500 ✗	2500 ∅	3000 C	—
Shirley and Son	1/4/X1	31/3/X2	12	40 000	✓ —	40 000 ⌒		40 000	—	3600 ∅	—	3600
Warner Corp.	1/10/X1	30/9/X3	12	20 000	✓ —	20 000 ⌒		20 000	—	600 ∅	—	600
					55 000 ✗	60 000	55 000	60 000 ∧	1750 ✗	7950	5500	4200 ∧
					F	F	F	FF FC	F	F	F	FF FC

✗   Agreed to 31.12.X0 working papers.
C   Traced collections to cash receipts and deposit slips.
∅   Verified computations.
✓   Examined note during cash count.
⌒   Confirmed with maker — no exceptions.
∧   Traced to ledger balance.
F   Footed.
FF   Footed and cross-footed.

Figure 6.6 *Notes receivable and interest working paper*

selected for sampling, enabling performance of the audit to be replicated if any query arises. It is also useful if documents and records sampled by the auditors are also marked to establish the proper conduct of the audit in the event of any inquiry.

Audit memoranda and corroborating information

Audit memoranda refer to written data in narrative form prepared by the auditors. Memoranda may include comments on the performance of auditing procedures and conclusions reached from the auditing work performed. Documentation of corroborating information includes extracts of minutes of the board of directors' meetings, confirmation responses, written representations from management and outside experts, and copies of important contracts.

Proposed adjusting and reclassifying entries

It is important to distinguish between adjusting entries and reclassifying entries. Audit adjusting entries are corrections of entity errors of omission or misapplication of Financial Reporting Standards. Thus, adjusting entries ultimately deemed to be material (individually or in the aggregate) are expected to be recorded by the entity. In contrast, reclassifying entries pertain to the proper financial statement presentation of correct account balances. Assume, for example, that the debtors' balance includes some customer accounts with credit balances pertaining to customer advances. Although it is not necessary for the entity to record the classifying entry on its books, for reporting purposes an entry should be made on the working trial balance in which debtors are debited to offset the customer advances and a liability account is credited. This is illustrated in Figure 6.4 and will result in the reclassification being reflected in the financial statements. As with adjusting entries, only reclassifications that have a material effect need be made.

In the working papers, each entry should be shown on (1) the schedule or analysis of the account, (2) the lead schedules, if any, (3) the summary of proposed adjusting or reclassifying entries and (4) the working trial balance. This is illustrated in Figure 6.5.

The summaries of adjusting and reclassifying entries are initially designated as 'proposed' entries because (1) the auditors' final judgement as to which entries must be made may not occur until the end of the audit and (2) the entity must approve them. The disposition of each proposed entry should ultimately be recorded on the working papers. If the entity declines to make adjusting or reclassifying entries that the auditors feel are necessary, then the auditors' report must be appropriately modified.

Audit programme

An audit programme is a listing of the auditing procedures to be performed. Audit programmes are used for the testing of internal controls and for substantive procedures. Examples of these audit programmes are included throughout this textbook, particularly in Chapters 10–13.

Preparing working papers

A number of basic techniques are used widely in preparing a working paper. These pertain to the mechanics of working paper preparation and include the following essential points.

HEADING
Each working paper should contain the name of the entity, a descriptive title identifying the content of the working paper (such as 'Bank Reconciliation – National Bank'), and the balance sheet date or the period covered by the audit.

INDEX NUMBERS
Each working paper is given an index or reference number – such as A-1, B-2 and so on – for identification purposes. Indexing facilitates the organisation and review of working papers. Most audit firms have standardised referencing systems so the organisation of audit files is consistent throughout the firm.

CROSS-REFERENCING
Data on a working paper that are taken from another working paper or that are carried forward to another working paper should be cross-referenced with the index numbers of those working papers, as illustrated in Figure 6.5.

EVIDENCE

The paper should document the evidence examined and the audit procedures applied to that evidence. A common practice is the use of tick marks (symbols such as check marks) to identify the different procedures applied. A legend on the working paper should explain the nature and extent of the work represented by each tick mark, or provide the additional information applicable to the items marked. Most firms use standardised tick marks to indicate common procedures such as adding columns and posting totals to ledgers.

Where the evidence is in the form of documents and records, it is usual to leave a trail of tick marks on those documents and records. This enables the work of the auditors to be traced back to the evidence if necessary.

CONCLUSION

The results of audit procedures should be summarised, indicating whether they confirm the particular assertion being tested.

SIGNATURE AND DATES

Upon completing their respective tasks, both the preparer and reviewer of a working paper should initial and date it. This establishes responsibility for the work performed and the review.

The partial working papers in Figure 6.5 do not show all of these essential elements because that figure was designed primarily to illustrate indexing and cross-referencing. Figure 6.6, however, illustrates all the above elements.

Reviewing working papers

There are several levels in the review of working papers within an audit practice. The first-level review is made by the preparer's supervisor, such as a manager. This review occurs when the work on a specific segment of the audit has been completed. The reviewer is primarily interested in the work done, the evidence obtained, the judgement exercised and the conclusions reached by the preparer of the working paper.

The working papers undergo other reviews when the audit has been completed. These reviews will be explained in Chapter 14.

Ownership and custody of working papers

The property rights of working papers rest with the auditors if they are acting as an independent 'contractor'. This was established in *Chantrey Martin & Co. v. Martin* (1953) 3 WLR 459. Working papers prepared at the auditors' request by the entity's staff also belong to the auditors. In certain circumstances auditors may be acting as an agent for other auditors. In the absence of any agreement to the contrary, the working papers belong to the principal auditors. In non-audit situations (for example, when the auditors are making representations on behalf of the client to the Inland Revenue), the auditors own the audit working papers but not the working papers relating to the representations to the Inland Revenue.

The auditors' ownership rights, however, are subject to constraints imposed by the auditors' own professional standards. ISA 230, Documentation, states that:

The auditor should adopt appropriate procedures for maintaining the confidentiality and safe custody of the working papers and for retaining them for a period sufficient to meet the needs of the practice and in accordance with legal and professional requirements of record retention.

Successor auditors may have access to the working papers of the predecessor auditors, with client approval. Working papers may also be made available during a practice review.
Physical custody of the working papers rests with the auditors, and they are responsible for their safekeeping. Working papers included in the permanent file are retained for as long as they are relevant; current working papers should be retained for as long as they are useful to the auditors in servicing an entity or needed to satisfy legal or professional requirements for record retention.

 ## LEARNING CHECK

6.16 Working papers contain the evidence collected by the auditors.

6.17 Working papers show that an audit was carried out in accordance with Auditing Standards.

6.18 Working paper files are classified into permanent and current files.

6.19 The permanent file contains information of a continuing nature.

6.20 The current file contains information relevant to the current period's audit.

6.21 Auditors own the working papers and are responsible for their safekeeping.

6.22 Auditors should adopt appropriate procedures to maintain confidentiality of information contained in the working papers.

SUMMARY

Prior to accepting an audit engagement, the auditors should ascertain that it could be completed in accordance with all applicable professional standards, including Auditing Standards and professional ethics. Important steps in accepting the engagement include evaluating the integrity of management, identifying any special circumstances and unusual risks, assessing competence, evaluating independence, determining that the engagement can be completed with due care, and issuing an engagement letter.

Proper planning and assessment of the risks of material misstatements is crucial in performing an efficient, effective audit. Planning steps include obtaining an understanding of the entity and the industry, performing analytical procedures, making preliminary judgements about materiality levels, considering audit risks, obtaining an understanding of the entity's internal control structure, and developing preliminary audit strategies for significant assertions. The next chapter will explain, in more detail, the procedures to be followed in obtaining the understanding of the internal control system and in assessing control risk. Chapter 9 will explain the design of substantive procedures and the development of an audit programme setting out the nature, timing and extent of audit procedures required to implement the audit plan.

The procedures performed, the evidence obtained and the auditors' evaluation of that evidence should be fully documented in working papers, which should provide the support for the auditors' report and evidence of the auditors' compliance with Auditing Standards.

FURTHER READING

Bodine, S., Pugliese, A. & Walker, P. 'A Road Map to Risk Management', *Journal of Accountancy* (December 2001), pp. 65–70.

Flesher, D. L. & de Magalhaes, R. 'Electronic Workpapers', *Internal Auditor* (August 1995), pp. 38–43.

Fraser, I. A. M., Hatherley, D. J. & Lim, K. Z. 'An Empirical Investigation of the Use of Analytical Review by External Auditors', *British Accounting Review* (March 1997), pp. 35–48.

Glover, S., Jiambalvo, J. & Kennedy, J. 'Analytical Procedures and Audit Planning Decisions', *Journal of Accountancy* (February 2001), p. 99.

Harper, R. M., Strawser, J. R. & Twang, K. 'Establishing Investigation Thresholds for Preliminary Analytical Procedures', *Auditing: A Journal of Practice & Theory* (Fall 1990), pp. 115–133.

Holder, W. W. 'Analytical Review Procedures in Planning the Audit: An Application Study', *Auditing: A Journal of Practice & Theory* (Spring 1983), pp. 100–107.

Hull, R. P. & Mitchem, C. 'Practitioners' Views on Communications Between Predecessor and Successor Auditors and Accountants', *Accounting Horizons* (June 1987), pp. 61–69.

Perkins, A. 'Put it in Writing', *Accountancy (International Edition)* (April 1996), p. 68.

Trotman, K. '*Analytical Review, Audit Monograph 1*', Australian Accounting Research Foundation, 1990.

Whittington, R. & Fischbach, G. 'The New Audit Documentation Requirements', *Journal of Accountancy* (April 2002), pp. 53–59.

Wright, A. & Ashton, R. H. 'Identifying Audit Adjustments with Attention-Directing Procedures', *Accounting Review* (October 1989), pp. 710–728.

APPENDIX 6A
Key financial ratios used in analytical procedures

Users of financial statements can obtain valuable insights into an entity's financial condition and performance through analysis of key financial ratios. The same analysis performed by auditors provides them with a better understanding of the entity.

Given that auditors already have some knowledge of the entity from other planning procedures, analytical procedures can also play a different role in the audit. Using prior knowledge, auditors can develop expectations as to whether current year ratios are expected to differ from those in prior years or from industry norms. When comparisons reveal unexpected fluctuations, or when expected fluctuations do not occur, the auditors will generally want to investigate whether the aberration is due to the misstatement of one or more variables used in calculating the ratio.

This appendix explains the calculation of 10 common ratios and comments on the purpose and interpretation of each. The comments on interpretation are general in nature and should be tailored according to a particular entity's circumstances, such as its recent experience and the industry in which it operates.

RATIO	CALCULATION	PURPOSE AND INTERPRETATION
Solvency		
Quick ratio	$\dfrac{\text{Cash} + \text{Debtors} + \text{Current asset investments}}{\text{Current liabilities}}$	To reveal protection afforded by cash or near-cash assets to short-term creditors – the larger the ratio, the greater the liquidity.
Current ratio	$\dfrac{\text{Total current assets}}{\text{Total current liabilities}}$	To measure the degree to which current liabilities are covered by current assets – the higher the ratio, the greater the assurance that current liabilities can be paid in a timely manner.
Debt to equity	$\dfrac{\text{Total liabilities}}{\text{Shareholders' equity}}$	To measure the extent to which a company is using its debt financing capacity. In general, this ratio should not exceed 100% because in such cases creditors will have more at stake than owners will.
Times interest earned	$\dfrac{\text{Operating profit before interest and tax}}{\text{Interest expense}}$	To measure the number of times a company can meet its fixed interest charges with earnings.
Efficiency		
Debtors' turnover	$\dfrac{\text{Sales}}{\text{Debtors}}$	To measure the number of times debtors are collected during the period. When used in analytical procedures, some auditors prefer to use the closing debtors' balance rather than average debtors, which would make a misstatement more difficult to detect. A variation, *the collection period*, is found by dividing the turnover ratio by 365. This ratio may be useful in evaluating the adequacy of the provision for doubtful debts.
Stock turnover	$\dfrac{\text{Cost of sales}}{\text{Stock}}$	To indicate how rapidly stock turns over. When using this calculation in analytical procedures, some auditors prefer to use the closing stock balance rather than average stock, which would make a misstatement more difficult to detect. Although the ratio varies widely among industries, low values may indicate excessively high stocks and slow-moving items; conversely, extremely high values may reflect insufficient merchandise to meet customer demand, resulting in lost sales.
Asset turnover	$\dfrac{\text{Sales}}{\text{Total assets}}$	To measure the efficiency with which a company uses its assets to generate sales. For the reasons noted above, some auditors prefer using closing rather than average assets to calculate this ratio.

RATIO	CALCULATION	PURPOSE AND INTERPRETATION
Profitability		
Return on sales	$$\frac{\text{Operating profit}}{\text{Sales}}$$	To reveal profits earned on sales. This ratio indicates ability to earn satisfactory profits for owners, as well as the entity's ability to withstand adverse conditions such as falling prices, rising costs and declining sales.
Return on assets	$$\frac{\text{Operating profit}}{\text{Total assets}}$$	To indicate profitability based on total assets available. Companies efficiently using assets will have a high ratio; less efficient companies will have a low ratio.
Return on shareholders' equity	$$\frac{\text{Operating profit after tax}}{\text{Ordinary shareholders' equity}}$$	To reveal management's ability to earn an adequate return on capital invested by owners. Generally, a minimum of 10% is considered desirable to provide funds for dividends and growth.

MULTIPLE-CHOICE QUESTIONS

Choose the best answer for each of the following.
(Answers are on pages 599–600)

6.1 Which of the following considerations on accepting a new client does not involve quality control:
  (a) availability of appropriately qualified staff to perform the audit.
  (b) previous auditors' advice as to whether audit fees are paid promptly.
  (c) provision of other services to the client that might impair independence.
  (d) previous auditors' communication as to possible illegal acts by the client.

6.2 Engagement letters are widely used in practice for professional engagements of all types. The primary purpose of the audit engagement letter is to:
  (a) remind management that the primary responsibility for the financial statements rests with management.
  (b) satisfy the requirements of the auditor's liability insurance policy.
  (c) provide a starting point for the auditor's preparation of the audit programme.
  (d) provide a written record of the agreement with the client as to the services to be provided.

6.3 When planning an audit an auditor would not normally be concerned with:
  (a) problems encountered on the previous year's audit.
  (b) changes in the company's accounting system.
  (c) the collection of the fee for the previous year's audit.
  (d) changes in the organisation of the internal audit department.

6.4 In the tour of the client's operations, the auditor noted two machines were not operating in the client's factory. This meant that production was 25% lower than normal. The factory manager informed the auditor that this was because the machine was being serviced; however, the auditor saw no evidence of this. How would this affect the audit plan?

(a) It would have no effect. The factory manager's explanation should be accepted.

(b) It would increase the amount of audit work on plant and machinery.

(c) It would be necessary to perform a more thorough review of sales for the year and the sales forecasts.

(d) It would be necessary to perform more work on stock to check for obsolescence.

6.5 Which of the following is not one of the uses of a time budget:

(a) determining the extent of reliance on internal control.

(b) controlling the efficiency of the performance of audit staff.

(c) planning the assignment of staff to jobs.

(d) negotiating the audit fee with the client.

6.6 Analytical procedures used in planning an audit should focus on identifying:

(a) material weaknesses in the internal control structure.

(b) the predictability of financial data from individual transactions.

(c) the various assertions that are embodied in the financial statements.

(d) areas that may represent specific risks relevant to the audit.

6.7 When preparing audit working papers it is important that:

(a) they be prepared in ink as a permanent record.

(b) they be prepared by the audit senior as junior staff do not have sufficient experience to prepare them.

(c) they be signed by the client as a precaution against the client subsequently claiming the auditor was negligent and the evidence recorded is incorrect.

(d) they indicate the name of the staff members responsible for preparing and reviewing them and any conclusions that may be drawn from the evidence.

6.8 Which of the following is not a function of the preparation of working papers:

(a) to provide a basis for an overall assessment of the audit and the evidence available to support the expression of an opinion.

(b) to provide a guide for the planning and performance of next year's audit.

(c) for use by the auditor on other engagements such as advising another client on the desirability of making a takeover bid for the audit client.

(d) to introduce a discipline into the performance of the audit.

6.9 Standardised working papers are useful because they:

(a) make sure that all of the firm's audits are done exactly the same way.

(b) facilitate the review of the audit since the reviewer will be accustomed to the layout, contents and purpose of such working papers.

(c) eliminate the need for junior audit staff to have to make decisions.

(d) eliminate the need for detailed planning since the only decision to be made is which strategy to adopt.

6.10 The auditor's permanent working paper file should not normally include:

(a) copies of the memorandum of association.

(b) extracts from the client's bank statements.

(c) details of mortgages.

(d) past years' financial statements.

DISCUSSION QUESTIONS

6.1 Discuss the suggestion that, if all auditors reject, as clients, entities identified as being too risky, those entities most in need of an audit will be unable to secure the services of an auditor? As professionals, should auditors be required to provide their services to any entity requiring an audit?

6.2 Identify factors that need to be considered in evaluating the auditor's ability to service a client.

6.3 Discuss the contention that the engagement letter understates the auditor's legal responsibilities in order to discourage litigation.

6.4 Would you agree with the argument that adoption of the lower assessed level of control risk audit strategy is driven by competitive pressures on auditors seeking cost savings and exposes auditors to excessive risks of audit failure?

6.5 Should the detailed audit programme be drafted for both tests of control and substantive procedures on completion of the planning phase or should the programme of substantive procedures be drawn up only after control risk had been assessed?

6.6 In the planning phase auditors use analytical procedures in much the same way as investors but, as a substantive procedure, the auditor knows the financial position and performance that ought to be shown by the analysis and uses analytical procedures to detect possible misstatements in the financial report. Explain.

6.7 Discuss the argument that time budgets put pressure on audit staff members to give priority to completing the audit within the budget at the expense of audit quality.

6.8 Discuss the role of working papers and tick marks on entity records in providing a 'trail' for the proper performance of the audit to be evidenced.

6.9 Discuss the respective merits of the use of standardised documentation by audit firms, such as pre-printed audit programmes, compared with tailoring all documentation for each separate audit engagement.

PROFESSIONAL APPLICATION QUESTIONS

(Suggested answers are on pages 616–620)

6.1 Client acceptance decision

You are a partner with a firm of Chartered Certified Accountants that has been invited, by the board of directors, to accept nomination as external auditors to Bondi plc. Bondi operates a number of car dealerships and has grown rapidly over the past two years through an aggressive take-over strategy.

You are aware that the company's existing auditors, a much smaller firm, qualified their last auditors' report. Over lunch with a number of your firm's partners, the company's finance director maintained that their existing auditors could not cope with the audit of a company their size and, in particular, were not equipped to audit the recently installed sophisticated computer accounting programme. He also suggests that they need a firm of your reputation in order to reassure the market as they intend to seek a public listing within two years.

The existing auditors, in response to your enquiry, advise against accepting the audit on the following grounds:

- Insufficient consideration has been devoted by management to developing the accounting system in line with the expanding business. In particular there is a lack of concern as to control. They detected a number of petty employee frauds as a result of control weaknesses. No action was taken against the employees identified as engaged in fraud. The attitude seems to be to encourage risk taking employees who make money on the side whilst securing good deals for the company. That is seen as a legitimate bonus.
- The newly installed computer accounting system is unreasonably complicated. Bondi claims this is necessary because of the need to maintain records to justify the company's claims for volume rebates, and bonuses under the complex incentive schemes by which car manufacturers reward dealers.
- They have no evidence of deliberate misrepresentation by the directors but audit staff were hindered in their audit work by a less than helpful attitude by senior management who adopted an aggressive stance whenever a query was raised. The finance director was constantly on the phone to the partner claiming the audit staff were incompetent and accusing them of wasting his time asking unnecessary questions.

At a partner's meeting a majority of partners accepted the story that the existing auditors were out of their depth and that their complaints were merely an attempt to cover up their own shortcomings. Your firm accepted nomination and was duly appointed as auditors.

Required
(a) State factors the partners should have considered for and against accepting nomination.
(b) Detail the matters you would be concerned about in obtaining the required knowledge of the business and in developing your audit plan.

(Adapted from Question 6, Audit Framework, June 1999. Reproduced by permission of ACCA)

6.2 Audit working papers
The preparation of working papers is an important part of the audit process. You have been asked to prepare a session introducing new recruits to your firm of Chartered Certified Accountants to the use of working papers. Amongst the topics you have been asked to cover are the distinction between working papers held in the permanent and current audit files, the design and use of audit programmes and the concept of an audit trail with respect to the conduct of the audit itself.

Required
(a) State four matters you would expect to find recorded in working papers in the permanent audit file and explain their purpose.
(b) Explain the design and use of audit programmes and the respective merits of standard and tailored audit programmes.

(c) Explain the importance of recording details of the actual evidence examined in the course of the audit on which the conclusions are drawn. Your explanation should include consideration of the details to be recorded in the working papers and of the audit trail to be left in the books and records of the entity being audited.

(Adapted from Question 1, Audit Framework, June 2000. Reproduced by permission of ACCA)

CHAPTER 7

INTERNAL CONTROL AND CONTROL RISK ASSESSMENT

DISCUSSION QUESTIONS

PROFESSIONAL APPLICATION QUESTIONS

LEARNING OBJECTIVES

After studying this chapter, you should be able to:

1 appreciate the importance of internal control to an entity and to its independent auditors

2 describe the components of internal control

3 state the inherent limitations of the internal control system

4 indicate the procedures to obtain and document an understanding of internal control

5 explain the purpose of making a preliminary assessment of control risk

6 describe the approach to evaluating the design effectiveness of control procedures

7 state the purpose of tests of controls and the nature of such tests

8 describe how the work of internal auditing may be used in tests of controls

9 explain the process of assessing control risk.

PROFESSIONAL STATEMENTS

ISA 315   Understanding the Entity and Its Environment and Assessing the Risks of Material Misstatement
ISA 330   The Auditor's Procedures in Response to Assessed Risks
ISA 260   Communications of Audit Matters with Those Charged with Governance
ISA 610   Considering the Work of Internal Auditing

One of the most important tasks in planning an audit engagement is obtaining an understanding of the entity's internal control. In Chapter 5 control risk was described as the risk that a misstatement that could occur will not be prevented or detected and corrected on a timely basis by the entity's internal control. Chapter 6 described procedures for obtaining an understanding of the entity sufficient to assess the risk that the financial statements could be materially misstated. Internal control is designed by management to ensure, among other matters, that material misstatements are either prevented or are detected in sufficient time for remedial action to be taken.

This chapter describes the nature of an entity's internal control and explains the auditors' responsibility for obtaining an understanding of that structure sufficient to assess the risk that control procedures may fail to prevent or detect, on a timely basis, material misstatements in the financial statements. The chapter describes how auditors test the design effectiveness of internal control to form a preliminary assessment of the level of control risk. Where that preliminary assessment is other than high, auditors could consider adopting the lower assessed level of control risk audit strategy described in Chapter 6. If this strategy is adopted, then it must be supported by more extensive tests of control.

Internal control is sometimes referred to as a 'risk management framework'. The term 'internal control' is more commonly used in auditing literature but students must be prepared to recognise either term.

INTERNAL CONTROL

We will begin by explaining the importance of internal control within an entity, and then describe the components of an entity's internal control.

The importance of internal control

The importance of internal control has been recognised in the professional literature for over half a century. As early as 1947 a US publication entitled *Internal Controls* cited the following factors as contributing to the expanding recognition of the significance of internal control:

- The scope and size of the business entity has become so complex and widespread that management must rely on numerous reports and analyses to effectively control operations.
- The checks and reviews inherent in a good system of internal control afford protection against human weaknesses and reduce the possibility that errors or irregularities will occur.
- It is impracticable for auditors to audit most companies within economic fee limitations without relying on the client's system of internal control.

The incidence of creative and even fraudulent accounting in the 1980s by large companies has led to internal control being elevated from a private concern of management and auditors to a matter of public interest. For example, the *Report of the Committee on Financial Aspects of Corporate Governance* (the Cadbury Report) published in 1992 recommended that directors be required to report publicly on the effectiveness of their system of internal control. This, in turn, led to the publication, in 1999, of *Internal Control – Guidance for Directors on the Combined Code* (the Turnbull Report). This report adopted a risk management approach that elevates internal control from being reactive to unwanted risks to a proactive component of value creation. It describes the role of internal control in the following terms.

In determining its policies with regard to internal control, and thereby assessing what constitutes a sound system of internal control in the particular circumstances of the company, the board's deliberations should include consideration of the following factors:

- the nature and extent of the risks facing the company;
- the extent and categories of risk which it regards as acceptable for the company to bear;
- the likelihood of the risks concerned materialising;
- the company's ability to reduce the incidence and impact on the business of risks that do materialise; and
- the costs of operating particular controls relative to the benefit thereby obtained in managing the related risks.

The Turnbull Report identifies the elements of a sound system of internal control as follows:

An internal control system encompasses the policies, processes, tasks, behaviours and other aspects of a company that, taken together:

- facilitate its effective and efficient operation by enabling it to respond appropriately to significant business, operational, financial, compliance and other risks to achieving the company's objectives. This includes the safeguarding of assets from inappropriate use or from loss and fraud, and ensuring that liabilities are identified and managed;
- help ensure the quality of internal and independent reporting. This requires the maintenance of proper records and processes that generate a flow of timely, relevant and reliable information from within and outside the organisation;
- help ensure compliance with applicable laws and regulations, and also with internal policies with respect to the conduct of business.

The US has taken the lead in this matter. In 1987, the National Commission on Fraudulent Financial Reporting (the Treadway Commission) re-emphasised the importance of internal control in reducing the incidence of fraudulent financial reporting. The Commission's final report included the following recommendation:

All public companies should maintain internal controls that will provide reasonable assurance that fraudulent financial reporting will be prevented or subject to early detection.

In implementing this recommendation, the Committee of Sponsoring Organisations (COSO) of the Treadway Commission issued a report in 1992 entitled *Internal Control – Integrated Framework*. The failure of the large US corporation Enron in 2001 and the subsequent collapse of its independent auditors, Andersens, led to a revision of this document in 2003 under the title of *Enterprise Risk Management Framework*. This document also emphasises the importance of risk management.

The underlying premise of enterprise risk management is that every entity, whether for-profit, not-for-profit, or a governmental body, exists to provide value for its stakeholders. All entities face uncertainty, and the challenge for management is to determine how much uncertainty the entity is prepared to accept as it strives to grow stakeholder value. Uncertainty presents both risk and opportunity, with the potential to erode or enhance value. Enterprise risk management provides a framework for management to effectively deal with uncertainty and associated risk and opportunity and thereby enhance its capacity to build value.

INTERNAL CONTROLS RELEVANT TO AN AUDIT

This chapter is primarily concerned with controls that have the objective of achieving reliable financial reporting. Other objectives and related controls may also be relevant if they pertain to data that auditors use in applying audit procedures, such as:

- non-financial data used in analytical procedures – for example, the number of employees, the volume of goods manufactured, and other production and marketing statistics; and
- financial data developed for internal purposes – for example, budgets and performance data that auditors use to obtain independent evidence about amounts in the financial statements.

As explained in Chapter 2, auditors have certain responsibilities for detecting errors and irregularities (including management and employee fraud) and particular illegal acts. Thus, any entity objectives and controls related to these matters are also relevant to auditors. Where non-compliance could have a direct and material effect on the financial statements, controls over 'compliance with applicable laws and regulations' are particularly relevant.

Operational effectiveness and efficiency controls that are designed to reduce the risk of bad operating decisions – such as selling a product at too low a price or failing to order replacement stock in time – are not usually considered relevant to a financial statement audit. Exceptions are controls that relate to the safeguarding of assets against unauthorised acquisition, use and disposition when these controls help to ensure that the entity's financial statements properly reflect related losses (such as from theft).

Components of internal control

The components of internal control identified by ISA 315, Understanding the Entity and Its Environment and Assessing the Risks of Material Misstatement, are:

- the control environment;
- the entity's risk assessment process;
- the information system;
- control activities; and
- monitoring of controls.

CONTROL ENVIRONMENT

The control environment means management's overall attitude, awareness and actions regarding internal control and its importance in the entity. Numerous factors comprise the control environment, including:

- integrity and ethical values;
- a commitment to competence;

- management's philosophy and operating style;
- organisational structure;
- the assignment of authority and responsibility;
- internal audit;
- the use of information technology;
- human resource policies and practices; and
- the board of directors and audit committee.

These factors are discussed in the following sections.

Integrity and ethical values

Increasingly, constituents of businesses – such as employees, customers, suppliers and the public – are demanding that business management exhibit integrity and ethical values. Managers of well-run entities are increasingly accepting the view that 'ethics pays' – that is, that ethical behaviour is good business.

To emphasise the importance of integrity and ethical values among all personnel of an organisation, the chief executive officer and other members of top management should:

- set the tone by example, by demonstrating integrity and practising ethical behaviour;
- communicate to all employees, verbally and through written policy statements and codes of conduct, that the same behaviour is expected of them – that each employee has a responsibility to report known or suspected violations to a higher level in the organisation, and that violations will result in penalties; and
- reduce or eliminate incentives and temptations that may lead individuals to engage in dishonest, illegal or unethical acts. Incentives for undesirable negative behaviour include placing undue emphasis on short-term results or on unrealistic performance targets, and offering bonus and profit-sharing plans that may, in the absence of necessary controls, encourage fraudulent financial reporting practices.

A commitment to competence

Personnel at every level in the organisation must possess the knowledge and skills needed to perform their jobs effectively. Meeting financial reporting objectives in a large publicly held company generally requires higher levels of competence on the part of chief financial officers and accounting personnel than would be needed for such personnel in a small, privately held company.

Management's philosophy and operating style

Characteristics that form part of a management's philosophy and operating style and that have an impact on the control environment include the management's:

- approach to taking and monitoring business risks;
- reliance on informal face-to-face contacts with key managers versus a formal system of written policies, performance indicators and exception reports;
- attitudes and actions towards financial reporting;

- conservative or aggressive selection of accounting principles from available alternatives;
- conscientiousness and conservatism in developing accounting estimates; and
- attitudes towards information processing and accounting functions and personnel.

The last four characteristics are particularly significant to an assessment of the control environment for financial reporting.

Organisational structure

An organisational structure contributes to an entity's ability to meet its objectives by providing an overall framework for planning, executing, controlling and monitoring the entity's activities. Developing an organisational structure for an entity involves determining the key areas of authority and responsibility and appropriate lines of reporting.

The assignment of authority and responsibility

The assignment of authority and responsibility is an extension of the development of an organisational structure. It includes the particulars of how, and to whom, authority and responsibility are assigned, and should enable each individual to know:

- how his or her actions contribute to the achievement of the entity's objectives; and
- for what he or she will be held accountable.

Internal audit

The establishment of an internal audit function strengthens the control environment. To be effective, internal audit personnel need to:

- be sufficiently skilled;
- possess integrity; and
- have appropriate access to the board of directors and the audit committee, and to the independent auditors.

The use of information technology

The use of information technology should be appropriate to the entity's size and complexity. The framework of overall control established by management should ensure that the general controls over information processing described on page 218 are achieved.

Human resource policies and practices

A fundamental concept of internal control is that it is effected or implemented by people. Thus, for the internal control structure to be effective, human resource policies and practices must ensure that entity personnel possess the expected integrity, ethical values and competence. Such practices include:

- developing appropriate recruiting policies;
- screening prospective employees;
- orienting new personnel to the entity's culture and operating style;
- developing training policies that communicate prospective roles and responsibilities;

- exercising disciplinary action for violations of expected behaviour;
- evaluating, counselling and promoting people based on periodic performance appraisals; and
- implementing compensation programmes that motivate and reward superior performance while avoiding disincentives to ethical behaviour.

Board of directors and audit committee

The composition of the board of directors and the audit committee, along with the manner in which they exercise their governance and oversight responsibilities, has a major impact on the control environment. Influential factors include:

- the proportion of non-executive directors and the establishment of an audit committee;
- the experience and stature of directors;
- the extent of their involvement with and scrutiny of management's activities;
- the degree to which they raise and pursue difficult questions with management; and
- the nature and extent of their interaction with internal and independent auditors.

RISK ASSESSMENT PROCESS

The entity should have a formal process for identifying risks and determining an appropriate strategy with regard to those risks. Auditors are particularly concerned with risks relevant to the truth and fairness of financial reporting, such as the possibility of unrecorded transactions or of unreliable accounting estimates. Internal control activities can only be designed to cope with identified risks.

It is particularly important that the entity be alert to changes that may render existing control activities inadequate such as rapid growth, changes in business activities, corporate restructuring and new financial reporting requirements.

INFORMATION SYSTEM

Before commencing an audit on an entity's financial statements, auditors must have a thorough understanding of its information system sufficient to plan the audit and develop an effective audit approach.

ISA 315 defines the information system as:

> the procedures and records established to initiate, record, process, and report entity transactions (as well as events and conditions) and to maintain accountability for the related assets, liabilities, and equity.

The quality of system-generated information affects management's ability to make appropriate decisions in controlling the entity's activities and to prepare reliable financial reports.

It is not only as auditors, however, that accountants need to have an understanding of information systems. As accountants, their prime function is to establish and maintain such a system to ensure that the financial reports they produce, whether for management or external parties, are accurate and reliable.

The focus of the information system is on transactions. Transactions consist of exchanges of assets and services between an entity and outside parties, and the transfer or use of assets and services within an entity. A major focus of controls in the information system is to ensure that transactions are initiated and processed in a way that prevents misstatements in financial statement assertions. An effective information system should:

- identify and record all valid transactions;
- describe the transactions on a timely basis and in sufficient detail to permit their proper classification for financial reporting;
- measure the value of transactions in a manner that permits recording their proper monetary value in the financial statements;
- determine the time period in which transactions occurred to permit recording of transactions in the proper accounting period; and
- present properly the transactions and related disclosures in the financial statements.

An entity's information system should provide a complete audit trail for each transaction. An audit trail is a chain of evidence provided by coding, cross-references and documentation that connects account balances and other summary results with original transaction data. Audit trails are essential to both management and auditors; for example, management uses the trail in responding to inquiries from customers or suppliers concerning account balances and auditors use the trail in vouching and tracing transactions. In computer information systems the audit trail may exist in electronic format only and sometimes may be deleted once the transaction has been verified (for example, when the personal identification number (PIN) is read and verified at the initiation of a credit or debit card transaction). Special audit techniques are required to verify the audit trail, such as the use of embedded audit facilities that trace the operation of controls electronically.

CONTROL ACTIVITIES

Control activities are detailed procedures that management establishes to ensure, as far as possible, that specific entity objectives will be achieved. Control activities that are relevant to a financial statement audit may be categorised as follows:

- information processing controls:
  - general controls;
  - application controls (proper authorisation; documents and records; independent checks);
- segregation of duties;
- physical controls; and
- performance reviews.

These categories are explained in the following sections.

Information processing controls

Of particular relevance to an audit are information processing controls that address risks related to the authorisation, completeness and accuracy of transactions. Most entities, regardless of size, now use computers for information processing in general and for accounting information in particular. In such cases, information processing controls are often further categorised as general controls and application controls.

GENERAL CONTROLS

General controls are those controls that apply to computer information systems (CIS) as a whole and include controls related to such matters as data centre organisation, hardware and systems software acquisition and maintenance, and backup and recovery procedures. Figure 7.3 lists the more important general controls.

APPLICATION CONTROLS

Application controls are those controls that apply to the processing of specific types of transaction, such as invoicing customers, paying suppliers and preparing payroll. Whether they are in a computerised or a manual environment, application controls may be further classified into the following categories:

- proper authorisation;
- documents and records; and
- independent checks.

Proper authorisation procedures ensure that transactions are authorised by personnel acting within the scope of their authority. Authorisations may be general or specific. General authorisation relates to the general conditions under which transactions are authorised, such as standard price lists for products and credit policies for charge sales. Specific authorisation is granted on a case-by-case basis and may apply in both non-routine transactions (such as major capital expenditures) and routine transactions that exceed the limits provided by the general authorisation (such as requisitioning goods or services other than replacement of stock).

Authorisation procedures are also important in limiting access to assets, documents and records, and to computer equipment, programs and files. These procedures will be explained in the section on physical controls (see page 220).

Documents and records are source documents, journals and ledgers. In computerised systems, some documents and records may exist only in electronic format. Documents provide evidence of transactions that have occurred and of the applicable price, nature and terms. Invoices, cheques and time tickets illustrate common types of document. When duly signed or stamped, documents also provide a basis for establishing responsibility for the execution and recording of transactions. Documents should be designed to encourage the capture of all relevant information and to provide for the required signatures and initials of those responsible for executing and recording the transaction. Employees are more likely to perform their duties reliably if their responsibility is evidenced on the document.

Pre-numbered documents are useful in maintaining control and accountability by providing a means for ensuring that:

- all transactions are recorded; and
- no transactions are recorded more than once.

Records include the primary accounting records (i.e. journals and ledgers) as well as other records of accumulated data, such as employee earnings records (which show cumulative payroll data for each employee) and perpetual stock records.

Independent checks involve the verification of work performed by other individuals or departments, or the proper measurement of recorded amounts. The following are examples of independent checks.

- A dispatch clerk verifies the agreement of goods received from the warehouse with the details on a duplicate copy of the approved sales order before shipping the goods.
- A sales supervisor checks prices on invoices prepared by invoicing clerks against an authorised price list before mailing them.
- A treasurer compares the amounts on cheques prepared by the accounts department with amounts on supporting documentation before signing the cheques.
- A routine in a computer program compares a computer-generated total of credits posted to the debtors master file with a manually prepared batch total keyed in at the beginning of the computer run, and prints the result.

Performance of independent checks should be evidenced in writing.

SEGREGATION OF DUTIES

Segregation of duties ensures that individuals do not perform incompatible duties. Duties are considered incompatible when it is possible for an individual to commit an error or irregularity and then be in a position to conceal it in the normal course of his or her duties. An individual who processes cash remittances from customers, for example, should not also have authority to approve and record credits to customers' accounts for sales returns and bad debt write-offs. In such a case, the individual could steal a cash remittance and cover the theft by recording a fictitious sales return or by writing off the balance. This reasoning supports segregation of duties in the following situations.

- *Responsibility for executing a transaction, recording the transaction and maintaining custody of the assets resulting from the transaction should be assigned to different individuals or departments.* As an example, purchasing department personnel should initiate purchase orders, accounting department personnel should record the goods received, and storeroom personnel should assume custody of the goods. Before recording the purchase, accounting personnel should ascertain that the purchase was authorised and that the goods ordered were received. The accounting entry, in turn, provides an accountability basis for the goods in the storeroom.
- *The various steps involved in executing a transaction should be assigned to different individuals or departments.* Thus, in executing a sales transaction, the entity should assign responsibility for authorising the sale, filling the order, shipping the goods and invoicing the customer to different individuals.
- *Responsibility for certain accounting operations should be segregated.* In a manual information system, for example, different personnel should maintain the general ledger and the sales ledger, and personnel involved in recording cash receipts and payments should not reconcile the bank accounts.

When duties are segregated such that the work of one individual automatically provides a cross-check on the work of another, the entity has the added benefit of an independent check. It should be noted that while an independent check always involves segregating duties, segregating duties does not always involve an independent check.

PHYSICAL CONTROLS

Physical controls limit access to assets and important records. Such controls may be direct or indirect. Direct controls include initiating measures for the safekeeping of assets, documents and records (such as fireproof safes and locked storerooms) and restricting access to storage areas to authorised personnel only. Indirect controls apply to the preparation or processing of documents (such as sales orders and payment vouchers) that authorise the use or disposition of assets. They involve the use of mechanical and electronic equipment such as cash registers, which help to assure that all cash receipt transactions are rung up and which provide locked-in summaries of daily receipts.

To be effective, physical controls must include periodic counts of assets and comparisons with the amounts shown on control records. Examples include petty cash counts and stock-takes.

Access controls, both physical and electronic, are particularly important in a computer information system. They should provide assurance that transactions being entered into the computer systems are appropriately authorised and that access to data and programs is restricted to authorised personnel.

Access to computer hardware should be limited to authorised individuals. Physical safeguards include housing the equipment in an area restricted by security guards, or using keys, badges or other automated security devices.

Access to data files and programs should be designed to prevent unauthorised use of such data. All computer users should have passwords for access to the computer network. Each user may have restricted access to specific programs and files. Access may be further designated as 'read only' or 'read and write'. The computer should also be programmed to record the names of all users who access the computer for the purposes of adding, altering or deleting data. If passwords are to provide for the security of data files and programs, then they should be changed regularly, not easily guessed, and secured by both the user and the system.

In systems with on-line entry of data, many users have direct access through remote input devices. Access often extends beyond the entity's employees to customers and suppliers through remote terminals such as automated teller machines or even via the Internet. To provide the necessary control, each user of a remote input device is provided with a key, code or card that identifies the holder as an authorised user.

Security packages can also provide access security. They can define the relationships of different types of user to the programs and data files stored in the computer. The software can detect access violations by logging all abortive access attempts.

PERFORMANCE REVIEWS

Examples of performance reviews include management review and analysis of:

- reports that summarise the detail of account balances such as an aged trial balance of debtors or reports of sales activity by region, division, salesperson or product line; and
- actual performance compared with budgets, forecasts or prior period amounts.

MONITORING

It is important that internal control is subject to regular management and supervisory review. Employees need to be aware that compliance with controls is monitored and non-compliance is likely to be detected. In larger organisations this function is entrusted to the internal audit department. Other important sources of information as to the operation of controls come from customers and regulatory agencies. Monitoring also provides feedback as to the effectiveness of controls and acts as a stimulus to reviewing controls and implementing changes.

Limitations of control

One of the fundamental concepts is that internal control can provide only reasonable assurance regarding the achievement of an entity's objectives. Reasons for this include the following inherent limitations in an entity's internal control structure:

- *Costs versus benefits*: The cost of an entity's internal control structure should not exceed the benefits that are expected to ensue. Because precise measurement of both costs and benefits is not usually possible, management must make both quantitative and qualitative estimates and judgements in evaluating the cost–benefit relationship.
- *Management override*: Management can overrule prescribed policies or procedures for illegitimate purposes, such as personal gain or enhanced presentation of an entity's financial condition (e.g. inflating reported earnings to increase a performance bonus or the market value of the entity's shares). Override practices include making deliberate misrepresentations to auditors and others, such as by issuing false documents to support the recording of fictitious sales transactions.
- *Mistakes in judgement*: Occasionally, as a result of inadequate information, time constraints or other pressures, management and other personnel may exercise poor judgement in making business decisions or performing routine duties.
- *Collusion*: Individuals acting together may evade the planned segregation of duties to perpetrate and conceal an irregularity (e.g. collusion among three employees from the personnel, manufacturing and payroll departments to initiate payments to fictitious employees, or 'kickback' schemes arranged between an employee in the purchasing department and a supplier, or between an employee in the sales department and a customer).
- *Breakdowns*: Breakdowns in established controls may occur because personnel mis-understand instructions or make errors as a result of carelessness, distractions or fatigue. Temporary or permanent changes in personnel, systems or procedures may also contribute to breakdowns.

Application to smaller entities

The information system, control activities and the control environment are applicable to entities of all sizes. However, the degree of formality and the manner in which the components are implemented may vary considerably for practical and sound reasons.

Smaller entities are less likely to have written codes of conduct, external directors, formal policy manuals, sufficient personnel to provide for optimal segregation of duties, or internal auditors. However, they can mitigate the absence of these safeguards by developing a culture that emphasises integrity, ethical values and competence. In addition, owner–managers can assume responsibility for certain critical tasks such as approving credit, signing cheques, reviewing bank reconciliations, monitoring customer balances and approving write-offs of bad debts. Moreover, the familiarity that managers of smaller entities can have with all critical areas of operation, and the simpler and shorter lines of communication, can obviate the need for the formalised control activities that are essential in larger entities.

Control in computer information systems

The general principles of control are the same in both computerised and manual information systems, but the effect of technology on the internal control structure must be recognised. Generally, computer information systems (CISs):

- consistently apply predefined business rules and perform complex calculations in processing large volumes of transactions or data;
- enhance the timeliness, availability, and accuracy of information;
- facilitate the additional analysis of information;
- enhance the ability to monitor the performance of the entity's activities and its policies and procedures;
- reduce the risk that controls will be circumvented; and
- enhance the ability to achieve effective segregation of duties by implementing security controls in applications, databases, and operating systems.

As the use of CISs becomes more common, their operation is becoming increasingly free of human intervention and greater reliance is being placed on them. Table 7.1 indicates that a well-designed CIS can significantly reduce errors. However, if the system is not well designed, then the impact of error is much greater.

 LEARNING **CHECK**

7.1 Internal control has long been recognised as vital to the conduct of business and the performance of an audit within economic fee limits.

7.2 This has more recently been emphasised by the findings of the Cadbury Report and Turnbull Report in the UK and the Committee of Sponsoring Organisations to the Treadway Commission in the US which locate internal control within an entity's risk management framework.

7.3 ISA 315 identifies the components of internal control as:

- the control environment;

- the entity's risk assessment process;

- the information system;

Table 7.1 Information technology (IT) systems versus manual processes

ATTRIBUTES OF IT SYSTEMS	ATTRIBUTES OF MANUAL PROCESSES	BENEFITS OF IT SYSTEM PROCESSES	POTENTIAL RISKS OF IT SYSTEM PROCESSES
More consistent processing	No real assurance as to consistency	Once right, always right; potentially fewer errors	If wrong, consistently wrong for that logical process; difficulty in detecting small but possibly significant individual discrepancies spread over a large volume of transactions
Often limited flexibility unless incorporated in design (which may change)	High dependence on individuals; high flexibility		Presumption by users that systems are right without sufficient review and testing. Major effort required for changes (e.g. new products). Where flexibility is incorporated in IT system design, potential for error arising from the increased complexity
Increased efficiency (in capacity and volume), because the volume of transactions that can be handled is increased	Effect of an increase in volume on timeliness and need for resources	Easier to maintain delivery, accuracy and timeliness requirements as volumes increase. Easier to maintain costs in the face of increasing volumes. Reduced ongoing operational costs	Higher up-front costs
Use of user-controlled parameters or key data for multiple transactions and calculations	Similar use of key data but needs to be examined for each transaction (e.g. the price list)	Use of data in this way, but data still examined each time, so as to ensure consistency of application (e.g. the consistent use of interest rates)	If key data are wrong or manipulated, potential effect on numerous transactions
Ability to review all transactions and report only exceptions	Only a sample of transactions reviewed. Possibility that the review may be limited to a scrutiny for reasonableness	Reduced number of items that require follow-up (increased efficiency). Ability to deal with all details of a transaction	Detection of potential problems only if programmed to do so. Possible inability to identify or deal with unexpected real or potential errors. Reliance on effective and timely manual follow-up of potential errors
Minimal manual interpretation or review	Need for detailed human knowledge of the process	Reduced cost. Reduced likelihood of disruption. Reduced reliance on operational staff	Possibility that users may no longer understand how the system works and, thus, may not be able to identify or deal with errors or operate without the system. Increased impact of disruption. The possibility that reduced intervention may reduce the levels of authorisation and increase exposure to fraud
Minimal visible evidence of the process that has been followed	Normally, physical evidence of the action taken	A reduced amount of information that is required to be reviewed manually	Possible difficulty in identifying the nature and extent of errors where they do arise. Reliance on the system documentation to define how the process works

Source: Adapted from Margaret Wright, *Audit Guide No. 5: Auditing in an IT Systems Environment*, Table 2.1. AARF, Melbourne, 1999. Reproduced with the joint permission of CPA Australia and the Institute of Chartered Accountants of Australia.

- control activities; and

- monitoring of controls.

7.4 The control environment relates to the attitude of management towards the importance of internal controls.

7.5 The prime function of the information system is to ensure that financial statements are accurate and reliable.

7.6 Control activities are established by management to ensure achievement of entity objectives. With respect to the accounting system, they consist of information processing controls, segregation of duties, physical controls and performance reviews.

7.7 Information processing controls may be general or they may be specific to an application. Specific controls are comprised of authorisations, documentation and independent checks.

7.8 Internal control provides only reasonable assurance, being subject to a number of inherent limitations.

7.9 Smaller entities need controls but they are likely to be less formal and to depend on the direct supervision of management.

PROCEDURES TO OBTAIN AN UNDERSTANDING

This section explains how auditors meet their responsibility for obtaining and documenting an understanding of the information system and internal control environment.

Obtaining an understanding

The procedures necessary to obtain an understanding consist of:

- reviewing previous experience with the entity;
- inquiring of appropriate management, supervisory and staff personnel;
- inspecting documents and records; and
- observing entity activities and operations.

REVIEW PREVIOUS EXPERIENCE

In a repeat engagement, the previous year's working papers contain a great deal of information relevant to the current year's audit. Auditors can use the previous year's recorded understanding and assessment of control risk as the starting point, making inquiries as to the changes that may have occurred in the current year. The working papers should also contain information about the types and causes of misstatements found in prior audits. Auditors can follow up on this information to determine whether management has taken corrective actions.

INQUIRING

Making inquiries of entity management and personnel is an important source of information. Types of inquiry are described in connection with documentation of internal control as described below.

INSPECTING DOCUMENTS AND RECORDS

Auditors should also inspect relevant documents and records of the entity, such as organisation charts, policy manuals, the chart of accounts, accounting ledgers, journals and source documents. These inspections will inevitably lead to additional inquiries about specific controls and changes in conditions.

OBSERVATION AND WALKTHROUGH

Observation commonly supplements inquiry by confirming the understanding of procedures as described. A particularly important form of inspection and observation is the walkthrough. To reinforce their understanding of the information system and control procedures or to confirm the absence of changes since the system was last reviewed, auditors perform a transaction walkthrough review by tracing one or a few transactions within each major class through the transaction trail to confirm the documented understanding. For example, auditors might select a few sales orders and follow these orders through delivery, invoicing, recording in the sales journal, posting to the sales ledger and subsequent receipt of cash and its proper recording. A few transactions might also be traced in the reverse direction, for example, from the credit entry in the sales ledger from cash receipts back to the sales order that initiated the transaction.

Documenting the understanding

Documenting the understanding of the information system is a requirement for all audits. Documentation may take the form of completed questionnaires, flow charts and/or narrative memoranda. In an audit of a large entity, involving a combination of audit strategies, all three types of documentation may be used for different parts of the understanding. In an audit of a small entity, a single memorandum may suffice to document the auditors' understanding of all the components. In a repeat engagement, it may be necessary only to update documentation from the prior year's working papers. Only those parts of the information system that are relevant to the audit need to be documented.

QUESTIONNAIRES

An internal control questionnaire (ICQ) consists of a series of questions about accounting and control policies and procedures that the auditors consider necessary to prevent material misstatements in the financial statements. The questions are usually phrased in such a way that a 'yes' answer indicates a favourable condition. Space is also provided on the questionnaire for comments such as who performs a control procedure and how often.

Standardised questionnaires are used for many audits. Some firms use quite different questionnaires for large versus small entities or for particular industries.

Excerpts from three questionnaires are illustrated in Figures 7.1, 7.2 and 7.3. These relate to parts of the control environment, to the cash payment activities of an information

CLIENT ___Amalgamated Products Ltd___	BALANCE SHEET DATE ___31/12/X1___
Completed by: ___RSC___ Date: ___12/9/X1___	Reviewed by: ___GEY___ Date: ___29/10/X1___

Internal Control Questionnaire Component: Control Environment

Question	Yes, No, N/A	Comments
Integrity and ethical values:		
1. Does management set the 'tone at the top' by demonstrating a commitment to integrity and ethics through both its words and deeds?	Yes	Management is conscious of setting an example. Entity does not have a formal code of conduct.
2. Have appropriate entity policies regarding acceptable business practices, conflicts of interest, and codes of conduct been established and adequately communicated?	Yes	Expectations of employees included in a policy manual distributed to all employees.
3. Have incentives and temptations that might lead to unethical behavior been reduced or eliminated?	Yes	Profit-sharing plan monitored by audit committee.
Board of directors and audit committee:		
1. Are there regular meetings of the board and are minutes prepared on a timely basis?	Yes	Board has nine inside members, three of whom serve on the audit committee. Considering adding three outside members to the board who would comprise the audit committee.
2. Do board members have sufficient knowledge, experience and time to serve effectively?	Yes	
3. Is there an audit committee composed of outside directors?	No	
Management's philosophy and operating style:		
1. Are business risks carefully considered and adequately monitored?	Yes	Management is conservative about business risks.
2. Is management's selection of accounting principles and development of accounting estimates consistent with objective and fair reporting?	Yes	
3. Has management demonstrated a willingness to adjust the financial statements for material misstatements?	Yes	Management has readily accepted all proposed adjustments in prior audits.
Human resource policies and practices:		
1. Do existing personnel policies and procedures result in the recruitment or development of competent and trustworthy people needed to support an effective internal control structure?	Yes	Formal job descriptions are provided for all positions.
2. Do personnel understand the duties and procedures applicable to their jobs?	Yes	
3. Is the turnover of personnel in key positions at an acceptable level?	Yes	Normal 'turnover'.

Figure 7.1 *Excerpt from internal control questionnaire – control environment*

system and to general controls over a computer information system respectively. In Figure 7.2, the questions relate to several possible categories of control activity: questions 1 and 4 relate to authorisation procedures; questions 2 and 6 relate to documents and records; questions 5, 8 and 9 relate to independent checks; question 3 relates to physical controls; and questions 7(a) and (b) relate to segregation of duties.

CLIENT ___Amalgamated Products Ltd___   BALANCE SHEET DATE ___31/12/X1___

Completed by: __RSC__ Date: __12/9/X1__   Reviewed by: __GEY__ Date: __29/10/X1__

Internal Control Questionnaire Component: Cash Payments

Question	Yes, No, N/A	Comments
Cash payments transactions:		
1. Is there an approved payment voucher with supporting documents for each cheque prepared?	Yes	
2. Are pre-numbered cheques used and accounted for?	Yes	
3. Are unused cheques stored in a secure area?	Yes	Safe in treasurer's office.
4. Are only authorised personnel permitted to sign cheques?	Yes	Only treasurer and assistant treasurer can sign.
5. Do cheque signers verify agreement of details of cheque and payment voucher before signing?	Yes	
6. Are vouchers and supporting documents cancelled after payment?	Yes	Vouchers and all supporting documents are stamped 'Paid'.
7. Is there segregation of duties for:		
(a) approving payment vouchers and signing cheques?	Yes	
(b) signing cheques and recording cheques?	Yes	
8. Are there periodic independent reconciliations of cheque accounts?	Yes	Performed by assistant controller.
9. Is there an independent check of agreement of daily summary of cheques issued with entry to cash payments?	No	Comparison now made by assistant treasurer; will recommend it be made by assistant controller.

Figure 7.2 *Excerpt from internal control questionnaire – control procedures*

Some auditing firms have automated their internal control questionnaires. The staff auditor enters the responses into a notebook computer as the information is obtained, using software that analyses the pattern of responses across related questions and guides the auditor through subsequent steps in assessing control risk and designing substantive audit procedures.

Some auditing firms also provide special training for staff in the interviewing skills needed to administer questionnaires. By being alert to non-verbal signals given by interviewees (such as a hesitancy to respond, an apparent lack of familiarity with controls, or undue nervousness during the interview), for example, auditors can significantly enhance their understanding.

As a means of documenting the understanding, questionnaires offer a number of advantages. They are developed by experienced professionals and provide guidance for less experienced staff who may be assigned to obtain the understanding on a particular

CONTROLS	YES	NO	COMMENTS

Organisational controls
1. Are the following duties segregated within the computer department:
   (a) systems design?
   (b) computer programming?
   (c) computer operations?
   (d) data entry?
   (e) custody of systems documentation, programs and files?
   (f) data control?
2. Are the following duties performed only outside the computer department:
   (a) initiation and authorisation of transactions?
   (b) authorisation of changes in systems, programs and master files?
   (c) preparation of source documents?
   (d) correction of errors in source documents?
   (e) custody of assets?			

Systems development and maintenance controls 1. Is there adequate participation by users and internal auditors in new systems development? 2. Is proper authorisation, testing and documentation required for systems and program changes? 3. Is access to systems software restricted to authorised personnel? 4. Are there adequate controls over data files (both master and transaction files) during conversion to prevent unauthorised changes?			
Access controls 1. Is access to computer facilities restricted to authorised personnel? 2. Does the librarian restrict access to data files and programs to authorised personnel? 3. Are computer processing activities reviewed by management?			
Other controls 1. Is there a disaster contingency plan to ensure continuity of operations? 2. Is there off-site storage of backup files and programs? 3. Are sufficient generations of programs, master files and transaction files maintained to facilitate recovery and reconstruction of computer processing? 4. Are there adequate safeguards against fire, water damage, power failure, power fluctuations, theft, loss, and intentional and unintentional destruction?			

Figure 7.3 *Excerpt from internal control questionnaire – general controls*

audit. They are relatively easy to use and reduce the possibility that auditors may overlook important internal control matters. Their disadvantage is that to cater for the varied types of information system, they may be long and unwieldy.

FLOW CHARTS

A flow chart is a schematic diagram that uses standardised symbols, interconnecting flow lines and annotations to portray the steps involved in processing information through the information system. Flow charts are prepared to depict the processing of individual classes of transaction, such as sales, cash receipts, purchases, cash payments, payroll and manufacturing.

Flow charts should depict:

- all operations performed in processing the class of transactions;
- the methods of processing (manual or computerised);
- the extent of segregation of duties (by identifying each operation with a functional area, department or individual); and
- the source, flow and disposition of the documents, records and reports involved in processing.

These essential components are illustrated in Figure 7.4, which is a partial flow chart of a system for processing cash (cheques) and accompanying remittance advices received from customers. (An example of a remittance advice is the portion of a telephone account or credit card statement that the customer returns with the payment.) The flow chart in Figure 7.4 displays four operations. The first two take place in the mail room – namely, (1) opening the mail and separating the cheques and remittance advices, and (2) preparing a prelist (in triplicate) of the cheques (to show the amount of each remittance and the grand total). The other two operations take place in sales ledger accounting – namely, (3) entering the remittance data into the computer for processing, and (4) reconciling a computer-generated summary with the input documents. The first, second and fourth operations involve manual processing, which is indicated by the use of a trapezoidal-shaped symbol. The third operation is represented in the flow chart by the symbol labelled 'On-line data entry' and the rectangular symbol labelled 'Receipts processing', which, together, indicate computer processes. The segregation of duties is indicated by the division of the flow chart into four vertical partitions, representing the four departments involved with the cash receipts processing. (The details of only two of these departments are shown, so as to keep the illustration simple.) Finally, the figure shows the source, flow and disposition of the following documents and records:

- the remittance advices and cheques received in the mail;
- the three copies of the prelist of cheques prepared in the mail room; and
- the two computer-generated reports that are produced when the remittance data are entered into the computer in sales ledger accounting.

The flow chart also shows that the computerised receipts processing results in the updating of three computer files maintained on disk (the symbols in the sales ledger accounting partition that look like cans).

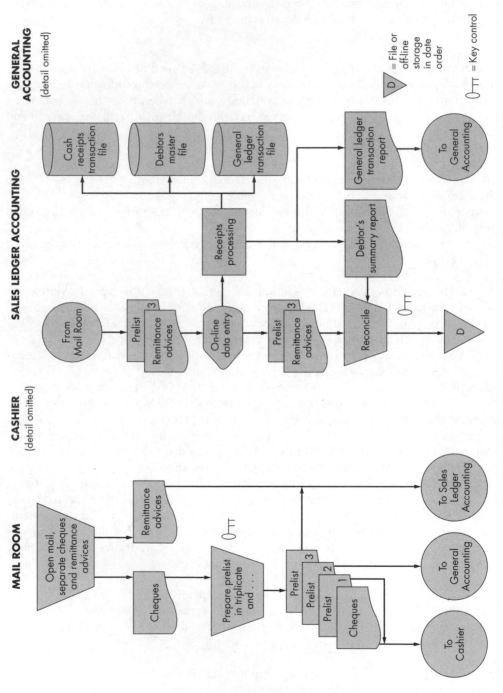

Figure 7.4 *Partial flow chart for processing of mail receipts transactions*

A more complete illustration of flow charting is presented in Appendix 7A. As well as extending the illustration of the system shown in Figure 7.4, Appendix 7A includes an explanation of additional standardised flow charting symbols and some helpful guidelines for preparing flow charts.

NARRATIVE MEMORANDA

A narrative memorandum may be used to supplement other forms of documentation by summarising the auditors' overall understanding of the information system or specific control policies or procedures. In audits of small entities, a narrative memorandum may serve as the only documentation of the auditors' understanding. Figure 7.5 illustrates this type of documentation for a small owner-managed company.

◁ LEARNING **CHECK**

7.10 In obtaining an understanding of the accounting system, the auditors call on any previous experience with the entity, the outcomes of inquiries of personnel, the inspection of documents, and personal observation.

7.11 The transaction walk-through review is a particularly important means of verifying the understanding by tracing a small number of transactions through the system.

7.12 The system may be documented at the time of obtaining the understanding by using internal control questionnaires. Alternatively, it may be documented in the form of flow charts or in memoranda prepared from notes made at the time of obtaining the understanding.

7.13 The internal control questionnaire is so designed that a 'yes' answer indicates satisfactory control procedures. In this way, the understanding and the preliminary assessment of control occur simultaneously.

7.14 The advantage of the internal control questionnaire is that it may be administered by relatively inexperienced staff. Its drawback is that it can often be extremely long.

7.15 Although experience is needed to present and interpret flow charts properly, they are particularly useful in presenting complex systems and in establishing the segregation of functions.

7.16 Narrative memoranda are simple to prepare. They are suitable for use with very small entities and to provide supplementary information to questionnaires and flow charts for larger entities.

PRELIMINARY ASSESSMENT OF CONTROL RISK

This section explains the role of the preliminary assessment of the risk of material misstatement arising out of the understanding of internal control and the nature of evidence used in making the assessment.

CLIENT _____ *Ownco, Ltd.*	BALANCE SHEET DATE _____ 31/12
Completed by: _m/w_ Date: 30/9/X5	Reviewed by: _ip_ Date: 01/11/X5
Updated by: _m/w_ Date: 15/9/X6	Reviewed by: _ip_ Date: 29/10/X6

Understanding of the Control Environment

The Company manufactures plastic fishing worms at one location and is managed by its sole owner, Ed Jones. Management of the company is dominated by Jones, who is responsible for marketing, purchasing, hiring and approving major transactions. He has a good understanding of the business and the industry in which it operates. Jones believes that hiring experienced personnel is particularly important because there are no layers of supervisory personnel and thus, because of limited segregation of duties, few independent checks of employees' work. Jones has a moderate-to-conservative attitude toward business risks. The business has demonstrated consistent profitability and, because Jones considers lower taxes to be as important as financial results, he has a conservative attitude toward accounting estimates.

Jones and Pat Willis, the book-keeper, readily consult with our firm on routine accounting questions, including the preparation of accounting estimates (tax accrual, stock obsolescence, or bad debts). Our firm also assists in assembling the financial statements.

The company's board of directors is composed of family members. The board is not expected to monitor the business or the owner-manager's activities.

Most of the significant accounting functions are performed by Willis, the book-keeper, and Jones's secretary, Chris Ross. Willis was hired by the company in 19X0, has a working knowledge of accounting fundamentals, and we have no reason to question her competence. Willis regularly consults with our firm on unusual transactions, and past history indicates that it is rare for adjustments to arise from errors in the processing of routine transactions.

Jones made the decision to purchase a microcomputer and a turnkey accounting software package. The source code is not available for this software. Access to the computer and computer files is limited to Willis, Ross and Jones, who effectively have access to all computer files.

The owner-manager carefully reviews computer-generated financial reports, such as reports on debtor's ageing, and compares revenues and expenses with prior year's performance. He also monitors the terms of the long-term debt agreement that requires certain ratios and compensating balances.

Source: AICPA Audit Guide, *Consideration of the Internal Control Structure in a Financial Statement Audit* (1990), pp. 117–118. © the American Institute of Chartered Public Accountants.

Figure 7.5 *Narrative memorandum documenting understanding of control environment*

The purpose of the preliminary assessment

Assessment of control risk is conducted in two phases: the effectiveness of the design of internal control and the effectiveness of its operation.

DESIGN EFFECTIVENESS

The preliminary assessment is made to obtain a reasonable expectation of the effectiveness of controls based on the understanding of their design. This assessment enables auditors to determine an appropriate audit strategy for each major transaction class assertion as explained in Chapter 6. Auditors then proceed to draw up the detailed audit programme combining tests of controls and substantive procedures, as explained in Chapter 5, consistent with the chosen audit strategy, such that the detailed audit programme can be designed in accordance with the assessed risks of material misstatement at the assertion level and the appropriate audit strategy. The reason for designing substantive procedures at this stage is because tests of control and substantive procedures are often conducted simultaneously, some as dual-purpose tests. It would add unduly to the cost and time of the audit if all tests of control were completed before commencing substantive procedures.

OPERATING EFFECTIVENESS

The second phase occurs on completion of all tests of control. If these tests do not support the preliminary assessment of control risk, then the auditors must perform additional substantive procedures. In most instances, however, the preliminary assessment is sufficiently reliable (especially for repeat engagements), such that the need to extend substantive procedures after completion of tests of control rarely arises.

Making the preliminary assessment of control risk

The preliminary assessment is the process of evaluating the effectiveness of the design of an entity's internal controls in preventing or detecting material misstatements in the financial statements.

The first step is to assess the control environment. A weak control environment can undermine the internal control. Strong individual control activities cannot compensate for a weak control environment. Assessment of the control environment is a matter for professional judgement, and is common to all assertions for all transaction classes.

The second step is to assess the design of the risk management framework and its ability to prevent or correct misstatements. The effectiveness of a control is ultimately limited by its design. Control risk is assessed in terms of individual financial statement assertions. Because the information system focuses on the processing of transactions, and because many control procedures pertain to the processing of a particular type of transaction, the auditors commonly begin by assessing control risk for transaction class assertions, such as the occurrence, completeness and accuracy assertions for cash receipts and cash payment transactions. It is important to keep in mind that control risk assessments are made for individual assertions, not for the information system as a whole.

In evaluating design effectiveness in order to make a preliminary assessment of control risk for an assertion, auditors:

- identify potential misstatements that could occur in the entity's assertion;
- identify the necessary controls that would be likely to prevent or detect any material misstatement; and
- evaluate the evidence and make the assessment.

IDENTIFYING THE POTENTIAL MISSTATEMENTS

If the auditors' understanding of the system has been obtained through the use of internal control questionnaires, then the 'yes' answers indicate the presence of effective controls and the 'no' answers indicate weaknesses. Some auditing firms use computer software to link responses to specific questions in computerised questionnaires to potential misstatements for particular assertions. However, most auditing firms have developed internal control evaluation checklists that enumerate the types of potential misstatement that could occur in specific assertions. Using either the computer software aid or checklists and the understanding of the entity's information system, the auditors identify the potential misstatements applicable to specific assertions, given the entity's circumstances. Examples of potential misstatements for several assertions pertaining to cash payments transactions are shown in the first column of Table 7.2.

IDENTIFYING THE NECESSARY CONTROLS

Whether by using computer software that processes internal control questionnaire responses or by manually analysing checklists, the auditors can identify the necessary controls that would be likely to prevent or detect specific potential misstatements. The second column in Table 7.2 illustrates a list of such controls.

Several controls may pertain to a given potential misstatement; in other instances, a single control may apply. In addition, a single control may pertain to more than one type of potential misstatement; for example, the control 'periodic independent bank reconciliations' (shown at the bottom of the second column in Table 7.2) may detect unrecorded cheques (completeness assertion) or cheques made out for the right amount but recorded in the cash payments journal at an incorrect amount (accuracy assertion).

Comparison of the information listed in the first and second columns of Table 7.2 with the questions presented in Figure 7.2 illustrates how a questionnaire that a staff auditor may be asked to administer can be developed by more experienced staff to facilitate analysis of potential misstatements and necessary controls. (*Note*: the questions in Figure 7.2 do not necessarily appear in the same order as the controls listed in Table 7.2 because some controls pertain to more than one assertion.)

Specifying necessary controls also requires judgement and a consideration of circumstances. Where there is a very high volume of cash payment transactions, for example, it may be critical to conduct an independent check of the agreement of a daily summary of cheques issued with the entry in the cash payments journal. In this way, errors will be quickly detected. When the volume of cash payments is light and timely detection of errors is not so essential, periodic independent bank reconciliations may compensate for the lack of a daily independent check. In such a circumstance, the bank reconciliation could be seen as a compensating control.

Where transactions are processed by a computer information system Table 7.3 provides an outline of the assessment of the design effectiveness of controls over the computerised application.

MAKING THE ASSESSMENT

The auditors can make a preliminary assessment of control risk from the knowledge acquired from (1) procedures to obtain an understanding and (2) the identification of potential misstatements and the necessary controls to prevent or detect those

Table 7.2 Potential misstatements, necessary controls, tests of controls – cash payments transactions

POTENTIAL MISSTATEMENT/ASSERTION	NECESSARY CONTROLS	TESTS OF OPERATING EFFECTIVENESS
A cash payment may be made for an unauthorised purpose (existence of valid transaction)	• Approved supplier's statement with matching supporting documents (supplier's invoice, goods received note, and approved purchase order) required for each payment transaction • Only authorised personnel are permitted to sign cheques • Segregation of duties required for approving suppliers' invoices and signing cheques	• For a sample of cash payment transactions, determine existence of approved supplier's invoice and matching supporting documents for each payment • Observe individuals signing cheques and identify them as authorised signatories • Observe segregation of duties
An invoice may be paid twice (occurrence of valid transaction)	• Stamp invoice and supporting documents 'Paid' when cheque is issued	• Observe documents being stamped and/or inspect sample of paid documents for presence of 'Paid' stamp
A cheque may be issued for the wrong amount (accuracy)	• Check that signers verify the agreement of cheque and invoice details before signing	• Observe cheque signers performing an independent check of the agreement of details and/or reperform an independent check
A cash payment transaction may not be recorded (completeness) or it may be recorded for the wrong amount (accuracy)	• All payment transactions are to be made by cheque • All cheques are to be pre-numbered and accounted for • Unused cheques are to be stored in a secure area • An independent check is to be made of the agreement of the daily summary of cheques issued with the entry in the cash payments journal • Periodic independent bank re-conciliations are to be performed	• Enquire about methods of making cash payments and/or inspect paid cheques for a sample of payment transactions • Examine evidence of use of, and accounting for, pre-numbered cheques and/or scan the sequence of cheque numbers in the cheque register or the cash payments journal • Observe the handling and storage of unused cheques • Observe the performance of an independent check and/or reperform an independent check • Observe the performance of bank reconciliations and/or inspect bank reconciliations

misstatements. The auditors' assessment must also consider the assessment of the control environment and the extent to which the design of the control activities is likely to be effective. The preliminary assessment is based on the presumption that further tests of control will provide evidence of the effective operation of the control.

If the assessed level of risk at the assertion level is less than high, auditors need to assess the level of risk as explained in Chapter 5. On the basis of the assessed level of control

Table 7.3 Control risk assessment considerations for application controls

POTENTIAL MISSTATEMENT/ASSERTION	NECESSARY CONTROLS	POSSIBLE TESTS OF CONTROL
Input controls		
Data for unauthorised transactions may be submitted for processing (occurrence).	Authorisation and approval of data in user departments, and screening of data by data control group.	Examine source documents and batch transmittals for evidence of approval; observe data control group.
Valid data may be incorrectly converted to machine-readable form (occurrence, completeness, accuracy).	Computer editing, and control totals.	Observe data verification procedures; use test data to test edit routines; examine control total reconciliations.
Errors on source documents may not be corrected and resubmitted (occurrence, completeness, accuracy).	Maintenance of error logs; return to user department for correction; follow-up by data control group.	Inspect logs and evidence of follow-up by data control group.
Processing controls		
Wrong files may be processed and updated (accuracy).	Use of external and internal file labels.	Observe use of external file labels; examine documentation for internal file labels.
Data may be lost, added, duplicated, or altered during processing (occurrence, completeness, accuracy).	Use of control totals; limit and reasonableness checks; sequence tests.	Examine evidence of control total reconciliations and use of test data.
Output controls		
Output may be incorrect (occurrence, completeness, accuracy).	Reconciliation of totals by data control group and user departments.	Examine evidence of reconciliations.
Output may be distributed to unauthorised users.	Use of report distribution control sheets; data control group monitoring.	Inspect report distribution control sheets; observe data control group monitoring.

risk (in conjunction with the assessed level of inherent risk) auditors will determine an appropriate audit strategy. If the auditors decide to adopt a lower assessed level of control risk strategy for that assertion, they would proceed to design an audit programme that incorporates tests of control.

There is a common misunderstanding that poor controls require auditors to extend the testing of controls. In fact the reverse applies. Where controls are poor the auditors proceed to plan an audit using a higher level of substantive procedures.

Discussion and documentation

As explained in Chapter 6, the assessment of the risks of material misstatements must be discussed among audit team members such that they have a sufficient awareness of the risks when performing further audit procedures. The matters discussed and the members of the audit team involved in the discussion should be documented in the working papers.

The working papers should also document the risk assessment process as applied to the assessment of control risk and results of the assessment in terms of the identified risks of material misstatements. This documentation is combined with the documentation described in Chapter 6 arising from understanding of the entity and the resultant assessment of risks of material misstatements developed during the planning process.

A common approach to documentation is a narrative memorandum organised by financial statement assertions. This approach is illustrated in Figure 7.6, which documents the control risk assessments for selected sales transaction assertions.

LEARNING **CHECK**

7.17 The preliminary assessment of control risk enables the independent auditors to determine the most appropriate audit strategy for each assertion, subject to confirmation of the assessment on completion of tests of control.

7.18 The preliminary assessment is based on knowledge obtained during the course of obtaining the understanding and is primarily based on the design effectiveness of controls.

CLIENT_____ Young Fashions, Ltd_____   BALANCE SHEET DATE_____ 30/9/x5

Completed by: _CRS_ Date: _19/05/x5_   Reviewed by: _RMT_ Date: _01/11/x5_

Control risk assessment for: Sales Transactions

COMPLETENESS

Entity internal control policies and procedures relevant to completeness relate primarily to the computer listing of unmatched sales orders, bills of lading, packing slips, and sales invoices. Based on discussions with sales ledger personnel on 11/5/x5 and with selected shipping personnel at Newton and Bytown locations on 18/4/x5, respectively, it normally can take up to two weeks between the placing of a sales order and shipment. It is rare, however, for an unmatched bill of lading or packing slip to remain on the unmatched documents report for more than two days (see W/P XX-4-2 [not illustrated here]) where the longest period a bill of lading or packing slip was outstanding was two days. Selected transactions on these reports were traced to underlying documents with no exceptions.

Based on this examination of audit evidence, combined with the results of inquiry of sales ledger and shipping personnel and corroborating observations, control risk is assessed as slightly lesss than high.

RIGHTS AND OBLIGATIONS

Control risk is assessed as high.

Source: AICPA Audit Guide, *Consideration of the Internal Control Structure in a Financial Statement Audit* (1990), p. 145
© the American Institute of Chartered Public Accountants.

Figure 7.6 *Partial documentation of control risk assessments*

7.19 Testing the design effectiveness of controls involves:

- first, identifying potential misstatements;

- second, identifying control procedures that prevent or detect such misstatements.

7.20 Tests of the design effectiveness of controls are facilitated by the use of internal control evaluation checklists.

TESTS OF CONTROL

As explained previously, tests of control are auditing procedures performed to determine the effectiveness of the operation of internal controls. ISA 330, The Auditor's Procedures in Response to Assessed Risks, states that:

> When the auditor's assessment of risks of material misstatement at the assertion level includes an expectation that controls are operating effectively, the auditor should perform tests of controls to obtain sufficient appropriate audit evidence that the controls were operating effectively at relevant times during the period under audit.

They are applied on controls whose design has been assessed as reliable and where the audit strategy intends placing reliance on those controls in reducing the level of substantive procedures. The auditors may conclude, for example, that management's plan to store stocks in locked warehouses should prevent or significantly reduce the risk of misstatements in the existence assertion for inventories. Tests of control pertaining to the operating effectiveness of the control procedures are concerned with whether controls are actually working. In the stock example, observing whether goods are actually stored in locked warehouses would provide a test of the effectiveness of operation.

Tests of operating effectiveness focus on three questions:

1. How was the control applied?
2. Was it applied consistently during the year?
3. By whom was it applied?

A control is operating effectively when it has been properly and consistently applied during the year by the employee(s) authorised to apply it. In contrast, failure to apply a control properly and consistently, or application of that control by an unauthorised employee, indicates ineffective operation. Such failures are referred to as deviations. This terminology is preferable to the term 'error' because a failure in performance indicates only that there may be an error in the accounting records. The failure, for example, of a second employee to verify the accuracy of a sales invoice is a deviation, but the document could still be correct if the first employee prepared it correctly.

Tests of control are included in the audit programme that is drawn up once the appropriate audit strategy is determined. They are mainly performed during the interim audit, but the auditors may conduct further tests at the final audit on significant controls for the period after the interim audit. These tests provide evidence of the proper and consistent application of a control throughout the year under audit, and support the preliminary assessment of control risk as being moderate or low and the corresponding planned level of substantive procedures.

Designing tests

In designing tests of the operating effectiveness of controls the auditors must decide their nature, timing and extent. The design may also be affected where there is no visible evidence of the performance of control procedures applied by computer to transactions processed by a computer information system.

NATURE OF TESTS
The auditors' choices in terms of the nature of tests of control are:

- inquiring of personnel about the performance of their duties;
- observing personnel perform their duties;
- inspecting documents and reports indicating performance of controls; and
- reperforming the control.

In performing the tests, auditors select the procedure that will provide the most reliable evidence about the effectiveness of the control.
Inquiring is designed to determine:

- an employee's understanding of his or her duties;
- how that employee performs those duties; and
- the frequency, cause(s) and disposition of deviations.

Unsatisfactory answers by an employee may indicate improper application of a control.
Observing the employee's performance provides similar evidence. Inquiring and observing are especially useful means of obtaining evidence about the control procedure of segregation of duties. However, evidence obtained from observation has the following limitations:

- the employee may perform the control differently when not being observed; and
- the evidence applies only to the time when the observation occurs.

Ideally, this procedure should be performed without the employee's knowledge or on a surprise basis.
Inspecting documents and records is applicable when there is a transaction trail of signatures and validation stamps that indicate whether the control was performed and by whom. Any document or record that fails to evidence the required performance is a deviation, regardless of whether the document is correct.

Dual-purpose tests

Reperformance is a dual-purpose test in that it provides evidence as both a test of control and a substantive test of detail. Where such a test reveals an error, it suggests the failure of controls intended to prevent such errors. Assume, for example, that the control procedure of independent checks requires a second clerk in the invoicing department to check the correctness of unit selling prices on sales invoices by comparing them to an authorised price list. On doing so, the employee initials a copy of the invoice to indicate performance of the independent check. In testing this control procedure, the auditors inspect invoices for the employee's initials and may reperform the process by comparing selling prices on invoices to the authorised price list. Such a test doubles as both a test of control and a substantive test of details, because any errors detected provide evidence both of a failure to perform the independent check properly and of monetary errors in the transactions recorded. When this type of testing is done, the auditors should exercise care in designing the tests to ensure that evidence is obtained as to both the effectiveness of controls and the monetary errors in the accounts. The auditors should also be careful in evaluating the evidence obtained.

TIMING OF TESTS OF CONTROL

The timing of tests of control refers to the part of the accounting period to which they relate. Planned tests of control are performed during interim work, which may be several months before the end of the year under audit. These tests, therefore, provide evidence of the effectiveness of controls only from the beginning of the year to the date of the tests.

The need to perform additional tests of control later in the year depends on:

- the length of the remaining period;
- the occurrence of significant changes in controls subsequent to interim testing, causing the auditors to revise their understanding of the internal control structure; and
- the decision to perform substantive tests of details on balances prior to the year-end (such as confirming debtors one month before the year-end), thus requiring assurance that control procedures remained effective in the period between the date of substantive procedures and the year-end.

EXTENT OF TESTS

More extensive tests of control provide more evidence of the operating effectiveness of a control. Asking more than one individual about the same control procedure, for example, will provide more evidence than a single inquiry; similarly, a more extensive inspection of documents for initials or signatures indicating performance of a control procedure provides more evidence than would examining fewer documents.

The extent of tests of control is determined by the auditors' planned assessed level of control risk. More extensive testing will be needed for a low assessed level of control risk than for a moderate level. This might seem contrary to common sense but remember that the assessment of control risk is ultimately limited by the control environment and the design of the control. Where control risk is moderate the appropriate audit strategy would be to obtain most assurance from the performance of substantive procedures with only limited reliance on controls.

TESTS OF CONTROL IN A COMPUTER INFORMATION SYSTEM

A particular problem arises with testing programmed application controls whose performance is invisible. In such situations auditors make use of a variety of computer-assisted audit techniques such as test data, integrated test facility (ITF) and parallel simulation.

Test data

Under the test data approach, dummy transactions are prepared by the auditors and processed under auditor control by the entity's software. The test data consist of one transaction for each valid or invalid condition that the auditors want to test. Payroll test data, for example, may include both a valid and an invalid overtime pay condition. The output from processing the test data is then compared with the auditors' expected output to determine whether the controls are operating effectively. This approach to testing is relatively simple, quick and inexpensive. However, the method has the following audit deficiencies:

- the method is a test only of the presence and functioning of controls in the program tested;
- there is no examination of documentation actually processed by the system;
- computer operators know that test data are being run, which could reduce the validity of the output; and
- the scope of the test is limited by the auditors' imagination and knowledge of the controls within the application.

Integrated test facility

The integrated test facility (ITF) approach overcomes some of the limitations of the use of test data. It requires the creation of a small subsystem (a mini-company) within the regular computer information system. This may be accomplished by creating dummy master files or appending dummy master records to existing entity files. Test data, specially coded to correspond to the dummy master files, are introduced into the system, together with actual transactions. The test data should include all kinds of transaction errors and exceptions that may be encountered. In this manner, the test data are subjected to the same programmed controls as placed on the actual data. A separate set of outputs is produced for the subsystem of dummy files. The results can be compared with those expected by the auditors.

A disadvantage of the ITF approach is the risk that errors could be created in entity data. In addition, the entity's programs may need to be modified to accommodate the dummy data.

Parallel simulation

Parallel simulation involves reprocessing actual entity data using auditor-controlled software. This method is so named because the software is designed to reproduce or simulate the entity's processing of real data. This approach does not corrupt the entity's files and may be conducted at an independent computer facility. It has the following advantages:

- because real data are used, the auditors can verify transactions by tracing them to source documents and approvals;
- the size of the sample can be expanded at relatively little additional cost; and
- the auditors can run the test independently.

If the auditors decide to use parallel simulation, they must take care to determine that the data selected for simulation are representative of actual entity transactions and include errors intended to be detected by the application of programmed controls. This could be a problem where the entity has corrected input data as a result of errors detected in processing.

Audit programmes for tests of control

The auditors' decisions regarding the nature, extent and timing of tests of control should be documented in an audit programme and related working papers. A sample audit programme for tests of control of cash payment transactions is illustrated in Figure 7.7. The programme lists the procedures to be used in performing the tests for indicated assertions. It also provides columns to indicate:

- cross-references to the working papers in which the test results are documented;
- who performed the tests; and
- the date on which the tests were completed.

Details concerning the extent and timing of the tests may be indicated in the audit programme or in the working papers, as assumed in Figure 7.7. The tests listed in the formal audit programme shown in Figure 7.7 are derived from the possible tests of control listed in column 3 of Table 7.2. Some of the tests have been rearranged and grouped by assertions. An alternative approach is to rearrange tests to facilitate their efficient performance – for example, grouping tests 1, 2 and 6 together such that tests on the sample selected in test 1 are performed together.

Using internal auditors

Companies with many divisions (such as Pearsons and Diageo) or many branches (such as Dixons and Abbey) usually employ internal auditors. Whenever an entity has an internal audit function, the auditors may co-ordinate their audit work with that of the internal auditors and/or use the internal auditors to provide direct assistance in the audit.

CO-ORDINATION WITH INTERNAL AUDITORS

Internal auditors will usually monitor internal control in each division or branch as part of their regular duties. The monitoring may include periodic reviews. In such cases, the independent auditors may co-ordinate work with the internal auditors and reduce the number of entity locations at which they would otherwise perform tests of control. The auditors must first consider the effectiveness of the internal auditors by:

- considering their organisational status:
  - Do they report to the highest level of management?
  - Are they free of operating responsibilities?
  - Are they free to communicate fully with the independent auditors?
- determining the scope of their work and, in particular, whether management acts on their recommendations;
- evaluating their technical competence; and
- ensuring that their work is performed with due professional care.

Amalgamated Products Limited		Prepared by: _____ Date: _____
Planned Tests of Controls — Cash Payments Transactions		Reviewed by: _____ Date: _____
Year Ending 31 December, 20X1		

Working Paper Reference	Assertion/Test of Control	Auditor	Date
	Existence or occurrence:		
	1. Select a sample of cash payment transactions from the cash payments journal and determine existence of matching approved payment vouchers and supporting documents.		
	2. Inspect paid invoices and supporting documents from (1) above for presence of "Paid" stamp.		
	3. Observe segregation of duties for approving suppliers' invoices and signing cheques.		
	4. Examine evidence of use of and accounting for pre numbered cheques and scan sequence of cheque numbers in cash payments journal.		
	5. Observe handling and storage of unused cheques.		
	Accuracy and valuation		
	6. For transactions selected in (1) above, examine evidence of independent verification of agreement of details of cheques with supporting suppliers' invoices and test by performance.		
	7. Select a sample of dates and examine evidence of independent check of agreement of daily summary of cheques issued with entry to cash payments and test by performance.		
	8. Inspect independent bank reconciliations. (Note: Steps 7 and 8 also provide evidence of control over completeness.)		

Figure 7.7 *Illustrative partial audit programme for tests of control*

When there is co-ordination of the work, the auditors should evaluate the quality of the internal auditors' work. ISA 610, Considering the Work of Internal Auditing, requires the independent auditors to confirm that:

- the work is performed by persons having adequate technical training and proficiency as internal auditors;
- the work of assistants is properly supervised, reviewed and documented;
- sufficient appropriate audit evidence is obtained to afford a reasonable basis for the conclusions reached;
- the conclusions reached are appropriate in the circumstances;
- any reports prepared by internal audit are consistent with the results of the work performed; and
- any exceptions or unusual matters disclosed by internal auditors are properly resolved.

In co-ordinating work with internal auditors, the auditors may find it efficient to have periodic meetings with them, review their work schedules, obtain access to their working papers and review internal audit reports.

Final assessment of control risk

The final assessment of control risk for a financial statement assertion is based on evaluating the evidence gained from (1) procedures to obtain an understanding of relevant internal control components and (2) related tests of control. When different types of evidence support the same conclusion about the effectiveness of a control, the degree of assurance increases. Conversely, when they support different conclusions, the degree of assurance decreases; for example, the initials of an employee may be consistently present on documents, indicating performance of a control procedure, but the auditors' inquiries of the person initialling the documents may reveal that employee's lack of understanding of the control procedure being applied. The oral evidence would reduce the assurance obtained from the inspection of initials on the documents.

The evaluation of evidence involves both quantitative and qualitative considerations. In forming a conclusion about the effectiveness of a control procedure, auditors often use guidelines concerning the tolerable frequency of deviations from the proper performance of a control (usually expressed as a percentage). If the results lead the auditors to conclude that the frequency of deviations is less than or equal to the tolerable level, then the operation of the control is considered effective. Before reaching this conclusion, the auditors should also consider the causes of the deviations; for example, the auditors may attach different significance to excessive deviations caused by a vacation replacement than to those caused by an experienced employee. It is also essential in reaching a conclusion about effectiveness to determine whether a deviation is attributable to unintentional errors or to deliberate misrepresentations (irregularities). Evidence of one deviation due to an irregularity may be more important to the auditors than are more frequent deviations caused by errors. When it is concluded that the nature and frequency of deviations exceeds the tolerable level, the preliminary assessed level of control risk is not confirmed. In this case the auditors must revise the audit programme for substantive procedures reflecting either a higher level of control risk than originally planned or the adoption of a predominantly substantive strategy for that particular assertion.

Communication of internal control matters

ISA 260, Communications of Audit Matters with Those Charged with Governance, requires auditors to report material weaknesses in internal control that have arisen from the risk assessment process. The form and content of such reports will be explained in Chapter 14.

 ## LEARNING **CHECK**

7.21 Tests of controls are designed to provide evidence as to the consistent and effective application of controls over the period under audit.

7.22 Planned tests of controls are performed where the preliminary assessment of control has assessed control risk as being less than high, and the auditors have adopted an audit strategy based on lower assessed level of control risk. Such planned tests are primarily aimed at assessing the operating effectiveness of the controls. The purpose of testing is to determine whether deviations from laid down controls invalidate the preliminary assessment of control risk.

7.23 Tests of controls may involve inquiry of personnel, observation of procedures, inspection of documents and reperformance of control procedures by the auditors.

7.24 Reperformance often provides substantive evidence as well as evidence as to the performance of controls.

7.25 Controls are normally tested during the interim audit. Significant controls or controls affected by changes in the accounting and internal control systems may also need to be tested later in the year.

7.26 The extent of testing is determined by the planned assessment of control risk. However, the planned level of control risk cannot exceed limitations determined by assessment of the control environment or the design effectiveness of individual controls.

7.27 The performance of tests of control is documented in working papers and recorded in the audit programme.

7.28 The work of internal audit may be taken into account in performing tests of control, providing the independent auditors are satisfied as to the effectiveness of the internal audit function.

7.29 Evaluation of control takes into consideration both the corroboratory effect of related evidence and the negative effect of inconsistent evidence.

7.30 Before reaching a final conclusion, deviations need to be assessed qualitatively as to whether or not they relate to the performance of the control generally.

SUMMARY

Internal control is important for the effective operation of entities. It is important for the auditors to obtain an understanding of internal control as a basis for planning the audit and for identifying particular problems relating to control risk. As a minimum, the auditors are required to obtain an understanding of the internal control system, and to make a preliminary assessment of control risk based primarily on their evaluation of the design effectiveness of control procedures.

Where preliminary assessment indicates that control risk for a particular assertion may be less than high, the auditors may choose to adopt a lower assessed level of control risk audit strategy. The auditors then proceed to test the operating effectiveness of controls as a basis for confirming that assessment and the consequent reduction in the level of substantive procedures.

An important side effect of tests of control is the opportunity to advise management of significant internal control weaknesses.

FURTHER READING

American Institute of Certified Public Accountants (AICPA) Control Risk Audit Guide Task Force. *Audit Guide: Consideration of the Internal Control Structure in a Financial Statement Audit.* AICPA, New York, 1990.

Bodine, S. W., Pugliese, A. & Walker, P. L. 'A Road Map to Risk Management', *Journal of Accountancy* (December 2001).

Committee of Sponsoring Organisations of the Treadway Commission (COSO). *Internal Control – Integrated Framework.* AICPA, 1992.

D'Aquila, J. M. 'Is the Control Environment Related to Financial Reporting Decisions?', *Managerial Auditing Journal* (Vol. 13, No. 8, 1998), pp. 472–478.

Lindow, P. E. & Race, J. D. 'Beyond Traditional Audit Techniques', *Journal of Accountancy* (July 2002).

Little, A. & Best, P. J. 'A Framework for Separation of Duties in an SAP R/3 Environment', *Managerial Auditing Journal* (Vol. 18, No. 5, 2003), pp. 419–430.

McKillop, G. & Shackall, M. 'Fraud Control: Best Practice in Business', *Australian Accountant* (October 1997).

Morrill, C. & Morrill, J. 'Internal Auditors and the External Audit: A Transaction Cost Perspective', *Managerial Auditing Journal* (Vol. 18, No. 6, 2003), pp. 490–504.

Myers, R. 'Ensuring Ethical Effectiveness', *Journal of Accountancy* (February 2003), pp. 28–33.

Spencer-Pickett, K. H. 'Diary of a Control Freak: The Manager's Guide to Internal Control', *Managerial Auditing Journal* (Vol. 13, No. 4/5, 1998), pp. 210–332.

Thomas, A. & Gibson, K. 'Management is Responsible Too', *Journal of Accountancy* (April 2003), pp. 53–55.

Turpen, R. 'Fraud Prevention and the Management Accountant', *Management Accounting (USA)* (February 1997), p. 34.

Vanasco, R. 'Fraud Auditing', *Managerial Auditing Journal* (Vol. 13, No. 1, 1998), pp. 4–71.

Well, J. T. 'Occupational Fraud: The Audit as Deterrent', *Journal of Accountancy* (April 2002), pp. 24–28.

Willingham, J. J. & Wright, W. F. 'Financial Statement Errors and Internal Control Judgments', *Auditing: A Journal of Practice and Theory* (Fall 1985), pp. 57–70.
York, D. 'Assessing Risk', *Accountancy* (February 1997), p. 76.

APPENDIX 7A
Flow charting guidelines

Flow charting is a creative task, making it unlikely that any two people would draw flow charts exactly alike for a given system. The more commonly used flow charting symbols are shown in Figure 7.8. Some firms supplement these basic symbols with more extensive sets of special-purpose symbols.

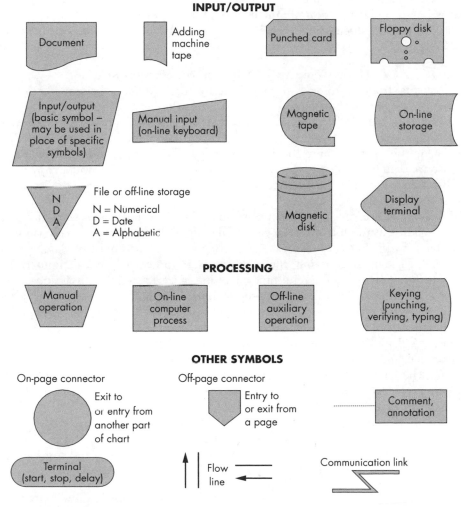

Figure 7.8 *Flow charting symbols*

In addition to the four essential components of flow charts listed on page 229, the following guidelines are helpful in preparing useful flow charts:

- Identify the class(es) of transaction to be included in a flow chart.
- Collect information through interviews, observations and the review of documents.
- Visualise an organisational format for the flow chart (e.g. the number and order of columns needed to represent departments, functions or individuals) and prepare a rough sketch.
- Prepare the flow chart, selecting the correct symbols carefully.
- Test the completeness and accuracy of the flow chart by tracing a hypothetical transaction through it.

To illustrate, assume the auditors wish to prepare a flow chart depicting the Hayes Company's processing of mail cash receipts. The following description of the processing system is based on information obtained through inquiries of entity personnel, observations, and review of documents. (*Note:* this is an extension of the system illustrated in Figure 7.4.)

Hayes Company – Mail cash receipts processing

All receipts from customers are received by mail and are accompanied by a preprinted remittance advice (bottom portion of the billing originally sent to the customer). In the Mail Room, the cheques and remittance advices are separated. The cheques are restrictively endorsed (For Deposit Only) and a listing (prelist) of the cheques is prepared in triplicate and totalled. The cheques and one copy of the prelist are then forwarded to the Cashier. The remittance advices and a copy of the prelist are sent to Sales Ledger Accounting, and another copy of the prelist is sent to General Accounting.

The Cashier prepares a bank deposit slip in duplicate and makes the daily bank deposit. The Cashier forwards the validated copy of the bank deposit (slip stamped and dated by the bank) to General Accounting and files the prelist by date.

In Sales Ledger Accounting, the remittances are processed on a computer. The Sales Ledger Clerk keys the remittance data into a cash receipts transaction file via an on-line terminal. This file is then processed to (1) update the debtor's master file, and (2) generate an entry in the general ledger transaction file, which is subsequently used to update the general ledger. This processing routine also generates two printed reports. A debtor's summary report shows the total credits posted to the debtor's master file and is reconciled to the total on the prelist received from the Mail Room. The remittance advices, prelist and summary report are then filed by date. The general ledger transaction report shows the daily totals for cash, discounts and debtors and is forwarded to General Accounting.

General Accounting compares the totals from the prelist received from the Mail Room, the validated deposit slip received from the Cashier and the general ledger transaction report received from Sales Ledger Accounting and resolves any discrepancies. The documents are then collated and filed by date.

After considering the above information, the auditors envision a flow chart with the following four columns: Mail Room, Cashier, Sales Ledger Accounting and General

Accounting. After first preparing a rough sketch, the flow chart depicted in Figure 7.9 is prepared.

It should be emphasised that a flow chart is a means to an end, not an end in itself. A flow chart should enable auditors to see the relationships that exist between controls, and facilitate the identification of key controls related to specific financial statement assertions. For example, from studying the flow chart in Figure 7.9, the following controls, among others, can be observed:

- Documents and records:
  - use of pre-printed remittance advices returned by customers with payments;
  - preparation of prelist of cash receipts in triplicate for use in subsequent control;
  - retention of validated (receipted) deposit slip for use in subsequent control;
  - generation of sales summary report and general ledger transaction report for use in subsequent controls;
  - segregation of handling cash (Mail Room and Cashier) from accounting for cash and debtors (General Accounting and Sales Ledger Accounting).
- Independent checks:
  - reconciliation of debtors summary report in Sales Ledger Accounting with total on prelist received from Mail Room;
  - reconciliation by General Accounting of amounts reported on prelist received from Mail Room, validated deposit slip received from Cashier, and general ledger transaction report received from Sales Ledger Accounting.
- Other control activities:
  - restrictive endorsement of cheques immediately upon receipt;
  - deposit of receipts intact daily.

Additional controls may be documented by making written notes on a flow chart. For example, in this illustration a note might be added to indicate that an independent monthly reconciliation is made of the bank account. Similarly, annotations about any observed weaknesses could be added to the flow chart.

MULTIPLE-CHOICE QUESTIONS

Choose the best answer for each of the following.

(Answers are on pages 600–601)

7.1 The primary objective of obtaining an understanding of the information system is to provide the auditor with:
   (a) audit evidence to use in forming an overall opinion on the company.
   (b) enough understanding to design procedures to gather sufficient audit evidence.
   (c) enough evidence to express an audit opinion.
   (d) enough understanding to express an opinion on the adequacy of the entity's internal controls.

7.2 Which of the following is not a method of documenting the understanding of the accounting system?
   (a) Internal control questionnaire.
   (b) Internal control evaluation checklist.

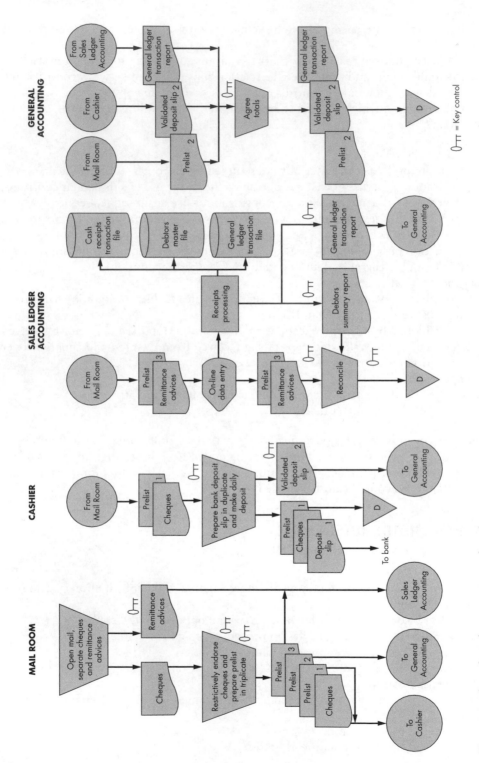

Figure 7.9 *Flow chart for processing of mail receipts*

(c)   Narrative description.

(d)   Systems flow chart.

7.3   An auditor's flow chart of an entity's information system is a diagrammatic representation that depicts the auditor's:

(a)   programme for tests of control.

(b)   understanding of the system.

(c)   understanding of the types of irregularity that are probable, given the present system.

(d)   documentation of the assessment of control risk.

7.4   Which of the following would not be relevant in obtaining an understanding of the control environment?

(a)   The existence of an internal audit department.

(b)   A need to demonstrate compliance with the requirements of a regulatory agency.

(c)   The existence of a sound budgetary control system.

(d)   Adoption of accounting policies in conformance with accounting standards.

7.5   Where the preliminary assessment of control risk is low for any particular audit objective:

(a)   the auditor must perform tests of control in order to confirm that controls are operating effectively.

(b)   the auditor may proceed directly to performing a reduced level of substantive testing.

(c)   the auditor may consider performing tests of controls to confirm the preliminary assessment if it would result in a reduction of the extent of audit effort.

(d)   the auditor may reduce the extent of tests of control otherwise necessary in confirming the assessment of control risk.

7.6   Segregation of duties is a means of ensuring that:

(a)   collusion between employees cannot take place.

(b)   performance and accuracy are independently checked.

(c)   management cannot override laid down controls.

(d)   employees cannot perpetrate and conceal errors or irregularities in the normal course of their duties.

7.7   The maximum reliance an auditor may place on control procedures in reducing the extent of substantive procedures is determined by:

(a)   the results of tests of control over operating effectiveness.

(b)   their design effectiveness in providing assurance that errors will be prevented or detected on a timely basis.

(c)   their design effectiveness subject to sufficient evidence from tests of control that they are operating effectively.

(d)   the reduction in audit effort that could be achieved through reliance on controls?

7.8   What would be an appropriate sample of invoices to gain reasonable assurance that all payments are properly authorised as part of the annual audit?

(a)   Randomly pick one month and select every invoice for that month.

(b)   Randomly select a sample of 100 invoices from throughout the financial year.

(c)   Select all invoices greater than £5,000 generated throughout the year.

(d)   Any of the above tests would be acceptable.

DISCUSSION QUESTIONS

7.1 The COSO guidelines on internal control have been described as providing a framework for generally accepted control policies similar to the financial reporting framework provided by accounting standards. Discuss the practicalities of prescribing such a framework in the light of the inherent limitations of control.

7.2 The auditor is primarily concerned with controls over financial reporting. Consider to what extent the auditor should consider controls over compliance with applicable laws and regulations and over the effectiveness and efficiency of operations.

7.3 Describe control problems faced by a small business all of whose accounting records are held on a single desktop computer.

7.4 Two of the problems associated with the use of internal control questionnaires (ICQs) are:
- the large number of questions to which the answer is 'not applicable'; and
- 'yes' answers may be too readily interpreted as indicating control strengths without adequate consideration being given to qualitative aspects.

Discuss the advantages and disadvantages of ICQs with particular reference to the above concerns.

7.5 Consider the possibility that, having adopted a lower assessed level control risk strategy, auditors will be tempted to ignore adverse findings from tests of control because of the consequences on the cost and time involved in extending substantive procedures.

7.6 Describe the extent to which auditors are currently responsible for detecting and reporting control weaknesses as part of a financial statement audit. Consider the argument that auditors should accept greater responsibility for detecting and reporting control weaknesses either to directors or to outside users of financial statements.

PROFESSIONAL APPLICATION QUESTIONS

(Suggested answers are on pages 620–624)

7.1 Accounting systems and internal controls

Fabulous Fashion Ltd (FF) runs four private colleges which provide education and training for people in the fashion industry. Its two-year course includes training in design, textiles, manufacture and retail of fashion garments. You are conducting the interim audit for the year ended 30 June 20X1. The tangible fixed assets of each college are recorded in an asset register which is maintained at each college location by each college manager. The system operates as described below:

- In order to obtain new assets, a purchase requisition form is completed and approved by the manager at each college.
- The requisition is sent to head office, where the purchasing officer checks the requisition for approval and completes a purchase order for the new asset.
- Assets costing more than £5,000 are approved by the financial accountant. All assets over £20,000 require board approval.
- The purchase order is then sent to the supplier and a copy is sent to the central store at the head office location.

- The asset is received by the central store where the receiving clerk checks that all the asset details agree with those on the goods received note and the copy of the purchase order. The receiving clerk will then issue the asset with its computer-generated sequential barcode number. This barcode is fixed to the asset and written on the goods received note and the supplier invoice.
- The relevant college manager inputs the new asset details into the asset register using a copy of the purchase order, the original requisition and the asset's barcode.
- For disposal or write-off of an asset, an asset disposal write-off form is completed by the relevant college manager, signed and sent to head office. Disposals and write-offs are approved by the financial accountant. A copy of the form is filed at head office and the approved original returned to the college manager for action. The college manager will then update the fixed asset register for the subsequent disposal.
- The asset register is maintained on FAST, a tailored fixed assets computer system, and reconciled to the general ledger by each college manager monthly.
- The FAST system calculates depreciation automatically each month using the rate input by the college manager at the time the asset was added to the register.

Required

(a) Identify five internal control strengths on which you would rely for your audit.
(b) Design tests of control to evaluate the effectiveness of each of the controls identified.

(This question is adapted from the Professional Year Programme of the Institute of Chartered Accountants in Australia – 1996, Accounting 2 Module)

7.2   Reliance on internal audit

Glebe, a listed company, is a retailer with its head office, principal store and warehouse in Bigtown and additional stores in 12 other cities. The company has developed its internal audit operation in recent years. Among the activities of the internal audit department are:

(i)   the documentation and evaluation of accounting and internal control systems, testing compliance with laid down procedures, identifying control weaknesses and recommending changes to control procedures;
(ii)   monitoring of computer operations through the use of embedded audit facilities;
(iii) routine visits to stores which include cash counts and observation of cyclical inventory counts as well as a range of tests of controls and of substantive procedures in areas such as purchasing, wages records and banking.

Glebe's Chief Financial Officer believes that the external audit fee could be significantly reduced if there was more effective co-ordination of work between the internal and external auditors and the elimination of unnecessary duplication. She is aware of the requirements of ISA 610 *Considering the Work of Internal Auditing.*

Required

(a) Describe the evaluation of the internal audit function that your firm would need to undertake;

(b) Assuming the evaluation confirms the adequacy of the internal audit function, explain
     the extent to which the external auditors could place reliance on the work of internal
     audit in the following areas:
   (i)   obtaining and documenting the understanding of the accounting and internal
         control systems;
   (ii) performing tests of controls;
   (iii) assessing inherent and control risk;
   (iv) performing procedures requiring the use of computer assisted audit techniques
         (CAATs);
   (v)   performing substantive tests on cash and inventory at the stores.

(Adapted from Question 4, Audit Framework, December 2000. Reproduced by permission of ACCA)

CHAPTER 8

AUDIT SAMPLING

DISCUSSION QUESTIONS

PROFESSIONAL APPLICATION QUESTIONS

LEARNING OBJECTIVES

After studying this chapter you should be able to:

1   define audit sampling and discuss its applicability

2   differentiate sampling and non-sampling risk and explain the types of sampling risk

3   explain the steps in planning a sample test

4   indicate the factors that affect sample size

5   describe the methods of selecting a sample

6   explain the steps in testing a sample and evaluating the results

7   describe the principal methods of statistical sampling used in auditing

8   explain the circumstances leading to the choice of specific statistical or non-statistical sampling plans.

PROFESSIONAL STATEMENT

ISA 530   Audit Sampling and Other Selective Testing Procedures

Sampling is well established as an audit procedure, but this was not always the case. A textbook published in 1881 contained the following statement:

> A thorough and efficient Audit should embrace an examination of all the transactions of a Company, and an auditor acting on this principle would ascertain that all had been duly entered and discharged.[1]

However, the changing size and complexity of business was causing this to become an unrealistic approach. Lindley LJ in *Re London and General Bank Ltd (No. 2)* (1895) 2 Ch 673 accepted sample testing as providing sufficient evidence for audit purposes. He said:

> Where there is nothing to excite suspicion, very little enquiry will be reasonable and quite sufficient; and in practice, I believe, businessmen select a few cases haphazard, see that they are right, and assume that others like them are correct also.

The importance of audit sampling in current practice is underscored by the issuance of ISA 530, Audit Sampling and Other Selective Testing Procedures.

This chapter explains the basic concepts of audit sampling and their application in tests of controls and substantive tests of details. The chapter is divided into four sections. The first section will explain how evidence obtained from sample testing introduces the risk that the evidence may not be representative of the population from which the sample is taken. This risk is known as sampling risk. The second section will describe the process of sampling in audit testing from the planning stage, through the selection and testing of the sample, to the evaluation of the results of sample tests. The third section will explain the use of different types of statistical sampling techniques and consider their relative merits. The final section will consider why many auditors continue to use non-statistical sampling rather than statistical sampling.

The four case studies attached as appendices to this chapter illustrate the use of sampling in the performance of auditing procedures. The first case study involves the use of non-statistical sampling while the remaining three illustrate the use of different statistical sampling plans in auditing.

BASIC CONCEPTS OF SAMPLING

Sampling is defined in ISA 530 as:

> ... the application of audit procedures to less than 100 per cent of items within an account balance or class of transactions such that all sampling units have a chance of selection.

Giving all items in the population a chance of selection enables auditors to obtain audit evidence to assist in forming a conclusion about the population from which the sample is drawn. Not all items must have an equal probability of selection but all items must have a determinable probability of selection for the selection method to be described as audit sampling.

Sampling may be used in tests of control or substantive testing. The sampling principles for both are essentially the same. The main difference is at the testing stage where the 'error' relates to control deviations when performing tests of control or misstatements when performing substantive procedures. An example of sampling in tests of control is the examination of a sample of purchase invoices to see that they have been initialled, by the employee responsible, as having been checked against the goods received note. The objective of the test is to confirm compliance with the laid down control procedure. As explained in Chapter 7, the proportion of deviations in the sample enables auditors to draw conclusions as to the effectiveness of the control procedure, contributing to the assessment of control risk. An example of sampling in substantive tests of details is the checking of a sample of invoices against goods received notes to verify the occurrence of recorded purchase transactions. The incidence of errors in the sample will enable auditors to draw conclusions as to the occurrence of recorded purchase transactions.

One of the most important issues for auditors to consider in audit sampling is the risk of drawing an incorrect conclusion from the sample selected. Another important consideration is the distinction between statistical sampling and non-statistical sampling.

Sampling risk and non-sampling risk

When sampling is used to obtain audit evidence, uncertainties may result from factors associated directly with the use of sampling (sampling risk) and from those unrelated to sampling (non-sampling risk).

SAMPLING RISK
Sampling risk is defined in ISA 530 as:

> ... the possibility that the auditor's conclusion, based on a sample, may be different from the conclusion reached if the entire population were subjected to the same audit procedure.

The following example illustrates this point: if a bag contains 80 red balls and 20 white balls, then a representative sample of 10 would contain eight red balls and two white balls. Sampling risk is the risk that a randomly selected sample of 10 would not consist of eight red and two white balls. The larger the sample, the more probable it is that it will consist of red and white balls in the same proportion as the population. Probability theory quantifies this risk and forms the basis of statistics. Sampling risk, therefore, is the risk that the auditors' conclusion about internal controls or the details of transactions and balances based on testing a sample may be different from the conclusion that would result from an examination of the entire population.

In performing tests of control and substantive tests of details, the following types of sampling risk – as outlined in ISA 530.07 – may occur (Figure 8.1):

- the risk the auditors will conclude, in the case of a test of control, that control risk is lower than it actually is (risk of overreliance), or in the case of a substantive test, that a material error does not exist when in fact it does (risk of incorrect acceptance). This type of risk affects audit effectiveness and is more likely to lead to an inappropriate audit opinion; and
- the risk the auditors will conclude, in the case of a test of control, that control risk is higher than it actually is (risk of underreliance), or in the case of a substantive test, that a material error exists when in fact it does not (risk of incorrect rejection). This type of risk affects audit efficiency as it would usually lead to additional work to establish that initial conclusions were incorrect.

These risks can have a significant impact on both the effectiveness and efficiency of the audit. The risk of overreliance and the risk of incorrect acceptance relate to audit effectiveness. When reaching either of these erroneous conclusions, the auditors may find that the combined procedures may be insufficient to detect material misstatements, and that they may not have a reasonable basis for an opinion. In contrast, the risk of underreliance and the risk of incorrect rejection relate to the efficiency of the audit. When reaching either of these erroneous conclusions, the auditors will increase substantive procedures unnecessarily. However, such effort will ordinarily lead to a correct conclusion, ultimately, and the audit will nevertheless be effective. The sampling risk associated with audit effectiveness is of much greater concern than the sampling risk associated with audit efficiency because it can lead to an inappropriate audit opinion.

TYPES OF SAMPLING RISK FOR TESTS OF CONTROL

True operating effectiveness of entity's internal control procedure

		Adequate for planned assessed level of control risk	Inadequate for planned assessed level of control risk
Assessed levels of control risk based on sample	Supports preliminary assessment of control risk →	Correct decision	Risk of overreliance (Audit ineffective)
	Does NOT support preliminary assessment of control risk →	Risk of underreliance (Audit inefficient)	Correct decision

TYPES OF SAMPLING RISK FOR SUBSTANTIVE TESTS OF DETAILS

True state of entity's recorded account balance

		Not materially misstated	Materially misstated
Sample estimate of account balance or error in account balance	Supports conclusion that recorded balance is not materially misstated →	Correct decision	Risk of incorrect acceptance (Audit ineffective)
	Supports conclusion that recorded balance is materially misstated →	Risk of incorrect rejection (Audit inefficient)	Correct decision

Figure 8.1 *Sampling risks for tests of controls and substantive tests of details*

Sampling risk in substantive procedures is effectively the same as detection risk for that particular audit procedure (see Chapter 9). The terms 'sampling risk' and 'detection risk' are used interchangeably throughout this chapter. Figure 8.1 is a summary of the types of sampling risk for tests of control and substantive tests of details, and their effects on the audit.

NON-SAMPLING RISK

Non-sampling risk refers to the component of audit risk that is not due to examining only a portion of the data. Therefore, even if the auditors selected 100%

of items within a population for testing, there would still be a risk of drawing an inappropriate conclusion. Sources of non-sampling risk include human mistakes (such as failing to recognise errors in documents, applying auditing procedures that are inappropriate to the audit objective, and misinterpreting the results of a sample) and reliance on erroneous information received from another party. Non-sampling risk can never be mathematically measured. However, by proper planning and supervision and adherence to the quality control standards described earlier, it can be held to a negligible level.

Statistical and non-statistical sampling

Statistical sampling has the following two characteristics according to ISA 530:

1. random selection of a sample; and
2. use of probability theory to evaluate sample results, including the measurement of the sampling risk.

Statistical sampling does not replace judgement. It provides a decision model within which the auditors' judgements as to the acceptable level of detection risk, testing materiality and other variables are the inputs. Given the acceptable level of both sampling risk and materiality for the audit procedure, the model specifies the sample size and evaluates the sample results in terms of sampling risk and materiality. The interpretation of the results is, therefore, only as reliable as the values placed on the sampling risk and testing materiality.

Non-statistical sampling is a sampling approach that does not have the second of the above characteristics of statistical sampling. In non-statistical sampling the auditors use judgement directly, both to determine sample size (given the planned level of detection risk and of testing materiality) and to interpret the results against the audit objective. Historically, non-statistical sampling was called judgement sampling; however, as revealed in the preceding discussion, both approaches require a significant amount of judgement. The main difference between the two is that sampling risk can be quantified when using statistical sampling.

The choice of non-statistical or statistical sampling does not affect the selection of auditing procedures to be applied to a sample. Moreover, it does not affect the appropriateness of evidence obtained about individual sample items or the appropriate response by the auditors to errors found in sample items. These matters require the exercise of professional judgement. Both statistical and non-statistical sampling require selection of the sample from the population by a means that is effectively random. (Appropriate methods of selecting a sample are described later in this chapter.) If the items to be tested are not selected in such a way, the approach is more properly referred to as selective testing, as described below.

Other types of selective testing

Selective testing is the examination of specific items within a population based on the auditors' knowledge of the business and the characteristics of the population being tested. ISA 530 outlines specific items that may be selected using this method:

- *High value or key items*. Individual items may be selected as being of high value or as being suspected to be prone to error, such as overdue debtors. The rest of the population, if material in the aggregate, may be subjected to testing by sampling.
- *All items over a certain amount*. These items may be selected to verify a large proportion of the total amount.
- *Items to obtain information*. The auditor may examine items to obtain information about the client's business, nature of transactions, accounting and internal control systems.
- *Items to test procedures*. The auditor may use judgement to select and examine a specific item to determine whether a particular procedure is being performed.

Selective testing may be an efficient way in which the auditors can collect audit evidence, but it does not constitute audit sampling. The characteristic that distinguishes selective testing from sampling, whether statistical or non-statistical, is that the results of verification of the selected items provide no information as to the probability of material misstatement in items not tested.

 LEARNING **CHECK**

8.1 Sampling is the testing of a representative sample to obtain evidence about a population.

8.2 Sampling may be used for tests of control and substantive tests of details.

8.3 Sampling risk is the risk that evidence derived from testing a sample may not reflect characteristics of the whole population.

8.4 With tests of control, sampling risk results in either overreliance or underreliance on the applicable control procedure.

8.5 With substantive tests of details, sampling risk results in incorrect acceptance of a population as being correctly stated and, more rarely, in incorrect rejection of a population.

8.6 Sampling risk may be assessed statistically, although auditors prefer non-statistical approaches.

8.7 Selection of individual items for verification is an appropriate audit procedure but is not to be confused with sampling.

USE OF SAMPLES FOR AUDIT TESTS

Regardless of whether statistical or non-statistical sampling is used, the auditors undertake some common steps:

- planning the sample;
- selecting and testing the sample; and
- evaluating the results.

Planning the sample

Once the auditors have decided that examining a sample will yield sufficient evidence on the operation of a control or on the absence of material misstatements in a transaction class or account balance, it is important that they plan the sample testing process properly if the results are to be projected to the entire population. Planning the sample involves the following steps:

- determining the objectives of the test;
- defining what errors or deviations are being sought;
- identifying the population and sampling unit; and
- deciding the size of the sample.

DETERMINING THE OBJECTIVES OF THE TEST

Auditors need to consider the specific objectives to be achieved and the combination of audit procedures that is most likely to achieve those objectives. Audit sampling is applicable to both tests of control and substantive procedures. However, it is not equally applicable to all the auditing procedures that may be used; for example, audit sampling is widely used in vouching, confirming and tracing, but it is rarely used in inquiring or observing and in analytical procedures.

Tests of control

The overall purpose of tests of control is to evaluate the effectiveness of the design and operation of internal controls. Sampling is applicable in testing the operation of controls only when there is a trail of documentary or electronic evidence of the performance of control procedures. Such control procedures normally fall into the categories of authorisation procedures, documents and records, and independent checks.

Sample testing of the performance of the control procedures is sometimes known as attribute sampling because each sample tested will have one of two attributes – either that the control has been properly performed or that it has not. The outcome of testing is known as a deviation rate, representing the proportion of transactions tested that have not been processed in accordance with laid down control procedures.

Substantive tests of details

Sampling plans for substantive tests of details may take one of two approaches. The first approach is to obtain evidence that an account balance is not materially misstated (for example, the book value of debtors). The second approach is to make an independent estimate of some amount (for example, to value stock for which no recorded book value exists). Variables sampling is sometimes used in substantive tests of details because it is a statistical technique to estimate the amount of an account balance or some other quantity.

DEFINING WHAT ERRORS OR DEVIATIONS ARE BEING SOUGHT

The auditors must consider what constitutes an error by referring to the objectives of the test. In tests of control, the test objective is the identification of 'deviations' from the laid down control procedure. In substantive testing, the test objective is the identification of 'errors or misstatements' in recorded transactions or balances.

The type of error or deviation expected will be related to the objective of the test. However, an audit procedure may also reveal errors that were not specifically being sought. When examining purchase invoices to verify that quantities invoiced agree with those on the goods received note, auditors might also notice some other defect in the invoice, such as errors in posting prices on the invoices. Sample evidence can be interpreted as evidence of the incidence of errors or deviations in the population as a whole only for those errors or deviations that are being sought. Other errors must be regarded as individual occurrences, which must be separately evaluated. It may be necessary for further tests to be carried out that are designed specifically to determine the extent of such errors. Of course, the auditors must never neglect an error simply because it was not what was being verified by that particular test. Cleverly concealed frauds are often discovered by such chance events.

IDENTIFYING THE POPULATION AND SAMPLING UNIT

Auditors must carefully identify the population and the sampling unit. In particular, they must consider the objective of the audit test to ensure that the population and sampling unit are appropriate.

Population

The first stage in planning the sample test is to identify the relevant population. ISA 530 defines a 'population' as:

> ... the entire set of data from which a sample is selected and about which the auditor wishes to draw conclusions.

Auditors must ensure that the population is:

- *appropriate* to the objective of the sampling procedure. When testing for overstatement of creditors, for example, auditors could define the population as the creditors' listing. However, when testing for understatement of creditors, it is inappropriate to use the creditors listing; the appropriate population is subsequent payments, unpaid invoices, suppliers' statements and unmatched goods received notes.
- *complete*. Ensuring completeness is important and requires particular care. It is made easier by the use of pre-numbering in recording transactions. For auditors to be able to make appropriate assessments of the level of monetary errors or of the application of a particular control, the population needs to include all relevant items from throughout the period. A complete population is particularly important when auditors are using computer-assisted audit techniques to perform sample selection – that is, they must use the correct file.

Sampling unit

A sampling unit means the individual items constituting a population – for example, sales invoices, debtors' balances, fixed assets on a register and a listing of suppliers. It will often appear to be self-evident but sometimes requires closer consideration. Creditors, for example, may be made up of a population of unpaid invoices or amounts owing to particular suppliers. The auditors will need to consider whether any particular advantage arises out of using a particular sampling unit. Sometimes, customers will be unable to respond to a request for confirmation of the balance owed, but they can confirm individual invoices outstanding; in such cases, the best sampling unit would be the unpaid invoices making up the balance.

When monetary unit sampling is used, the sampling unit is an individual £1 (or other monetary unit) contained in the population. This method will be discussed later in the chapter (see page 274).

Stratification

A common approach to increasing audit efficiency in sampling is stratification. Stratification is defined in ISA 530 as:

> ... the process of dividing a population up into sub-populations, each of which is a group of sampling units which have similar characteristics (often monetary value).

The objective of stratification is to focus greater audit work on areas that are of higher risk of being materially misstated. Monetary value is the most common method of stratifying a population, particularly for asset balances. The auditors' main risk with asset balances is overstatement, so they will want to place more emphasis on testing large value items. In a fixed asset register, for example, the assets may be split into three strata:

1. balances greater than £2,000,000;
2. balances of £100,000 to £2,000,000; and
3. balances less than £100,000.

Auditors may choose to perform tests on a random sample of 50% of items in group 1, on a random sample of 20 items in group 2, and on a random sample of 10 items in group 3. When using computer-assisted audit techniques, stratification of the population and sample selection can be performed by most auditing software packages according to whatever criteria are specified by the auditors.

Where individual items are selected for 100% testing on the grounds of materiality or otherwise, the results of testing such items must be separated from the results of sample testing the remaining items in the population.

Stratification is a means of reducing audit costs while increasing the efficiency of the audit. It is a very popular technique to assist in audit sampling, particularly in the audit areas of debtors, stock and property, plant and equipment.

DECIDING THE SIZE OF THE SAMPLE

In determining an appropriate sample size, the auditors' main concern is with reducing sampling risk to an acceptably low level. The level of sampling risk that auditors are willing to accept will have an inverse relationship with the sample size required. The sample size can be determined by the application of a statistically based formula or through the exercise of professional judgement.

Sampling, as an audit procedure, is valid only if the sample selected for testing is representative of the population from which it is drawn, such that the incidence of errors or deviations in the sample closely approximates the incidence of errors or deviations in the population. The larger the sample, the more representative of the population it is likely to be. However, only a 100% sample will be completely representative. Given that the purpose of sampling is to save time and cost, it would be pointless to audit a larger sample than necessary. Table 8.1 outlines factors that influence sample size for tests of control and Table 8.2 outlines factors that influence sample size for substantive procedures.

Table 8.1 Examples of factors influencing sample size for tests of control

The following are factors that the auditor considers when determining the sample size for a test of control. These factors need to be considered together.

FACTOR	EFFECT ON SAMPLE SIZE
An increase in the auditor's intended reliance on accounting and internal control systems	Increase
An increase in the rate of deviation from the prescribed control procedure that the auditor is willing to accept	Decrease
An increase in the rate of deviation from the prescribed control procedure that the auditor expects to find in the population	Increase
An increase in the auditor's required confidence level (or conversely, a decrease in the risk that the auditor will conclude that the control risk is lower than the actual control risk in the population)	Increase
An increase in the number of sampling units in the population	Negligible effect

1. *The auditor's intended reliance on accounting and internal control systems.* The more assurance the auditor intends to obtain from accounting and internal control systems, the lower the auditor's assessment of control risk will be, and the larger the sample size will need to be. For example, a preliminary assessment of control risk as low indicates that the auditor plans to place considerable reliance on the effective operation of particular internal controls. The auditor therefore needs to gather more audit evidence to support this assessment than would be the case if control risk were assessed at a higher level (that is, if less reliance were planned).

2. *The rate of deviation from the prescribed control procedure the auditor is willing to accept (tolerable error).* The lower the rate of deviation that the auditor is willing to accept, the larger the sample size needs to be.

3. *The rate of deviation from the prescribed control procedure the auditor expects to find in the population (expected error).* The higher the rate of deviation that the auditor expects, the larger the sample size needs to be so as to be in a position to make a reasonable estimate of the actual rate of deviation. Factors relevant to the auditor's consideration of the expected error rate include the auditor's understanding of the business (in particular, procedures undertaken to obtain an understanding of the accounting and internal control systems), changes in personnel or in the accounting and internal control systems, the results of audit procedures applied in prior periods and the results of other audit procedures. High expected error rates ordinarily warrant little, if any, reduction of control risk, and therefore in such circumstances tests of controls would ordinarily be omitted.

4. *The auditor's required confidence level.* The greater the degree of confidence that the auditor requires that the results of the sample are in fact indicative of the actual incidence of error in the population, the larger the sample size needs to be.

5. *The number of sampling units in the population.* For large populations, the actual size of the population has little, if any, effect on sample size. For small populations however, audit sampling is often not as efficient as alternative means of obtaining sufficient appropriate audit evidence.

Source: ISA 530, Audit Sampling and Other Selective Testing Procedures, Appendix 1. Copyright © International Federation of Accountants.

Table 8.2 Examples of factors influencing sample size for substantive procedures

The following are factors that the auditor considers when determining the sample size for a substantive procedure. These factors need to be considered together.

FACTOR	EFFECT ON SAMPLE SIZE
An increase in the auditor's assessment of inherent risk	Increase
An increase in the auditor's assessment of control risk	Increase
An increase in the use of other substantive procedures directed at the same financial statement assertion	Decrease
An increase in the auditor's required confidence level (or conversely, a decrease in the risk that the auditor will conclude that a material error does not exist, when in fact it does exist)	Increase
An increase in the total error that the auditor is willing to accept (tolerable error)	Decrease
An increase in the amount of error the auditor expects to find in the population	Increase
Stratification of the population when appropriate	Decrease
The number of sampling units in the population	Negligible effect

1. *The auditor's assessment of inherent risk.* The higher the auditor's assessment of inherent risk, the larger the sample size needs to be. Higher inherent risk implies that a lower detection risk is needed to reduce the audit risk to an acceptable low level, and lower detection risk can be obtained by increasing sample size.
2. *The auditor's assessment of control risk.* The higher the auditor's assessment of control risk, the larger the sample size needs to be. For example, an assessment of control risk as high indicates that the auditor cannot place much reliance on the effective operation of internal controls with respect to the particular financial statement assertion. Therefore, in order to reduce audit risk to an acceptably low level, the auditor needs a low detection risk and will rely more on substantive tests. The more reliance that is placed on substantive tests (that is, the lower the detection risk), the larger the sample size will need to be.
3. *The use of other substantive procedures directed at the same financial statement assertion.* The more the auditor is relying on other substantive procedures (tests of detail or analytical procedures) to reduce to an acceptable level the detection risk regarding a particular account balance or class of transactions, the less assurance the auditor will require from sampling and, therefore, the smaller the sample size can be.
4. *The auditor's required confidence level.* The greater the degree of confidence that the auditor requires that the results of the sample are in fact indicative of the actual amount of error in the population, the larger the sample size needs to be.
5. *The total error the auditor is willing to accept (tolerable error).* The lower the total error that the auditor is willing to accept, the larger the sample size needs to be.
6. *The amount of error the auditor expects to find in the population (expected error).* The greater the amount of error the auditor expects to find in the population, the larger the sample size needs to be in order to make a reasonable estimate of the actual amount of error in the population. Factors relevant to the auditor's consideration of the expected error amount include the extent to which item values are determined subjectively, the results of tests of control, the results of audit procedures applied in prior periods, and the results of other substantive procedures.
7. *Stratification.* When there is a wide range (variability) in the monetary size of items in the population, it may be useful to group items of similar size into separate sub-populations or strata. This is referred to as stratification. When a population can be appropriately stratified, the aggregate of the sample sizes from the strata generally will be less than the sample size that would have been required to attain a given level of sampling risk, had one sample been drawn from the whole population.
8. *The number of sampling units in the population.* For large populations, the actual size of the population has little, if any, effect on sample size. Thus, for small populations, audit sampling is often not as efficient as alternative means of obtaining sufficient appropriate audit evidence. (However, when using monetary unit sampling, an increase in the monetary value of the population increases sample size, unless this is offset by a proportional increase in materiality.)

Source: ISA 530, Audit Sampling and Other Selective Testing Procedures, Appendix 2. Copyright © International Federation of Accountants.

Population size

Population size, commonly presumed to be the major influence on sample size, in fact has no effect on sample size for populations over 5,000. This is true whether statistical or non-statistical sampling is being used. This is demonstrated in Table 8.3.

The case study in Appendix 8A provides a formula that could be used to determine sample size based on judgements concerned with required assurance, tolerable error and expected error.

Selecting and testing the sample

The test objectives and sample size are often determined during audit planning and are detailed in the audit plan. The staff member responsible is then required to select the required number of individual members of the population for testing, perform the test and evaluate the results.

SELECTING THE SAMPLE

The fundamental principle in selecting the sample is that each item in the population must have a chance of being selected, but not necessarily an equal chance. Statistical sampling requires random selection so each sampling unit has a known chance of being selected.

A sample can be selected in a number of ways. The selection approaches suggested in ISA 530, Appendix 3, include:

- random;
- systematic; and
- haphazard.

Another type of selection is called block selection. This is not considered a method of audit sampling because most populations are structured such that items in a sequence can be expected to have similar characteristics. Given this problem, it is difficult to draw valid inferences about the population based on the sample selected. However, this method of selection may be appropriate; for example, if the auditors suspect fraud in creditors, then they may decide to review all transactions for a particular month.

Table 8.3 Illustrative relationship between population size and sample size

POPULATION SIZE	SAMPLE SIZE
50	45
500	87
5,000	93
100,000	93

Note: other factors also affect sample size. This illustration is based on a test of controls with a 5% risk of overreliance, a 1% expected deviation rate and a 5% tolerable deviation rate.

Random selection

Random selection is generally considered to be the best method of obtaining a sample to evaluate the results statistically. A computer may be used to generate random numbers to test. Alternatively, if computer-assisted audit techniques are being used and the population is on the auditors' computer, then most auditing software packages will allow an audit sample to be selected at random. The advantage of this method is that it does not allow auditor bias to affect the selections of the sample, either knowingly or not. Random selection is generally associated with statistical sampling, but is often used in non-statistical sampling as well.

Historically, auditors used random number tables to generate random samples. Use of these tables, which requires each item in the population to have a unique number, is facilitated when the population items are numbered consecutively. In using these tables, the auditors must pick a starting point – either by making a 'blind stab' or arbitrarily choosing a point to start – and then determine the direction or route (top to bottom, left to right, etc.) to be used in reading them. The route selected must be followed consistently.

A random number table is shown in Table 8.4. You will note that the 'random numbers' are shown in five-digit groupings. To illustrate its use, assume that a sample is desired from a population of sales invoices numbered 0001 to 4000. Assume further that the auditors elect to use the first four digits of each five-digit random number, start with row six of column one, and read from top to bottom. In this case, the first 10 invoices in the sample would be those shown in bold. Note that the starting number, 9287, is rejected because it falls outside the range of sales invoice numbers in the population (0001 to 4000). Similarly, the numbers 7748 and 4837 are rejected, and so on.

There are two problems with the use of random number tables:

1. They require populations that are individually and uniquely numbered within a reasonably consistent sequence.
2. The random numbers drawn from the table are not in sequence, which makes drawing a sample from a sequentially ordered file a time-consuming task.

Table 8.4 Partial random number table

| ROW | COLUMNS | | | | |
	(1)	**(2)**	**(3)**	**(4)**	**(5)**
1	04734	*439426*	91035	54839	76873
2	10417	*519688*	83404	42038	48226
3	07514	48374	*1035658*	38971	53779
4	52305	86925	16223	25946	90222
5	96357	*611486*	30102	82679	57983
6	Start → 92870	*705921*	65698	27993	86406
7	*100500*	75924	38803	05386	10072
8	*234862*	93784	52709	15370	96727
9	*325809*	*821860*	36790	76883	20435
10	77487	*938419*	20631	48694	12638

For samples that have to be extracted manually from the records, the auditors usually prefer an alternative method of sample selection.

Systematic selection

Systematic selection is the process of dividing the number of sampling units in the population by the sample size to give a sampling interval. It is generally considered to be the most widely used sample selection technique in auditing.[2] The population – say 8,200 – is divided by the sample size – say 40 – to obtain the sampling interval – 205 in this case. Every 205th item is then selected, starting from a randomly selected point between 1 and 205. To be able to evaluate the results statistically, the auditors must randomly select the starting point, not using the haphazard method of selection.

The criticism of systematic selection is that the population may have a fixed pattern. For example, employee numbers of supervisors may always end in 0, such that a sampling interval which is a multiple of 10 will result in a sample of supervisors only, or one that excludes supervisors. The auditors should have sufficient knowledge of the population to make sure this does not happen. When this problem could arise, the auditors should use random selection to select the sample.

Haphazard selection

Haphazard selection is the selection of a sample without following a structured technique. Sometimes, this is the only practical method when the population is not ordered in any numerical sequence, such as postings to the repairs and maintenance expense account in the ledger. The auditors must take care to avoid any bias (such as avoiding the first or last entry on each page of the ledger) particularly conscious bias (such as avoiding difficult-to-locate items). The method is not recommended where other methods are available, because the absence of bias cannot be subsequently evidenced. Haphazard selection is inappropriate when the auditors are using statistical sampling because they cannot measure the probability of an item being selected.

TESTING THE SAMPLE

Having drawn the sample, the auditors should then perform audit procedures that are appropriate to the test objective on each item selected. In the case of missing documents or similar difficulties encountered in completing the test, the auditors must consider the item to be misstated or to represent a deviation from laid down controls, and evaluate the sample evidence accordingly.

Evaluating the results

Each error or deviation discovered will need to be examined for its implications (i.e. its qualitative aspects). Errors or deviations that appear to be consistent with those anticipated during the procedure's planning can then be projected to consider the effect on the population. Given the planned level of sampling risk, it is assumed that the deviation or error rate in the sample is representative of the rate of deviation or errors in the population.

Both non-statistical and statistical sampling require the sample results to be projected on the population. The key difference with non-statistical sampling is that sampling risk is not mathematically quantified, but assessed on a more qualitative basis.

QUALITATIVE ASPECTS OF ERRORS OR DEVIATIONS

In analysing errors, the auditors must consider whether the error or deviation:

- has an effect on the whole population; or
- is an isolated or localised occurrence.

An error due to posting a sales invoice to the wrong customer's account will not affect the total balance of debtors. Similarly, a control deviation properly authorised by management will not affect the assessed level of control risk.

Errors related to events that can be specifically identified (such as payroll errors occurring when the computer broke down and payrolls had to be prepared manually) may be regarded as localised and not affecting the population as a whole.

PROJECTING THE ERROR TO THE POPULATION

Where the qualitative analysis identifies deviations or errors consistent with the objective of the test, the auditors then draw conclusions about the population, based on the results of testing the sample.

Tests of control

The rate of deviations in the sample may be taken to be the rate of deviations in the population. If, of a sample of 60, three deviations from laid down control procedures are discovered, then the projected deviation rate for the population can be estimated as 3/60 or 5%. If this is no worse than the tolerable deviation rate, then it is appropriate to confirm the preliminary assessment of control risk. However, if the deviation rate is much lower than expected, then this cannot be interpreted as justifying a lower assessed level of control risk. This level of risk has been determined from an evaluation of the overall effectiveness of controls.

If the projected deviation rate exceeds the tolerable deviation rate, then the preliminary assessment of control risk is not confirmed. Depending on qualitative considerations of actual deviations or on the existence of compensating controls, the auditors must reassess control risk at a higher level, thus reducing the acceptable detection risk. This means that the auditors have to revise the audit programme to increase the level of substantive procedures.

Substantive tests

The projection of errors in substantive testing depends on whether the object of the test is to estimate (1) the population mean (mean-per-unit method) or (2) the relative differences between recorded and audited amounts (difference estimation). Each of these methods requires a different projection from sample results to estimated population values. (Both methods are discussed in more detail later in this chapter.)

Where a population has been subdivided or stratified, the projected error must be related to the specific sub-population. Errors in items singled out for selective testing must be omitted from the errors projected to the population. This is illustrated in Table 8.5, based on a confirmation of debtors.

- Out of 1,000 accounts, three are individually material and are specifically selected for confirmation.

Table 8.5 Sample calculation of projected error for an account balance

		INDIVIDUALLY MATERIAL	OVERDUE	CURRENT	TOTAL
(a)	Number of accounts	3	200	797	1,000
(b)	Recorded value	£5,000	£10,000	£40,000	£55,000
(c)	Confirmed – number	3	20	20	43
(d)	Confirmed – recorded value	£5,000	£1,000	£1,000	£7,000
(e)	Overstatement errors	£500	£100	£25	£625
(f)	Ratio of errors (e/d×100)	n/a	10%	2.5%	–
(g)	Projected error (f×b)	£500	£1,000	£1,000	£2,500

- Of the remainder, 200 contain overdue balances and a sample of 20 of these is confirmed.
- A further sample of 20 of the remaining 797 current due accounts is confirmed. The relatively smaller sample size for current due balances is due to the lower expected error rate.

Table 8.5 then illustrates how errors discovered are projected to the population and a total projected error determined. It will be noted that the total projected error is the actual error in individually selected accounts confirmed, plus the separate projected errors of overdue and current due accounts.

Where the entity corrects the specific errors discovered in the sample, projected error may be reduced by the amount of those corrections.

In reaching a conclusion, the auditors will need to consider:

- how close the projected error is to the predetermined tolerable error;
- whether the nature of errors has any special significance; and
- the relationship to other evidence pertaining to the same audit objective.

Where sample error approaches or exceeds tolerable error, the auditors will need to consider carefully whether additional evidence might be necessary. In most cases, it would normally be appropriate to select a further sample, thus reducing sampling risk. (Note, however, that where statistical sampling is employed, certain sampling plans do not provide for extension of the existing sample.) If the further sample confirms the projected results indicating a substantial error, the auditors will request management to revise the recorded amount. If the projected error is only slightly greater than the tolerable error and management is unwilling to make any corrections, the error will be carried forward to the aggregate likely misstatements working paper described in Chapter 14, Completing the Audit.

◁ LEARNING **CHECK**

8.8 Where sample testing is considered appropriate, the auditors must consider the objectives of the test, the appropriate population from which the sample is to be selected, the errors or deviations being sought, and the size of the sample.

8.9 For tests of control, the objective of the sample test is to estimate the deviation rate; that is, the extent to which a particular control procedure has not been properly applied.

8.10 For substantive tests of details, the objective is usually to estimate the extent to which recorded amounts are misstated.

8.11 It is important that the population from which the sample is selected is one that the auditors believe to be consistent as far as the likelihood of deviation or misstatement of the type being sought is concerned.

8.12 For substantive tests of details, the apparent population (such as customer balances on debtors) may need to be subdivided for sampling. This could arise where balances differ as to assessed control risk (such as customer accounts processed at different locations) or as to the likelihood of misstatement (such as overdue accounts).

8.13 In sample testing, it is important to distinguish between those errors or deviations being sought and all other errors or deviations discovered during the course of testing the sample. Since the sample is representative of the population, only those errors the sample is designed to discover may be regarded as errors likely to be present to the same extent in the population.

8.14 The sample tested must be sufficiently large as to reduce sampling risk to an acceptable level. For tests of control, this is primarily dependent on the level of the preliminary assessment of control risk the test is intended to confirm. For substantive tests, it depends on the combination of detection risk applicable to that particular test and the materiality of the account balance or transaction class being tested.

8.15 Sample size is additionally dependent on the importance attached to the less critical risks of assessing control risk too high or of incorrectly rejecting properly stated balances. It also is affected by the number of deviations or errors expected and, for substantive procedures, by the variability of the population.

8.16 Only if the population is less than 5,000 does population size affect sample size.

8.17 In selecting the sample, each member of the population must have an equal chance of selection. Commonly used methods are (1) random selection by computer, (2) the use of random number tables and (3) systematic selection where every nth item is selected. It is important that the auditors avoid subjectivity. Wherever practicable, the selection process should be recorded so as to enable its replication.

8.18 Where statistical sampling is being used, the sampling plan will indicate the implications of the sample results for the population. For non-statistical sampling, it is usual to project the sample deviation or error rate to the population.

STATISTICAL SAMPLING TECHNIQUES

The major statistical sampling techniques used by auditors are:

- attribute sampling;
- variables sampling; and
- monetary unit sampling.

Attribute sampling plans

Attribute sampling plans refer to three different methods of sampling that are used to test the operating effectiveness of controls by estimating the rate of deviation:

1. *Attribute sampling.* This is the most common attribute sampling plan. It is a statistical sampling plan to estimate the proportion of a characteristic in a population. In relation to testing controls auditors determine the effectiveness of a control in terms of deviations from a prescribed internal control policy. An example of this method is shown in Appendix 8C.
2. *Sequential sampling.* This method is used to improve audit efficiency when it is expected that there will be relatively few deviations in the population. The auditors may stop testing as soon as they obtain enough assurance to assess that the control being tested is operating effectively.
3. *Discovery sampling.* This method is used when the expected rate of error occurrence in the population is extremely low and the expected error rate can be set at zero.

Variables sampling plans

The main difference between attribute sampling and variables sampling is that the auditors estimate the error in terms of a quantity rather than an occurrence rate. Variables sampling is generally used in substantive testing to estimate a monetary misstatement in an account balance. The different types of variables sampling plan include the following three plans:

1. *Unstratified mean-per-unit method.* When using this approach the auditors estimate a total population amount by calculating the mean for items in the sample and projecting the mean to the number of items in the population. This method is illustrated in Appendix 8D.
2. *Stratified mean-per-unit method.* This method is essentially similar in approach to the unstratified mean-per-unit, except that the population is stratified into two or more sub-populations. The rationale for adopting this approach is to improve audit efficiency.
3. *Difference estimation.* Using this approach, the auditors calculate the mean difference between audited and recorded amounts of the sample items, and projects the mean difference to the population. The estimated population difference between audited values and recorded (book) values is added or subtracted from the total recorded value to produce an estimate of the true population total.

Monetary unit sampling

The most commonly used statistical sampling technique for substantive testing is based on attribute sampling and not, as might reasonably be expected, on variables sampling. This technique is known as monetary unit sampling. Monetary unit sampling takes each £1 of the population as the sampling unit and tests to see whether it is correctly stated, not correctly stated or tainted. Incorrectly stated and tainted £1s are then projected to the number of £1s recorded as the population to estimate the extent of monetary error in the population.

The principal feature of this technique is the manner in which the £1s sampled are selected. If a sample of 100 £1s is required from a population of 10,000 £1s, it is drawn systematically by taking each 100th £1. The audit test is then applied to the item (such as the customer's account or stock item) containing that £1. The technique is sometimes called probability proportionate to size sampling, referring to the fact that the more £1s an item contains (i.e. the larger the customer's account balance), the more likely one of its £1s will be selected for sampling, thus drawing the entire account with it. The proportion of incorrect £1s to the recorded number of £1s (i.e. the recorded account balance) becomes the percentage tainting of that £1 being sampled. Application of this sampling plan is illustrated in the case study in Appendix 8B.

Choice of statistical sampling method

If statistical sampling is to be used for tests of control, then the auditors must use one of the attribute sampling plans. However, if substantive testing is being done, then there is a choice of either monetary unit sampling or variables sampling. Here, the relative merits and drawbacks of each method will be considered.

MONETARY UNIT SAMPLING
The advantages of monetary unit sampling over variables sampling are that:

- it is not affected by variability and, therefore, it is easy to determine sample size;
- it is mathematically simple and, therefore, easy to apply, especially if computer assistance is not available;
- it usually enables conclusions to be drawn on the basis of small sample sizes where the auditors expect no or few errors; and
- individually material items are automatically selected for sampling.

The disadvantages of monetary unit sampling are that:

- it is unsuitable for detecting errors of understatement because understated items, being smaller than they ought to be, are less likely to be selected for sampling. Special considerations are needed where a monetary unit sample detects understated items;
- if detected errors exceed those expected when the sampling plan is developed, then the auditors are likely to be forced to conclude that the population is materially misstated and to have to conduct further audit work;

- as expected error increases, sample size is likely to exceed that required by variables sampling; and
- the required cumulative addition of the population for the purposes of drawing the sample may not be convenient.

Audit situations in which monetary unit sampling will produce sufficient evidence using smaller sample sizes are those where:

- few errors are expected;
- the auditors are principally concerned with overstatement;
- understatement errors are unlikely; and
- it is convenient to obtain a cumulatively added listing of the population.

The technique is most useful for verifying the existence of assets and the occurrence of recorded transactions where sampling risk is moderate to low. Many audit tests where sampling is appropriate fall into this category, such as stock pricing and debtors' circularisation.

VARIABLES SAMPLING
Variables sampling is preferable where:

- errors of understatement are expected or are being sought;
- the population includes zero and negative balances;
- many errors are expected; and
- it may be necessary to extend the sample to estimate the population value more reliably.

Difference estimation techniques work reliably only where 50 or more errors are found. Where fewer errors are expected, the choice is between monetary unit sampling and the mean-per-unit methods of variables sampling.

Variables sampling is most likely to be useful in the audit of large computerised accounting systems with the assistance of computer audit software. This will be the case especially when most of the testing can be performed directly on the computer. In such circumstances, however, the auditors must consider whether the time spent planning and evaluating a sample may be better spent using the computer audit software to perform a 100% test.

◿ LEARNING **CHECK**

8.19 Statistical sampling techniques relate to sampling for attributes, as in the case of tests of control, and sampling for variables as is commonly the case in substantive testing.

8.20 Variables sampling is the most widely used variables sampling technique outside of auditing. It is used by auditors in either of the mean-per-unit, ratio or difference methods.

8.21 Monetary unit sampling is the most widely used statistical sampling technique in auditing.

8.22 Monetary unit sampling is preferred when testing for overstatement errors and where few errors are expected. Classical variables sampling is used when errors are expected to be numerous and expected to be a mixture of overstatements and understatements.

8.23 The advantages of statistical sampling are that:

- samples are determined and evaluated in accordance with probability theory;

- it provides a uniform framework for making consistent judgements; and

- it requires explicit consideration of relevant factors.

8.24 Statistical sampling is more likely to be appropriate where:

- the sample test is significant, relative to the expression of an opinion;

- the population is held on computer;

- qualitative considerations of test results are unlikely to dominate the evaluation; and

- the audit firm and staff are familiar with statistical techniques.

NON-STATISTICAL SAMPLING TECHNIQUES

The evidence suggests that non-statistical sampling is much more widely used than statistical sampling. Given that non-statistical sampling is less rigorous than statistical sampling, why would auditors use non-statistical sampling?

Why use non-statistical sampling?

Part of the reason for the prevalence of non-statistical sampling is probably found in ISA 500, which states that:

> The auditor needs to consider the relationship between the cost of obtaining audit evidence and the usefulness of the information obtained.

The rationale for non-statistical sampling is often that it is less costly and less time consuming but can be just as effective in satisfying audit objectives. This advantage is explained by the following:

- The lower training costs of non-statistical sampling. It usually takes less time to learn non-statistical sampling methods.
- The ease of implementation of non-statistical sampling. These methods are less complex, which makes them easier and quicker to apply in the field and also reduces the risk that staff will misuse the method.

- The impracticality of random selection. In some cases it is impractical to apply random selection – for example, where the population of source documents is large and unnumbered.
- Proposed adjustment based on qualitative analysis. The increased precision of a statistical estimate is often not needed because the proposed audit adjustment is based on the auditor's qualitative analysis of sample results rather than a mathematical calculation.[3]

An example of non-statistical sampling of substantive tests of details is shown in Appendix 8A.

Formal and informal non-statistical sampling

A formal non-statistical sampling plan uses a structured approach to determine the sample size and evaluate sample results. The main differences from a statistical sampling plan is that the selection of sample items may be haphazard and the level of sampling risk is not precisely quantified.

An informal approach is an unstructured approach to determining the sample size and evaluating the results. Sample size and results are determined on an entirely qualitative basis, so any conclusions about the population are also qualitative. Disadvantages with informal non-statistical sampling include the following:

- There is no systematic way to train staff in this approach, which requires experience and, therefore, is problematic for junior staff.
- Auditors in the same circumstances may reach significantly different judgements about the scope of audit work necessary on an engagement.
- There may not be enough documentation to prove that the auditors have complied with Auditing Standards on sampling.
- The unstructured approach increases the likelihood that the auditors will fail to recognise an unacceptable level of sampling risk.

◁ LEARNING **CHECK**

8.25 The advantages of non-statistical sampling are that it:

- is likely to be less time-consuming;

- does not require specially trained staff; and

- recognises the significance of qualitative judgements in sampling.

SUMMARY

The purpose of sampling is to obtain evidence about an account balance or transaction class without examining each individual item or transaction. The risk is that the sample examined might not be representative of the population from which the sample is drawn. Increasing the size of the sample reduces this risk. Sample size in auditing is a function of:

- the risk the auditors are willing to accept, based on the audit risk model;
- the magnitude of control deviations or errors that are considered material; and
- the level of expectation that deviations or errors do exist in the population.

Statistics tells us much about how to make sure that our sample is sufficiently large to provide the required level of knowledge about the account balance or transaction class. Auditors sometimes use statistical sampling techniques in their sample tests. However, non-statistical sampling is also commonly adopted, often using the principles of statistical theory in the planning of the sample test. In selecting the sample from the population, the technique adopted should provide reasonable assurance that the sample is representative and unaffected by selection bias. Random sampling is required for statistical sampling, but less rigorous techniques may be applied for non-statistical sampling.

In examining the sample, it must be remembered that it is representative of the population and that its purpose is to assess the extent to which deviations or errors could be present in the population from which the sample is drawn. The major statistical sampling techniques used by auditors are attribute sampling plans, variables sampling plans and monetary unit sampling. Attribute sampling is used for compliance testing, while the other two techniques are used for substantive testing.

Non-statistical sampling is widely used and, if undertaken properly, provides valid evidence. Reasons for its widespread use include its lower training costs, its ease of use and the fact that the auditors often base adjustments on a qualitative assessment irrespective of the sampling method employed.

NOTES

[1] Pixley, F. W. *Auditors: Their Duties and Responsibilities*, Effingham, Wilson, London, 1881.
[2] Hitzig, N. B. 'Audit Sampling: A Survey of Current Practice', *CPA Journal* (July 1995), p. 56.
[3] Guy, D., Carmichael, D. & Whittington, O. R. *Audit Sampling: An Introduction*, 5th edn. John Wiley & Sons, New York, 2002, p. 222.

FURTHER READING

American Institute of Certified Public Accountants. *Audit Sampling*, AICPA, 2001.

Colbert, J. L. 'Audit Sampling', *Internal Auditor* (February 2001), pp. 27–29.

Elder, R. J. & Allen, R. D. 'An Empirical Investigation of the Auditor's Decision to Project Errors', *Auditing: A Journal of Practice and Theory* (Fall 1998), pp. 71–87.

Gillett, P. R. & Srivastava, R. P. 'Attribute Sampling: A Belief-Function Approach to Statistical Audit Evidence', *Auditing: A Journal of Practice and Theory* (Spring 2000), pp. 145–155.

Guy, D. M., Carmichael, D. & Whittington, O. R. *Audit Sampling: An Introduction*, 5th edn. John Wiley & Sons, New York, 2002.

Hall, T. W., Herron, T. L., Pierce, B. J. & Witt, T. J. 'The Effectiveness of Increasing Sample Size to Mitigate the Influence of Population Characteristics in Haphazard Sampling', *Auditing: A Journal of Practice and Theory* (March 2001), pp. 169–185.

Hall, T. W., Herron, T. L. & Pierce, B. J. 'The Use of and Selection Biases Associated with Non-statistical Sampling in Auditing', *Behavioral Research in Accounting* (2000), pp. 232–255.

Hall, T. W., Herron, T. L. & Pierce, B. J. 'Sampling Practices of Auditors in Public Accounting, Industry, and Government', *Accounting Horizons* (June 2002), pp. 125–136.

Jones, P. *Statistical Sampling and Risk Analysis in Auditing.* Gower Publishing Limited, Hampshire, England, 1999.

Manson, S. 'Statistical Sampling', in M. Sherer & S. Turley (eds), *Current Issues in Auditing*, 3rd edn. Paul Chapman Publishing, London, 1997, pp. 234–253.

Messier, W. F., Kachelmeier, S. J. & Jensen, K. L. 'An Experimental Assessment of Recent Professional Developments in Nonstatistical Audit Sampling Guidance', *Auditing: A Journal of Practice and Theory* (March 2001), pp. 81–96.

APPENDIX 8A
Non-statistical sampling of substantive tests of details

FACTS OF THE CASE

Objective	Circularisation of debtors to confirm existence.
Population	Debtors (excluding credit balances) £4,250,000.
Sampling unit	Account balances 1,100.
Variability	£100 to £140,000.

JUDGEMENTS

Five accounts over £50,000 totalling £500,000 were considered to be individually material, leaving a population of 1,095 accounts with a value of £3,750,000 to be sampled.

Tolerable error	£130,000
Control risk assessment	Moderate
Effect on detection risk of other substantive procedures	Analytical procedures provide moderate assurance. Cut-off test provides moderate assurance.
Acceptable level of sample risk	Moderate
Expected errors	Few or none

SAMPLE SIZE

Using the formula:

$$\frac{\text{Population value}}{\text{Tolerable error}} \times \text{Reliability factor}$$

where the reliability factor is determined using the data in Table 8.6, produces a sample size of:

$$\frac{3,750,000}{130,000} \times 2.3 = 66$$

Table 8.6 Reliability factors for non-statistical sampling

REQUIRED LEVEL OF ASSURANCE	RELIABILITY FACTOR	
	FEW OR NO ERRORS EXPECTED	SOME ERRORS EXPECTED
Substantial	3.0	6.0
Moderate	2.3	4.0
Little	1.5	3.0

Source: Adapted from *Audit and Accounting Guide: Audit Sampling*, p. 59. © The American Institute of Chartered Public Accountants.

SAMPLE SELECTION

The sample was selected systematically from a listing of debtors' balances that had been tested to and from the sales ledger, and had been added and agreed in total to the balance on the control account in the general ledger.

SAMPLE RESULTS

Replies were received from the five large customers and from 60 of those sampled. The accounts of the six customers failing to reply were verified by other tests and found to be correctly stated. The reported errors were considered qualitatively. Those considered to reflect errors in the population are detailed in Table 8.7 below.

PROJECTED ERROR

Using the ratio method, the projected error is:

$$\frac{£3,000}{£180,000} \times £3,750,000 = £62,500$$

CONCLUSION

The entity corrected the £3,000 errors found in the sample, but disputed the £1,000 error on the large accounts resulting in a net projected population error of:

$$£62,500 - £3,000 + £1,000 = £60,500.$$

Table 8.7 Errors considered to reflect errors in the population

	POPULATION		SAMPLE	
	RECORDED AMOUNT (£)	RECORDED AMOUNT (£)	AUDITED AMOUNT (£)	OVERSTATEMENT ERRORS (£)
Material items	500,000	500,000	499,000	1,000
Sampled items	3,750,000	180,000	177,000	3,000

This is significantly lower than the tolerable error, so the auditor concluded that the recorded existence of debtors is not materially misstated.

APPENDIX 8B
Monetary unit sampling

FACTS OF CASE

Objective	To verify that standard costs used in valuing closing stock have been accurately determined.
Population	Stock, all of which is valued at standard cost, has a recorded value of £1,375,000 and consists of 320 different items.
Sampling unit	Individual £1s of recorded value.

JUDGEMENTS

Tolerable error	£53,500
Internal control	Not assessed as there are no procedures for checking the accuracy of standard costs. Control risk is, therefore, 100%.
Other substantive procedures	The operation of the costing system has been tested, particularly the determination of variances, all of which are immaterial. Analytical procedures confirm that stock appears to be properly valued. Allowing for reliance on other substantive procedures, detection risk is judged to be 70%.
Inherent risk	Inherent risk, overall, is judged to be low and no material errors have been detected by this test in previous years. Inherent risk is assessed at 70%.
Assurance required	Audit risk is set at 5%. Using the audit risk model, risk for this particular test is determined as being:

$$\frac{\text{Audit risk}}{\text{Inherent risk} \times \text{Control risk} \times \text{Detection risk}}$$

$$\frac{0.05}{0.7 \times 1.0 \times 0.7} = 0.102 \text{ or } 10\%$$

Ninety per cent assurance is, therefore, required from this particular test.

Expected errors	Two errors are expected on items not individually material.

SAMPLE SIZE

Using the formula:

$$\frac{\text{Population value}}{\text{Tolerable error}} \times \text{Reliability factor}$$

Table 8.8 Table of reliability factors for attribute sampling

NUMBER OF SAMPLE ERRORS	CONFIDENCE LEVEL	
	90%	95%
0	2.31	3.00
1	3.89	4.75
2	5.33	6.30
3	6.69	7.76
4	8.00	9.16

Based on Poisson distribution

where the reliability factor is determined as per the data in Table 8.8, sample size is calculated as being:

$$\frac{1,375,000}{53,500} \times 5.33 = 137$$

The sample interval is $\dfrac{1,375,000}{137} = 10,036$ (say 10,000).

SAMPLE SELECTION
The sample is selected from stock listings that have been printed out from the computer with a running cumulative total. The listing is test-added to verify its completeness, and the sample is selected as shown in Table 8.9 for the first 20 items on the list. A random start below £10,000 is selected, say 4,000, and every 10,000th £1 is then systematically selected and used as a hook to catch the stock item containing that £1.

SAMPLE RESULTS AND PROJECTED ERROR
Three alternative scenarios will be considered:

1. No errors were found.
2. Two errors were found in items with a recorded value less than the sampling interval.
3. Three errors were found including one error in an item with a recorded value above the sampling interval.

Scenario 1 – no errors
In this scenario, the monetary precision is better than tolerable error. When determining sample size, the auditor expected two errors and used a reliability factor of 5.33. As it turned out, the auditor could have used a reliability factor of 2.31. The extra sample size enables the auditor to conclude, with 90% assurance, that the maximum possible error in the population is:

Reliability factor × Sampling interval = Upper error limit

which gives

$$2.31 \times £10,000 = £23,100.$$

This figure is known as basic error or basic precision.

Table 8.9 Details of first 20 items selected

STOCK NO.	QTY	UNIT COST (£)	TOTAL VALUE (£)	CUMULATIVE VALUE (£)	HOOK (£)	SAMPLE (£)
1100	20	100	2,000	2,000		
1101	400	20	8,000	10,000	4,000	8,000
1102	100	5	500	10,500		
1103	1,000	7	7,000	17,500	14,000	7,000
1104	10	50	500	18,000		
1105	300	40	12,000	30,000	24,000	12,000
1200	1,500	3	4,500	34,500	34,000	4,500
1201	7	1,200	8,400	42,900		
1202	300	20	6,000	48,900	44,000	6,000
1203	20	5	100	49,000		
1204	200	5	1,000	50,000		
1205	30	50	1,500	51,500		
1206	20	75	1,500	53,000		
1207	500	4	2,000	55,000	54,000	2,000
1208	11	1,200	13,200	68,200	64,000	13,200
2100	300	4	1,200	69,400		
2101	20	10	200	69,600		
2102	50	5	250	69,850		
2103	100	15	1,500	71,350		
2104	50	10	500	71,850		

Scenario 2 – two errors

The upper error limit is determined as being basic error plus the projected error plus the precision gap widening.

Basic error is the upper error limit if no errors were found (i.e. £23,100 as in scenario 1).

Projected error is based on the assumption that the £1 being sampled is tainted by the extent of any error in the item of which it forms part. Thus, a £200 error in an item with a recorded amount of £1,000 taints the £1 being sampled by 20%. This tainting percentage is then projected to all those £1s of which the £1 is a representative sample (i.e. the sampling interval). Projected error is calculated as follows:

BOOK VALUE (£) (BV)	AUDITED VALUE (£) (AV)	TAINTING % (TP)*	SAMPLE INTERVAL (£) (SI)	PROJECTED ERROR (£) TP × SI
1,000	800	20	10,000	2,000
8,000	4,000	50	10,000	5,000
			Projected error	7,000

$$*TP = \frac{(BV - AV)}{BV}$$

For precision gap widening, the projected errors are ranked and the calculation is as follows:

NO. OF ERRORS	RF @ 90% (TABLE 8.8)	INCREMENTAL CHANGE (IC)	PROJECTED ERROR (£) (PE)	PRECISION GAP WIDENING (£) (IC × PE) − PE
0	2.31			
1st	3.89	1.58	5,000	2,900
2nd	5.33	1.44	2,000	880
				3,780

The upper error limit can now be calculated.

Basic error	£23,100
Projected error	7,000
Precision gap widening	3,780
	£33,880

If both errors were 100%, then:

Projected error would have been:	2 × 100% × £10,000	= £20,000
Precision gap widening would have been:	£10,000 × 0.58 plus £10,000 × 0.44 = £5,800 + £4,400	= 10,200
Basic error as before:		= £23,100
Upper error limit:	= tolerable error	= **£53,300**

In other words, if our worst expectations as to expected errors are confirmed, our sample size would be just sufficient to provide us with the required level of assurance.

Scenario 3 – three errors

The calculation of projected error and precision gap widening for the two errors in items with recorded values below the sampling interval is exactly the same as for Scenario 2 above. The actual error in the item whose recorded value is above the sampling interval is not subjected to a precision gap widening calculation, and is simply added to the other figures in determining the upper error limit.

If an item with a recorded value of £14,000 was found to be overstated by £3,000, the upper error limit would be:

As previously calculated	£33,880
Error in material item	3,000
Upper error limit	**£36,880**

CONCLUSION

The auditor would conclude, with 90% confidence, that the stock is not overstated because of errors in standard costs by more than:

- Scenario 1 – £23,100
- Scenario 2 – £33,880
- Scenario 3 – £36,880.

All of these are below the tolerable error for this particular test. Because of assurance from other procedures, the auditor has, in fact, 95% confidence that the stock is not materially misstated.

APPENDIX 8C
Test of control using attribute sampling

FACTS OF THE CASE

Objective	To test compliance of invoicing procedures, with laid down controls as a basis for confirming a preliminary assessment of control risk as moderate.
Population	8,190 credit sale invoices issued in the year.
Attributes being tested	1. Authorisation of order.
	2. Shipment of goods agreed with order.
	3. Invoices agreed with dispatch note.
	4 Invoice pricing verified.
	5. Mathematical accuracy of invoice verified.

JUDGEMENTS

Confidence level	95%
Tolerable deviation	7% (Also referred to as the upper error limit or UEL.)

SAMPLE SIZE

The auditor can determine sample size in a number of ways.

Sample plan 1

The auditor can estimate the likelihood of deviations being found in the sample. If the auditor expects two deviations, the required sample size is determined by the formula:

$$\frac{\text{Reliability factor (see Table 8.8)}}{\text{Tolerable deviation rate}} = \frac{6.3}{0.07} = 90$$

This approach is complicated by the fact that, without knowing the sample size, it is difficult to estimate how many deviations it is expected to contain.

Sample plan 2

If the auditor is reasonably confident that no deviations will be found, then he or she can take the minimum sample size possible of $3/0.07 = 43$, using the same formula as shown in Sample plan 1 above. This approach is also known as discovery sampling.

Sample plan 3

A third approach is to use a standard sample size, say 75, for all tests of control and determine, retrospectively, what assurance as to control effectiveness can be obtained.

SAMPLE SELECTION

Sales invoices for sampling are selected from the sales transaction file on the computer using computer-generated random numbers. The same sample will be used for testing each of the attributes.

SAMPLE RESULTS

Two orders not evidenced as being authorised, and one invoice not evidenced as being checked either for pricing or for mathematical accuracy, are found. No other deviations are found.

PROJECTED DEVIATION RATE

Sample plan 1

If two deviations are found, the auditor can calculate the upper error limit using the following formula:

$$\frac{\text{Reliability factor}}{\text{Sample size}} = \frac{6.3}{90} = 0.07$$

Since the sample size was determined on the basis that, if no more than two deviations are found, there is a 95% probability that the upper error limit will not exceed 7%, it is hardly surprising that, if two deviations are found, the auditor can conclude that the level of compliance is just acceptable. For the attributes where one deviation was found, the auditor can conclude that the level of compliance is well within the tolerable range.

Sample plan 2

Since the discovery sample was based on the expectation that no errors would be found, the finding of even one error means that the auditor must conclude that there is a more than 5% probability that the deviation rate could exceed 7%. Using the above formula, there is a 5% probability that the deviation rate could be as high as:

$$\frac{6.3}{43} = 14.65\%$$

The calculation is not necessary as the finding of any deviation means that there is a better than 5% probability that the deviation rate exceeds the tolerable rate. The problem with discovery sampling is that, unless the auditor is confident that no errors will be found, it can lead to underreliance being placed on internal control, with consequent overauditing in substantive procedures.

Sample plan 3

Using the formula, the auditor finding two deviations in a sample of 75 can determine that the upper error limit with 95% assurance could be $6.3/75 = 8.4\%$. However, since this approach is relatively informal, the auditor might consider whether a 90% assurance that the upper error limit does not exceed $5.33/75 = 7.1\%$ would be sufficient to support the preliminary assessed level of control risk, or at least an assessed level higher than planned, but still less than high.

CONCLUSION

With the second, and probably the third approaches, the auditor would be required to conclude that the preliminary assessment of control risk used in planning the level of substantive procedures on debtors cannot be supported on the basis of the results of tests of those controls. With the second method, discovery sampling, the sample results do not provide sufficient information to support some higher assessed level of control risk. The auditors could always use their judgement as to the importance of orders being approved in the overall context of controls over debtors, and might conclude that the final assessed level of control risk is still sufficient to support the planned programme of substantive procedures.

APPENDIX 8D
Classical sampling for variables using the mean-per-unit method

FACTS OF THE CASE

Objectives	Circularisation of loans receivable by a finance company.
Population	Loans receivable £1,340,000.
Sampling unit	3,000 accounts, all below £500.

JUDGEMENTS

Tolerable error	£60,000.
Risk of incorrect rejection	This judgement, which is not necessary in monetary unit sampling, allows the auditors to control the risk that the sample results show the population as being misstated when it is not. The trade-off facing the auditors is of increased sample size against reduced possibility of unnecessary audit work if the sample results in incorrect rejection. This risk is typically set at 5%.
Risk of incorrect acceptance	This is the same as the sampling risk in monetary unit sampling and is the same as detection risk. Using the audit risk model, this risk is put at 20%.

SAMPLE SIZE

The above factors were fed into a computer program which calculated the required sample size as 184. In the process, the computer estimated standard deviation at £100.

SAMPLE SELECTION

The sample was selected from files held on computer by means of a random number generator.

SAMPLE RESULTS

The 184 accounts confirmed had a total audited value of £81,328. Details of the audited value of each account confirmed were fed into the computer program. As this is a mean-per-unit sample, the auditor was not interested in errors.

POPULATION PROJECTION

The computer calculated population value as being £1,326,000 with an 'achieved allowance for sampling risk' of £37,803.

CONCLUSION

Since the recorded value lies within the range £1,326,000 plus or minus £37,803, the auditor may conclude that the recorded value is confirmed by the sample results.

MULTIPLE-CHOICE QUESTIONS

Choose the best answer for each of the following.
(Answers are on page 601)

8.1 Which of the following does not constitute sampling?
   (a) Select all payments made during the year greater than £10,000 and ensure they have supporting documentation.
   (b) Select 50 purchase orders from all purchases made during the year using a random number table.
   (c) Randomly pick a number of assets from the fixed assets register to inspect to ensure existence.
   (d) Select every tenth payment made during the year from the cash payments journal.

8.2 An advantage of using statistical sampling techniques is that such techniques:
   (a) mathematically measure risk.
   (b) eliminate the need for judgemental decisions.
   (c) define the values of tolerable error and risk of incorrect acceptance required to provide audit satisfaction.
   (d) have been established in the courts to be superior to judgemental sampling.

8.3 What would most effectively describe the risk of incorrect rejection in terms of substantive audit testing?
   (a) The auditor has ascertained that the balance is materially correct when in actual fact it is not.
   (b) The auditor has rejected an item from his or her sample and later found the item was materially incorrect.
   (c) The auditor concludes that the balance is materially misstated when in actual fact it is not.
   (d) The auditor decides to perform a predominantly compliance-based audit due to an evaluation that the controls were effective within the company. Midway through the audit, the auditor realises the controls are not good, and decides to expand substantive testing.

8.4 An advantage in using statistical sampling over non-statistical sampling methods in tests of control is that statistical methods:

(a)   eliminate the need to use judgement in determining appropriate sample sizes.
(b)   can more easily convert the sample into a dual-purpose test useful for substantive testing.
(c)   provide an objective basis for quantitatively evaluating sample risks.
(d)   afford greater assurance than a non-statistical sample of equal size.

8.5   If all other factors remained constant, changing the tolerable deviation rate from 10% to 12% would mean:
(a)   that the sample size would increase.
(b)   that the sample size would remain the same – there would be no effect on the sample size.
(c)   that the sample size would decrease.
(d)   that the sample size could not be determined without knowing the size of the population.

8.6   An underlying feature of random-based selection of items is that each:
(a)   stratum of the accounting population must be given equal representation in the sample.
(b)   item in the accounting population must be randomly ordered.
(c)   item in the accounting population should have an opportunity to be selected.
(d)   item must be systematically selected using replacement.

8.7   Which of the following methods of sample selection is the least desirable in terms of extrapolating results to the population?
(a)   Systematic selection.
(b)   Random selection.
(c)   Block selection.
(d)   Haphazard selection.

8.8   What audit tests do you think would be most appropriate for monetary unit sampling?
(a)   To select a sample of debtors to confirm their balances.
(b)   To ensure an appropriate level of management has reviewed all invoices.
(c)   To select a sample of creditors to circularise.
(d)   To check that all wages payments made during the year are bona fide.

DISCUSSION QUESTIONS

8.1   Discuss the risk of overreliance and its potential implications for an audit.
8.2   Explain the difference between statistical and non-statistical sampling.
8.3   Discuss the benefits to the auditor from using statistical sampling.
8.4   Explain the difference between selective testing and stratification in selecting items for audit testing.
8.5   Discuss the factors that will affect the sample size for tests of control and substantive tests.
8.6   Consider the appropriateness of using haphazard selection for statistical sampling.
8.7   Explain how errors should be projected to the population for tests of control and substantive testing.
8.8   Discuss the advantages and disadvantages of using probability-proportional-to-size sampling rather than variables sampling plans.
8.9   Explain why an auditor may decide to use non-statistical sampling.

8.10 Discuss some of the potential problems associated with using informal non-statistical sampling methods.

PROFESSIONAL APPLICATION QUESTIONS

(Suggested answers are on pages 624–628)

8.1 Evaluating results of sample testing

The recorded value of debtors in the sales ledger of Strathfield Ltd as at 31 December 1998, was £2,350,000.

Out of the 5,350 debtor's accounts, Sarah Jones selected 120 accounts for confirmation as part of the external audit of the company.

In selecting accounts for confirmation Sarah picked the 10 largest accounts totalling £205,000 and 110 other accounts selected haphazardly. Her working paper states that she rejected any accounts that were less than £100 as not being worth confirming and accounts with government bodies since she knew they never bother replying to confirmation requests.

Each of the 10 largest accounts was satisfactorily confirmed. Sarah analysed the responses to the confirmation of the other 110 accounts as follows:

RESULT OF CONFIRMATION	NUMBER OF ACCOUNTS	RECORDED AMOUNT £	AMOUNT CONFIRMED £
Satisfactorily confirmed	75	245,000	245,000
Confirmation returned marked 'gone away–address unknown'	4	950	0
Cut-off differences due to cash or goods in transit	8	6,800	5,750
Invoicing errors	4	2,800	2,200
Invoices posted to the wrong customer's account	2	1,300	980
Disputed as to price or quantity or quality of goods	3	2,800	1,300
Not confirmed – verified by alternative procedures	14	5,800	5,800
Totals	110	265,450	261,030

Sarah is about to draw up her working paper in which she reaches a conclusion as to whether the results of the confirmation of debtors enables her to conclude that the recorded balance is not materially misstated. She is aware that ISA 530 *Audit Sampling and Other Selective Testing Procedures* requires her to:

- consider the qualitative aspects of errors and whether any of these relate to a sub-population and not to debtors as a whole; and

- project the error results of the sample to the population from which the sample was selected.

Required

(a) Discuss Sarah's method of selecting items to be confirmed. Your answer should:
- (i) identify any aspects of her approach that might be considered inconsistent with sampling;
- (ii) suggest alternative means of selecting a sample ensuring that the more material balances stand the greatest chance of selection;
- (iii) compare and contrast the haphazard method of selection with random selection and systematic selection.

(b) Consider qualitative aspects of each of the five categories of error or other reported differences analysed by Sarah. Suggest which of them should be included in arriving at an estimate of population error.

(c) Calculate the projected error in debtors based on the results of the sample test consistent with the qualitative considerations in your answer to (b).

(Adapted from Question 6, Audit Framework, December 1999. Reproduced by permission of ACCA)

8.2 Determining sample size

As the senior in charge of the audit of Killara, a listed company, you are planning appropriate non-statistical sample sizes for tests specified in the audit programme. In accordance with the guidance provided in ISA 530 *Audit Sampling and Other Selective Testing Procedures*, you have identified the relevant factors to be taken into consideration in the following tests of control and substantive tests of details.

Tests of control

Test 1 Purchase Invoices

Select a sample of purchase invoices and see that they are initialled by the accounts payable clerk as having been checked with the goods received note.

Test 2 Sales Invoices

Select a sample of sales invoices and see that a second clerk has initialled them for checking prices against the approved price list.

Sample size factor	Test 1 Purchase invoices	Test 2 Sales invoices
Number of invoices processed in the year	6,000	20,000
Preliminary assessment of control risk	low at 30%	moderate at 60%
Tolerable deviation rate	2%	5%
Expected deviation rate based on last year's audit	0.1%	3%

Substantive tests of detail

Test 1 Inventory

Test pricing of inventory items against costing records.

Test 2 Accounts receivable
  Test the ageing of balances in the aged listing of accounts receivable balances.

Sample size factor	Test 1 Inventory	Test 2 Accounts receivable
Combined assessment of inherent and control risk	moderate at 50%	low at 20%
Tolerable error as percentage of recorded balance	2%	0.5%
Expected error rate based on last year's audit	2%	0%

Required
(a) For each pair of tests, discuss the effect of each of the factors referred to in the tables above.
(b) When subsequently performed, the sample tests of control indicated a deviation rate of 2.1% for test (1) and a deviation rate of 0.5 for test (2). Comment on these results.

(Adapted from Question 4, Audit Framework, June 2001. Reproduced by permission of ACCA)

CHAPTER 9

DESIGNING SUBSTANTIVE PROCEDURES

DISCUSSION QUESTIONS

PROFESSIONAL APPLICATION QUESTIONS

LEARNING OBJECTIVES

After studying this chapter you should be able to:

1   explain the process for determining the appropriate level of substantive procedures based on the assessment of inherent and control risk

2   indicate how the nature, timing, and extent of substantive procedures are varied to achieve an acceptable level of detection risk

3   discuss the relationships among assertions, specific audit objectives, and substantive procedures

4   state the nature and uses of audit programmes for substantive procedures

5   describe and apply a general framework for developing audit programmes for substantive procedures

6   indicate special considerations in designing substantive procedures for selected types of accounts

7   contrast tests of controls and substantive procedures.

PROFESSIONAL STATEMENTS

ISA 200   Objectives and General Principles Governing an Audit of Financial Statements
ISA 230   Documentation
ISA 500   Audit Evidence
ISA 510   Initial Engagements – Opening Balances
ISA 520   Analytical Procedures
ISA 540   Audit of Accounting Estimates
ISA 545   Auditing Fair Value Measurements and Disclosures

Chapter 5 explained that auditors assess the level of inherent risk at the entity level and at the level of individual assertion, at the planning stage of the audit. Chapter 7 considered how auditors (1) obtain and document an understanding of internal control and (2) assess control risk for significant transaction class and account balance assertions, based on the understanding of internal control and the results of tests of control.

This chapter explains how the assessment of inherent risk and the assessment of control risk impact on the required level of detection risk, which will affect the design of substantive procedures. The acceptable level of detection risk influences the auditors' assessment of the nature, timing and extent of the procedures that need to be performed to gain sufficient appropriate audit evidence.

DETERMINING DETECTION RISK

Detection risk is the risk that the auditors' substantive procedures will not detect a material misstatement. It is therefore directly related to the substantive procedures performed as part of the audit. The relationship between detection risk, inherent risk and control risk can be expressed by the audit risk model, as represented in the equation below, which was introduced in Chapter 5.

$$DR \frac{AR}{IR \times CR}$$

The model shows that for a given level of audit risk (AR) specified by the auditors, detection risk (DR) is inversely related to the assessed levels of inherent risk (IR) and control risk (CR). Auditors normally make a preliminary assessment of inherent risk and control risk for each financial statement assertion, as explained in Chapter 5. Where the auditors' assessment of inherent risk and control risk is high, detection risk must be low if the desired level of audit risk is to be attained. A low level of detection risk requires auditors to adopt a predominantly substantive audit strategy (as explained in Chapter 6), whereby evidence, obtained through the performance of substantive procedures, enables the auditors to minimise the risk of failure to detect such material misstatements as might exist.

Assessing control risk as being less than high means that the auditors are confident that the entity's own procedures reduce the likelihood of material misstatement in that particular financial statement assertion. The auditors need to obtain less evidence from substantive procedures to achieve the desired level of audit risk, and may adopt a lower assessed level of control risk audit strategy, as explained in Chapter 7. In such situations, the auditors are said to tolerate a higher level of detection risk. Where tolerable or planned detection risk is high, the auditors obtain less evidence from substantive procedures than where planned detection risk is low. This can appear confusing, and it is important to understand the logic underlying the terminology of ISA 200, Objectives and General Principles Governing an Audit of Financial Statements. It is re-emphasised below:

- When the acceptable detection risk is high it means that auditors are prepared to accept a high risk that material errors will not be picked up by substantive audit tests. This means that relatively less evidence needs to be collected by substantive audit procedures.
- When the acceptable detection risk is low it means that auditors require a low risk that material errors will not be picked up by substantive audit tests. This means that relatively more evidence needs to be collected by substantive audit procedures.

Since detection risk is the only component of audit risk controlled by the auditors, the term 'planned detection risk' is sometimes used to refer to that level of detection risk, after performing substantive procedures, that will reduce overall audit risk to the desired level. Sometimes the term 'assessed level of risk of material misstatement' will be used to

Table 9.1 The relationships between the audit strategy, detection risk, and the level of substantive procedures

AUDIT STRATEGY	DETECTION RISK	LEVEL OF SUBSTANTIVE PROCEDURES
Predominantly substantive approach	Low or very low	Higher level
Lower assessed level of control risk approach	Moderate or high	Lower level

reflect the joint assessment of inherent and control risk. Where this is low, a higher level of detection risk can be tolerated, and conversely.

It is important to note that auditors should perform some substantive tests for material balances and transactions and disclosures, regardless of the assessed levels of inherent and control risks.

The relationships between the audit strategy, detection risk and the level of substantive procedures that were explained in Chapter 5 are summarised in Table 9.1.

Assessing control risk for account balances

The internal control system usually applies controls at the time the relevant transaction is first recognised and recorded. For many financial statement assertions, therefore, control risk is assessed by reference to transaction classes. Where substantive procedures are to be applied to account balances and disclosures, the assessed level of control risk applicable to the account balance or disclosure has to be derived from the assessed control risk of the relevant transaction classes. For the balance of creditors, for example, this would be controls over purchase and payment transactions. The relationship between transaction class control risk and account balance control risk will now be considered for (1) account balance assertions affected by a single transaction class and (2) for account balance assertions affected by more than one transaction class.

ACCOUNT BALANCE ASSERTIONS AFFECTED BY A SINGLE TRANSACTION CLASS

The process of assessing control risk for account balance assertions is straightforward for accounts that are affected by a single transaction class. This is the case for most profit and loss statement accounts. The balance on the sales account, for example, is the cumulative effect of credits for sales transactions. Similarly, many expense accounts reflect the cumulative effect of debits for purchase transactions. In these cases, the auditors' control risk assessment for each account balance assertion is the same as the control risk assessment for the related transaction class assertion. For example, if the control risk assessment for the occurrence assertion for sales transactions is low, the same assessment will apply to the existence assertion for the sales account balance. Similarly, the control risk assessment for the accuracy assertion for purchases transactions is the same as the control risk assessment for the valuation assertion for many expenses account balances.

ACCOUNT BALANCE ASSERTIONS AFFECTED BY MULTIPLE TRANSACTION CLASSES

Most balance sheet accounts are affected by more than one transaction class. For example, the cash balance is increased by cash receipt transactions and decreased by cash payment transactions. In these cases, assessing control risk for an account balance assertion requires consideration of the relevant control risk assessments for each transaction class. Thus, the control risk assessment for the valuation assertion for the cash balance is based on the control risk assessments for the accuracy assertions for both cash receipt and cash payment transactions.

For an account affected by more than one transaction class, the control risk assessment for a particular account balance assertion is based on the control risk assessment for the same assertion pertaining to each transaction class that affects the account balance – with one major exception. The control risk assessments for the occurrence and completeness assertions for a transaction class that decreases an account balance relate to the opposite assertion for the account balance affected. This perhaps unexpected relationship is illustrated in Table 9.2, which shows the relevant control risk assessments for transaction class assertions that are used to assess control risk for the existence and completeness assertions for the cash balance.

A summary of the relationships between account balance assertions and transaction class assertions is presented in Figure 9.1.

When the control risk assessments for the relevant transaction class assertions differ, the auditors may judgementally weigh the significance of each assessment in arriving at a combined assessment. The auditors may consider the significance of a transaction class to the balance or, alternatively, whether one of the assessments was less persuasive. Some audit firms elect to use the most conservative (highest) of the relevant assessments. The existence assertion for the cash balance, for example, is affected by the occurrence of cash receipts and the completeness of cash payments. If the control risk for occurrence is

Table 9.2 Relevant control risk assessments for transaction classes that affect the cash balance

CASH BALANCE ASSERTION FOR WHICH CONTROL RISK IS BEING ASSESSED	RELEVANT CONTROL RISK ASSESSMENTS FOR TRANSACTION CLASSES THAT AFFECT THE CASH BALANCE	EXPLANATION
Existence	Occurrence of cash receipts that increase the balance	If some recorded cash receipts did not occur, part of the cash balance does not exist
	Completeness of cash payments that decrease the balance	If some cash payments have not been recorded, part of the cash balance no longer exists
Completeness	Completeness of cash receipts that increase the balance	If some cash receipts have not been recorded, the cash balance is not complete
	Occurrence of cash payments that decrease the balance	If some recorded cash payments did not occur, the cash balance is not complete

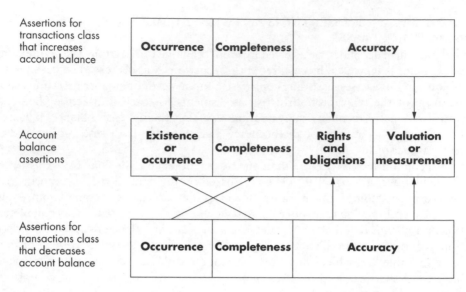

Figure 9.1 *Summary of relationships between account balance assertions and transaction class assertions*

assessed as being low, and completeness is assessed as being moderate, then the auditors would assess the control risk for the existence of cash as being moderate.

Effects of preliminary audit strategies

After making a preliminary assessment of the risk of material misstatement the auditors need to determine the appropriate strategy for the audit. As explained in Chapter 6, these strategies can be classified as being either a predominantly substantive approach or a lower assessed level of control risk approach. Regardless of the audit strategy chosen for a particular part of the audit, the auditors need to identify types of potential misstatement in the assertions.

PREDOMINANTLY SUBSTANTIVE APPROACH

The auditors may assess control risk as being high and adopt the predominantly substantive approach where:

- there are no significant control procedures that pertain to the assertion;
- relevant control procedures are ineffective; and
- it would not be efficient to perform tests of controls.

In making this decision, the auditors consider the costs of performing the higher level of substantive procedures required by the predominantly substantive approach to be less than the combined costs of performing sufficient tests of control to support a lower assessed level of control risk approach and the reduced level of substantive procedures that would be appropriate, assuming a lower control risk assessment were supported.

This may happen more commonly when auditing smaller entities because small entities may not have adequate resources to implement all appropriate controls, the controls may not be as effective (often as a result of problems due to a lack of segregation of duties) and the size of the entity may make it inefficient for the auditors to rely on these controls in performing the audit. In these cases, the level of detection risk (i.e. the amount of substantive procedures) is the only part of the audit risk model that the auditors can vary.

LOWER ASSESSED LEVEL OF CONTROL RISK APPROACH

Use of this approach requires the auditors to plan and perform tests of control. On completion of these tests, the auditors must consider whether the actual assessed level of control risk supports the planned level of substantive procedures, determined on the basis of the preliminary assessment. If the results of tests of control do not support the preliminary assessed level of control risk, then the auditors must increase the planned level of substantive procedures. For example, the auditors might have made a preliminary assessment of control risk as being low, resulting in the lowest planned level of substantive procedures. If evidence from tests of control (including dual-purpose tests) fails to support the assessment of control risk as being low, then revision of the planned level of substantive procedures to a higher level would be appropriate.

The auditors may assess the controls as being low if the controls are effectively designed and the auditors perform adequate tests of their operating effectiveness. However, if the controls are not designed effectively, then no amount of audit testing can change the assessment of control risk as being high. Thus, the assessed level of control risk is outside of the auditors' control. The only aspects of the audit risk model that are completely within the auditors' control are the assessment of audit risk and the amount of substantive work performed to vary detection risk.

Detection risk for individual substantive procedures

The term 'detection risk' as used in the preceding sections refers to the risk that all the substantive procedures used to obtain evidence about an assertion will collectively fail to detect a material misstatement. Typically, auditors will apply analytical procedures as early in the audit as practicable as being the most cost-effective substantive procedures. In designing substantive tests of details, auditors will assume that analytical procedures will not reveal any unexpected differences. If analytical procedures do reveal unexpected differences, then tests of details will need to be amended to enable the planned level of detection risk to be achieved. In summary, the lower the risk that analytical procedures will not detect material misstatements, the higher the detection risk can be for the tests of details that follow.

◁ LEARNING **CHECK**

9.1 Detection risk is determined by considering the assessment of inherent and control risk.

9.2 The level of detection risk determines the mix of tests of control and substantive procedures.

9.3 The preliminary assessment of control risk must be reviewed on completion of tests of control.

9.4 Control risk for account balance assertions is determined by the control risk of transaction classes making up that account balance.

9.5 Detection risk is often the combined effect of several types of substantive procedure.

9.6 Analytical procedures are typically performed first, and planned tests of details are based on the presumption that analytical procedures will not reveal unexpected differences.

DESIGNING SUBSTANTIVE PROCEDURES

Having determined the appropriate audit strategy, auditors need to design substantive audit procedures that will provide them with sufficient appropriate audit evidence as required by ISA 500, Audit Evidence. Substantive procedures either provide evidence that supports the truth and fairness of each significant financial statement assertion or, conversely, reveal monetary errors or misstatements in the recording or reporting of transactions and balances. Designing substantive procedures involves the following considerations:

- their nature, timing and extent should be responsive to the assessed risks of material misstatement at the assertion level; and
- they should be specifically responsive to significant assessed risks of material misstatement.

This section will explain considerations to be made by auditors in determining the nature, timing and extent of substantive procedures to be performed.

Nature

The nature of substantive procedures refers to the type and effectiveness of the auditing procedures to be performed. When the assessed risk of material misstatement is high, auditors must use more effective and usually more costly procedures; when it is low, less effective and less costly procedures can be used. As explained in Chapter 5, the types of substantive procedure are:

- analytical procedures;
- tests of details of transactions; and
- tests of details of balances.

These procedures and their relative effectiveness and cost will be discussed in the following sections.

ANALYTICAL PROCEDURES
The use of analytical procedures in audit planning to identify areas of greater risk of misstatement is explained in Chapter 6. ISA 520, Analytical Procedures, suggests that

analytical procedures should be used at the planning and overall review stage of the audit. However, it also notes that analytical review may be used at other stages of the audit as a substantive procedure to reduce detection risk. Analytical procedures are often the least costly to perform. Thus, consideration should be given to the extent to which these procedures can contribute to achieving the planned level of detection risk, thus reducing the extent of tests of details. For most assertions, analytical procedures are considered to be less effective than tests of details, so they are used as a supplement to tests of details. However, the opposite is true in a few cases, in which analytical procedures provide most (if not all) of the required evidence. When the results of the analytical procedures are as expected and the assessed risk of material misstatement is low, it may not be necessary to perform tests of details.

In the hotel industry, for example, relatively small amounts of revenue are billed to and collected from many customers each month. Tests of details of these high-volume, low-value revenue transactions would be tedious and costly. But, revenues in such cases can often be estimated fairly precisely using independent variables such as the occupancy rate and average room rate. The auditors could multiply the average occupancy rate for each month (probably monthly, given seasonal variations) by the average room rate by the number of rooms to estimate the revenue for every month. The auditors' estimated balance for room revenue can then be compared with the reported balance as part of the evidence used in determining whether revenues are fairly stated. Reasons for substantial differences would need to be discussed with management to determine whether alternative procedures need to be performed.

In other cases, auditors may use the expected relationship of one account balance to another. Total sales commission expense, for example, could normally be estimated from total sales revenue, rather than from the details of entries to sales commissions.

ISA 520 indicates that the extent of reliance on analytical procedures depends on:

- *materiality*: *Ceteris paribus*, the more material a balance is, the less likely it is that auditors would rely solely on the results of analytical procedures to audit the balance;
- *other audit procedures*: If other audit procedures are directed towards the same audit objective and similar results are found, then more reliance can be placed on the analytical procedures;
- *accuracy of predicted results*: The more accurate the results that can be predicted, the more reliance that can be placed on the analytical procedures. Greater accuracy can be expected, for example, for balances where interrelationships are expected to be constant over time (such as gross profit margin percentages); and
- *inherent and control risks*: If these risks are high, then more reliance will be placed on tests of details than on analytical procedures.

TESTS OF DETAILS OF TRANSACTIONS

Tests of details of transactions are tests to obtain evidence of a sample (or all) of the individual debits and credits that make up an account to reach a conclusion about the account balance. These tests primarily involve inspection of documents including tracing and vouching as explained on pages 159–160.

The details of transactions may be traced, for example, from source documents (such as sales and suppliers' invoices) to entries in accounting records (such as the sales and purchase journals). Or, the details of entries in accounting records (such as the cash payments journal and perpetual stock records) can be vouched to supporting documents (such as suppliers' invoices). The auditors' focus in performing these tests is on finding monetary errors rather than deviations from controls. As noted in Chapter 5, tracing is useful in testing for understatements, and vouching is useful in testing for overstatements.

In tests of details of transactions, auditors use evidence obtained about some (a sample) or all of the individual debits and credits in an account to reach a conclusion about the account balance. These tests generally use documents available in entity files, although sometimes documents will be obtained from external sources. The effectiveness of the tests depends on the particular procedure and documents used. For example, externally generated documents are more reliable than internally generated documents.

Although tests of details of both transactions and balances may be performed in an audit, the former will provide most of the evidence for account balances affected by few transactions during the year, such as tangible fixed assets or investments. For account balances affected by many transactions, such as cash and debtors, it is more effective to apply tests of details to the balances. For the same account balance, some assertions may be tested by tests of details of transactions, such as existence, and other assertions by tests of details of balances, such as valuation. Often, because the same documentation may be required, tests of details of transactions may be performed in conjunction with tests of control. This dual-purpose testing increases the cost-efficiency of such tests of details of transactions.

Cut-off tests are a special category of tests of details of transactions that are related more to the closing balance than to transactions. It is much more important at balance sheet date to ensure that transactions are recorded on the correct date, given the impact on the financial statements. Although cut-off is important for periodic reports it is critical only once a year. Control procedures are rarely effective and cut-off is usually monitored directly by senior accounting personnel. The purpose of cut-off tests is to ensure that transactions are recorded in the correct accounting period. Cut-off errors can significantly affect profit. For example, goods received before balance sheet date and included in stock, but not recorded in purchases until after the year-end, will overstate profit by the amount of the purchases.

Cut-off testing is needed for many accruals that will have a direct impact on profit, including electricity, telephone, gas, wages, advertising, etc. Often, the amount of these accruals is not confirmed until the receipt of an invoice, which may be several weeks after the balance sheet date.

TESTS OF DETAILS OF BALANCES

Tests of details of balances focus on obtaining evidence directly about an account balance rather than the individual transactions that are debited and credited to the account. Auditors may, for example, verify amounts owed by individual customers making up the balance on debtors by requesting confirmation of balances from the customers. Auditors may also inspect tangible fixed assets, observe the entity's stock-taking and perform pricing tests of the closing stock.

The effectiveness of these tests depends on the particular procedure performed and the type of evidence obtained. The information in the tabular layout below illustrates how the effectiveness of tests of balances can be tailored to meet different detection risk levels for the completeness assertion for creditors.

DETECTION RISK	TEST OF DETAILS OF BALANCES
High	Inspect suppliers' statements held by the entity and consider reasonableness of explanations of differences.
Low	Confirm amount owing directly with the suppliers and investigate reported differences.

Note in the above example that when the assessed risk of material misstatement is low, auditors use documentation held by the entity and perform limited auditing procedures. In contrast, when the assessed risk of material misstatement is high, auditors use documentation obtained from third parties directly and perform extensive auditing procedures.

ILLUSTRATION OF THE USE OF TYPES OF SUBSTANTIVE PROCEDURES

The application of the three types of substantive procedure may be illustrated in the context of the following accounts (see Figure 9.2).

Debtors

To simplify Figure 9.2, only one debtor's account is shown; in practice, there would typically be a control account backed up by a subsidiary ledger of customer accounts containing the individual debits and credits for transactions affecting each customer. The opening balance of debtors would have been verified as true and fair in the prior year's audit. To determine that the closing balance of debtors is true and fair, auditors may consider obtaining evidence from any of the following substantive procedures:

- analytical procedures, such as:
  - comparing this year's closing balance in the control account with the prior year's balance, a budgeted amount or other expected value;
  - using the closing balance to determine the percentage of debtors to current assets for comparison with the prior year's percentage or industry data;
  - using the closing balance to calculate the debtors' turnover ratio for comparison with the prior year's ratio, industry data or other expected value;
- tests of details of transactions, such as:
  - vouching a sample of the individual debits and credits in customer accounts, for the transaction classes indicated, to the entries in journals (for example, vouching the debits to the sales journal) and supporting documentation (such as sales invoices);
  - tracing transactions data from source documents (such as remittance advices) and journals (such as the cash receipts journal) to the corresponding entries in the customer accounts for the transaction classes indicated;

DEBTORS			
Opening balance	x		
Credit sales transactions	x	Collections from customers	x
	x		x
	x		x
		Write-offs	x
			x
			x
		Returns and allowances	x
Closing balance	x		

SALES REVENUE			
		Credit sales transactions	x
			x
			x
			x
			x
			x
			x
		Closing balance	x

COMMISSIONS EXPENSE			
Commissions accrual	x		
	x		
	x		
	x		
	x		
	x		
	x		
Closing balance	x		

Note: The number of entries shown by crosses above is arbitrary. In reality, there would probably be many more than these.

Figure 9.2 *General ledger accounts illustrating the processing of sales transactions to debtors*

- tests of details of balances, such as:
  - determining that the closing balances in the individual customer accounts add up to the control account balance;
  - confirming the balances for a sample of customer accounts with the customers.

In the case of debtors, it is common to apply each of the three types of substantive procedure to some extent. For other accounts, only one or two of the types of test may be performed in obtaining sufficient evidence to meet the planned level of detection risk.

Sales revenue

For simplicity, the sales revenue account shown in Figure 9.2 shows the credits representing the individual sales transactions. In practice, the sales revenue account may show only daily, weekly or monthly totals posted from the sales journal. In either case, to determine that sales revenue is true and fair, auditors may obtain evidence from any of the following:

- analytical procedures, such as:
  - comparing the closing balance with the prior year's balance, a budgeted amount or other expected value;
  - comparing the closing balance with an independent estimate of the closing balance (as illustrated previously for a hotel's revenues – see page 301);
- tests of details of transactions, such as:
  - vouching the individual credits to the sales journal and to supporting documentation such as sales invoices, shipping documents and sales orders;
  - tracing transactions data from source documents such as shipping documents, to sales invoices, to the sales journal, and then tracing postings from the sales journal to the sales account;
- tests of details of balances (this type of test is unlikely to be applicable).

In many cases, both analytical procedures and tests of details are applied to the sales revenue account to achieve the acceptable level of detection risk. In some cases, analytical procedures alone may suffice, as we will discuss in a later section (see page 317).

Commissions expense

The commissions expense account shown in Figure 9.2 is a good example of a situation in which analytical procedures alone may be all that is needed to achieve the planned level of detection risk. Examining source documents and recalculating the individual commissions could test the details of the individual debits to the account. However, for this type of account, it may be sufficient simply to calculate an estimate of the total for commissions expense using an expected relationship with the sales revenue account balance, such as 3%, and then to compare the estimate with the recorded balance for commissions expense.

Timing

Often, many of the entities audited by an audit firm have similar year-ends. In the UK a common year-end is 31 March. The result is that the months of April to June are commonly referred to as the 'busy season', when resources are often stretched to ensure that all audits are completed on a timely basis. To reduce this pressure auditors will try to perform as much work as possible in the 'quieter' time before the audit busy season. This has the dual advantage of (1) putting less pressure on resources during the busy season and (2) helping to complete audits on a timely basis. The assessed risk of material misstatement has an impact on the extent to which auditors can alter the timing of substantive procedures.

If the assessed risk of material misstatement is low, then certain procedures (typically tests of details of balances) may be performed several months before the end of the year. At the end of the year the auditors can conduct roll-forward testing to verify the account balance as at the year-end, using analytical procedures or tests of details of transactions applied to transactions in the intervening period. In contrast, when the assessed risk of material misstatement for an assertion is high, all substantive procedures relating to account balances will ordinarily be performed at or near the balance sheet date.

SUBSTANTIVE PROCEDURES PRIOR TO BALANCE SHEET DATE

Substantive procedures commonly performed prior to the balance sheet date are (1) the confirmation of debtors, (2) the observation of stock-take and (3) the physical inspection of investments.

Performing substantive procedures prior to the balance sheet date may be more cost-effective but only if it does not increase the audit risk that material misstatements existing in the account at the balance sheet date will not be detected by the auditors beyond an acceptable level. This risk becomes greater as the time period remaining between the date of the interim audit and the balance sheet date is lengthened.

The potential increased audit risk can be controlled if:

- internal control during the remaining period is effective;
- there are no conditions or circumstances that may predispose management to misstate the financial statements in the remaining period;
- the year-end balances of the accounts examined at the interim date are reasonably predictable; and
- the entity's accounting system will provide information concerning significant unusual transactions and significant fluctuations that may occur in the remaining period.

If these conditions do not exist, then the account should be examined at the balance sheet date. In practice, early substantive testing of account balances is not done unless tests of control have provided convincing evidence that internal controls are operating effectively. Substantive procedures prior to the balance sheet date do not completely eliminate the need for substantive procedures at the balance sheet date. Such procedures (roll-forward testing) ordinarily should include:

- a comparison of the account balances at the two dates and of the totals of transactions making up the difference to identify amounts that appear to be unusual, and the investigation of such amounts; and
- other analytical procedures or other substantive tests of details to provide a reasonable basis for extending the interim audit conclusions to the balance sheet date.

When properly planned and executed, the combination of substantive procedures prior to the balance sheet date and substantive procedures for the remaining period should provide auditors with sufficient appropriate audit evidence to have a reasonable basis for an opinion on the entity's financial statements.

Extent

Auditors can vary the amount of evidence obtained by changing the extent of substantive procedures performed. 'Extent' means the number of items or sample size to which a particular test or procedure is applied. More evidence is needed to achieve a low planned level of detection risk than a high planned level of detection risk.

The extent will therefore relate to the size of the samples selected by the auditors. Thus, more extensive substantive procedures are being performed when the auditors confirm 200 debtors' accounts rather than 100 accounts, or vouch 100 sales journal entries to supporting documents rather than 50 entries. The sample size to which a particular test is applied can be determined statistically or non-statistically. Reference to Table 8.2 on page 266 will reveal that the first two factors affecting sample size are the assessments of inherent and control risk. As the assessment of these risks increases a lower level of detection risk is required, which means a larger sample size is needed.

Audit risk and choice of substantive procedures

A graphic summary of several important relationships between the audit risk components and the nature, timing and extent of substantive procedures is presented in Figure 9.3. As noted earlier, designing substantive procedures involves determining the nature, timing and extent of substantive procedures for significant financial statement assertions. The next section considers how auditors relate assertions, specific audit objectives and substantive procedures in developing written audit programmes for substantive procedures.

Computer-assisted audit techniques as substantive procedures

In designing substantive audit procedures auditors may decide to use computer-assisted audit techniques (CAATs) as an audit tool. This will generally be done when the auditors decide that it is effective and efficient to use these audit techniques in the performance of

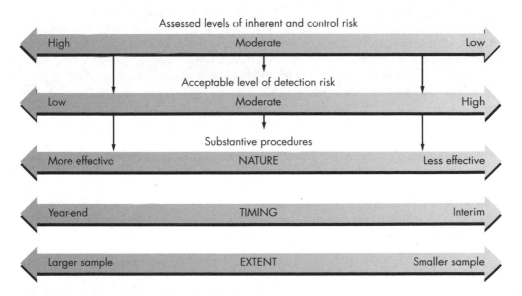

Figure 9.3 *Risk components and the nature, timing and extent of substantive procedures*

the audit. This is particularly so where there are no input documents or a visible audit trail, or where population and sample sizes are very large.

Their use in tests of control was described in Chapter 7. The focus of this discussion is on the use of CAATs in performing substantive tests. Using CAATs for substantive testing involves analysis of the entity's data files, either the master files or transaction files. Some of the types of substantive auditing procedures that can be performed or assisted by the use of CAATs include:

- tests of details of transactions and balances, for example the use of audit software for recalculating interest or the extraction of invoices over a certain value from computer records;
- analytical procedures, for example identifying inconsistencies or significant fluctuations;
- sampling programs to extract data for audit testing and evaluating the implications of the results of testing the sample; and
- reperforming calculations performed by the entity's accounting systems.

There are three main categories of audit software that are used to perform substantive audit testing:

1. Generalised audit software (GAS).
2. Customised audit software.
3. Utility programs.

Generalised audit software is the most commonly used audit software. It is designed for ease of use on many different computers and operating systems. Examples of this type of software include ACL and IDEA. It can be used for many different functions in performing the audit, including: performing calculations; selecting samples; identifying records meeting specified criteria; comparing data in different fields; and producing reports.

Customised audit software is developed for the audit of entity specific computer applications that are not compatible with the GAS or where the auditors need to perform a specialised function unavailable in GAS. This is much more costly than the use of GAS. They are most commonly used in very large entities where they are designed in conjunction with the entity's internal auditors and thus form part of the entity's own monitoring procedures.

Utility programs are commonly included within database management systems and are readily available as part of the entity's own computer system. They are not specifically designed for audit purposes but can perform such tasks as sorting, creating and printing files from data held on the entity's database.

As GAS is the most commonly used audit software, the next section will discuss issues associated with its usage.

GENERALISED AUDIT SOFTWARE

Depending on the application, the following distinct phases are involved in using generalised audit software:

- identifying the audit objective and the tests to be performed;
- determining the feasibility of using a software package with the entity's system;
- designing the application, which may include the logic, calculations and the output; and
- processing the application on entity file data and reviewing the results.

The use of generalised audit software enables auditors to deal effectively with large quantities of data. This may permit the accumulation of either the same quantity of evidence at less cost, or more evidence at an economical cost. The main cost associated with using this type of software is on an audit for the first time (i.e. start-up costs). Depending on the entity's computer system, the software may be designed to perform many of the auditing procedures that auditors might perform manually. Generalised audit software can be used for tests of control, as described in Chapter 7. However, in practice they are most commonly used for substantive procedures.

Its use in the audit of debtors will be illustrated with reference to a sample customer file held in the accounts receivable master file as shown in Figure 9.4. Using GAS the auditors may perform the following tests on the records:

- recalculate the balance on each customer file in each category (Fields 4, 5, 6 and 7) checking that it equals the total (Field 8);
- sum the totals for each customer file (Field 8) to check the overall total for accounts receivable;
- select all accounts where the balance is over 60 days (from Field 7) and print out the results as the basis of a test on collectability;
- select all accounts where the total balance is negative (from Field 8) and print out the results for further audit testing as negative balances are unusual;

FIELD	TYPE	NAME	DETAILS
1	N	Customer Number	0003
2	A	Customer Name	Company X
3	A	Address	34 King Edward Road
4	N	Current Balance	5800
5	N	Balance <30 days	0
6	N	Balance 30<60 days	2200
7	N	Balance >60 days	1100
8	N	Total Balance	9100
9	N	Credit Limit	10000

Figure 9.4 *Sample file from the accounts receivable master file*

- select a random sample of all customer files for circularisation and print out confirmation letters using data from the following fields: customer number (Field 1); customer name (Field 2); address (Field 3); total balance (Field 8);
- select all accounts where the total balance (Field 8) exceeds the credit limit (Field 9) and print out the results as the basis of a test on collectability; and
- calculate the percentage of total amounts in each ageing category (sum of Fields 4, 5, 6 and 7) and compare the result with similar percentages calculated in the previous year's audit.

◿ LEARNING **CHECK**

9.7 Substantive procedures include analytical procedures and tests of details of transactions and balances.

9.8 Analytical procedures are usually the least effective but also the least costly, and are often performed first in order to reduce the extent of tests of details. They may provide sufficient evidence on their own where the risk of material misstatement is low.

9.9 Tests of details of transactions are often performed as dual-purpose tests with tests of control.

9.10 Tests of details of transactions are usually most efficient for account balances affected by few transactions during the year, and tests of details of balances are most efficient for account balances affected by many transactions.

9.11 Substantive procedures may be performed at or prior to the year-end.

9.12 Procedures applied prior to the year-end are less costly, but provide sufficient evidence for assertions only where control risk is low and there is little risk of misstatement between the date of audit and the balance sheet date.

9.13 Increasing the extent of individual substantive procedures, such as by testing a larger sample, is the commonest way of reducing detection risk.

DEVELOPING AUDIT PROGRAMMES FOR SUBSTANTIVE PROCEDURES

As previously stated, the overall objective of a financial statement audit is the expression of an opinion on whether the entity's financial statements give a true and fair view, in accordance with applicable Financial Reporting Standards. Furthermore, as noted in Chapter 5, it is necessary to develop specific audit objectives for each account balance, based on each of the financial statement assertions. In designing audit programmes auditors also use the understanding of the entity's business and of its information system obtained as described in Chapters 6 and 7, incorporating procedures that address specific risks of material misstatement discovered during that process. Finally, the auditors should determine that appropriate procedures have been identified to achieve each of the specific audit objectives pertaining to each assertion. If this is done for each account, then the overall objective will be met.

Assertions, audit objectives and substantive procedures

Table 9.3 illustrates the relationships between assertions, specific audit objectives and substantive procedures for the stock of a manufacturing company. Study of the procedures shown in the second column indicates that a mix of analytical procedures and tests of details of both transactions and balances is included. In some cases, a procedure is listed more than once because the evidence from the procedure relates to more than one specific audit objective or assertion. Table 9.3 is not intended to include a listing of all possible substantive procedures that may be used in auditing stock, and nor should it be inferred that all the listed procedures would be performed in every audit. The next section illustrates how these procedures are incorporated into the audit programme.

Illustrative audit programme

As required by ISA 230, Documentation, auditors' decisions regarding the design of substantive procedures must be documented in the working papers in the form of written audit programmes. An audit programme is a list of audit procedures to be performed. As a working tool it is set out in a manner that facilitates the conduct of the audit. You will note, for example, that many of the procedures listed in Table 9.3 are common to several assertions. Clearly each procedure needs to be performed only once so Figure 9.5 illustrates how the programme of audit procedures may be listed in a sequence that is logical for the development of the programme and/or performance of the procedures

In addition to listing audit procedures, each audit programme should have:

- columns for a cross-reference to other working papers detailing the evidence obtained from each procedure (when applicable);
- the initials of the audit team member who performed each procedure; and
- the date performance of the procedure was completed.

These features are also illustrated in Figure 9.5.

Details of procedures given in Figure 9.5 are only an outline. Such an outline would form part of an audit firm's standard documentation to be tailored for each engagement. In a tailored audit programme, the details would refer to the entity's specific information system and portions of the audit trail applicable to processing the transactions. They would also identify the particular documents and records involved, and may specify the extent of each procedure.

Audit programmes should be sufficiently detailed to provide:

- an outline of the work to be done;
- a basis for co-ordinating, supervising and controlling the audit; and
- a record of the work performed.

The audit programme shown in Figure 9.5 is presented to illustrate the format of audit programmes for substantive procedures and how they can be developed. The application

Table 9.3 Relationships between assertions, specific audit objectives and substantive procedures

SPECIFIC AUDIT OBJECTIVE	EXAMPLES OF SUBSTANTIVE PROCEDURES
For the existence assertion:	
Stocks included in the balance sheet physically exist. Stocks represent items held for sale or use in the normal course of business.	Observe and test physical stock-take. Obtain confirmation of stocks at locations outside the entity. Review perpetual stock records and purchasing records for indications of current activity. Compare stocks with a current sales catalogue and subsequent sales and despatch notes.
For the rights and obligations assertion:	
The entity has legal title or similar rights of ownership to the stocks.	Observe stock-take. Obtain confirmation of stocks at locations outside the entity. Examine paid suppliers' invoices, consignment agreements and contracts.
Stocks exclude items billed to customers or owned by others.	Examine paid suppliers' invoices, consignment agreements and contracts. Test shipping and receiving cut-off procedures. Compare stocks with a current sales catalogue and subsequent sales and delivery reports.
For the completeness assertion:	
Stock quantities include all products, materials and supplies on hand.	Observe and test physical stock-take. Account for all stock-taking tags and count sheets used in making the physical stock-take. Analytically review the relationship of stock balances to recent purchasing and sales activities. Test shipping and receiving cut-off procedures.
Stock quantities include all products, materials and supplies owned by the company that are stored at outside locations. Stock listings are accurately compiled and the totals are properly included in the stock accounts.	Obtain confirmation of stocks at locations outside the entity. Trace test counts recorded during the physical stock-take observation to the stock listing. Test the clerical accuracy of stock listings. Reconcile physical counts to perpetual records and general ledger balances and investigate significant fluctuations.
For the valuation assertion:	
Stocks are properly stated at cost (except when net realisable value is lower). Slow-moving, excess, defective and obsolete items included in stock are properly identified.	Examine suppliers' invoices. Inquire of sales personnel concerning possible excess or obsolete stock items. Examine an analysis of stock turnover. Review industry experience and trends. Analytically review the relationship of stock balances to anticipated sales volume.
Stocks are reduced, when appropriate, to net realisable value.	Review estimates of realisable values.
For the transparency assertion:	
Stocks are properly classified in the balance sheet as current assets.	Review drafts of the financial statements.
The basis of valuation is adequately disclosed in the financial statements.	Compare the disclosures made in the financial statements with the requirements of the Companies Act and applicable Accounting Standards.
The pledge or assignment of any stock is appropriately disclosed.	Obtain confirmation of stock pledged under loan agreements.

		Reviewed by: _____ Date: _____		
		Prepared by: _____ Date: _____		

XYZ Company Ltd

Audit programme for substantive procedures of stocks
31 December 20X1

SUBSTANTIVE PROCEDURE	W/P REF.	AUDITOR	DATE
1. Verify totals and agreement of stock balances and records that will be subjected to further testing:			
(a) Trace opening stock balances to prior year's working papers.			
(b) Review activity in stock accounts and investigate unusual items.			
(c) Verify totals of perpetual records and other stock schedules and their agreement with closing general ledger balances.			
2. Perform analytical procedures:			
(a) Review industry experience and trends.			
(b) Examine an analysis of stock turnover.			
(c) Review relationship of stock balances to recent purchasing and sales activities.			
(d) Compare stock balances to anticipated sales volume.			
3. Test details of stock transactions:			
(a) Vouch additions to stock records to suppliers' invoices.			
(b) Trace data from purchases to stock records.			
(c) Test cut-off of purchases (receiving) and sales (shipping).			
4. Observe physical stock-take:			
(a) Make test counts.			
(b) Look for indications of slow-moving, damaged or obsolete stocks.			
(c) Account for all stock-taking tags and count sheets used in physical count.			
5. Test clerical accuracy of stock records:			
(a) Recalculate extensions of quantities times unit prices.			
(b) Trace test counts to records.			
(c) Vouch items on stock listings to stock-taking tags and count sheets.			
6. Test stock pricing:			
(a) Examine supplier's paid invoices for purchased stock.			
(b) Obtain market quotations and perform lower of cost or net realisable value test.			
(c) Review perpetual stock records and purchasing records for indications of current activity.			
(d) Compare stocks with current sales catalogue and sales reports.			
(e) Inquire about slow-moving, excess, or obsolete stocks and determine need for write-downs.			
7. Confirm stocks at locations outside the entity.			
8. Examine consignment agreements and contracts.			
9. Confirm agreements for assignment and pledging of stocks.			
10. Review disclosures for stocks in drafts of the financial statements and determine conformity with the Companies Act and applicable Accounting Standards.			

Figure 9.5 *Illustrative audit programme for substantive procedures on stocks*

of substantive procedures in the audit of stock will be developed in more detail in Chapter 12.

Framework for developing audit programmes

Referring again to Figure 9.5 and to the previous discussion on designing substantive procedures, it is possible to construct a general framework for developing audit programmes for substantive procedures. Such an approach is described in Figure 9.6.

The steps listed in the upper portion of Figure 9.6 summarise the application of several important concepts and procedures explained in Chapters 5–7. Note that the first step listed in the lower portion of the figure corresponds to the first step in Figure 9.5. Because subsequent substantive procedures are often performed on the subsidiary records or supporting schedules prepared by the entity, or samples drawn therefrom, it is logical to start by ascertaining that the supporting records do tie in with the general ledger. When applicable, it is also logical to establish the agreement of opening balances with audited amounts in the prior year's working papers, so procedures performed in the current audit can be focused on the effects of transactions that occurred in the current period and the closing balance.

The specification of analytical procedures is considered next because, if effective procedures are available, they may reduce or eliminate the need for more expensive tests of details. Note that even though there are several analytical procedures listed in Step 2 of Figure 9.5, in the case of stocks, the normal requirement to observe stock-taking means tests of details cannot be entirely eliminated.

Tests of details of transactions are ordinarily considered next because they are usually performed during the interim audit at the same time as tests of control, often as dual-purpose tests. Finally, the programme should specify tests of details of balances, special requirements not previously addressed and procedures relating to the disclosure assertions. In specifying the latter procedures, auditors use knowledge of relevant business practices and financial reporting disclosure requirements such as, in the case of stocks, those pertaining to the method of valuation.

The general framework for developing audit programmes described in Figure 9.6 underpins the illustrations of audit programmes for substantive procedures presented in subsequent chapters of this text. Auditors generally adopt a consistent approach in developing audit programmes for recurring engagements, but there are some special considerations in developing audit programmes for initial engagements.

Often many of the choices in the preliminary planning part of Figure 9.6 will be input into a computer program designed to assist with developing audit programmes. The program will tailor procedures to the audit engagement based on the information entered, reducing the number of decisions required by the auditors in the second part of Figure 9.6, which specifies the substantive procedures.

Audit programmes in initial engagements

ISA 510, Initial Engagements – Opening Balances, identifies two matters as requiring special consideration during the design of audit programmes for initial engagements. These are:

GENERAL FRAMEWORK

Complete preliminary planning

1. Develop specific audit objectives for each financial statement assertion pertaining to closing stock balances (as illustrated in Table 9.3).

2. Assess inherent and control risk and determine the acceptable level of detection risk for each assertion consistent with the overall level of audit risk and applicable materiality level.

3. From knowledge acquired from procedures to obtain an understanding of the accounting and internal control systems, envision the accounting records, supporting documents, accounting process (including the audit trail), and financial reporting process pertaining to the assertions.

4. Consider options regarding the design of substantive procedures:

    • Alternatives for accommodating varying acceptable levels of detection risk:
        − Nature
            • Analytical procedures
            • Tests of details of transactions
            • Tests of details of balances
        − Timing: interim versus year-end
        − Extent: sample size.
    • Possible types of corroborating evidence available:

Analytical	Documentary	Mathematical	Physical
Confirmations	Electronic	Oral	Written representations

    • Possible types of audit procedures available:

Analytical procedures	Confirming	Observing
Computer-assisted	Counting	Reperforming
audit techniques	Inquiring	Tracing
	Inspecting	Vouching

Specify substantive procedures to be included in audit programme

1. Specify initial procedures to:

    (a) trace opening balances to prior year's working papers (if applicable);
    (b) review activity in applicable general ledger accounts and investigate unusual items;
    (c) verify totals of supporting records or schedules to be used in subsequent procedures and determine their agreement with general ledger balances, when applicable, to establish tie-in of detail with control accounts.

2. Specify analytical procedures to be performed.

3. Specify tests of details of transactions to be performed.

4. Specify tests of details of balances (in addition to 1(a), (b), and (c) above) to be performed.

5. Consider whether there are any special requirements or procedures applicable to assertions tested in the circumstances, such as procedures required by Auditing Standards or by regulatory agencies that have not been included in (3) and (4) above.

6. Specify procedures to determine that disclosure is in accordance with Companies Act and applicable Accounting Standards.

Figure 9.6 *General framework for developing audit programmes for substantive procedures*

1. determining the fairness of the account balances at the beginning of the period being audited; and
2. ascertaining the accounting principles used in the preceding period as a basis for determining the consistency of application of such principles in the current period.

The auditors will need to review the audit working papers of the predecessor auditor to ascertain whether they can rely on the previous work. If this is not possible, the auditors will need to attempt to gather information on the opening assets and liabilities as part of the current year's audit. If sufficient evidence cannot be gathered, the auditors may need to qualify the auditors' report based on a limitation of scope.

LEARNING **CHECK**

9.14 The audit programme details substantive procedures required to provide sufficient appropriate audit evidence for each material account balance assertion.

9.15 The written audit programme is listed in a sequence logical for performance of the audit, instead of by assertion, since many procedures provide evidence pertaining to more than one assertion.

9.16 Most audit firms have outline programmes which are tailored by reference to the details of the entity's documents and records and its audit trail, based on the understanding of the accounting system.

9.17 The audit programme has columns for recording references to working papers detailing the evidence obtained and results of tests, the initials of the staff member performing the procedures, and the date.

9.18 In developing the audit programme, auditors first identify the audit objectives, the primary evidence available from the accounting system and the alternative types of substantive procedure.

9.19 The auditors next consider the types of corroborating evidence available and methods of obtaining that evidence.

9.20 The finished programme will detail initial procedures, the separate analytical procedures and tests of details, special procedures required by regulations (if any), and procedures relevant to disclosure.

9.21 Additional procedures are required in initial engagements relating to opening balances and consistency of accounting principles.

SPECIAL CONSIDERATIONS IN DESIGNING SUBSTANTIVE PROCEDURES

The foregoing discussions of assessing detection risk, designing substantive procedures and developing audit programmes apply to all accounts. In this section we will note some special considerations relevant to designing substantive procedures.

Profit and loss statement accounts

Traditionally, tests of details of balances have focused more on financial statement assertions that pertain to balance sheet accounts than on profit and loss statement accounts.

This approach is both efficient and logical because each profit and loss statement account is inextricably linked to one or more balance sheet accounts. Examples are shown below.

BALANCE SHEET ACCOUNT	RELATED PROFIT AND LOSS STATEMENT ACCOUNT
Debtors	Sales
Stocks	Cost of sales
Prepaid expenses	Various related expenses
Investments	Investment income
Tangible fixed assets	Depreciation expense
Interest-bearing liabilities	Interest expense

The assertions for the accounts are linked as well. Evidence that debtors do not exist, for example, may indicate that sales did not occur (although it could also mean the entity failed to record a payment remitted by the customer). Similarly, if interest-bearing liabilities are not complete, then interest expense may not be complete, and so on. Generally, if there is an error or deliberate misstatement in profit and loss accounts, then there is a higher likelihood that it has occurred towards the end of the year and it will, therefore, affect the related balance sheet account.

Given these relationships, evidence obtained through substantive procedures applied to balance sheet accounts also provides much of the evidence required to achieve the desired level of detection risk for profit and loss account balances. For this reason, analytical procedures are frequently the only substantive procedures that must be specifically applied in verifying profit and loss statement account balances.

ANALYTICAL PROCEDURES FOR PROFIT AND LOSS STATEMENT ACCOUNTS

Analytical procedures can be a powerful audit tool in obtaining audit evidence about profit and loss statement balances. This type of substantive procedure may be used directly or indirectly. Direct tests occur when a revenue or an expense account is compared with other relevant data to determine the reasonableness of its balance. The ratio of sales commissions to sales, for example, can be compared with the ratios for prior years and with budget data for the current year. Comparisons can also be made with non-financial information, as shown in the following two examples.

ACCOUNT	ANALYTICAL PROCEDURE
Hotel room revenue	Number of rooms × occupancy rate × average room rate revenue
Wages expense	Average number of employees per pay period × average pay per period × number of pay periods

Indirect tests occur when evidence concerning profit and loss statement balances can be derived from analytical procedures applied to related balance sheet accounts. Debtors' turnover may be used in verifying debtors, for example, and the findings may have an impact on whether bad-debts expense and sales are fairly stated.

TESTS OF DETAILS FOR PROFIT AND LOSS STATEMENT ACCOUNTS
When the evidence obtained from analytical procedures and from tests of details of related balance sheet accounts does not reduce detection risk to an acceptably low level, direct tests of details of assertions pertaining to profit and loss statement accounts are necessary. This may be the case when:

- inherent risk is high, as in the case of assertions affected by non-routine transactions and management's judgements and estimates;
- control risk is high, such as when related internal controls for non-routine and routine transactions are ineffective, and when the auditors elect not to test the internal controls;
- analytical procedures reveal unusual relationships and unexpected fluctuations; or
- the account requires analysis – for example, legal expenses and professional fees, corporation tax, maintenance and repairs expenses, travel and entertainment expenses, and directors' remuneration.

Accounts involving accounting estimates

An accounting estimate is an approximation of a financial statement item in the absence of exact measurement. Examples of accounting estimates include depreciation, the provision for bad debts, and the provision for warranty claims. Management is responsible for establishing the process and controls for preparing accounting estimates. Judgement is required in making an accounting estimate as it may have a significant effect on an entity's financial statements.

ISA 540, Audit of Accounting Estimates, states that the auditors' objective in evaluating accounting estimates is to obtain sufficient appropriate audit evidence to provide reasonable assurance that the accounting estimates are reasonable in the circumstances and that they are appropriately disclosed.

In determining whether all necessary estimates have been made, the auditors should consider the industry in which the entity operates, its methods of conducting business, and any financial reporting pronouncements.

An entity's internal controls may reduce the likelihood of material misstatements of accounting estimates and thereby reduce the extent of substantive procedures. To evaluate the reasonableness of an estimate, ISA 540 explains that the auditors should normally concentrate on the key factors and assumptions used by management, including those that are significant to the accounting estimate; are sensitive to variations, and to deviations from historical patterns; and are subjective and susceptible to misstatement and bias.

Evidence of the reasonableness of an estimate may be obtained by the auditors from one or a combination of the following approaches:

- performance of procedures to review and test management's process in making the estimate;
- preparation of an independent estimate; or
- review of subsequent transactions and events that pertain to the estimate occurring prior to completing the audit.

The procedures to be performed include:

- considering the relevance, reliability and sufficiency of the data and other factors used by management;
- evaluating the reasonableness and consistency of the assumptions; and
- reperforming the calculations made by management.

In some cases, it may be useful to obtain the opinion of a specialist regarding the assumptions.

Fair value measurements and disclosures

On initial recognition assets and liabilities are valued at cost. They may be subsequently remeasured at fair value where fair value can be reliably determined. In the past this has rarely been the case. The increasing use by business entities of financial instruments which are usually capable of remeasurement, however, has increased the extent to which remeasurement is being applied.

ISA 545, Auditing Fair Value Measurements and Disclosures, outlines the auditors' responsibilities. They should obtain an understanding of the process of determining fair values and assess the risks of material misstatement. Further audit procedures are likely to include, in the first instance, making inquiry as to published price quotations in an active market. Where there is no active market the fair value may be based on a discounted cash flow analysis or a comparative transaction model. These approaches require assumptions to be made by management, the reasonableness of which must be evaluated by the auditors. The auditors then test the data used by management in developing the fair value measurements and disclosures. The final audit procedure is verifying that the fair value measurements have been properly derived from the data in accordance with management's assumptions.

Comparison of tests of control and substantive procedures

As indicated in Chapter 6, the third phase of an audit is performing audit procedures. These audit procedures consist of tests of control and substantive procedures. Table 9.4 on page 320 presents a summarised comparison of the two classes of test, including the types of test in each class, their purpose, and the risk component to which each class relates, among other factors.

 LEARNING **CHECK**

9.22 Much of the evidence for profit and loss account balances is derived from procedures applied to related balance sheet accounts. Otherwise, analytical procedures normally provide sufficient evidence directly related to profit and loss account balances.

9.23 A few profit and loss account balances require more specific evidence from tests of details.

Table 9.4 Summary of audit tests

	TESTS OF CONTROL	SUBSTANTIVE PROCEDURES
Types	Design effectiveness Operating effectiveness	Analytical procedures Tests of details of transactions Tests of details of balances
Purpose	Determine effectiveness of design and operation of the internal control structure	Determine truth and fairness of significant financial statement assertions
Nature of test measurement	Frequency of deviations from control structure policies and procedures	Monetary errors in transactions and balances
Applicable audit procedures	Inquiring, observing, inspecting, reperforming, and computer-assisted audit techniques	Same as tests of control, plus analytical procedures, counting, confirming, tracing and vouching
Timing	Primarily interim work(1)	Primarily at or shortly after balance sheet date(2)
Audit risk component	Control risk	Detection risk

Notes:
(1) Tests of the design effectiveness of controls are performed in audit planning with procedures to obtain an understanding of the internal control structure. Tests of the operating effectiveness of controls are performed during interim fieldwork.
(2) Tests of details of transactions may also be performed with tests of control as dual-purpose tests during interim fieldwork.

9.24 Account balances determined by management require special considerations including reviewing procedures adopted by management, independently determining the estimate, and confirming estimates by way of subsequent events.

SUMMARY

After obtaining an understanding of internal control relevant to an assertion and making a preliminary assessment of control risk, the auditors determine the preliminary audit strategy and the associated acceptable level of detection risk and level of substantive procedures. The auditors then plan specific substantive procedures to achieve the acceptable level of detection risk by exercising judgements about the nature, timing and extent of such procedures. The auditors also relate the tests to specific audit objectives to ensure that they meet the overall objective of rendering an opinion on the financial statements as a whole.

The types of substantive procedure performed on particular transaction classes, account balances and disclosures are discussed in more detail in the following chapters:

- Chapter 10 – Auditing sales and debtors;
- Chapter 11 – Auditing purchases, creditors and payroll;
- Chapter 12 – Auditing stocks and tangible fixed assets;
- Chapter 13 – Auditing cash and investments.

The auditors' decisions about the design of substantive procedures are documented in the form of written audit programmes, which provide an outline of the work to be done and a means for controlling the audit and recording the work performed. A general framework may be used in developing effective and efficient audit programmes for substantive procedures tailored to the entity's circumstances. There are special considerations in designing substantive procedures for selected types of account, including profit and loss accounts and accounts requiring estimation and remeasurement at fair value. Ultimately, for most audits, the performance of these substantive procedures will provide a large part of the audit evidence that auditors use to form an opinion on the financial statements (discussed further in Chapter 15).

FURTHER READING

Beasley, M. S., Carcello, J. V. & Hermanson, D. R. 'Top 10 Audit Deficiencies', *Journal of Accountancy* (April 2001).

Bell, T. B. & Wright, A. M. 'When Judgment Counts', *Journal of Accountancy* (November 1997), pp. 73–77.

Biggs, S. F., Mock, T. J. & Simnett, R. 'Analytical Procedures: Promise, Problems and Implications for Practice', *Australian Accounting Review* (Vol. 9, No. 1, 1999), pp. 42–52.

Blocher, E. & Patterson, G. F. Jr. 'The Use of Analytical Procedures', *Journal of Accountancy* (February 1996), pp. 53–55.

Colbert, J. L. 'International and US Standards – Audit Risk and Materiality', *Managerial Auditing Journal* (Vol. 11, No. 8, 1996), pp. 31–35.

Lin, K. Z., Fraser, I. A. M & Hatherly, D. J. 'Auditor Analytical Review Judgement: A Performance Evaluation', *British Accounting Review* (Vol. 35, Issue 1, 2003), pp. 19–35.

Menelaides, S., Graham, L. & Fischbach, G. 'The Auditor's Approach to Fair Value', *Journal of Accountancy* (June 2003), pp. 73–76.

Mock, T. J. & Wright, A. 'An Exploratory Study of Auditors' Evidential Planning Judgments', *Auditing: A Journal of Practice and Theory* (Fall 1993), pp. 39–61.

Mock, T. J. & Wright, A. 'Are Audit Program Plans Risk Adjusted?', *Auditing: A Journal of Practice and Theory* (Spring 1999), pp. 55–74.

Quadackers, L. M., Theodore, J. & Maijoor, S. 'Audit Risk and Audit Programmes: Archival Evidence from Four Dutch Audit Firms', *The European Accounting Review* (Vol. 5, No. 2, 1996), pp. 217–237.

Srinidhi, B. N. & Vasarhelyi, M. A. 'Auditors Judgment Concerning Establishment of Substantive Tests Based on Internal Control Reliability', *Auditing: A Journal of Practice and Theory* (Spring 1986), pp. 64–76.

Wright, A. & Wright, S. 'The Relationships Between Assessments of Internal Control Strength and Error Occurrence, Impact and Cause', *Accounting & Business Research* (Winter 1996), pp. 58–71.

MULTIPLE-CHOICE QUESTIONS

Choose the best answer for each of the following.
(Answers are on pages 601–602)

9.1 Which of the following is the only risk that can be manipulated by the auditors?
   (a) Control risk.
   (b) Detection risk.
   (c) Inherent risk.
   (d) Sampling risk.

9.2 If the acceptable level of detection risk decreases, the assurance directly provided from:
   (a) substantive procedures should increase.
   (b) substantive procedures should decrease.
   (c) tests of control should increase.
   (d) tests of control should decrease.

9.3 The auditor assesses control risk because it:
   (a) includes the aspects of non-sampling risk that are controllable.
   (b) indicates where inherent risk may be the greatest.
   (c) affects the level of detection risk the auditors may accept.
   (d) needs to be reported on in the auditors' report.

9.4 The auditor is more likely to use analytical review as a substantive test when:
   (a) planned detection risk is high.
   (b) inherent risk is assessed as high.
   (c) control risk is assessed as low.
   (d) planned audit risk is high.

9.5 Which of the following analytical procedures should be applied to the profit and loss statement?
   (a) Select sales and expense items and trace amounts to related supporting documents.
   (b) Ascertain that the net profit in the statement of cash flows agrees with the net profit in the profit and loss statement.
   (c) Obtain from the entity the opening and closing stock amounts that were used to determine the cost of sales.
   (d) Compare the actual revenues and expenses with the corresponding figures of the previous year, and investigate significant differences.

9.6 As the acceptable level of detection risk decreases, an auditor may change the:
   (a) assessed level of inherent risk to a lower amount.
   (b) timing of tests of control by performing them at several dates rather than at one time.
   (c) nature of substantive procedures, from a less effective to a more effective procedure.
   (d) timing of substantive procedures by performing them at an interim date rather than at year-end.

9.7 The procedures specifically outlined in an audit programme are primarily designed to:
   (a) protect the auditor in the event of litigation.
   (b) detect errors or irregularities.
   (c) test internal control structures.
   (d) gather evidence.

9.8 When would tests of details of profit and loss statement accounts be more likely to be required?

(a) When control risk is low.
(b) When substantial analytical procedures have been performed.
(c) When the auditor decides not to test the company's internal controls.
(d) When the analytical procedures do not show any unexpected relationships.

DISCUSSION QUESTIONS

9.1 Explain how the planned level of detection risk has an impact on the nature, timing and extent of substantive procedures.

9.2 Identify situations in which analytical procedures may provide sufficient substantive evidence for specific account balances.

9.3 Explain why cut-off tests are a special category of tests of details of transactions.

9.4 Explain why it is sometimes convenient for auditors to perform substantive procedures prior to the year-end, what additional procedures may need to be performed and under what conditions such a practice may provide sufficient evidence.

9.5 Identify situations when an auditor may perform tests of details on profit and loss statement balances instead of relying solely on analytical procedures.

9.6 Describe the nature of accounting estimates and consider why their audit constitutes a special challenge for the auditor.

9.7 There is general agreement that current values are preferable to historic costs providing there is sufficient evidence to determine their reliability. In practice, current values are rarely used. Is there more that auditors could do to encourage the remeasurement of assets at fair value?

PROFESSIONAL APPLICATION QUESTIONS

(Suggested answers are on pages 628–631)

9.1 Audit programme framework for substantive procedures

Buildwell Manufacturing Company was formed 10 years ago. At that time it took out a 30-year mortgage to purchase land and a factory building that continues to house all of its manufacturing, warehousing and office facilities. It also owns various manufacturing and office equipment acquired at various dates. It is in the process of constructing an addition to the factory building to provide more warehouse space. The addition is approximately 50% complete and should be completed during the next financial year. The general ledger for Buildwell includes the following accounts for plant assets: Land, Factory Building, Manufacturing Equipment, Office Equipment, and related accumulated depreciation control accounts for each of the last three accounts. The details of the cost and accumulated depreciation for each item of the manufacturing and office equipment are maintained in separate sections of a plant ledger. There is also a Construction-in-Progress account for the accumulated costs of the warehouse addition.

Buildwell is a new audit client for your accounting firm that has never been audited before. You have completed the preliminary planning for the audit of plant assets and are about to design substantive procedures. Under the circumstances, you have assessed both inherent and control risk as high for all fixed asset assertions.

Required

(a) Using only your general knowledge of accounting for property, plant and equipment assets and the general framework for developing an audit programme for substantive procedures described in this chapter, develop an audit programme for your first audit of the property, plant and equipment asset accounts of Buildwell Manufacturing Company.

(b) Following each procedure in your audit programme, indicate the assertion (or assertions) to which it applies by using the letters E, C, RO, V, and D for the existence, completeness, rights and obligations, valuation, and presentation and disclosure assertions, respectively.

9.2 Audit of accounting estimates

Coogee Ltd is a medium sized engineering company with an annual turnover of £23 million. Most of its sales are on credit. At its financial year-end of 31 December 1998 its sales ledger contained 2,000 accounts with balances ranging from £50 to £10,000 and totalling £2,300,000. As a staff member of Coogee's external auditors you have been assigned to the audit of the provision for bad and doubtful debts which has been set at £120,000. Your initial enquiries establish that £80,000 relates to the provision against specific bad and doubtful debts and £40,000 is a general provision determined as a percentage of overdue debtors with an increasing percentage being applied against the longest overdue accounts.

You are aware that ISA 540 *Audit of Accounting Estimates* is likely to be relevant to your audit of the provision for bad and doubtful debts.

Required

(a) Explain the approaches adopted by auditors in obtaining sufficient appropriate audit evidence regarding accounting estimates.

(b) Describe the procedures you would apply in verifying the general provision for bad and doubtful debts.

(c) Describe the procedures you would apply in verifying the specific provision for bad and doubtful debts.

(Adapted from Question 5, Audit Framework, June 1999. Reproduced by permission of ACCA)

CHAPTER 10

AUDITING SALES AND DEBTORS

OVERVIEW

AUDIT OBJECTIVES

SALES, CASH RECEIPTS AND SALES ADJUSTMENT TRANSACTIONS
Credit sales transactions
Cash receipts transactions
Sales adjustment transactions

DEVELOPING THE AUDIT PLAN
Audit strategy considerations
The control environment
Assessment of control risk
Final assessment

SUBSTANTIVE PROCEDURES
Determining detection risk
Designing substantive procedures

SUMMARY

FURTHER READING

MULTIPLE-CHOICE QUESTIONS

DISCUSSION QUESTIONS

PROFESSIONAL APPLICATION QUESTIONS

LEARNING **OBJECTIVES**

After studying this chapter, you should be able to:

1   identify the audit objectives applicable to sales and debtors

2   describe the functions and control procedures normally found in information systems for processing sales, cash receipts and sales adjustment transactions

3   apply the concepts of materiality and inherent risk to the audit of sales and debtors

4   discuss considerations relevant to determining the audit strategy for sales and debtors

5   design and execute tests of control over sales, cash receipts and sales adjustment transactions in order to assess control risk

6   indicate the factors relevant to determining an acceptable level of detection risk for the audit of sales and debtors

7   design a substantive audit programme for sales and debtors

8   explain the procedures for undertaking a confirmation of debtors' balances.

PROFESSIONAL STATEMENTS

ISA 315   Understanding the Entity and Its Environment and Assessing the Risks of Material Misstatement

ISA 505   External Confirmations

ISA 540   Audit of Accounting Estimates

The next four chapters apply the procedures explained in the preceding chapters to specific transaction classes, account balances and disclosures. This chapter examines the audit of the transaction classes of sales, cash receipts and sales adjustments and of the balance in the debtors (accounts receivable) account and the related disclosures.

This chapter is organised as follows:

- First, it identifies the audit objectives that apply to the relevant transaction classes, the account balance and related disclosures for each of the financial statement assertions explained in Chapter 5.
- Second, it describes (1) the procedures involved in sales, cash receipts and sales adjustment transactions, and (2) the internal control commonly associated with these procedures that will be identified in the course of 'obtaining the understanding' required by ISA 315, Understanding the Entity and Its Environment and Assessing the Risks of Material Misstatement.
- Third, it considers factors relevant to developing the audit plan, including determining the risks of material misstatement and using that knowledge to determine the appropriate audit strategy (see Chapter 6).
- Fourth, it explains the design of the audit programme including tests of control as described in Chapter 7 and substantive procedures, using the methodology introduced in Chapter 9.

AUDIT OBJECTIVES

The audit objectives for sales and debtors relate to obtaining sufficient appropriate evidence about each significant assertion for the applicable transactions and balances. The

Table 10.1 Selected specific audit objectives for sales and debtors

ASSERTION CATEGORY	TRANSACTION CLASS AUDIT OBJECTIVES	ACCOUNT BALANCE AUDIT AND DISCLOSURE OBJECTIVES
Existence or occurrence	Recorded sales transactions represent goods shipped (**EO1**) Recorded cash receipts transactions represent cash received (**EO2**) Recorded sales adjustment transactions represent authorised discounts, returns and allowances, and bad debts (**EO3**)	Debtors' balances represent amounts owed by customers at the balance sheet date (**EO4**)
Completeness	All sales (**C1**), cash receipts (**C2**) and sales adjustment (**C3**) transactions that occurred have been recorded	Debtors include all claims on customers at the balance sheet date (**C4**)
Rights and obligations	The entity has rights to the debtor's balance (**RO1**) and cash (**RO2**) resulting from recorded sales transactions	Debtors at the balance sheet date represent legal claims of the entity on customers for payment (**RO3**)
Accuracy, classification and valuation	All sales (**ACV1**), cash receipts (**ACV2**) and sales adjustment (**ACV3**) transactions are correctly journalised, summarised and posted to the correct accounts	Debtors represent gross claims on customers at the balance sheet date and agree with the sum of the sales subsidiary ledger (**ACV4**) The provision for bad debts represents a reasonable estimate of the difference between gross debtors and their net realisable value (**ACV5**)
Cut-off	All sales (**C-O1**), cash receipts (**C-O2**) and sales adjustment transactions (**C-O3**) are recorded in the correct accounting period	
Presentation and disclosure	The details of sales (**PD1**), cash receipts (**PD2**) and sales adjustment (**PD3**) transactions support their presentation in the financial statements, including their classification and related disclosures	Debtors are properly identified and classified in the balance sheet (**PD4**) Appropriate disclosures have been made concerning debts that have been factored or otherwise assigned (**PD5**)

principal audit objectives for these transaction classes and account balances are shown in Table 10.1. These objectives are those that would apply to most merchandising entities selling on credit; they are not intended to apply to all entity situations.

To achieve each of these specific audit objectives, auditors employ a combination of tests of control (as described in Chapter 7) and substantive procedures (as described in Chapter 9) as determined by the audit strategy adopted (as described in Chapter 6). Each audit objective is numbered (**EO1, EO2, Cl,** and so on) in Table 10.1. Specific controls and audit procedures described in this chapter will be referenced, using this numbering system, to the applicable audit objective.

◁ LEARNING **CHECK**

10.1 The debtors' balance is determined by transactions relating to sales, cash receipts and sales adjustments.

10.2 Audit objectives for sales and debtors relate to each assertion for each of the three transaction classes and for the balance of debtors and related disclosures.

SALES, CASH RECEIPTS AND SALES ADJUSTMENT TRANSACTIONS

These transactions arise out of the processes of selling goods and services to customers and collecting the revenue in cash. The three principal functions are those of sales, cash receipts and sales adjustments, and their related information systems and control procedures are described in the following sections. Where sales are made on credit, the information system also needs to maintain records of debtors. The use of a sales ledger will also be described as appropriate. Where applicable, control functions are keyed to the audit objectives identified in Table 10.1 using the bold symbols (such as **EO1**). The discussions and illustrations in this section are based on a company selling goods. However, much of the commentary can easily be adapted to other types of entity.

Credit sales transactions

Sales orders may be taken over the counter, via the telephone, by mail order, through sales representatives, by facsimile or by electronic data interchange. The goods may be picked up by the customer or shipped by the seller. The accounting for sales transactions may be done manually or with a computer – in real time or batch processing mode. This section begins by identifying the separate functions involved in making credit sales transactions; the documents and records that are used in processing the transactions; and the control procedures that are interwoven into each to reduce the risk of misstatements in the financial statements. As was explained in Chapter 7, control activities include information processing controls, physical controls, the segregation of duties and performance reviews. Information processing controls specific to credit sales transactions include, in addition to documents and records, proper authorisation and independent checks.

FUNCTIONS

The processing of credit sales transactions involves a sequence of steps or credit sales functions as follows:

- accepting customer orders;
- approving credit;
- filling and dispatching sales orders;
- invoicing customers; and
- recording the sales.

Accepting customer orders

Sales orders need to be checked for their authenticity, the acceptability of terms and conditions, and the availability of stock. Orders submitted in writing on a customer order provide ready evidence of authenticity. Telephone orders from businesses are sometimes authenticated by requiring an order number, even though no written order is submitted. Specification of an order number provides reasonable assurance that the order has been issued in accordance with the customer's purchasing procedures, as will be described in Chapter 11. Terms and conditions relate to matters such as prices, delivery dates, modifications, etc. Sales clerks will accept only orders that meet the entity's normal terms. In some businesses, it is necessary to check the availability of the goods in stock before accepting an order. Any orders not meeting the above checks need to be referred to a supervisor with the authority to accept orders that depart from normal entity policy.

Once accepted, the order is recorded on a multi-copy sales order, which is a form showing the description of the goods, the quantity ordered and other relevant data. It is signed by the clerk accepting the order and serves as the basis for internal processing of the customer order. Sales orders are commonly pre-numbered in case they are mislaid and thus business is lost. This represents the start of the transaction trail of documentary evidence and confirms the existence of a valid order. It thus relates to audit objectives **EO1** and **RO1** in Table 10.1. Information on open (unfilled) and filled sales orders is usually maintained in hard-copy files in the sales order department and/or in computer files.

External auditors have little interest in the acceptance of orders. Potential risks are the loss of business and the acceptance of unprofitable business, which are unlikely to lead to misstatements in recorded transactions.

Approving credit
Order acceptance is normally entrusted to the sales department. However, although the sales department is unlikely to accept unprofitable orders, because they will have an adverse effect on departmental performance, the department may accept orders from customers who are poor credit risks. Debt collection is normally an accounting function; bad debt losses are not recognised until months after the sale, and responsibility for the loss is rarely blamed on the sales department. For these reasons, credit approval is separated from sales order acceptance, and it is the responsibility of an independent credit department. This prevents sales personnel from subjecting the entity to undue credit risks to boost sales.

A credit check is made of any new customer, which may include obtaining a credit report from a rating agency such as Experian. The credit supervisor would then determine an appropriate credit limit and record this on a newly created customer record. For existing customers, a credit department employee compares the amount of the order with the customer's authorised credit limit and the current balance owed by the customer. Credit approval would normally be refused if the order would take the balance over the customer's credit limit or if the account were overdue. To indicate approval (or non-approval) of credit, an authorised credit department employee signs or initials the sales order form and returns it to the sales order department.

For auditors, controls over credit approval reduce the risk of a sales transaction being initially recorded in an amount in excess of the amount of cash expected to be realised, and thus contributes to audit objective **ACV1**. The expectations of realisability for some of these amounts will change over time, resulting in the need for a provision for bad debts. Controls over credit approval enable management to make a more reliable estimate of the size of the provision needed (**ACV5**).

Filling and dispatching sales orders
A copy of the approved sales order form is usually sent to the warehouse as authorisation to fill the order and release the goods to the shipping department (or dispatch area).

Because the order form constitutes the source of credits to stock records, the issue of goods by the storekeepers without such authorisation will result in an apparent stock shortage for which they are held accountable. Segregation of the custody of stock from the maintenance of stock records and the physical check of verifying recorded accountability reduces the risk of stock shortages caused by the unrecorded (and possibly unauthorised) release of stock. Control over stock will be described in Chapter 12.

Segregating responsibility for dispatch from responsibility for approving and filling orders prevents dispatch clerks from making unauthorised shipments (**EO1**). In addition, dispatch clerks are normally required to make independent checks to determine that goods received from the warehouse are accompanied by an approved sales order form.

The dispatch function involves preparing multi-copy dispatch notes. Dispatch notes can be prepared manually on pre-numbered forms or produced by the computer using order information already logged into the computer, with appropriate delivery data added (such as quantities shipped, carrier details, freight charges and so on). In a manual system, the multi-copy sales order documentation may include a copy to act as a dispatch note, thus retaining the same numerical control. In any event, the dispatch note must be pre-numbered. Subsequent checks of the numerical continuity of dispatch notes invoiced ensure completeness of recorded sales transactions (**Cl**). Pre-numbering dispatch notes also helps in establishing cut-off at the year-end (**C-O1**). Gatekeepers are sometimes required to check that drivers of all vehicles leaving the premises possess dispatch notes for the goods in their vehicle, as a double-check against failure to record deliveries.

Dispatch notes provide evidence that goods were shipped and thus of the occurrence of the credit sale (**EO1**), giving rise to a claim against the customer within debtors (**RO1**). Some entities obtain a copy of the dispatch note, signed by the customer on receipt of the goods, as evidence of the claim on the customer.

Invoicing customers

The invoicing function involves preparing and sending sales invoices to customers. Applicable control objectives for invoicing are that:

- all deliveries are invoiced to customers;
- only actual deliveries are invoiced (and there should be no duplicate invoices or fictitious transactions); and
- deliveries are invoiced at authorised prices and the invoice amount is accurately calculated.

Control procedures designed to achieve these objectives are likely to include the following:

- segregating invoicing from the foregoing functions (**EO1, Cl**);
- checking the existence of a dispatch note and matching the approved sales order before each invoice is prepared (**EO1**);
- using an authorised price list in preparing the sales invoices (**ACV1**);
- performing independent checks on the pricing and mathematical accuracy of sales invoices (**ACV1**); and

- comparing control totals for dispatch notes with corresponding totals for sales invoices (**EO1, CI**).

File copies of the sales invoices are usually maintained in the invoicing department.

Recording the sales

The primary control objective is to ensure that sales invoices are recorded accurately and in the proper period, which is usually when the goods are shipped.

In a manual system, the recording process involves entering sales invoices in a sales journal, posting the invoices to the sales subsidiary ledger, and posting the sales journal totals to the general ledger. It is common practice for invoices to be entered separately in the sales journal and the sales ledger. The sales ledger balance is periodically agreed with the general ledger control account (**ACV4**). Failure of the balances on the sales ledger to agree in total with the control account in the general ledger indicates that an error has been made. A further control is the use of prelists, whereby the total of invoices entered in the sales journal is agreed with the total of sales invoices posted to the sales ledger (**ACV1**). Sales invoices should also be entered in numerical sequence and a check should be made on missing numbers (**CI**). A monthly customer statement must be sent to each customer to provide the customer with an opportunity to alert a designated accounting supervisor, who is not otherwise involved in the execution or recording of sales transactions, if the balance does not agree with the customer's records (**EO1, RO1**).

As indicated above, balances on the sales ledger should be regularly and independently agreed to the balance on the control account in the general ledger. Periodic performance reviews by sales executives of sales analysed by product, division, salesperson or region, along with comparisons with budgets, contribute to controls over sales transactions.

Computer information systems

In on-line systems, once an order has been entered into the computer, the computer can be programmed to validate the customer credit, check stock availability and issue the necessary instructions to the dispatch department. On delivery, the dispatch department can enter the necessary shipping details and the computer will automatically produce the invoice and update the accounts receivable master file, as well as the related stock and general ledger files. Additionally, the computer information system will maintain a sales transactions file or equivalent data within a database system. Important controls in such a system include access controls, programmed application controls and controls over standing data files.

Access controls should permit read-only access to transaction and master files except for authorised individuals. Those with authority should have prescribed limits to that authority. For example, the credit controller may have the right to override rejections of orders when an order marginally breaches a customer's credit limit, and the sales manager may have the right to amend price or discount rates for individual customers or sales transactions.

Programmed application controls should include checks to ensure that:

- only orders from customers on the accounts receivable master file are accepted;
- only orders for goods in the entity's product range are accepted;

- the numerical continuity of documents is assured;
- transactions are chased at regular intervals;
- duplicate document numbers are rejected; and
- unreasonable quantities, amounts and dates are queried.

The correctness of standing data is of particular significance in a computer information system. Standing data in a sales system include authorised customers, their credit limits and product sales prices. Access controls should ensure that only authorised officers can amend standing data. For example, only the credit controller can add new customers and vary the credit limits of existing customers, and only the sales director can amend selling prices. As an added precaution, standing data should be periodically printed out for approval.

ILLUSTRATIVE SYSTEM FOR PROCESSING CREDIT SALES

There are many variations in the systems used to perform the functions involved in processing credit sales transactions. Figure 10.1 shows a flow chart of an on-line/batch-entry processing system that incorporates most of the controls discussed in the preceding sections.

In the illustrated system, as orders are received, sales order clerks use on-line terminals and an order program to determine that the customer has been approved and that the order will not cause the customer's balance to exceed the customer's authorised credit limit. The program also checks the stock master file to determine that goods are on hand to fill the order. If the order is accepted, the computer enters it into an open order file and produces a multi-copy sales order form on a printer in the sales order department. When an order is not accepted, a message is displayed on the terminal, indicating the reason for rejection.

Copies of the approved sales order are forwarded to the warehouse as authorisation to release goods to dispatch. In dispatch, personnel make an independent check on the agreement of the goods received with the accompanying sales order form. They then use their on-line terminals and a dispatch program to retrieve the corresponding sales order from the open order file and add appropriate dispatch data. Next, the computer transfers the transaction from the open order file to a dispatch file and produces a dispatch note on the printer in the dispatch department.

As matching dispatch notes and sales order forms are received in the invoicing department, they are batched and batch totals are manually prepared. Using their on-line terminals and an invoicing program, invoicing department personnel first enter the manually prepared batch totals. Next, they retrieve the previously entered order and dispatch data for each transaction from the dispatch file, and generate a sales invoice using prices from the master price file. As each invoice is completed, the computer enters it into a sales transactions file. After all the transactions in a batch have been processed in this manner, the invoicing program compares a computer-generated batch total with the manual batch total previously entered by the invoicing clerk. Discrepancies are displayed on the terminal and corrected by the invoicing clerks before processing continues. Finally, sales invoices for the batch are printed in the computer department and distributed as shown in the flow chart.

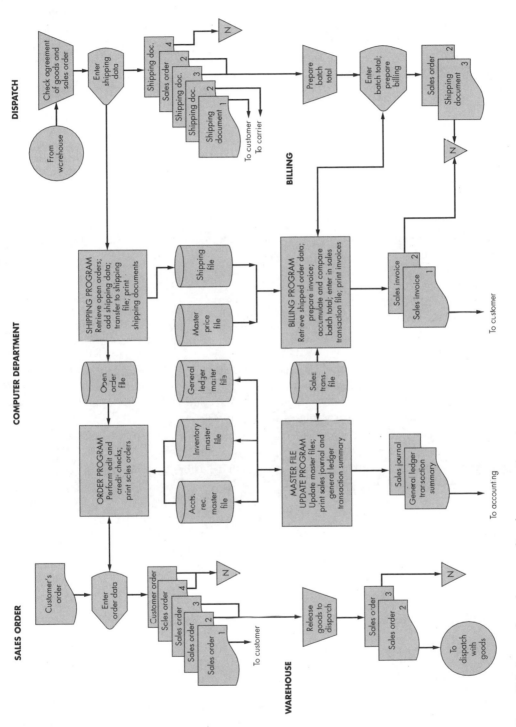

Figure 10.1 *System flow chart – credit sales transactions*

The recording of sales transactions is completed at the end of each day when the computer department runs the master file update program. As shown in Figure 10.1, this program updates three master files and produces a sales journal and a general ledger transaction summary, which are sent to accounting. The use of separate programs to produce monthly customer statements and periodic sales analyses for use in performance reviews is not shown in the flow chart.

Cash receipts transactions

Cash receipts result from a variety of activities. The scope of this section is limited to the information systems for processing and recording cash receipts from cash sales and collections from customers on credit sales.

FUNCTIONS
The processing of receipts from cash and credit sales involves the following cash receipts functions:

- receiving cash;
- depositing cash in bank; and
- recording the receipts.

Receiving cash
A major risk is that cash being paid by customers is stolen before it is recorded. For control purposes, accountability measures must be in place from the moment cash is received, and the cash must be subsequently safeguarded. A second risk is the possibility of errors occurring in the subsequent processing of the receipts.

OVER-THE-COUNTER RECEIPTS
For over-the-counter receipts, the use of a cash register or point-of-sale terminal is indispensable. These devices provide:

- immediate visual display, for the customer, of the amount of the cash sale and the cash tendered;
- a printed receipt for the customer and an internal record of the transaction on a computer file or a tape locked inside the register; and
- printed control totals of the day's receipts.

The customer's expectation of a printed receipt and supervisory surveillance of over-the-counter sales transactions helps to ensure that all cash sales are processed through the cash registers or terminals (C2). In addition, there should be an independent check of the agreement of cash on hand with the totals printed by the register or terminal (EO2, C2, ACV2). The cash is then forwarded to the cashier's department for deposit in the bank, together with the register or terminal-printed totals.

Increasingly, customers pay by use of credit or debit cards. These payments are processed via on-line terminals linked to the bank or other card issuer, which validates the transaction. Staff need to be properly trained in the use of such terminals and in procedures to be followed where the transaction is refused. Procedures must be in place for reconciling card sales with cash register totals as part of the daily agreement of cash on hand. Amounts due from card issuers also need to be recorded and agreed with subsequent payments. The use of credit and debit cards also facilitates the acceptance of mail or telephone orders from customers without the need for creditworthiness checks once the card transaction has been validated. Because no cash handling is involved, such transactions reduce the costs of banking and the risks of misappropriations, and are often preferred despite the commission payable to the card issuer.

MAIL RECEIPTS

There should always be at least two clerks responsible for mail opening so they would need to be in collusion if they were to misappropriate any cash receipts in the mail. They should immediately restrictively endorse cheques for deposit only, which is done by impressing a rubber stamp imprinted with the words 'for deposit to the account of …' on the face of the cheques. If it falls into the wrong hands, such a cheque cannot subsequently be endorsed for payment to the person acting fraudulently. All cash received through the mail should be listed, such as in a rough cash book. This record then serves for use in independent checks on the completeness and accuracy of processing. All of these procedures ensure that mail receipts are not misappropriated (**C2**).

Most cash receipts will be attached to or accompanied by a remittance advice indicating the payee and the particulars of the payment being made. The cheques will be forwarded to the cashier's department for banking, with a copy of the listing made referred to as a prelist. Remittance advices (or other details of the payment enclosed with the cash receipt) are forwarded to sales ledger accounting for posting to the sales ledger.

Major suppliers also pay by credit transfer. Such payments may be identified as part of the bank reconciliation process (see Chapter 13). Because this can lead to delays in recording receipts, entities receiving payments this way usually have on-line access to their bank account, linked to the accounts receivable master file which automatically detects credit transfers and updates the accounts receivable records.

Depositing cash in bank

All cash receipts must be deposited intact daily. Intact means all receipts should be deposited, not used to make payments. This reduces the risk that cash receipts will not be recorded (**C2**) and the resulting bank deposit record establishes the occurrence of the transactions (**EO2**).

When the cashier receives over-the-counter and mail receipts, he or she should check that the cash agrees with both the accompanying register total and the prelist (**EO2, C2, ACV2**). Details of cash receipts are then entered on a daily cash summary and the bank deposit slip is prepared in duplicate. The cash is deposited in the bank and the copy of the deposit slip is receipted by the bank and retained by the cashier. The daily cash summary is forwarded to the general accounting department.

Recording the receipts

To ensure that only valid transactions are entered, access to the accounting records or computer program should be restricted to authorised personnel (**EO2**). In manual systems, the duties of journalising the cash receipt and of posting the receipt to customer accounts are segregated. The daily cash summary is used to enter the cash receipts journal, distinguishing between receipts from cash sales and from credit sale customers. Posting the receipts to the sales ledger may be done in sales ledger accounting, based on the remittance advices received from the mail room (**ACV2**). In computerised processing, it is common for accounts receivable ledger clerks to use a terminal to enter mail receipts into a cash receipts transactions file, which is subsequently used in updating both the accounts receivable and general ledger master files.

To ensure the completeness and accuracy of recording mail receipts, independent checks are made of:

- the agreement of the amounts journalised and posted with the amounts shown in the rough cash book kept by the mail room; and
- the agreement of total amounts journalised and posted for over-the-counter and mail receipts with the daily cash summary and receipted deposit slips retained by the cashier (**C2, ACV2**).

In addition, an employee not otherwise involved in executing or recording cash transactions should perform periodic bank reconciliations.

Computer information systems

Opportunities for automating accounting for cash receipts involving currency and cheques are limited, which is why many companies are moving to on-line banking and direct debit and credit transfer systems. However, the use of point-of-sale cash register terminals provides controls over the pricing of goods sold and over stock management.

ILLUSTRATIVE SYSTEM FOR PROCESSING CASH RECEIPTS

There are many variations in systems for processing cash receipts. A flow chart for an illustrative system of processing mail receipts is presented in Figure 7.9 on page 250. Readers should review this flow chart and the accompanying narrative before proceeding further.

Sales adjustment transactions

Sales adjustment transactions involve the following functions:

- granting cash discounts;
- allowing sales returns and allowances; and
- determining bad debts.

The number and value of these transactions vary significantly among entities. However, where material, the potential for misstatements resulting from errors and irregularities in the processing of these transactions is considerable. Of primary concern is the possibility of fictitious sales adjustment transactions being recorded to conceal misappropriations of cash receipts. An employee may, for example, conceal misappropriation of cash received from a customer by writing the customer's account off against the provision for bad debts, or by overstating cash discounts or sales returns and allowances. Controls useful in reducing the risk of such frauds focus on establishing the validity of such transactions (EO3). They include:

- the proper authorisation of all sales adjustment transactions, such as requiring treasurer's office authority for the write-off of bad debts (EO3);
- the use of appropriate documents and records – in particular, an approved credit memo for granting credit for returned or damaged goods, and an approved write-off authorisation memo for writing off bad debts; and
- the segregation of the duties of authorising sales adjustment transactions and of handling and recording cash receipts.

◁ LEARNING **CHECK**

10.3 In accepting customer orders, laid down procedures should ensure that only those orders meeting the entity's normal terms of business are accepted.

10.4 Credit approval must be segregated from order acceptance.

10.5 Procedures should ensure that goods are delivered only to those customers whose orders have been properly approved.

10.6 The completeness of records of dispatch is important in ensuring that all goods delivered are invoiced.

10.7 The reconciliation of sales ledger balances with the general ledger control account, the sending of monthly statements to customers and the comparison of sales with budgets are all important independent checks in ensuring the accuracy of recording of the related transactions and balances.

10.8 Controls over the completeness of recorded cash receipts are of great importance. For over-the-counter sales, this is achieved by using cash registers and, for postal receipts, by segregating mail opening from the recording of cash receipts and posting to the sales ledger.

10.9 The nature and materiality of sales adjustments vary widely between entities. In general, controls should ensure that only properly authorised adjustments may be made.

DEVELOPING THE AUDIT PLAN

This section explains how auditors develop the audit plan for sales and debtors. This requires an assessment of the risks of material misstatement. First, we will illustrate how the auditors use the concepts of materiality and inherent risk. Second, we will describe factors to be considered by the auditors, in assessing the control environment within which the information system and control procedures operate. Third, we will illustrate the assessment of inherent and control risks using tests of design effectiveness and tests of operating effectiveness. Finally, we will explain how the procedures result in the development of the detailed audit programme (described in Chapter 9) used in directing audit staff and controlling their work.

Audit strategy considerations

Audit strategy refers to the mix of tests of control and substantive procedures to be applied in the audit. The main determinants of the mix are the assessed levels of inherent and control risks. Materiality considerations also influence the level of substantive procedures. This section will begin by considering the materiality of the relevant transactions and balances. Factors related to inherent and control risks, and the implications of both materiality and inherent and control risks in determining the audit strategy, will then be considered.

MATERIALITY

Sales transactions are the principal source of operating revenue for most business enterprises. The debtors' balance produced by credit sales transactions is material to the balance sheet for all businesses except those transacting most of their sales for cash. Cash balances at a particular balance sheet date may not be material, but the flow of cash associated with sales transactions is nearly always material. The significance of sales adjustment transactions varies considerably from one entity to another. However, the bad debts expense is often material to the profit and loss of entities that sell to customers on credit. Most of the audit objectives for sales and debtors that are depicted in Table 10.1 are important in arriving at an opinion on the financial statements as a whole.

INHERENT AND CONTROL RISKS

In assessing inherent risk for financial statement assertions, auditors should consider pervasive factors that may affect assertions in many transaction classes and account balances, as well as factors that may only pertain to specific assertions affecting sales and debtors. These factors include:

- pressure to overstate sales so as to report that announced sales or profitability targets were achieved when they were not. Such reporting includes:
  - recording fictitious sales;
  - holding the books open to record subsequent period sales in the current year (improper cut-off);
  - shipping unordered goods to customers near the year-end and recording them as sales in the current period only to have them returned in the subsequent period;
- pressure to overstate cash and debtors or understate the provision for bad debts, in order to report a higher level of working capital in the face of liquidity problems or going-concern doubts.

Other factors that could contribute to the possibility of misstatements in sales and debtors' assertions include:

- the volume of sales, cash receipts and sales adjustment transactions, resulting in numerous opportunities for errors to occur;
- contentious issues relating to the timing of revenue recognition, such as the effect of purchasers' rights of return;
- susceptibility to misappropriation of liquid assets generated by cash receipts; and
- the use of sales adjustment transactions to conceal thefts of cash received from customers by overstating discounts, recording fictitious sales returns or writing off customers' balances as uncollectable.

Recognising these risks, management usually adopts extensive internal controls to address them. Thus, auditors need also to consider the extent to which inherent risks are properly addressed by the internal control structure in deciding on the appropriate audit strategy for sales and debtors' assertions.

AUDIT STRATEGY

Given the materiality of sales and debtors, auditors must take care in assessing inherent and control risks, and in determining the audit strategy. The principal inherent risk is that of overstatement of sales revenue and debtors' balances. In the audit of transaction classes, this relates to the occurrence, cut-off and accuracy assertions for sales transactions, and to the completeness assertion for cash receipts and sales adjustments. In most entities, controls relative to these assertions for sales and cash receipts are effective and auditors are able to adopt a lower assessed level of control risk strategy for these transaction classes. Given the variety of sales adjustment transactions in some entities (and their infrequency in others), control risk may be higher for all assertions applicable to such transactions, requiring a predominantly substantive audit strategy.

Although controls over occurrence and completeness assertions of sales transactions are normally effective, this may not extend to the case of balance sheet date cut-off because this is only of significance at that particular date. A predominantly substantive approach is, therefore, commonly adopted in verifying cut-off.

In the design of substantive audit procedures, the large volume of sales and cash receipt transactions means that it is normally cost-effective to obtain most of the evidence from the application of substantive procedures to the debtors' balance.

The control environment

The control environment may contain several factors that may mitigate several of the inherent risks discussed earlier in this chapter. In addition, the control environment may enhance or negate the effectiveness of other internal control components in controlling the risk of misstatements in sales and debtors' assertions.

Management's adoption of and adherence to high standards of 'integrity' and 'ethical values' is a key control environment factor in reducing the risk of fraudulent financial reporting through the overstatement of sales and debtors. Related aspects include the elimination of incentives for dishonest reporting – such as undue emphasis on meeting sales or profit targets – and of temptations – such as an indifferent or ineffective board of directors and audit committee.

Inherent risks related to contentious accounting issues may be controlled if management has made the appropriate 'commitment to competence' on the part of chief financial officers and accounting personnel. In obtaining an understanding of this factor, the auditors will make inquiries of personnel, review personnel files and consider prior experience with the entity.

'Management's philosophy and operating style' are defined by a number of factors. These include its propensity for either conservative or aggressive selection from alternative accounting policies, and its conscientiousness and conservatism in developing accounting estimates, such as the provisions for bad debts and sales returns.

The control environment is enhanced when the 'assignment of authority and responsibility' for all activities in the revenue cycle is clearly communicated, such as through written job descriptions.

A number of special 'personnel policies and practices' are often adopted for employees who handle cash receipts. These include having such employees take mandatory vacations and periodically rotating their duties. The thrust of these controls is to deter dishonesty by making employees aware that they may not be able to conceal their misdeeds permanently. Some embezzlements from banks and other entities, for example, have been traced to the seemingly dedicated employee who held the same job without taking a vacation for 10, 20 or more years so as not to disrupt his or her routine of concealment.

Assessment of control risk

As explained in Chapter 7, this procedure initially involves evaluating the design of internal controls and considering their effectiveness in preventing or detecting any material misstatements that might occur. If the auditors consider that a lower assessed level of control risk strategy is appropriate, they will also plan and perform tests of control to determine that they are operating effectively.

The auditors must also identify any areas where substantive procedures alone would be unlikely to provide sufficient evidence. This is commonly the case with the completeness of receipts from cash sales. In such cases auditors must test the operating effectiveness of such controls even if no other tests of controls are performed.

SALES
This section is concerned with credit sales. We will consider the assessment of control risk for cash sales in the next section on cash receipts.

Tests of design effectiveness
Table 10.2 contains a partial listing of possible misstatements, necessary controls, potential tests of the operating effectiveness of controls, and the specific transaction class audit objectives for credit sales to which each relates. Using the understanding of the information system the auditors will identify the presence of necessary controls and make a preliminary assessment of control risk.

Where transactions are processed by a computer information system, the auditors will also need to consider the effectiveness of general controls over computer operations. Refer to Figure 7.3 on page 228, which describes control risk assessment considerations for general controls over computer information systems.

Table 10.2 Control risk assessment considerations – credit sales transactions

FUNCTION	POTENTIAL MISSTATEMENT	NECESSARY CONTROL	POSSIBLE TEST OF OPERATING EFFECTIVENESS	RELEVANT TRANSACTION CLASS AUDIT OBJECTIVE (FROM TABLE 10.1)				
				EO1	C1	RO1	ACV1	PD1
Accepting customer orders	Sales may be made to unauthorised customers	Determination that customer is on approved customer list	Observe procedure; reperform	✓				
		Approved sales order form for each sale	Examine approved sales order forms	✓				
Approving credit	Sales may be made without credit approval	Credit department credit check on all new customers	Inquire about procedures for checking credit on new customers				✓	
		Check on customer's credit limit prior to each sale	Examine evidence of credit limit check prior to each sale				✓	
Filling sales orders	Goods may be released from warehouse for unauthorised orders	Approved sales order for all goods released to dispatch	Observe warehouse personnel filling orders	✓				
Shipping sales orders	Goods dispatched may not agree with goods ordered	Independent check by dispatch clerks of agreement of goods received from warehouse with approved sales order	Examine evidence of performance of independent check	✓	✓			
	Unauthorised shipments may be made	Segregation of duties for filling and dispatching orders	Observe segregation of duties	✓				
		Preparation of dispatch note for each shipment	Inspect dispatch notes	✓				
Invoicing customers	Invoices may be made for fictitious transactions, or duplicate invoices may be made	Matching dispatch note and approved sales order for each invoice	Vouch invoices to dispatch notes and approved sales orders	✓				

(continued overleaf)

341

Table 10.2 (*continued*)

FUNCTION	POTENTIAL MISSTATEMENT	NECESSARY CONTROL	POSSIBLE TEST OF OPERATING EFFECTIVENESS	RELEVANT TRANSACTION CLASS AUDIT OBJECTIVE (FROM TABLE 10.1)				
				EO1	C1	RO1	ACV1	PD1
	Some shipments may not be invoiced	Matching sales invoice for each dispatch note	Trace dispatch notes to sales invoices *		✓			
		Periodic accounting for all dispatch notes	Observe procedure; reperform		✓			
	Sales invoices may have incorrect prices	Independent check on pricing of invoices	Inspect copy invoice for evidence of performance Reperform check on accuracy of pricing *				✓	
Recording the sales	Fictitious sales transactions may be recorded	Sales invoice and matching documents required for all entries	Vouch recorded sales to supporting documents *	✓		✓	✓	
	Invoices may not be journalised or posted to customer accounts	Independent check of agreement of sales journal entries and amounts posted to customer accounts with control totals of invoices	Review evidence of independent check; reperform check; trace sales invoices to sales journal and customer accounts *		✓		✓	
		Periodic accounting for all sales invoices	Observe procedure; reperform *		✓			
	Invoices may be posted to wrong customer account	Chart of accounts and supervisory review	Observe procedures; reperform *					✓
		Mailing of monthly statements to customers with independent follow-up of customer complaints	Observe mailing and follow-up procedures *	✓	✓	✓	✓	✓

Note: *Tests are sometimes performed as part of dual-purpose tests.

Tests of operating effectiveness

Tests of control designed to provide evidence of operating effectiveness involve a variety of audit procedures, including reperformance of certain control procedures by the auditors. Statistical or non-statistical sampling procedures (see Chapter 8) may be applied in the performance of some tests. In designing tests, the auditors need to remember that the direction of testing should be backward along the audit trail when the objective is to test controls over the occurrence assertion, and forward along the audit trail when the objective is to test controls over the completeness assertion. As an example, a sample of invoices from the sales journal would be vouched back to sales orders or shipping documents to test occurrence; to test completeness, a sample of sales orders or shipping documents would be traced to the sales journal to determine that all the transactions were recorded. The auditors must document the tests of controls performed, the evidence obtained and the conclusions reached. A formal audit programme that incorporates several of the tests from Table 10.2 is presented in Figure 10.2. As explained in Chapter 7, certain tests of operating effectiveness simultaneously provide substantive evidence as to the correctness of recorded amounts, and these are known as dual-purpose tests. Auditors must be particularly careful in drawing conclusions from such tests. As substantive tests, it may be concluded that misstatements are only significant if material. However, all misstatements suggest that control procedures have not been properly performed. These deviations from prescribed procedures could have caused misstatements in transactions of any size. Therefore, as a test of control, it is the number of misstatements that is important, not their size. Detection of misstatements of any size, therefore, may require the assessment of control risk to be revised.

Computer information systems

Tests of the operating effectiveness of controls over a computer information system are usually undertaken by computer-assisted audit techniques (CAATs). The two main categories of CAATs are:

1. those that test the operation of programs and related programmed application controls directly; and
2. those that test data held on computer files.

In the first category, the most common techniques used for testing controls over the processing of sales transactions are the test data approach and the use of embedded audit facilities. Test data are composed of simulated transactions. One batch of data will consist of transactions replicating the normal types of transaction processed by the system. A second batch will consist of transactions that should activate those programmed application controls of significance to the audit, such as orders exceeding credit limits. Both batches are processed against a copy of the program, and the results are compared with expected results determined manually. Test data are best suited to batch processing systems where the relevant program can be isolated and a copy can be taken for audit purposes. With real-time processing it is less satisfactory and most such systems incorporate embedded audit facilities. One kind of embedded audit facility is the integrated test facility (ITF) based on dummy accounts to which test data can be processed on a real-time basis. Another embedded audit facility is a systems control and audit file (SCARF).

Prepared by:_____ Date:_____
Reviewed by:_____ Date:_____

Amalgamated Products Ltd
Planned tests of control – Credit sales transactions
Year ending 31 December 20X1

Assertion/Test of control	W/P ref.	Auditor	Date
Occurrence 1. Observe procedures, including segregation of duties, for: • approving sales orders; • filling sales orders; • dispatching sales orders; • invoicing customers; • mailing monthly statements to customers and following up on customer complaints. 2. Select a sample of sales transactions from the sales journal and verify transaction dates, customer names, and amounts by vouching entries to the following matching supporting documents: • sales invoices; • dispatch notes; • approved sales orders. *Completeness* 3. Examine evidence of use of and accounting for pre-numbered sales orders, dispatch notes and sales invoices. Scan sequence of sales invoice numbers in sales journal. 4. Select a sample of approved sales orders and trace to matching: • dispatch notes; • sales invoices; • entries in the sales journal. *Accuracy* 5. For the sample in Step 2 above, examine evidence of: • proper credit approval for each transaction; • independent check on proper pricing of invoices; • independent check on mathematical accuracy of invoices. 6. For sales invoices processed in batches, examine evidence of independent check on agreement of totals for sales journal entries and amounts posted to customer accounts with batch totals.			

Figure 10.2 *Partial audit programme for tests of controls – credit sales*

This facility enables auditors to specify parameters of interest, such as orders where credit limits are overridden by the credit controller. The facility will then log all such transactions and record them on a special audit file for subsequent review by the auditors.

For tests applied to sales transactions held on computer files, the auditors can use generalised audit software (GAS) for large computer systems and proprietary database packages for smaller, PC-based systems. Both techniques can be used to access data on computer files according to criteria specified by the auditors and to perform a wide range of mathematical functions on that data. For tests involving the inspection of documents, the software can be programmed to select a sample of documents. If statistical sampling techniques are being used, as described in Chapter 8, the software can be programmed with the sampling parameters, such as the preliminary assessment of inherent and control risk and the tolerable deviation rate. The software will select a suitably random sample and, after testing by the auditors, will calculate the achieved deviation rate. For reperformance, the software can be programmed to perform the entire test. In reperforming invoice pricing, for example, the auditors can program the software to select a sample of invoices and compare unit sales prices on those invoices with sales prices held on the price file, and to report differences.

CASH RECEIPTS

Table 10.3 illustrates a partial listing of potential misstatements, necessary controls, possible tests of the operating effectiveness of controls, and related transaction class audit objectives for cash receipt transactions. The particulars of the items listed in this table would vary among entities, based on such factors as the method of data processing used. As was explained for credit sales, the potential misstatements and necessary controls would be the basis of a checklist used to assess design effectiveness. Similarly, an audit programme for tests of the operating effectiveness of controls for cash receipts transactions can be prepared based on the potential tests of control shown in Table 10.3.

SALES ADJUSTMENTS

Sales adjustment information systems are more diverse than sales and cash receipt systems, so it is not practicable to illustrate typical potential misstatements and necessary controls. However, tests of control that are likely to be appropriate include:

- recalculating cash discounts and determining that the payments were received within the discount period;
- inspecting credit memoranda for sales returns for indication of proper approval and accompanying receiving reports for evidence of the actual return of goods; and
- inspecting written authorisations and supporting documentation (such as correspondence with the customer or collection agencies) for the write-off of bad debts.

Final assessment

Based on the evidence obtained from the procedures to obtain an understanding of internal control and related tests of control, the auditors make a final assessment of inherent and control risks. This assessment must be documented. Figure 7.6 on page 237 illustrates such documentation in the form of a memorandum.

Table 10.3 Control risk assessment considerations – cash receipts

FUNCTION	POTENTIAL MISSTATEMENT	NECESSARY CONTROL	POSSIBLE TEST OF OPERATING EFFECTIVENESS	RELEVANT TRANSACTION CLASS AUDIT OBJECTIVE (FROM TABLE 10.1)				
				EO2	C2	RO2	ACV2	PD2
Receiving cash receipts	Cash sales may not be registered	Use of cash registers or point-of-sale devices	Observe cash sales procedures		✓			
		Periodic surveillance of cash sales procedures	Inquire of supervisors about results of surveillance		✓			
	Mail receipts may be lost or misappropriated after receipt	Restrictive endorsement of cheques immediately on receipt	Observe mail opening, including endorsement of cheques		✓			
		Immediate preparation of rough cash book or prelist of mail receipts	Observe preparation of records	✓	✓			
Depositing cash in bank	Cash and cheques received for deposit may not agree with cash count list and prelist	Independent check of agreement of cash and cheques with register totals and prelist	Examine evidence of independent check*	✓	✓		✓	
	Cash may not be deposited intact daily	Independent check of agreement of validated deposit slip with daily cash summary	Reperform independent check*	✓	✓			
Recording the receipts	Some receipts may not be recorded	Independent check of agreement of amounts journalised and posted with daily cash summary	Reperform independent check*		✓			
	Errors may be made in journalising receipts	Preparation of periodic independent bank reconciliations	Examine bank reconciliations*	✓	✓	✓	✓	
	Receipts may be posted to the wrong customer account	Mailing of monthly statements to customers	Observe mailing of monthly statements	✓	✓		✓	✓

Note: *Tests marked with an asterisk are sometimes performed as part of dual-purpose tests.

This assessment enables auditors to plan the level of substantive procedures to be performed. The understanding of the information system also assists in the design of tests making the best use of data available within the entity's records. Where significant risks are identified it is important that the design of tests is tailored to meet those specific risks. For example, a sales promotion policy may entitle customers to extra discounts if they meet specified conditions. There may be a risk that cash receipts may be misappropriated by staff falsely recording a lower cash receipt and ascribing the shortfall to discount entitlement. Specific substantive procedures may need to be designed to verify the authenticity of such discounts allowed.

Because many tests of control are dual-purpose tests, providing evidence of errors in amounts as well as deviations from controls, the auditors usually draw up the detailed audit programme based on the preliminary assessment of control risk. This improves audit efficiency in that tests of the operating effectiveness of controls that use sources of evidence on which the substantive tests of details are also based are performed simultaneously with those substantive procedures. The auditors must ensure that control deviations are properly identified and that their implications for the assessment of control risk are properly considered in terms of whether further substantive procedures need to be performed.

 ## LEARNING **CHECK**

10.10 In developing the audit plan, the auditors need to have (1) obtained the understanding of the accounting and internal control systems and control environment, (2) assessed inherent risk both for the entity and for the specific transactions and balances, and (3) assessed control risk based on the results of tests of control.

10.11 Sales and cash receipt transactions are always material and debtors are nearly always material to an entity, making the audit of this area important to the audit overall.

10.12 The greatest inherent risk is the overstatement of sales transactions and the debtors' balance and the understatement of cash receipts and the provision for bad debts. Because of the volume of transactions, most entities ensure that their internal controls relating to such matters are effective.

10.13 It is nearly always advantageous to adopt a lower assessed level of control risk strategy in order to reduce the level of costly substantive procedures.

10.14 The control environment is generally common to the entity and must be sound if control risk is to be less than high.

10.15 The testing of the design effectiveness of controls is achieved by evaluating the system with the aid of a list of potential misstatements and suggested control procedures.

10.16 The testing of the operating effectiveness of controls is achieved by examining evidence of the performance of control procedures.

10.17 The audit programme is usually determined on the basis of the preliminary assessment of controls, which typically consists of the assessment of design effectiveness. The audit plan may need to be revised if tests of operating effectiveness fail to confirm the preliminary assessment.

SUBSTANTIVE PROCEDURES

The primary consideration here is the gross amount due from customers on credit sales and the related provision for bad debts. To design substantive procedures for these accounts, auditors must first determine the risk of material misstatement for each significant related assertion. Given that the verification of debtors requires consideration of sales, sales adjustment and cash receipts transactions, the procedures also contribute to the profit and loss account balance of sales, and to the balance of cash on hand and at bank in the balance sheet.

Determining detection risk

As was explained in Chapter 5, for a specified level of audit risk, detection risk is inversely related to the assessed levels of inherent risk and control risk. Thus, the auditors must consider these assessments when determining the planned level of detection risk for each debtors' assertion. Several pervasive inherent risk and control environment factors that affect sales and debtors' transactions and balances were discussed earlier. The combined effects of these factors, especially those contributing to the risk of credit sales being overstated, may result in assessments of inherent risk as being high for:

- the existence and valuation assertions for debtors; and
- the valuation assertion for the related provision account.

Assessments of inherent risk as being lower may be appropriate for the other assertions.

Control risk assessments for debtors' assertions depend on the related control risk assessments for the transaction classes (credit sales, cash receipts and sales adjustments) that affect the debtors' balance. As was explained in Chapter 9, the assessments for transaction class assertions affect the same account balance assertions for accounts affected by the transactions, with the following exception: control risk assessments for the occurrence and completeness assertions for a transaction class that decreases an account balance affect the assessments for the opposite account balance assertions. Thus because both cash receipts and sales adjustment transactions decrease the debtors' balance, the assessment for the occurrence assertion for these transaction classes affects the assessment for the completeness assertion for the debtors' balance. Similarly, the assessment for the completeness assertion for these transaction classes affects the assessment for the existence assertion for the debtors' balance.

The audit programme will be based on the preliminary assessment of control risk. If tests of control subsequently lead to a revised assessment of control risk, then the design of substantive procedures in terms of their nature, timing or extent will need to be revised. Some auditors use a matrix similar to the one illustrated in Table 10.4 to document and correlate the various risk components that must be considered in the design of substantive

Table 10.4 Correlation of risk components – debtors

RISK COMPONENT	EXISTENCE OR OCCURRENCE	COMPLETENESS	ACCURACY, CLASSIFICATION AND VALUATION	PRESENTATION AND DISCLOSURE
Audit risk	Low	Low	Low	Low
Inherent risk	High	Moderate	High	Moderate
Control risk – sales transactions	Low	Low	Moderate	Moderate
Control risk – cash receipts	Low	Low	Low	Low
Control risk – sales adjustments	Moderate	Low	High	Moderate
Combined control risk [1]	Low	Moderate	High	Moderate
Acceptable detection risk [2]	Moderate	Moderate	Low	Moderate

Notes: [1]This is the most conservative (highest) of transaction class control risk assessments used as the combined risk assessment as per the methodology discussed in Chapter 9 on page 297.
[2]Determined from risk components matrix shown in Table 5.2 on page 138, based on levels of audit risk, inherent risk and combined control risk indicated above for each assertion category.

procedures for each account balance assertion. The risk levels specified in this matrix are illustrative only and would vary based on the entity's circumstances. Alternatively, when the risk components are quantified, the audit risk model can be solved mathematically for the acceptable levels of detection risk.

Designing substantive procedures

The next step is to finalise the audit programme to achieve the specific audit objectives for each account balance assertion. The specific audit objectives addressed here are the ones listed in the 'Account balance audit and disclosure objectives' column of Table 10.1. Chapter 9 introduced a general framework for developing audit programmes for substantive procedures. Of the steps listed under the heading 'Complete preliminary planning' in Figure 9.6, the application of items to debtors has already been considered in this chapter. This section considers the options for designing the substantive procedures for debtors, following the sequence suggested in the lower portion of Figure 9.6.

Table 10.5 lists possible substantive procedures to be included in an audit programme developed on this basis. This table does not represent a formal audit programme because: it is not tailored to any specific information system; there is no working paper heading; and there are no columns for supporting working paper references, initials and dates. Instead, for instructional purposes, there are columns to indicate the categories of substantive procedure (referred to in Figure 9.6) and the specific account balance audit objectives from Table 10.1 to which each procedure applies. Several of the procedures apply to more than one audit objective, and each objective is addressed by multiple possible procedures. Each of the procedures will be explained in the sections that follow, including comments on how some procedures can be tailored, based on the planned level of detection risk to be achieved.

INITIAL PROCEDURES

The starting point for verifying debtors and the related provision account is to trace the current period's opening balances to the closing audited balances in the prior year's working papers (when applicable). Next, the auditors should review the current period's activity in the general ledger control account and related provision account for any significant entries that are unusual in nature or amount, and that require special investigation.

A sales ledger trial balance (listing all customer balances) is obtained, usually from the entity. To determine that it is an accurate and complete representation of the underlying accounting records, the auditors should add this listing and compare the total with the total of the subsidiary ledger from which it was prepared and with the general ledger control account balance. The auditors should also compare a sample of the customer details and balances shown on the trial balance with those in the subsidiary ledger, and vice versa. The trial balance can then serve as the physical representation of the population of debtors to be subjected to further substantive procedures.

An example of an aged sales ledger trial balance working paper is presented in Figure 10.3. This working paper not only provides evidence of performance of the initial procedures just described, but of several of the other substantive procedures discussed in subsequent sections. The initial procedures in verifying the accuracy of the trial balance and determining its agreement with the control account in the general ledger relate primarily to the accuracy assertion.

Computer information systems

Where accounts receivable data are held on computer files, auditors can use computer-assisted audit techniques to perform substantive procedures. This is likely to involve the use of computer audit software. Both generalised audit software (GAS) and database packages can be used to print a trial balance directly from the accounts receivable master file, test the ageing of a sample of accounts, and verify the total and its agreement with the control account in the general ledger.

ANALYTICAL PROCEDURES

Tests of details are usually planned on the basis that the analytical procedures confirm expectations. It is preferable to perform analytical procedures early in the final audit, so

Table 10.5 Possible substantive procedures for trade debtors assertions

CATEGORY	SUBSTANTIVE PROCEDURE	ACCOUNT BALANCE AUDIT OBJECTIVE (FROM TABLE 10.1)					
		EO4	C4	RO3	ACV#	PD#	C-O#
Initial procedures	1. Perform initial procedures on debtors balances and records that will be subjected to further testing. (a) Trace opening balances for debtors and related provision to prior year's working papers. (b) Review activity in general ledger accounts for debtors and related provision, and investigate entries that appear unusual in amount or source. (c) Obtain sales ledger trial balance and determine that it accurately represents the underlying accounting records by: • adding trial balance and determining agreement with the total of the subsidiary ledger or debtors master file and the general ledger balance; • testing agreement of customers and balances listed on the trial balance with those included on the subsidiary ledger or master file.				√4,5		
Analytical procedures	2. Perform analytical procedures. (a) Determine expectations. (b) Compare current and prior year balances. (c) Compute significant ratios such as: • gross profit; • days' sales in debtors. (d) Obtain explanations for unexpected changes. (e) Corroborate explanations.	√	√		√4,5		
Tests of details of transactions	3. Vouch a sample of recorded debtors transactions to supporting documentation (see also Step 6(c) below). (a) Vouch debits to supporting sales invoices, dispatch notes and sales orders. (b) Vouch credits to remittance advices or sales adjustment authorisation for sales returns and allowances or bad debt write-offs.	√	√	√	√4		
	4. Perform cut-off tests for sales and sales returns. (a) Select a sample of recorded sales transactions from several days before and after year-end, and examine supporting sales invoices and dispatch notes to determine that sales were recorded in the proper period. (b) Select a sample of credit memos issued after year-end, examine supporting documentation such as dated goods inward notes, and determine that the returns were recorded in the proper period. Also, consider whether volume of sales returns after year-end suggests the possibility of unauthorised shipments before year-end.						√1,3

(continued overleaf)

Table 10.5 (*continued*)

CATEGORY	SUBSTANTIVE PROCEDURE	ACCOUNT BALANCE AUDIT OBJECTIVE (FROM TABLE 10.1)					
		EO4	C4	RO3	ACV#	PD#	C-O#
	5. Perform cash receipts cut-off test. (a) Observe that all cash received before the close of business on the last day of the financial year is included in cash on hand or deposits in transit, and that no receipts of the subsequent period are included; or (b) review documentation such as daily cash summaries, duplicate deposit slips, and bank statements covering several days before and after the year-end date to determine proper cut-off.						√2
Tests of details of balances	6. Confirm debtors. (a) Determine the form, timing and extent of confirmation requests. (b) Select and execute a sample and investigate exceptions. (c) For positive confirmation requests for which no reply was received, perform alternative follow-up procedures: • Vouch subsequent payments identifiable with items comprising account balance at confirmation date to supporting documentation as in Step 3(b) above. • Vouch items comprising balance at confirmation date to documentary support as in Step 3(a) above. (d) Summarise results of confirmation and alternative follow-up procedures.	√		√	√4		√1,2
	7. Evaluate adequacy of provision for bad debts. (a) Add and cross-add aged sales ledger trial balance and agree total to general ledger. (b) Test ageing by vouching amounts in ageing categories for sample of accounts to supporting documentation. (c) For past-due accounts: • Examine evidence of collectability such as correspondence with customers and outside collection agencies, credit reports and customers' financial statements. • Discuss collectability of accounts with appropriate management personnel. (d) Evaluate adequacy of provision component for each ageing category and in the aggregate.				√5		
Presentation and disclosure	8. Compare report presentation with applicable Financial Reporting Standards and regulatory requirements such as the *Companies Act 1985*. (a) Determine that debtors are properly classified as to type and expected period of realisation. (b) Determine whether there are credit balances that are significant in the aggregate and should be reclassified as liabilities. (c) Determine the appropriateness of presentation and disclosure and accounting for related party or factored debts.				√4	√4,5	

Bates Company
Aged trial balance — Debtors — Trade
31 December 20X1

(PBC)

Account no. 120

		W/P ref:	B–1
Prepared by:	A.C.E.	Date:	5/1/X2
Reviewed by:	P.A.R.	Date:	20/1/X2

	Account name	Over 90 days	Past due over 60 days	Over 30 Days	Current	Balance per books 31/12/X1	Adjustments	Balance per audit 31/12/X1	
ø	Ace Engineering		2529.04	2016.14	11875.90	16421.08✓		16421.08	
	Applied Devices	1088.92↑	15938.89↑	27901.11↑	43840.00✓		43840.00	C1
ø	Barry Manufacturing	501.10↑	743.12↑	3176.22↑	8993.01↑	14001.27↑		14001.27	C2
ø	Brandt Electronics		7309.50↑	33948.01↑	24441.25↑	63199.86✓		63199.86	C3
ø	Cermetrics Ltd			3813.76	8617.30	12431.06✓		12431.06	
ø	Columbia Components				4321.18↑	4321.18✓		4321.18	
	Drake Manufacturing		739.57	2953.88	3693.45✓		3693.45	
ø	EMC		1261.01	1048.23	16194.76	18504.00✓		18504.00	
	Groton Electric		7799.36↑	2C006.63↑	89017.15↑	116823.14↑		116823.14	C4
ø	Harvey Industries		1709.16	6111.25	18247.31	26067.72✓		26067.72	
	Jed Ltd	2615.87↑	12098.00↑	15434.46↑	56536.88↑	86685.21↑	(9416.96)	77268.25	C5
	Jericho Electric		1198.72	13123.14	14321.86✓		14321.86	
ø	W & M Manufacturing Corp.	814.98	1904.65↑	2166.78↑	28389.69↑	32461.12✓		32461.12	C60
	Yancey Corp.		2861.05	9574.13	13561.80	27111.96✓		27111.96	
		10157.46	56705.59	160537.28	392136.41	619536.74	(9416.96)	610119.78	
		✓	✓	✓	✓	B	B	B	

✓ Added or cross-added
ø Customer name and balance per books agreed to subsidiary ledger
↑ Ageing verified by examining transaction dates of related unpaid sales invoices in subsidiary ledger
C Account selected for confirmation — see W/P B–2

Figure 10.3 *Aged sales ledger trial balance working paper*

any necessary changes to tests of details can be determined prior to the commencement of that part of the audit.

The first stage in applying analytical procedures is to review the understanding of the entity, obtained during the planning phase, as to whether any changes to sales and debtors' balances are to be expected.

The second stage is to identify absolute changes in amounts between this year and prior years. This is normally done in the course of preparing the lead schedule for sales and debtors, as was explained in Chapter 6. On this schedule, prior and current year ledger balances making up the financial statement disclosures are recorded side by side, making any differences readily apparent.

The third stage involves the use of more sophisticated relationships such as ratios and trends. This procedure can be performed on accounting data held on computer files, using computer audit software. Significant ratios are gross profit and days' sales in debtors. If gross profit is higher than expected, it could be that sales have been overstated to boost revenue, such as by a deliberate cut-off error. An increase in days' sales in debtors indicates potential problems in collecting debtors, with the consequent need for a greater provision.

Wherever a change in relationships cannot be readily explained, auditors must seek an explanation from management and corroborate that explanation, usually by performing more tests of details. For debtors and sales, analytical procedures can provide evidence pertaining to the existence, completeness, and valuation assertions.

TESTS OF DETAILS OF TRANSACTIONS

Where balances result from the effects of numerous transactions, it is normally more efficient to concentrate substantive procedures on tests of details of balances, and not tests of details of transactions. The latter are not unimportant, but serve to corroborate tests of details of balances. In the main, the tests of transactions will be performed during the interim audit, commonly in the form of dual-purpose tests. The cut-off tests that will be described in subsequent sections are always performed as part of year-end work and, although they are tests of transactions, serve to verify the recorded balance at the balance sheet date.

Vouching recorded debtors to supporting transactions

This procedure involves vouching a sample of debits to customers' accounts to supporting sales invoices and matching documents to provide evidence relevant to the existence, accuracy and classification assertions. It also involves vouching a sample of credits to remittance advices and sales adjustment authorisations to provide evidence relevant to the completeness assertion for debtors that reductions in customer balances are legitimate.

Performing sales cut-off test

The sales cut-off test is designed to obtain reasonable assurance that:

- sales and debtors are recorded in the accounting period in which the transactions occurred; and
- the corresponding entries for stock and cost of goods sold are made in the same period.

The sales cut-off test is made as of the balance sheet date. Given the greater risk of overstatement, the emphasis is on verifying the occurrence of recorded sales before the year-end. Auditors usually record the number of the last issued dispatch note during attendance at stock-take and agree it to the cut-off established for stock purposes. For sales of goods from stock, the procedure involves comparing a sample of recorded sales from the last few days of the current period with dispatch notes numbered prior to the cut-off number to determine that the transactions occurred before the balance sheet date. A smaller number of sales recorded after the balance sheet date are vouched to dispatch notes numbered subsequently to the cut-off, to ensure that none was delivered before the balance sheet date.

The sales return cut-off test is similar and particularly directed towards the possibility that returns made prior to the year-end are not recorded until after the year-end, resulting in the overstatement of debtors and sales. Auditors can determine the correct cut-off by examining dated goods received notes for returned merchandise and correspondence with customers. Auditors should also be alert to the possibility that an unusually heavy volume of sales returns shortly after the year-end could signal unauthorised shipments before the year-end to inflate recorded sales and debtors.

Performing cash receipts cut-off test

The cash receipts cut-off test is designed to obtain reasonable assurance that cash receipts are recorded in the accounting period in which they are received. A proper cut-off at the balance sheet date is essential to the correct presentation of both cash and debtors. If the auditors are present at the year-end date, then they can observe that all collections received prior to the close of business are included in cash on hand or in deposits in transit, and are credited to debtors. An alternative to personal observation is to review supporting documentation such as the daily cash summary and a validated deposit slip for the last day of the year. The objective of the review is to determine that the deposit slip total agrees with the receipts shown on the daily cash summary. In addition, auditors should determine that the receipts were recorded on the closing date.

TESTS OF DETAILS OF BALANCES

As explained above, most of the audit effort on debtors is obtained through tests of details of balances, of which the most important is the confirmation of debtors and related follow-up procedures. Confirmation provides evidence as to existence, rights and valuation. It does not provide evidence of completeness, because customers are unlikely to admit to owing more than their recorded balance. The other major test of details of balances is an evaluation of the adequacy of the provision for bad debts.

Confirming debtors

Confirmation of debtors involves direct written communication by the auditors with individual customers. The test is often referred to as a debtors' circularisation.

ACCEPTED AUDIT PROCEDURE

The confirmation of debtors is an accepted audit procedure when they are material and it is reasonable to presume the debtors will respond (ISA 505, External Confirmations).

Confirmation is usually the most efficient procedure for obtaining sufficient appropriate audit evidence to support the existence and rights assertions of debtors. There are circumstances, however, in which the auditors conclude that confirmation is unlikely to be effective and that sufficient appropriate audit evidence can be achieved through the performance of alternative audit procedures. Based on the prior year's audit experience on that engagement, the auditors might expect, for example, that responses would be unreliable in the current year or that the response rates would be inadequate. Also, in some cases, customers may be unable to confirm balances if they use voucher systems that show the amount owed on individual transactions, but not the total amount owed to one creditor. This is often true of governmental agencies. The auditors may be able to overcome this problem by confirming individual transactions rather than balances.

As written evidence from third parties, responses to confirmation requests constitute highly reliable evidence. Against this, it must be remembered that:

- where customers are largely small businesses or private individuals, they are less likely to maintain sufficiently accurate bought ledger records to provide a reliable response;
- even larger businesses generally maintain less effective controls over the completeness of liabilities recorded in the bought ledger;
- customers are unlikely to admit to owing more than is shown on the monthly statement, limiting the evidence to that of existence, rights and, to a lesser extent, valuation;
- many trivial differences are likely to be reported as a result of goods and cash in transit; and
- the non-response rate may be high.

Given that dealings between the entity and its customers are confidential, the entity must authorise its customers to disclose details of the outstanding balance to its auditors. Occasionally, entities have prohibited auditors from confirming certain debtors. The effect of prohibition should be evaluated on the basis of management's reasons, with the auditors determining whether they can obtain sufficient evidence from other auditing procedures. If the auditors regard management's reasons as unacceptable, then there has been a limitation on the scope of the audit that might result in a qualified auditors' report.

FORM OF CONFIRMATION

There are two forms of confirmation request:

- the positive form, which requires the debtor to respond whether or not the balance shown is correct; and
- the negative form, which requires the debtor to respond only when the amount shown is incorrect.

The two forms are illustrated in Figures 10.4 and 10.5. The positive confirmation request is usually made in the form of a separate letter on entity letterhead, but it may also be printed on the customer's monthly statement. The negative request is usually in the form of a rubber stamp or sticker attached to, or a request printed on, the statement of account routinely sent by the entity to each customer. The positive form generally produces statistically valid evidence, providing non-responses are verified by other means.

BATES COMPANY
4 Queensland Road
Eastville

Ace Engineering Service
New Road
Westville   6 January 20X2

Dear Sir or Madam,
This request is being sent to you to enable our independent auditors to confirm the correctness of our records. It is not a request for payment.

Our records on 31 December 20X1 showed an amount of £16,421.08 receivable from you. Please confirm whether this agrees with your records on that date by signing this form and returning it directly to our auditors. An addressed envelope is enclosed for this purpose. If you find any difference, please report details directly to our auditors in the space provided below.

Yours faithfully
Controller

The above amount is correct [   ]. The above amount is incorrect for the following reasons:

....

....

(Individual or company name)
By: ....

Figure 10.4 *Positive confirmation request – letter form*

With the negative form, it is impossible to determine whether a lack of response indicates agreement with the balance or simply a failure to reply. The positive form is used when planned detection risk is low or individual customer balances are relatively large. The negative form should be used only when the following conditions apply:

- planned detection risk is moderate or high;
- there is a large number of small balances in the population; or
- the auditors have no reason to believe that the respondents are unlikely to give the request due consideration.

Frequently, a combination of the two forms is used in a single engagement. In the audit of a public utility, for example, auditors may elect to use the negative form for residential

> Please examine this monthly statement carefully
> and advise our auditors
>
> **Reddy & Abel**
> **Certified Public Accountants**
> **465 City Centre Building**
> **Perth**
> as to any exceptions.
>
> A self-addressed stamped envelope is
> enclosed for your convenience.
>
> THIS IS NOT A REQUEST FOR PAYMENT.

Figure 10.5 *Negative confirmation request – stamp form*

customers and the positive form for commercial customers. When the positive form is used, auditors should generally follow up with a second and sometimes an additional request to those debtors that fail to reply.

TIMING AND EXTENT OF REQUESTS

When the planned level of detection risk is low, auditors ordinarily confirm debtors as at the balance sheet date. Otherwise, the confirmation date may be one or two months earlier. In such case, the auditors must conduct roll-forward tests such as:

- performing analytical procedures on entries to the debtors' control account in the period between the date of confirmation and the balance sheet date, and obtain a satisfactory explanation for any unexpected changes; and
- performing tests of control in the intervening period to ensure that the assessment of control risk leading to a decision to accept a high level of detection risk continues to apply.

The extent of requests or sample size is determined by the criteria that were described in Chapter 8 on audit sampling. Debtors may be divided into distinct populations for sampling. For example, different categories of debtor – such as wholesale and retail – may be subject to different information systems and control activities and, thus, different control risks. Also, individually material balances are often confirmed directly and the remainder subdivided into either overdue accounts or other, with a proportionately larger number of the former selected for confirmation as presenting a greater risk of misstatement. Sample size may be determined judgementally or with the aid of a statistical sampling plan. Apart from the exceptions noted, selection of accounts for confirmation should be effectively random, such as through use of a sequential sampling plan.

CONTROL OF THE REQUESTS

The auditors must control every step in the confirmation process. This means:

- prior to selecting the sample for confirmation, performing the initial procedures described above to ensure the list of balances is complete and accurate;
- drawing up a list of selected accounts and verifying that confirmation requests, prepared and signed by entity management at the auditors' request, are in complete agreement with that list;
- ascertaining that the amount, name and address on the confirmation agree with the corresponding data in the customer's account;
- maintaining custody of the confirmations until they are mailed;
- using the audit firm's own return address envelopes for the confirmations;
- personally depositing the requests in the mail; and
- requiring that the replies be sent directly to the auditors.

A working paper should list each account selected for confirmation and the results obtained from each request, cross-referenced to the actual confirmation response (which should also be filed with the working papers). A confirmation control working paper is illustrated in Figure 10.6.

DISPOSITION OF EXCEPTIONS

Confirmation responses will inevitably contain some exceptions. Exceptions may be attributable to goods in transit from the entity to the customer, returned goods or payments in transit from the customer to the entity, items in dispute or errors and irregularities. The auditors should investigate all exceptions and record their resolution in the working papers, as illustrated in Figure 10.6.

COMPUTER INFORMATION SYSTEMS

Computer audit software may assist the auditors in the process of confirming receivables held on an accounts receivable master file. As explained above in our discussion of initial procedures, the software can be programmed to test the completeness and accuracy of receivables listed on the master file. Software can also be used to select accounts on bases as discussed above, print the letters for circularisation and prepare a working paper for recording responses. A detailed illustration of the use of computer audit software in confirming receivables can also be found in Chapter 9 on pages 308–310.

ALTERNATIVE PROCEDURES FOR DEALING WITH NON-RESPONSES

When no response has been received after the second (or third) positive confirmation request to a customer, auditors should perform alternative procedures. The two main alternative procedures are examining subsequent collections and vouching unpaid invoices and supporting documentation comprising customer balances.

The best evidence of existence and collectability is the receipt of payment from the customer. Before the conclusion of the auditors' examination, the entity will receive payments from many customers on amounts owed at the confirmation date. The matching

Bates Company

Debtors confirmation control

31 December 20X1

W/P Ref: _B-2_
Prepared by: _A.C.E._ Date: _28/1/X2_
Reviewed by: _P.A.R._ Date: _31/1/X2_

Account no. 120

Conf. no.	Customer	Book value	Confirmed value ø	Audited value	(Over) Under statement	Subsequent collections examined through 28/1/X2
1	Applied Devices	43 480.00	43 480.00	43 480.00		
2	Barry Manufacturing	14 001.27	NR	14 001.27		14 001.27 ✓
3	Brandt Electronics	63 199.86	63 199.86	63 199.86		
4	Groton Electric	116 823.14	116 823.14	116 823.14		
5	Jed Ltd	86 685.21	77 268.25	77 268.25	(9 416.96) Ⓧ	
60	W & M Manufacturing Corp.	32 461.12	NR	32 461.12↑		4 071.43 ✓
	Totals	470 847.92	414 968.57	461 430.96	(9 416.96)	

Response recap:

	# Items	
Value of confirmations mailed	60	£470 847.92
Value of confirmations received	58	£414 968.57
Response	97%	88%

Summary of results:

	# Items	
Value of account total	300	£619 536.74
Book value of confirmation sample	60	£470 847.92
Coverage of book value		76%
Audited value of sample		£461 430.96
Ratio of audited value to book value of sample		98%

ø   Signed confirmation response attached for confirmed values

NR   No response — alternative procedures performed

✓   Examined entries in cash receipts journal and related remittance advices for total collections indicated

↑   Examined supporting documentation for portion of book value remaining uncollected as of 28/1/X2

Ⓧ   Credit memo issued 12/1/X2 for merchandise returned 28/12/X1. Adjusting entry:

Dr: sales returns   9416.96

Cr: debtors   9416.96   } See W/P B-1 and AE-1

Figure 10.6 *Confirmation control working paper*

of such cash receipts to unpaid invoices at the confirmation date, evidenced by the remittance advice accompanying the cash receipt, establishes the existence and collectability of the accounts.

Vouching open invoices comprising balances is a variation of Step 3(a) in Table 10.5. Preferably, the unpaid item should be traced to a dispatch note signed by the customer acknowledging receipt of the goods, or to a written order from the customer.

SUMMARY AND EVALUATION OF THE RESULTS

The auditors' working papers should contain a summary of the results from confirming debtors. (The lower portion of Figure 10.6 illustrates how such data may be presented.) The auditors may use statistical or non-statistical procedures to project misstatements found in the sample to the population. It must not be forgotten, for a sample test, that it is not sufficient merely to correct errors detected by the confirmation, but that the implications for the entire population of debtors must also be considered.

The auditors evaluate combined evidence from the confirmations, alternative procedures performed on non-responses, and other tests of details and analytical procedures to determine whether sufficient evidence has been obtained to support management's assertions about debtors.

Evaluating adequacy of the provision for bad debts

Most entities determine the provision for bad debts by:

- making a general provision, such as a percentage of balances overdue by more than a specified period; or
- making a specific provision, by identifying customers who are known to be in financial difficulty or who are in dispute as to payment.

The provision is an estimate that the auditors will verify in accordance with ISA 540, Audit of Accounting Estimates. Auditors adopt one or more of the following approaches:

- reviewing and testing the process used by management;
- using an independent estimate; or
- reviewing subsequent events.

Auditors usually follow the first approach in verifying the general provision, and it involves:

- ascertaining management's procedures for determining the estimate and considering their reliability;
- ensuring that the procedures have been properly followed and that the estimate has been approved;
- identifying the assumptions underpinning the estimate and considering their reasonableness;
- verifying the reliability of the data (such as the aged analysis of debtors) on which the estimate is based;

- checking the calculations (such as the percentages applied to each overdue category) in determining the general provision; and
- considering the reliability of prior year provisions.

Auditors usually apply second and third approaches suggested by ISA 540 when considering the specific provision. In arriving at an independent estimate, the auditors will examine correspondence with customers and outside collection agencies, review customers' credit reports and financial statements, and discuss the collectability of the account with appropriate management personnel. This review will include a consideration of subsequent events, such as news of a customer's financial difficulties or payment of a disputed amount.

Disclosure

Auditors must be knowledgeable about the disclosure requirements for debtors and sales under the *Companies Act 1985* or other regulatory framework. A review of the sales ledger trial balance may indicate amounts due from employees, officers, other group entities and related parties that should be specifically identified if material. The same source may reveal credit balances in customer accounts that may warrant classification as current liabilities. There should also be disclosure of the pledging, assigning or factoring of debtors. The auditors should be able to obtain evidence of such activities from a review of the minutes of the board of directors' meetings and from inquiry of management. As one of the final steps in the audit, the auditors should obtain management's representations on these matters in writing in a representation letter (see Chapter 14).

 LEARNING **CHECK**

10.18 The nature, timing and extent of substantive procedures is determined by the planned level of detection risk which, in turn, is a function of the assessed levels of inherent and control risks.

10.19 In determining the detection risk for tests of details of assertions for debtors' balances:

- the assessed control risk over the completeness of cash receipts and sales adjustment transactions relates to control risk as to the existence of the balance;

- the assessed control risk over the occurrence of cash receipts and sales adjustment transactions relates to control risk as to the completeness of the balance.

10.20 Initial procedures ensure the accuracy of the list of debtors' balances used as the basis for tests of the debtors' balance.

10.21 Analytical procedures require the determination of expectations and the comparison of amounts, trends and ratios, particularly the gross profit ratio and days' sales in debtors ratio.

10.22 Tests of details of transactions are largely dual-purpose tests performed at the interim audit except for cut-off tests of transactions either side of the balance sheet date.

10.23 The principal test of details of balances is the debtors' confirmation, which provides third party evidence of the balance.

10.24 The other major test of details of balances is of the reasonableness of the provision for bad debts.

SUMMARY

Sales and cash receipts from sales are the most important transaction classes for a commercial entity. For businesses selling on credit, maintaining records over the debtors' balance is also highly important. In auditing these transactions and the debtors' balance, the auditors use techniques explained in Chapters 5–9.

This chapter followed the audit approach required by ISA 315. It described the information system and related control procedures typically employed by entities in processing the relevant transaction classes. The audit process commences with obtaining the understanding of this system. The auditors also consider issues relating to materiality, inherent risk and the control environment, prior to assessing the risk of material misstatement and determining the appropriate audit strategy. For sales and debtors, materiality is invariably high. For audit purposes, the most significant inherent risk is that of overstatement of sales transactions and debtors' balances to boost reported profits and assets. For the entity, the greatest inherent risk is that of misappropriation of cash arising from sales transactions. In evaluating the control environment, the auditors consider each of the control environment factors – integrity and ethical values, commitment to competence, management's philosophy and operating style, the assignment of authority and responsibility, and personnel policies and practices – as they relate to sales and debtors.

The next stage of the audit is determining the audit strategy, which, for sales and debtors, is likely to be one based on a lower assessed level of control risk. The first stage in assessing control risk is evaluating design effectiveness. This chapter illustrated the use of evaluation checklists which hypothesise potential misstatements for each function in the processing of sales and cash receipt transactions. In assessing design effectiveness, the auditors compare the control procedures in the entity's information system with necessary controls identified by the checklist. At this point, the auditors draft the audit programme based on the preliminary assessment of control risk, identifying both tests of the operating effectiveness of controls and the reduced level of substantive procedures relevant to the assessed level of control risk. The auditors confirm the assessed level of control risk on completion of the tests of operating effectiveness.

The final stage of the audit is performing substantive procedures. It is usually cost-effective to test the balance of debtors rather than the transactions making up that balance. The most important test of transactions is that of cut-off at the year-end. The major test of balances is the confirmation of debtors. Given that customers are third parties, such evidence is highly reliable. This chapter explained the process of performing the confirmation, procedures to be followed where the test is performed prior to the year-end, and alternative procedures for verifying balances where no reply to the request for confirmation is received. Finally, procedures necessary to verify the estimated provision for bad debts were explained.

FURTHER READING

Allen, R. D. & Elder, R. J. 'An Empirical Investigation of Balance and Invoice Confirmations', *Journal of Forensic Accounting* (Vol. 11, 2001), pp. 219–234.

American Institute of Certified Public Accountants. '*Confirmation of Accounts Receivable*'. Auditing Procedures Study, New York, 1984.

Bailey, C. D. & Ballard, G. 'Improving Response Rates to Accounts Receivable Confirmations: An Experiment Using Four Techniques', *Auditing: A Journal of Practice & Theory* (Spring 1986), pp. 77–85.

Beran, D. & Evans, R. 'Auditing for Sales Adjustment Fraud', *Internal Auditor* (February 1990), pp. 51–56.

Caster, P. 'The Role of Confirmations as Audit Evidence', *Journal of Accountancy* (February 1992), pp. 73–76.

Engle, T. J. & Hunton J. E. 'Confirmation of Accounts Receivable Balances', *Journal of Accountancy* (May 2001), p. 91.

McConnell, Jr., D. K. & Banks, G. Y. 'A Common Peer Review Problem', *Journal of Accountancy* (June 1998).

O'Leary, C. 'Debtors' Confirmations – Handle with Care', *Australian Accountant* (May 1993), pp. 35–37.

Swearingen, J. G., Wilkes, J. A. & Swearingen, S. L. 'Confirmation Response Differences Between Businesses, Clerks and Consumers', *The CPA Journal* (May 1991), pp. 58–60.

MULTIPLE-CHOICE QUESTIONS

Choose the best answer for each of the following.
(Answers are on page 602)

10.1 Which of the following controls would most likely ensure that all deliveries are invoiced?
   (a)   The invoicing department supervisor matches pre-numbered shipping documents with entries in the sales journal.
   (b)   The accounting department supervisor controls the mailing of monthly statements to customers, and investigates any differences reported by customers.
   (c)   Customers are required to acknowledge receipt of the goods by signing a copy of the delivery note.
   (d)   All orders are required to be approved by the credit controller before the goods are delivered.

10.2 Which of the following internal control procedures would most likely assure that all receipts from cash sales are recorded?
   (a)   The bank account is independently reconciled monthly.
   (b)   Two persons are present at the opening of the mail.

(c)   Sales are rung up on a cash register which displays the sale amount and issues a printed receipt.

(d)   Daily sales summaries are compared with daily postings to the accounts receivable ledger.

10.3   For which of the following reasons might inherent risk over the occurrence of sales transactions be assessed as high?

(a)   There is a large volume of such transactions during the year.

(b)   Sales department staff earn a bonus if they achieve annual sales targets.

(c)   Cash from sales transactions is easily misappropriated.

(d)   There are poor controls over the year-end cut-off of sales transactions.

10.4   Sales revenue is usually a material balance within the financial statements of a company. Why would an auditor mainly focus his or her work on sales transactions occurring at the end of the year rather than throughout the year?

(a)   There are usually larger sales transactions occurring at the end of the financial year.

(b)   The auditor is concerned that the company may attempt to bring forward sales into the current year.

(c)   This work will provide some evidence to verify the existence of debtors.

(d)   The auditor can review these sales transactions when they actually occur during his or her interim visit to the client.

10.5   Which of the following tests of control would provide audit evidence for the financial statement assertion of the completeness of sales transactions?

(a)   Check to ensure that all dispatch orders have been properly matched to a sales invoice.

(b)   Ensure customer's credit limit is checked prior to each sale.

(c)   Reperform the pricing of sales invoices.

(d)   Observe separation of duties between sales order acceptance and dispatching orders.

10.6   If the auditor assesses control risk over the completeness of cash receipts transactions to be high, the control risk assessment would be high for the debtors' balance assertion of:

(a)   completeness.

(b)   existence.

(c)   rights and obligations.

(d)   valuation.

10.7   After completing the testing of controls over cash receipts and sales adjustments, the auditor assesses the level of control risk to be higher than expected. How would this affect the auditor's substantive audit work on debtors?

(a)   More work would need to be performed to ensure that the provision for doubtful debts is fairly stated.

(b)   Less work would need to be performed on following up non-responses from the debtors' circularisation.

(c)   The auditor may consider changing the date of the debtors' circularisation from one month before the year-end to the actual year-end date.

(d)   More analytical review tests could be performed on debtors as a substitute for other substantive tests.

10.8 Which of the following would give the most assurance concerning the existence assertion of debtors?
(a) Tracing amounts in the subsidiary ledger to details on shipping documents.
(b) Comparing debtors' turnover ratios with industry statistics for reasonableness.
(c) Sending a debtor's confirmation letter.
(d) Ensuring the sales subsidiary ledger has been correctly added.

DISCUSSION QUESTIONS

10.1 Identify application controls that could be programmed into a computer system for processing credit sales transactions.

10.2 Discuss situations where sales adjustments might be necessary and identify necessary controls to ensure that only genuine adjustments are recognised by the accounting system.

10.3 Identify situations leading to an inherent risk that an entity might wish (a) to overstate sales revenue, and (b) understate sales revenue.

10.4 Explain the kinds of fraud that could be anticipated in sales, cash receipts and sales adjustment transactions in the absence of adequate internal control procedures and consider the importance of the segregation of duties in preventing such frauds.

10.5 Explain why existence is often regarded as the assertion presenting the greatest degree of inherent risk.

10.6 In the absence of effective controls, consider whether it is possible for the auditor to verify the completeness of cash receipts using substantive procedures? Is there a distinction between the ability to verify the completeness of cash receipts from sales transactions and the completeness of donations to a charity?

10.7 Explain what is meant by 'cut-off' and why it is important to auditors in establishing the fairness of financial statements.

10.8 Identify situations where the negative form of debtors' confirmation might be appropriate.

10.9 Consider reasons why management might not wish particular debtors to be circularised. Which of these reasons might be regarded as acceptable by the auditor?

10.10 ISA 530 distinguishes between sampling and other selective testing procedures. Explain the application of the requirements of this standard to the selection of debtors' balances for confirmation.

PROFESSIONAL APPLICATION QUESTIONS

(Suggested answers are on pages 631–636)

10.1 Accounts receivable circularisation

Your firm is the external auditor of Southwood Trading Limited and you are auditing the financial statements for the year ended 30 November 20X2. Southwood Trading has a turnover of £25 million and trade debtors at 30 November 20X2 were £5.2 million.

The engagement partner has asked you to consider the relative reliability and independence of evidence from third parties and certain matters relating to a debtors' circularisation.

In relation to part (b)(ii) of the question the partner has explained that judgement would be used to select debtors which appear doubtful and those which would not be selected using the monetary unit sampling technique described in part (b)(i).

Required
(a) Consider the relative reliability and independence of the following types of evidence from third parties:
   (i)   replies to a debtors' circularisation to confirm trade debtors;
   (ii)   suppliers' statements to confirm purchase ledger balances.
(b) In relation to selecting debtors for circularisation:
   (i)   explain how you would use monetary unit sampling to select the debtors to circularise;
   (ii)   consider the criteria you would use to select individual debtors for circularisation using judgement;
   (iii) discuss the advantages and disadvantages of using monetary unit sampling (in (i) above) as compared with judgement (in (ii) above) to select the debtors to circularise. Your answer should consider the reasons why it is undesirable only to use judgement to select the debtors for circularisation.
(c) Describe the audit work you would carry out in following up the responses to a debtors' circularisation where:
   (i)   the debtor disagrees the balance and provides a different balance;
   (ii)   no reply to the circularisation has been received from the debtor and all attempts at obtaining a reply have failed.

(Adapted from Question 2, Audit Framework, December 1998. Reproduced by permission of ACCA)

10.2 Control procedures – cash receipts and debtors
Bardwell Ltd operates a garage which repairs and services motor vehicles. Most customers are required to pay by cash or cheque on collecting their vehicle. Credit accounts are available to business customers. These customers sign the invoice on collection of the vehicle and the business is billed monthly. Separate series of prenumbered invoices are drawn up by the foreman for cash sales and for credit sales. All customer accounts are maintained by the receptionist. His duties include the following:

Cash sales
   i.   Collect cash or cheques from customers on collecting their vehicle.
   ii.   At the end of the day, check the numerical sequence of cash sales invoices, add the sales total and agree the total to the amount of cash and cheques received.
   iii. Record the total cash sales in the cash receipts book.

Credit sales
   i.   Obtain the customer's signature on the copy invoice of business account customers.
   ii.   Enter the invoices in numerical sequence in the sales journal and post the customer's account in the sales ledger.
   iii. Send monthly statements to credit account customers and follow up overdue accounts.

   iv. List the balances on the sales ledger at the end of the month and reconcile the total with the control account in the general ledger.

   v. Write off uncollectible balances to bad debts.

Cash receipts

   i. Open the mail, extract cheques from credit account customers, record them in the cash receipts book and post the sales ledger.

   ii. Make up the day's banking of cash (and cheques) from both cash and credit sales, prepare the deposit slip and bank the cash.

   iii. All other accounting duties are the responsibility of two further accounts clerks and all are subject to supervision by the garage manager.

Required

(a) Explain in what way the functions assigned to the receptionist result in an inadequate segregation of duties. Your explanation should identify misstatements that could occur and indicate how those duties could be reassigned to other staff members.

(b) Identify other control procedures you would consider necessary to ensure the completeness of the recorded cash receipts and debtors.

(Adapted from Question 1, Audit Framework, June 2001. Reproduced by permission of ACCA)

CHAPTER 11

AUDITING PURCHASES, CREDITORS AND PAYROLL

◿ LEARNING **OBJECTIVES**

After studying this chapter, you should be able to:

1   identify the audit objectives applicable to purchases, creditors and payroll

2   describe the functions and control activities normally found in information systems for processing purchase, payment and payroll transactions

3   apply the concepts of materiality and inherent risk to the audit of purchases, creditors and payroll

4   discuss considerations relevant to determining the audit strategy for purchases, creditors and payroll

5   design and execute tests of control over purchase, payment and payroll transactions in order to assess control risk

6   indicate the factors relevant to determining an acceptable level of detection risk for the audit of purchases, creditors and payroll

7   design a substantive audit programme for purchases, creditors and payroll

8   explain the use of suppliers' statements in verifying the completeness of recorded liabilities.

PROFESSIONAL STATEMENTS

ISA 315   Understanding the Entity and Its Environment and Assessing the Risks of Material Misstatement

This chapter examines the audit of:

- the account balances of creditors (accounts payable) and of accruals related to payroll; and
- the transaction classes of purchases, payments and payroll.

Purchases and payments are for the acquisition of goods and services from outside suppliers, while payroll relates to the acquisition of, and payment for, labour services from employees. Together, they represent the major expenditures of most entities. There are similarities between the two in that both involve the acquisition of resources and payment to the suppliers. However, the nature of the employment contract between the entity and its employees is such that payroll transactions are always processed separately, including the payment of salaries and wages.

This chapter follows a similar structure to that of the previous chapter on auditing sales and debtors. It begins by identifying the audit objectives for each of the financial statement assertions that applies to the transaction classes mentioned above and to the creditors' and accrued payroll liability balances and related disclosures. In the rest of the chapter we will follow the audit process from obtaining the understanding of the internal control structure, through the assessment of the inherent and control risks to the design and execution of substantive procedures.

AUDIT OBJECTIVES

The audit objectives for purchases, payables and payroll relate to obtaining sufficient appropriate evidence about each significant financial statement assertion for the applicable transactions and balances. Table 11.1 lists the primary objectives for each assertion that apply in most audits of these transactions and balances.

Table 11.1 Selected specific audit objectives for purchases, creditors and payroll

ASSERTION CATEGORY	TRANSACTION CLASS AUDIT OBJECTIVES	ACCOUNT BALANCE AUDIT OBJECTIVES
Existence or occurrence	Recorded purchase transactions represent goods and services received (**EO1**) Recorded payment transactions represent payments made to suppliers and creditors (**EO2**) Recorded payroll expenses relate to employee services received (**EO3**)	Recorded trade creditors represent amounts owed by the entity at the balance sheet date (**EO4**) Accrued payroll liability balances represent amounts owed at the balance sheet date (**EO5**)
Completeness	All purchase (**C1**) and payment (**C2**) transactions that occurred have been recorded Recorded payroll expenses include all such expenses incurred (**C3**)	Trade creditors include all amounts owed by the entity to suppliers of goods and services at the balance sheet date (**C4**) Accrued payroll liabilities include all amounts owed in respect of payroll and deductions therefrom at the balance sheet date (**C5**)
Rights and obligations	Recorded purchase (**RO1**) and payroll (**RO2**) transactions represent the liabilities of the entity	Trade creditors (**RO3**) and accrued payroll liabilities (**RO4**) are liabilities of the entity at the balance sheet date
Accuracy, classification and valuation	Purchase transactions (**ACV1**), payment transactions (**ACV2**) and payroll transactions (**ACV3**) are correctly recorded in the accounting system	Trade creditors (**ACV4**) and accrued payroll liabilities (**ACV5**) are stated at the correct amount owed Related expense balances conform with applicable Accounting Standards (**ACV6**)
Cut-off	All purchase (**C-01**), payment (**C-02**) and payroll transactions (**C-03**) are recorded in the correct accounting period	
Presentation and disclosure	The details of purchase (**PD1**), payment (**PD2**) and payroll (**PD3**) transactions support their presentation in the financial statements, including their classification and disclosure	Trade creditors (**PD4**), accrued payroll liabilities (**PD5**) and related expenses (**PD6**) are properly identified and classified in the financial statements Disclosures pertaining to commitments, contingent liabilities and related party creditors are adequate (**PD7**)

To achieve each audit objective, auditors employ a combination of tests of control and substantive procedures (as determined by the audit strategy adopted), following the audit planning and testing methods described in Chapters 5–9. The procedures are much the same as those illustrated for sales and debtors in Chapter 10. Each audit objective is numbered in Table 11.1 (e.g. the first objective is numbered EO1). Specific controls and audit procedures described in this chapter will be referenced, using this numbering system, to the applicable audit objective.

◁ LEARNING CHECK

11.1 The balance of trade creditors is determined by transactions relating to purchases and payments, and accrued payroll liabilities are determined by payroll transactions.

11.2 Audit objectives for purchases, creditors and payroll relate to each assertion for purchase, payment and payroll transactions for trade creditors and to payroll liability accrual balances.

PURCHASE, PAYMENT AND PAYROLL TRANSACTIONS

This section describes features of internal control components typically employed by entities in processing and recording purchase, payment and payroll transactions. It describes information systems likely to be identified by auditors in obtaining the understanding of internal control. Control activities normally found in such systems are also described and referenced to the assertions and audit objectives (identified in Table 11.1) to which they relate. Identifying the presence of these control activities and evaluating their design effectiveness enables auditors to make the preliminary assessment of control risk.

Purchase transactions relate to the purchase (from outside entities) of (1) goods including stocks (inventory), fixed assets (plant and equipment), and supplies, and (2) services, such as the supply of utilities and advertising, and the rent of premises. Payment transactions relate to the payment for such goods and services. In this chapter it will be presumed that most purchases are on credit and that payment is of balances recorded in the bought (accounts payable) ledger. Figure 11.1 presents a flow chart that shows the basic features of manual and computer systems for processing purchase and payment transactions. The flow chart is not intended to show every document, record, process or account involved. More detailed flow charts are presented later in the chapter.

Variations in purchase information systems include the use of either a purchase journal or a voucher register for recording purchases. Use of a purchase journal system is assumed in this chapter. Thus, the key accounting records shown in the flow chart in Figure 11.1 are the purchase journal (or purchase day book) for recording purchases and the cash book (or cheque register) for recording payments to suppliers. As with sales transactions, recorded purchases occasionally need to be adjusted to take account of claims for credit in respect of returned goods and invoicing errors. Unlike sales adjustments, the extent of such transactions relating to purchases is rarely material, and this chapter does not consider such adjustments as a separate class of transaction.

Payroll relates to payment for the services of employees. Most entities have a detailed information system and related internal control procedures for recording labour services

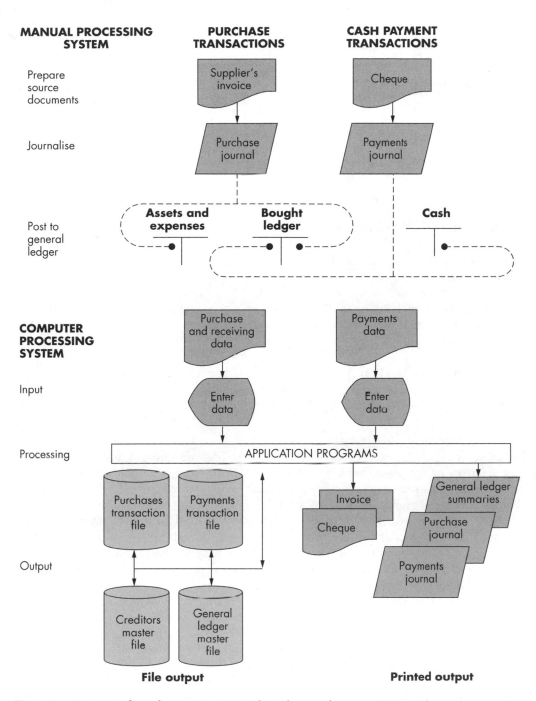

Figure 11.1 *Overview flow chart – processing of purchase and payment transactions*

(typically in the form of hours worked) and ensuring that payment is only made to current employees in respect of labour services actually provided.

Purchase transactions

We begin by identifying the separate functions involved in making purchases, the documents and records that are used in processing the transactions, and the control activities commonly applied to reduce the risk of fraud or error. Among the control activities considered here are information processing controls, the segregation of duties, physical controls and performance reviews.

FUNCTIONS

The processing of purchase transactions involves the following functions:

- requisitioning goods and services;
- preparing purchase orders;
- receiving the goods;
- storing goods received for stock;
- checking and approving the supplier's invoice; and
- recording the liability.

When practicable, each of these functions should be assigned to a different individual or department. In such cases, the work of one employee or department can provide an independent check on the accuracy of the work of another.

Requisitioning goods and services

Purchase requisitions may originate from stores (the warehouse) for stock or from any department for other items. For stock items, computerised stock records are often programmed to issue requisitions automatically when predetermined reorder levels are reached. For purchases other than stock replenishment, requisitioning authority is granted to specific individuals. This authority is usually restricted in value and to the types of goods and services applicable to the individual's function and level of authority. A stationery clerk may requisition sundry stationery supplies, for example, but only the office manager may requisition a photocopier service contract. Special procedures usually apply for requisitioning plant and equipment or for entering into lease contracts.

Purchase requisition forms may be prepared manually or electronically. Manually prepared forms should be signed by a person with the appropriate requisitioning authority. The requisition will normally indicate the general ledger account coding for the purchase, being one over which the person making the requisition has budgetary responsibility.

Purchase requisitions are usually pre-numbered within each originating department as a control over outstanding requisitions to ensure that goods requisitioned are duly ordered and received. The purchase requisition represents the start of the transaction trail of documentary evidence in support of management's assertion as to the occurrence of purchase transactions. Thus, it provides evidence that relates to the specific audit objective coded **EO1** in Table 11.1.

Preparing purchase orders

The purchasing department should issue purchase orders only on the receipt of requisitions properly approved by an employee having appropriate requisitioning authority (except for programmed stock replenishment). Before placing an order the purchasing department personnel should ascertain the best source of supply and, for major items, should obtain competitive bids.

Segregating requisitioning from ordering achieves two controls. It restricts the opportunity for those making requisitions to issue fraudulent orders, such as for goods for their own use. Purchasing department personnel are less likely to issue improper orders because they do not normally have access to goods delivered. The second control is improved efficiency through the centralisation of purchasing in a specialised department. The purchasing department is better able to negotiate more favourable terms and prices and, by amalgamating orders, can obtain better volume discounts.

Purchase orders should contain a precise description of the goods and services required, quantities, price, delivery instructions and the supplier's name and address. Purchase orders should be pre-numbered and signed by an authorised purchasing officer. The original is sent to the supplier and copies are distributed internally to the receiving department, the accounting department and the requisitioner.

The purchase orders also become part of the transaction trail of documentary evidence that supports the occurrence assertion for purchase transactions (**EO1**). A file of unfilled purchase orders is generally maintained on the computer or as a hard copy. A subsequent independent check on the disposition of purchase orders to determine that the goods and services were received and recorded relates to the completeness assertion for purchase transactions (**C1**).

Receiving the goods

A valid purchase order represents the authorisation for the receiving department to accept goods delivered by suppliers. The quantity ordered is sometimes obliterated to ensure that receiving clerks will make careful counts when the goods are received. Receiving department personnel should compare the goods received with the description of the goods on the purchase order, count the goods and inspect them for damage. Delivery of unordered goods should be refused.

The segregation of receiving from requisitioning and purchase ordering prevents those making requisitions from ordering goods directly from suppliers. It also prevents the purchasing department from gaining access to goods improperly ordered.

A pre-numbered goods received note should be prepared for each delivery. In a computer information system, it may be prepared by adding the appropriate receiving data to order details held on file. The goods received note is an important document in supporting the occurrence assertion for purchase transactions (**EO1**). A copy of the goods received note is forwarded to accounts. A periodic independent check on the sequence of pre-numbered goods received notes (to determine that a supplier's invoice has been recorded for each) relates to the completeness assertion (**C1**).

Storing goods received for stock

On delivery of the goods to stores or other requisitioning department, receiving clerks should obtain a signed receipt on the copy of the goods received note retained by the receiving department. This provides further evidence for the occurrence assertion for the purchase transaction (**EO1**). The signed receipt also establishes subsequent accountability for the purchased goods. The physical safekeeping of stock and the maintenance of records over stock quantities will be considered in Chapter 12.

Checking and approving the supplier's invoice

For goods and services supplied on credit, the supplier is usually instructed by the purchase order to send the invoice directly to the entity's accounting department. Prior to being recorded suppliers' invoices are checked and approved. Procedures applicable to this function include:

- serially numbering suppliers' invoices on receipt so that subsequent checks of numerical continuity can confirm that all invoices are recorded (**C1**);
- establishing the agreement of the details of suppliers' invoices with the related goods received notes and purchase orders to ensure that all invoices relate to valid purchase transactions (**EO1**);
- determining the mathematical accuracy of the suppliers' invoices (**ACV1**);
- coding the account distributions on the suppliers' invoices (i.e. indicating the asset and expense accounts to be debited) (**ACV1, PD1**);
- approving the invoices for payment by having an authorised person sign the invoice (**EO1, RO1**); and
- preparing a daily prelist of suppliers' invoices approved for payment (**EO1, C1, ACV1**).

A common practice is to stamp a grid on the supplier's invoice. The grid has boxes in which to record the serial numbers of purchase orders and goods received notes, the account codes and the initials of the clerk performing the check. Invoices, purchase orders and goods received notes are commonly stapled together to support the subsequent payment and are then filed by supplier.

Other kinds of supporting documentation (such as copies of contracts) may be required when the invoice relates to certain types of service or to leased assets. In other cases, such as for monthly utility bills, the supplier's invoice alone may suffice because there is no purchase order and goods received note. Other forms of verification will be required, such as a check of utility bills against meter readings recorded in a special register.

Unpaid suppliers' invoices and supporting documentation are held in a file in the accounts department pending their subsequent payment. Properly approved suppliers' invoices provide the basis for recording purchase transactions.

Recording the liability

In manual systems, the approved suppliers' invoices are entered in the purchase journal, the monthly totals of which are posted to the creditors' control account in the general ledger. The approved suppliers' invoices are sent daily, with a prelist, to the accounting department for recording in the bought ledger. An accounting supervisor should perform an independent check of the agreement of the total of the invoices recorded by accounting personnel with the daily prelist. Furthermore, a supervisor should check, each month, that the total of balances on the bought ledger agrees with the control account in the general ledger. A discrepancy will indicate the presence of errors in the recording of suppliers' invoices in either the purchase journal or the bought ledger (**EO1, C1, ACV1**).

In batch processing computer information systems, personnel in the accounts department either send approved suppliers' invoices to the computer department or enter the data via terminals. Programmed edit checks are made for such matters as valid suppliers and the reasonableness of amounts. When the data for a supplier's invoice are accepted by the computer, the accounts payable master file for that supplier is updated and the invoice is added to the purchase transactions file. Additional controls over the accuracy of the data entry process include the use of batch totals and exception reports (**EO1, C1, ACV1**).

The purchase transactions file is used to update the stock and general ledger master files. Print-outs of the purchase journal and a general ledger summary showing the amounts posted to general ledger accounts are produced by the update program and sent to accounting. An accounting supervisor determines the agreement of the print-outs with the prelist prepared.

In on-line systems the invoice is entered immediately on receipt, automatically approved by reference to order and receiving details, and coded by reference to information recorded on the order. The accounts payable, inventory and general ledger files are immediately updated. Manual verification is required only if programmed application controls reject the invoice.

Monthly statements received from suppliers should be reconciled with the recorded supplier balances. Periodic performance reviews by management, in the form of comparisons of asset, liability and expense balances with budgeted amounts, can provide a means of both controlling expenditures and detecting misstatements in recorded purchase transactions.

ILLUSTRATIVE SYSTEM FOR PURCHASE TRANSACTIONS

A flow chart of a representative system for processing purchase transactions is shown in Figure 11.2. In this system, purchase orders are prepared in the purchasing department using on-line terminals. Multi-copy purchase orders are printed and distributed, as shown in the flow chart, and an open purchase order file is maintained on the computer. When goods arrive in the receiving department, a copy of the matching purchase order is pulled from the file. The goods are then counted, inspected and compared against relevant details on the copy of the purchase order. Next, receiving clerks use their computer terminals to retrieve the computer record of the purchase order from the open purchase order file. After a clerk keys in the quantities received, the computer produces a multi-copy goods received note and transfers the record from the open purchase order file to the goods received note file. The copies of the goods received note are distributed as shown in the flow chart.

Copies of the purchase order and goods received note for each transaction are placed in a holding file in the accounts department pending arrival of the supplier's invoice. Once the supplier's invoice arrives, an accounts clerk checks its mathematical accuracy and compares it with the purchase order and goods received note.

Batches of approved matched documents are assembled and a batch total is calculated manually. Data keyed in from the suppliers' invoices, together with matching data extracted by the computer from the goods received note file, are then used to create the purchase transactions file. The batch total is printed out and compared with the manual

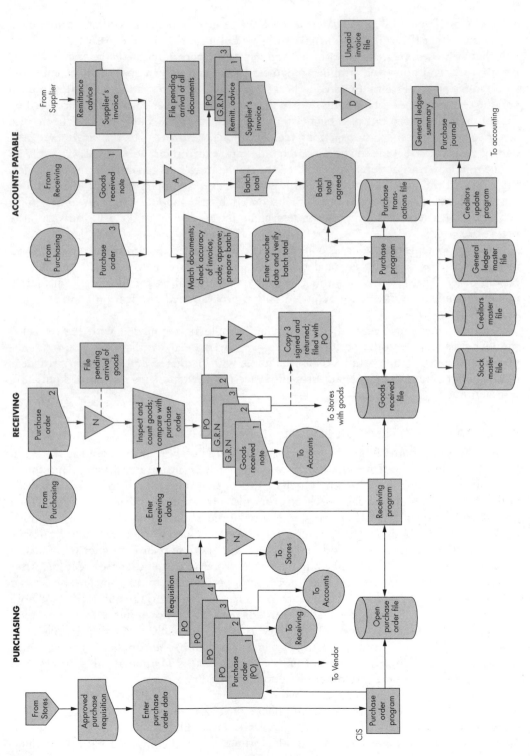

Figure 11.2 *System flow chart – purchase transactions*

batch total in accounts, and any differences are resolved. The unpaid suppliers' invoices are collated with the supporting documents and filed by due date in the accounts department.

The purchase transactions file is subsequently used to update the creditors, stock and general ledger master files. Outputs of that run include a purchase journal listing the newly processed invoices and a general ledger summary showing the totals posted to the general ledger accounts.

Payment transactions

This section considers the common documents and records, functions and control activities for payment transactions.

FUNCTIONS

The two payments functions are:

- paying the liability; and
- recording the payments.

These functions should not be performed by the same department or individual.

Paying the liability

The accounts department is responsible for ensuring that suppliers' invoices are processed for payment on their due dates. Payment is normally required within 30 days and, in practice, most entities pay the unpaid creditors' balance at the end of each calendar month. Where prompt payment discounts are allowed, such as a 2% discount on invoices paid within 10 days, and where it is entity policy to take them up, relevant invoices need to be scheduled for payment within the allowed period.

Payments are normally by cheque, although regular suppliers may be paid by credit transfer. In a manual system, a cheque requisition is prepared and forwarded to the treasurer's department for preparation of the cheques. The requisition is usually accompanied by supporting documentation consisting of the supplier's statement and related invoices (including the attached orders and goods received notes).

In a batch computer system, the computer can be programmed to extract the payments due on each day from the accounts payable master file, produce the cheques and a cheque summary (or a credit transfer list), and enter the payment data in a payment transactions file. The cheques (and credit transfer list) are then forwarded to the accounts department, where they are physically matched with the supporting documents before being forwarded to the treasurer's office for signing.

Where controls over input to the accounts payable master file are strong, computer-produced cheques may be mechanically signed using a signature plate. The signatory should maintain physical custody of the signature plate and release it only after scrutiny of the list of cheques to be signed. In such systems, cheques must be mailed directly from the computer department and not returned to the accounts department. With on-line banking, credit transfer details may be electronically transmitted to the bank. Access controls should restrict this function to approved signatories.

Controls over the preparation and signing of the cheques and related specific audit objectives include the following:

- authorised personnel in the treasurer's department, who otherwise have no responsibility for initiating or processing purchase transactions, should be responsible for signing the cheques (**EO2**);
- authorised cheque signers should determine that each cheque is accompanied by properly approved suppliers' invoices, and that the name of the payee and amount on the cheque agree with details on the invoice (**ACV2**);
- the suppliers' invoices and supporting documents should be stamped (or otherwise cancelled) with the date or the cheque number when the cheque is signed to prevent resubmission for duplicate payment (**EO2**);
- the cheque signer should control the mailing of the cheques to reduce the risk of theft or alterations (**EO2**);
- no cheques should be made payable to 'cash' or 'bearer' and no blank cheques should be issued (**EO2**);
- pre-numbered cheques should be used (**C2**); and
- access to blank cheques and to signature plates should be limited to authorised personnel (**C2**).

Cheques generally include a perforated attachment known as a remittance advice which identifies the serial numbers of the invoice(s) being paid. Alternatively, copies of the supplier's statement or remittance advice provided by the supplier can be enclosed with the cheques mailed to suppliers.

Recording the payments

In manual systems, accounting personnel journalise the payments from the cheques issued to the payments journal or the cheque register. These personnel should not participate in the execution of purchase transactions such as checking, approving or recording suppliers' invoices, or in the preparation of the cheques. In computer systems, the payment transactions file created when cheques are prepared is used to update the accounts payable master file and general ledger accounts. The update program also produces the payments journal and a general ledger summary, which are forwarded to accounting.

Controls over the recording of payments include:

- an independent check by an accounting supervisor of the agreement of the amounts journalised and posted to the bought ledger with the cheque summary received from the treasurer (**EO2, C2, ACV2**); and
- independently prepared bank reconciliations (**EO2, C2, ACV2**).

Payroll transactions

An entity's payroll transactions include salaries, hourly and incentive (piecework) wages, commissions, bonuses and employee benefits (e.g. health insurance and paid holidays). This section will focus on hourly paid employees. The payroll transactions also record deductions from payroll in determining net pay. These deductions may be statutory (such as taxation) or by agreement (such as employee contributions to a pension scheme). Deductions are recorded as liabilities for payment to the appropriate body.

FUNCTIONS

The relevant functions are those of:

- hiring employees;
- authorising payroll changes;
- preparing attendance and timekeeping data;
- preparing the payroll;
- recording the payroll; and
- paying the payroll and protecting unclaimed wages.

Below we will explain each function. Where applicable, we will refer to the flow chart in Figure 11.3, which shows a representative system for processing payroll transactions. In this case, the entity is using on-line entry/on-line processing for payroll authorisation changes and batch entry/batch processing for preparing the payroll.

It is evident from the flow chart that responsibility for executing and recording payroll is spread over several departments. This segregation of duties significantly contributes to reducing the risk of payments to fictitious employees and the risk of excessive payments to actual employees due to inflated rates or hours.

Hiring employees

Employees are hired by the personnel department. Details are documented on a personnel authorisation form which should indicate the job classification, starting wage rate and authorised payroll deductions. In the system shown in Figure 11.3, data on new employees are entered in the personnel data master file. Access to data entry to this file is restricted, by password, to authorised individuals in the personnel department. One copy of the personnel authorisation form is placed in the employee's personnel file in the personnel department. Another copy is sent to the payroll department. Periodically, a computer-generated log of all changes to the master file is printed and independently checked by a personnel manager not involved in entering the data into the computer.

Segregating the functions of personnel and payroll reduces the risk of payments to fictitious employees because only the personnel department may add new employees to the personnel master file and only the payroll department may process the payment of wages (EO3, RO2). This segregation of function is also an important control in the next function – authorising payroll changes. Thus, personnel department employees cannot benefit from falsifying personnel records, while payroll department employees can process payroll only for employees listed in the personnel records and at the wage rates specified therein.

Authorising payroll changes

The request for a change in job classification (or a wage rate increase) may be initiated by the employee's supervisor. However, all changes should be authorised in writing by the personnel department before being entered in the personnel data master file. Other

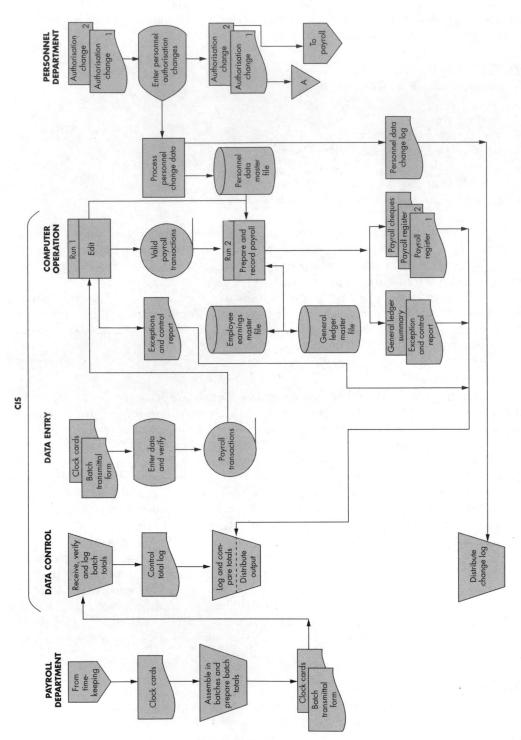

Figure 11.3 *System flow chart – payroll transactions*

controls over entering the changes in the computer and distributing the change forms are the same as those for new employees. These controls over payroll changes help to ensure the accuracy of the payroll (**RO2, ACV3**).

The personnel department should also issue a termination notice on completion of an individual's employment. It is vital that the payroll department is promptly notified of such terminations to prevent payment continuing to be made to employees after they have left (**EO3**).

Preparing attendance and timekeeping data

In many entities, a timekeeping department is responsible for this function for hourly paid employees. Time clocks are frequently used to record time worked. Each employee 'clocks on' and 'clocks off' by inserting a clock card or employee identity card in the clock. To prevent one employee from 'punching in' for another, the time clock should be located in view of supervisory or security personnel. It may also be used to record direct labour charged to individual jobs within work in progress, thus ensuring the reliability of costing records and stock valuation.

All time worked that has been recorded on clock cards should be approved in writing by a supervisor, particularly with regard to the authorisation of overtime. The timekeeping department then forwards the clock cards to the payroll department for use in preparing the payroll. In modern systems the time clock is electronically linked to the computer. Approval of hours worked is signalled by the supervisor using his or her personal access code. These controls ensure that payment is made only for hours worked (**EO3, RO2**).

Preparing the payroll

Figure 11.3 illustrates typical controls in a basic system for preparing the payroll. Clock cards are batched in the payroll department and a batch total is prepared of hours worked. The documents and a batch transmittal form are then sent to data control in the computer department. Data control verifies the information on the batch transmittal form, enters the batch totals in a control log, and forwards the documents to data entry where they are keyed into the system. The resulting payroll transactions data are then used in preparing the payroll.

In run 1 (see Figure 11.3), the payroll transactions are subjected to an edit check routine, including a check for a valid employee number and a limit or reasonableness check on the hours worked. The output of this run consists of a valid payroll transactions file and an exceptions and control report that is sent to data control. Data control compares the control totals with the batch control log, informs the payroll department of exceptions discovered by the edit routine, and follows up to see that the payroll department submits corrected data. In the system shown in Figure 11.3, the calculation of the payroll and the preparation of the payroll register and payroll cheques occur in run 2. The program uses data from the valid payroll transactions file, the personnel data master file and the employee earnings master file(s). This run also records the payroll, as described in the next section.

Recording the payroll

Using calculated gross pay, deductions and net pay for each employee from run 2, the program updates the employee earnings master file and accumulates totals for the payroll journal entry that is generated and entered in the general ledger master file at the end of the run. The following printed outputs of this run are sent to data control:

- an exceptions and control report that data control reviews before distributing the other printed output;
- a copy of the payroll register that is returned to the payroll department for comparison with the original batch transmittal data;
- a second copy of the payroll register and pre-numbered payroll cheques that are sent to the treasurer's office (or pay slips and a cheque for total net pay if wages are paid in cash); and
- a general ledger summary that is sent to accounting, showing the payroll entry generated by the payroll program.

Proper review of each of these outputs by the appropriate personnel contributes to control over misstatements (**EO3, C3, RO2, ACV3**).

In manual systems, it is common practice for a senior accounting officer to approve the payroll before payroll cheques are prepared. In smaller entities, the authorising officer could verify payroll by reconciling it with the previous period's payroll, allowing for hirings, terminations, changes in hours worked, etc. In any event, the payroll should be independently checked against personnel records at regular intervals.

Paying the payroll and protecting unclaimed wages

These functions are not shown in Figure 11.3. However, the preceding section shows that the payroll cheques and a copy of the payroll register are sent to the treasurer's or chief accountant's office where these functions are commonly performed. Applicable controls include the following:

- Treasurer's office personnel should check the agreement of the names and amounts on cheques with payroll register entries (**EO3, C3, ACV3**).
- Payroll cheques should be signed by treasurer's office personnel not involved in preparing or recording the payroll, using cheque-signing machines and signature plates.
- Access to cheque-signing machines and signature plates should be restricted to authorised individuals.
- Payroll cheques should be distributed to employees by treasurer's office personnel not involved in preparing or recording the payroll, who should require proper identification of employees (**EO3, ACV3**).
- Unclaimed payroll cheques should be stored in a safe or vault in the treasurer's office (**EO3, C3**).

Another important control over paying the payroll in many large entities is the use of an imprest payroll bank account on which all payroll cheques are drawn. This account is funded with the amount of net pay. Any errors in preparing payroll cheques or deliberate falsification of payroll cheques would soon be detected because cheques paid in would exceed the account balance, causing the bank to refuse acceptance (**EO3, ACV3**). Increasingly, entities are paying wages by direct credit transfer to employee bank accounts, eliminating the need for cheques and the associated risks of their misuse.

Some entities pay wages in cash. The payroll system is designed to produce pay slips instead of pay cheques, and a single cheque is produced for the total net pay. The exact amount of cash should be drawn from the bank, and the pay envelopes should be filled and distributed by authorised treasurer's office personnel not involved in preparing or recording the payroll. A preferred system is to arrange for a security company to collect the cash from the bank and make up the pay envelopes, which are then delivered to the entity ready for distribution. Unclaimed wage packets should be returned immediately to a safe in the accounting office and recorded in an unclaimed wages book. If unclaimed by the end of the day, the wages should be rebanked.

LEARNING **CHECK**

11.3 Purchasing involves the functions of:

- requisitioning;

- ordering;

- receiving;

- storing goods;

- approving the invoice; and

- recording the liability.

11.4 An important control is the segregation of each of these functions.

11.5 Requisitioning is either automatic on reaching the stock reorder point, or by authorised individuals.

11.6 The purchasing department obtains goods and services on the best terms, and issues purchase orders to suppliers.

11.7 The receiving department only accepts goods as ordered, and issues goods received notes.

11.8 Goods are sent to the warehouse which is responsible for the safe custody of stock.

11.9 The accounts department approves invoices by verifying details against orders and goods received notes.

11.10 Approved suppliers' invoices are recorded in the purchase journal and bought ledger with appropriate controls to ensure completeness and accuracy.

11.11 Payment involves the functions of:

- paying the liability; and

- recording the payment.

11.12 In manual systems, the cheque signer verifies supporting documents and cancels them to prevent reuse.

11.13 In computer systems, reliance may be placed on controls over the existence of liabilities entered in the accounts payable master file. Cheques are produced by the computer and mechanically signed. It is vital that cheques are not returned to the purchasing and accounts departments.

11.14 Payroll transactions involve the functions of:

- hiring;

- authorising changes;

- timekeeping;

- preparing the payroll;

- recording the payroll; and

- distributing pay.

11.15 It is important to segregate the personnel functions of hiring and authorising changes from all other payroll functions.

11.16 The greatest risk is of payments to fictitious employees, either through entering details of fictitious employees in the records, or by failing to remove details of employees who have left.

DEVELOPING THE AUDIT PLAN

In the previous section, we illustrated features of the internal control structure relating to purchase, payment and payroll transactions typically identified and recorded by auditors in obtaining the understanding as required by ISA 315, Understanding the Entity and Its Environment and Assessing the Risks of Material Misstatement. The next phase of the audit is to assess inherent and control risk to assess the risk of material misstatement at the assertion level. This phase commences with the auditors considering materiality and inherent risk and making a preliminary assessment of control risk based mainly on evaluating the design effectiveness of the internal controls. This enables the auditors to determine the audit strategy and to plan an appropriate mix of tests of control and substantive procedures. Tests of control confirm (or otherwise) the auditors' preliminary assessment of control risk by testing operating effectiveness. Results of the tests of control may require a reassessment of control risk and a revision of the planned level of substantive procedures.

Audit strategy considerations

Audit strategy refers to the mix of tests of control and substantive procedures to be applied in the audit. The main determinants of the mix are the assessed levels of inherent and control risks. Materiality considerations also influence the level of substantive procedures. This section will begin by considering the materiality of the relevant transactions and balances. Factors related to inherent and control risks, and the implications of both materiality and inherent and control risks in determining the audit strategy will then be considered.

MATERIALITY

Purchase and payroll transactions account for the major expenses incurred by a business, so are a major component in the determination of net profit. They also relate to the acquisition of major classes of asset (notably stocks and plant and machinery), which are also individually material. Moreover, the balance on trade creditors produced by credit purchase transactions is nearly always material to the balance sheet. Thus, auditors seek to achieve a low level of risk that errors in purchase and payroll transactions could cause material misstatements in the financial statements.

INHERENT AND CONTROL RISKS

In assessing inherent risk for purchase and payroll assertions, auditors should consider pervasive factors that could motivate management to misstate expenditure. These may include:

- pressures to understate expenses in order to report, falsely, the achievement of announced profitability targets or industry norms; or
- pressures to understate payables in order to report a higher level of working capital in the face of liquidity problems or going-concern doubts.

These factors primarily affect the completeness assertion and reduce the acceptable detection risk, particularly in testing for understatement of liabilities.

Other factors that may contribute to misstatements include:

- the high volume of transactions, which affects all assertions;
- temptations for employees to make unauthorised purchases and payments, or to misappropriate purchased assets, which relate to the occurrence assertion;
- contentious accounting issues such as whether a cost should be capitalised or expensed (for example, the treatment of repairs and maintenance costs or the classification of a lease as an operating or finance lease), which relate to the classification assertion; and
- the complexity of payroll computations for factory workers whose gross earnings may be based on time and/or productivity, affecting the classification of payroll costs.

Payroll fraud is a major concern for auditors. Employees involved in preparing and paying the payroll may process data for fictitious employees or for employees whose services have already been terminated, and then divert the wages for their own use. This affects the auditors' assessment of risk for the occurrence assertion for payroll.

In most well-established entities, management's own risk assessment procedures will have led it to adopt control activities to reduce the risk of misstatements occurring in the processing and recording of transactions. However, the existence and effectiveness of controls pertaining to different transaction class assertions for purchases, payments and payroll can vary considerably among entities and even among assertions for the same entity. Moreover, auditors must remain mindful of the inherent limitations of internal control, including the possibility of management override, collusion, errors due to fatigue or misunderstanding, and failure to adapt the control structure for changed circumstances.

AUDIT STRATEGY

The high volume of transactions, combined with the likely existence of effective control activities over these transactions, means that it is normally appropriate to adopt an approach based on a lower assessed level of control risk, particularly in respect to the occurrence, accuracy and classification assertions. For other assertions, the audit strategy may vary with the assessed risk of material misstatement. The volume of transactions, however, means that the lower assessed level of control risk approach is preferred wherever the assessment of risk can support such a strategy.

Control environment

Factors relating to the control environment that auditors need to consider when assessing control risk for purchase, payment and payroll transactions include those described below:

- *Integrity and ethical values* are important because there are numerous opportunities for employee fraud in processing purchase, payment and payroll transactions, and for fraudulent financial reporting by management of expense account balances. Purchasing agents may be subjected to pressures from solicitous suppliers, for example, including offers of 'kickbacks' for transacting more business with those suppliers.
- Management's *commitment to competence* should be reflected in the assignment and training of personnel involved in processing purchasing, payment and payroll transactions. In particular, individuals involved in payroll functions should be knowledgeable about employment laws and regulations, and the applicable provisions of labour contracts.
- The entity's *organisational structure* and management's *assignment of authority and responsibility* over purchase, payment and payroll transactions should be clearly communicated and provide for clear lines of authority, responsibility and reporting relationships. As an example, purchasing, receiving, and stores or warehousing activities may fall under the duties of the production director; accounting may be the responsibility of the finance director; and payments may be supervised by the treasurer. Overall responsibility for personnel matters is often assigned to a director or manager of human or personnel resources. Officers' salaries and other forms of compensation are usually set by the board of directors.

Assessment of control risk

Assessment of control risk is normally undertaken in two phases. On obtaining the understanding of internal control, auditors will normally test the design effectiveness of controls and form a preliminary assessment. Where the design effectiveness of control risk is assessed as being less than high and a lower assessed level of control risk strategy adopted, tests of the operating effectiveness of controls will be included in the audit programme to confirm the preliminary assessment. Tests of both the design and operating effectiveness of control for each of the three transaction classes are described below.

PURCHASE TRANSACTIONS

Table 11.2 contains a partial listing of potential misstatements, necessary controls, potential tests of the operating effectiveness of those controls, and the specific transaction class audit objective for purchases to which each belongs.

Table 11.2 Control risk assessment considerations – purchase transactions

FUNCTION	POTENTIAL MISSTATEMENT	NECESSARY CONTROL	POSSIBLE TEST OF OPERATING EFFECTIVENESS	RELEVANT TRANSACTION CLASS AUDIT OBJECTIVE (FROM TABLE 11.1)					
				E01	C1	R01	ACV1	PD1	C-01
Requisitioning goods and services	Goods may be requisitioned for unauthorised purposes	General and specific authorisation procedures	Inquire about procedures	√					
Preparing purchase orders	Purchases may be made for unauthorised purposes	Approved purchase requisition for each order	Examine purchase orders for approved requisitions	√					
Receiving goods	Goods received may not have been ordered	Approved purchase order for each shipment	Examine goods received note for matching purchase order	√					
	Incorrect quantities, damaged goods, or incorrect items may be received	Receiving clerks to count, inspect and compare goods received with purchase order	Observe performance by receiving clerks	√					
Storing goods received for stock	Stores clerks may deny taking custody of purchased goods	Obtain signed receipt upon delivery of goods from Receiving to Stores	Inspect signed receipts	√					

(continued overleaf)

Table 11.2 (*continued*)

FUNCTION	POTENTIAL MISSTATEMENT	NECESSARY CONTROL	POSSIBLE TEST OF OPERATING EFFECTIVENESS	RELEVANT TRANSACTION CLASS AUDIT OBJECTIVE (FROM TABLE 11.1)					
				E01	C1	R01	ACV1	PD1	C-01
Approving the invoice	Invoices may be recorded for goods not ordered	Matching purchase order and goods received note with supplier's invoice	Examine supporting documentation for invoices*	✓	✓	✓	✓	✓	
Recording the liability	Invoices may be recorded incorrectly or not recorded	Independent check of agreement of prelist against amounts recorded in purchase journal	Examine evidence of independent check; reperform independent check*	✓	✓		✓	✓	
		Periodic accounting for pre-numbered goods received notes and purchase orders	Observe procedure; reperform		✓				
		Periodic performance reviews by management of reports, comparing actual asset, creditor and expense balances with budgeted amounts	Inquire of management about results of performance reviews; inspect reports*	✓	✓	✓	✓	✓	

Note: *Tests are sometimes performed as a part of dual-purpose tests.

Preliminary assessment – design effectiveness

The potential misstatements and necessary controls listed in Table 11.2 form the basis of internal control evaluation checklists. As explained in Chapter 10 on sales and debtors, auditors apply this checklist to the documented information system and reach a conclusion as to the effectiveness of controls relative to each potential misstatement. The basis for this conclusion is normally explained on the checklist, which thus forms part of the necessary documentation of the assessment of inherent and control risk. Where the auditors' understanding of the system is obtained and recorded by means of internal control questionnaires, this process simultaneously assesses and documents control effectiveness. Where controls over a particular assertion are judged to be effective and the auditors adopt a moderate or high planned level of detection risk for that assertion, the audit programme must incorporate tests of operating effectiveness.

Tests of operating effectiveness

The extent of tests of controls will vary inversely with the auditors' preliminary assessment of control risk. Statistical or non-statistical attribute sampling procedures (see Chapter 8) may be applicable to certain tests. Recall that the direction of testing must be compatible with the specific audit objective to which the test relates – vouching for occurrence and tracing for completeness. Evidence applicable to other assertion categories can be obtained from testing in either direction. Also, recall that some tests, particularly those pertaining to checking and approving suppliers' invoices and recording the liability, may be performed as dual-purpose tests. In these tests, evidence is obtained about the effects, measured in money, of processing errors on account balances, as well as about the frequency of deviations from controls. These tests are marked with an asterisk in Table 11.2. Based on the evidence obtained from procedures to obtain an understanding of internal control and related tests of control, the auditors make a final assessment of control risk for each significant assertion related to purchase transactions.

When the processing of purchase transactions is computer assisted, the auditors may use the computer in performing tests of control, using techniques similar to those described for sales transactions in Chapter 10. In particular, tests of effectiveness must be performed for any controls that serve as the basis for a control risk assessment at a reduced level. This includes making inquiries and inspecting documentation concerning general controls over changes to programs and master files used in processing purchase transactions.

Tests of application controls may include the use of test data to determine whether expected results are produced by the entity's program for accepting and recording data for unpaid suppliers' invoices in circumstances such as the following:

- a missing or invalid supplier number;
- a missing or invalid account classification code number;
- a missing or unreasonable amount;
- a missing due date or payment terms; or
- alphabetical characters in a numeric field.

Examples of other possible computer-assisted audit tests are:

- using generalised audit software or a database program to perform sequence checks in designated computer files and print exception reports of gaps in the sequence of purchase orders, goods received notes or invoices; and
- designing, selecting and evaluating an attribute sample of goods received notes or unpaid invoices.

PAYMENT TRANSACTIONS

Table 11.3 contains a partial listing of potential misstatements, necessary controls, possible tests of the operating effectiveness of those controls, and the specific transaction class audit objective for payments to which each belongs. As explained for purchases, the potential misstatements and necessary controls would be the basis of a checklist used to assess design effectiveness. Similarly, an audit programme for tests of the operating effectiveness

Table 11.3 Control risk assessment considerations – payment transactions

FUNCTION	POTENTIAL MISSTATEMENT	NECESSARY CONTROL	POSSIBLE TEST OF OPERATING EFFECTIVENESS	RELEVANT TRANSACTION CLASS AUDIT OBJECTIVE (FROM TABLE 11.1)					
				E02	C2	R02	ACV2	PD2	C-02
Paying the liability	Cheques may be issued for unauthorised purchases	Cheque signers review supporting documentation for completeness and approval	Observe cheque signers performing independent check of supporting documentation	✓		✓			
	An invoice may be paid twice	'Paid' stamp placed on invoice and supporting documents when cheque issued	Examine paid invoices for 'paid' stamp	✓					
	A cheque may be altered after being signed	Cheque signers mail cheques	Inquire about mailing procedures; observe mailing				✓		
Recording the payment	A cheque may not be recorded	Use of and accounting for pre-numbered cheques	Examine evidence of use of and accounting for pre-numbered cheques		✓		✓		
	Errors may be made in recording cheques	Independent check of agreement of amounts journalised and posted with cheque summary	Observe procedure; reperform*	✓	✓		✓		
		Periodic independent bank reconciliations	Examine bank reconciliations*	✓	✓		✓	✓	
	Cheques may not be recorded promptly	Independent check of dates on cheques with dates recorded	Reperform independent check	✓	✓				

Note: *Tests are sometimes performed as a part of dual-purpose tests.

of controls for payment transactions can be prepared, based on the potential tests of control in Table 11.3. Possible computer-assisted tests of control arc also similar to those for purchase transactions. Thus, for example, test data can be used to test programmed controls pertaining to the preparation and recording of cheques. Computer assistance can also be used to design, select and evaluate an attribute sample for payments.

PAYROLL TRANSACTIONS

The process of assessing the control risk for payroll transactions begins, as for purchases and payments, with identifying potential misstatements and necessary controls. These steps are shown in the second and third columns of Table 11.4. Possible tests of control are shown in the fourth column.

Table 11.4 Control risk assessment considerations for payroll transactions

FUNCTION	POTENTIAL MISSTATEMENT	NECESSARY CONTROL	POSSIBLE TEST OF OPERATING EFFECTIVENESS	RELEVANT TRANSACTION CLASS AUDIT OBJECTIVE (FROM TABLE 11.1)					
				EO3	C3	RO3	ACV3	PD3	C-03
Hiring employees	Fictitious employees may be added to the payroll	Personnel department authorisation for all new hires	Examine authorisation forms for new hires	✓		✓			
Authorising payroll changes	Employees may receive unauthorised rate increases	Personnel department authorisation for all rate changes	Inquire about procedures for authorising rate changes			✓	✓		
	Terminated employees may remain on the payroll	Personnel department notification to payroll department of all terminations	Examine termination notices in payroll department	✓					
Preparing attendance and time keeping data	Employees may be paid for hours not worked	Use of time clock procedures and supervisory approval of time tickets	Observe time clock procedures; examine time tickets for supervisory approval	✓	✓		✓	✓	
Preparing the payroll	Payroll data may be lost during submission to computer department	Batch totals of hours worked prepared by payroll department and verified by data control	Examine evidence of preparation and use of batch totals		✓				

(continued overleaf)

Table 11.4 (*continued*)

FUNCTION	POTENTIAL MISSTATEMENT	NECESSARY CONTROL	POSSIBLE TEST OF OPERATING EFFECTIVENESS	RELEVANT TRANSACTION CLASS AUDIT OBJECTIVE (FROM TABLE 11.1)					
				EO3	C3	RO3	ACV3	PD3	C-03
	Payroll transactions file may include incorrectly keyed or invalid data	Edit checks of data on payroll transactions file	Observe data entry procedures; examine exceptions and control report*	✓	✓		✓	✓	
Recording the payroll	Processing errors may occur in recording the payroll	Exceptions and control report reviewed by data control	Inquire about preparation and use of exceptions and control report*	✓	✓	✓	✓	✓	
	Unauthorised changes may be made to payroll data in computer department	Payroll department comparison of payroll register with original batch transmittal data	Reperform comparison*	✓	✓	✓	✓	✓	
Paying the payroll and protecting unclaimed wages	Payroll cheques may be distributed to unauthorised recipients	Employee identification on distribution	Witness distribution of payroll	✓	✓	✓	✓	✓	

Note: *Tests are sometimes performed as a part of dual-purpose tests.

In computer information systems (CIS), access controls over changes to personnel data are important. In the testing of controls in a CIS, test data can be used to test programmed controls pertaining to the preparation and recording of payroll. Where time recording is computerised, test data can also be used in testing programmed controls over time-keeping.

In assessing control risk, auditors realise that misstatements in payroll may result from intentional errors or fraud. Of particular concern is the risk of overstatement of payroll through:

- payments to fictitious employees;
- payments to actual employees for hours not worked; and
- payments to actual employees at higher than authorised rates.

The first two risks relate to the occurrence assertion. The third risk relates to the accuracy assertion.

The risk of understatement (the completeness assertion) is of minimal concern because employees will complain when they are underpaid. Accordingly, many tests of payroll controls are directed at controls that prevent or detect overstatements. The direction of testing for these controls is from the recorded payroll data to source documents; for example, the auditors may vouch data for a sample of employees in a payroll register to approved clock card data and authorised pay rates and deductions.

Two tests of control pertaining to the control risk for the occurrence assertion are the test for terminated employees and witnessing a payroll distribution. The former represents an exception to the normal direction of testing for payroll, in that the auditors select a sample of termination notices and scan subsequent payroll registers to determine that the terminated employees did not continue to receive pay cheques. In witnessing the distribution of payroll cheques or envelopes, the auditors observe that:

- segregation of duties exists between the preparation and payment of the payroll;
- each employee is identified by a badge or employee identification card;
- each employee receives only one cheque or pay envelope; and
- there is proper control and disposal of unclaimed wages.

Final assessment

Based on the evidence obtained from the procedures to obtain an understanding of internal control and related tests of control, the auditors make a final assessment of inherent and control risk. This assessment enables the auditors to confirm the planned level of substantive procedures to be performed. The auditors must ensure that control deviations are properly identified and that their implications for the assessment of control risk are properly considered as to whether further substantive procedures need to be performed.

 LEARNING **CHECK**

11.17 In developing the audit plan, auditors need to have:

- obtained the understanding of the accounting system, control procedures and control environment;

- assessed inherent risk both for the entity and for the specific transactions, balances and disclosures; and

- assessed control risk based on the results of tests of control.

11.18 Purchase, payment and payroll transactions are always material and trade creditors are nearly always material to an entity, making the audit of this area important to the audit overall.

11.19 The greatest inherent risks are those of fraudulent purchases for private use by an employee, understatement of credit purchase transactions and of the creditors' balance, and payments to fictitious employees. Because of the volume of transactions, most entities ensure their internal control system relating to such matters is effective.

11.20 It is nearly always advantageous to assess inherent and control risk as less than high in order to reduce the level of costly substantive procedures.

11.21 Testing the design effectiveness of controls is achieved by evaluating the system with the aid of a list of potential misstatements and suggested control procedures. Possible misstatements include payment for goods not ordered or received, and payment to fictitious employees.

11.22 Tests of the operating effectiveness of controls involve the examination of evidence of the performance of control procedures.

11.23 The audit programme is usually determined on the basis of the preliminary assessment of controls, which typically consists of the assessment of design effectiveness. The audit plan may need to be revised if tests of operating effectiveness fail to confirm the preliminary assessment.

SUBSTANTIVE PROCEDURES

Trade creditors are usually the largest current liability in a balance sheet and a significant factor in the evaluation of an entity's short-term solvency. Like debtors, it is affected by a high volume of transactions and thus is susceptible to misstatements. However, whereas with debtors the auditors are concerned with overstatement, with creditors, understatement is the greatest risk. The reason is that management, if motivated to misrepresent creditors, would be likely to understate them in order to report a more favourable financial position. Compared with the audit of asset balances, the audit of creditors places more emphasis on gathering evidence about the completeness assertion than the existence assertion.

Determining detection risk

Trade creditors are affected by purchase transactions that increase the account balance and payment transactions that decrease the balance. Thus, detection risk for creditor assertions is affected by the inherent and control risk factors related to both of these transaction classes. Auditors use the methodology explained in Chapter 9 for combining control risk assessments for transaction class assessments to arrive at control risk assessments for creditors' balance assertions. Auditors then use the methodology explained in Chapter 5, involving the audit risk model or a risk matrix, to determine acceptable levels of detection risk in planning the audit. The application of this process for creditors is summarised in Table 11.5. The risk levels specified in this matrix are only illustrative and would vary based on the entity's circumstances. Furthermore, note that the acceptable detection

Table 11.5 Correlation of risk components – trade creditors

RISK COMPONENT	EXISTENCE OR OCCURRENCE	COMPLETENESS	ACCURACY, CLASSIFICATION AND VALUATION	PRESENTATION AND DISCLOSURE
Audit risk	Low	Low	Low	Low
Inherent risk	Moderate	High	High	Low
Control risk – purchase transactions	Low	High	High	Moderate
Control risk – payments	Moderate	Low	Low	Low
Combined control risk[1]	Low	High	High	Moderate
Acceptable detection risk[2]	High	Low	Low	High

Notes

[1]This is the most conservative (highest) of transaction class control risk assessments used as the combined risk assessment as per the methodology discussed in Chapter 9.

[2]Determined from risk components matrix shown in Table 5.2, based on levels of audit risk, inherent risk and combined control risk indicated above for each assertion category.

risk levels shown in Table 11.5 indicate the need for more persuasive evidence for the completeness accuracy and classification assertions than for the other assertions.

As noted above, payroll is subject to high inherent risks for the occurrence and classification assertions. For this reason, however, controls are usually effective and control risk is low. Substantive procedures for payroll balances predominantly involve the application of analytical procedures to the expense accounts and related accruals with only limited tests of details.

Designing substantive procedures

The general framework for developing audit programmes for substantive procedures, which was explained in Chapter 9 and illustrated in Chapter 10 for debtors, is used in designing substantive procedures for creditors and payroll liabilities. Table 11.6 lists substantive procedures that could be included in an audit programme developed on this basis. Note that each test in the table is linked to one or more of the specific account balance audit objectives from Table 11.1.

Each of the procedures is explained in a following section, including comments on how some tests can be tailored based on the planned level of detection risk to be achieved.

Table 11.6 Possible substantive procedures for creditors assertions

CATEGORY	SUBSTANTIVE PROCEDURE	ACCOUNT BALANCE AUDIT OBJECTIVE (FROM TABLE 11.1)					
		EO4	C4	RO3	ACV4	PD#	C-O#
Initial procedures	1. Perform initial procedures on creditors' balances and records that will be subjected to further testing. (a) Trace opening balance for creditors to prior year's working papers. (b) Review activity in general ledger account for creditors, and investigate entries that appear unusual in amount or source. (c) Obtain listing of trade creditors at balance sheet date and determine that it accurately represents the underlying accounting records by: • adding the listing and determining agreement with the total of the subsidiary ledger, or creditors master file and the general ledger control account balance; • testing agreement of suppliers and balances on the listing with those included in the underlying accounting records				✓		
Analytical procedures	2. Perform analytical procedures. (a) Determine expectations. (b) Compare current and prior year balances. (c) Compute significant ratios such as: • gross profit; • trade creditors' turnover. (d) Obtain explanations for unexpected changes. (e) Corroborate explanations.	✓	✓		✓		
Tests of details of transactions	3. Vouch a sample of recorded creditor transactions to supporting documentation. (a) Vouch credits to supporting suppliers' invoices, goods received notes and purchase orders or other supporting documents. (b) Vouch debits to payments. 4. Perform purchases cut-off test. (a) Select a sample of recorded purchase transactions from several days before and after year-end and examine supporting vouchers, suppliers' invoices and goods received notes to determine that purchases were recorded in the proper period; or (b) Observe the number of the last goods received note issued on the last business day of the audit period and trace a sample of lower and higher numbered goods received notes to related purchase documents to determine whether transactions were recorded in the proper period.	✓	✓	✓	✓	✓4 ✓1	

Table 11.6 (*continued*)

CATEGORY	SUBSTANTIVE PROCEDURE	ACCOUNT BALANCE AUDIT OBJECTIVE (FROM TABLE 11.1)					
		EO4	C4	RO3	ACV4	PD#	C-O#
	(c) Examine subsequent payments between the balance sheet date and the end of fieldwork and, when related documentation indicates the payment was for an obligation in existence at balance sheet date, trace to the trade creditors listing.						
	(d) Investigate unmatched purchase orders, goods received notes and suppliers' invoices at year-end.						
	5. Perform payments cut-off test by tracing dates cheques were presented for payment on the subsequent period's bank statement to dates recorded						√ 2
Tests of details of balances	6. Reconcile creditors to monthly statements received by entity from suppliers.	√	√		√		√ 1,2
	(a) Identify major suppliers by reviewing purchases subsidiary ledger or creditors master file.						
	(b) Investigate and reconcile differences.						
	7. Confirm creditors with major suppliers whose monthly statements are unavailable.	√	√	√	√	√ 4	√ 1,2
	8. Perform a search for unrecorded liabilities.		√				√ 1
	(a) Investigate differences identified by analytical procedures.						
	(b) Review agreements and long-term contracts entered into that require periodic payments for evidence of unrecorded liabilities.						
	9. Recalculate accrued payroll liabilities.				√		
	10. Verify directors' and officers' remuneration	√	√	√	√	√ 6	
Presentation and disclosure	11. Compare financial statement presentation with applicable regulations and Accounting Standards.				√	√ 4,7	
	(a) Determine that creditors are properly identified and classified as to type and expected period of payment.						
	(b) Determine whether there are debit balances that are significant in the aggregate and that should be reclassified.						
	(c) Determine the appropriateness of disclosures pertaining to related party creditors.						
	(d) Inquire of management about existence of undisclosed commitments or contingent liabilities						

INITIAL PROCEDURES

The starting point for verifying creditors is to:

- trace the opening balance to the prior year's working papers, when applicable;
- review activity in the general ledger account for any unusual entries; and
- obtain a listing of amounts owed at the balance sheet date.

Usually the listing is prepared by the entity from the bought ledger. The auditors must verify the mathematical accuracy of the listing by adding the total and verifying that it agrees with the underlying accounting records and the general ledger control account balance. In addition, the auditors selectively compare details for suppliers and amounts on the listing with the underlying records to determine that it is an accurate representation of the records from which it was prepared.

ANALYTICAL PROCEDURES

Tests of details are usually planned on the basis that the analytical procedures confirm expectations. It is preferable to perform analytical procedures early in the final audit so that any necessary changes to tests of details can be determined prior to commencing that part of the audit.

As explained in the case of debtors in Chapter 10, the first stage in applying analytical procedures is to review the understanding of the entity obtained during the planning phase as to whether any changes to creditors' balances are to be expected. The second stage is to identify absolute changes in amounts between this year and prior years. This is normally done in the course of preparing the lead schedules for creditors' and payroll balances, as was explained in Chapter 6. The third stage involves the use of more sophisticated relationships such as ratios and trends. As with debtors, the gross profit ratio is important. If it is higher than expected, then one explanation could be an understatement of purchases (such as by a deliberate cut-off error) in order to boost revenues.

Analysis of expense accounts is also important. This is usually undertaken by comparing the ratio of each expense to sales in the current and previous years. In this way, the effect of changes in the level of activity is largely eliminated. An unusually low expense account may indicate unrecorded liabilities such as through cut-off error. For example, if the final quarter's electricity account has neither been paid nor accrued for, then the current year's electricity expense would appear unusually low compared with that for the previous year. Wherever a change in relationships cannot be readily explained, the auditors must seek an explanation from management and corroborate it, usually by conducting additional tests of details.

Analytical procedures are significant in achieving the desired level of detection risk for payroll balances. Particularly useful ratios are those of the average wages per employee, which should not be dissimilar from prior years, subject only to known wage rises, and payroll expenses as a percentage of sales.

TESTS OF DETAILS OF TRANSACTIONS

As was explained in Chapter 10 in the case of debtors, balances affected by numerous transactions are more efficiently verified by testing the closing balance and not the transactions making up that balance. In the main, the tests of details of transactions will be performed during the interim audit, commonly in the form of dual-purpose tests. For this reason, no substantive tests of details of payroll transactions are described here, because the tests of control described earlier also constitute, as dual-purpose tests, the primary sources of substantive evidence for payroll transactions. The cut-off tests described in subsequent sections are always performed as part of year-end work and, although tests of transactions, they serve to verify the recorded balance at balance sheet date.

Vouching recorded payables to supporting documentation

The emphasis of these tests is on vouching purchase transactions to supporting documentation in the entity's files, such as purchase orders, goods received notes and suppliers' invoices, to verify their occurrence as legitimate transactions. It is equally important, however, to test the numerical continuity of purchase orders and goods received notes, and to trace them to suppliers' invoices and creditors to verify completeness.

Performing purchases cut-off test

The purchases cut-off test involves determining that purchase transactions occurring near the balance sheet date are recorded in the proper period. Most entities hold their books open for a certain period to ensure that purchase transactions are recorded in the correct accounting period. When the books are closed, unmatched goods received notes and purchase orders are scrutinised and, if they relate to the current period, they are recorded by way of journal entry.

Unlike debtors, it may take several weeks for transactions occurring before the balance sheet date to be invoiced by the suppliers. Because cut-off is significant only at the balance sheet date, most entities do not have effective controls to ensure an accurate distinction between the recording of transactions before and after that date. Acceptable detection risk is likely to be low, and extensive tests of details will be performed. The emphasis is on completeness, which is achieved by tracing goods received notes issued in the days immediately prior to the balance sheet date to purchase journal entries or to the closing journal entry of purchase accruals. This procedure provides evidence that they are recorded in the current accounting period.

After balance sheet date purchases that do not result in the issue of a goods received note (such as services) are vouched to supporting documentation to ensure that they do not relate to goods or services received prior to balance sheet date.

Although the emphasis of the test is on completeness, some goods received notes issued after the year-end will be traced to suppliers' invoices to ensure that they are recorded in the subsequent period's purchase journal. In addition, recorded purchases prior to the balance sheet date will be vouched to goods received notes dated prior to the balance sheet date, to ensure that no transactions that occurred after the end of the period are recorded prior to the balance sheet date. This provides evidence as to the occurrence assertion. These tests usually cover a period of five to 10 business days before the balance sheet date and as long after as appears necessary. In performing this test, the auditors should determine that a proper cut-off is achieved at stock-take (as will be explained in Chapter 12) as well as in the recording of the purchase transactions. Where stock is counted other than at the balance sheet date, cut-off for purchases of stock will need to be checked at the stock-take date as well as at the balance sheet date.

Performing payments cut-off test

A proper cut-off of payment transactions at the year-end is essential to the correct presentation of cash and creditors at the balance sheet date. The usual method of verifying payments cut-off is to examine the date of presentation of cheques outstanding as at balance sheet date. This test is normally performed as part of the test of the bank reconciliation and the use of the subsequent period's bank statement (see Chapter 13).

Tests of details of balances

The three tests included in this category for creditors are:

- reconciling creditors to monthly statements received by the entity from suppliers;
- confirming creditors; and
- searching for unrecorded liabilities.

The two tests for payroll balances are:

- recalculating payroll liabilities; and
- verifying directors' and executive officers' remuneration.

Reconciling payables with suppliers' statements

In many cases, suppliers provide monthly statements that are available in entity files. As documentary evidence originating outside the entity, suppliers' statements provide reliable evidence as to suppliers' balances. However, because they are obtained from the entity, the auditors need to be cautious that the statements have not been altered. Photocopied and faxed statements should not be relied on. Where there is doubt, the auditors should request a copy directly from the supplier or confirm the balance directly with the supplier.

In the selection of accounts for testing, the criterion should be the volume of business during the year, not the balance shown in the entity's creditors' listing, because the prime concern is that the recorded balance may be understated.

Discrepancies between suppliers' statements and the bought ledger need to be investigated. Most differences are likely to be due to goods and cash in transit and to disputed amounts. This procedure provides evidence as to the existence, completeness and valuation assertions.

Confirming creditors

Unlike the confirmation of debtors, the confirmation of creditors is performed less frequently because:

- confirmation offers no assurance that unrecorded liabilities will be discovered; and
- external evidence in the form of invoices and suppliers' monthly statements should be available to substantiate the balances.

Confirmation of creditors is recommended (1) when detection risk is low and (2) for suppliers with which the entity undertook a substantial level of business during the current or prior years and that do not issue monthly statements, and for suppliers for which the statement at the balance sheet date is unexpectedly unavailable.

As in the case of confirming debtors, auditors must control the preparation and mailing of the requests and should receive the responses directly from the supplier. The positive form should be used in making the confirmation request, as illustrated in Figure 11.4. Note that the confirmation does not specify the amount due. In confirming a creditor, auditors prefer to have the creditor indicate the amount due because that is the amount to be reconciled to the entity's records. Information is also requested regarding purchase

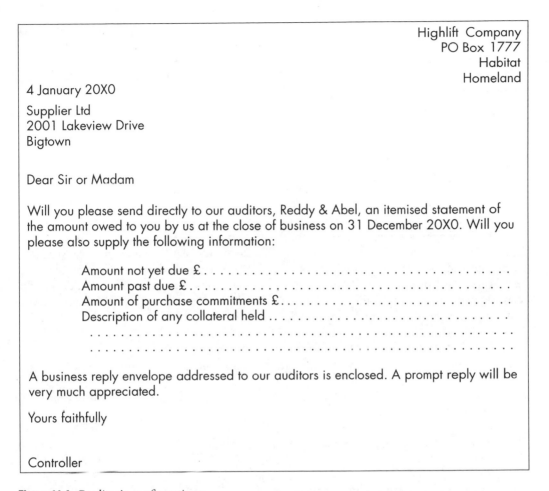

Highlift Company
PO Box 1777
Habitat
Homeland

4 January 20X0

Supplier Ltd
2001 Lakeview Drive
Bigtown

Dear Sir or Madam

Will you please send directly to our auditors, Reddy & Abel, an itemised statement of the amount owed to you by us at the close of business on 31 December 20X0. Will you please also supply the following information:

Amount not yet due £ . . . .
Amount past due £ . . . .
Amount of purchase commitments £ . . . .
Description of any collateral held . . . .
. . . .
. . . .

A business reply envelope addressed to our auditors is enclosed. A prompt reply will be very much appreciated.

Yours faithfully

Controller

Figure 11.4 *Creditor's confirmation*

commitments of the entity and any collateral for the amount due. This test produces evidence for all creditors' balance assertions. However, only limited evidence pertaining to the completeness assertion is provided, given the possible failure to identify and send confirmation requests to suppliers with which the entity has unrecorded obligations.

Searching for unrecorded liabilities

The major procedure for identifying unrecorded liabilities is the examination of the subsequent period's purchase and payment transactions as described earlier under cut-off tests. Analytical procedures may also identify unexpected differences between this year's and the prior year's expense or liability balances, which could indicate the presence of unrecorded liabilities. An analysis of rent expense, for example, may indicate that only three quarterly payments have been made, suggesting that the fourth quarter's rent needs to be accrued. Similarly, a comparison of accruals and prepayments may identify differences due to the failure to make a closing accrual in the current year.

An examination of contractual commitments may also alert auditors to the existence of liabilities not yet provided for, such as progress payments on long-term contracts, or amounts accrued but not yet due or invoiced under a franchise agreement.

Procedures known as the subsequent-events review and the review for contingent liabilities will be described in Chapter 14. Both of these procedures contribute to the search for unrecorded liabilities.

Recalculating payroll liabilities

It is necessary for many entities to make a variety of accruals at the balance sheet date for amounts owed to officers and employees for salaries and wages, commissions, bonuses, vacation pay and so on, and for amounts owed to government agencies for income tax deductions. Although the auditors' primary concern for payroll expenses for the year is with overstatement, the primary concern for the year-end accruals is with understatement. Also of concern is consistency in the methods of calculating the accruals from one period to the next. In obtaining evidence concerning the reasonableness of management's accruals, the auditors should review management's calculations or make independent calculations. Additional evidence can be obtained by examining subsequent payments made on the accruals prior to the completion of fieldwork. Evidence obtained from these procedures primarily pertains to the valuation assertion.

Verifying directors' and executive officers' remuneration

Directors' and executive officers' remuneration is audit sensitive for the following reasons:

- directors' remuneration must be disclosed in the financial statements of all companies under the Companies Act; and
- directors and executive officers may be able to override controls and receive salaries, bonuses, share options and other forms of compensation in excess of authorised amounts.

For these reasons, the auditors should compare the recorded amounts with authorisations of the remuneration committee for directors' and executive officers' salaries and other forms of compensation. This procedure relates to all assertions.

DISCLOSURE

Each major class of creditors and borrowings must be disclosed. These are likely to include bank overdrafts, bank loans, trade creditors, lease liabilities, taxation and employee entitlements. In addition, disclosure must be made of the amount of each class of liability secured by a charge and the nature of the security. If creditors' balances include material advance payments for future goods and services, such amounts should be reported as advances to suppliers and classified under current assets.

◁ LEARNING CHECK

11.24 The nature, timing and extent of substantive procedures is determined by the planned level of detection risk which, in turn, is a function of the assessed levels of inherent and control risks. For tests of details of purchase, payment and payroll transactions, the related assessed level of control risk for each assertion applies. For tests of details of creditors' balances:

- control risk as to the completeness of payment transactions relates to control risk as to the existence of the balance; and

- control risk as to the occurrence of payment transactions etc., relates to control over the completeness of the creditors' balance.

11.25 Initial procedures ensure the accuracy of the list of creditors' balances used as the basis for tests of the balance.

11.26 Analytical procedures require the determination of expectations and the comparison of amounts, trends and ratios, particularly the gross profit ratio and analysis of expense accounts. For payroll balances, analytical procedures may be sufficient without the need for further tests of details. An important payroll ratio is that of average wages per employee.

11.27 Tests of details of transactions are largely dual-purpose tests performed at the interim audit, except for cut-off tests of transactions either side of the balance sheet date. Unlike sales, cut-off tests for purchases need to be extended considerably into the subsequent period.

11.28 The principal test of details of balances is the comparison of bought ledger balances with suppliers' statements. Only if suppliers' statements are unavailable would auditors obtain confirmation directly from the supplier.

11.29 The other major test of details of balances is verifying directors' and executive officers' remuneration.

SUMMARY

Purchase and payroll transactions constitute the major source of expenditure for most entities, and the balance of creditors constitutes a major liability. In auditing these transactions and the account balances, auditors use techniques explained in Chapters 5–9. This chapter followed the audit approach required by ISA 315. The information system and related control procedures typically employed by entities in processing the relevant transactions classes are described. The audit process commences with obtaining the understanding of this system. The auditors also consider issues relating to materiality, inherent risk and the control environment, prior to assessing the risks of material misstatement and determining the appropriate audit strategy. For purchase and payroll transactions, materiality is invariably high. For audit purposes, the most significant inherent risk is that of understatement of purchase transactions and creditors' balances in order to boost reported profits and enhance liquidity. For the entity, the greatest inherent risk is that of improper purchasing and payments to fictitious employees. This chapter illustrated how the control environment factors of integrity and ethical values, commitment to competence, management's philosophy and operating style, assignment of authority and responsibility, and personnel policies and practices apply to the control environment relating to purchases and payroll.

The next stage of the audit is the determination of an audit strategy which, for purchases and payroll, is likely to be one based on a lower assessed level of control risk. The first step in assessing control risk is to evaluate design effectiveness. The chapter illustrated the use of evaluation checklists which hypothesise potential misstatements for each function in the processing of purchases, payments and payroll. The auditors then compare the control activities in the entity's information system with necessary controls identified by the checklist in assessing design effectiveness. At this point, the auditors draft the audit programme based on the preliminary assessment of control risk, identifying both tests of the operating effectiveness of controls and the reduced level of substantive procedures relevant to the assessed level of control risk. The assessed level of control risk is confirmed on completion of the tests of operating effectiveness. The final stage of the audit is the performance of substantive procedures. It is usually more cost-effective to test the balance of creditors than to test the transactions making up that balance.

The most important test of transactions is that of cut-off at the year-end. The major test of balances is the examination of suppliers' statements. As documentary evidence received from third parties, it is moderately reliable. However, auditors need to be alert to the possibility that such statements may be forged or altered by the entity. Finally, the chapter explained the importance of verifying directors' and officers' salaries.

FURTHER READING

Saunders, G. D. & Munter, P. 'The Search for Unrecorded Liabilities – The Implications of Maislin', *The CPA Journal* (February 1991), pp. 48–51.

Schwersenz, J. 'Accounts Payable Confirmations: Why and How Used', *The CPA Journal* (May 1987), pp. 93–101.

MULTIPLE-CHOICE QUESTIONS

Choose the best answer for each of the following.
(Answers are on pages 602–603)

11.1 Which of the following controls would be most effective in assuring that only purchases that properly occurred are recorded for payment?
  (a) Suppliers' invoices are independently matched with purchase orders and goods received notes.
  (b) Goods received notes require the signature of the individual who authorised the purchase.
  (c) Suppliers' invoices are serially numbered on receipt.
  (d) Suppliers' invoices are mathematically checked.

11.2 On receipt of a supplier's invoices the purchases clerk should:
  (a) prepare a cheque in payment of the invoice.
  (b) match the invoice with the goods received note and purchase order.
  (c) send it to the purchasing officer for approval.
  (d) ignore it as payments are based on the statement amount.

11.3 Internal control is not strengthened when the following functions are segregated:
   (a)   requisitioning from purchasing.
   (b)   receiving from purchasing.
   (c)   approving suppliers' invoices and recording the liability.
   (d)   recording the liability and paying the liability.

11.4 An auditor wants to perform tests of control on an entity's computerised cash disbursement procedures. If the control procedures leave no audit trail of documentary evidence, the auditor most likely will test the procedures by:
   (a)   inspection of documents.
   (b)   observation.
   (c)   analytical procedures.
   (d)   the use of test data.

11.5 Which of the following is a test of control over payroll transactions?
   (a)   Identifying changes in employees between two payrolls in successive months and verifying the start date of newly hired employees and the termination date of employees leaving, with personnel records.
   (b)   Vouching wage rates for a sample of employees to personnel records.
   (c)   Vouching hours worked for a sample of employees to approved time records.
   (d)   Observing procedures performed at a payroll distribution.

11.6 The sampling unit in an audit procedure providing evidence as to the occurrence of payroll transactions ordinarily is:
   (a)   a clock card.
   (b)   a group certificate.
   (c)   the employee's personnel record.
   (d)   a payroll register entry.

11.7 To ensure the completeness of recorded liabilities at the balance sheet date the auditor should:
   (a)   select a sample of transactions from the bought ledger immediately after the year-end and vouch them to goods received notes.
   (b)   select a sample of transactions from the bought ledger and vouch them to suppliers' invoices.
   (c)   perform a bank reconciliation.
   (d)   select a sample of invoices received before the year-end and ensure that they are appropriately recorded in the bought ledger.

11.8 The principal reason for the auditor to examine suppliers' statements at balance sheet date is to obtain evidence that:
   (a)   the supplier exists.
   (b)   recorded purchases actually occurred.
   (c)   there are no unrecorded liabilities.
   (d)   payment transactions were properly made.

DISCUSSION QUESTIONS

11.1 Explain how the purchasing function can be fully automated from identifying the need for stock replacement through to payment of the liability using modern information technology. What manual intervention would still be required in such a fully integrated system.

11.2 It is increasingly common for companies to program their computer systems to print and distribute cheques without further authorisation. As auditor, describe controls you would expect to find in place over such a system.

11.3 Consider how a payroll fraud might be perpetrated if personnel and payroll functions were not adequately segregated.

11.4 Describe programmed application controls you would expected to find in a computerised payroll function and explain audit procedures for testing those controls.

11.5 Explain why an unexpected change in the gross profit ratio leads the auditor to suspect a wide range of possible misstatements in recorded transactions and balances.

11.6 Cut-off procedures can be applied to goods received notes issued before the year-end or to liabilities recorded after the year-end. Consider the separate merits of each approach in assuring the completeness of recorded liabilities.

11.7 Discuss reasons why auditors rarely confirm creditors and yet nearly always confirm debtors.

11.8 Explain why achieving an accurate cut-off of purchase and sale transactions is of critical importance in assuring the fairness of financial statements, illustrating your explanation with examples of the effect of cut-off errors.

11.9 Describe as many different kinds of unrecorded liability as possible and, for each, explain audit procedures you would perform for its detection.

PROFESSIONAL APPLICATION QUESTIONS

(Suggested answers are on pages 636–640)

11.1 Creditors' substantive procedures

Oatley is a small privately incorporated manufacturing business of which your firm of Accountants is the external auditor. You have been assigned to the audit of creditors for the year ended 30 September 20x2.

The audit file indicates that control risk for purchase and payment transactions is assessed as slightly less than high, not because of any identified control problems or prior year audit problems, but because of limitations in the extent of segregation of duties due to the small number of accounts personnel.

Narrative notes on the accounting system contain the following description.

- Purchases are requisitioned by the user department and ordered, using prenumbered order forms, by the purchasing manager.
- Raw materials and manufacturing supplies are delivered to the receiving department of the factory where the receiver issues prenumbered goods received notes (GRNs).
- Purchases of other goods and services are delivered directly to the requisitioning department and no GRNs are issued.
- The accounts department checks suppliers' invoices with purchase orders, and

- for production department purchases, with GRNs
- for other purchases, sends the invoices to the requisitioning department manager who initials the invoice to indicate that it is appropriate to pay.
- Invoices are then processed to the accounting records using proprietary software.
- All accounts payable are paid at the end of the month following the month of receipt of the invoice.

Creditors at 30 September 20x2, therefore, represent goods and services invoiced in September. In addition, invoices received between 1 and 15 October 20x2 were divided into those relating to goods received or services provided before and after 30 September, the former being recorded in the accounting records before the September trial balance was produced. On 15 October 20x2, any unmatched GRNs relating to deliveries before 30 September were posted to the accounts as at 30 September at the estimated amounts of the invoices.

Suppliers' invoices are filed alphabetically with supporting documentation, all of which is cancelled with the date of payment when the cheque is issued. Supplier's monthly statements are also filed with the invoices. These are scrutinised by the accounts department for unusual items, such as overdue invoices, but are not regularly reconciled with the company's own records.

Required

(a) In your audit of creditors in the 30 September 20x2 financial statements explain which of the financial statement assertions you would regard as presenting the greatest inherent risk.

(b) Discuss the reasons for undertaking or not undertaking a creditors' circularisation.

(c) Outline substantive procedures you would apply in your audit of creditors relating to production department purchases.

(d) Explain additional procedures you would perform in verifying the completeness of non-production department creditors.

(Adapted from Question 2, Audit Framework, December 1999. Reproduced by permission of ACCA)

11.2 Payroll controls

You are the audit senior in charge of the audit of payroll for Ned's Trailers Ltd (NT), a company that manufactures trailers and caravans for the family market. Employees of NT are paid on the basis of hours worked and quantities produced. The hours worked are recorded on clock cards and the quantities produced are confirmed by the supervisor. Wages are paid in cash each Friday for the previous week's work. Appointments of employees are authorised by the managing director, and the personnel department maintains employees' records and their rates of pay. The cashier is separate from the wages department. Previous years' audits have highlighted weaknesses in internal controls on the company's payroll. This has allowed an employee in the wages department to perpetrate a fraud by creating fictitious employees on the payroll and misappropriating wages. Thus, some of your audit tests have been designed to detect whether this fraud is still taking place.

Required

(a) State the principal controls you would expect to exist in the above payroll system, and explain their purpose.
(b) How might you test to ensure that all employees exist?
(c) Describe three analytical review techniques you might use to audit payroll.

(Adapted from Question 3, Audit Framework, December 1994. Reproduced by permission of ACCA)

CHAPTER 12

AUDITING STOCKS AND TANGIBLE FIXED ASSETS

OVERVIEW

STOCK
Audit objectives
Recording stock transactions
Developing the audit plan
Substantive procedures for stocks

TANGIBLE FIXED ASSETS
Audit objectives
Developing the audit plan
Substantive procedures for fixed assets

SUMMARY

FURTHER READING

MULTIPLE-CHOICE QUESTIONS

DISCUSSION QUESTIONS

PROFESSIONAL APPLICATION QUESTIONS

LEARNING **OBJECTIVES**

After studying this chapter you should be able to:

1   identify the audit objectives applicable to stocks

2   explain the nature of stock records

3   describe procedures to be followed at a stock-take

4   discuss considerations relevant to determining the audit strategy for stocks

5 describe procedures to be followed when observing stock-taking

6 explain the audit procedures for verifying stock pricing

7 identify the audit objectives applicable to tangible fixed assets

8 discuss considerations relevant to determining the audit strategy for tangible fixed assets

9 design a substantive audit programme for tangible fixed assets.

PROFESSIONAL STATEMENTS

ISA 501   Audit Evidence – Additional Considerations for Specific Items, Part A: Attendance at Physical Inventory Counting
ISA 510   Initial Engagements – Opening Balances
ISA 540   Audit of Accounting Estimates
ISA 600   Using the Work of Another Auditor
ISA 610   Considering the Work of Internal Auditing
ISA 620   Using the Work of an Expert
IAS 2   Inventories
IAS 16   Property, Plant and Equipment
IAS 17   Accounting for Leases
IAS 36   Impairment of Assets

The first half of this chapter deals with the audit of stocks (inventories) and the second half with the audit of tangible fixed assets (property, plant and equipment). Audit considerations of the internal control components of the principal transaction classes affecting both account balances have already been described: purchases in the case of both stocks and tangible fixed assets, and also sales in the case of stocks. For this reason, the organisation of the chapter differs from that of the two previous chapters. There is no separate section describing the functions and control procedures for either stock or tangible fixed asset transactions. For stock, there is a section describing functions and control procedures associated with the custody of stock and the maintenance of stock records. In the section on developing the audit plan, the significance of assessing the effectiveness of controls over stock records is discussed in the context of determining the audit strategy.

For tangible fixed assets, auditors adopt a predominantly substantive approach to the audit and rarely consider it necessary to examine controls over fixed asset records. The nature of such records is described in the section on developing the audit plan, but there is no assessment of control. The explanation of the audit of fixed assets then proceeds to the design and execution of substantive audit procedures. This text uses the term 'fixed assets' in the customary sense of referring to tangible fixed assets. Given the complex nature of intangible fixed assets, their audit is not dealt with in this text. The audit of fixed asset investments is the subject of Chapter 13.

A feature of both classes of asset is the inherent risk as to their valuation. Thus, verification of the valuation assertion for these assets receives special consideration during the audit.

STOCK

In a merchandising entity, stock consists of goods acquired for resale. In a manufacturing entity, stock can be in one of three stages:

- raw materials awaiting processing;
- partly manufactured items known as work in process (or work in progress); or
- finished goods awaiting sale.

Smaller entities, particularly those not engaging in manufacturing, may not maintain stock records. Instead, stock is determined at or near the balance sheet date by physical count known as a stock-take. The principal audit procedure in such cases is observation of that stock-take. At the other extreme, large manufacturing entities maintain comprehensive stock records, with subsidiary stock ledgers integrated with the general ledger. These records may be used as the basis for determining both the quantity and value of stock at the balance sheet date. To obtain sufficient audit evidence in such cases, auditors must perform extensive tests of control over the recording of stock transactions and the maintenance of stock records.

Obtaining evidence of the existence of stock through physical observation is a required audit procedure. Auditors may meet this requirement by observing a number of cyclical counts that the entity undertakes during the year as part of its control procedures over the maintenance of stock records. Alternatively, where the entity determines stock by physical count at or close to the year-end, auditors meet the requirement by attendance at that count.

Verifying the valuation assertion for stock is also an important audit procedure. This involves verifying both cost and net realisable value and the judgement by management as to which basis is relevant for each item of stock.

Audit objectives

Table 12.1 lists the primary audit objectives for each assertion, referencing them to specific controls and audit procedures.

Recording stock transactions

The process of obtaining evidence relating to purchase and sale transactions has been described in the previous two chapters. For entities that rely entirely on stock-take at or near the balance sheet date, the auditors will adopt a predominantly substantive approach in obtaining evidence as to the existence and completeness assertions. Where perpetual stock records are used wholly or partly in determining stock at the balance sheet date, it is necessary for the auditors to obtain an understanding of the accounting and internal control procedures relating to such records. For non-manufacturing entities, the auditors

Table 12.1 Selected specific audit objectives for stock

ASSERTION CATEGORY	TRANSACTION CLASS AUDIT OBJECTIVES	ACCOUNT BALANCE AUDIT OBJECTIVES
Existence or occurrence	Recorded purchase transactions represent stocks acquired (**EO1**) Recorded transfers represent stocks transferred between locations or categories (**EO2**) Recorded sales transactions represent stocks sold (**EO3**)	Stocks included in the balance sheet physically exist (**EO4**)
Completeness	All purchases (**C1**), transfers (**C2**) and sales (**C3**) of stocks that occurred have been recorded	Stocks include all materials, products and supplies on hand at balance sheet date (**C4**)
Rights and obligations	The entity has rights to the stocks recorded during the period (**RO1**)	The entity has rights to the stocks included in the balance sheet (**RO2**)
Accuracy, classification and valuation	The costs of materials purchased and of labour and overheads applied have been accurately determined and are in accordance with applicable Accounting Standards (**ACV1**)	Stocks are properly stated at the lower of cost or net realisable value, determined in accordance with applicable Accounting Standards (**ACV2**)
Cut-off	All purchases, transfers and sales of stocks are recorded in the correct accounting period (**C-O1**)	
Presentation and disclosure	Transactions relating to stocks have been properly identified and classified in the financial statements (**PD1**)	Stocks are properly identified and classified in the financial statements (**PD2**) Disclosures pertaining to the classification, basis of valuation and the pledging of stocks are adequate (**PD3**)

can rely on records of purchase transactions in obtaining sufficient evidence as to accuracy and classification. For manufacturing entities, even where perpetual stock records are not maintained, the auditors need to obtain an understanding of the procedures for determining and recording costs of production.

MAINTAINING STOCK RECORDS

The increasing use of computer information systems has made it much easier for entities to maintain perpetual stock records which are now relatively common. If the recording of sales and purchases is computerised, it is a relatively simple procedure to extend the system to record the input and removal of goods from stock. Simpler systems maintain records of quantity only. More sophisticated systems maintain stock records by quantity and value which are fully integrated with the accounting records in a stock master file. For merchandising entities, a single stock record is required, although this may be subdivided by location. Manufacturing entities need to maintain separate stock records of raw materials, work in process and finished goods, and to establish procedures for recording the movement of goods through production.

An important control over maintaining stock records is the segregation of this function from the physical custody of the stock. The custodian will then have no opportunity to conceal a stock shortage by manipulating the stock records.

The separate functions are:

- recording the movement of goods into stock;
- recording the movement of goods from stock;
- recording transfers of stock; and
- physically comparing stock with stock records.

Movement of goods into stock

In all cases, the initial entry into stock will be through the purchasing system (see Chapter 11). The storekeeper acknowledges receipt of the goods by initialling a copy of the goods received note. The goods received note then provides the source of entry of the quantity and cost in the appropriate stock record. These procedures relate primarily to the occurrence and completeness assertions (**EO1, C1**), but also contribute to the rights and obligations assertion (**RO1**).

Movement of goods from stock

When merchandise stocks or finished goods are sold, the dispatch note serves as the basis for authorisation of the release of the goods from stock, and for the entry in stock records reducing the quantity on hand. In retail stores, the use of barcodes or security tags scanned at the cash register provides data for reducing recorded stock. Control procedures as to the occurrence and completeness of sales transactions (see Chapter 10) also relate to the occurrence and completeness of recorded stock movements (**EO3, C3**).

Transfers of stock

Further procedures are necessary where goods are transferred from one stock location to another. In manufacturing entities, *production move orders* control the movement of goods from raw materials, through work in process to finished goods. These pre-numbered documents are issued by production control and represent authorisation to issue raw materials and to apply direct labour to process materials to produce the finished goods. Each move order consists of tickets identifying the specific material and labour requirements for the goods to be produced. Initialled copies of tickets represent acknowledgement, by stock custodians, of the receipt of goods, or evidence of their proper delivery. They also provide the basis for accounting entries, relieving one stock location and charging the other. Similar procedures, on a less elaborate scale, are required in retailing entities to record and control internal transfers. These procedures relate to the occurrence and completeness assertions for internal stock movements (**EO2, C2**).

Physical comparison of stock with stock records

Perpetual stock records need to be compared with physical stock at regular intervals. The two functions involved are:

1. a stock count (cyclical stock-take); and
2. a comparison with records.

STOCK COUNT

Procedures for stock-taking are similar, whether the purpose is to determine stock at the balance sheet date or to compare stock with stock records at an intermediate date. This section describes procedures applicable to a full stock-take. Procedures for cyclical stock counts may be less thorough and involve counting only a sample of stock items. The sample selected for counting may be organised systematically, through different sections of the warehouse or different types of stock, or by random sampling. A further approach is to count items whose levels have reached reorder point when stock levels will be low, thus reducing both the cost of the count and the likelihood of count errors.

The procedures for stock-taking involve:

- assigning and communicating responsibility;
- preparation;
- identification;
- counting;
- checking;
- clearing;
- recording; and
- cut-off.

- *Assigning and communicating responsibility.* Overall responsibility for the count should be assigned to an individual who has no responsibility for either the custody of stock or the maintenance of stock records. Persons involved in the count should also be suitably independent, although storekeepers may be involved if supervised. The area containing stock should be subdivided, with count teams assigned to specific sections. Stock-taking instructions should be drawn up, and individual responsibilities should be clearly explained to each person involved.
- *Preparation.* Prior to the count, areas such as the warehouse and shop floor should be tidied, with stock neatly stacked and items not to be counted (such as scrap or goods held for third parties) removed or clearly marked. Arrangements need to be made to cease production, if possible, and receiving and shipping departments need to be alerted so as to avoid movement of goods to or from these departments during the count. In this way, cut-off errors can be avoided. If an accurate cut-off is not achieved, the physical count may include, for example, goods for which the purchase or production cost is not recorded by the information system until after the count. This could result in an overstatement of stock.
- *Identification.* Stock to be counted must be properly identified. This is a particular problem with specialised items or work in process. With work in process, the problem

is with identifying the stage of completion, which determines the costs accumulated against the items. Either the goods must be tagged in advance or count teams knowledgeable in the stock must be assigned to the count in appropriate sections.

- *Counting.* Count teams usually work in pairs where any lifting or moving of items is necessary to ascertain the quantity. Forklift trucks and weighing scales may also need to be available. Instructions should ensure that count teams understand the unit of measurement (e.g. 25-kilogram bags). The degree of thoroughness also needs to be considered. For example, whether cartons need to be opened at random or weighed to verify that they are full and the contents are as described.

- *Checking.* Sometimes all counts are double-checked and all discrepancies are recounted. Where errors are unlikely, only spot checks need to be performed and only counts by those count teams making errors need to be double-checked.

- *Clearing.* As each item is counted, the count team should leave a mark to avoid duplicating the count. On completion of a section, a supervisor should tour the area to ensure no items appear to be uncounted.

- *Recording.* Control over count sheets is particularly important. Three systems are commonly used. Where stock items are standardised, pre-printed stock count sheets containing descriptions are issued to the count teams, who then complete the sheets by entering the quantity. Another system is to issue blank, pre-numbered count sheets. The serial numbers issued to each count team must be noted and checked on completion to ensure that no sheets are missing. Half-filled sheets should be ruled off, and unused sheets should be identified as such to prevent items being added after the count. The third method involves attaching pre-numbered, three-part stock tags to each stock item prior to the count. The count team enters the description and quantity on the first part of the tag and removes it. The checkers do likewise with the second part, which is compared with the first part. The third part, the stub of the tag, remains attached to the item to enable the supervisor to verify completeness of the count. Again, serial numbers should be fully accounted for. In each case, counters and checkers should be required to sign or initial each count sheet or tag.

- *Cut-off.* Serial numbers of the last pre-numbered goods received notes, dispatch notes and production move orders issued prior to stock-take need to be recorded to ensure that the count is compared with stock records that are based on the same documents.

COMPARISON WITH RECORDS

Comparison with records is of greater importance for cyclical counts, where the aims are to ensure the reliability of the stock records and to ascertain the effectiveness of procedures designed to ensure accountability for custodianship and record-keeping. With counts undertaken at or near the balance sheet date, comparison with the records will assist in identifying any major errors in quantities ascertained by count.

Procedures should require a recount of material differences. If the difference remains, further investigation is required to ascertain if the stock records are in error and why. A record should be maintained of differences and the cause (if known), and the stock records should be adjusted to agree with the count. This list of errors provides evidence as to the reliability of the records and the possibility of reliance on book stock in determining stock at the balance sheet date, without the need for a further count.

These procedures relate primarily to the existence, accuracy, classification and cut-off assertions (**EO4, ACV2, C-O1**) but also contribute to the completeness assertion (**C4**).

DETERMINING AND RECORDING STOCK COSTS

For merchandise stock, procedures relating to accuracy and classification in the recording of purchase transactions ensure that proper costs are recorded in stock records. On sale, the cost of sale should be determined in accordance with the appropriate cost flow assumption, which would normally be either first-in first-out (FIFO) or weighted average. Entities recording cost of sales on a continuing basis will usually rely on computer information systems, which should be programmed to determine the appropriate cost.

Costing of manufactured stock is far more complex. Procedures are required to:

- determine the cost of material entered into raw materials;
- determine the cost of raw materials transferred to work in process at first-in first-out or weighted average cost;
- record costs of direct labour applied to work in process;
- identify abnormal waste or spoilage in the production process;
- identify manufacturing overhead costs and apportion costs to production departments;
- assign overhead costs to work in process using an appropriate absorption rate;
- apportion costs to by-products;
- relieve work in process and charge finished goods on completion of manufacturing, based on costing procedures such as batch or process costing; and
- relieve finished goods with the cost of goods sold at first-in first-out or weighted average.

Some entities record stock at standard cost and identify differences between standard and actual costs as variances.

In obtaining the understanding of the accounting system, auditors need to identify the entity's accounting policy and ascertain the procedures for ensuring that costs are recorded in accordance with that policy. It is also necessary for the auditors to ensure that the policy is consistent with the requirements of IAS 2, Inventories. These procedures relate to the valuation assertion (**ACV2**) and contribute to the disclosure assertion (**PD1**).

Developing the audit plan

The selected approach to the audit of stock depends on the availability and reliability of stock records. Consideration of internal control relating to stock records, which are described in the previous section, is necessary only where such records exist. In all audits, consideration of the determination of cost records is important.

MATERIALITY AND RISK

In a manufacturing entity, stocks and cost of goods sold are usually significant to both the entity's financial position and the results of its operations. Moreover, numerous factors contribute to the risk of misstatements in the assertions for these accounts, including those described below:

- The volume of purchase, manufacturing and sale transactions that affect these accounts is generally high, increasing the opportunities for misstatements to occur.

- There are often contentious valuation and measurement issues such as:
  - the identification, measurement and allocation of indirect materials, labour and manufacturing overhead;
  - joint product costs;
  - the disposition of cost variances;
  - accounting for scrap and wastage.
- Special procedures are sometimes required to determine stock quantity or value, such as geometric volume measurements of stockpiles using aerial photography, and estimation of value by experts.
- Stocks are often stored at multiple sites, leading to difficulties in maintaining physical control over theft and damage, and in accounting for goods in transit between sites.
- Stocks are vulnerable to spoilage, obsolescence and general economic conditions that may affect demand and saleability, and thus their valuation.
- Stocks may be sold subject to right of return and repurchase agreements.

In planning the audit, the auditors will be aware that the inherent risks are greater with respect to the existence and valuation assertions. Being an asset, management has a greater incentive to overstate stock than to understate it. This may be done by inflating the quantity or by overstating its value. There are numerous instances of such frauds discovered (and not discovered) by auditors. A lack of third party evidence means it is also often easier to overstate stocks than assets such as cash or debtors. Stock is also subject to theft both by employees and outsiders. The depletion of stock as a consequence of shoplifting is well known.

AUDIT STRATEGY

In verifying the existence (and completeness) assertions, auditors have the choice of three audit strategies depending on the entity's policy for determining stock quantity. The options are:

1. stock quantity determined by perpetual stock records where the entity does not intend to count stock at or close to the balance sheet date. This strategy requires that control risk over stock records is assessed as low;
2. stock quantities determined by stock-take near the balance sheet date, adjusted to balance sheet quantities by reference to perpetual stock records. This strategy requires that control risk over stock records, or of purchases and sales cut-off, is not assessed as high; or
3. stock quantities determined by stock-take at or within a few days of the balance sheet date. This is a predominantly substantive approach in which the auditors would not test control over stock records, which may not even exist.

An entity may use each of the three methods for different categories of stock or for stock at different locations. For example, a manufacturing entity may determine the quantity of raw materials and finished goods at a year-end stock-take, but rely on perpetual records in determining the work in process stock.

In developing the audit plan, auditors will need to discuss the approach that management intends to take. If management intends to rely solely on stock records, then more extensive tests of control will be necessary to confirm the required assessment of control risk. Moreover, this assessment must be completed before the balance sheet date in the event that tests of control fail to confirm the assessment of control risk as being low, and the auditors are required to advise management to count stock at or near the balance sheet date.

Specialised stocks may require the assistance of experts in determining either the quantity (as in the case of aerial measurement of stockpiles) or value (as in the case of antiques). In accordance with ISA 620, Using the Work of an Expert, the auditors must discuss use of experts with management to ensure that persons acceptable to both management and the auditors are employed.

For merchandise stock, a predominantly substantive approach is usually more efficient in verifying the valuation assertion. For manufacturing entities, it is usually necessary for the auditors to have assessed control risk over the maintenance of costing records (used as the basis for costing closing stock) as being less than high. This is an area that frequently receives insufficient audit attention owing to a reluctance to unravel the complexities of the costing system.

ASSESSMENT OF CONTROL RISK

Assessment of control risk over stock records is important where the entity does not intend to count stock at or near the year-end. In this case, a satisfactory assessment is vital. Otherwise, assessment of control risk over stock records is unimportant. Assessment of control risk over the cost of stock is always important for manufacturing entities.

Control risk over stock records

Table 12.2 contains a partial listing of potential misstatements, necessary controls, possible tests of the operating effectiveness of those controls, and the specific audit objective to which each belongs. As explained above, auditors would assess control risk over perpetual stock records only where they are used in determining stock at the balance sheet date. If the preliminary assessment, based on the design effectiveness of controls, is that control risk is likely to be high, then the auditors would advise management not to rely on the records in determining stock at the balance sheet date.

If the preliminary assessment supports management's intended reliance on stock records, then the auditors would proceed to draw up an audit programme incorporating possible tests of the operating effectiveness of controls such as those identified in Table 12.2.

Many of these tests are in the form of dual-purpose tests. It is important to remember that ISA 501, Audit Evidence – Additional Considerations for Specific Items, Part A: Attendance at Physical Inventory Counting, requires that, where reliance is placed entirely on perpetual stock records in determining stock at the balance sheet date, the auditors must additionally perform substantive procedures to:

- verify the physical existence of stocks by inspection and performing test counts, usually in conjunction with observing cyclical counts; and
- investigate significant differences between the physical count and the perpetual stock records, and confirm that the records are properly adjusted.

Table 12.2 Control risk assessment considerations – stock records

FUNCTION	POTENTIAL MISSTATEMENT	NECESSARY CONTROL	POSSIBLE TEST OF OPERATING EFFECTIVENESS	RELEVANT AUDIT OBJECTIVE (FROM TABLE 12.1)					
				EO	C	RO	ACV	PD	C-O
Recording movement of goods into stock	Goods may not be recorded	Use of pre-numbered goods received notes and production move orders	Reperform test of numerical continuity		√1,2				
		Independent reconciliation of stock records with control account in general ledger	Reperform*	√1,2,3	√1,2,3		√1		√1
Recording movement of goods from stock	Unauthorised removal of goods	Custodian required to acknowledge responsibility for receipt of goods into store	Inspect goods received notes and production move orders for custodian's initials	√1,2					
		Custodian required to obtain receipt for all deliveries from store	Vouch recorded removals with properly authorised dispatch notes and production move orders*	√2,3					
		Physical comparison of stock with stock records	Observe Reperform*	√1,2,3	√1,2,3				√1
Physical comparison of stock with stock records	Count procedures may be unreliable	Responsibility independent from maintenance of stock records and custodianship of stock	Observe	√4	√4				
		Adequate instructions properly issued and followed	Observe Reperform*	√4	√4				
	Inadequate investigation and correction	Proper record maintained of differences and their correction	Inspect Reperform*	√4	√4				√1
	Extent of comparison insufficient	Laid down procedures for systematic counts	Inspect	√4	√4				

(*continued overleaf*)

Table 12.2 (*continued*)

FUNCTION	POTENTIAL MISSTATEMENT	NECESSARY CONTROL	POSSIBLE TEST OF OPERATING EFFECTIVENESS	RELEVANT AUDIT OBJECTIVE (FROM TABLE 12.1)					
				EO	C	RO	ACV	PD	C-O
Determining stock costs	Inappropriate basis	Approved by finance director	Enquire Compare with Accounting Standards				√ 1,2	√ 1,2	
	Improper calculation	Consistent with engineering specification	Inspect Reperform*				√ 1,2		
		Program controls	Use test data*				√ 1,2		

Note: *Tests are usually performed as part of dual-purpose tests.

Close to the balance sheet date, the auditors will need to consider the extent of test counts relative to total stock, and to review the recorded differences between test counts and stock records over the year and the explanations of those differences. If the auditors are not satisfied that results of test counts support an assessment of control risk as low, then they must discuss with management the need for a complete stock-take.

Control risk over costing stock

In a manufacturing entity, assessment of the reliability of the costing system in providing accurate costs of production that are correctly determined in accordance with applicable Financial Reporting Standards can constitute a substantial component of the interim audit. Manufacturing costs are nearly always determined through the computer information system, and test data can be used to test the accuracy of processing and recording cost information. Where standard costs are intended to be used as the basis for valuing stocks, the tests must extend to the procedures employed in developing standards from the engineering specifications as to:

- the quantities of labour and material required; and
- the determination of standard prices for labour and materials.

 LEARNING **CHECK**

12.1 Where perpetual stock records are used to determine stock at balance sheet date, auditors need to obtain an understanding of the accounting and internal control systems and perform tests of control.

12.2 There should be segregation between the duties of record-keeping and custody.

12.3 There should be adequate procedures for recording movement of stock. For purchases and deliveries on sale, these procedures are linked with the control structure for purchase and sale transactions. There also needs to be a procedure for recording movement of stock through the production process and between locations.

12.4 The most important test of control is evaluation of the design effectiveness of test counts of physical stock and comparison with the records. Assessment of control risk is critically dependent on the extent and results of such test counts performed by the entity.

12.5 For manufacturing entities, auditors need to assess cost accumulation procedures and their reliability as a basis for determining stock cost.

12.6 Stock is material to many entities.

12.7 Principal inherent risks are those of existence and valuation.

- Management has an incentive to overstate the quantity and/or value of stocks.

- Stock is subject to theft.

- Valuation of stock involves judgement, estimation and contentious accounting treatments.

Substantive procedures for stocks

Except where perpetual records are used as the basis for determining stock at the balance sheet date, the audit is primarily based on substantive procedures applied to the account balance at the balance sheet date. The emphasis is on the assertions of existence and valuation, because the inherent risk of their misstatement is always high. Acceptable detection risk for these two assertions is usually assessed as being low, with detection risk for other assertions being low to moderate.

DESIGNING SUBSTANTIVE PROCEDURES
A listing of possible substantive procedures to be included in the audit programme appears in Table 12.3, with each test referenced to the audit objectives shown in Table 12.1.

Initial procedures
In tracing opening stock balances to prior year working papers, the auditors should make certain that any audit adjustments, agreed upon in the prior year, were recorded. In addition, where perpetual stock records are maintained, entries to the control accounts in the general ledger should be scanned to identify any postings that are unusual in amount or nature and thus require special investigation. Where perpetual stock records are to be used as the basis for determining stock at the balance sheet date, the stock listing must be test checked to and from the records, added, and agreed with the balance in the control account. Additional work on stock listings is described later in the tests of details of balances.

Table 12.3 Possible substantive procedures for tests of stock assertions

CATEGORY	SUBSTANTIVE PROCEDURE	RELEVANT AUDIT OBJECTIVE (FROM TABLE 12.1)					
		EO4	C4	RO2	ACV2	PD#	C-01
Initial procedures	1. Perform initial procedures on stock balances and records that will be subjected to further testing. (a) Trace opening stock balances to prior year's working papers. (b) Review activity in stock accounts and investigate entries that appear unusual in amount or source. (c) Verify totals of perpetual stock records and their agreement with closing general ledger balances				✓		
Analytical procedures	2. Perform analytical procedures. (a) Review industry experience and trends. (b) Examine an analysis of stock turnover and gross profit. (c) Review relationships of stock balances to recent purchasing, production and sales activities	✓	✓		✓		
Tests of details of transactions	3. Test entries in stock records to and from supporting documentation	✓	✓	✓	✓		
	4. Test cut-off of purchases, stock transfers and sales	✓	✓				✓
Tests of details of balances	5. Observe entity's stock-taking. (a) Evaluate adequacy of entity's stock-taking plans. (b) Observe stock-take and test compliance with laid down procedures. (c) Make test counts. (d) Look for indications of slow-moving, damaged or obsolete stock. (e) Account for all stock-taking tags and count sheets used in physical count. (f) Record cut-off data	✓	✓	✓	✓		
	6. Test clerical accuracy of stock listings. (a) Recalculate totals and extensions of quantities times unit prices. (b) Trace test counts (from item 5(c)) to listings. (c) Vouch items on listings to and from count sheets and stock-taking tags. (d) Compare physical counts to perpetual stock records. (e) Verify adjustment of amounts for movements between date of stock-take and balance sheet date				✓ ✓		
	7. Test stock pricing. (a) Examine suppliers' invoices for purchased stocks.						

(*continued overleaf*)

Table 12.3 *(continued)*

CATEGORY	SUBSTANTIVE PROCEDURE	RELEVANT AUDIT OBJECTIVE (FROM TABLE 12.1)					
		EO4	C4	RO2	ACV2	PD#	C-O1
	(b) Examine propriety of costing information, standard costs, and disposition of variances pertaining to manufactured stocks. (c) Perform a lower of cost or net realisable value test. 8. Confirm stocks at locations outside the entity. 9. Examine consignment agreements and contracts	√	√	√ √		√ 3	
Presentation and disclosure	10. Compare report presentation with applicable Accounting Standards. (a) Confirm agreements for assignment and pledging of stocks. (b) Review disclosures for stocks in drafts of financial statements and determine conformity with applicable Accounting Standards					√ 2,3	

Analytical procedures

The application of analytical procedures to stocks is often extensive. A review of industry experience and trends is useful in developing expectations to be used in evaluating analytical data for the entity. For example, knowledge of an industry-wide fall in turnover will enable the auditors to expect a fall in the entity's stock turnover ratio. If the ratio does not show the expected fall, then the auditors may suspect errors as to the existence of the stock balance, or in the completeness of the turnover balance used in calculating the ratio. A review of relationships of stock balances with recent purchasing, production and sales activities also aids auditors in understanding changes in stock levels. For example, an increase in the reported level of finished goods stock when purchasing, production and sales levels have remained steady, could indicate misstatements related to the existence or valuation of the finished goods stock.

Important ratios are those of stock turnover and gross profit. The use of the gross profit ratio has previously been explained with respect to the audits of sales and purchases. An unexpectedly high stock turnover ratio, or an unexpectedly low gross profit ratio, might be caused by an overstatement of cost of goods sold and a corresponding understatement of stocks. Conversely, conformity of these ratios with expectations provides assurance of the fairness of the data used in the calculations.

Where stock-take is other than at the year-end, totals of transactions in the intervening period should be analysed for reasonableness.

Tests of details of transactions

With the exception of cut-off tests, tests of details of transactions will be performed only where stock at the balance sheet date is determined wholly or partly from perpetual stock records.

TESTING ENTRIES IN STOCK RECORDS

Where stock at the balance sheet date is determined wholly by reference to perpetual stock records, the tests of details of stock transactions will be those described in Table 12.2 as dual-purpose tests. Where stock at the balance sheet date is determined by count other than at the year-end and adjusted by reference to stock records in the intervening period, such tests of details of transactions may be confined to the period between the date of stock-take and the balance sheet date.

TESTING CUT-OFF OF PURCHASE, MANUFACTURING AND SALES TRANSACTIONS

The purpose and nature of sales and purchases cut-off tests are explained in Chapters 10 and 11 respectively, in connection with the audit of debtors' and creditors' balances. Both tests are important in establishing that transactions occurring near the end of the year are recorded in the correct accounting period. For example, purchases in transit at the year-end should be excluded from stock and creditors, and stock in transit to customers at the year-end should be included in sales and excluded from stock. In a manufacturing entity, it must also be determined that entries are recorded in the proper period for the allocation of labour and overhead costs to work in process and for goods moved between raw materials, work in process and finished goods.

In each case, the auditors must ascertain, through inspection of documents and physical observation, that the paperwork cut-off and the physical cut-off for stock-take are co-ordinated. For example, if the auditors determine that an entry transferring the cost of the final completed batch of the period to finished goods has been recorded, then they should determine that the goods, even if in transit, were included in the stock-take of finished goods and that they were neither counted as part of work in process, nor missed altogether. During their attendance at the count, the auditors should note details of documentation relating to the movement of goods at the date of stock-take. Where stock-taking is other than at the balance sheet date, the auditors must also check cut-off at the date of stock-take to ensure that movements between that date and the balance sheet date exclude transactions prior to the count.

Tests of details of balances

As already explained, auditors reduce audit risk in the audit of stocks to the desired level primarily through the performance of substantive tests of details of balances.

OBSERVING THE ENTITY'S STOCK-TAKE

During the 1930s, audit evidence for stocks was usually restricted to obtaining a certificate from management as to the correctness of the stated amount. In 1938, the discovery of a substantial fraud in the McKesson & Robbins Company, a major US pharmaceutical corporation, caused a reappraisal, in the US, of auditors' responsibilities for stocks. The company's December 1937 financial statements, 'certified' by a national public accounting firm, reported $87 million of total assets. Of this amount, $19 million was subsequently determined to be fictitious: $10 million in stock and $9 million in debtors. The auditors were exonerated of blame because they had complied with existing Auditing Standards. However, promptly thereafter, US Auditing Standards were changed to include a requirement for the physical observation of inventories.

The observation of stock-take is now required by ISA 501 whenever stocks are material to an entity's financial statements, and observation is not impracticable. The observation of stock-take may prove to be inconvenient, time consuming and difficult for the auditors, but it is seldom impracticable. When stocks are material and the auditors do not observe the stock-take, the auditors may perform alternative procedures, such as verifying sales transactions after the stock-take date of items included in stock. However, such procedures may not provide the auditors with sufficient appropriate audit evidence as to applicable assertions.

In observing stock-take, the auditors have no responsibility to take or supervise the taking of the stock. From this procedure, the auditors obtain direct knowledge of the reliability of management's stock-take procedures and, thus, the reliance that may be placed on management's assertions as to the quantities and physical condition of the stocks. In some cases, the entity may hire outside stock-taking specialists to take stock. Where the outside stock-taking specialists have no particular expertise in the type of stock being counted, the auditors must be present to observe their counts too because, from an auditing standpoint, they are basically the same as entity employees. Where the specialists are experts in the particular type of stock (such as precious stones), the auditors may be in a position to place a degree of reliance on the work of the expert in accordance with ISA 620, Using the Work of an Expert.

As has been explained, the timing of stock-take is negotiated with management in accordance with the entity's stock system and the assessment of control risk. Except where reliance is placed wholly on perpetual stock records, quantities are determined by physical count as of a specific date. The date should be at or near the balance sheet date, and the auditors should be present on the specific date. For a multi-site entity, the auditors may vary locations attended each year, so long as they observe a sufficiently sized sample of stock each year. In such cases, the auditors may consider relying on internal audit for attendance at locations not visited, subject to the requirements of ISA 610, Considering the Work of Internal Auditing. Such reliance, however, does not replace the requirement for the auditors to undertake sufficient personal observation of inventories. Other firms of auditors may also be engaged to observe stock-take at inconvenient locations, subject to the requirements of ISA 600, Using the Work of Another Auditor.

Attendance at stock-take involves the performance of tests of control over entity procedures and of substantive procedures applied directly by the auditors. Because both procedures are performed simultaneously, both types of audit procedure are usually included within the programme of substantive procedures. Moreover, because there is no alternative audit strategy if the entity's stock-take procedures are found to be inadequate, the auditors should review and evaluate the entity's stock-taking plans well in advance of the counting date. With ample lead time, the entity should be able to respond favourably to suggested modifications in the plans before the count is begun. It is common for the auditors to assist the entity in designing a stock-taking plan that will facilitate both the taking and the observing of the stock.

Procedures are the same as for test counts in respect of perpetual stock records (see pages 416–417), except that the count is of all stock, not just a sample thereof.

In observing stock-take the auditors should ensure that laid down procedures are being properly followed by:

- observing entity employees performing their laid down procedures;
- determining that pre-numbered count sheets or stock tags are properly controlled;
- being alert to the existence of empty containers and hollow squares (empty spaces) that may exist when goods are stacked in solid formations;
- observing that cut-off procedures are being followed and that the movement of goods, if any, is properly controlled; and
- seeing that all goods are marked as having been counted.

In addition, the auditors should perform substantive procedures, including:

- making test counts and agreeing quantities with the entity's count;
- recording details of serial numbers of count sheets or tags, used and unused (or take copies of all used count sheets);
- ensuring that partly used count sheets are ruled off to prevent additional entries being made;
- appraising the general condition of the stock, noting damaged, obsolete and slow-moving items; and
- identifying and noting the last receiving, production and dispatch documents used, and determining that goods received during the count are properly segregated.

The extent of the auditors' test counts partly depends on the nature and composition of the stock. Prior to stock-take, the auditors will identify high-value items for test counting in addition to counting a representative sample of other items. In making test counts, the auditors should record the count and give a complete and accurate description of the item (identification number, unit of measurement, location, etc.) in the working papers, as shown in Figure 12.1. Such data are essential for the auditors' comparison of the test counts with the entity's counts, and for the subsequent tracing of the counts to stock summary sheets and perpetual stock records.

On conclusion of the observation procedure, a designated member of the audit team should prepare a working paper detailing such matters as listed below, before reaching a conclusion as to the reliability of the count:

- departures from the entity's stock-taking plan;
- the extent of test counts and any material discrepancies resulting therefrom;
- conclusions on the accuracy of the counts; and
- the general condition of the stock.

In the initial audit of an established entity, it is clearly impracticable for the auditors to have observed the stock-take at the previous year-end that establishes the opening stock. ISA 510, Initial Engagements – Opening Balances, permits auditors to verify the stocks by other auditing procedures. When the entity has been audited by another firm of auditors in the prior period, the auditors may review working papers of the predecessor audit firm and consider its competence and independence. If the entity has not been audited

Highlift Company
Raw Materials Test Counts
31/12/X1

Prepared by: __L.R.S.__ Date: __31/12/X1__
Reviewed by: __B.E.M.__ Date: __7/1/X2__

Tag no.	Stock sheet no.	Stock		Count		
		Number	Description	Company	Auditor	Difference
6531	15	1-42-003	Back plate	1 2 5 ✓	1 2 5	
8340	18	1-83-012	5 mm copper plate	9 3 ✓	9 3	
1483	24	2-11-004	Single-end wire	1 3 2 1 m✓	1 3 2 5 m	4 m
4486	26	2-28-811	Copper tubing	2 2 0 m✓	2 2 0 m	
3334	48	4-26-204	Side plate	4 2 4 ✓	4 2 4	
8502	64	7-44-310	10 mm copper wire	2 7 6 m✓	2 7 6 m	
8844	68	7-72-460	20 mm copper wire	4 1 9 m✓	4 1 9 m	
6285	92	3-48-260	Front plate	9 6 ✓	6 9	2 7

Each difference was corrected by the company and the net effect
of the corrections was to increase stock by £840. Total
stock values for which test counts were made and
traced to stock summaries without exemption = £210 460
or 22% of the total. In my opinion, errors were immaterial.

✓ = Traced to company's stock summary
sheets (F-4), noting corrections for all differences

Figure 12.1 *Stock-taking test counts working paper*

previously, the auditors may be able to obtain audit satisfaction by testing prior period transactions, reviewing the records of prior counts or applying analytical procedures.

When sufficient evidence has not been obtained as to the existence of opening stocks, or when the auditors are unable to observe the closing stock-take or to obtain sufficient evidence from alternative procedures, they are precluded from issuing an unqualified auditors' report. The specific effects on the auditors' report will be considered in Chapter 15. Like the confirmation of debtors, the observation of the entity's stock-take applies to many assertions. It is the primary source of evidence that the stock exists and also provides evidence as to the assertions detailed in Table 12.4.

Table 12.4 Assertions for which attendance at stock-take provides evidence

ASSERTION	APPLICATION
Completeness	Procedures provide assurance that no items were omitted from the count
Valuation	Observation of the condition of goods as being damaged, obsolete or apparently slow-moving and which may need to be valued at net realisable value
Rights and obligations	Possession of goods on entity premises provides some evidence as to ownership

TESTING CLERICAL ACCURACY OF STOCK LISTINGS

After the stock-take, the entity uses the count sheets or stock tags to prepare a listing of all items counted. The stock items are then priced to arrive at the total value of stock. Because this listing serves as the basis for the recorded stock balance, the auditors must ensure that the listing is clerically accurate and that it accurately represents the results of the physical count by:

- testing their own test counts to the stock listings;
- identifying count sheets or tags used in the stock-take according to records made by the auditors at the time of attendance, and testing items on those count sheets or tags to and from the listings;
- comparing the count, on a test basis, with amounts per perpetual records, when applicable, and inquiring into any differences noted; and
- testing the clerical accuracy by recalculating the extensions of quantities times unit prices on a test basis, and the totals shown on the stock listings.

TESTING STOCK PRICING

This procedure involves verifying the cost of stock and the net realisable value of those items that management has determined need to be written down. It also involves considering whether other items need to be written down whose net realisable value may be below cost. Thus, it relates to the valuation assertion.

Stock at cost. For merchandise stock and raw materials valued on a first-in first-out basis, this test involves examining suppliers' invoices covering the quantity in stock.

For work in process and finished goods stocks, the auditors must test cost against costing records. The entity's costing system will have been evaluated during the interim audit, and controls over the determination of product cost assessed. The dual-purpose tests listed in Table 12.2 should provide sufficient evidence as to the reliability of product cost data. The auditors then vouch the costs that are applied to physical stock to the costing records.

Where stock is costed at standard cost, variances for the year need to be analysed. When a variance account has a large balance, the auditors must consider whether fair presentation requires a pro rata allocation of the variance to stocks and to costs of goods sold, instead of charging the entire variance to the cost of goods sold. For example, a large adverse material price variance may indicate that the true cost of stock is greater than the standard cost. If the variance is written off, then the cost of stock is understated.

Stock at net realisable value. IAS 2 requires stock to be written down to net realisable value where below cost. The write-down constitutes an accounting estimate and the auditors must follow the procedures in ISA 540, Audit of Accounting Estimates. This requires auditors to perform some or all of the following:

- review and test the process used by management;
- use an independent estimate; or
- review subsequent events.

For items priced at net realisable value, the auditors must verify the basis for arriving at that value. In some cases, it will be the actual, current or contracted selling price less an estimate of costs to be incurred in completion and selling. In other cases, a formula may be used, taking into account the age, past movement and expected future movement of the stock items. The auditors must examine the data and assumptions on which the estimates are based, check the calculations, consider prior period experience, and see that the estimates are properly approved by management.

In view of the inherent risk of understatement of the required write-down, the auditors should also carry out substantive procedures to identify the need for further write-downs. IAS 2 specifically identifies the following situations in which a write-down may be necessary:

- a fall in selling price;
- physical deterioration of inventories;
- obsolescence;
- a decision to sell at a loss; or
- purchasing or production errors.

Specific procedures normally adopted by the auditors include:

- reviewing sales after the balance date;
- observing signs of deterioration or obsolescence during the attendance at stock-take;
- analysing of stock holdings relative to recent or future budgeted turnover to identify excessive holdings. This analysis is often performed with the use of generalised audit software;
- making inquiry of management and of sales and production personnel; and
- reviewing the minutes of the board of directors and executive committees.

Use of an expert. When entity assertions about the value of the stock pertain to highly technical matters, auditors may require the assistance of an outside expert. This may occur, for example, in an oil company with different grades of petrol and motor oil, or in a jewellery shop with different carat diamonds. As explained in Chapter 6, auditors may rely on the work of an expert in obtaining sufficient appropriate audit evidence when they are satisfied as to the qualifications and independence of the expert.

CONFIRMING INVENTORIES AT LOCATIONS OUTSIDE THE ENTITY

When stocks are stored in public warehouses or with other third parties, auditors should obtain evidence as to the existence of the stock by direct communication with the custodian. This type of evidence is deemed sufficient except when the amounts involved represent a significant proportion of current or total assets. When this is the case, the auditors should:

- consider the integrity and independence of the third party;
- observe (or arrange for another auditor to observe) physical counts of the goods;
- obtain another auditors' report on the warehouse's control procedures relevant to physical counting and to custody of goods; and
- if warehouse receipts have been pledged as collateral, confirm with lenders the pertinent details of the pledged receipts.

Confirmation of stocks at outside locations also provides evidence about the rights and obligations assertion. In addition, it will result in evidence as to the completeness assertion if the custodian confirms more goods on hand than stated in the confirmation request. It does not provide any evidence about the value of the stock because the custodian is not asked to report on the condition of the goods stored in the warehouse.

EXAMINING CONSIGNMENT AGREEMENTS AND CONTRACTS

Goods on hand may be held for customers, at their request, after a sale has occurred, and goods belonging to others may be held on consignment. A consignment 'sale' is one made on a sale or return basis. Payment for the goods is required only on subsequent sale to a third party. For accounting purposes, such goods are included in the 'seller's' stock. Thus, management is requested to segregate goods not owned during the stock-take. In addition, auditors usually request a written assertion on ownership of stocks in the representation letter. This letter is illustrated in Chapter 14 (page 496).

The auditors should also inquire whether any of the entity's own goods are held on consignment and included in stock. If so, the auditors should review the documentation or, if the goods are material, confirm the existence of such goods directly with the other party.

Goods may also be assigned or pledged, usually as security for loans. Auditors must inquire of management as to the existence of such agreements and check that appropriate disclosure is made in the financial statements. Auditors must also consider the possibility of window dressing. Substantial sales immediately prior to the year-end, to an unlikely customer, of goods that are not required to be delivered may, in reality, be a loan by the 'customer', secured by the transfer of title to specified goods. Such a 'transaction' enables the entity to reduce its stocks and increase its cash, thus enhancing the quick or acid test ratio. Further inquiry may reveal an agreement, by the entity, to repurchase the goods after the year-end. Such a transaction should be accounted for in accordance with its substance: a loan secured by stock.

Evidence obtained from this procedure relates to the rights and obligations assertion and the disclosure assertion.

DISCLOSURE

It is appropriate to identify the major stock categories in the balance sheet. In addition, there should be disclosure of the stock costing method(s) used, the pledging of stocks and the existence of major purchase commitments.

Inquiry of management is used to determine the existence of binding contracts for future purchases of goods. When such commitments exist, auditors should examine the terms of the contracts and evaluate the fairness of the entity's accounting and reporting. When material losses exist on purchase commitments, they should be recognised in the financial statements, together with a disclosure of the attendant circumstances as noted in the discussion of creditors in the previous chapter.

The substantive procedures described above provide evidence as to financial statement disclosure. Further evidence may be obtained, as needed, from a review of the minutes of board of directors meetings and from inquiries of management. Based on the evidence, and on a comparison of the entity's financial statements with the Companies Act (or other regulatory frameworks) and with applicable Financial Reporting Standards, the auditors determine the truth and fairness of the disclosures.

◁ LEARNING **CHECK**

12.8 Analytical procedures of stock turnover and gross profit contribute evidence as to the reasonableness of the stock balance.

12.9 Physical observation of stock is a required audit procedure whether by attendance at cyclical counts of perpetual stock records or at a balance date count.

12.10 Physical observation involves:

- considering the adequacy of management plans;

- observing compliance with laid down procedures; and

- performing substantive procedures in the form of inspecting and test counting stock, noting usage of count sheets and obtaining cut-off information.

12.11 Stock listing must be checked:

- against count sheets recorded as used at stock-taking;

- against test counts; and

- as to clerical accuracy.

12.12 Pricing of stock involves testing against costing records and verifying write-downs to net realisable value.

12.13 An independent consideration of the need for further write-downs to net realisable value should also be performed.

12.14 Stock held elsewhere is verified by confirmation with the custodian.

12.15 Inquiry must be made of stock held for others and stock assigned or pledged.

TANGIBLE FIXED ASSETS

Tangible fixed assets are tangible assets intended to be retained for use in the entity's operations. This category, on the balance sheet, includes land and buildings, plant and equipment, and the related accumulated depreciation. Land and buildings may be freehold or leasehold, and plant and equipment may include assets held under finance leases. The principal related profit and loss accounts are depreciation expense, repairs expense, finance charges on finance leases and rent on operating leases.

The principal transaction class relating to fixed asset balances is that of purchases. The information system and internal control procedures relating to purchases were explained in Chapter 11. This chapter considers issues relating to developing the audit plan and designing substantive procedures relating to the account balance and disclosure assertions.

Audit objectives

The relevant audit objectives are presented in Table 12.5.

Developing the audit plan

This section will consider materiality and inherent risk and the development of an appropriate audit strategy. Because transactions relating to fixed assets are few and

Table 12.5 Selected specific audit objectives for tangible fixed assets

ASSERTION CATEGORY	TRANSACTION CLASS AUDIT OBJECTIVES	ACCOUNT BALANCE AUDIT OBJECTIVES
Existence or occurrence	Recorded additions represent fixed assets acquired during the period under audit (**E01**) Recorded disposals represent fixed assets sold or scrapped during the period under audit (**E02**)	Recorded fixed assets represent productive assets that are in use at the balance sheet date (**E03**)
Completeness	All additions (**C1**) and disposals (**C2**) that occurred during the period have been recorded	Fixed asset balances include all applicable assets used in operations at balance sheet date (**C3**)
Rights and obligations	The entity has rights to the fixed assets resulting from recorded purchase transactions (**R1**)	The entity owns or has rights to all recorded fixed assets at the balance sheet date (**R2**)
Accuracy classification and valuation	Additions (**ACV1**) and disposals (**ACV2**) are correctly journalised, and posted	Fixed assets are stated at cost or valuation less accumulated depreciation (**ACV3**)
Presentation and disclosure	The details of additions (**PD1**) and disposals (**PD2**) of fixed assets support their classification and disclosure in the financial statements	Disclosures as to: • cost or valuation • depreciation methods and useful lives of each major class • the pledging as collateral, and • the major terms of finance lease contracts of fixed assets are adequate (**PD3**)

usually individually material, a predominantly substantive audit strategy is normally cost-effective. Additionally, the use of a plant register will be explained. Although auditors rarely assess controls over recording fixed asset transactions in the register, the existence of the register is a source of evidence used in substantive procedures.

MATERIALITY

Fixed assets often represent the largest category of assets on the balance sheet, and the related expenses such as depreciation and repairs and maintenance are material factors in the determination of net profit.

INHERENT RISK

There may be significant variations in the inherent risk assessments for assertions pertaining to different fixed asset accounts. For example, inherent risk for the existence assertion may be low in a merchandising entity because the plant and equipment are not normally vulnerable to theft. However, it may be moderate or high in a manufacturing entity because scrapped or retired machinery may not be written off the books, or small tools and equipment used in production may be stolen. Similarly, the inherent risk in the valuation assertions may be low when equipment items are purchased for cash, but high when items are acquired under finance leases. In the same way, the inherent risk may be high for the rights and obligations assertion and disclosure assertion for plant and equipment acquired under finance leases.

AUDIT STRATEGY

Although material, the verification of fixed assets typically involves significantly less time and cost than the verification of current assets. Unlike debtors or cash balances, control risk assessments for fixed asset balances are usually less dependent on controls over major transaction classes.

The only transaction class with a significant effect on fixed asset balances is that of purchases, which was considered in Chapter 11. When expenditures for smaller items (such as furniture, fixtures and equipment) are processed as routine purchase transactions, auditors may elect to use a lower assessed level of control risk approach. In such cases, the auditors' tests of control of purchase transactions should include a sample of such assets. In assessing control risk for plant and equipment assertions, the control risk assessments for purchase transactions are applicable. Other expenditures for land, buildings and major capital improvements tend to occur infrequently and are not subject to the routine purchasing controls. These transactions may be subject to separate controls, including capital budgeting and specific authorisation by the board of directors. Because such transactions are often individually material, a predominantly substantive approach is often adopted for the fixed assets, resulting in low planned levels of detection risk.

In determining detection risk for the valuation assertion for depreciation expense and accumulated depreciation, it should be recognised that inherent risk is affected by both the degree of difficulty in estimating useful lives and residual values, and the complexity of the depreciation methods used. Control risk may be affected by the effectiveness of any controls related to these estimates and calculations.

FIXED ASSET REGISTER

Entities frequently maintain a fixed asset register as a subsidiary ledger detailing individual items of plant and equipment. The register records the cost of each asset and of any additions or alterations, and the accumulated depreciation charged against it. Balances in the register reconcile with the written-down value of the plant and equipment account in the general ledger. The register also contains additional information, such as the serial number, the supplier or manufacturer, the insurance cover, the maintenance record and the location, as well as other information relevant to management of the portfolio of plant and equipment. From time to time, the entity may carry out an inventory of plant and equipment. Among other benefits, this helps in revealing unrecorded disposals of fully depreciated items.

Control over maintenance of the register is only of audit significance for assets that are vulnerable to misappropriation. Regular physical inventory of such assets provides evidence as to their existence and may be sufficient to enable the auditors to forgo the need to inspect such assets physically at the balance sheet date. Procedures for understanding internal control procedures and assessing control risk are similar to those for perpetual stock records described in the first part of this chapter.

Substantive procedures for fixed assets

As explained earlier, the performance of substantive procedures achieves the required reduction in audit risk of misstatements in tangible fixed asset balances whatever the assessed level of inherent and control risk. Substantive procedures must, therefore, be designed and performed so as to achieve the desired low level of detection risk. The design of substantive procedures will also be guided by the understanding of the entity and of its internal control and the resultant assessment of any specific risks of material misstatement.

DESIGNING SUBSTANTIVE PROCEDURES

In the first audit, evidence must be obtained as to the truth and fairness of the opening balances and the ownership of the assets comprising the balances. When the entity has previously been audited by another firm of auditors, this evidence may be obtained from a review of the predecessor auditors' working papers. If the entity has not been previously audited, the auditors must undertake an investigation of the opening balances. Information concerning opening balances obtained in the initial audit is usually recorded in the permanent audit file. This record is updated annually to record changes in the major assets, particularly property, including details of title deeds and registered charges such as mortgages.

In a recurring engagement, the auditors concentrate on the current year's transactions. The opening balances have been verified through the preceding year's audit, and changes in the balance are usually few. This contrasts with the audit of current assets, which are subject to numerous transactions and for which the audit effort is concentrated on the closing balance. The auditors rely on the inspection of documentary evidence in verifying additions and disposals, and on mathematical evidence in verifying depreciation.

Possible substantive procedures for fixed asset balances, and the specific account balance audit objectives to which the tests relate, are shown in Table 12.6. Risk considerations usually result in greater emphasis being placed on the existence and valuation assertions. We will explain each substantive procedure in a later section.

Table 12.6 Possible substantive procedures for tangible fixed asset assertions

CATEGORY	SUBSTANTIVE PROCEDURE	ACCOUNT BALANCE AUDIT OBJECTIVE (FROM TABLE 12.5)				
		E03	C3	R2	ACV3	PD3
Initial procedures	1. Perform initial procedures on fixed asset balances and records that will be subjected to further testing. (a) Trace opening balances for fixed assets and related accumulated depreciation accounts to and from prior year's working papers. (b) Review activity in general ledger, accumulated depreciation and depreciation expense accounts, and investigate entries that appear unusual in amount or source. (c) Obtain entity-prepared schedules of additions and disposals and determine that they accurately represent the underlying accounting records by: • adding and cross-adding the schedules and reconciling the totals with increases or decreases in the related general ledger balances during the period; • testing agreement of items on schedules with entries in related general ledger accounts.	✓	✓	✓	✓	✓
Analytical procedures	2. Perform analytical procedures. (a) Calculate ratios. (b) Analyse ratio results relative to expectations based on prior years, industry data, budgeted amounts, or other data.	✓	✓		✓	
Tests of details of transactions	3. Agree asset addition with supporting documentation.	✓		✓	✓	✓
	4. Agree asset disposals with supporting documentation.	✓	✓	✓	✓	✓
	5. Review repairs and maintenance and rental expense.		✓			✓
Tests of details of balances	6. Examine title documents and contracts.	✓		✓		
	7. Review provisions for depreciation.				✓	
	8. Consider the possibility of impairment.				✓	✓
	9. Inquire into the valuation of fixed assets.				✓	✓
Presentation and disclosure	10. Compare statement presentation with applicable Accounting Standards. (a) Determine that fixed assets and related expenses, gains and losses are properly identified and classified in the financial statements. (b) Determine the appropriateness of disclosures pertaining to the cost, value, depreciation methods and useful lives of major classes of asset, the pledging of assets as collateral and the terms of lease contracts.					✓

Initial procedures

Before performing any of the other steps in the audit programme, the auditors determine that the opening general ledger balances agree with the prior period's audit working papers. This comparison will confirm that any adjustments determined to be necessary at the conclusion of the prior audit and reflected in the prior period's published financial statements were also properly booked and carried forward. Next, the auditors test the mathematical accuracy of entity-prepared schedules of additions and disposals, and reconcile the totals with changes in the related general ledger balances for fixed assets during the period. In addition, the auditors test the schedules by vouching items on the schedules to entries in the ledger accounts, and tracing ledger entries to the schedules to determine that they are an accurate representation of the accounting records from which they were prepared. The schedules may then be used as the basis for several other audit procedures. Figure 12.2 illustrates an auditors' lead schedule for fixed assets and accumulated depreciation.

Analytical procedures

Analytical procedures are less useful as a source of evidence as to fixed asset balances than they are for current assets and liabilities. This is because the balance can vary substantially as the result of relatively few transactions of which the auditors are already likely to be aware. A comparison of the annual depreciation charge with the cost or written-down value of the relevant class of assets should yield a measure comparable to the depreciation rate. Such evidence could provide some of the required evidence as to the valuation assertion. Comparison of repairs and maintenance expense with that for prior years or with net sales may indicate the possibility that some maintenance expenditures have not been recorded or that they have been capitalised in error.

Tests of details of transactions

These substantive procedures cover three types of transaction related to tangible fixed assets: additions, disposals, and repairs and maintenance.

AGREEING ADDITIONS

The auditors need first to ascertain management's policy with regard to the distinction between capital and revenue expenditure. Most entities specify a cut-off value below which purchases are expensed regardless of their nature. A consistent policy also needs to be followed in distinguishing improvements, which prolong the life or enhance the usefulness of existing assets, from repairs and maintenance, which are necessary for the asset to continue to function over its expected useful life, subject to the guidance provided by IAS 16, Property, Plant and Equipment. The auditors must ensure that additions are properly capitalised and that a consistent policy is being followed.

The recorded amounts should be vouched to supporting documentation in the form of authorisations in the minutes, suppliers' invoices and contracts. If there are numerous transactions, the vouching may be done on a test basis. In performing this test, the auditors ascertain that the amount capitalised includes installation, freight and similar costs, but excludes expenses included on the supplier's invoice, such as a year's maintenance charge. For construction in progress, the auditors may review the contract and documentation in

Highlift Company
Fixed asset and accumulated depreciation
Lead schedule
31 December 20X1

Prepared by: C.J.G. W/P ref.: G
Reviewed by: R.C.P. Date: 4/2/X2
  Date: 12/2/X2

W/P ref.	Acct. no.	Account title	Asset Cost					Accumulated depreciation				
			Balance 31/12/X0	Additions	Disposals	Adjustments DR/(CR)	Balance 31/12/X1	Balance 31/12/X0	Provisions	Disposals	Adjustments (DR)/CR	Balance 31/12/X1
G–1	301	Land	450 000√				450 000					
G–1	302	Buildings	2 108 000√	125 000		②(25 000)	2 208 000	379 440√	84 320		②(1 000)	462 760
G–3	303	Mach. and equip.	3 757 250√	980 000	370 000	②25 000	4 392 250	1 074 210√	352 910	172 500	②1 000	1 255 620
G–4	304	Furn. and fixtures	853 400√	144 000	110 000		887 400	217 450√	43 250	21 000		239 700
			7 168 650	1 249 000	480 000	0	7 937 650	1 671 100	480 480	193 500	0	1 958 080
			F	F	F	F	FF	F	F	F	F	FF

√ Traced to general ledger and 31/12/X0 working papers

F Footed

FF Cross-footed and footed

② To reclassify cost and related accumulated depreciation for purchased addition recorded in Buildings account that should have been recorded in Machinery and Equipment account. See adjusting entry #21 on W/P AE–4.

Figure 12.2 *Fixed asset and accumulated depreciation lead schedule*

support of construction costs. Major items should be physically inspected, ensuring that details of the asset inspected (such as its description and the manufacturer's serial number) agree with the documentation.

The auditors also need to inquire about leases for tangible fixed assets entered into during the period. Lease agreements convey, to a lessee, the right to use assets, usually for a specified period of time. For accounting purposes, leases may be classified as either finance leases or as operating leases. The auditors should read the lease agreement to determine its proper accounting classification in accordance with IAS 17, Accounting for Leases. When a finance lease exists, both an asset and a liability should be recognised in the accounts and financial statements. The cost of the asset and the related liability should be recorded at the present value of the future minimum lease payments. The accuracy of the entity's determination of the present value of the lease liability should be verified by recomputation.

The vouching of additions provides evidence about the occurrence, rights and obligations, accuracy and classification assertions. In addition, the examination of lease contracts pertains to the disclosure assertion, due to the disclosures that are required under IAS 17.

AGREEING DISPOSALS

Evidence as to the occurrence of sales, disposals and trade-ins is obtained by vouching recorded transactions to cash remittance advices, written authorisations and sales agreements. Such documentation should be carefully examined to determine the accuracy and propriety of the accounting records, including the recognition of any gain or loss. This procedure additionally provides evidence as to the accuracy and rights assertions.

The following procedures may be used by auditors in determining the completeness of recorded disposals:

- analysing the miscellaneous revenue account for proceeds from sales of fixed assets;
- investigating the disposition of facilities associated with discontinued product lines and operations;
- tracing disposal work orders and authorisations for disposals to the accounting records;
- reviewing insurance policies for termination or reductions of coverage; and
- inquiring of management as to disposals.

Reconciling the results of any physical inventory of plant and equipment undertaken by the entity with the general ledger accounts provides further evidence that all disposals have been recorded.

REVIEWING REPAIRS AND MAINTENANCE AND RENTAL EXPENSES

The auditors' objective in reviewing repairs and maintenance expenses is to determine the propriety and consistency of the charges to this expense. Auditors scan the individual charges, in excess of the entity's cut-off value for capitalisation, to ensure that they are properly expensed. This procedure is related to the examination of additions to ensure that they are properly capitalised.

This substantive procedure provides important evidence concerning the completeness assertion for fixed assets because it reveals expenditures that should be capitalised. In addition, the analysis may reveal misclassifications in the accounts that relate to the disclosure assertion.

Rental expenses are reviewed to ensure that such rents relate to assets under operating leases. Documentary evidence needs to be tested for evidence of leases that should be accounted for as finance leases. This procedure provides evidence as to the completeness assertion in that all assets acquired under finance leases are properly accounted for as additions to tangible fixed assets.

Tests of details of balances

The auditors usually conclude that the closing balance is correctly stated, with respect to the assertions of existence, completeness, and rights and obligations, after having tested the opening balance with the prior year's working papers and verified additions and disposals.

The principal tests of balances relate to valuation and disclosure. These tests are reviewing the provision for depreciation, considering the need for provision for impairment and determining the appropriateness of any revaluation. The other test of balances involves examining documentary evidence of title as to the rights and obligations assertions of the recorded balance.

REVIEWING PROVISIONS FOR DEPRECIATION

In this test, the auditors seek evidence as to the reasonableness, consistency and accuracy of depreciation charges.

- *Reasonableness.* The auditors determine the reasonableness of depreciation provisions by considering such factors as the entity's past history in estimating useful lives and the remaining useful lives of existing assets. The auditors must also ensure that management has reviewed the depreciation rates during the year and adjusted the rates as necessary in accordance with IAS 16, Property, Plant and Equipment.
- *Consistency.* The auditors can ascertain the depreciation methods used by reviewing depreciation schedules prepared by the entity and by inquiry of management. The auditors must then determine whether the methods in use are consistent with those used in the preceding year. On a recurring audit, this can be established by a review of the previous year's working papers.
- *Accuracy.* The auditors verify accuracy through recalculation. Ordinarily, this is done on a selective basis by recomputing the depreciation on major assets and testing depreciation taken on additions and disposals during the year.

These substantive procedures provide evidence about the valuation assertion.

CONSIDERING THE POSSIBILITY OF IMPAIRMENT

The auditors must be satisfied that the carrying value of fixed assets does not exceed the greater of their realisable value or value in use in accordance with IAS 36, Impairment of Assets.

Evidence of overvalued assets may be derived by observing obsolete or damaged units during a tour of the plant; by identifying assets associated with discontinued activities but not yet disposed of; and by inquiring of management as to budgets and forecasts for specific activities in relation to the carrying value of assets associated with those activities.

Where amounts have been written off the carrying value of any fixed asset, the auditors must be satisfied, by inquiring of management as to future plans, that the write-down is reasonable.

INQUIRING INTO THE VALUATION

Management may also choose to revalue fixed assets so as to reflect more fairly their value to the business. IAS 16, Property, Plant and Equipment, requires that any revaluation must be applied to a class of assets, not to individual assets within a class. The auditors would need to be satisfied as to the skill, competence and objectivity of the valuer as an expert in accordance with ISA 620, Using the Work of an Expert. Auditors would need to be particular careful in placing reliance on a valuation where the valuer is an employee of the entity. In particular, it would be necessary for the auditors to:

- sight a copy of the valuer's report;
- pay regard to the basis of valuation stated therein; and
- consider its appropriateness as the basis for determining the carrying amount of that class of assets in the financial statements.

This substantive procedure provides evidence about the valuation assertion and the disclosure assertion.

EXAMINING TITLE DOCUMENTS AND CONTRACTS

Auditors may verify the ownership of vehicles by inspecting registration certificates and insurance policies. For plant and equipment, the 'paid' invoice may be the best evidence of ownership. Evidence of ownership of freehold property is found in title deeds, property rates bills, mortgage payment receipts and fire insurance policies. Auditors can also verify ownership of freehold property by reviewing public records. When this form of additional evidence is desired, the auditors may seek the help of a solicitor. The examination of ownership documents relates to the rights and obligations assertion and contributes to the existence assertion for tangible fixed assets.

Disclosure

The financial statement presentation requirements for fixed assets are extensive. The financial statements should show the depreciation expense for the year and the depreciation method(s) used; the opening and closing value and additions and disposals for each class of fixed assets. For assets carried other than at cost, information that must be disclosed includes (1) the names and qualifications of the valuers and whether they are internal or independent, (2) the basis of valuation and (3) the date and amounts of the valuation. Auditors acquire evidence concerning these matters through the substantive procedures described in the preceding sections.

Property pledged as security for loans should be disclosed. Information on pledging may be obtained by reviewing the minutes, the register of charges and long-term contractual agreements; by confirming debt agreements; and by making inquiries of management.

The appropriateness of the entity's disclosures related to assets under lease can be determined by referring to the authoritative accounting pronouncements and the related lease agreements.

 LEARNING **CHECK**

12.16 Transactions involving fixed assets are infrequent and, where material, are usually subject to special treatment. For this reason, auditors rarely test controls over fixed asset transactions or the fixed asset register, preferring to adopt a predominantly substantive approach.

12.17 The principal inherent risks are those for existence and valuation, namely:

- management has an incentive to overstate the existence and/or value of fixed assets; and

- valuation requires considerable estimation and judgement.

12.18 Because transactions are few and the make-up of the balance is relatively constant, substantive procedures concentrate on verifying transactions which reconcile the opening balance with the closing balance.

12.19 Valuation requires:

- consideration of the reasonableness, consistency and accuracy of the year's depreciation provision;

- consideration of the need for an impairment provision; and

- verification of revaluations.

12.20 Presentation and disclosure requirements are extensive and require special consideration.

SUMMARY

Stocks and fixed assets are the major non-monetary assets in most entities' financial statements. Misstatements in these balances are frequently a major cause of audit failure. There are many similarities in the audit of these balances, but also some significant differences. For both balances, the primary inherent risks are misstatements in the existence and valuation assertions. In verifying the existence of stocks, auditors rely on physical inspection, whether through observation of cyclical counts verifying perpetual stock records or through attendance at an annual stock-take.

However, in verifying fixed assets, auditors rely on verifying changes in the recorded balance, including an inspection of additions, and rarely inspect assets making up the balance, reflecting the infrequency of transactions. In contrast, the high incidence of stock transactions, being a current asset, makes it more convenient to verify the closing balance by inspection, and not by verifying transactions.

Given that stocks and tangible fixed assets are non-monetary assets, the valuation of both is determined by the application of accounting procedures involving a high degree of judgement. For stocks, the auditors need to understand the costing system to determine its appropriateness and its accuracy in accumulating cost data. For fixed assets, the principal judgements involve estimating useful economic lives, residual values and the basis of depreciation that best reflects benefits derived from the use of fixed assets. Again, the auditors need to determine the appropriateness of the judgements made and the accuracy of the resulting computations. For both asset classes, auditors need to ensure that the accounting basis adopted complies with applicable Financial Reporting Standards and that required disclosures are properly made in the financial statements.

FURTHER READING

Peress, M. 'Be Sceptical of Barter Transactions', *The CPA Journal* (January 1990), p. 56.

Sarasohn, L. & Luehlfing, M. 'Fixed Assets Don't Squeak', *Management Accounting (US)* (November 1996), pp. 29–36.

Wells, J. T. 'Ghost Goods: How to Spot Phantom Inventory', *Journal of Accountancy* (June 2001).

Windsor, S. 'The Use of Audit Sampling Techniques to Test Inventory', *Journal of Accountancy* (January 1991), pp. 107–111.

MULTIPLE-CHOICE QUESTIONS

Choose the best answer for each of the following.

(Answers are on pages 603–604)

12.1 If an entity maintains perpetual stock records the appropriate audit strategy for determining stock at balance sheet date would be to:

    (a) insist on a stock-take at or close to the year-end as required by Auditing Standards.

    (b) rely on book stock if its reliability is confirmed by substantive tests of transactions.

    (c) rely on book stock if its reliability had been confirmed by cyclical counts throughout the year confirmed by both tests of controls and substantive procedures.

    (d) insist on a stock-take at or close to the year-end because perpetual stock records are never sufficiently reliable to dispense with the count.

12.2 The primary objective of an auditor's observation of an entity's stock-take is to:

    (a) allow the auditor to supervise the conduct of the count to obtain assurance that stock quantities are reasonably accurate.

    (b) provide an appraisal of the quality of the merchandise on hand on the day of the stock-take.

    (c) obtain direct knowledge that the stock exists, and has been properly counted.

    (d) discover whether the entity has counted a particular stock item or group of items.

12.3 An entity maintains perpetual stock records in both quantities and value. If the preliminary assessed level of control risk is high, an auditor would probably:
- (a) insist that the entity performs physical counts of stock several times during the year.
- (b) apply gross profit tests to ascertain the reasonableness of the physical counts.
- (c) increase the extent of tests of control over stock records.
- (d) request the entity to schedule the stock-take at the end of the year.

12.4 Which of the following procedures would not be appropriate for an auditor in discharging his or her responsibilities concerning the existence of the entity's stocks?
- (a) Obtaining written representation from the entity as to the existence, quality and value of the stocks.
- (b) Carrying out stock-taking procedures at an interim date.
- (c) Supervising the annual stock-take.
- (d) Confirming the goods in the hands of public warehouses.

12.5 If the client maintains perpetual stock records and performs cyclical counts of stock rather than one major stock-take at the end of the year, what should the auditor do?
- (a) Suggest to the client that it performs a full year-end stock-take.
- (b) Review one or two of the cyclical counts – and not request a full stock-take if there is evidence of adequate procedures.
- (c) Attend all of the cyclical stock-takes and ensure that they have been performed correctly – using the same procedures as are used for the normal year-end stock-take.
- (d) Perform only his or her own full stock-take at year-end.

12.6 What should an auditor do to ensure that stock is stated at the lower of cost and net realisable value?
- (a) Select a sample of stock purchases made during the year and check the associated invoice to ensure they are not recorded at more than that value.
- (b) Select a sample of stock items held at year-end and compare their value with that for subsequent sales of similar items.
- (c) Ensure that all stock items on hand at year-end have been properly recorded at cost when purchased.
- (d) Ensure that stock that is not saleable is disclosed separately in the financial statements.

12.7 In auditing fixed assets, why might the auditor decide to assess control risk at the maximum and perform predominantly substantive testing?
- (a) The number of additions to/disposals of fixed assets is usually not a material number – therefore, it is not of concern to the auditor.
- (b) Fixed assets in total are material. All material balances should be tested using a substantive approach.
- (c) The controls over fixed assets for most companies are usually poor.
- (d) It is more economical to audit fixed assets using substantive testing because of the relatively few associated transactions compared with other balances.

12.8 What audit procedure would most likely detect the incorrect capitalisation of an expense to fixed assets?
- (a) Checking a sample of repairs and maintenance expenses to supporting documentation.

(b)   Selecting a sample of additions to fixed assets, and ensuring that they have adequate supporting documentation.

(c)   Discussing the capitalisation policy with the manager.

(d)   Selecting a sample of large assets, and sighting them.

DISCUSSION QUESTIONS

12.1 Consider the impact the development of barcodes has had on the ability to maintain proper stock records. Might there be any problems associated with reliance on barcodes?

12.2 Discuss the many different ways of identifying production overheads and methods of apportionment to determine the cost of stock. Consider the audit implications involved.

12.3 Many companies use standard costing as the basis for stock costing. What audit procedures might be appropriate for establishing the fairness of the standard costs, for testing the maintenance of the standard cost records and for determining the disposition of variances?

12.4 Overhead is to be absorbed into the cost of stock on the basis of the normal level of activity. What evidence is available to the auditor in verifying management's determination of what that level of activity is?

12.5 Is attendance at stock-take more appropriately seen as a test of controls or as a substantive procedure?

12.6 Consider the cut-off implications where stock-take is before or after the year-end and closing stock is determined by adjusting the count by reference to purchases and sales records in the intervening period.

12.7 Consider the problems confronting the auditor in verifying both the rate and method of depreciation.

12.8 What steps can the auditor take to ensure that the disposal of fully depreciated assets is properly recorded? What are the implications if such assets are retained in the accounts?

12.9 One of the bases of valuation required by the proposed accounting standard on impairment is that of 'present value'. What does this involve and why might it cause difficulties for auditors?

PROFESSIONAL APPLICATION QUESTIONS

(Suggested answers are on pages 640–646)

12.1 Perpetual stock records and the audit of stock

For several years Pyrmont plc has maintained perpetual records of stock at each of its ten shoe shops. Nevertheless, it has continued to determine closing stock by stocktaking at or near the year end. As the senior in charge of Pyrmont's external audit for the year ending 31 December 20x1, you are in the process of planning the audit. In discussions with the company's chief accountant she informs you that the company is intending to dispense with the annual stocktaking and to rely on the perpetual records in determining closing stock.

The company operates a centralised computer system networked to terminals and point of sale registers in each shop. Last year's audit file indicates that control risks over purchase and sale transactions were assessed as low for occurrence, completeness and measurement assertions. However, the control risk assessment did not extend to the recording of sale and purchase transactions into the stock records since stock was determined by physical count. The description of the accounting system shows stock as being delivered directly to each shop. The manufacturers attach a bar-coded tag to each pair of shoes. On delivery, shop personnel physically check each pair of shoes with the description coded on the tag. They then scan the tags. The networked computer verifies the goods against the order and records them on the shop's stock records. At the point of sale the tag is again scanned which both records the sale and removes the item from stock records.

During the past year the company's computing department has rewritten the stock control system to incorporate stock costs as well as quantities. The computer system now records cost at the point of delivery. On sale the computer determines cost of sale on a first in first out (FIFO) basis and recalculates the cost of stock on hand at each shop.

Required

(a) (i)   Describe the control procedures you would need to identify in order to accept book stock as the basis for determining the quantity of stock on hand at the year end.

    (ii)   Describe how you would test those controls.

    Assume your assessment of control risk over recorded stocks is sufficiently low for you to plan substantive procedures that do not require observation of the stocktaking at or near the year end.

(b)   Describe the substantive procedures you would perform, both during the year and as at the year end, in order to verify the completeness and existence of stocks.

(c)   State the systems development controls you would expect to find applied to the rewriting of the stock control system.

(Adapted from Question 1, Audit Framework, June 1999. Reproduced by permission of ACCA)

12.2   Tangible fixed assets

As a staff member of Reddy and Abel, Chartered Certified Accountants, you are assigned to the audit of tangible fixed assets of Redfern Limited for the year ended 30 September 20x1. Reddy and Abel have been the auditors of Redfern for many years. You obtain the following schedule of fixed asset movements and analysis of additions from the company's accountant.

	PROPERTY	PLANT AND MACHINERY	TOTAL
COST OR VALUATION	£000	£000	£000
1 October 20x0	340	275	615
Additions		123	123
Disposals		(72)	(72)
Revaluations	120		120
30 September 20x1	460	326	786

Accumulated depreciation

1 October 20x0	24	213	237
Provision	5	30	35
Written back on disposal		(65)	(65)
Adjustment on revaluation	(24)		(24)
30 September 20x1	5	178	183
Written down value	455	148	603

Schedule of additions (plant and machinery)

SUPPLIER	DESCRIPTION	COST £
New Models Ltd	Milling machine Model 38	55,000
Drill Suppliers	Power drill Type 45 C	34,000
Hoist Co Ltd	Electric hoist No 722	18,000
Sundry below £1,000		16,000
		123,000

The company's accountant also advises you that the property was revalued following a valuation by the company's property manager who is a professionally qualified valuer.

During your verification of depreciation you discover that most plant and machinery is fully depreciated. Moreover, you discover that, due to oversight, depreciation has continued to be provided on fully depreciated items. As at the beginning of the year the amount of overstatement was £ 43,000. The accountant suggests the correction be made by reducing the current year's charge for depreciation.

Required
(a) State, with reasons, the first audit procedures you would perform on the schedules provided by the company's accountant.
(b) Outline the substantive audit procedures you would apply in verifying plant and machinery additions. Your answer should identify procedures applicable to each of the financial statement assertions.
(c) Describe the audit procedures applicable to verifying the revaluation of property.
(d) With respect to the correction to accumulated depreciation, and assuming the amount to be material, discuss the accountant's proposed treatment. If you disagree with the accountant's proposal, state, with reasons, the correct accounting treatment.

CHAPTER 13

AUDITING CASH AND INVESTMENTS

LEARNING **OBJECTIVES**

After studying this chapter you should be able to:

1   identify the audit objectives applicable to cash

2   discuss considerations relevant to determining the audit strategy for cash

3   design and execute an audit programme for cash balances

4 explain procedures for confirming bank balances

5 describe the irregularity known as teeming and lading and how auditors can detect it

6 identify the audit objectives applicable to investments

7 describe control procedures applicable to investments

8 design and execute an audit programme for investments

9 explain the special considerations applicable to the audit of investments in subsidiaries, associates and joint ventures.

PROFESSIONAL STATEMENTS

ISA 600 (Revised) The Work of Related Auditors and Other Auditors in the Audit of Group Financial Statements (Exposure draft)
IAS 7 Cash Flow Statements
IAS 21 The Effects of Changes in Foreign Exchange Rates
IAS 22 Business Combinations
IAS 27 Consolidated Financial Statements and Accounting for Investments in Subsidiaries
IAS 28 Accounting for Investments in Associates
IAS 31 Financial Reporting of Interests in Joint Ventures

Information systems and control procedures for transactions affecting both cash and investment assets have already been described in connection with the audits of sales and purchases in Chapters 10 and 11. This chapter is concerned with the planning and application of substantive audit procedures aimed at verifying these account balances. However, consideration will be given to control procedures over the safekeeping of these assets: (1) the use of bank reconciliations in the case of cash; and (2) the maintenance of an investment register.

For each of these account balances, this chapter will:

- identify the audit objectives;
- describe controls over safekeeping;
- discuss considerations relating to the audit plan; and
- explain applicable substantive procedures.

Special consideration will be given, in the audit of cash, to audit procedures designed to detect a fraud known as 'teeming and lading' (or 'lapping') and to the audit of petty cash balances and imprest bank accounts.

A particular feature of the audit of investments is the special disclosure requirement for investments in subsidiaries, associates and joint ventures. It is usually in the form of consolidated financial statements. This chapter also explains the additional audit responsibilities in verifying investments in group entities, and the responsibilities for the consolidated financial statements.

CASH

Cash balances include cash on hand and at bank or on deposit at similar financial institutions. Cash on hand includes undeposited receipts and petty cash. Cash at bank includes cash held in current and savings accounts and in imprest accounts such as payroll bank accounts, which is available on demand. IAS 7, Cash Flow Statements, has an intermediate category of investments referred to as cash equivalents. Cash equivalents are highly liquid investments readily convertible to known amounts of cash within three months. Although separately disclosed as current asset investments, such funds are usually verified as part of the audit of cash itself.

Other balances at bank that are not readily available and do not meet the definition of cash equivalents (such as debenture sinking fund cash and other accounts that have restrictions on their use) should ordinarily be classified as investments, rather than as part of cash balances. Unlike any other balance sheet account balance, cash may be either an asset or a liability. The latter arises where the bank or other institution with which the entity holds an account allows the entity to write cheques in excess of the balance in the account up to an agreed limit known as an overdraft.

Audit objectives

Internal control considerations and the related audit objectives for cash receipts and payments are addressed in Chapters 10 and 11. For cash receipts, you should refer to pages 334–336 for internal control considerations; to page 345 for tests of control and dual-purpose tests; and to page 355 for a description of substantive tests of cash receipts cut-off.

For cash payments, you should refer to pages 379–380 for control procedures; to pages 392–393 for tests of control and dual-purpose tests; and to page 401 for substantive tests of payments cut-off. Table 13.1 includes only account balance audit objectives.

Table 13.1 Selected specific audit objectives for cash balances

ASSERTION CATEGORY	ACCOUNT BALANCE AUDIT OBJECTIVE
Existence	Recorded cash balances exist at the balance sheet date (**E1**)
Completeness	Recorded cash balances include the effects of all cash transactions that have occurred (**C1**) Year-end transfers of cash between banks are recorded in the proper period (**C2**)
Rights and obligations	The entity has legal title to all cash balances shown at the balance sheet date (**RO1**)
Valuation	Recorded cash balances are realisable at the amounts stated on the balance sheet and agree with supporting schedules (**V1**)
Presentation and disclosure	Cash balances are properly identified and classified in the balance sheet (**PD1**) Lines of credit, loan guarantees and other restrictions on cash balances are appropriately disclosed (**PD2**)

Developing the audit plan

Before planning the audit, it is necessary to consider the effectiveness of control procedures designed to ensure the correctness of the recorded balance by way of regular bank reconciliations and the use of imprest accounts. Materiality and risk will then be considered before identifying factors applicable to determining a strategy for the audit of cash.

SAFEKEEPING OF CASH

Although auditors adopt a predominantly substantive approach to the audit of cash balances, an understanding of procedures for maintaining accountability over cash is necessary in designing the substantive tests of details. The principal procedures are:

- independently performed bank reconciliations; and
- the use of imprest accounts.

Bank reconciliations

In the audit of cash receipts (see Chapter 10) and cash payments (see Chapter 11), the auditors will have obtained an understanding of bank reconciliations and tested controls relating to their preparation and use. This involves an independent comparison of the balance shown on the bank statement with the balance recorded in the entity's records. The difference between the two is reconciled by listing outstanding deposits and cheques. Verifying the reconciliation of the bank account at the balance sheet date is an important substantive procedure. The extent of the auditors' procedures depends on whether there is an entity-prepared reconciliation for the auditors to verify.

Imprest accounts

An imprest petty cash fund is established by transferring a specified amount of cash, such as £200 or £500, to a petty cash box. When cash is paid out of the fund, an authorised voucher is placed in the petty cash box in its place. This voucher could be a supplier's invoice or a special petty cash voucher authorised by a responsible official. When the cash is getting low, the vouchers will be used as support for a cheque requisition to replenish the fund. On replenishment, the cash in the petty cash box will be restored to its imprest level. The following internal control features apply to the management of an imprest petty cash fund:

- The fund should be maintained at the imprest level; that is, cash in the fund plus vouchers for payments should always equal the imprest amount.
- The fund should be in the custody of one individual.
- The fund should be kept secure and stored in the safe when not in use.
- Payments from the fund should be for small amounts, and documentation should support each payment.
- The fund should not be mingled with other cash.
- Replenishment of the fund should be based on a review of supporting documentation.
- Upon payment, supporting documents should be stamped 'PAID' to prevent their reuse.

Certain bank accounts are sometimes also set up on an imprest basis such as payroll and dividend bank accounts. The imprest bank account is opened, or replenished with the net payroll, dividend, etc. When all cheques written on the account have been presented, the balance will be zero. Until such time, reconciliation can be achieved by agreeing the balance as per the bank statement with outstanding cheques. Internal controls over an imprest bank account include the following:

- An individual, such as a paymaster or assistant treasurer, should be authorised to sign cheques drawn on the account.
- Only payroll cheques, dividend cheques, etc. should be written against the account.
- Each pay/dividend period, funds equal to the total net amount payable should be transferred into the imprest bank account.
- The imprest bank account should be independently reconciled each month.

MATERIALITY AND RISK

For many entities, cash balances represent only a small proportion of assets. However, the amount of cash flowing through the accounts over a period of time is usually greater than for any other account in the financial statements. Moreover, cash is vital to the survival of the business as a going concern. The inability of an entity to pay its debts as they fall due because it has a shortage of cash can render a company insolvent, despite the profitability of its operations. Cash, therefore, has a materiality that is greater (relative to its balance) than any other account balance.

The high volume of transactions contributes to a significant level of inherent risk for cash balance assertions, particularly existence and completeness. In addition, the nature of cash balances makes them susceptible to theft, as evidenced by numerous kinds of fraudulent schemes involving cash. In contrast to debtors or stocks, however, the risks pertaining to the rights and obligations, valuation and disclosure assertions for cash are minimal, given the absence of complexities involving these assertions.

AUDIT STRATEGY

Given the large volume of cash transactions and the small account balance, the audit strategy is invariably to concentrate on verifying the account balance. Moreover, given the significance of cash to an entity's liquidity, auditors tend to plan their procedures to detect much smaller levels of misstatements than for other accounts. The small balance means that it is usually more cost-effective to obtain the required overall reduction in audit risk by performing substantive tests of details of balances.

That is not to say that the verification of cash transactions is unimportant. It has a significant impact on recorded sales and purchase balances. The assessment of control risk and the description of substantive tests of details of cash transactions have already been considered in relation to sales and purchases. Nevertheless, even when the lower assessed level of control risk approach is applied in the audit of cash transactions, auditors tend to perform a significant level of substantive procedures in verifying cash balances.

In verifying cash, auditors must remember that the closing balance may be an overdraft. The assertions of existence and completeness are thus equally important, given that the balance may be either an asset or a liability.

◁ LEARNING **CHECK**

13.1 A high volume of cash transactions results in a high inherent risk.

13.2 Controls over cash transactions are usually strong and are tested in connection with the audits of sales and purchases.

13.3 Regular bank reconciliations are an important control over the prevention and detection of fraud and error.

13.4 The use of 'imprest' accounts for petty cash and for payroll and dividend cheques is a further control over safeguarding cash balances.

13.5 Cash balances are usually relatively small but significant because of their importance for liquidity.

13.6 The small balance means that auditors tend to adopt a predominantly substantive approach to the audit of cash balances.

Substantive procedures for cash balances

Procedures described in this section exclude those for petty cash and imprest bank accounts. The audit of these two accounts will be considered separately on pages 465–466.

DETERMINING DETECTION RISK

As explained above, the significance of cash to the entity's liquidity and the fact that the balance is relatively small require that the acceptable level of detection risk in verifying cash balances is invariably set as low.

DESIGNING SUBSTANTIVE PROCEDURES

Table 13.2 lists possible substantive procedures to achieve the specific audit objectives for cash balances. The list is organised in accordance with the general framework for developing audit programmes for substantive procedures, which is explained in Chapter 9. Each of the procedures is explained in a following section including comments on how some tests can be tailored based on applicable risk factors.

Initial procedures

The starting point for verifying cash balances is tracing the current period's opening balances to the closing audited balances in the prior year's working papers. Next, the current period's activity in the general ledger cash accounts is reviewed for any significant entries that are unusual in nature or amount and that may require investigation.

In addition, any schedules that might have been prepared by the entity showing summaries of undeposited cash receipts at different locations and/or summaries of bank balances are obtained. The auditors should determine the mathematical accuracy of such schedules and check their agreement with related cash balances in the general ledger. This test provides evidence about the valuation assertion.

Table 13.2 Possible substantive procedures for cash balance assertions

| CATEGORY | SUBSTANTIVE PROCEDURE | CASH BALANCE AUDIT OBJECTIVE (FROM TABLE 13.1) | | | | |
		E1	C#	RO1	V1	PD#
Initial procedures	1. Perform initial procedures on cash balances and records that will be subjected to further testing: (a) Trace opening balances for cash on hand and in bank to prior year's working papers (b) Review activity in general ledger accounts for cash and investigate entries that appear unusual in amount or source (c) Obtain entity-prepared summaries of cash on hand and in bank, verify mathematical accuracy, and determine agreement with general ledger				√	
Analytical procedures	2. Perform analytical procedures: (a) Compare cash balances with expected amounts	√	√1		√	
Tests of details of transactions	3. Perform cash cut-off tests (note – these tests may have been performed as part of the audit programmes for debtors and creditors): (a) Observe that all cash received by the close of business on the last day of the fiscal year is included in cash and that no receipts of the subsequent period are included, or (b) Review the documentation such as daily cash summaries, duplicate deposit slips, and bank statements covering several days before and after the year-end date to determine proper cut-off (c) Observe the last cheque issued and mailed on the last day of the fiscal year and trace to the accounting records to determine the accuracy of the cash payments cut-off, or (d) Compare dates on cheques issued for several days before and after the year-end date to the dates the cheques were recorded to determine proper cut-off	√	√1			
	4. Trace bank transfers before and after balance sheet date to determine that each transfer is properly recorded as a payment and a receipt in the same accounting period	√	√2			
Tests of details of balances	5. Count undeposited cash on hand	√	√1	√	√	
	6. Confirm bank balances	√	√1	√	√	
	7. Confirm other arrangements with banks	√	√1	√	√	√1,2
	8. Verify reconciliations as appropriate	√	√1, 2	√	√	

(*continued overleaf*)

Table 13.2 (*continued*)

CATEGORY	SUBSTANTIVE PROCEDURE	CASH BALANCE AUDIT OBJECTIVE (FROM TABLE 13.1)				
		E1	C#	RO1	V1	PD#
	9. Obtain and use subsequent period's statements to verify bank reconciliation items and look for evidence of window dressing	√	√1,2	√	√	
Presentation and disclosure	10. Compare statement presentation with applicable Financial Reporting Standards:					
	(a) Determine that cash balances are properly identified and classified					√1
	(b) Determine that bank overdrafts are reclassified as liabilities					√1
	(c) Make inquiries of management, review correspondence with banks, and review minutes of board of directors meetings to determine matters requiring disclosure, such as lines of credit, loan guarantees, compensating balance agreements, or other restrictions on cash balances					√2

Analytical procedures

Cash balances do not normally show a stable or predictable relationship with other current or historical financial or operating data. However, cash balances can be compared with amounts expected from cash flow forecasts.

Tests of details of transactions

Tests of details of cash receipt and payment transactions are described in Chapters 10 and 11. This chapter looks at tests of transactions around the balance sheet date that assist in verifying the balance as at that date.

CASH CUT-OFF TESTS

A proper cut-off of cash receipts and cash payments at the end of the year is essential to the proper statement of cash at the balance sheet date. Two cash cut-off tests are performed:

- a cash receipts cut-off test (see Chapter 10); and
- a cash payments cut-off test (see Chapter 11).

The use of the subsequent period's bank statement (described below) is also helpful in determining whether a proper cash cut-off has been made.

TRACING BANK TRANSFERS

Many entities maintain accounts with more than one bank. An entity with multiple bank accounts may transfer money between bank accounts. For example, money may be transferred from a general bank account to a payroll bank account for payroll cheques that are to be distributed on the next pay day. The funds may be transferred by drawing a cheque on the general account and depositing it in the bank in which the payroll account is held. Several days will elapse before the cheque clears the bank on which it is drawn. Thus, cash on deposit as per bank records will be overstated during this period because the cheque will be included in the balance of the bank in which it is deposited and will not be deducted from the bank on which it is drawn. Where the transfer is effected electronically using on-line banking services, the opposite problem may occur in that, using the above example, the amount will be deducted from the general bank account immediately but will not be credited to the payroll bank account for several days. Thus cash on deposit as per bank records will be understated. Bank transfers may also result in a misstatement of the bank balance as per books if the payment and receipt are not recorded in the same accounting period.

Auditors must identify bank transfers around the year-end and trace them through the books to ensure that all are properly recorded in the same accounting period. The tracing of bank transfers provides reliable evidence concerning the cut-off assertion.

Tests of details of balances

There are five commonly used substantive tests for cash balances in this category:

1. counting cash on hand;
2. confirming bank balances;
3. confirming other arrangements with banks;
4. verifying bank reconciliations; and
5. obtaining and using the subsequent period's bank statement.

COUNTING CASH ON HAND

Cash on hand consists of undeposited cash receipts and change funds. To perform cash counts properly, the auditors should:

- control all cash and negotiable instruments held by the entity until all funds have been counted;
- insist that the custodian of the cash be present throughout the count;
- obtain a signed receipt from the custodian on return of the funds; and
- ascertain that all undeposited cheques are payable to the order of the entity, either directly or through endorsement.

The control of all funds is designed to prevent transfers, by entity personnel, of counted funds to uncounted funds. The sealing of funds and the use of additional auditors are often required when cash is held in many locations. Having the custodian present and requiring his or her signature on return of the funds minimises the possibility, in the event of a shortage, of the custodian claiming that all cash was intact when released to the auditors for counting.

This procedure provides evidence of each of the financial statement assertions except disclosure. It should be noted that the evidence about rights is weak because the custodian of the fund may have substituted personal cash to cover a shortage.

CONFIRMING BANK BALANCES

It is customary for the auditors to obtain a bank confirmation for cash on deposit and loan balances at balance sheet date. Figure 13.1 illustrates the form of the Bank Confirmation Request to be sent on the auditors' letterhead at least two weeks before the confirmation date. The letter identifies the information required. Four categories of information have been agreed between the Auditing Practices Board and the British Bankers Association and the confirmation letter states which category or categories are required. One of these is described as standard and is likely to apply to most situations where entities have a simple banking relationship. The other three categories refer to supplementary information relating to trade finance, derivative and commodity trading and custodian arrangements. The information applicable to each of these categories is also illustrated in Figure 13.1.

The confirmation provides evidence of cash on deposit and of overdraft and loan balances. Primarily it provides evidence of the existence of cash at bank, overdrafts and loans (because there is written acknowledgement that the balance exists), of rights and obligations of cash, overdrafts and loans (because the balances are in the name of the entity) and the valuation of loans. The response from the bank also provides some evidence for the valuation assertion for cash at bank and overdrafts, in that the confirmed balance is used in arriving at the correct cash or overdraft balance at the balance sheet date. Furthermore, it contributes to the completeness assertion; however, it cannot be relied on entirely because the bank confirmation contains a disclaimer in favour of the bank. The bank cannot be held liable if the information supplied is incomplete or inaccurate.

CONFIRMING OTHER ARRANGEMENTS WITH BANKS

The confirmation of other arrangements with the bank, such as acceptances held by the bank for collection, bills discounted with recourse, guarantees of loans to third parties and unused facilities, is especially helpful in meeting the presentation and disclosure assertion. It also provides evidence for each of the other assertions. However, the evidence for the completeness assertion is limited to information known by the branch officer completing the confirmation.

VERIFYING BANK RECONCILIATIONS

When the entity prepares bank reconciliations on a regular basis that are expected to be reliable, the auditors will test the reconciliations prepared as at the balance sheet date. The test normally includes:

- comparing the closing bank balance with the balance confirmed on the bank confirmation form;
- verifying the validity of deposits in transit and outstanding cheques;
- establishing the mathematical accuracy of the reconciliation;
- vouching reconciling items such as bank charges and credits and errors to supporting documentation; and
- investigating old items, such as cheques outstanding for a long period of time, and unusual items.

BANK CONFIRMATION REQUEST LETTER – ILLUSTRATION

[xxxx Bank PLC
25 xxx Street
Warrington
Cheshire
WA1 1XQ]

Dear Sirs

In accordance with the agreed practice for provision of information to auditors, please forward information on our mutual client(s) as detailed below on behalf of the bank, its branches and subsidiaries. This request and your response will not create any contractual or other duty with us.

COMPANIES OR OTHER BUSINESS ENTITIES
(attach a separate listing if necessary)

[Parent Company Ltd
Subsidiary 1 Ltd
Subsidiary 2 Ltd]

AUDIT CONFIRMATION DATE *[30 APRIL 1998]*

Information Required	Tick
Standard Trade finance Derivative and commodity trading Custodian arrangements Other information (see attached)	

The Authority to Disclose Information signed by your customer is attached / already held by you (delete as appropriate). Please advise us if this Authority is insufficient for you to provide full disclosure of the information requested.

The contact name is *[John Caller]*   **Telephone** *[01 234 5678]*

Yours faithfully

[XXX Accountants]

Source: APB Practice Note 16, Bank Reports for Audit Purposes

Figure 13.1 *Bank confirmation request. Form of letter and details of standard and trade finance information.*

STANDARD REQUEST FOR INFORMATION

The following is an extract from the BBA instruction to banks regarding receipt of a standard request for information for audit purposes.

The following information must always be disclosed upon receipt of a request for information for audit purposes. Responses must be given in the order as below and if no information is available then this must be stated as 'None' in the response.

1	**Account and Balance Details**
	• Give full titles of all Bank accounts including loans, (whether in sterling or another currency) together with their account numbers and balances. For accounts closed during the 12 months up to the audit confirmation date give the account details and date of closure.
	Note. Also give details where your Customer's name is joined with that of other parties and where the account is in a trade name.
	• State if any account or balances are subject to any restriction(s) whatsoever. Indicate the nature and extent of the restriction e.g. garnishee order
2	**Facilities**
	Give the following details of all loans, overdrafts, and associated guarantees and indemnities:
	• term
	• repayment frequency and/or review date
	• details of period of availability of agreed finance i.e. finance remaining undrawn
	• detail the facility limit.
3	**Securities**
	With reference to the facilities detailed in (2) above give the following details:
	• Any security formally charged (date, ownership and type of charge). State whether the security supports facilities granted by the Bank to the customer or to another party.
	Note. Give details if a security is limited in amount or to a specific borrowing or if to your knowledge there is a prior, equal or subordinate charge.
	• Where there are any arrangements for set-off of balances or compensating balances e.g. back to back loans, give particulars (i.e. date, type of document and accounts covered) of any acknowledgement of set-off, whether given by specific letter of set-off or incorporated in some other document.
4	**Additional Banking Relationships**
	State if you are aware of the customer(s) having any additional relationships with branches or subsidiaries of the Bank not covered by the response. Supply a list of branches etc.

REQUEST FOR SUPPLEMENTARY INFORMATION

The following is an extract from the BBA instruction to banks regarding receipt of a supplementary request for information for audit purposes.

Request for Trade Finance information

On occasion Auditors may request Trade Finance information. Responses must be given in the order as below and if no information is available then this must be stated as 'None' in the response.

1	**Trade Finance**
	Give the currencies and amounts of the following:
	a) Letters of Credit
	b) Acceptances
	c) Bills discounted with recourse to the customer or any subsidiary or related party of the customer.
	d) Bonds, Guarantees, Indemnities or other undertakings given to the Bank by the customer in favour of third parties (including separately any such items in favour of any subsidiary or related party of the customer). Give details of the parties in favour of whom guarantees or undertakings have been given, whether such guarantees or undertakings are written or oral and their nature.
	e) Bonds, Guarantees, Indemnities or other undertakings given by you, on your customer's behalf, stating whether there is recourse to your customer and/or to its parent or any other company within the group.
	f) Other contingent liabilities not already detailed.
	Note. For each item state the nature and extent of any facility limits and details of period of availability of agreed facility.
2	**Securities**
	With reference to the facilities detailed in the above section give the following:
	• Details of any security formally charged (date, ownership and type of charge). State whether the security supports facilities granted by the Bank to the customer or to another party.
	Note. Give details if a security is limited in amount or to a specific borrowing or if to your knowledge there is prior, equal or subordinate charge.
	• Where there are any arrangements for set-off of balances or compensating balances e.g. back to back loans, give particulars (i.e. date, type of document and accounts covered) of any acknowledgement of set-off, whether given by specific letter of set-off or incorporated in some other document.

Figure 13.1 (*continued*)

Verifying the validity of deposits in transit and outstanding cheques involves:

- tracing or test tracing entries in the bank statement for the last month of the fiscal year to the cash book or bank reconciliation at the beginning of the month, marking them off in the process;

- identifying deposits and cheques recorded in the cash book for the last month of the fiscal year, or in the reconciliation at the beginning of that month not marked as appearing on the bank statement, and tracing them through to the closing reconciliation; and
- clearing the bank reconciliation to ensure that all applicable outstanding deposits and outstanding cheques are marked as having been traced from the cash book.

If there are large numbers of transactions, the test may be restricted to items over a certain amount.

The working paper for an auditor test of an entity-prepared bank reconciliation is illustrated in Figure 13.2.

When the entity does not prepare a bank reconciliation or when control risk over entity-prepared reconciliations is high (such as when it is prepared by the cashier), the auditors may prepare the bank reconciliation. When the auditors suspect possible material misstatements, the auditors may obtain the year-end bank statement directly from the bank for use in preparing the bank reconciliation, rather than relying on the copy of the bank statement held by the entity. This procedure will prevent the entity from making alterations to the data to cover any misstatements.

It is also necessary to verify deposits in transit and outstanding cheques by tracing them to the subsequent period's bank statement. When the next period's bank statement validates these and other reconciling items, the reliance that auditors can place on a bank reconciliation is significantly enhanced.

Testing or preparing a bank reconciliation establishes the correct cash at bank (or overdraft) balance at the balance sheet date. Thus, it is a primary source of evidence for the valuation assertion. This test also provides evidence for the existence, completeness, and rights and obligations assertions.

OBTAINING AND USING THE SUBSEQUENT PERIOD'S BANK STATEMENT

The subsequent period's bank statement would normally be issued at the end of the month following the entity's financial year-end. The entity should be requested to instruct the bank to send a copy of the subsequent period's bank statement directly to the auditors. If the audit deadline does not permit waiting for the issue of this statement, post-year-end transactions as recorded by the bank can be downloaded from the entity's on-line access to their bank account under the auditors' control to ensure details of transactions are not manipulated by entity personnel. On receipt of the subsequent period's bank statement or other record of post-year-end transactions as recorded by the bank, the auditors should:

- trace all prior year dated cheques to the outstanding cheques listed on the bank reconciliation;
- trace deposits in transit on the bank reconciliation to deposits on the statement; and
- scan the statement for unusual items.

The tracing of cheques is designed to verify the list of outstanding cheques. In this step, the auditors may also find that a prior period cheque not on the list of outstanding cheques has cleared the bank and that some of the cheques listed as outstanding have not cleared

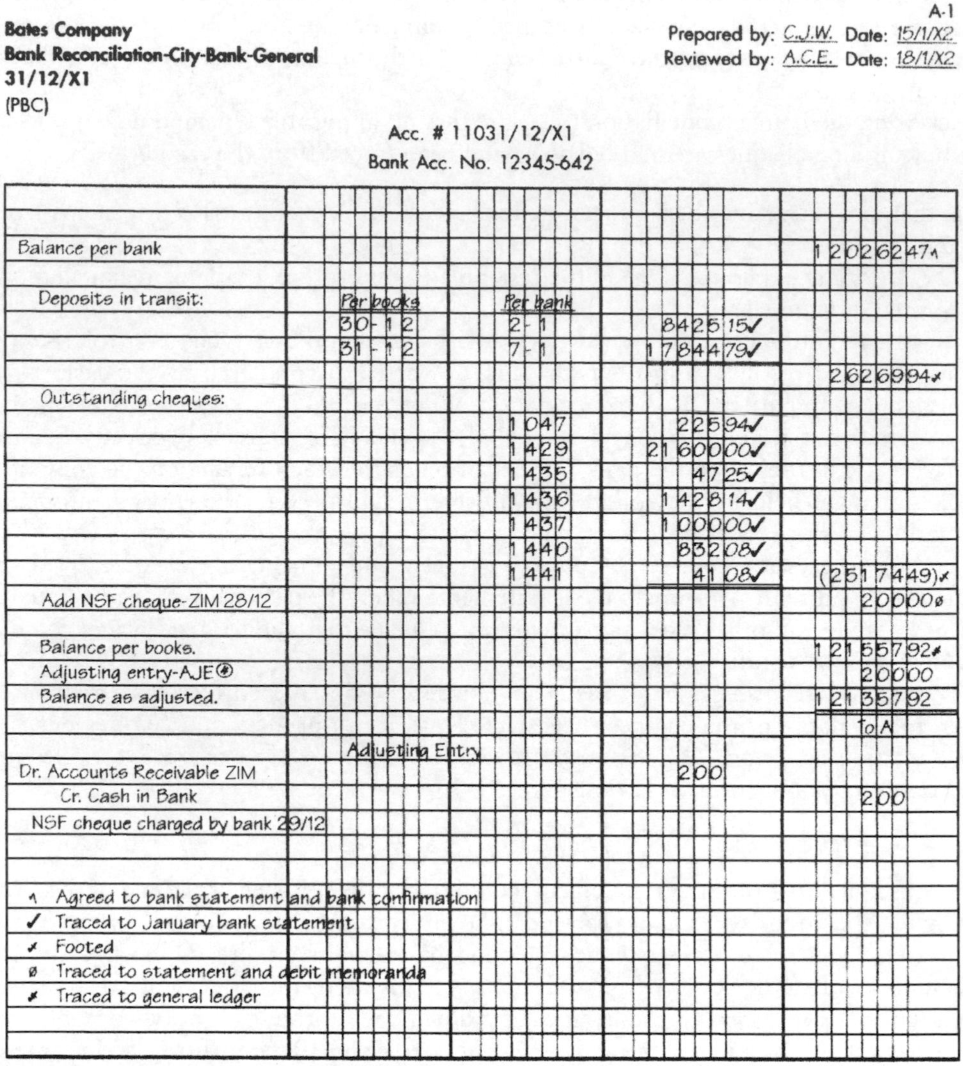

A-1

Bates Company
Bank Reconciliation-City-Bank-General
31/12/X1
(PBC)

Prepared by: _C.J.W._ Date: _15/1/X2_
Reviewed by: _A.C.E._ Date: _18/1/X2_

Acc. # 11031/12/X1
Bank Acc. No. 12345-642

	Per books	Per bank			
Balance per bank					1 202 624 7↰
Deposits in transit:					
	30-12	2-1	842 515 ✓		
	31-12	7-1	1 784 479 ✓		
					2 626 994 ⤬
Outstanding cheques:					
		1 047	225 94 ✓		
		1 429	21 600 00 ✓		
		1 435	47 25 ✓		
		1 436	1 428 14 ✓		
		1 437	1 000 00 ✓		
		1 440	832 08 ✓		
		1 441	41 08 ✓	(251 744 9) ⤬	
Add NSF cheque- ZIM 28/12					200 00 ∅
Balance per books.					1 21 557 92 ⤬
Adjusting entry-AJE④					200 00
Balance as adjusted.					1 21 357 92
					To A
	Adjusting Entry				
Dr. Accounts Receivable ZIM				200	
Cr. Cash in Bank					200
NSF cheque charged by bank 29/12					

↰ Agreed to bank statement and bank confirmation
✓ Traced to January bank statement
⤬ Footed
∅ Traced to statement and debit memoranda
⤬ Traced to general ledger

Figure 13.2 *Review of entity-prepared bank reconciliation*

the bank. The latter may be due to delays in the entity mailing the cheques or in the payees depositing the cheques. The auditors should investigate any unusual circumstances.

When the aggregate effect of uncleared cheques is material, it may indicate an irregularity known as window dressing. This is a deliberate attempt to enhance a company's apparent short-term solvency. (Assume that the entity's balances at the balance sheet date show current assets of £800,000 and current liabilities of £400,000. If £100,000 of cheques to short-term creditors have been prematurely entered, then the correct totals are current assets of £900,000 and current liabilities of £500,000, which results in a 1.8:1 current ratio instead of the reported 2:1.) Window dressing is normally perpetrated by writing cheques on the last day of the financial year but not mailing them until several weeks later, when cleared funds are available at the bank to meet those cheques. If none of a sequence of cheques is presented for payment on the bank statement for more than two weeks after the balance sheet date, then the auditors should make inquiries of the treasurer. Recipients do not usually delay banking cheques once received, and it is normal for most cheques to clear the bank statement within a week of issue.

The tracing of deposits in transit to the subsequent period's bank statement is normally a relatively simple matter because the first deposit on that statement should be the deposit in transit shown on the reconciliation. When this is not the case, the auditors should determine the underlying circumstances for the time lag from the treasurer, and corroborate his or her explanations. Delays in depositing cash receipts could indicate the practice of a fraud known as 'teeming and lading' (see pages 464–465).

In scanning the subsequent period's statement for unusual items, the auditors should be alert for such items as unrecorded bank debits and credits, and bank errors and corrections. For example, Figure 13.2 illustrates a deposit made prior to the year-end that is returned by the drawer's bank after the year-end, marked 'not sufficient funds' (NSF) and requiring adjustment.

By obtaining the subsequent period's statement directly from an independent source, the auditors secure a high degree of competent corroborating information about the validity of the year-end bank reconciliation and the existence, completeness, rights and obligations, and valuation assertions for cash in bank.

Disclosure

Cash should be correctly identified and classified in the balance sheet. Cash on deposit, for example, is a current asset, but debenture sinking fund cash is a long-term investment. A bank overdraft is normally reported as a current liability. In addition, there should be appropriate disclosure of arrangements with banks, such as lines of credit, compensating balances and contingent liabilities. Responses to the Request for Supplementary Information in the bank confirmation request illustrated in Figure 13.1 (pages 459–460) are matters that may require disclosure as contingent liabilities.

The auditors determine the appropriateness of the report presentation from a review of the draft of the entity's financial statements and the evidence obtained from the foregoing substantive procedures. In addition, the auditors should review the minutes of meetings of the board of directors and inquire of management for evidence of restrictions on the use of cash balances.

 LEARNING **CHECK**

13.7 Analytical procedures are little used in the audit of cash balances.

13.8 Cut-off tests are performed in connection with the cut-off of sales and purchases and with the cash count.

13.9 It is important to check the cut-off of bank transfers.

13.10 Principal substantive audit procedures applied to balances are:

- counting cash;

- confirming balances with banks;

- testing the closing bank reconciliation; and

- tracing outstanding items in the reconciliation to the next period's bank statement.

13.11 In counting cash, the auditors should control all cash funds and count them in the presence of the custodian.

13.12 In examining the subsequent period's bank statement, the auditors must consider the possibility of window dressing.

Other issues

This section covers three topics: (1) testing to detect an irregularity known as teeming and lading (or lapping); (2) auditing imprest petty cash funds; and (3) auditing imprest bank accounts.

DETECTING TEEMING AND LADING

Teeming and lading is an irregularity that results in the deliberate misappropriation of cash receipts, either temporarily or permanently, for the personal use of the individual perpetrating the unauthorised act. Teeming and lading is usually associated with collections from customers, but it may also involve other types of cash receipt. Conditions conducive to teeming and lading exist when the same individual handles cash receipts and maintains the sales ledger. Auditors assess the likelihood of teeming and lading by obtaining an understanding of the segregation of duties in the receiving and recording of collections from customers.

An example of teeming and lading

Assume, on a given day, that cash register receipts totalled £600 and mail receipts opened by the defrauder consisted of one payment on account by cheque for £200 from customer A. The perpetrator would steal £200 in cash and destroy all evidence as to the mail receipt, except for the customer's cheque. The cash receipts journal entry would agree with the register (£600), and the deposit slip would show cash of £400 and customer A's cheque for £200. These facts can be tabulated as follows:

ACTUAL RECEIPTS		DOCUMENTATION		CASH RECEIPTS JOURNAL ENTRY		BANK DEPOSIT SLIP	
Cash	£600	Cash tape	£600	Cash sales	£600	Cash	£400
Customer A's cheque	200					Customer A's cheque	200
	£800		£600		£600		£600

To conceal the shortage, the defrauder usually attempts to keep bank and book amounts in daily agreement so a bank reconciliation will not detect the irregularity. The defrauder also corrects the customer's account within three to four days of actual collection so any apparent discrepancy in the customer's account can be explained as a delay in receiving the money or in posting. To accomplish the latter, the amount stolen is shifted to another customer's account (customer B) several days later as follows:

ACTUAL RECEIPTS		DOCUMENTATION		CASH RECEIPTS JOURNAL ENTRY		BANK DEPOSIT SLIP	
Cash	£500	Cash tape	£500	Cash sales	£500	Cash	£400
Customer B's cheque	300	Customer A's cheque	200	Customer A's cheque	200	Customer B's cheque	300
	£800		£700		£700		£700

The total shortage is now £300 – £200 from the first example plus £100 from the second example.

Auditing procedures

Tests to detect teeming and lading are performed only when the control risk for cash receipts transactions is moderate or high. There are three procedures that should detect teeming and lading:

1. *Confirm accounts receivable on a surprise basis at an interim date.* Confirming at this time will prevent the individual engaged in teeming and lading from bringing the accounts up to date. Confirmation at the balance sheet date may be ineffective because the 'defrauder' may anticipate this procedure and adjust the accounts to their correct balances at this date.
2. *Make a surprise cash count.* The cash count will include coin, currency and customer cheques on hand. The auditors should oversee the deposit of these funds. Subsequently, the auditors should compare the details of the deposit shown on the duplicate deposit slip with cash receipts journal entries and postings to the customers' accounts.
3. *Compare details of cash receipts journal entries with the details of corresponding daily deposit slips.* This procedure should uncover discrepancies in the details such as those shown in the above two examples.

AUDITING IMPREST PETTY CASH FUNDS

The balance of petty cash is rarely material. Some auditors audit petty cash only if the total petty cash payments and replenishments throughout the year are material. Even then, the degree of misstatement would need to be substantial to have a material effect on the financial statements. Other auditors, however, believe that entities expect the auditors to verify petty cash and that it is important for the auditors to be seen to do this.

Substantive procedures

In auditing petty cash, auditors perform tests of details of transactions and tests of balances. The auditors will test a number of replenishing transactions, including reviewing supporting documentation, accounting for all pre-numbered receipts, and determining that the reimbursement cheque was for the correct amount. The test of balances involves counting the fund. The count is usually made on a surprise basis at an interim date rather than at the balance sheet date. The auditors may also count the fund at the balance sheet date, along with all other cash funds, to avoid the possibility that petty cash may be used to conceal a shortage elsewhere.

AUDITING IMPREST BANK ACCOUNTS

As explained above, an entity may use an imprest bank account for payroll and dividends.

Substantive procedures

The tests should include confirming the balance with the bank, reviewing the reconciliation prepared by the entity, and using the subsequent period's bank statement. The adjusted or true cash balance at the balance sheet date should be the imprest amount. The only reconciling items on the bank statement will be outstanding payroll or dividend cheques.

Employees usually cash their pay cheques promptly, so all the outstanding cheques should clear the bank on the subsequent period's bank statement. Unpaid dividends are more likely to be a problem. However, larger entities with quoted share capital (which are more likely to experience outstanding dividend cheques) usually employ an independent share registrar – one of whose functions is to distribute dividends. In such cases, the entity pays the total dividend to the registrar in a single cheque, and it is the registrar's responsibility to pay individual dividends and to maintain records of outstanding dividend cheques

◿ LEARNING **CHECK**

13.13 Teeming and lading is the concealment of the misappropriation of cash by the use of subsequent receipts.

13.14 Teeming and lading is facilitated where one individual handles cash and maintains the sales ledger.

13.15 The auditors should be alert to delays in crediting cheques to debtors and to discrepancies between duplicate deposit slips and cash receipts journal details.

13.16 Petty cash need not be audited where the petty cash transactions are immaterial, although many auditors still do so as a matter of routine.

13.17 Auditing petty cash involves vouching reimbursements and counting the balance.

13.18 Imprest bank accounts are usually audited by reconciling the balance.

INVESTMENTS

An entity's investment balances constitute of the ownership of securities issued by other entities. The securities may be in the form of certificates of deposit, preferred and ordinary shares, corporate debentures or government bonds. Consideration is given here to investments in ordinary shares and corporate debentures. Investments may be held for a variety of reasons, with the principal reasons being:

- to hold surplus funds or funds earmarked for a future purpose; and
- to secure a long-term relationship with the other party.

A special category of investments held for the second reason is investment for the purpose of acquiring influence or control over the activities of the other entity. Such entities may be classified as subsidiaries, associates or joint ventures, and are regarded as part of the reporting entity. The financial statements of the investing or 'parent' entity are required to include appropriate balances relating to these other entities, so as to present a consolidated picture of the group or reporting entity. The audit of such investments extends to the verification of the balances in group entity financial statements, which are consolidated with the parent entity's accounts. The final section of this chapter will explain auditors' responsibilities in connection with consolidated financial statements.

Investment transactions involve cash receipts, such as dividends and interest received on investments, and proceeds on their disposal. Control risk considerations for cash receipts are considered in Chapter 10. Investment transactions also involve cash payments for the purchase of investments. Control risk considerations for payment transactions are considered in Chapter 11. This chapter considers additional controls applicable to investing transactions only. These will be considered in the course of discussing the development of the audit plan.

Audit objectives

For each of the relevant categories of financial statement assertion Table 13.3 lists specific account balance audit objectives pertaining to accounts affected by investing transactions. Considerations and procedures relevant to meeting these objectives are explained in the following sections.

Developing the audit plan

Before planning the audit, it is necessary to consider the effectiveness of control structure components designed to ensure that investment transactions are properly supervised and that the investments are subject to adequate safeguards over misappropriation. Materiality and risk will then be considered before identifying factors applicable to determining a strategy for the audit of investments.

SAFEKEEPING OF INVESTMENTS
Because the purchase and sale of investments are often processed separately from other purchases and sales, and the certificates of title may be readily negotiable, entities holding substantial investment portfolios usually adopt specific control procedures over investments.

Control environment
The understanding of several control environment factors is relevant to the audit of the investments. The authority and responsibility for investing transactions, for example,

Table 13.3 Selected specific audit objectives for investments

ASSERTION CATEGORY	ACCOUNT BALANCE AUDIT OBJECTIVE
Existence	Recorded investment balances represent investments that exist at the balance sheet date (**E1**) Investment revenues, gains and losses resulting from transactions and events that occurred during the period (**E2**)
Completeness	All investments are included in the balance sheet investment accounts (**C1**) The profit and loss statement effects of all investment transactions and events during the period are included in the profit and loss statement accounts (**C2**)
Rights and obligations	All recorded investments are owned by the reporting entity (**RO1**)
Valuation	Investments are reported on the balance sheet at valuation, lower of cost or net realisable value or cost, as appropriate for particular investments (**V1**) Investment revenues, gains and losses are reported at proper amounts (**V2**)
Presentation and disclosure	Investment balances are properly identified and classified in the financial statements (**PD1**) Appropriate disclosures are made concerning (1) related party investments, (2) the bases for valuing investments, and (3) the pledging of investments as collateral (**PD2**)

should be assigned to a company officer such as the treasurer. This individual should be a person of integrity, with appropriate knowledge and skills, who realises the importance of observing all prescribed control procedures and who can assist other participating members of management in making initial and ongoing assessments of the risks associated with individual investments.

The information system must include provision for capturing the data required for accounting for the various categories of investment in equity and debt securities, both at acquisition and subsequent reporting dates. Accounting personnel must be familiar with these requirements and capable of implementing them.

In addition, internal auditors and the audit committee of the board of directors should closely monitor the effectiveness of controls over investing activities.

Common documents and records

Title to investments is normally evidenced by a document such as a share or debenture certificate. Arrangements need to be made to ensure their safe custody. They may be held in a bank safe deposit box or directly by the bank or other financial institution as nominees for the entity. In addition, an important document specific to the investment cycle is the broker's advice or contract note issued by a broker specifying the exchange price of investing transactions; it is the primary source document for recording investing transactions.

Where substantial investments are held, a separate investment subsidiary ledger or investment register may be maintained. This records details of acquisitions and disposals, of the receipt of interest and dividends, and of market values.

Functions and related controls

Activities in the investing cycle include the following investing functions and related controls:

- Purchases and sales should be made in accordance with management's authorisations. The purchase and sale of investments intended to be retained as non-current assets would normally require board approval.
- Dividend and interest cheques must be promptly deposited, and the completeness of recorded investment income must be independently verified.
- Transactions should be recorded on the basis of appropriate supporting documentation, and the duties of recording of transactions and custody of the securities should be segregated.
- Securities should be stored in safes or vaults, with access restricted to authorised personnel. Periodically, relevant documents should be independently compared against recorded balances.
- Changes in value and in circumstances pertaining to the appropriate classification of investments should be periodically analysed.
- Management should undertake performance reviews to detect poor investment performance and/or erroneous reporting.
- The classification of individual investments should be periodically reviewed.

Auditors obtain an understanding of the entity's laid down procedures to assess the risks of material misstatements that could occur in investment balances and to design substantive procedures accordingly. For example, if investment certificates are kept in the entity's safe and not independently verified, the audit programme must call for physical inspection at or close to the balance sheet date.

MATERIALITY, RISK AND AUDIT STRATEGY

Securities held as short-term investments may be material to an entity's short-term solvency, but income from such securities is seldom significant to the results of operations of entities outside the financial services sector. Securities held as non-current investments may be material to both the balance sheet and the profit and loss statement.

Many factors affect the inherent risk for investments. The volume of investing transactions is generally quite low. However, securities are susceptible to theft, and the accounting for investments can become complex. In addition, certain inherent risks are more challenging to address with controls, giving management an opportunity to manipulate the reporting for investments. Specifically, the proper classification of an investment may be contentious, which affects the valuation method, income effects and disclosure requirements applicable to the investment. Investments classified as current assets must be carried at the lower of cost and net realisable value. Falls in their market value must be recognised, but gains can be recognised only on realisation. For investments classified as being non-current, falls in value need be recognised only if they are expected to be permanent. Moreover, the entity may choose to carry such assets at valuation and thus recognise unrealised gains as increases in equity, although not as income.[1] Valuation of unquoted investments is subjective and may contribute to high levels of inherent risk for the valuation and disclosure assertions.

The low volume of investing transactions means that it is generally cost-efficient to use the predominantly substantive strategy in auditing investment balances. However, auditors must still obtain an understanding of the internal control components applicable to investments and assess the risks of material misstatements before designing substantive procedures. As with cash, the significant controls are those ensuring the safe custody of investment assets.

◿ LEARNING **CHECK**

13.19 Investments are holdings of securities such as shares and debentures issued by other entities.

13.20 The purpose of holding investments may be to provide a home for funds currently surplus to operating needs or to secure a relationship with the other entity.

13.21 Investments in group entities are required to be consolidated with the financial statements of the parent entity to produce group financial statements.

13.22 Inherent risks include the negotiability of documents of title and the proper classification of securities dependent on management intent.

13.23 The infrequency of investment transactions leads to a predominantly substantive approach to their audit.

13.24 The principal controls relate to those over safekeeping and the maintenance of an investment register.

Substantive procedures for investments

For most entities, investment transactions are infrequent, but individual transactions are usually for substantial amounts. Investment transactions rarely present cut-off problems so the auditors may perform many substantive procedures before or after the balance sheet date. Profit and loss statement balances relating to investments are usually verified at the same time.

DETERMINING DETECTION RISK

Relevant inherent risk and control risk assessments can vary widely, owing to the variety of types of investment and circumstance across entities. However, the small number of transactions means that planned detection risk is usually set as low, with evidence being obtained through the performance of substantive procedures.

DESIGNING SUBSTANTIVE PROCEDURES

Table 13.4 lists possible substantive procedures for investment balances and the specific audit objectives to which they relate. Each of the procedures is explained in a following section.

Table 13.4 Possible substantive procedures for investment balance assertions

CATEGORY	SUBSTANTIVE PROCEDURE	INVESTMENT BALANCE AUDIT OBJECTIVE (FROM TABLE 13.3)				
		EO#	C#	RO1	V#	PD#
Initial procedures	1. Perform initial procedures on investment balances and records that will be subjected to further testing: (a) Trace opening balances for investment accounts to prior year's working papers (b) Review activity in all investment-related balance sheet and profit and loss statement accounts, and investigate entries that appear unusual in amount or source (c) Obtain entity-prepared schedules of investments and determine that they accurately represent the underlying accounting records from which they are prepared by: • adding and cross-adding the schedules and reconciling the totals with the related subsidiary and general ledger balances; • testing agreement of items on schedules with entries in related subsidiary and general ledger accounts				√1,2	
Analytical procedures	2. Perform analytical procedures by analysing interest and dividend yields relative to expectations	√1,2	√1,2		√1,2	
Tests of details of transactions	3. Vouch entries in investment and related profit and loss and equity accounts	√1,2	√1,2	√	√1,2	√1
Tests of details of balances	4. Inspect and count securities on hand 5. Confirm securities held by others 6. Recalculate investment revenue earned 7. Review documentation concerning fair values	√1 √1 √2	√1 √1 √2	√ √	√2 √1,2	√1
Presentation and disclosure	8. Compare financial statement presentation with the *Companies Act 1985* and applicable Financial Reporting Standards: (a) Determine that investment balances are properly identified and classified in the financial statements (b) Determine the appropriateness of disclosures concerning the valuation bases for investments, realised and unrealised gains or losses, related party investments, and pledged investments					√1 √2

Initial procedures

Procedures in this category (as shown in Table 13.4) follow the pattern established for other account balances. First, the auditors agree opening investment balances with audited amounts in the prior year's working papers. Next, the auditors review the activity in investment-related accounts to identify entries that are unusual in nature or amount that need to be investigated. Then, entity-prepared schedules of investment additions and disposals in the period are checked for mathematical accuracy and agreement with the underlying accounting records. The latter procedure includes determining that schedules and subsidiary investment ledgers agree with related general ledger control account balances. The schedules can then serve as the basis for additional substantive procedures.

Analytical procedures

Current asset investments tend not to have any predictable relationship with other balances, while non-current investments are subject to so few transactions that it is easier to proceed directly to tests of details. Analytical procedures can be applied in comparing interest and dividend revenues to investment balances. Unexpected differences in interest or dividend yields may indicate misstatements; for example, a higher-than-expected rate of return may be found to have been caused by erroneous recording of the unrealised gain from an increase in the value of non-current securities in the profit and loss account rather than as a revaluation reserve.

Tests of details of transactions

Purchases and sales of investments are vouched by inspecting brokers' advices and evidence of appropriate approval. Purchases and sales of non-current investments, for example, should be vouched to authorisations in the minutes of directors' meetings. These tests provide evidence about the occurrence of transactions, the transfer of ownership of securities, and the valuation of the securities at the transaction date. For sales, the gain or loss recorded in the profit and loss account can be verified by referring to the carrying value in the investment register.

Evidence as to the completeness of recorded purchases is determined through verification of purchase and payment transactions, as described in Chapter 11. Evidence as to the completeness of sales of investments is determined through verification of the existence of recorded investment assets (as one of the tests of details of balances) and inquiring into the disposition of investments included in the opening balance but not in the closing balance.

Dividend and interest receipts are vouched to remittance advices accompanying the payment. This provides evidence as to the occurrence, accuracy and classification assertions. The completeness of interest received can be verified by computation (the par value of the debt times the annual interest rate) or by confirmation with the issuer of the debt security. The completeness of dividends received can be checked with the investees' financial statements, copies of which should be held by the investor.

Tests of details of balances

Tests of details of balances involve inspecting or confirming recorded investments, verifying income from investments and checking their market value.

INSPECTING AND COUNTING SECURITIES ON HAND

Securities held at the entity's own premises should be inspected and counted at the same time as the count of cash and other negotiable instruments. In performing the test, the custodian of the securities should be present throughout the count, a receipt should be obtained from the custodian when the securities are returned, and the auditors should control all securities until the count is completed.

For securities stored for safekeeping in bank safety deposit boxes, the banks will generally seal the boxes on the nominated date of the count at the entity's request and will confirm to the auditors that there was no access to the box, other than by the auditors, until all locations have been counted. When the count is not made on the balance sheet date, the auditors should prepare a reconciliation from the date of the count to the report date by reviewing any intervening security transactions.

In inspecting securities, the auditors should observe such matters as:

- the certificate number on the document;
- the name of the owner (which should be the entity, either directly or through endorsement);
- the description of the security;
- the number of shares (or debentures);
- the par or face value of the shares (or debentures); and
- the name of the issuer.

These data should be recorded as part of the auditors' analysis of the investment account. Figure 13.3 illustrates an audit working paper for quoted equity securities. All securities should be checked against the records in the investment register and, for

---

Williams Company
Quoted Equity Securities
31 December 20X1

W/P ref: _H-2_
Prepared by: _A.E.R_ Date: _3/1/X2_
Reviewed by: _R.C 91_ Date: _10/1/X2_

Accounts 115 and 425

Description	Certificate no.	Date acquired	No. of shares	Cost per share	Balance 1/1/X1	Purchases	Sales	Balance 31/12/X1	Market price at 31/12/X1 per share	Total	Dividend Income
General Manufacturing	C2779	21/4/X0	900ᴎ	22.00	19 800 ✓			19 800 ✗	24.50 ✔	22 050 ʌ	675 ⓧ
Metropolitan Edison Ltd	M82931	21/9/X0	500	33.20	16 600 ✓		16 600 ø	ʌ			127 ⓧ
Pacific Papers	54942	14/2/X1	200ᴎ	18.50		3 700 ø		3 700 ✗	17.00 ✔	3 400 ʌ	
Warrenton Corp. Ltd	7336	19/7/X0	400ᴎ	27.25	10 900 ✓			10 900 ✗	29.25 ✔	11 700 ʌ	120 ⓧ
					47 300 ✓	3 700	16 600	34 400		37 150	922
					F	F	F	FF To H-1		F	F To R-1

ᴎ Examined stock etc. at Federal Trust Co.
✓ Traced to prior year's working papers
✗ Traced to general ledger balance
F Added
FF Added and cross-added
ʌ Extension checked
ø Vouched to broker's advices and board of director's authorisations
✔ Per market quotation in 2/1/X2 Stock Exchange Journal
ⓧ Dividend rates checked to Standard and Poors; dividends received traced to cash receipts journal.
Aggregate market value exceeded aggregate cost of securities at both beginning and end of year. Therefore, no allowance for declines in market value.

Figure 13.3 *Quoted equity securities working paper*

securities purchased in prior years, the details should be compared with those shown on the prior year's working papers. A lack of agreement between the certificate numbers may indicate unauthorised transactions for those securities.

This substantive procedure provides evidence about the existence, completeness, rights and obligations, and disclosure assertions.

CONFIRMING SECURITIES HELD BY OTHERS

Securities held by outsiders for safekeeping must be confirmed as of the date on which securities held by the entity are counted. As with the confirmation of debtors, the auditors must control the mailings and receive the responses directly from the custodian. The data confirmed are the same as the data that should be noted when the auditors are able to inspect the securities.

Securities may also be held by creditors as collateral against loans. In such cases, the confirmation should be sent to the indicated custodian. The confirmation of securities held by third parties provides evidence as to the existence or occurrence, and rights and obligations assertions. It will also furnish evidence about the completeness assertion if the confirmation response indicates more securities on hand than recorded.

RECALCULATING INVESTMENT REVENUE EARNED

Procedures described under tests of details of transactions above provide evidence as to the existence, completeness and valuation of revenue balances. The verification of dividend income is usually incorporated into the schedule of investments, as illustrated in Figure 13.3.

REVIEWING DOCUMENTATION CONCERNING MARKET VALUES

Where held as current assets, quoted equity securities and marketable debt securities (such as ordinary shares, government bonds and corporate debentures) are normally valued at the lower of the aggregate cost or market value. Investments held as fixed or non-current assets are usually stated at the lower of the cost or impaired value, but may be carried at valuation. Whatever the carrying value, disclosure is also required of the valuation of quoted securities. The auditors verify market quotations by referring to published security prices on stock exchanges. For infrequently traded securities, it may be necessary to seek advice from an independent broker as to the estimated market value at the balance sheet date. Market quotations based on a reasonably broad and active market constitute sufficient appropriate audit evidence as to the current value of the securities.

Audited financial statements of the entity in which investments are held assist in the valuation of unquoted shares, debentures and similar debt obligations. Audited financial statements also represent appropriate evidence as to the adequacy of provisions against cost, if any. This substantive test relates to the valuation assertion.

DISCLOSURE

To conform to the requirements of the Companies Act and Financial Reporting Standards, the presentation of investments in securities in the financial statements requires:

- an analysis of investments as between current and non-current;
- a classification of investments into appropriate classes;

- the recognition of dividends, interest and realised gains and losses in the profit and loss statement;
- the recognition of impairment write-offs in the profit and loss statement;
- disclosure of the basis and methods of accounting;
- disclosure of the market value of quoted investments; and
- disclosure of any liens.

Substantive procedures already described provide evidence for most of the above items. Inspection of the minutes, loan agreements and register of charges should reveal the existence of liens. Inquiry of management as to its intent in holding the securities provides evidence as to their proper classification.

 LEARNING **CHECK**

13.25 Tests of details of transactions are relevant in verifying the occurrence of recorded investment balances.

13.26 Securities on hand at the year-end are verified by count or confirmation.

13.27 The count of securities on the entity's premises should be conducted at the same time as the count of cash.

13.28 Securities held in bank safety deposit boxes may be counted before or after the year-end, with reliance placed on bank records to assure there was no entity access between the date of the count and year-end.

13.29 The count should confirm all details of security certificates to ensure that there is no unrecorded substitution.

13.30 Investment income can be verified by recalculation for interest and, for dividends, by referring to the audited financial statements of investees.

13.31 Market values are verified by referring to official stock exchange quotations.

Substantive procedures for consolidated financial statements

Where a company (or other entity) controls another company (or other entity), consolidated financial statements must be prepared for the group. The group comprises both the parent company and the controlled entities (unless the company or entity is itself a controlled entity) (IAS 27, Consolidated Financial Statements and Accounting for Investments in Subsidiaries). Auditors of parent entities are required to report on the consolidated financial statements. To do so, they must identify the controlled companies (or other entities) comprising the group, verify the amounts pertaining to the other companies (or entities) to be consolidated, and verify the accuracy of the preparation of the consolidated financial statements.

Similar but less extensive disclosure requirements apply in respect of investments in associates (IAS 28, Accounting for Investments in Associates) and in joint ventures (IAS

31, Financial Reporting of Interests in Joint Ventures). The same audit procedures with respect to subsidiaries also apply to investments in associates and joint ventures. The parent entity and its subsidiaries, associates and joint ventures are referred to collectively as group entities.

DETERMINING DETECTION RISK

Inherent risk is normally low for all related account balance assertions, except where the nature of the relationship with related entities is unusually complex. This gives rise to uncertainty as to the existence of control over the other entities, in which case the inherent risk for the completeness assertion may be high.[2] Sometimes, too, the consolidation adjustments may be particularly complex and involve a significant degree of management estimation. This can happen with the consolidation of foreign group entities whose financial statements may be prepared on accounting bases different from those appropriate to the parent entity, or with new acquisitions requiring determination of the fair value of their net assets at the date of acquisition. In such cases, the inherent risk as to the valuation or measurement assertion may be moderate.

Given the materiality of the amounts involved, the audit approach will be predominantly substantive. Little or no reliance will be placed on controls, which are unlikely to be strong. Detection risk will, therefore, be inversely related to the relevant inherent risk assessments.

A special problem arises where the accounts of one or more of the group entities are audited by another auditor, because it may be risky to rely on work performed by another person.

DESIGNING SUBSTANTIVE PROCEDURES

Table 13.5 shows a list of possible substantive procedures for the consolidated financial statements, together with the assertions to which each test relates.

Identifying the group

Where a reporting entity has investments in entities that it controls (or over which it exercises significant influence), it must prepare consolidated financial statements of the group comprising the parent entity and its subsidiaries, associates and joint ventures. The auditors must ensure that all entities included in the consolidated financial statements are properly recognised as subsidiaries, associates or joint ventures of the parent entity, and that no such entities are excluded.

Table 13.5 Possible substantive tests of consolidated financial statement assertions

SUBSTANTIVE PROCEDURE	ASSERTIONS				
	E	C	RO	V	PD
Identify the reporting entity	√	√	√		
Verify the financial statements of other group entities	√	√			
Verify the consolidating adjustments				√	
Compare statement presentation with applicable Accounting Standards				√	√

Control or influence by one entity over another is most likely to arise where the parent has an investment in another entity greater than 50% for it to be accounted for as a subsidiary, or greater than 20% for consideration to be given to accounting for it as an associate. For joint ventures, the relationship is determined by contractual arrangements with the other venturers. For such investments, the auditors verify that the investment in those entities does provide the parent with the required degree of control or influence. For subsidiaries in which the parent entity does not own a majority of the voting rights, the auditors will need to obtain and verify management's explanation as to the basis on which control is secured.

The auditors also investigate the possibility that cumulative investments by the entity and its subsidiaries enable the group to exercise control or significant influence over other entities. If, for example, the parent holds 15% of the shares of another entity and one of its subsidiaries also holds 40%, then that other entity is controlled by the group and is to be accounted for as a subsidiary. In obtaining an understanding of the business in the planning stage and in reviewing related party transactions, the auditors should be alert for evidence of the existence of control over other entities other than through ownership of voting rights. The auditors will need to obtain and verify an explanation as to why any such entities are excluded from the consolidation.

This procedure provides evidence as to the existence and rights and obligations assertions with respect to entities consolidated as controlled entities, and as to the completeness assertion that all controlled entities are included in the consolidation.

Verifying the financial statements of other group entities

To verify the amounts included in the consolidated financial statements, the auditors must obtain and verify the financial statements of each group entity. Where the auditors are not also the auditors of another group entity, consideration must be given as to the extent of reliance to be placed on the work of the other auditors. ISA 600 Revised, The Work of Related Auditors and Other Auditors in the Audit of Group Financial Statements (Exposure draft), recommends that the group auditors:

- obtain information regarding the professional competence of the other auditors;
- advise the other auditors of the independence requirements and obtain representation as to the other auditors' compliance;
- advise the other auditors of the reliance to be placed on their work and of any special requirements, such as identification of intercompany transactions;
- advise the other auditors as to applicable accounting and auditing requirements and obtain representation as to the other auditors' compliance; and
- consider the findings of the other auditors.

Where the group auditors are unable to rely on the work of the other auditors, the group auditors have the statutory right of access, under the Companies Act, to the accounting and other records of any entity controlled by the parent entity. The group auditors can require any information and explanations necessary to report on the consolidated financial statements from any officer or auditors of that entity.

This procedure provides evidence as to the existence assertion and the completeness assertion with respect to assets, liabilities and transactions with entities consolidated with those of the parent entity.

Verifying the consolidating adjustments

Consolidation adjustments fall into four categories: (1) acquisitions and disposals, (2) the elimination of inter-entity balances and transactions, (3) the standardisation of accounting policies, and (4) the translation of foreign currencies.

ACQUISITIONS AND DISPOSALS

On the acquisition of an interest in an associate or subsidiary, its assets are consolidated (directly or by way of equity accounting) in the group accounts at their fair value at the date of acquisition (IAS 22, Business Combinations). The difference between the fair value of the parent entity's ownership interest in the net assets and the consideration paid constitutes purchased goodwill. It is important that auditors verify the amounts recorded as fair value. This involves testing management estimates and evaluating the work of experts. Of particular concern are valuations placed on intangibles not recorded in the books of the controlled entity.

Adjustments on the disposal of a controlling interest must be verified against the carrying value of the controlled entity's net assets immediately prior to disposal.

ELIMINATION OF INTER-ENTITY BALANCES AND TRANSACTIONS

In the course of auditing each group entity, auditors ensure that inter-entity transactions are properly identified and recorded. Where group entities are audited by other auditors, they must be requested to ensure that all such transactions are properly accounted for. At the year-end, the auditors obtain an analysis of inter-entity balances, verify their reconciliation with each other and ensure that they are properly eliminated. The auditors should also ensure that any inter-entity profit in assets held by any of the group entities is properly identified and eliminated on consolidation.

STANDARDISATION OF ACCOUNTING POLICIES

Where the financial statements of group entities have been prepared using accounting policies inconsistent with those of the reporting entity, appropriate adjustments must be made on consolidation. When auditing group entities or when communicating with other auditors of group entities, the auditors must identify any accounting policies inconsistent with those of the reporting entity, and verify the consolidating adjustment.

TRANSLATION OF FOREIGN CURRENCIES

Where a group entity's financial statements are prepared in a foreign currency, they must be translated for purposes of consolidation. The auditors must verify the exchange rates used, check the translations and ensure that the accounting treatment conforms to the requirements of IAS 21, The Effects of Changes in Foreign Exchange Rates.

These substantive procedures provide evidence as to the existence, completeness and valuation assertions.

Comparison of report presentation with applicable Accounting Standards

The auditors should ensure that the disclosures in the consolidated financial statements conform to the requirements of applicable Financial Reporting Standards and the Companies Act. Particular requirements are explanations as to why control exists over entities in which the parent entity's ownership interest is 50% or less, and why control does not exist over entities in which the ownership interest is greater than 50%.

 LEARNING **CHECK**

13.32 The auditors of the parent entity are responsible for reporting on the consolidated financial statements and must obtain evidence relating to relevant balances of other group entities.

13.33 The first requirement is to identify group entities and their classification as sub-sidiaries, associates or joint ventures.

13.34 Where group entities are audited by other firms, the parent entity's auditors must perform procedures to determine the reliability of those financial statements for the purpose of including them in the consolidated financial statements.

13.35 Consolidation adjustments need to be verified. These include:

- fair value adjustments of acquisitions and the determination of goodwill;

- elimination of inter-entity balances and transactions;

- standardisation of accounting policies; and

- translation of foreign currency balances.

SUMMARY

The verification of cash balances is an important part of a financial statement audit because, even though the balances at the balance sheet date may appear immaterial relative to other assets, the amount of cash flowing through the accounts during the audit period can be very material. In addition, cash is susceptible to misappropriation and is involved in many fraudulent schemes, such as teeming and lading. For these reasons, extensive substantive procedures to test cash balances are performed during most audits. These include cash cut-off tests, tracing bank transfers, counting cash on hand, confirming balances and other arrangements with banks, reviewing bank reconciliations, obtaining and using subsequent period bank statements, and determining the adequacy of management's disclosures for cash balances.

Although internal control over the processing of investment transactions is gener-ally good, because transactions are infrequent and usually individually significant, it is common for the auditors to use a predominantly substantive audit strategy in verify-ing investment balance assertions. Important among audit procedures is the physical inspection of certificates of title of investments, or their confirmation with indepen-dent custodians.

Auditors also employ a predominantly substantive approach in verifying the consol-idation of investments in group entities in the consolidated financial statements of the economic entity.

NOTES

[1] The accounting treatment of investments is under review. IAS 39, Financial Instruments: Recognition and Measurement, requires remeasurement of all equity investments, except those in subsidiaries and associates, at fair value.

[2] The exclusion of 'special purpose entities' from the consolidated financial statements of Enron was one of the most controversial aspects revealed by the failure of Enron in 2001.

FURTHER READING

Braid, M. 'Counting the Cash', *The CPA Journal* (September 1979), pp. 82–84.

Carmichael, D. R. 'Audit Reporting Considerations for the New Statement of Cash Flows', *The CPA Journal* (June 1988), pp. 72–73.

Compton, J. C. & Van Son, W. P. 'Check Truncation: The Auditor's Dilemma', *Journal of Accountancy* (January 1983), pp. 36–38.

Doppelt, A. B. 'The Telltale Signs of Money Laundering', *Journal of Accountancy* (March 1990), pp. 31–33.

Fensome, M. 'Statement of Auditing Practice AUP 1, Bank Confirmation Requests', *Australian Accountant* (August 1993), pp. 54–55.

Locke, C. 'Auditing Issues – Bank Confirmation Requests', *Charter* (March 1998), pp. 76–77.

Mills, J. 'Controlling Cash in Casinos', *Management Accounting (USA)* (May 1996), pp. 38–40.

Morris, D. M. & Fisher, D. J. 'Investment vs. Trading – A Misnomer', *The CPA Journal* (May 1990), pp. 28–37.

Patterson Jr., G. F. 'New Guide on Auditing Investments', *Journal of Accountancy* (February 1997), pp. 65–67.

Pomeroy, H. 'Restrictive Covenants: What the CPA Should Know', *Journal of Accountancy* (February 1981), pp. 61–68.

Sauls, W. S. 'Developing a Kite-Detection System', *The Internal Auditor* (December 1984), pp. 39–42.

MULTIPLE-CHOICE QUESTIONS

Choose the best answer for each of the following.
(Answers are on page 604)

13.1 The balance of cash is often only 1% of total assets.
   (a) Cash is always qualitatively material no matter how small the balance and should always be audited.
   (b) No audit of the balance is needed where cash is less than 2% of total assets.
   (c) The cash balance need only be audited if the balance is in overdraft.
   (d) The balance need not be audited if control risks over cash receipts and payments have been assessed as less than high.

13.2 When counting cash on hand the auditor should:
   (a) obtain a receipt from the custodian as to its return.
   (b) have two audit staff present to minimise the risk of its being stolen.
   (c) note the details of cash and cheques making up the balance.

(d) perform the count on the same date as the receivables' confirmation to ensure a reliable cut-off.

13.3 In reviewing the bank reconciliation prepared by the cashier, the auditor finds a 'miscellaneous reconciling item'. From discussion with the cashier, the auditor is told that this relates to correction of a bank error. What should the auditor do?

(a) Accept the cashier's explanation.

(b) Accept the cashier's explanation – provided it is also noted in the management representation letter.

(c) Perform tests to detect for teeming and lading.

(d) Note the details for checking against the subsequent period's bank statement.

13.4 Which of the following would be the best protection for an entity that wishes to prevent the 'teeming and lading' of trade debtors?

(a) Request that customers' payment cheques be made payable to the entity and addressed to the treasurer.

(b) Have customers send payments directly to the entity's bank.

(c) Segregate duties so that no employee has access to both the cheques from customers and currency from daily cash receipts.

(d) Segregate duties so that the book-keeper in charge of the general ledger has no access to incoming mail.

13.5 Consider which of the following statements, with respect to the bank confirmation, is least appropriate.

(a) The confirmation is reliable because banks usually maintain reliable records.

(b) The confirmation is reliable because it is received directly from the bank.

(c) The confirmation is reliable because its accuracy is guaranteed by the bank.

(d) The confirmation is reliable because the request is made on a form specially designed for that purpose.

13.6 The auditor usually adopts a predominantly substantive approach to the audit of investments because:

(a) with few transactions there would be no saving in audit effort from testing controls in order to reduce the level of substantive procedures.

(b) the auditor has no duty to advise management on control weaknesses on investments.

(c) inherent risks for investments are high and rarely compensated by adequate controls.

(d) it is a requirement of Auditing Standards.

13.7 Which of the following controls would be the most effective in assuring that the proper custody of investment assets is maintained?

(a) The purchase and sale of investments are executed on the specific authorisation of the board of directors.

(b) The recorded balances in the investment subsidiary ledger are periodically compared with the contents of the safety deposit box by independent personnel.

(c) Direct access to securities in the safety deposit box is limited to only one corporate officer.

(d) Personnel who post investment transactions to the general ledger are not permitted to update the investment subsidiary ledger.

13.8 The following investment ratio is most likely to be of audit relevance.
  (a) Investment income to sales.
  (b) Non-current investments to equity.
  (c) Interest income to investments in debentures and other interest-bearing securities.
  (d) Divided income to investments in equity shares.

13.9 Which of the following is least likely to require special attention when auditing consolidated financial statements?
  (a) Subsidiaries audited by other auditors.
  (b) Fair values of the assets of subsidiaries acquired during the year.
  (c) 100% owned subsidiaries.
  (d) Subsidiaries located and operating in foreign countries.

DISCUSSION QUESTIONS

13.1 Why is it important for the auditor to identify and confirm all bank accounts operated by the entity during the year and how can the auditor be satisfied that all accounts have been confirmed?

13.2 Consider the implications of on-line banking with respect to control over banking transactions and the maintenance of cash and bank records.

13.3 Where petty cash transactions are quantitatively immaterial, discuss arguments for and against its audit by the independent auditor.

13.4 The effort involved in perpetrating a teeming and lading fraud never justifies its rewards. Discuss.

13.5 Consider the audit implications of the introduction of paperless share trading and the elimination of share certificates.

13.6 Discuss the approach to ascertaining the value of investments in private companies and in unquoted public companies.

13.7 Cash and investments now represent only part of sum total of financial assets held by most companies. Apart from debtors, what other financial assets might a company hold and are there any specific accounting and audit requirements for them?

13.8 Discuss the problems associated with reliance on the work of other auditors. Should groups be required to appoint a single firm of auditors?

PROFESSIONAL APPLICATION QUESTIONS

(Suggested answers are on pages 646–653)

13.1 Substantive procedures for cash balances

The firm of Chartered Certified Accountants you are employed by is the external auditor of Villawood Computers Ltd.

Accounting records are maintained on a computer using proprietary software.

You have worked on the audit for three years and this year you are in charge of the audit. Your assistant is a newly recruited business graduate who has done an accounting course but has no practical experience.

Because of the small size of the company there is limited opportunity for segregation of duties. You decide, as in previous years, that the appropriate audit strategy is to obtain evidence primarily through the performance of substantive procedures. However, you are satisfied that there are no special risks of misstatement. You also plan to perform the audit around the computer as the proprietary software is known to be reliable and details of all transactions and balances can be readily printed out.

On arriving at the company's premises in December 1999 to perform the final audit on the 31 October 1999 financial statements, you obtain a copy of the year end bank reconciliation prepared by the bookkeeper and checked by the managing director. This is reproduced below.

VILLAWOOD COMPUTERS LTD BANK RECONCILIATION 31 OCTOBER 1999	£	£
Balance per bank statement 31 October 1998		18,375.91
Deposits outstanding		
30 October	1,887.00	
31 October	1,973.00	3,860.00
		22,235.91
Outstanding cheques		
2696	25.00	
2724	289.40	
2725	569.00	
2728	724.25	
2729	1,900.00	
2730	398.00	
2731	53.50	
2732	1,776.00	
2733	255.65	5,990.80
		16,245.11
Cheque returned 'not sufficient funds' 29 October		348.00
Bank charges October		90.00
Balance per books 31 October 1998		£16,683.11

You have already obtained the bank confirmation and lists of cash (and cheque) receipts and payments printed out from the computer. These lists have been added and the totals agreed with ledger postings. You decide the first task to set for your assistant is the verification of the bank reconciliation.

Required

(a) (i) List the audit procedures to be followed by your assistant in verifying the bank reconciliation in sufficient detail for an inexperienced staff member to follow.

    (ii) Explain the purpose of each procedure in terms of audit objectives.

(b) Discuss the reliability of bank statements as audit evidence. What steps can be taken if it is considered desirable to increase their reliability?

(c) (i) Distinguish between 'auditing around the computer' and 'auditing through the computer'.

    (ii) Explain the circumstances when it would be inappropriate for the auditor to rely on auditing around the computer.

(Adapted from Question 1, Audit Framework, December 1999. Reproduced by permission of ACCA)

13.2 Audit of consolidated financial statements

The Mighty Company Limited is a reporting entity of which your firm of accountants is the auditor. Mighty's consolidated financial statements incorporate the financial statements of its four subsidiaries. Three subsidiaries are incorporated in the UK and audited by your firm. The fourth subsidiary is located in another country and audited by another firm of professional accountants.

Required

(a) Explain how you would verify the intercompany balances.
(b) Describe other audit adjustments you would expect to find and explain how you would verify each of them:
   (i) where the subsidiary had been acquired prior to the financial year being audited; and
  (ii) where the subsidiary had been acquired during the financial year under audit.
(c) Describe the procedures necessary to determine the level of reliance to be placed on the audited financial statements of the foreign subsidiary.

CHAPTER 14

COMPLETING THE AUDIT

LEARNING **OBJECTIVES**

After studying this chapter, you should be able to

1   describe the types of responsibility the auditor has in completing the audit

2   enumerate the procedures in completing fieldwork

3   understand the auditors' responsibilities with respect to events up to the date of the auditors' report

4   describe and state the purpose of a solicitor's representation letter

5   describe and state the purpose of a management representation letter

6   identify the steps in evaluating audit findings

7   indicate the communications with the entity at the conclusion of the audit

8   state the auditors' post-audit responsibilities.

PROFESSIONAL STATEMENTS

ISA 220   Quality Control for Audit Engagements (Exposure draft)
ISA 260   Communication of Audit Matters with those Charged with Governance
ISA 501   Audit Evidence – Additional Considerations for Specific Items, Part C: Inquiry Regarding Litigation and Claims
ISA 520   Analytical Procedures
ISA 560   Subsequent Events
ISA 570   Going Concern
ISA 580   Management Representations
IAS 10   Contingencies and Events Occurring After Balance Sheet Date
IAS 37   Provisions, Contingent Liabilities and Contingent Assets

Many aspects of interim and year-end audit testing have been discussed in previous chapters. This chapter is concerned with two important additional areas of activity in a financial statement audit. The major part of the chapter considers steps involved in completing the audit. These steps are: (1) completing the audit procedures, (2) evaluating the findings and (3) communicating with the entity. The procedures performed in these activities have the distinctive characteristics described below:

• They do not pertain to specific transaction classes or accounts.
• They are performed after the balance sheet date.
• They involve many subjective judgements by the auditors.
• They are usually performed by audit managers or other senior members of the audit team who have extensive audit experience with the entity.

The adage 'last but not least' applies to completing the audit. Indeed, the decisions made by the auditors in this part of the audit are usually crucial to the ultimate outcome of the audit. For example, in determining the procedures to be used and in evaluating the evidence obtained, the auditors must be fully aware of the audit risks associated with the engagement. Moreover, the conclusions reached by the auditors in completing the audit often have a direct impact on the opinion to be expressed on the entity's financial statements.

In completing the audit, the auditors frequently work under tight time constraints, particularly as entities seek the earliest possible date for the issuance of the auditors' report. Although time may not be the ally of the auditors, the auditors must take the time to make sound professional judgements and to express the opinion appropriate in the circumstances.

After explaining the activities involved in completing the audit, consideration is then given in this chapter to the auditors' post-audit responsibilities. These responsibilities pertain to events occurring after the date of the auditors' report.

COMPLETING THE AUDIT PROCEDURES

In completing the audit, the auditors perform specific auditing procedures to obtain additional audit evidence pertaining to (1) subsequent events, (2) minutes of meetings, (3) contingencies, (4) the going-concern assumption, (5) management representations, and (6) financial statement analysis. The procedures do not have to be performed in the foregoing sequence. Each procedure is explained in a subsequent section.

Undertaking a subsequent-events review

Subsequent events, as described in ISA 560, Subsequent Events, refer both to events occurring between the end of the period and the date of the auditors' report, and to facts discovered after the date of the auditors' report. Facts discovered after the date of the auditors' report are further classified into those that are (1) known before the issuance of the financial statements and (2) not discovered until after the issuance of the financial statements.

IAS 10, Events After the Balance Sheet Date, refers to events occurring after the reporting date but prior to the date the financial statements are authorised for issue such as being adopted and signed by the board. The auditors' responsibility extends to the date the auditors' report is issued. The auditors can only issue their report once the entity has finalised and formally adopted the financial statements. However, to avoid any confusion as to responsibility for events occurring between adoption of the financial statements and the issue of the auditors' report, the auditors' report should be signed on the same day.

Auditing Standards require the auditors to apply procedures designed to provide reasonable assurance that all significant events occurring up to the date of the auditors' report are identified. As is shown in Figure 14.1, there is also a further period that extends from the date of the auditors' report. The auditors' responsibility with respect to subsequent events in this period is considered later in this chapter.

TYPES OF EVENT

IAS 10 distinguishes between two types of event occurring after the reporting date:

- *type 1 event:* provides evidence with respect to conditions that existed at the reporting date, and affects the estimates inherent in the process of preparing the financial statements; and

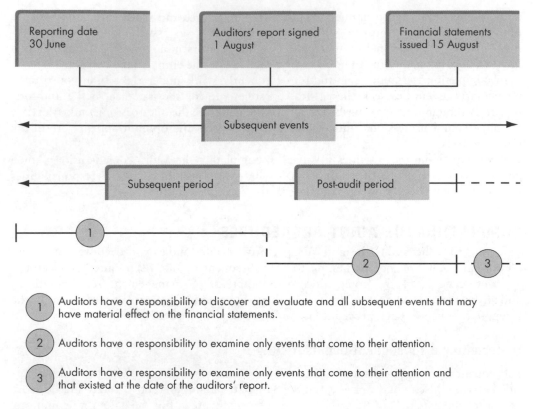

1. Auditors have a responsibility to discover and evaluate and all subsequent events that may have material effect on the financial statements.

2. Auditors have a responsibility to examine only events that come to their attention.

3. Auditors have a responsibility to examine only events that come to their attention and that existed at the date of the auditors' report.

Figure 14.1 *Subsequent-events time dimension*

- *type 2 event:* provides evidence with respect to conditions that did not exist at the reporting date but which arose subsequent to that date.

Type 1 events require adjustment of the financial statements; type 2 events may require disclosure in the statements. The examples in Table 14.1 illustrate the two types of event.

A specific example may help to distinguish further between these two types of event. Assume that a major customer becomes bankrupt on 1 February 20X1. Assume further that the entity considered the customer's balance to be totally collectable in estimating its provision for bad debts in its 31 December 20X0 financial statements. If, on review of the subsequent event, the auditors determine that the bankruptcy was attributable to the customer's deteriorating financial position (which existed, but was unknown to the entity, at the balance sheet date), the entity should be asked to adjust the 31 December 20X0 financial statements for the loss. If, on the other hand, the auditors determine that the customer was financially sound at 31 December and the bankruptcy resulted from a fire or similar catastrophe that occurred after the balance sheet date, only disclosure in the notes to the 31 December financial statements is needed. Ordinarily, type 1 events require adjustment because they typically represent conditions that have accumulated over an extended period of time.

Table 14.1 Examples of events occurring after balance sheet date

TYPE 1 EVENT	TYPE 2 EVENT
Realisation of recorded year-end assets, such as debtors and stocks, at a different amount than recorded	Issuance of preferred or ordinary shares
Settlement of recorded year-end estimated liabilities, such as litigation and product warranties, at a different amount than recorded	Purchase of a business Insurance losses resulting from fire or flood

AUDITING PROCEDURES IN THE SUBSEQUENT PERIOD

The auditors should identify and evaluate subsequent events up to the date of the auditors' report. This responsibility is discharged by the auditors in the following two ways: (1) by being alert for subsequent events in performing year-end substantive procedures (such as cut-off tests and the search for unrecorded liabilities); and (2) by performing the following auditing procedures at or near the completion of the examination:

- reviewing procedures that management has established to ensure that subsequent events are identified;
- reading minutes of the meetings of shareholders and of the board of directors and audit and executive committees for the period after the balance sheet date, and inquiring about matters discussed at meetings for which minutes are not yet available;
- reading the entity's latest available interim financial statements and, as considered necessary and appropriate, budgets, cash flow forecasts and other related management reports;
- inquiring (or adding to previous oral or written inquiries) of the entity's lawyers;
- inquiring of management as to whether any subsequent events have occurred that could affect the financial statements. Examples of specific inquiries that might be made of management are:
  - the current status of items that were accounted for on the basis of tentative, preliminary or inconclusive data;
  - whether new commitments, borrowings or guarantees have been entered into;
  - whether sales of assets have occurred or are planned;
  - whether the issue of new shares or debentures, or an agreement to merge or to liquidate, has been made or is planned;
  - whether any assets have been appropriated by government or destroyed (for example, by fire or flood);
  - whether there have been any developments regarding contingencies;
  - whether any unusual accounting adjustments have been made or are contemplated;
  - whether any events have occurred or are likely to occur which will bring into question the appropriateness of accounting policies used in the financial statements, as would be the case, for example, if such events call into question the validity of the going-concern assumption.

The procedures pertaining to lawyers, inquiry of management (management representations) and the going-concern concept are explained later in the chapter.

In addition to the above, many audit procedures described in the previous chapters refer to subsequent events. Cut-off, for example, is often verified by examining transactions recorded after balance sheet date. The net realisable value of stock is often determined by examining after balance date sales; the collectability of debtors is confirmed by subsequent payments by customers and the correctness of the closing bank reconciliation is confirmed by examining the subsequent period's bank statement.

If the audit procedures identify events that could affect the financial statements, the auditors should carry out further procedures to assess whether such events are appropriately reflected in the financial statements.

EFFECTS ON THE AUDITORS' REPORT

Improper treatment of subsequent events will mean that the auditors' report will have to be modified when the effect on the financial statements is material. Depending on materiality, either an 'except for – disagreement' or an adverse opinion should be issued, as explained in Chapter 2.

Reading the minutes of meetings

The minutes of meetings of the board of directors, and its subcommittees (such as the finance committee and the audit committee) may contain matters that have audit significance. For example, the board of directors may authorise a new debenture issue, the buy-back of shares, payment of a cash dividend or the discontinuance of a product line. Each of these circumstances affects management's assertions in the financial statements. The auditors should determine that all minutes of board meetings held during the period under audit and during the period from the balance sheet date to the end of the audit have been provided for their review. The auditors must review the original set of minutes, signed by authorised officers. Copies or extracts are not acceptable. The reading of minutes is ordinarily done as soon as they become available, to give the auditors the maximum opportunity to assess their significance to the audit. For example, information learned from the minutes might cause the auditors to modify planned substantive procedures, or to request the entity to include the disclosure of a subsequent event in the financial statements. The auditors' reading of the minutes should be documented in the working papers.

Obtaining evidence on contingencies

A contingency is a possible asset or liability that arises from past events whose existence will be confirmed by the occurrence or non-occurrence of one or more uncertain future events not wholly within the control of the entity. Auditors are primarily concerned with contingent liabilities since contingent assets are only required to be disclosed if the future event is likely to occur. IAS 37, Provisions, Contingent Liabilities and Contingent Assets, however, requires that contingent liabilities be recognised as provisions if they can be reliably measured and it is probable that the future event will occur. Even if the contingent liability cannot be reliably measured or is unlikely to occur, it must still be disclosed in the notes. The nature of contingencies is that they are unlikely to be recorded by the information system until the occurrence of the uncertain future event. Discovery of contingencies, therefore, requires the performance of specific audit procedures. These obligations include potential liabilities from tax disputes, product warranties, guarantees of obligations of others, and law suits.

Auditors should be alert for the possibility of contingent liabilities throughout the audit process and particularly when searching for unrecorded liabilities (see Chapter 11) and confirming banks (see Chapter 13). However, more specific procedures are performed when completing the audit because the auditors want to obtain the evidence as close to the date of the auditors' report. The most common contingencies are those relating to unresolved legal disputes. The most appropriate audit procedure relating to contingencies, therefore, is inquiring of the entity's solicitor(s). Additionally, in reading the minutes of board of directors meetings and in reviewing contracts, the auditors should look for circumstances that may indicate contingencies that should be investigated.

AUDIT CONSIDERATIONS

Auditors must obtain sufficient appropriate audit evidence as to (1) whether all appropriate legal matters have been identified, (2) the probability of any material revenue or expense and (3) the adequacy of the accounting treatment and disclosure.

Management represents the primary source of information about the existence of such matters. Thus, the auditors should review and discuss procedures for identifying such matters, and obtain from management:

- a description and estimate of the financial consequences of legal matters; and
- an assurance (preferably in writing) of the completeness of such information.

Other auditing procedures that may disclose outstanding litigation as well as other contingent liabilities include reading the minutes of board of directors' meetings; reviewing contracts and loan agreements, particularly those outside the normal course of business; and reviewing solicitors' fee accounts and correspondence.

LETTER OF AUDIT INQUIRY

The auditors should examine supporting documentation in the entity's files pertaining to all such matters that have come to their attention. It should be recognised, however, that the auditors normally do not possess sufficient legal skill to make an informed judgement on all these matters. Accordingly, the auditors need the assistance of an outside specialist. A solicitor's representation letter to the entity's outside solicitor(s) is the auditors' primary means of obtaining corroborating information about management's assertions concerning the existence and status of legal claims against the entity. This is required by ISA 501, Audit Evidence – Additional Considerations for Specific Items, Part C: Inquiry Regarding Litigation and Claims. An example of such a letter is shown in Figure 14.2.

It should be noted that, in the UK, the Law Society has indicated that it would normally only advise on matters specifically identified by the auditor. Primary evidence as to the existence of contingencies must come from inquiry of management and the inspection of documents held by the entity.

CLIENT COMPANY LIMITED

Letterhead

Messrs ABC & Co. Solicitors

(Address)

Dear. . . . .

In connection with the audit of the financial statements of. . . . . .for the financial period ending . . . ., we request that you provide to this company, at our cost, the following information:

1. Confirmation that you are acting for the company in relation to the matters mentioned below and that the directors' descriptions and estimates of the amounts of the financial settlement (including costs and disbursements) which might arise in relation to those matters are in your opinion reasonable.

Name of company	Directors' description of matter (including current status)	Directors' estimate of the financial settlement (inclusive of costs and disbursements)

2. Should you disagree with any of the information included in 1 above, please comment on the nature of your disagreement.
3. In addition to the above, a list of open files that you maintain in relation to the company.
4. In relation to the matters identified under 2 and 3 above, we authorise you to discuss these matters with our auditors, if requested, and at our cost.
   It is understood that:
   (a) the company may have used other solicitors in certain matters;
   (b) the information sought relates only to information relating to legal matters referred to your firm, which were current at any time during the reporting period, or have arisen since the end of the reporting period and up to the date of your response;
   (c) unless separately requested in writing, you are not responsible for keeping the auditors advised of any changes after the date of your reply;
   (d) you are required to respond only on matters referred to you as solicitors for the company;
   (e) your reply is sought solely for the information of, and assistance to, this company in connection with the audit of the financial statements of the company, and will not be quoted or otherwise referred to in any financial statements or otherwise disclosed, subject to specific legislation requirements, without the prior written consent of your firm.

Your prompt assistance in this matter will be appreciated.

Would you please forward a signed copy of your reply directly to our auditors.

Yours sincerely

CLIENT COMPANY LIMITED

per. . . . .

Secretary

Figure 14.2 *Solicitor's representation letter*

EFFECTS OF RESPONSE ON AUDITORS' REPORT

When the solicitors' responses, together with other audit procedures, provide sufficient appropriate audit evidence on which to form an opinion as to the fairness of financial statement presentation, the auditors may issue an unqualified auditors' report. Where the solicitor's response indicates significant uncertainty about the likelihood of an unfavourable outcome of legal claims, or the amount or range of potential loss, the auditors may conclude that the financial statements are affected by an inherent uncertainty that is not susceptible to reasonable estimation at the balance sheet date. For example, the matter may be only in the initial stage of litigation and there may be no historical experience of the entity in similar litigation. In this situation if the uncertainty is adequately disclosed in the financial statements, the auditors' report should contain an unqualified opinion. If the matter is considered to be fundamental the uncertainty should be further explained in a paragraph contained within the basis of opinion section of the auditors' report. If in the auditors' opinion the disclosure of the uncertainty is inadequate or unreliable, an 'except for' or an adverse opinion would be expressed on the basis of a disagreement with management.

A solicitor's refusal to respond to a letter of audit inquiry is a limitation on the scope of the audit. Depending on the materiality of the items, the auditors should express an 'except for' or disclaimer of opinion on the financial statements. The auditors may obtain assistance about contingencies from the entity's legal department. However, because of possible management bias, such help is unlikely to be a substitute for corroborating information that an outside solicitor refuses to furnish.

Considering the appropriateness of the going-concern assumption

Where financial statements are prepared on a going-concern basis, as would normally be the case, the auditors must consider whether applying this basis is appropriate in the valuation and measurement of items appearing in the financial statements. ISA 570, Going Concern, requires the auditors, when planning the audit, to identify risks that the entity's ability to continue as a going concern may be uncertain and to include appropriate audit procedures in the audit programme. Additionally the auditor needs to:

- evaluate management's assessment of the entity's ability to continue as a going concern; and
- be alert for evidence of events or conditions that may cast doubt on the entity's ability to continue as a going concern;

and it is these procedures that are considered below.

In making inquiry of the directors the auditors will consider the period to which the directors have paid attention and the procedures adopted by the directors for identifying going-concern problems. It is normally expected that directors and auditors consider a period of one year from the date of approval of the financial statements. Where directors assess going concern for a lesser period, such as due to the size and complexity of the entity, the auditors will need to be satisfied as to the directors' reasoning and that adequate disclosure is made in the financial statements as to the applicability of the going-concern assumption.

In evaluating the procedures adopted by management the auditors will consider:

- formal and informal systems for identifying risks;
- budgetary system;
- appropriateness of key assumptions;
- sensitivity of the budget to variable factors;
- obligations to other entities such as guarantees;
- existence of borrowing facilities; and
- plans for resolving matters giving rise to going-concern doubts.

Additionally the auditors will consider the implications of other matters of which they have become aware at the planning stage, and again during the final review. Indications that continuance as a going concern should be questioned may be financial (such as material operating losses), operating (such as the loss of key management personnel) or other (such as changes in legislation).

When a question arises regarding the going-concern basis, additional procedures may be necessary. Most of these are performed during the period of completion of the audit. The auditors will need to discuss, with management, its plans for alleviating the problem; for example, by raising additional finance or the presence of other mitigating factors such as disposal of surplus assets or sale of loss-making business operations. The auditors will need to obtain written representation concerning such plans, and should consider their feasibility by analysing their effect on cash flow or other relevant forecasts. Where appropriate, written confirmation will need to be obtained from third parties, such as banks or creditors, as to the existence of:

- their commitment to additional lending or to a scheme of reconstruction; and
- their willingness to be identified in the financial statements as having entered into such arrangements.

EFFECTS OF GOING CONCERN ON AUDITORS' REPORT

The auditors' report on the financial statements may be qualified because of going-concern problems. If the going-concern assumption is inappropriate, an adverse opinion is required. If an entity has going-concern problems, which are adequately disclosed, an unqualified opinion can be issued.

Adequate disclosure includes:

- a statement that the financial statements are prepared on a going-concern basis;
- a statement as to the facts, the nature of concern and assumptions made by the directors; and
- directors' plans and other relevant actions for resolving the matters.

If disclosures are inadequate, then an 'except for – disagreement' or adverse opinion is required.

Obtaining the management representation letter

ISA 580, Management Representations, requires auditors to obtain certain written representations from management. The objectives of these representations are to:

- confirm oral representations given to the auditors;
- document the continuing appropriateness of such representations;
- reduce the possibility that there might be misunderstandings concerning management's representations; and
- impress upon management that it has the primary responsibility for the financial statements.

As has been described in the preceding sections, a management representation letter may complement other auditing procedures (for example, in connection with (1) the completeness of identified contingent liabilities and (2) the existence of mitigating factors in the presence of going-concern problems). In some cases, however, a representation letter may be the primary source of audit evidence. For instance, when a client plans to discontinue a line of business, the auditors may not be able to corroborate this event through other auditing procedures. Accordingly, the auditors should ask management to indicate its intent in the representation letter.

CONTENTS OF MANAGEMENT REPRESENTATION LETTER

Written representations from management, where they pertain directly to financial statement amounts, should be limited to matters that either individually or collectively are considered to be material to the financial statements. Representation letters should be prepared on the entity's stationery, addressed to the auditors, signed by appropriate officers (usually the senior executive officer and the senior financial officer), and dated with the date of the auditors' report. In many audits, the auditors will draft the representations, which subsequently become the responsibility of the officers who sign the letter. A management representation letter is illustrated in Figure 14.3.

EFFECTS ON THE AUDITORS' REPORT

A management representation letter is not a substitute for any auditing procedures necessary to provide a reasonable basis for an opinion on the financial statements. The representation is a form of documentary evidence from an internal source. Such evidence is judged to have relatively low reliability because of possible management bias. Whether it represents sufficient, appropriate evidence for the matters concerned depends on:

- the materiality of the matters concerned, the availability of other evidence and the cumulative effect of the representation and other evidence (not forgetting that representation would not have been requested if other evidence, on its own, were sufficient);
- whether the representations are consistent with such other audit evidence as is available; and
- the auditors' assessment of management integrity and the degree of professional scepticism appropriate to the engagement.

CROPWELL ENGINEERING PLC

CROPWELL HOUSE

CROPWELL

25 October 20xx

Smith and Co., Chartered Certified Accountants,

Professional Chambers,

Cropwell.

Sirs,

Financial Statements 30 June 20xx

This representation letter is provided in connection with your audit of the financial statements of Cropwell Engineering PLC for the year ended 30 June 20xx, for the purpose of expressing an opinion as to whether the financial statements give a true and fair view of the financial position of Cropwell Engineering PLC as of 30 June 20xx and of the results of its operations and its cash flows for the year then ended in accordance with the *Companies Act 1985*.

On behalf of the Board of Directors we acknowledge our responsibility for the fair presentation of the financial statements in accordance with the *Companies Act 1985*.

We confirm, to the best of our knowledge and belief, the following representations:

[Include here representations relevant to the entity. Such representations may include:]

- There have been no irregularities involving management or employees who have a significant role in the accounting and internal control systems or that could have a material effect on the financial statements.
- We have made available to you all books of account and supporting documentation and all minutes of meetings of shareholders and the board of directors (namely those held on 15 March 20xx and 30 September 20xx, respectively).
- We confirm the completeness of the information provided regarding the identification of related parties.
- The financial statements are free of material misstatements, including omissions.
- The Company has complied with all aspects of contractual agreements that could have a material effect on the financial statements in the event of non-compliance.
- There has been no non-compliance with requirements of regulatory authorities that could have a material effect on the financial statements in the event of non-compliance.
- The following have been properly recorded and when appropriate, adequately disclosed in the financial statements:
  a   The identity of, and balances and transactions with, related parties.
  b   Losses arising from sale and purchase commitments.
  c   Agreements and options to buy back assets previously sold.
  d   Assets pledged as collateral.

Figure 14.3 *Management representation letter*
(Adapted from ISA 580, Management Representations, Appendix. Copyright © International Federation of Accountants)

- We have no plans or intentions that may materially alter the carrying value or classification of assets and liabilities reflected in the financial statements.

- We have no plans to abandon lines of product or other plans or intentions that will result in any excess or obsolete inventory, and no inventory is stated at an amount in excess of net realisable value.

- The Company has satisfactory title to all assets and there are no liens or encumbrances on the company's assets, except for those that are disclosed in Note X to the financial statements.

- We have recorded or disclosed, as appropriate, all liabilities, both actual and contingent, and have disclosed in Note X to the financial statements all guarantees that we have given to third parties.

- Other than ... described in Note X to the financial statements, there have been no events subsequent to period end which require adjustment of or disclosure in the financial statements or Notes thereto.

- The ... claim by XYZ Company has been settled for the total sum of XXX which has been properly accrued in the financial statements. No other claims in connection with litigation have been or are expected to be received.

- There are no formal or informal compensating balance arrangements with any of our cash and investment accounts. Except as disclosed in Note X to the financial statements, we have no other line of credit arrangements.

- We have properly recorded or disclosed in the financial statements the capital stock repurchase options and agreements, and capital stock reserved for options, warrants, conversions and other requirements.

Signed on behalf of the Board of Directors,

    J. Butler

    Managing Director

    J. Bishop

    Company Secretary

The letter should be signed immediately prior to the date of the auditors' report since it constitutes part of the evidence on which the opinion is based.

Figure 14.3 (*continued*)

The refusal of management to furnish a written representation constitutes a limitation on the scope of the auditors' examination. In such circumstances, the auditors may express an 'except for – scope limitation' or a disclaimer of opinion. At the same time, the auditors may draw management's attention to the statutory and regulatory provisions that give the auditors access to records and information and the penalty for providing false or misleading information (s.389A of the *Companies Act 1985*). A scope limitation may also exist when the auditors are not able to perform audit procedures considered necessary in the circumstances to verify essential data in the management representation letter.

Performing analytical procedures

Earlier chapters have explained and illustrated the application of analytical procedures in audit planning and in performing year-end substantive procedures. It will be recalled that analytical procedures involve the use of ratios and other comparative techniques. Analytical procedures are also used in undertaking the overall review of the financial statements. ISA 520, Analytical Procedures, states that the objective of the overall review is to corroborate conclusions formed during the audit on individual elements of financial statements and to assist in arriving at the overall conclusion as to whether the financial statements as a whole are consistent with the auditors' knowledge of the entity's business. In carrying out an overall review, the auditors read the financial statements and accompanying notes. In so doing, they consider the adequacy of the evidence gathered for unusual or unexpected balances and relationships that have been either anticipated in planning or identified during the audit through substantive procedures. Analytical procedures are then applied to the financial statements to determine if any additional unusual or unexpected relationships exist. If such relationships exist, additional auditing procedures should be performed in completing the audit.

Analytical procedures in the overall review should be performed by an individual having comprehensive knowledge of the entity's business, such as a partner or the manager on the audit. A variety of analytical procedures may be used. The procedures should be:

- applied to critical audit areas identified during the audit; and
- based on financial statement data after all audit adjustments and reclassifications have been recognised.

As in earlier applications of analytical procedures, entity data may be compared with expected entity results, available industry data and relevant non-financial data such as units produced or sold and the number of employees.

LEARNING **CHECK**

14.1 The auditors are required to identify and evaluate events occurring up to the date of the auditors' report.

14.2 Events occurring after the reporting date can be classified as:

- type 1 events, which require adjustment of the financial statements; and
- type 2 events, which require disclosure.

14.3 A representation letter obtained from the entity's outside solicitor(s) is the primary means of obtaining corroborating information as to management's assertions in relation to the status of litigation, claims and unrecorded or contingent liabilities.

14.4 The auditors should assess the appropriateness of the going-concern assumption during the final review. Additional audit procedures must be performed if it is questioned.

14.5 A management representation letter:

- impresses upon management that it has the primary responsibility for the financial statements; and

- may be the primary source of audit evidence, where appropriate audit evidence cannot reasonably be expected to exist.

14.6 Analytical procedures performed in completing the audit help the auditors to conclude that the financial information as a whole is consistent with their knowledge of the entity's business.

14.7 The auditors should read all minutes of board meetings held during the period under audit and during the period from the reporting date to the end of the audit examination.

EVALUATING THE FINDINGS

The auditors have the following two objectives in evaluating the findings: (1) determining the type of opinion to be expressed; and (2) determining whether Auditing Standards have been complied with. To meet these objectives, the auditors complete the following steps:

- make the final assessment of materiality and audit risk;
- undertake the technical review of the financial statements;
- formulate an opinion and draft the auditors' report; and
- undertake the final review/s of working papers.

These steps are performed in the order in which they are listed.

Making the final assessment of materiality and audit risk

In formulating an opinion on the financial statements, the auditors should assimilate all the evidence gathered during the examination. An essential prerequisite in deciding on the opinion to express is a final assessment of materiality and audit risk. The starting point in this process is to total the misstatements found in examining all accounts that were not corrected by management. In some cases, the uncorrected misstatements may have been individually immaterial so that no correction was requested by the auditors. In other cases, management may have been unwilling to make the corrections that were requested by the auditors. The next step in the process is to determine the effects of the total misstatements on net profit and other financial statement totals to which the misstatements pertain, such as current assets or current liabilities.

The auditors' determination of misstatements in an account should include the following components:

- uncorrected errors specifically identified through substantive tests of details of transactions and balances (referred to as known misstatements);
- projected uncorrected errors estimated through audit sampling techniques; and
- estimated errors detected through analytical procedures and quantified by other auditing procedures.

'Likely misstatement' is the term used to refer to the total of these components, and 'aggregate likely misstatement' to the sum of likely misstatements in all accounts. The auditors' assessment of aggregate likely misstatement may also include the effect on the current period's financial statements of any uncorrected likely misstatements from a prior period. Including likely misstatements from a prior period may lead to the conclusion that there is an unacceptably high risk that the current period's financial statements are materially misstated. A working paper illustrating one approach to analysing aggregate likely misstatement is shown in Figure 14.4.

The data that have been accumulated are then compared with the auditors' preliminary judgements concerning materiality that were made in planning the audit. As explained in Chapter 5, planning materiality extends to both the individual account and the financial statement levels. If any adjustments in planning materiality have been made during the course of the examination, they should, of course, be included in this assessment.

Consider that, in planning the audit, the auditors have specified an acceptable level of audit risk. As aggregate likely misstatement increases, the risk that the financial statements may be materially misstated will also increase. When the auditors conclude that audit

---

W/P ref: S-1

Ambient Ltd
Analysis of aggregate likely misstatement
31 December 20X1

Prepared by: _C.J.G._ Date: 12/2/X2
Reviewed by: _R.C.P._ Date: 16/2/X2

| W/P Acct. Ref. No. | Description | Debit (Credit) | | | | Shareholders' equity | Pre-tax profit | Tax expense |
| | | Assets | | Liabilities | | | | |
		Current	Non-current	Current	Non-current			
Uncorrected known misstatements:								
D 1 1590	Accumulated depreciation		3 500.00					
4590	Depreciation expense					(3 500.00)	(3 500.00)	
2295	Taxes payable			(1750.00)		1750.00		1750.00
	Overstatement of depreciation expense							
Uncorrected projected misstatements:								
C 1 4200	Cost of goods sold					8 000.00	8 000.00	
1200	Stock	(8 000.00)						
2295	Taxes payable			4 000.00		(4 000.00)		(4 000.00)
	Overstatement of closing stock projected from statistical sample							
Other estimated misstatements:								
	None							
Aggregate likely misstatement		(8 000.00)	3 500.00	2 250.00	0.00	2 250.00	4 500.00	(2 250.00)
Final balance from trial balance		400 000.00	735 000.00	225 000.00	375 000.00	535 000.00	150 000.00	75 000.00
Aggregate likely misstatement %		2%	0.5%	1%	0%	0.4%	3%	3%

Conclusion: The likely misstatments listed above are deemed not to be material, either individually or in their aggregate effects on the individual accounts, the financial statement categories, or the financial statement totals to which they relate.

Figure 14.4 *Analysis of likely misstatements working paper*

risk is at an acceptable level, they can proceed to formulate the opinion supported by the findings. However, if the auditors believe audit risk is not acceptable, they should either perform additional substantive procedures or convince management to make the corrections necessary to reduce the risk of material misstatement to an acceptable level.

Undertaking the technical review of the financial statements

Many public accounting firms have detailed financial statement checklists that are completed by the staff member who performs the initial review of the financial statements. Once completed, the checklist is reviewed by the manager and partner in charge of the engagement. Prior to the release of the auditors' report on a publicly held client, there may also be a technical review of the report by a partner who was not a member of the audit team.

The checklists include matters pertaining to the form and content of each of the basic financial statements, in accordance with:

- the requirements of applicable Financial Reporting Standards and other required disclosures;
- other matters as required by the *Companies Act 1985*; and
- the Combined Code on Corporate Governance (where this applies).

The completed checklist and the findings of the reviewers should be included in the working papers.

Formulating an opinion and drafting the auditors' report

During the course of an audit engagement, a variety of audit tests are performed. These are often performed by staff personnel whose participation in the audit may be limited to a few areas or accounts. As the tests for each functional area or statement item are completed, the staff auditors are expected to summarise their findings. These findings may include identifying monetary errors and proposed adjustments, or qualitative factors such as on matters of principle.

In completing the audit, the separate findings need to be summarised and evaluated so as to express an opinion on the financial statements as a whole. The ultimate responsibility for these steps rests with the partner in charge of the engagement. In some cases, the audit manager makes the initial determinations, which are then carefully reviewed by the partner.

Before reaching a final decision on the opinion, a conference is held with management. At this meeting, the auditors report the findings orally and attempt to provide a rationale for proposed adjustments and/or additional disclosures. Management, in turn, may attempt to defend its position. In the end, some agreement is generally reached on the changes to be made and the auditors can proceed to issue an unqualified opinion. When such an agreement is not obtained, the auditors may have to issue another type of opinion. Communication of the auditors' opinion is made through an auditors' report. The various types of auditors' report are discussed in Chapter 15.

Undertaking final review/s of working papers

In Chapter 6 the first-level review of working papers by a supervisor was explained. The review is made to evaluate the work done, the evidence obtained and the conclusions reached by the person preparing the working paper. Additional reviews of the working papers are made on completion of audit procedures by members of the audit team. The levels of review that may be made in completing the audit are shown in Table 14.2.

The partner's review of the working papers is designed to obtain assurance that:

- the work done by subordinates has been accurate and thorough and in accordance with the audit programme;
- the judgements exercised by subordinates were reasonable and appropriate in the circumstances and have been properly documented;
- the audit engagement has been completed in accordance with the conditions and terms specified in the engagement letter;
- all significant accounting, auditing and reporting questions raised during the audit have been properly resolved;
- the working papers support the auditors' opinion; and
- Auditing Standards and the firm's quality control policies and procedures have been met.

Detailed checklists covering the above matters are commonly used in performing the review of working papers.

A quality control (hot) review of the working papers by a partner who did not participate in the audit is required for listed company audits by ISA 220, Quality Control for Audit Engagements (Exposure draft), and in other situations if required by the firm's quality control procedures. The rationale for this review is based on the objectivity of the reviewer who may challenge matters approved by earlier reviewers. Thus, the review provides additional assurance that all Auditing Standards and the firm's quality control standards have been met in the engagement.

Table 14.2 Levels of review in completing the audit

REVIEWER	NATURE OF REVIEW
Manager	Reviews working papers prepared by seniors, and reviews some or all of the working papers reviewed by seniors.
Partner in charge of the engagement	Reviews working papers prepared by managers and other working papers on a selective basis.
Quality control review	Reviews significant judgements and conclusions in reaching an opinion.

◁ LEARNING **CHECK**

14.8 The purposes of the auditors' final assessment of materiality and risk are to determine whether (1) the auditors' preliminary judgements concerning materiality have been met, and (2) audit risk is at an acceptable level to warrant the expression of an opinion.

14.9 The technical review of the financial statements includes a review of matters pertaining to the form and content of each of the basic financial statements, in accordance with the requirements of applicable Accounting Standards and other required disclosures.

14.10 The type of audit opinion to be expressed is determined by the partner in charge of the engagement.

14.11 Audit working papers are reviewed by the audit manager, the partner in charge of the engagement and, for listed entity audits, an independent partner.

COMMUNICATING WITH THE ENTITY

The auditors have no duty to design audit procedures for identifying matters that may be appropriate to report to management unless specifically agreed upon in the engagement letter or elsewhere in the terms of appointment. However, ISA 260, Communication of Audit Matters with those Charged with Governance, requires auditors to report, to an appropriate level of management, any significant matters identified as a result of audit procedures performed. Such matters may include:

- difficulties encountered in performing the audit such as limitations in scope;
- the selection and application of accounting policies for material unusual transactions or in controversial areas;
- audit adjustments that have a significant effect on the financial statements;
- events and conditions that cast doubt on the entity's ability to continue as a going concern;
- disagreements with operational management that could have a significant effect on the entity's financial statements;
- expected modifications of the auditors' report;
- reasons for assessing inherent and control risk as high for specific financial statement assertions, notably internal control weaknesses;
- irregularities, including fraud and non-compliance with laws and regulations; and
- any other matters, including those falling outside the scope of the audit (for example, inefficiencies), which may usefully be brought to management's notice.

Communicating matters with management

The auditors must consider to what level of management the report should be made and whether to report verbally or in writing. Certain matters may be so significant that they require reporting to the audit committee or governing body. Less significant matters may be reported to a level of management with authority to take appropriate action. For example, weaknesses in specific control activities or irregularities involving non-management employees may be reported to the appropriate line manager. Shortcomings in the control environment or irregularities involving senior management should be communicated to the highest level of management and possibly also to the audit committee. In the interests of time and expediency, the initial communication may be with the line manager concerned or, for more significant matters, with the chief executive. In the former case, it may sometimes be necessary to advise senior management about the matters raised with line management. In the latter case, if the auditors believe the content of the communication could be withheld from the audit committee, the auditors may consider it necessary to communicate directly with individual members.

Less significant matters may be appropriately dealt with by verbal discussion, with a record of the discussion being included in the working papers. Other matters may initially be communicated verbally, in order to save time and to clarify the situation before the matter is put in writing. For example, a control weakness may be discussed with the relevant line manager in order to determine the means of correcting the weaknesses most likely to be acceptable.

Preparing the management letter

During the course of an audit engagement, auditors observe many facets of the entity's business organisation and operations. At the conclusion of an audit, it is desirable to write a letter to management (known as a management letter or letter of weaknesses) that contains recommendations for improving the efficiency and effectiveness of those matters noticed during the course of the audit. The principal purpose of such a letter is to advise management of weaknesses in the internal control structure. It also tangibly demonstrates the auditors' continuing interest in the welfare and future of the entity. The issuance of management letters has now become an integral part of the services rendered by many auditors.

The audit plan should contain a separate section on management letters. Where feasible, the plan should indicate areas of the entity's operations and controls that might be included in management letters. As the audit progresses, matters that are relevant to management letters should be noted in the audit working papers to ensure that they are not overlooked. Subsequently, the working papers should provide adequate documentation of the comments contained in the management letter. Such support will also be useful in any discussions with management about the comments. Management letters should be carefully prepared, well organised, and written in a constructive tone. The contents of the draft letter should be discussed with the company official responsible for the accounting system (for example, the finance director). In particular, the practicality of implementing the suggested changes to the existing system should be discussed. However, absence of agreement should not inhibit the inclusion of recommendations that the auditors consider desirable. In order to avoid misunderstanding, management letters should contain a paragraph advising management that the auditors' examination is made in order to form an opinion on the financial statements and that the report to management should not be regarded as a statement of all matters that may exist. The letter should also prohibit disclosure of its contents to third parties without the auditors' consent. This is to prevent the letter being used, by the entity, as proof of the soundness of its control procedures, exposing the auditors to liability to third parties relying on the letter.

Prompt issuance of management letters on completion of the audit creates a favourable impression and may encourage both an early and a positive response by management. Where the interim audit reveals material weaknesses in internal control, it may be desirable to issue a management letter on completion of that phase of the audit as well as on completion of the final audit.

The letter should request a written reply indicating the action taken or intended to be taken on the matters raised. If no response is received, the auditors should consider whether to raise the matter directly with the audit committee. In any event, if no action is taken by management, the auditors should consider raising the matter again in, for example, subsequent management letters.

A summary of the auditors' responsibilities in completing the audit is presented in Figure 14.5.

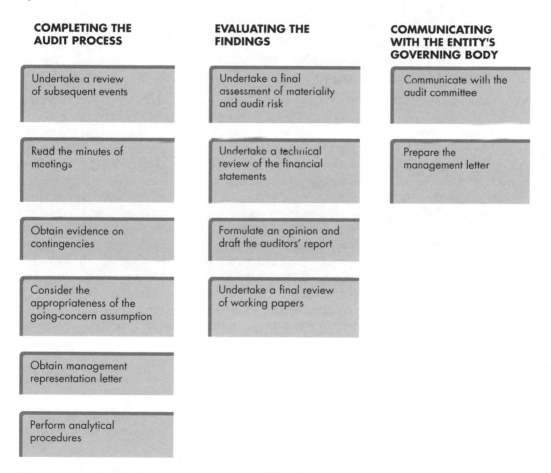

COMPLETING THE AUDIT PROCESS	EVALUATING THE FINDINGS	COMMUNICATING WITH THE ENTITY'S GOVERNING BODY
Undertake a review of subsequent events	Undertake a final assessment of materiality and audit risk	Communicate with the audit committee
Read the minutes of meetings	Undertake a technical review of the financial statements	Prepare the management letter
Obtain evidence on contingencies	Formulate an opinion and draft the auditors' report	
Consider the appropriateness of the going-concern assumption	Undertake a final review of working papers	
Obtain management representation letter		
Perform analytical procedures		

Figure 14.5 *Summary of auditors' responsibilities in completing the audit*

◁ LEARNING **CHECK**

14.12 Auditing Standards require that significant matters identified as a result of audit procedures are reported to the audit committee or the governing body. Less significant matters may be reported to a level of management with authority to take appropriate action.

14.13 The principal purpose of the management letter is to advise management of weaknesses in the internal control structure.

POST-AUDIT RESPONSIBILITIES

This section pertains to the auditors' responsibilities following the completion of the audit examination. Post-audit responsibilities include a consideration of:

- subsequent events occurring between the date of the auditors' report and the issue of the financial statements; and
- the discovery, after issuing the financial statements, of facts that were unknown at the time of issuance.

Occurrence of subsequent events

As shown in Figure 14.1, several weeks may elapse between the end of the audit and the issue of the financial statements. The auditors have no responsibility to make an inquiry or to perform auditing procedures during this time to discover any material after-balance-date events. However, during this period, management is responsible for informing the auditors of any events that may affect the financial statements. The need to amend the financial statements should be considered and discussed with management. If the financial statements are amended, the auditors must carry out any necessary auditing procedures, including extending the review of after-balance-date events, and reissue the auditors' report at the date of approval of the amended financial statements. Management may, in an exceptional circumstance, issue the financial statements as originally prepared together with the original auditors' report, notwithstanding the auditors' dissent as to the truth and fairness of the financial statements in the light of knowledge of events occurring in this period. In this event, the auditors should take action to prevent reliance on the auditors' report. This can be done, for example, by exercising the auditors' right to be heard at the general meeting at which the audited financial statements are presented to members.

Discovery of previously unknown facts

Auditors have no responsibility to make an ongoing inquiry on the financial statements after they have been issued. However, an event may have existed at the date of the auditors' report that materially affects the financial statements and becomes known to the auditors after the financial statements were issued.

As the event in question occurred before the auditors' report was signed, the auditors had a responsibility to detect this event. The auditors should discuss the matter with management and take steps to prevent future reliance on the auditors' report. The preferred result is the preparation of revised financial statements by the entity and the issuance of a revised auditors' report as soon as practicable. Again, prior to the issuance of a revised auditors' report the auditors should extend the review of subsequent events up to the date of the issuance of the revised report. The new report should include a paragraph referring to the note in the financial statements that provides an explanation for the revision of the previously issued financial statements and the earlier auditors' report.

The new report should be dated not earlier than the date the revised financial statements are approved. If the issuance of the following period's financial statements are imminent, the revised financial statements may not be issued. However, appropriate disclosures are required in these circumstances in the following period's report.

LEARNING **CHECK**

14.14 Should an event that occurs between the date of the auditors' report and the issue of the financial statements become known, the auditors should discuss this with management and consider the need to amend the financial statements.

14.15 If subsequent events affecting the financial statements are discovered after the report's issue, the preferred procedure is for management to prepare revised financial statements, and for a revised auditors' report to be issued as soon as practicable.

SUMMARY

This chapter described several key responsibilities of auditors in completing an audit of financial statements. Steps performed in completing the examination include making the after-balance-date review, obtaining evidence concerning contingent liabilities, considering the applicability of the going-concern basis, obtaining the letter of management representations, and performing analytical procedures. Steps involved in evaluating the auditors' findings include making a final assessment of materiality and audit risk, making a technical review of the financial statements, formulating an opinion and drafting the auditors' report, and making a final review of the working papers.

Auditors are required to communicate with the entity's governing body details of significant problems encountered during the audit and other matters of concern such as internal control weaknesses. The management letter details control weaknesses and other concerns and offers recommendations regarding the efficiency and effectiveness of the entity's operations.

Finally, auditors have certain post-audit responsibilities relating to subsequent events that occur between the date of the auditors' report and the issue of the financial statements, and the subsequent discovery of facts existing at the report date.

FURTHER READING

Jiambalvo, J. & Wilner, N. 'Auditor Evaluation of Contingent Claims', *Auditing: A Journal of Theory and Practice* (Fall 1985), pp. 1–11.

Rezaee, Z., Olibe, K. O. & Minmier, G. 'Improving Corporate Governance: The Role of Audit Committee Disclosures', *Managerial Auditing Journal* (Vol. 18, No. 6, 2003), pp. 530–537.

Wright, A. & Ashton, R. H. 'Identifying Audit Adjustments with Attention-Directing Procedures', *The Accounting Review* (October 1989), pp. 710–728.

MULTIPLE-CHOICE QUESTIONS

Choose the best answer for each of the following.
(Answers are on pages 604–605)

14.1 In the auditors' completion of the audit, which of the following is not a subsequent event procedure?
  (a) Read available minutes of meetings of directors.
  (b) Make enquiries with respect to the previously audited financial statements to establish whether new information has become available that might affect that report.
  (c) Read available interim financial statements.
  (d) Discuss with officers the current status of items in the financial statements that were accounted for on the basis of inconclusive data.

14.2 Which of the following would an auditor ordinarily perform during his or her review of after-balance-date events?
  (a) Analyse related party transactions to discover possible irregularities.
  (b) Investigate control weaknesses previously reported to management.
  (c) Inquire of the entity's solicitor concerning litigation.
  (d) Review the bank statements for the period after the year-end.

14.3 The auditors are concerned with completing various phases of the examination after the balance sheet date. This period extends to:
  (a) the date of the final review of the audit working papers.
  (b) the date of the auditors' report.
  (c) the issue of the financial statements.
  (d) five months after the entity's year-end.

14.4 The following matters came to the attention of the auditors before the audit fieldwork was completed. Which one would require an adjustment to be made to the financial statements?
  (a) A discussion by management to change the main operations of the company.
  (b) A major lawsuit against the company, with proceedings commencing after the end of the financial year.
  (c) The bankruptcy of a major customer of the client.
  (d) The application for a government export grant.

14.5 Auditors should send a letter of inquiry to those solicitors who have been consulted concerning litigation or claims. The primary reason for this request is to provide:
  (a) corroborative evidential matter.
  (b) information concerning the progress of cases to date.
  (c) an estimate of the amount of the probable loss.
  (d) an expert opinion as to whether a loss is possible, probable or remote.

14.6 Which of the following is ordinarily included among the written management representations obtained by the auditors?

(a) Sufficient audit evidence has been made available to permit the issue of an unqualified opinion.

(b) All books of account and supporting documentation have been made available.

(c) Management acknowledges that there are no material weaknesses in internal control.

(d) Management acknowledges responsibility for illegal actions committed by employees.

14.7 Six months after issuing an unqualified opinion on a set of financial statements, the audit partner discovered that the engagement personnel on the audit failed to confirm several of the client's material debtor's balances. The audit partner should first:

(a) inquire whether there are persons currently relying, or likely to rely, on the unqualified opinion.

(b) assess the importance of the omitted procedures to the auditor's ability to support the previously expressed opinion.

(c) perform alternative procedures to provide a satisfactory basis for the unqualified opinion.

(d) request permission of the entity to undertake the confirmation of debtors.

14.8 Subsequent to the issuance of the auditors' report, the auditors became aware of facts existing at the report date that would have affected the report had the auditors then been aware of them. After determining that the information is reliable, the auditors should next:

(a) notify the board of directors that the auditors' report must no longer be associated with the financial statements.

(b) determine whether there are persons relying, or likely to rely, on the financial statements who would attach importance to the information.

(c) request that management discloses the effects of the newly discovered information by adding a note to subsequently issued financial statements.

(d) issue revised pro-forma financial statements, taking into consideration the newly discovered information.

DISCUSSION QUESTIONS

14.1 Explain the auditors' responsibility for identifying and acting on after-balance-date events. Is there an 'end point' to the auditors' responsibilities?

14.2 Can facts discovered after the issue of the financial statements have an impact on the audit report? Discuss.

14.3 What is the possible effect on the auditors' report of a solicitor's failure to respond to a request for representation?

14.4 Can a management representation letter be a substitute for auditing procedures? Discuss.

14.5 Explain the purpose of the performance of analytical procedures at the end of the audit.

14.6 Describe the various steps required in evaluating the findings of the audit.

14.7 Discuss the audit engagement partner's responsibilities in evaluating the findings of the audit.

14.8 Explain the purpose of preparing a management letter at the end of the audit.

14.9 Is a management letter required when only minor problems are discovered during the audit? Discuss.

14.10 Describe the responsibility of the auditors to communicate with the audit committee.

PROFESSIONAL APPLICATION QUESTIONS

(Suggested answers are on pages 653–656)

14.1 Letter of Representation and Management Report

Two important communications between the auditors and the management or Board of Directors of the client entity are commonly referred to as the *Letter of Representation* and the *Management Letter* (or Letter of Weaknesses). Both letters are referred to in ISA 210 *Terms of Audit Engagements*. The letter of representations is, additionally, the subject of ISA 580 *Management Representations* and the letter of weaknesses is the subject of ISA 260 *Communication of Audit Matters with Those Charged with Governance*.

Required

(a) Letter of representation
   (i) Explain the purpose of the letter of representation and the extent to which it constitutes sufficient appropriate audit evidence.
   (ii) Describe three matters you might find in a letter of representation (other than the acknowledgement by management of its responsibility for the financial statements).
   (iii) Explain the effect, on the audit, if management refuse to make one or more of the representations requested.
(b) Management letter
   (i) Describe the procedures associated with the communication of control weaknesses to management relating to:
      • timing of the communication,
      • method of communication,
      • level of management to which communication should be made.
   (ii) Discuss the extent of the auditors' responsibility for detecting and reporting internal control weaknesses.

(Adapted from Question 3, Audit Framework, June 2001. Reproduced by permission of ACCA)

14.2 After balance sheet date events

Reddy and Co., Chartered Certified Accountants, are the external auditors of Drummoyne, a listed company. On completing the audit for the year ended 31 March 2000 the following list of matters was prepared for the partner's attention.

(a) On May 25 2000 Drummoyne agreed to a pay rise of 5% for all of its employees backdated to 1 January 2000. No provision for this has been made in the financial statements.
(b) The draft Chairman's Statement states that the profits have increased by 25%. It is true that operating profit has increased by 25% but, after deducting reorganisation

costs and losses on disposals of property, plant and equipment, profit on ordinary activities, both before and after tax, has increased by only 4% over the previous year.

(c) The audit revealed a major control weakness in the management of investments. The company recently recruited a financial analyst, as an employee, to manage the investment of surplus funds. Company policy is to invest in the shares of large quoted companies. The audit discovered a number of situations where the financial analyst had made substantial profits for the company by speculating in risky investments such as derivatives. Such investments could result in massive losses. The matter was reported in writing to the chief financial officer four months ago but no action has yet been taken.

(d) One of the company's oil tankers has just run aground on the coast of California. There is a risk of a serious oil spill which could have a significant effect on the future of the company. Further information will not be available until after the auditor's report has been signed.

Assume that each of these matters is potentially material and is to be considered independently of each of the others.

Required
Consider what further action Reddy and Co. should take with respect to each of the matters listed.

(Adapted from Question 3, Audit Framework, December 2000. Reproduced by permission of ACCA)

REPORTING ON AUDITED FINANCIAL STATEMENTS

DISCUSSION QUESTIONS

PROFESSIONAL APPLICATION QUESTIONS

 LEARNING **OBJECTIVES**

After studying this chapter, you should be able to:

1   explain the requirements of the reporting standard

2   prepare an unqualified auditors' report

3   enumerate the circumstances that result in the issue of a qualified opinion

4   describe how each circumstance affects the auditors' report's form and content

5   describe the effects on auditors' reports of uncertainties

6   explain how the international reporting standard differs from the UK standard

7   explain reporting considerations for consolidations, comparatives and opening balances.

PROFESSIONAL STATEMENTS

APB Bulletin	1998/1 The Auditors' Association with Preliminary Announcements
APB Bulletin	1999/4 Review of Interim Financial Information
APB Bulletin	1999/6 The Auditors' Statement on the Summary Financial Statement
APB Bulletin	2001/1 The Electronic Publication of Auditors' Reports
APB Bulletin	2001/2 Revisions to the Wording of Auditors' Reports on Financial Statements and the Interim Review Report
IAPS 1014	Reporting by Auditors on Compliance with International Financial Reporting Standards
ISA 560	Subsequent Events
ISA 510	Initial Engagements – Opening Balances
ISA 700	The Auditor's Report on Financial Statements
ISA 710	Comparatives
ISA 720	Other Information in Documents Containing Audited Financial Statements
SAS 600	Auditors' Reports on Financial Statements

The final phase of the auditing process is reporting the findings. This chapter expands on the explanation of the auditors' report provided in Chapter 2.

To meet their reporting responsibilities, auditors must have a thorough understanding of the reporting requirements of Auditing Standards pertaining to auditors' reports. First, they must know the required contents of the auditors' report expressing an unqualified opinion and the conditions that must be met for it to be issued. They must also understand the types of departure from an unqualified report and the circumstances when each is appropriate. Lastly, they must be knowledgeable about their reporting responsibilities under the *Companies Act 1985*, and other special reporting considerations. Each of these topics is explained in this chapter.

Throughout the chapter it should be assumed that the auditors are reporting on an engagement to perform an audit, in accordance with Auditing Standards, to render an opinion as to whether management's financial statements give a true and fair view.

Unlike the rest of this text, which is based on International Auditing Standards, this chapter will be based on UK Auditing Standard SAS 600, Auditors' Reports on Financial Statements. At the date of publication the IAASB was working on a project for the revision of its statement on Auditors' Reports reflecting its adoption as the required standard in member states of the European Union and in many other countries. However, the requirements of existing ISA 700, The Auditor's Report on Financial Statements, will be described at the end of the chapter with an overview of changes under consideration.

STANDARDS OF REPORTING

SAS 600, Auditors' Reports on Financial Statements, states that:

> Auditors' reports on financial statements should contain a clear expression of opinion, based on review and assessment of the conclusions drawn from evidence obtained during the course of the audit.

Financial statements

Financial statements are intended to meet the information needs common to users who are unable to command the preparation of statements tailored to specifically satisfy all of their information needs. For this reason they are often referred to as general-purpose financial statements. The disclosure and presentation requirements for such reports are determined by Financial Reporting Standards and only financial statements prepared in accordance with a recognised financial reporting framework are likely to give a true and fair view. The financial statements include:

- a balance sheet as at the end of the year;
- a statement of total recognised gains and losses;
- the profit and loss statement for the year;
- a statement of cash flows for the year; and
- notes to the financial statements covering:
    - disclosures required by regulations;
    - notes required by Financial Reporting Standards; and
    - any other information necessary to give a true and fair view.

Financial Reporting Standards

Financial Reporting Standards refer to:

- Accounting Standards, being standards issued by the Accounting Standards Board; or
- Financial Reporting Standards issued by the International Accounting Standards Committee.

The Foreword to Accounting Standards states that:

Members of the accounting profession are required to use their best endeavours to ensure that accounting standards are observed and that significant departures found to be necessary are adequately disclosed and explained in the financial statements. Where members act as auditors, they should be in a position to justify significant departures to the extent that their concurrence with the departures is stated or implied.

When dealing with matters not covered by a specific Financial Reporting Standard, the policies used should be those generally accepted by the accounting profession and business community. Moreover, all accounting policies (especially when there is a choice between alternatives permitted from within specific Financial Reporting Standards) should be selected and applied with regard to relevance, reliability, materiality, and substance over form.

The International Accounting Standards Board is concerned that entities preparing financial statements in accordance with national Financial Reporting Standards (such as those issued in the UK by the ASB) are claiming conformance with International Financial Reporting Standards subject to exceptions or additional disclosures such as a reconciliation. International Auditing Practice Statement IAPS 1014, Reporting by Auditors on Compliance with International Financial Reporting Standards, only allows an unqualified opinion to be given if the financial statements comply simultaneously with both financial reporting frameworks.

Relevant statutory and other requirements

Where the audit is being conducted in accordance with statutory and other requirements such as the *Companies Act 1985*, the auditors usually have an additional responsibility to report on compliance with relevant sections of the regulations or statutory requirements. Reporting on such matters may be explicit or on an exception basis. The opinion on such requirements may be separated from the opinion on truth and fairness. That is, the report may be qualified with respect to other requirements, but unqualified as to presentation (or vice versa). This is further considered in the following sections.

REPORTING REQUIREMENTS OF THE COMPANIES ACT 1985

Section 235 of the *Companies Act 1985* prescribes the auditors' reporting duties. In addition to reporting positively on truth and fairness it requires auditors to state whether the financial statements have been properly prepared in accordance with the Act. Section 235 also requires auditors to report on part of the Directors' Remuneration Report required for quoted companies. Section 237 introduces a negative reporting responsibility where:

- proper accounting records and returns from branches adequate for their audit have not been kept;
- the financial statements are not in agreement with the accounting records; or
- they have not received information and explanations necessary for the purposes of their audit.

515

Furthermore, if the financial statements do not meet requirements as to the disclosure of directors' remuneration, the auditors must provide the required information within their report.

Expression of opinion

SAS 600 requires a '... clear expression of opinion on the financial statements ...'. Where the opinion is qualified, the reasons for the qualification and its effect on the information in the financial statements must also be provided (in quantified terms) wherever practicable. SAS 600 reiterates the requirement laid down in the London and General Bank case described in Chapter 4 that it is the duty of the auditors to convey information, not merely to arouse enquiry.

The auditors' opinion refers to the financial statements as a whole. While the audit examination is performed item by item, the auditors must consider whether the impression created by the financial statements taken as a whole is consistent with their intimate knowledge of the entity and its financial condition.

TRUTH AND FAIRNESS

Truth refers to the correctness of those matters capable of being determined with precision, such as the balance of cash at bank. The concept of fairness is linked with a set of standards which provide a framework within which judgement can be exercised to report on the entity's economic condition and fairness.

UNQUALIFIED AUDITORS' REPORT

The concept of an unqualified audit opinion on financial statements was introduced in Chapter 2. The wording of the report is not standardised. SAS 600 requires that auditors draft each section of their report to reflect the requirements which apply to the particular audit engagement, but adds that the uses of common language in auditors' reports assists the reader's understanding. In reality, this means that the example of an unqualified report illustrated in SAS 600 should normally be followed, modified as necessary for the particular circumstances of each audit. An unqualified report, as illustrated in SAS 600, is reproduced in Figure 15.1.

The basic elements of an unqualified auditors' report are as described below:

- *Title*: This identifies the auditors' report and to whom it is addressed.
- *Introductory section*: The introductory section identifies the financial statements and the accounting convention.
- *Responsibility section*: This section identifies the respective responsibilities of directors and auditors.
- *Scope of the audit*: In essence, it describes the nature of the audit, stating that it was conducted in accordance with a prescribed set of Auditing Standards. In lay terms, this phrase means that it was undertaken in accordance with established professional standards. Any departure from these must be indicated in this section of the auditors' report, with the auditors' opinion being qualified as appropriate. This section also identifies several limitations of an audit in that an audit includes examining evidence

---

INDEPENDENT AUDITORS' REPORT TO THE SHAREHOLDERS OF XYZ PLC

We have audited the financial statements of (name of entity) for the year ended ... which comprise [state the primary financial statements such as the Profit and Loss Account, the Balance Sheet, the Cash Flow Statement, the Statement of Total Recognised Gains and Losses] and the related notes. These financial statements have been prepared under the historical cost convention [as modified by the revaluation of certain fixed assets] and the accounting policies set out therein. We have also audited the information in the Directors' Remuneration Report that is described as having been audited.

Respective responsibilities of directors and auditors

The directors' responsibilities for preparing the Annual Report, the Directors' Remuneration Report and the financial statements in accordance with applicable law and United Kingdom Accounting Standards are set out in the Statement of Directors' Responsibilities.

Our responsibility is to audit the financial statements and the part of the Directors' Remuneration Report to be audited in accordance with relevant legal and regulatory requirements and United Kingdom Auditing Standards.

We report to you our opinion as to whether the financial statements give a true and fair view and whether the financial statements and the part of the Directors' Remuneration Report to be audited have been properly prepared in accordance with the Companies Act 1985. We also report to you if, in our opinion, the Directors' Report is not consistent with the financial statements, if the company has not kept proper accounting records, if we have not received all the information and explanations we require for our audit, or if information specified by law regarding directors' remuneration and transactions with the company is not disclosed.

We review whether the Corporate Governance Statement reflects the company's compliance with the seven provisions of the Combined Code specified for our review by the Listing Rules of the Financial Services Authority, and we report if it does not. We are not required to consider whether the board's statements on internal control cover all risks and controls, or form an opinion on the effectiveness of the company's corporate governance procedures or its risk and control procedures.

We read other information contained in the Annual Report and consider whether it is consistent with the audited financial statements. The other information comprises only the Directors' Report, the unaudited part of the Directors' Remuneration Report, the Chairman's Statement, the Operating and Financial Review and the Corporate Governance Statement. We consider the implications for our report if we become aware of any apparent misstatements or material inconsistencies with the financial statements. Our responsibilities do not extend to any other information.

Basis of audit opinion

We conducted our audit in accordance with United Kingdom Auditing Standards issued by the Auditing Practices Board. An audit includes examination, on a test basis, of evidence relevant to the amounts and disclosures in the financial statements and the part of the Directors' Remuneration Report to be audited. It also includes an assessment of the significant estimates and judgements made by the directors in the preparation of the financial statements, and of whether the accounting policies are appropriate in the company's circumstances consistently applied and adequately disclosed.

Figure 15.1 *Example of an unqualified auditors' report for a quoted company without subsidiaries (Adapted from APB Bulletin 2001/2, Revisions to the Wording of Auditors' Reports on Financial Statements and the Interim Review Report, Appendix 1)*

We planned and performed our audit so as to obtain all the information and explanations which we considered necessary in order to provide us with sufficient evidence to give reasonable assurance that the financial statements and the part of the Directors' Remuneration Report to be audited are free from material misstatement, whether caused by fraud or other irregularity or error. In forming our opinion we also evaluated the overall adequacy of the presentation of information in the financial statements and the part of the Directors' Remuneration Report to be audited.

Opinion

In our opinion:

- the financial statements give a true and fair view of the state of the company's affairs as at . . . and of its profit [loss] for the year then ended; and
- the financial statements and the part of the Directors' Remuneration Report to be audited have been properly prepared in accordance with the Companies Act 1985.

Registered auditors   *Address*

Date

Figure 15.1 (*continued*)

on a test basis and thus only provides reasonable, not absolute, assurance and only with respect to an absence of material, and not all, misstatements. Additionally, by referring to the evaluation of accounting policies used, and significant estimates made, by management, it is made clear that financial statements are a matter of judgement, not fact. The degree of responsibility for the audit and the opinion is indicated through the use of such wording as 'we have audited', 'our audit', and in 'our opinion'. The use of these words without qualification means that the auditors are assuming full or complete responsibility for the work done and the opinion rendered.

- *Opinion section*: An opinion is expressed as to the truth and fairness of the view given by the financial statements and on other matters required by statute.
- *Signature*: The report is signed by the audit firm or the individual audit partner as appropriate.
- *Date the auditors' report is signed*: The auditors' report is dated after the financial statements have been signed by the governing body. The auditors have responsibility for subsequent events up to this date. Backdating does not change the responsibility.

◁ LEARNING **CHECK**

15.1 The disclosure and presentation requirements of financial statements are determined by Financial Reporting Standards and statutory and other requirements.

15.2 Financial Reporting Standards must be consistently applied in the preparation and presentation of financial statements.

15.3 The auditors should express a clear written opinion on the financial statements.

15.4 The independent auditors' report has a standardised format.

TYPES OF QUALIFIED OPINION

Qualified opinions are expressed when the auditors have reservations on the financial statements. The types of qualified opinion permitted by Auditing Standards are:

- an 'except for' opinion;
- an adverse opinion; and
- a disclaimer of opinion.

A qualified auditors' report should refer to all relevant matters. Qualification of one matter is not a reason to exclude another. A combined opinion is possible. Other reporting mechanisms are not a substitute for qualified auditors' reports (for example, a report directly to management or a regulatory agency does not justify the omission of a matter from the auditors' report). A qualified auditors' report may necessitate additional considerations or action by the auditors such as inclusion of other matters in the auditors' report.

The auditors make a judgement within the framework of Financial Reporting Standards and other regulatory requirements in determining whether financial statements give a true and fair view. In deciding on the appropriate opinion, the auditors consider if there is (1) any disagreement with management, pertaining to the financial statements, and (2) sufficient appropriate evidence to have a reasonable basis for an opinion.

Materiality is an important consideration in arriving at an appropriate opinion, given a set of circumstances. When the effect of the matter is immaterial, an unqualified opinion is appropriate. When the effect is material, an 'except for' opinion is expressed. When the effect on the financial statements is extremely material, the auditors are likely to issue an adverse opinion. A disclaimer of opinion is appropriate when the effect of the lack of evidence is extremely material, and the auditors are unable to form an opinion. Table 15.1 gives an interpretation of the types of audit opinion.

A corollary to the concept of materiality is the concept of pervasiveness. Pervasiveness relates to the number of financial statement items affected by a circumstance. When a small number of items are affected, the auditors will usually render an 'except for' opinion because the effects can be adequately explained in the Qualification section and the overall financial statements will still be useful. Conversely, when a large number of items are affected, it may be impractical to attempt to explain all the effects in the Qualification section, and an inability to form an opinion or adverse opinion will be issued. For example, inappropriate application of the going-concern assumption will probably mean that most assets and many liabilities are stated at incorrect amounts. The number of such items affected thus means that an adverse opinion will need to be issued.

Since the auditors have a duty to form an opinion, a report disclaiming an opinion should be issued only after the auditors have exhausted all reasonable means of obtaining sufficient appropriate evidence. In addition, before issuing a qualified opinion of any kind, the auditors should do everything reasonably possible to express an unqualified

Table 15.1 Types of audit opinion and their interpretation

TYPE OF OPINION	SIGNAL	INTERPRETATION
Unqualified	Favourable	The financial statements give a true and fair view of the state of the company's affairs and of its profit (loss) and have been properly prepared in accordance with the *Companies Act 1985*.
'Except for'	Favourable, with a qualification	Except for the specific reservation, deficiency, shortcoming or scope limitation, the financial statements give a true and fair view.
Adverse	Unfavourable	The financial statements do not give a true and fair view. They are misleading and are of no use.
Disclaimer of opinion	Neither favourable nor unfavourable	The auditors are unable to express an opinion on the financial statements owing to audit limitations.

opinion. (An unqualified opinion is in the best interests of the readers of the audited financial statements.) Conversely, the auditors should not shirk from issuing a qualified opinion should this be necessary. This is particularly so should there be a disagreement with management. Such a qualified opinion does not necessarily impugn the integrity of management; rather, it reflects the exercise of independent judgement by the auditors on matters where differences of opinion might properly exist.

Instances requiring issue of a qualified opinion

Instances or circumstances requiring the issue of a qualified opinion on the auditors' report of those instances will now be explained together with illustrations as to the effect on the auditors' report. The issue of a qualified opinion may be necessary if there is:

- a disagreement with management; or
- a scope limitation.

DISAGREEMENT WITH MANAGEMENT
The auditors may disagree as to the truth and fairness of the financial statements prepared by management over matters such as the following:

- the relevance, reliability, comparability, and understandability of the accounting policies selected including, but not restricted to, non-adherence with Financial Reporting Standards;
- the estimation techniques employed in the application of accounting policies and the reasonableness of the resulting accounting estimates;
- the adequacy of disclosures in the financial statements (including disclosures regarding inherent uncertainties); and
- the compliance of the financial statements with relevant statutory and other requirements.

The auditors must undertake all reasonable steps to overcome the cause of the disagreement. However, truth and fairness of presentation is a matter of judgement, and occasional disagreements are the essence of an independent audit.

Effects of disagreement on the auditors' report

Where the nature of the disagreement and its impact on the financial statements can be readily explained by the auditors in their report, an 'except for' opinion will normally be issued. Where the disagreement is such that the report as a whole might be misleading, even when read in conjunction with the auditors' report, the auditors should issue an adverse opinion.

Where the auditors disagree over accounting treatment or disclosure, the opinion section of their report should:

- describe the factors giving rise to the disagreement;
- explain the implications for the financial statements; and
- quantify the effect on the financial statements wherever practicable.

A disagreement with management resulting in the issue of an 'except for' opinion is illustrated in Figure 15.2 and a disagreement with management resulting in an adverse opinion is illustrated in Figure 15.3. Where the disagreement affects only one of the statements, such as the classification of closing balances in the balance sheet, an unqualified opinion may still be expressed on the other statements.

Disagreements over statutory and other requirements

When an audit is conducted in accordance with statutory and other requirements, the auditors usually have an additional responsibility to report on compliance with relevant sections of statutory and other requirements. Statutory requirements may apply to an entity by an Act of Parliament, including rules, regulations and directives pursuant to an Act (e.g. the *Companies Act 1985*). Other requirements may be those of a regulatory body such as the UK Listing Authority, a contract or by the constitution of the entity.

Qualified opinion arising from disagreement about accounting treatment

Included in the stocks shown on the balance sheet are items carried at their cost of £X which we believe are unlikely to be sold at an amount in excess of cost. In our opinion the net realisable value of these items is £Y. The value of stocks shown in the balance sheet should be reduced by £X – Y reducing profit before tax and net assets by that amount.

Except for this overstatement in the value of stocks, in our opinion, the financial statements give a true and fair view of the state of the company's affairs as at 31 December 20XX and of its profit for the year then ended and have been properly prepared in accordance with the *Companies Act 1985*.

The other sections of the auditors' report are unaltered.

Figure 15.2 *An 'except for' opinion arising from disagreement with management*

Adverse opinion

Included in the financial statements as a fixed asset investment is an investment in [subsidiary entity], recorded at a cost of £xxx. The company has not presented consolidated financial statements which combine the financial statements of [subsidiary entity] with its own. In our opinion consolidated financial statements are required because the company has the capacity to dominate [subsidiary entity's] decision-making in relation to its financial and operating policies.

The audited financial statements of [subsidiary entity] for the year ended 30 June 20X1 disclosed an operating loss after tax of £xxx (20X0 – £xxx) and a net liability position of £xxx (20X0 – £xxx). As there were no signicant transactions between the company and [subsidiary entity] during the year and no significant inter-entity balances at balance date, had consolidated financial statements been presented, it would disclose an operating loss after tax attributable to members of the company of approximately £xxx (20X0 – £xxx) and a net liability position of approximately £xxx (20X0 – £xxx).

In view of the failure to present consolidated financial statements as described above, in our opinion the financial statements do not give a true and fair view of the state of the company's affairs as at 31 December 20XX and of its loss for the year then ended. In all other respects, in our opinion, the financial statements have been properly prepared in accordance with the *Companies Act 1985*.

The other sections of the auditors' report are unaltered.

Figure 15.3 *An adverse opinion arising from a disagreement with management*

Auditors will form an opinion on statutory and other requirements only if required by the audit mandate, or if the financial statements include an assertion that those requirements have been complied with. A qualified opinion is expressed when there is non-compliance with relevant statutory or other requirements. The opinion may be either explicit or on an exception basis. The opinion on such requirements may be separated from the opinion on truth and fairness as to the state of affairs and profit or loss: that is, the report may be qualified with respect to statutory or other requirements, but unqualified as to presentation (or vice versa).

SCOPE LIMITATION

In undertaking an examination in accordance with Auditing Standards, it is expected that the auditors will obtain sufficient appropriate audit evidence to have a reasonable basis for expressing an opinion on the financial statements. When the auditors cannot perform the necessary procedures or the procedures do not provide sufficient evidence, the auditors are said to have a scope limitation.

The terms of the engagement may prohibit the auditors from carrying out specific audit procedures or impose restrictions on the type of opinion the auditors might express. If in the auditors' judgement the outcome of such restrictions is a disclaimer of opinion, the audit engagement should be declined. The audit should also be declined when known limitations impinge on the auditors' legal duties, or ethical or other professional responsibilities. Examples of scope limitations imposed during the course of the audit include a refusal to permit confirmation of debtors, sign a management representation letter, or give the auditors access to the minutes of board of directors' meetings. An example of a restriction attributable to circumstances is the timing of procedures (for example, appointing the auditors too late to perform procedures considered necessary in the circumstances). Scope limitations also exist when, in the opinion of the auditors, the entity's accounting records are inadequate or the auditors are unable to carry out a desirable audit procedure. The auditors should attempt to carry out reasonable audit procedures to overcome the scope limitation. When a scope limitation exists, the auditors should:

- describe the factors leading to the limitation; and
- express an 'except for' opinion or disclaim an opinion in the qualified audit opinion section.

The importance of the missing evidence and the materiality of the effects of the item(s) in question on the financial statements are factors the auditors should consider in deciding whether to qualify or express an disclaimer of an opinion. When the scope limitation extends to many financial statement items, there is a greater probability that a disclaimer of an opinion will be necessary.

The wording of the Opinion section should refer to the potential effects on the financial statements of the items for which the auditors have not obtained audit satisfaction, rather than to the scope limitation itself. This is because the auditors' opinion relates to the financial statements. A scope limitation resulting in an inability to form an opinion is illustrated in Figure 15.4.

◁ LEARNING **CHECK**

15.5   The auditors' report may be qualified.

15.6   The types of qualified opinion are:

- an 'except for' opinion;

- an adverse opinion; and

- a disclaimer of opinion.

15.7   Materiality is an important consideration in arriving at an appropriate opinion. A corollary to the concept of materiality is pervasiveness. This relates to the number of financial statement items affected by a circumstance.

15.8   In deciding on the appropriate opinion, the auditors consider if there is (1) a disagreement with management, and (2) sufficient appropriate audit evidence to form an opinion.

15.9   When a qualified audit opinion is expressed, the opinion section of the auditors' report is modified with the inclusion of a heading summarising the qualification which is described in the opinion section if it is a disagreement, and within the basis of opinion section if it is a scope limitation.

Basis of opinion

We conducted our audit in accordance with United Kingdom Auditing Standards issued by the Auditing Practices Board except that the scope of our work was limited as explained below. An audit includes examination, on a test basis, of evidence relevant to the amounts and disclosures in the financial statements. It also includes an assessment of the significant estimates and judgements made by the directors in the preparation of the financial statements, and of whether the accounting policies are appropriate in the company's circumstances consistently applied and adequately disclosed.

We planned and performed our audit so as to obtain all the information and explanations which we considered necessary in order to provide us with sufficient evidence to give reasonable assurance that the financial statements are free from material misstatement, whether caused by fraud or other irregularity or error. However, as stated in Note X to the financial statements, a fire at the company's computer centre destroyed many of the accounting records. The fire occurred prior to the completion of our audit. As the remaining accounting records are not adequate to permit the application of necessary auditing procedures, we are unable to obtain all the information and explanations we require in order to form an opinion on the financial statements. In forming our opinion we also evaluated the overall adequacy of the presentation of information in the financial statements.

Opinion: disclaimer on view given by financial statements

Because of the possible effect of the limitation in evidence available to us we are unable to form an opinion as to whether the financial statements give a true and fair view of the state of the company's affairs as at 31 December 20XX or of its profit for the year then ended. In all other respects, in our opinion the financial statements have been properly prepared in accordance with the Companies Act 1985.

The other sections of the auditors' report are unaltered.

Figure 15.4 *Qualified auditors' report including a disclaimer of opinion*

15.10 Disagreements with management could relate to the selection of and/or the method of application of accounting policies, the adequacy of disclosure and compliance with relevant statutory and other requirements.

15.11 The audit mandate (or circumstances) may impose scope limitations. If, in the auditors' judgement, the outcome of such limitations is necessarily a disclaimer of opinion, the audit engagement should be declined.

FURTHER DISCLOSURES WITHIN THE AUDITORS' REPORT

Further disclosures may be required where the financial statements are subject to a fundamental uncertainty, where there are inconsistencies with other information in the annual report and where the report is on revised financial statements following the discovery of material subsequent events.

Fundamental uncertainty

The term 'inherent uncertainty' applies to the outcome of any report item or disclosure contingent upon future events that is not capable of reasonable estimation at the date of the auditors' report. Uncertainties differ from accounting estimates in that the latter are capable of reasonable determination by management in the preparation of the financial statements. Uncertainties may range from a single event, where the effect on the financial statements can be isolated and understood, to multiple events whose possible effects on the financial statements are complex and difficult to assess. The former includes the outcome of a lawsuit; the latter include recurring operating losses and major financial problems that affect the ability of the entity to continue as a going concern. The procedures necessary to evaluate the appropriateness of the going-concern basis are discussed in Chapter 14.

Uncertainties present a special problem for auditors because evidence of their resolution does not exist prior to completing the examination. On the basis of available evidence, auditors are responsible for determining whether the uncertainties are properly accounted for and disclosed. Auditors are not expected to predict the outcome of the uncertainties.

An inherent uncertainty may be accompanied by inadequate disclosure. This may arise where amounts recognised for inclusion in the financial statements do not meet the criteria for recognition as a result of the uncertainty. It could also arise where disclosures in the notes are insufficiently informative. Such matters constitute a disagreement with management and the appropriate form of qualification is either an 'except for' or an adverse opinion.

A fundamental uncertainty is one that, in the auditors' opinion, involves significant concern as to the validity of the going-concern assumption or otherwise has, potentially, a highly significant effect on the financial statements. An uncertainty is more likely to be fundamental where the range of possible outcomes is sufficiently great as to have the potential for fundamentally affecting the entity.

Where there is such a fundamental uncertainty, auditors need to draw users' attention to it by an appropriately headed paragraph within the Basis of opinion section of their report. By including such a paragraph within the Basis of opinion section of their report the auditors make it clear that the uncertainty has been taken into consideration in arriving at their opinion. Nevertheless, many auditors specifically state that their reference to the fundamental uncertainty does not constitute a qualification. An example of such a paragraph is illustrated in Figure 15.5.

Inconsistent other information

The audited financial statements are often bound together with other unaudited statements and reports to comprise the entity's annual report. Some of this other information,

---

Fundamental uncertainty

The company is the defendant in litigation alleging an infringement of patent rights with respect to the company's principal product. The claim for royalties and damages amounts to £xxx. The circumstances of the case are such that the outcome of the litigation cannot presently be determined with an acceptable degree of reliability and, accordingly, no provision for any liability that may result has been made in the financial statements. Moreover, if the case were to be lost, manufacture of the product would need to be discontinued with indeterminable consequences for the future of the company. Details of this fundamental uncertainty are described in note . . . Our opinion is not qualified in this respect.

Figure 15.5 *Paragraph describing a fundamental uncertainty for inclusion in the Basis of opinion section of the auditors' report*

such as the directors' report, may be required to be included by relevant regulations or statutes. The auditors have a statutory responsibility under the *Companies Act 1985* to consider whether the directors' report is consistent with the financial statements with which it is issued. Other information, such as the operating and financial review, may be recommended by the Accounting Standards Board, while yet other information, such as a chairperson's address or a five-year financial summary, is provided voluntarily. ISA 720, Other Information in Documents Containing Audited Financial Statements, requires auditors to obtain details of other information intended for inclusion in the annual report that may have a relationship with information in the audited financial statements. This should be reviewed for inconsistency with the audited financial statements and for material misstatements of fact, before signing the auditors' report. An inconsistency may cause a reader to doubt the reliability of the information in the audited financial statements, while a misstatement of fact might cause harm to readers, who mistakenly interpret the auditors' opinion as extending to the entire document.

When the auditors become aware of an inconsistency between the financial statements being reported on and other information contained in the same document, it is necessary to determine whether it is the financial statements or the other information that needs revision. The matter should be discussed with management. If the financial statements require revision and management refuses to revise the statements, an 'except for' or an adverse opinion should be expressed. If it is the directors' report that is inconsistent the auditors must make reference to the inconsistencies in their report. If it is the other information that requires revision, and management refuses to do so, the auditors need to consider referring to the matter in their report or using their right to address shareholders at the annual general meeting. Before doing so, however, they would need to seek legal advice as to the possible consequences, such as an action for defamation. As a last resort the auditors could resign and use the required statement on ceasing to hold office as a means for informing shareholders.

ISA 720 also discusses material misstatements of fact. These misstatements concern matters not related to the financial statements. If the auditors believe the other information contains a misstatement, he or she must discuss the matter with management. After discussion, if the auditors are satisfied that there is a material misstatement of fact, the entity should be notified in writing and legal advice sought as to further appropriate action should management refuse to correct the misstatement.

Subsequent events

This issue was considered in Chapter 14 (for which ISA 560, Subsequent Events, applies). It is sufficient here to say that when management prepares revised financial statements as a consequence of discovery of a material fact after the financial statements and the auditors' report have been issued, the revised financial statements and the new auditors' report should refer to the earlier report and to the note to the financial statements giving reasons for the revision of the previously issued financial statements.

△ LEARNING **CHECK**

15.12 Inherent uncertainties are not capable of reasonable estimation. Where these are fundamental the uncertainty must be referred to in the Basis for opinion section of the auditors' report.

15.13 An inconsistency causes the reader to doubt the reliability of information in the financial statements. A misstatement of fact causes harm to readers.

15.14 Subsequent events requiring issue of revised financial statements should be referred to in the reissued auditors' report.

OTHER REPORTING CONSIDERATIONS

This section discusses reporting responsibilities relating to additional situations: reporting under International Standards on Auditing; consolidated financial statements; comparatives; initial engagements – opening balances; interim reports and reports available on the Internet.

International Standards on Auditing

When reporting under International Auditing Standards, the form of report required by SAS 600 described above is consistent with the requirements of ISA 700, The Auditor's Report on Financial Statements, in all situations except that of a fundamental uncertainty. Whereas, in the UK a fundamental uncertainty is dealt with by way of modifying the Basis of opinion section of the report, International Auditing Standards use a form of disclosure known as *Emphasis of Matter*.

Auditors may add an Emphasis of matter section to an auditors' report under ISA 700 while still expressing an unqualified opinion on the financial statements. The purpose of this is to draw the attention of users of the auditors' report to relevant information that is adequately disclosed within the notes to the financial statements. Circumstances in which an emphasis of matter is appropriate are:

- a material matter regarding a going-concern problem; and
- an inherent uncertainty other than a going-concern problem.

An emphasis of matter paragraph may also be included where there is an inconsistency with other information included with the audited financial statements. An emphasis of matter should be included after the opinion paragraph and it should be made clear that the contents of the Emphasis of matter section do not constitute a qualification (for example, by use of an opening phrase such as: 'Without qualifying our opinion we draw attention to ...').

To avoid confusion ISA 700 uses the term 'unmodified' to refer to auditors' reports that are neither qualified nor contain an emphasis of matter. Note, however, that the term 'qualified' is restricted to situations that ISA 600 refers to as *'except for' qualifications*. An opinion may be *'modified'* in situations that:

- do not affect the auditors' opinion by way of an emphasis of matter; or
- do affect the auditors' opinion in the form of:
  - a qualified opinion,
  - a disclaimer of opinion, or
  - an adverse opinion.

Proposals for modifying ISA 700 include a suggestion that, wherever practicable, the main body of the auditors' report should be restricted to reporting on the financial statements. Other matters that are required to be reported on by the auditors, such as the Corporate Governance Statement and the Directors' Remuneration Report, should be included after expressing an opinion on the financial statements themselves.

Consolidated financial statements

The opinion expressed on the consolidated financial statements is the sole responsibility of the auditors of the parent company, the principal auditors. When a reporting entity has one or more subsidiaries, more than one auditing firm may be involved. This arises where, for whatever reason, the directors of the parent entity appoint firms other than the auditors of the parent company as auditors to the subsidiaries.

Section 389A of the *Companies Act 1985* provides the auditors of a reporting entity, for which consolidated financial statements are required, with the right of access to the accounting records and registers of controlled entities and the right to require from their officers and auditors such information and explanation as is needed. In many cases, auditors build up a continuing formal relationship with other auditors. Such relationships may include inter-firm reviews, for example, of compliance with quality control procedures. Evaluation of the work of the other auditors need not be applied on each specific engagement. In the case of branches or divisions, the other auditors would be appointed by the principal auditors and thus act as an agent. The other auditors would therefore normally be one with whom the principal auditors have built up a formal relationship. Such relationships also commonly exist between auditors of parent and subsidiary companies where the directors of the parent company recognise the advantages when appointing auditors of subsidiaries.

In order that the principal auditors may obtain the necessary assurance as to the financial statements of subsidiaries not audited by them, it is necessary that they undertake certain steps with respect to the work of the other auditors as explained in Chapter 13. If the auditors conclude that reliance cannot be placed on the work of another auditor and are unable to perform satisfactory alternative procedures, they should qualify the auditors' report with respect to limitation of the scope of the audit. For example, should the auditors of a subsidiary not co-operate fully with the auditors of the parent company, a qualification relating to the failure to receive adequate information and explanations would be required.

Comparatives

Comparatives refer to amounts or disclosures of one or more prior periods that are presented on a comparative basis with those of the current period. Comparatives form an integral part of the current period's financial statements. As such, reporting standards apply not only to the amounts and disclosures of the current period, but also to comparatives.

The auditors have a responsibility to obtain sufficient appropriate audit evidence to ensure comparatives are not materially misstated (ISA 710, Comparatives) and that (1) comparatives agree with those in the prior period financial statements and (2) accounting policies used for comparatives are consistent with those of the current period. During the audit of the current year, the auditors should be alert to circumstances and events relating to the prior period financial statements. The circumstances considered in ISA 710 are (1) prior period opinion was qualified, (2) subsequent events, (3) change of auditors and (4) unaudited prior period financial statements.

PRIOR PERIOD REPORT IS QUALIFIED

It is possible that a prior period audit opinion may be qualified, but an unqualified opinion is expressed for the current year. However, the auditors' report for the current year will be qualified if (1) the matter which gave rise to a qualification for the prior period also results in a qualification of the auditors' report in the current period's financial information or (2) the unresolved matter, while not resulting in a qualification of the current period's financial information, is material in relation to amounts and disclosures in the current period.

SUBSEQUENT EVENTS

A material misstatement may be discovered in prior period financial statements on which the auditors previously expressed an unqualified opinion. In such circumstances, if the report has been revised and reissued with a new auditors' report, the auditors should satisfy themselves that comparatives agree with the new financial statements. If the prior period report is not revised, but the comparatives have been properly accounted for and disclosed in accordance with Financial Reporting Standards, the auditors should express an unqualified opinion.

The auditors should express a qualified opinion if the prior period financial statements were not revised and the misstatement has not been properly accounted for and is material in respect to the current period's amounts.

CHANGE OF AUDITORS

Additional reporting requirements must be met when there has been a change in auditors during the period covered by the comparative financial statements. If the incoming auditors are unable to obtain sufficient appropriate audit evidence regarding the comparatives, the current auditors' report is qualified on the basis of scope limitations. The successor auditors should refer to the predecessor's auditors' report in the qualification section and state:

- that the financial statements of the prior period were audited by another auditor (and provide the name of the auditor);
- the date of the predecessor auditors' report;
- the type of opinion expressed by the predecessor; and
- what the substantive reasons are if the report was qualified.

UNAUDITED PRIOR PERIOD FINANCIAL STATEMENTS

If the prior period report is unaudited, the auditors have a responsibility to seek sufficient appropriate audit evidence to assess if the comparatives are misstated. If there is persuasive evidence that there are no material misstatements, an unqualified opinion should be expressed.

Initial engagements

In an initial audit engagement the auditors need to:

- determine the propriety of account balances at the beginning of the period being audited;
- ascertain the accounting policies used in the preceding period and determine if these policies are consistently applied in the current period; and
- ascertain that opening balances do not contain material misstatements that affect the current period's financial statements.

The auditors should obtain sufficient appropriate audit evidence in relation to the above matters. ISA 510, Initial Engagements – Opening Balances, suggests that reliance may be placed on the work of another auditor if the prior period financial statements were audited by other auditors. Other procedures need to be performed if prior period accounts were unaudited. The sufficiency or lack thereof of appropriate audit evidence may lead to the reporting conclusions described below.

- If the auditors are unable to obtain sufficient appropriate audit evidence, there is a limitation on the scope of the audit work. Accordingly, an 'except for' opinion or a statement of inability to form an opinion should be expressed.
- If accounting policies are not consistently applied or the change has not been properly accounted for and adequately disclosed, an 'except for' (disagreement) or adverse opinion should be expressed owing to lack of consistency or inadequate disclosure.
- If material misstatements in opening balances affect the current period's financial statements, an 'except for' (disagreement) or adverse opinion should be expressed.

Electronic publication of financial statements

Entities are now allowed to distribute financial statements electronically via the Internet to shareholders wishing the receive them in this way. This raises a number of concerns as to the auditors' report attached to those financial statements. Guidance issued by the APB contained in Bulletin 2001/1, The Electronic Publication of Auditors' Reports, raises the following issues.

- Except where the electronic publication is by way of a pdf file, which retains the original page numbering, the auditors' report needs to identify the audited financial statements by name and date instead of using page numbers as is usually the case with printed versions.

- Because such financial statements are available internationally and the shareholders or other users may be unaware of the audited entity's domicile, references to Financial Reporting and to Auditing Standards should specify the relevant nationality.
- Care must be taken to ensure that the documents loaded onto the Web are identical to the hard-copy version.
- Care must be taken to ensure that the use of hyperlinks does not inappropriately link the auditors' report to non-audited data.

Operating and financial review

In 2002 the government published a White Paper *Modernising Company Law* setting out its proposals for the revision of the Companies Act. A major proposal is for the introduction of a mandatory requirement for significant economic entities to publish an Operating and Financial Review[1] and for the auditors to review the adequacy of the procedures adopted by the directors in its preparation. In their review the auditors must consider whether:

- the information in the operating and financial review is consistent with the financial statements and with any other information of which they have become aware in the performance of the audit; and
- the review and the manner of its preparation comply with the applicable rules.

Summary financial statements, interim reports and preliminary announcements

In the UK companies issue financial reports in forms other than the annual financial statements with which auditors may have some level of involvement.

SUMMARY FINANCIAL STATEMENTS
SAS 600 (as amended by APB Bulletin 1999/6, The Auditors' Statement on the Summary Financial Statement) states that auditors' reports on summary financial statements should state that the full financial statements have been audited, whether or not the auditors' report on those financial statements was qualified (and, if so, repeating the qualification) and expressing an opinion that the summary financial statement is consistent with the full financial statements. By virtue of its being a summary, the summary financial statements, on their own, cannot be said to give a true and fair view.

INTERIM REPORTS
Auditors have no statutory responsibility for the interim financial reports. However, in many companies, the directors request that the auditors perform a review and report their findings. The nature of the review and of the limited assurance expressed in their report is along the lines described on page 8 (Chapter 1). The procedures are explained in an APB Bulletin 1999/4, Review of Interim Financial Information.

PRELIMINARY ANNOUNCEMENTS
Auditors are required to communicate to directors their consent to the publication of the preliminary announcement. However, there is no overt statement as to the auditors'

involvement. The required procedures are described in APB Bulletin 1998/1, The Auditors' Association with Preliminary Announcements.

 LEARNING **CHECK**

15.15 The principal effects of International Auditing Standards on the auditors' report are:

- use of 'emphasis of matter' for referring to uncertainties and other modifications to the auditors' report that do not constitute a qualification; and

- reference to auditors' reports as being modified or unmodified where modified includes inclusion of an emphasis of matter.

15.16 The auditor has a responsibility to obtain sufficient appropriate evidence to ensure comparatives are not misstated.

15.17 For opening balances in initial engagements, an unqualified opinion is expressed if:

- there is propriety of opening balances;

- there are no misstatements in opening balances; or

- accounting policies are consistently applied.

15.18 Special conditions apply where financial statements are published electronically and for reports on summary financial statements, interim reports and preliminary announcements.

SUMMARY

Reporting the findings is the final phase of a financial statement audit. The auditors must comply with relevant Auditing Standards when reporting on audited financial statements. Depending on the circumstances, the auditors may issue an unqualified auditors' report or a qualified auditors' report that expresses one of three other types of opinion. Where financial statements are subject to fundamental uncertainty, readers' attention is drawn to the fact in a special paragraph in the Basis of opinion section of the auditors' report but without qualifying the opinion. When expressing a qualified opinion, the report must contain a clear statement as to the reasons for the qualification and the effect thereof. The reporting requirements under International Standards of Auditing are similar except that the terminology relating to qualifications is different. Special considerations pertain to audits of consolidated financial statements and to comparatives and opening balances. The auditors must exercise due care in conducting the audit so as to obtain a reasonable basis for an opinion and to express the opinion justified by the findings.

NOTE

[1] Accounting Standards Board Statement, *Operating and Financial Review*, ASB 1993.

FURTHER READING

Hatherly, D. J., Innes, J. & Brown, T. 'The Expanded Audit Report – An Empirical Investigation', *Accounting and Business Research* (Autumn 1991), pp. 311–319.

Gangolly, J. S., Hussein, M. E., Seow, G. S. & Tam, K. 'Harmonization of the Auditor's Report', *International Journal of Accounting* (Vol. 37, Issue 3, 2002), pp. 327–347.

King, C. G. 'The Measurement of Harmonization in the Form and Content of the Auditor's Report in the European Union', *Journal of International Accounting Auditing & Taxation* (Vol. 8, Issue 1, 1999), pp. 23–43.

Nugent, M. 'Uncertain About What Type of Audit Report to Issue?', *Charter* (August 1997), pp. 84–85.

Petravick, S. 'Online Financial Reporting', *The CPA Journal* (February 1999).

Willis, D. M. & Lightle, S. S. 'Management Reports on Internal Controls', *Journal of Accountancy* (October 2000).

MULTIPLE-CHOICE QUESTIONS

Choose the best answer for each of the following.
(Answers are on pages 605–606)

15.1 What is an auditor required to state on completion of the audit?
(a) A statement of fact in relation to whether the financial statements represent a 'true and fair' view.
(b) A detailed analysis of items the auditor has become aware of that have aroused his or her interest.
(c) A statement of opinion about the firm's compliance with all statutory requirements.
(d) A statement of opinion about the truth and fairness of the financial statements.

15.2 If the auditor believes that management should disclose further information about directors' remuneration but management does not agree to do this, what should the auditor do?
(a) Report the breach to the appropriate regulatory authority and issue an 'except for' audit opinion.
(b) Report the breach to the appropriate regulatory authority and issue an unqualified auditors' report.
(c) Disclose the information within the auditors' report.
(d) Issue an unqualified audit opinion.

15.3 Consider the following scenario. Restrictions imposed by the entity prohibit the observation of stock-take, which accounts for about 40% of all assets. Alternative audit procedures cannot be applied, although the auditor was able to obtain satisfactory evidence for all other items in the financial statements. The auditor should issue:
(a) an unqualified opinion.
(b) an adverse opinion.
(c) a disclaimer of opinion.
(d) an 'except for' opinion.

15.4 In reviewing subsequent events, the auditor reviewed a number of sales transactions that raised serious concerns in relation to the recorded value of stocks. The auditor believes that stock should be written down by 15% in the financial statements, but management is satisfied that stock is stated fairly. The auditor should issue:
   (a)   an unqualified opinion.
   (b)   an adverse opinion.
   (c)   a disclaimer of opinion.
   (d)   an 'except for' opinion.

15.5 The auditor has serious concerns about the going concern of the company. The company's going concern is dependent on obtaining a large sales contract that is still under negotiation at the time of signing the auditors' report. The management of the company has made full disclosure of this situation in the notes to the accounts. The auditor is satisfied with the level of disclosure. The auditor should issue:
   (a)   an unqualified opinion.
   (b)   an unqualified opinion with reference to the notes to the accounts.
   (c)   a disclaimer of an opinion.
   (d)   an 'except for' opinion.

15.6 The auditor concludes that there is a material inconsistency in the other information in an annual report to shareholders containing audited financial statements. If the auditor concludes that the financial statements do not require revision, but the directors refuse to revise or eliminate the material inconsistency in the other information, the auditor should issue:
   (a)   an unqualified opinion.
   (b)   an unqualified opinion with an explanatory paragraph.
   (c)   a disclaimer of an opinion.
   (d)   an 'except for' opinion.

15.7 You have accepted the appointment to audit the financial statements of Hippo Ltd for the year ended 31 December 20X1. The financial statements of the company for the year ended 31 December 20X0 were unaudited. In relation to the opening balances in the 31 December 20X1 financial statements, you need to issue:
   (a)   a disclaimer of opinion where you cannot obtain sufficient appropriate audit evidence on the opening balances.
   (b)   an adverse opinion where you cannot obtain sufficient appropriate audit evidence on opening balances.
   (c)   an unqualified report because of representations of management.
   (d)   an unqualified report after advising the appropriate regulatory authority that the previous year's report was unaudited.

DISCUSSION QUESTIONS

15.1 Until about 10 years ago the auditors' report consisted simply of an opinion. Does the inclusion of scope and responsibility sections improve their value to users or merely protect the auditors?

15.2 Terminology in the UK auditors' report refers to the report as being qualified when, in fact, it may be an adverse opinion or a disclaimer of opinion. The IAASB preferred terminology is for a modified report, but this could include a report containing an emphasis of matter but where the opinion is unaffected. How can the terminology be improved to remove such ambiguities?

15.3 The UK auditors' report combines the opinion on truth and fairness of the financial statements with compliance with a range of regulatory requirements. The IAASB proposes separating the two sets of opinions. Which approach is best?

15.4 The meaning of 'truth and fairness' has long been debated. In some jurisdictions the term 'fair presentation' is used to avoid the implications that financial statements contain elements of absolute truth. In the post-Enron USA the notion of 'fairness' is being emphasised as more than compliance with the financial reporting framework (see also Chapter 4). What do you think 'fairness' means?

15.5 What concerns might you have if a company you have audited proposes placing its annual report, including your auditors' report, on its web site which includes a wide range of other information on the company?

15.6 If the financial statements give a true and fair view, including the threat of fundamental uncertainties, is it necessary for auditors to highlight such matters in their report?

15.7 Following a recent court case, the Institute of Chartered Accountants in England & Wales advised its members to add to their auditors' reports a disclaimer of liability to third parties. Is this sensible or does it devalue the audit?

15.8 Students sometimes confuse the term 'pervasive' in the context of requiring an adverse or disclaimer of opinion, with 'materiality'. What do you understand by the term 'pervasive'?

PROFESSIONAL APPLICATION QUESTIONS

(Suggested answers are on pages 656–658)

15.1 Effect of circumstances on audit opinion

Assume that the following separate circumstances could be sufficiently material to require the expression of a qualified opinion.

1. The company sacked its computer systems controller during the year. Before she left, she corrupted the system and consequently destroyed all financial records.
2. The cash flow statement does not conform to the requirements of IAS 7.
3. Finished goods stored in Singapore were not observed or test-counted. The items constituted 10% of closing stock.
4. The entity is the defendant in a major litigation that has not been settled at the report date.
5. Profits on long-term construction contracts are recognised by a method inconsistent with IAS 11.
6. The continuation of the company as a going concern is in doubt.
7. Another firm of auditors audited a subsidiary that accounted for 5% of the consolidation's total assets and 10% of the total revenues.
8. The entity changed its stock valuation method from average cost to first-in first-out, necessitating a restatement of prior years' statements.

Required

Indicate the effect of the above eight circumstances on the auditors' report.

15.2 Going-concern issues, audit opinion

Fly-By-Night Ltd is a listed public company that manufactures highly sophisticated navigation equipment for defence force aircraft and Navy ships. The company has a 30 June 20X0 year-end, and the statutory accounts are due to be signed one week after the board of directors' meeting on 5 August 20X0. During the course of the audit, you become aware that the government has reviewed its budget in an effort to reduce the growing deficit. As a result, defence expenditure had major cuts.

One of the major projects to be scrapped as a result of these cuts is the planned upgrading of the navigation equipment for the Navy's submarine fleet. You are aware that the company's budget for this year includes a major subcontract to the Department of Defence and the Navy for this project.

The company has been experiencing cash flow difficulties and has recently applied for a significant increase to a borrowing facility that is already fully drawn. Management is adamant that the company will continue to be viable. If necessary, it claims it can resort to cutbacks in its future capital expenditure programme, seek additional off-balance sheet financing, and/or reschedule existing debt arrangements.

Required
(a) What does the going-concern concept mean? Discuss the reporting options open to an auditor when going-concern issues arise.
(b) Discuss the potential auditors' report options in relation to Fly-By-Night Ltd.

(This question is adapted from the Professional Year Programme of the Institute of Chartered Accountants in Australia – 1996, Advanced Audit Module)

E-COMMERCE AND AUDITING

LEARNING **OBJECTIVES**

After studying this chapter, you should be able to:

1   describe the business environment in the information economy

2   appreciate the nature and development of strategic issues relating to e-commerce

3   assess the knowledge, risk and control matters in an e-commerce environment

4   discuss the objectives and approach of forensic auditing, with an emphasis on Internet fraud.

PROFESSIONAL STATEMENTS

ISA 250   Consideration of Laws and Regulations in an Audit of Financial Statements
ISA 315   Understanding the Entity and Its Environment and Assessing the Risks of Material Misstatement
ISA 402   Audit Considerations Relating to Entities Using a Service Organisation
ISA 620   Using the Work of an Expert
IAPS 1001 IT Environments – Stand-alone Personal Computers
IAPS 1002 IT Environments – On-line Computer Systems
IAPS 1003 IT Environments – Database Systems
IAPS 1013 Electronic Commerce – Effect on the Audit of Financial Statements

> No accountant can afford to ignore the influence of the Internet altogether. Developing a certain familiarity with the workings of the Internet and e-commerce should be high on the agenda of every accountant, in business or in practice[1]

In the information economy, the use, by organisations, of emerging forms of information technology is of increasing importance to their management, control and competitiveness. Information and communication technologies are key enabling tools in the process of commercial and technological change. This chapter introduces the nature, development and business models of electronic commerce (e-commerce), increasingly encountered by auditors, and considers the implications for the audit process. The chapter commences with a brief review of the current electronic business environment, leading to a more detailed description of e-commerce and various business models. This is followed by an explanation of some of the key audit risk and control considerations, based on IAPS 1013, Electronic Commerce – Effect on the Audit of Financial Statements. Trends in the methods of auditing e-commerce business cycles will then be explained including the emerging areas of on-line and continuous auditing. The final part of the chapter discusses one of the major risks in e-commerce – cyber crime – and the approaches adopted in the assurance service of forensic auditing.

THE INFORMATION ECONOMY AND BUSINESS ENVIRONMENT

The development of the information economy is related to the process of business transformation within modern economies. Through the increased use of information and

Table 16.1 A profile of business transformation

ASPECTS OF OPERATIONS	TRADITIONAL ECONOMY	INFORMATION ECONOMY
Organisations	Inwardly focused entities	Extended network
Market	Distinctive marketplace	Unlimited market space
Infrastructure	Physical, hierarchical infrastructure	Integrated, digital infrastructure using communication technology
Resources	Functional, hierarchical use of resources	Shared use of *knowledge-based* resources
Business emphasis	Local outlook, visible returns	Global outlook, empowerment, enhanced relationships
Access	Arm's length operations	Direct, on-line operations in real time

associated technologies by businesses and other users, new industrial structures, systems, patterns and trends emerge alongside new products and services. Complicated networks of enterprises replace the traditional entities, and business is performed using information and communication technologies. Customers, suppliers and other intermediaries are drawn together under processes conducted through the Internet, with an unlimited market space. Internal employees are less hierarchically managed, cross-functional relationships are used, and business innovation is enhanced through empowerment and knowledge management strategies. Businesses are linked by way of strategic partnerships and have direct access to global resources. Table 16.1 illustrates the different aspects of business transformation.

The information economy is not a synonym for the commercial evolution of the Internet. Apart from reflecting the commercial impact of technology, the information economy is concerned with the use of information and communication technologies in business processes, including the continuous growth of innovative methods such as outsourcing and quality assurance services. It is a pragmatic phenomenon as a response to the needs of businesses and economies when knowledge and information are the key drivers to business success and survival.

A conceptual model of the information economy

A conceptual model developed by the Austin Centre for Research into Electronic Commerce[2] uses four layers of commercial activity that characterise such an information economy. Each layer illustrates the respective business motivations in the new information economy and reflects the commercial opportunities and challenges. Businesses transform to meet the needs of the information economy, so as to maintain their competitive advantages. The four layers are: the infrastructure layer, the applications layer, the intermediary layer and the e-commerce layer.

THE INFRASTRUCTURE LAYER
This layer consists of enterprises that supply products and services that aid the development of a network infrastructure based on the Internet. The infrastructure comprises Internet backbone and service providers, networking hardware and software, server and PC

manufacturers, and security suppliers. These parties support the basic components of business transmission and provide the capability to process information.

THE APPLICATIONS LAYER

The components of the applications layer are developed as the existing Internet protocol is built on to satisfy certain business uses, such as on-line business activities. They include parties such as Internet consultants, e-commerce applications, multimedia applications, web-development software, search engine software and on-line training.

THE INTERMEDIARY LAYER

Intermediaries in on-line business smooth and augment the market and transaction process by bringing together buyers and sellers through networks. They enable applications and infrastructure to be translated and used in business transactions. Examples of intermediaries are on-line travel agents, on-line brokers, on-line libraries and media publications providers, and on-line advertising and electronic auctions.

THE E-COMMERCE LAYER

This layer represents the transactions of goods and services between businesses and consumers over the Internet. It includes electronic retailers, manufacturers selling on-line, fee/subscription-based enterprises, on-line entertainment and professional services.

Enterprises are not normally limited to a particular layer; instead, they operate across different layers. As technology and commercial activities converge, the above model conceptualises the development of an emerging Internet ecosystem which becomes the backbone of the information economy. It signifies the evolution of the electronic business models in the development of on-line commerce. Figure 16.1 shows the conceptual model of commercial activity that characterises information economy.

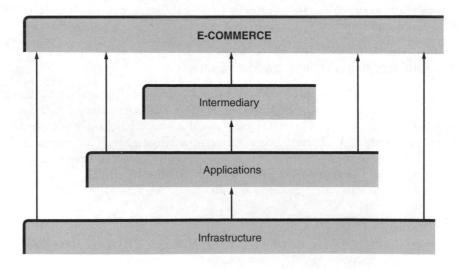

Figure 16.1 *Layers in an information economy*

The information economy represents a fundamental change in the business environment globally. Its evolution is largely based on the impact of information and communication technology (notably through the development of the Internet) on commercial activity. The result is a reorganisation of economic activity involving increased use of information as a key resource and the wider deployment of technology. E-commerce has become the integral part of the information economy, meaning that all aspects of business need to be redesigned. Existing businesses need to review their business processes and explore how these could be improved by using the latest technologies. This chapter focuses on the impact of e-commerce and the implications for auditors.

THE NATURE AND DEVELOPMENT OF E-COMMERCE

Following on from the conceptual framework of the information economy, e-commerce activities can be regarded as an integral process of the modern economy, which combines the layers of infrastructure, applications and intermediaries to achieve the optimum performance of business transactions. E-commerce has tremendous scope for strategic impact across an enterprise. The extent to which it is adopted across functions depends on the form and nature of the enterprise and the commercial environment within which it operates. The functions affected by e-commerce may include product development, resourcing, promotion, marketing, sales, contracting, financing, transaction processing, system procurement, transport and logistics, accounting and administration, financing, reporting and insurance. Thus, to appreciate its impact, we must understand the strategic implications of e-commerce.

The core of e-commerce lies in its commercial transaction cycle. Surrounding this core is the use of electronic methods to advertise and promote products, the facilitation of contracts, market intelligence and sales support. The full development of e-commerce requires giving users certain guarantees in respect of privacy, information security and integrity.

Managers of organisations need to assess the strategic impact of e-commerce. They must possess the business knowledge that helps them to assess the best strategy as well as gauge the knowledge of competitors and the changes in the markets. They will rely on the following core information resources to identify the relevant strategic implications:

- Human resources and management embody corporate knowledge, intellectual property and project/product-based knowledge. Having knowledge of its human resources can help an entity formulate policies relating to its workforce, skilling, staff recruitment and retention policies, and supporting structures.
- Market and product knowledge encompasses knowledge of the value chain concept, production costs, productivity, competitive dynamics, partnerships, market locations, operational strategies and workplace support.
- Infrastructure and structural support comprises support activities used in Porter's value chain.[3] An entity's infrastructure includes firm infrastructure such as accounts, finance and quality management; technology development and procurement; physical processes such as inventory; data storage; product development; hardware, software and electronic data links; and security systems.

- The customer/supplier element concerns all the entity's interactions with customers, prospective markets, suppliers and banks, along with its relationship enhancement programmes and databases.

E-commerce builds on the structures of traditional commerce by adding the flexibilities offered by electronic networks. In turn, electronic networks create new opportunities so commercial transactions can be conducted more efficiently, involving more interactive activities among interested groups and using more innovative processes. This section discusses the nature and development of e-commerce with a view to identifying the implications for auditors.

The evolution of e-commerce

With its fast-developing features, e-commerce has evolved through many forms and there is little agreement on what constitutes electronic commerce. For some time, large business enterprises have used e-commerce to conduct their business-to-business (B2B) transactions. Electronic data interchange (EDI) on private networks began in the 1960s, and banks have been using dedicated networks for electronic funds transfer (EFT) for almost as long. However, with the increased awareness and popularity of the Internet, e-commerce now also encompasses individual customers in business-to-consumer (B2C) transactions with businesses of all sizes.

E-commerce can be defined as the use of electronic networks to facilitate commercial transactions. It includes:

- on-line purchasing of tangible and intangible products, including on-line ordering (with or without on-line access to catalogues) and direct delivery to the customer, bypassing traditional retailers. Such activity includes the direct sale of intangible and digitised content of items where payment and delivery are made via the personal computer at home;
- on-line advertising and marketing for purposes of promoting sales;
- fund management and transfers via the Internet;
- on-line transactions and information transfers between information aggregators and intermediaries, including business-to-business transactions; and
- on-line catalysts for commercial transactions such as telecommunications systems, facilitating hardware and software, Internet access services, information accreditation agencies and on-line service providers.

SPECIFIC THEMES IN E-COMMERCE

To help managers evaluate their business positions. Merrill Lynch identified specific themes that tend to characterise electronic marketplaces.[4] These themes can be described as improved customer status, low entry barriers, the disintermediation of business processes, and the scaling of matters. Let us look at these in more detail.

- Customers are powerful on the Internet because they can gather and demand information about rival products.

- Entry to the market is relatively easy, although a real cost is the cost of sustainable development.
- Intermediaries, such as the distributor, can be easily eliminated, to be replaced by new informediaries, who find products and aggregate resources for potential customers.
- Because the incremental cost of the incremental transaction is negligible, matters are scaled to allow for the incremental transaction.

DIFFERENT BUSINESS MODELS OF E-COMMERCE

There are broadly two types of e-commerce: business-to-business and business-to-consumer. For purposes of simplicity, we will not discuss the regulatory aspects, such as on-line filing of tax returns.

Business-to-business applications include the sell side where goods or services are sold to business customers to create revenue. These applications provide the capability to integrate inventory and production systems with ease of use and access. The buy side focuses on helping enterprises make procurements, and these applications are designed primarily for internal staff so they can process spending and acquisitions more efficiently. Marketplace applications bring together both sell and buy sides, using a community of network and common resources.

Business-to-consumers commerce is considered secondary to business-to-business commerce in terms of volume. The impact of business-to-consumers applications can be seen in the volume of digital content available free of charge to the public. The offer of on-line content is mostly a complement to the physical form of businesses, with some providers offering additional advantages from on-line transacting. Common applications are travel reservations, banking, insurance, on-line securities trading and investment, and retail such as books, compact discs, apparel and cars. However, in many cases, e-commerce in consumer markets encounters impediments to its growth, including concerns regarding the security of payment, the potential for fraud, the privacy of personal data, and problems in assessing on-line merchants. The take-up in the market for business-to-consumer transactions has been slow, and its future development depends on a maturing of a generation who possess a strong familiarity with information and communication technologies.

DISINTERMEDIATION AND THE EMERGENCE OF INFORMEDIARIES

The Internet can effectively remove bottlenecks (as represented in the past by intermediaries such as distributors), so it stimulates disintermediation by decreasing search costs, reducing user entry barriers and automating activity. Enterprises are bypassing the need for sales representatives and costly house calls; for example, Encyclopaedia Britannica effectively disintermediated its door-to-door sales force when it offered its product free over the Internet. Internally, people can share information and corporate knowledge more readily and act on it more quickly through the Internet and intranet. Consequently, adjusting systems to take disintermediation into consideration may prove essential to sustaining a competitive advantage in the long term.

On the other hand, there is also the emergence of reintermediation – an altered model of intermediation which uses the critical mass concept of information aggregators and providers (called 'informediaries'). An informediary is a web site that provides specialised, up-to-date information on behalf of producers of goods and services and potential customers. Informediaries gather, analyse and redistribute information using information and communication technologies. They create new services and add value to potential information users. They may even be able to organise exchanges and resales, on-line auctions, etc. Banks, travel agents and airlines, music stores and large publishing organisations offer services for sale as well as informediaries.

SMALL AND MEDIUM-SIZED ENTERPRISES

Small and medium-sized enterprises (SMEs) are usually more innovative in applying e-commerce models. There are two kinds of SMEs in terms of e-commerce applications: (1) those SMEs whose existence depends on the Internet and, therefore, that generate all their sales and customer communications through this medium; and (2) those that are experimenting with the new distribution channel as a means of complementing their existing capabilities. Typically, SMEs face many problems in implementing and developing new technological systems. The most significant issue of implementation is the sheer cost of investment. Other problems include cultural factors (especially for family businesses that are used to doing business in conventional ways), the cost of and changes in infrastructure, the divergence of business applications and technology, a lack of knowledge and awareness, the uncertainty of benefits, the nature of the products to be sold on line, a lack of maturity of e-commerce, security, the absence of a legal framework concerning e-commerce, the cost of consumer access, and the lack of human resource.

 LEARNING **CHECK**

16.1 The information economy does not only concern technology, but also the use of information and communication technologies in business processes, including a continual growth of innovative methods.

16.2 The conceptual model of the information economy consists of four key layers: the infrastructure layer, the applications layer, the intermediary layer and e-commerce layer. The e-commerce layer combines all aspects of the information economy and uses both internal networks (intranets) and external networks (the Internet).

16.3 To identify the relevant strategic implications, e-commerce relies on core information resources such as those concerning human resources, management, market and product knowledge, infrastructural supports and customer/supplier relationships.

16.4 The implementation of e-commerce involves many strategic issues, which include satisfying various corporate objectives or incentives, identifying the extent of intermediation required, selecting different business models, and understanding the costs, constraints and benefits for the business concerned.

E-COMMERCE – AUDIT AND ASSURANCE SERVICES

In identifying the nature and extent of audit in an e-commerce environment, we will consolidate the earlier discussions concerning the business process and strategies of e-commerce. Figure 16.2 denotes an e-commerce environment with the relevant business processes and related audit and assurance services. There are many in the accounting profession who

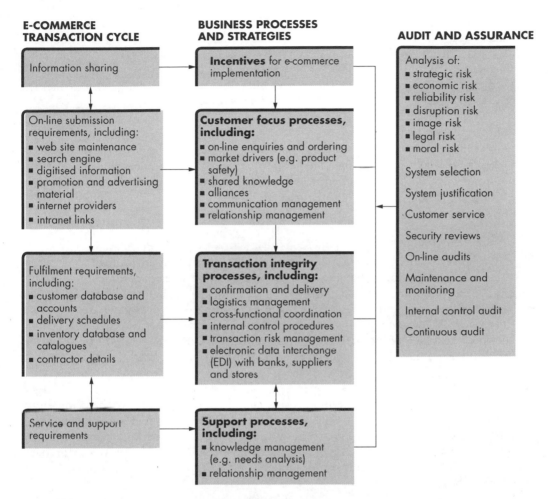

Figure 16.2 *An e-commerce environment analysis*

see the development of wide-ranging applications of e-business as providing an expanding opportunity in the demand for audit and assurance services. In the USA, the American Institute of Certified Public Accountants (AICPA) has set up a 'Vision Project' to identify emerging opportunities for audit and assurance services in the e-commerce environment.

An e-commerce environment

An e-commerce transaction can be effected through four main steps: information sharing, on-line submissions, fulfilment, and service and support. Each step involves a part of the business strategy and an operational process.

INFORMATION SHARING
This step involves using the entity's infrastructure or information systems to address the goals of the entity and its customers. An enterprise can use the Internet to provide

information about its products, services and related news, while also learning about its markets. On the other hand, this is the initial stage when customers get to know about the entity and its products. A large number of web sites are aimed at the general public, but a significant number of sites are aimed at business markets. Intermediaries or informediaries and brokers often offer sites that allow buyers and sellers in a particular market to interact, trade information, bid and make sales.

Business processes and strategies
The entity designs a web site, including a web page, survey/enquiry forms, e-mail services that use network communities, and data monitor systems that track and follow up visitors and enquiries. It can identify its own niche market by gathering competitive information, evaluating the various incentives for embarking on e-commerce activities, and developing its implementation strategy.

ON-LINE SUBMISSIONS
This step involves potential customers electronically ordering either through the Internet or by e-mail. Thus, on-line submission refers to the ordering stage or transaction initiation stage. The entity gathers electronic forms (i.e. order forms) or digitised information. The web site maintenance and support systems must be reliable to handle electronic forms and the information secured therein. Other web sites and intranet (if applicable) search engines may also be incorporated within the web site, and the reliability of these links is essential to ensure that promotional and personal information is kept intact.

Business processes and strategies
The on-line submission and ordering process signifies the first impression of the entity for customers. The entity must adhere to the concept of customer focus when using its intelligence on market drivers, ascertaining the level of shared knowledge, assessing the possibility of alliances and enhancing relationships with external parties. Moreover, this is the initial stage of a transaction and must be supported by sound communication technology.

FULFILMENT
This step involves confirming orders, delivering goods and ensuring payment on accounts. This part of e-commerce activities is very much related to the effectiveness and efficiency of the entity's internal control systems. The entity has to confirm transactions with customers; update and interrogate the inventory database and customer database; use EDI to communicate with shippers, suppliers and distributors; provide delivery schedules; and print pro forma invoices and delivery notes. In some cases, the entity may need to prepare banking instructions and details to set up direct debits/credits. Other tasks may be the preparation of daily/weekly reports of sales/purchases activities and the updating of accounting records.

Business processes and strategies
The entity must be able to maintain effective logistics management methods, cross-functional procedures, and sufficient internal controls to minimise risks, and to use EDI to interact with the bank regarding secured information.

Payment over the Internet is the most fluid and fast-developing aspect of e-commerce. Consumers and businesses can use credit cards, electronic cheques, digital cash (micro-cash) or electronic transfers to make payments. EDI is one technique, while some suppliers offer commerce-server software specifically designed to handle accepting web payments. Security and controls are the key issues in the fulfilment stage of an e-commerce transaction.

SERVICE AND SUPPORT

This step entails a range of activities by the entity to monitor and use the corporate knowledge and experience about customers, products, discrepancies in systems, customer services and maintenance. The supplier may enter into some contracting arrangements with other businesses or customers, as a part of the maintenance service. Otherwise, technical notes to track the features of 'frequently asked questions', common complaints, product shortages and discrepancies can be built in for product development projects. Enterprises often use maintenance and support services to enhance customer relationships.

Business processes and strategies

E-commerce systems should interface with corporate strategies regarding knowledge management, resource planning and customer relationship management. Management should continually monitor the features and performance of e-commerce activities, because opportunities and threats are changing rapidly – an environment that results from the development in information and communication technology.

Audit and assurance services

Electronic commerce provides organisations and enterprises with new tools and techniques for reducing costs, communicating more effectively, promoting and increasing sales, and improving operational efficiency and effectiveness. To keep pace with the electronic revolution in business, auditors must acquire an understanding of new technologies. New audit approaches should be developed to ensure the enterprise's e-commerce objectives are achieved in an adequate manner. For independent auditors, an entity's e-commerce environment will most likely require electronic audit tools. Audit plans must be developed with a clear understanding of the e-commerce characteristics and their limitations. Internal auditors, on the other hand, must be fully involved in the e-commerce system from the outset of implementation to maintenance and support. Both types of auditor are also concerned with the reliability of the management and financial reports generated on the e-commerce transactions.

The e-commerce environment opens up enormous opportunities for professional accountants in the range of assurance services they can provide. Types of audit and assurance services related to the e-commerce environment are described below. Note, however, that the following discussions pertain to a scope beyond the financial statement audit.

RISK ANALYSIS

Enterprises and organisations may choose to participate in different levels of e-commerce activities. Lower involvement is about a basic network presence, entity promotion, and pre- and post-sales support. These services often rely on web hosting services, which are convenient and cheap for small enterprises. They typically provide the speed, reliability and scalability of the powerful web servers, but with minimal administrative support. The more advanced e-commerce services are used by expanding enterprises that are concerned with building a customer base and retaining relationships with existing customers. Control systems, technical support and an understanding of the technical aspects, together with legal and cultural developments, are essential.

At the information sharing stage, a professional accountant may add value by conducting a risk analysis. Security and operational issues are the key aspects of risk analysis. An enterprise initiating an e-commerce system must determine how it is going to assure the confidentiality of information such as prices, inventory quantities and other trading data of value to competitors. The integrity of the transaction details must be maintained so only authorised personnel have access to the identity of customers and users, and so the transmission of data is secured and not vulnerable to tampering.

The key operational concern is that investment in e-commerce should be justified from a cost and strategic perspective. Web site design issues such as speed, currency of information, follow-up of enquiries, excessive information, lack of resources, and an inability to protect customers from intruders are the related risks. Powell identifies a number of e-commerce risks: strategic risk, economic risk, reliability risk, disruption risk, image risk, legal risk and moral risk.[5] Strategic risk concerns the use of the Internet to gain a competitive advantage. Economic risk refers to the justifiable returns on the cost of investment in e-commerce. Reliability risk is about the adequacy of a well-tested and monitored e-commerce system. Disruption risk relates to the probability of the integrity of the system being disrupted. Image risk arises from the fear of hackers vandalising the web sites, and requires proof that security measures are competent and protected. Thus, legal compliance and attention to staff capability are necessary to overcome such risks in implementing e-commerce.

SYSTEM SELECTION AND JUSTIFICATION

The professional accountant or auditor should be involved during the early stages of the e-commerce project by performing reviews of the proposed internal control systems, carrying out pilot tests, assessing the e-commerce business model, and participating in project management. Specific areas for assessment include the proposed communication system, the network data generation and maintenance system, access controls, change authorisation and controls, physical controls and contingency planning. In reviewing the possible e-commerce business models, the professional accountant should ensure that the financial and operational feasibility of the proposed initiatives have been well researched and that the model details the financial resources needed to implement the staffing, technical and equipment requirements. The business model should also identify the strengths and weaknesses (or risks) of e-commerce, detailing the changes that the business processes will undergo and the expected timing or staging of those changes. The model should also consider working conditions, job specifications, and the physical layout of office and operational areas. The professional accountant should assess how well the emerging e-commerce model will interact with future business models or existing ones during the transitional period.

Project management tasks should include verifying that the organisation has established a skilled project team representing the entity's and information technology personnel. The team must have a thorough understanding of the legal and security implications of the proposed system. Interactions with other business partners may also be essential when shared knowledge and linked networks are involved.

CUSTOMER SERVICE

Interactions with customers are an essential part of e-commerce. Applications should be as self-service oriented as possible. Customer service may include users' ability to:

- review the customer database to identify changes in personal information, banking instructions, etc.;
- enter their own orders and receive confirmations;
- carry out claims on line speedily;
- propose changes to delivery dates and order quantities, with amended confirmations;
- review the transaction/account status;
- check shipment details;
- access accounts receivable details;
- search for, request and download on-line information and documentation; and
- download reports.

The system should be able to review pricing and other procedures for follow-up inquiries by customers.

SECURITY REVIEWS

The professional accountant carrying out security reviews should examine procedures surrounding the confidentiality of data, transmission of information, periodical reconciliation procedures, authenticating procedures, and the arrangements with outside contractors such as information aggregators and brokers. He or she should also conduct server security reviews. Web-based information may be certified using products such as Webtrusts. The examination of on-line security is an ongoing procedure, which sometimes becomes part of the on-line auditing.

ON-LINE AUDITS

The professional accountant may provide on-line audit. Such an audit evaluates the likely acceptance of on-line sites or services among targeted users. It includes:

- on-line market analysis and overview;
- marketing and communication goals implementation;
- technology evaluation;
- on-line content audit;
- target audience identification and analysis;
- site upgrade and enhancement recommendations;
- ongoing competitive analysis; and
- traffic monitoring and server log analysis.

The components of an on-line content audit comprise the review of the content or service offering, review of the competitors' content or service offering, a site review with the entity, a joint audit with a review questionnaire, and recommendations for content or service improvements.

An on-line audit is appropriate both before and after a web site for on-line service is built. It involves checking each on-line activity against set goals to provide for specific and actionable recommendations in terms of communication, security and customer relationships.

The on-line auditor should be familiar with software copyright information and ensure compliance is achieved. Audit software is available in the market for auditors to integrate entities' systems with that of the auditor's so they can interact on line. Based on Microsoft Access, Audit Leverage is an example of a package designed for internal auditors. This audit software enables all audit work to be done on line.

MAINTENANCE AND MONITORING

The professional accountant's review should confirm that the enterprise is monitoring its web site performance in terms of criteria such as download time, transaction time, availability and access. Errors such as failed connection, missing information or pages, and broken links must be listed and investigated. The accountant may use or prepare comparative web performance statistics to evaluate overall performance. Also relevant is a review of other web information to ascertain its currency, the accuracy of management reports and data for analysis. The accountant may recommend a reference material repository. This is a part of the web site that contains information related to the business cycle, econometric reports and forecasts, industry trends, media releases and/or links to other relevant web sites. The presence of the repository may enhance customer relationships and maintain competitive advantage.

INTERNAL CONTROL AUDIT

This is a typical audit examination of the adequacy of internal controls within the e-commerce environment. The audit may encompass the control environment, the control features relating to transaction details and transmission security; risk assessment and controls to minimise such risks, information and communication technology, and the competency and sufficiency of human resources. The approach to this audit is similar to that for normal business, only the audit or examination focuses more on the risks associated with e-commerce.

CONTINUOUS AUDIT

Continuous auditing was named one of the top five emerging issues for 1999, selected by the task force charged with defining the American Institute of Certified Public Accountants' Top Technology Lists.[6] The electronic revolution has created a demand for more timely assurance on a broader range of information than that provided by the annual audit of historical financial statements.

In a continuous audit, entity information would be released in a very short time frame (via the Internet) and audit reports on that information would follow the release of the information almost immediately. Thus, a continuous audit is a process or method that enables independent auditors to provide written assurance on a subject matter using a series of auditors' reports issued simultaneously with, or a short time after, the occurrence of events underlying the subject matter. It would be conducted on continuous financial and non-financial information made available to users in formats defined by management.

Auditors could be requested to continuously audit and report on:

- financial statements available on demand via a web site;
- specific financial information in conjunction with a debt covenant agreement;
- compliance with published policies and practices regarding e-commerce transactions (e.g. reliance on secure encrypted systems for credit card processing); and
- the effectiveness of controls operating in key systems or processes.

A continuous audit presents a number of auditing issues. There would be little time for the auditors to gather audit evidence in verifying and substantiating the subject matter(s) concerned. The auditors could not rely on normal audit procedures such as obtaining independent confirmations and addressing material misstatements, so a reliable and well-controlled application system would be vital. The auditors would have to employ fully automated audit software such as IDEA or ACL to read, manipulate and generate the information required. Other conditions necessary to ensure a successful continuous audit would be:

- effective communication (and technology) between the entity and the auditors;
- prior agreement as to the form, content and scope of the audit; and
- a sound knowledge by the auditors of the operating systems employed by the entity.

The above discussion examines the e-commerce environment in terms of the implications of e-commerce and the related strategies and business processes. The above introduction to e-commerce audit and assurance services enables the emerging role of the accountant in this environment to be appreciated.

AUDIT RISK AND CONTROL CONSIDERATIONS

In view of the increasing likelihood that auditors will be working in an Internet-driven environment, this section offers a framework for the conduct of auditing and assurance services in e-commerce. IAPS 1013, Electronic Commerce – Effect on the Audit of Financial Statements, provides the backbone of this section. It describes the skills and knowledge required of auditors in establishing the knowledge of the business and its internal control and assessing the risks of material misstatements.

The key audit planning procedures identified in Chapter 6 apply in an e-commerce environment. Where other parties are involved (e.g. an outsourced party in the electronic transaction cycle), further considerations will be necessary to evaluate the security infrastructure.

IAPS 1013 identifies five areas of concern for the auditor. They are: skills and knowledge, knowledge of the business, risk identification, internal control considerations, and the effect of electronic records on audit evidence. Each of these areas is discussed below.

Skills and knowledge

In planning the audit where e-commerce has a significant effect on the entity's business, the auditors need to consider the required information technology and Internet business knowledge which involves:

- understanding the impact of the entity's e-commerce strategy and activities, the technology used, and the risks involved on the financial statements;
- determining the nature and extent of audit procedures and the methods used to evaluate audit evidence; and
- considering the extent of e-commerce activities and their potential risk on the entity's ability to continue as a going concern.

If the auditors decide to use the work of an expert, for example regarding IT security and controls, such work must be adequate and sufficient for the purposes of the audit. ISA 620, Using the Work of an Expert, should be used as a guide. The auditors should integrate, if necessary, the work of the expert within their own tests, and establish supporting procedures to minimise risks identified through the expert's work.

Knowledge of the business

The auditors should obtain sufficient knowledge of the entity's e-commerce business, so that they can identify and understand the events, transactions and practices which may have a significant impact on the financial statements. These include the entity's:

- business activities and industry;
- e-commerce strategy;
- extent and risks of e-commerce activities; and
- outsourcing arrangements.

The auditors should assess the model and extent of the entity's e-commerce activities as described in the previous section of this chapter. Industries such as computer software, securities trading, travelling, banking and advertising are more likely to have extensive Internet activities. The geographical and operational aspects of e-commerce activities should also be ascertained to identify regulatory risks, systems risks, etc. The entity's e-commerce strategy may affect the generation and adequacy, completeness and reliability of the accounting records. The auditors should assess how the IT strategy is aligned with the business overall strategy, sources of support and revenue, management evaluation of risks and revenue, development of e-commerce systems, identification of risks and risk management policies, and the management's commitment to best practice.

The extent of e-commerce activities affects the nature of risks. The security infrastructure and related controls should be expected to be more complex and extensive where the Internet is used for transacting with business partners and consumers, and are highly integrated. Development of new activities should be aligned with existent systems to minimise system failures.

Where outside parties are involved, such as Internet Service Providers (ISPs), Application Service Providers (ASPs), data hosting agencies, or other informediaries, the auditors should consult ISA 402, Audit Considerations Relating to Entities Using a Service Organisation, to provide guidance on assessing the effect that the service entity has on control risk.

Risk identification

The business risks identified in IAPS 1013 include:

- loss of transaction integrity resulting in loss of audit trail;
- security risks such as virus attacks or e-frauds;
- improper accounting policies relating to, for example, web site development expenditure, recognition of revenue relating to Internet sales, and cut-off;
- non-compliance with taxation and other regulatory matters such as privacy issues and legal protection requirements across international boundaries;
- failure to ensure contracts evidenced only by electronic means are binding;
- overreliance on e-commerce when placing significant business systems or transactions on the Internet; and
- systems and infrastructure failures or breakdowns.

Related controls over the systems infrastructure are, therefore, important. These include:

- authentication or identity verification of customers or authorised entries;
- agreement to specified terms of delivery, trading processes, dispute and credit arrangements, payment forms, and secure credit facilities; and
- privacy and protocol protection.

The auditors need to judge if the protection and controls in place are comparable to the complexity and requirements of the e-commerce platform. Moreover, the auditors should be familiar with the legal and regulatory issues relating to the entity's business. While there is not yet a comprehensive international legal framework for e-commerce, the recognition of e-commerce transactions varies in different jurisdictions. The auditors should consider the factors which might give rise to e-commerce taxes and other legal issues, including the place of registration of the business, the location of the web server, the place of supply of goods, and the delivery location of the customers. The auditor should also consider other legal pronouncements such as privacy law, the enforceability of e-contracts, Internet gambling regulations, money laundering and intellectual property rights. ISA 250, Consideration of Laws and Regulations in an Audit of Financial Statements, should be used in the planning and performance of an audit.

INTERNAL CONTROL CONSIDERATIONS

ISA 315, Understanding the Entity and Its Environment and Assessing the Risks of Material Misstatement, requires the auditors to obtain an understanding of the business and its internal control. This understanding is then used to assess the risks of material misstatements and the effectiveness of the design of internal controls to prevent or detect such misstatements. The understanding is then used to plan the audit and to determine the appropriate strategy for each assertion. In view of the highly automated procedures and the lack of valid audit trail auditors may choose a predominantly substantive approach to the audit of transactions associated with e-commerce. Alternatively in view of the high volume of e-commerce activities auditors may choose to test controls with the assistance of computer-assisted audit techniques (CAATs) and to adopt a lower assessed level of control risk audit strategy. Relevant control considerations are considered below.

SECURITY CONTROLS

The security of transactions through the Internet should be established by the implementation of various security measures. The types of security infrastructure include:

- logical and physical security measures such as firewalls, encryption, physical controls over password issues, authorisation, etc. The IBM SecureWay Firewall version 4.1 for Windows NT, for example, offers a combination of advanced e-mail protection features alongside other firewall architectures (such as filtering, proxy and a circuit level gateway), to provide customers with a high level of security for controlling communication and business;
- internal and external security measures (the latter relating to interfaces with external parties, Internet security and virus protection);
- user profiles, including authorisation and review procedures for users, password security, and logical controls over access;
- information protection, which relates to all measures used to safeguard the integrity of files, virus protection, transmission security, and programmed controls such as check digits and reasonableness checks;
- privacy issues relating to customer information; and
- potential liabilities arising from a breach of legislation, copyright issues, etc.

The auditors consider the various security measures to ensure that the controls are properly incorporated within the e-commerce system. Auditors should refer to IAPSs 1001, 1002 and 1003, which provide guidance on IT environments concerning stand-alone microcomputers, on-line computer systems and database systems respectively. The entity's information technology staff must carefully monitor additional interface controls between the Internet and intranet, along with the entire e-commerce design. The auditors may be involved in the development and design of the system with management to ensure proper safeguards are incorporated and documented.

TRANSACTION INTEGRITY

The security infrastructure described above considers the information sharing and monitoring aspects of the e-commerce environment, while controls relating to transaction integrity safeguard the ordering or transaction initiation stage and the execution or fulfilment stage. Transaction integrity relates to the completeness, accuracy and reliability of the information provided for recording and processing financial records and annual financial statements.

Systems controls for transaction integrity include:

- controls for remote locations (controls on ordering, delivery, authorisation procedures and the accuracy of information);
- identity controls for authorised personnel or businesses;
- processing controls to ensure the completeness and accuracy of transactions and to identify irregularities;
- records controls such as reconciliations between systems and subsystems, timely and accurate reporting, and distribution controls;
- monitoring procedures to ensure all discrepancies are followed up immediately and resubmissions are processed; and
- authenticity, accuracy and reasonableness controls on the customers' database, inventory levels, catalogues and prices, etc., which should be similar to normal computer information system controls.

PROCESS ALIGNMENT

The auditors are concerned with the alignment process between the on-line shopfront and the internal reporting systems (or the back office systems) so that Internet transactions are captured accurately and completely in the entity's reports. The auditors should ascertain, for example, when a transaction takes place through the Internet and is subsequently recognised in the system. They will need to review any disputed transactions and follow up system changes. Training of information technology staff for both on-line operations and back office systems is essential.

The effect of electronic records on audit evidence

The verification procedures for transactions should include an examination of proper information policies and proper implementation of security controls to prevent unauthorised access or changes to the financial records. The auditors should consider the controls incorporated during system design – such as integrity checks, electronic date stamps using digital signatures, version controls on electronic evidence, and transmission controls on real-time transactions – to ensure they are regularly maintained and periodically reviewed.

Audit and assurance issues

Owing to the nature of e-commerce, auditors will consider other key issues that may have an impact on their approach to audit (and other assurance) engagements. These issues include:

- information technology issues such as the technical competence of management and staff, the obsolescence of technology, system integrity and the overall complexity of the electronic environment;
- the combination of the components of internal control (the control environment, the risk assessment process, the information system, control activities and monitoring, as described in Chapter 7) in the e-commerce system. It is important for the auditors to understand the information technology security and system controls to minimise risks;

- frequent monitoring by management to ensure that irregular, improper, unusual and abnormal items are investigated, so the system can be improved and updated regularly. Furthermore, the entity may experience different types of problem in various sectors, or different rates of growth, so it needs to scale its e-commerce operations and development to reflect the resources required;
- management's attitude to, awareness of, and actions regarding internal control and maintenance of the e-commerce environment;
- system failures either at the organisational level or from outsourced operations, which may have a significant impact on the entity's earnings and reputation. The auditors should consider the risks relating to the business continuity aspects of the e-commerce environment;
- matters such as those affected by disintermediation (e.g. inventory held, overdue accounts, forecasts and budgets), the difficulties of relying on data produced for e-commerce, and going-concern issues;
- materiality issues, which involve not only quantitative measures but also qualitative matters. Auditors will consider the materiality of financial data on e-commerce without traditional benchmarks; and
- the fact that many e-businesses report a financial loss during their initial stage of e-commerce. The auditors should consider the economic impact of the e-commerce activities, the integrity and reliability of the entity's financial data, and the viability of maintaining continuous on-line activities. They must use professional judgement to assess the appropriateness of the going-concern assumptions of the financial statements and the adequacy of disclosures.

CYBER CRIMES AND FORENSIC AUDITING

The cyber world is a new arena for risk managers and businesses – one in which the risks are unclear yet dwarf exposures in the physical sense. Distributed denial-of-service (DDOS) attacks, like the ones launched by hackers against Yahoo! and other sites in February 2000, are more than just tremendous business interruption losses. Such events are an emerging area of concern called downstream liability. Some of the new e-commerce insurance policies offer coverage (up to US$25 million) at a price somewhere between 2 and 3.5% of the limits purchased, yet the potential policy holder must undergo an extensive audit of its computer systems, networks, on-line marketplaces, security measures, etc.

In this section we will offer a basic appreciation of (1) the extent and nature of electronic crimes that impose significant risks on e-commerce activities, and (2) the objectives of forensic auditing.

Cyber crimes and electronic crimes

The complexity of the information economy, the reliance of business on technology, and the increasing amount of interconnectivity among organisations are a result of and a driver for e-commerce. These widespread developments have created opportunities for theft, fraud and other forms of exploitation by offenders both outside and inside organisations. As businesses grow, their networked systems become increasingly sophisticated and less dependent on human intervention. Monitoring individual behaviour becomes difficult and vulnerability to electronic crimes (e-crimes) grows as organisations are increasingly connected to, and reliant on, individuals and systems outside their control. Most are alert to the risks posed by electronic viruses.

Denial-of-service attacks, including the launch of viruses, can be perpetrated internally or externally. They disable network and e-commerce services. These attacks use the large-scale communications bandwidth of an intermediary to overwhelm their victims' systems with meaningless service requests, thereby degrading or denying legitimate users any service. But criminals are doing much more – everything from stealing intellectual property and committing fraud to unleashing viruses and committing acts of cyber terrorism in which political groups or unfriendly governments disseminate crucial information. As the broadband technology catches on, the Internet will go from being the occasional dial-up service to being 'always on', much like the telephone. That concept may be beneficial to e-tailers, but could pose a real danger to consumers and e-commerce activities.

Ernst & Young, in an international survey conducted in October 1999, found that computer fraud was viewed as a threat to organisations more than any other type of fraud and 60% of respondents feared that such fraud was likely or very likely to occur within their organisation. The kinds of computer frauds that presented the greatest concern were those that involved manipulation of data records or computer programs to disguise the true nature of transactions, hacking into an organisation's computer system to steal or to manipulate business information, and unauthorised transfers of funds electronically. Similarly, KPMG, in a Global eFraud survey, found that 39% of respondents said that security and privacy issues prevented their company from implementing an electronic commerce system. Seventy-nine per cent of respondents indicated that a security breach to their electronic commerce system would most likely result from a breach caused via the Internet or other external access.

Not all computer crimes are Internet related. E-crime perpetrators can be either external or internal, or they can be just computer-systems related. External attackers are either sophisticated 'crackers' who develop and use technology-based tools that facilitate illegal entry into a victim's network system or other technologies, or just 'cookbook' crackers. ('Cookbook' crackers, who lack the knowledge, skills and abilities to create and use more sophisticated tools, seek out such tools to launch attacks.) Internal attackers, on the other hand, can include dissatisfied current employees working alone or with other insiders or ex-employees. Some experts consider that organisations face greater risk from the fraudulent acts of their own employees or former employees with knowledge of their systems.

In a publication by KPMG, a number of factors were cited as giving rise to the increase of e-commerce frauds. These include:

- poor security of access devices and passwords;
- the ease with which valuable products and funds can be moved around the globe;
- the breakdown of traditional internal controls which were replaced by poorly understood systems controls; and
- the growing acceptance of certain levels of fraud in doing business.

KPMG also listed a number of e-frauds and suggested mitigation strategies. These are summarised in Table 16.2.

Table 16.2 Common e-frauds encountered by businesses

E-FRAUD TYPE	DESCRIPTION	MITIGATION STRATEGY
False Internet shopfront	False website offerings which can only accept orders upon credit card details. Fraudsters process credit cards and close down site before investigation.	Verification of supplier before making purchase.
Trafficking in credit card numbers	Increased amount of trades in credit card details easily spread in the Internet, and small amount not requiring authorisation is a major threat.	Anti-fraud systems to detect unusual spending pattern by card holder; validity of card number checks.
Fictitious merchant	Fraudster establishes a merchant facility with the bank or credit card service, then processes claims for goods purchased using stolen or fabricated credit card numbers.	Verification of bona fide applicants for new merchant facilities by banks.
Fraudulent purchase orders	Fictitious orders for the supply of goods or electronic transfers of valuables, with a stolen credit card and a false address.	Verification of identity of customers by e-tailers.
Privacy	Purchasers of downloadable product can electronically copy the purchased item and offer it for resale.	Electronic security, hardware solutions, dial up password, etc. should be used.
On-line funds transfer	An employee who gains access to on-line banking system of employer and transfers sums to accounts controlled by him/her.	Compliance procedures with ID and password for on-line banking, regular audit of compliance and investigation of breaches. Daily bank reconciliation.
Internet banking fraud	Fraudsters gain access to individual banking facilities and transfer funds to a controlled account.	Strict confidentiality and security over banking details.

Source: adapted from KPMG, 'e-Commerce Fraud Uncovered', *Fighting Fraud: Forensic Accounting* (issue 9, 2001), pp. 3–5.

Forensic auditing

A forensic audit is an effective investigative tool to help combat fraudulent claims. Such an audit investigates the causes and effect of possibly fraudulent activities or system failures that may be the consequences of fraud. The forensic auditor looks for evidence of fraud, documents system failures and identifies the extent of losses incurred. A forensic audit may be held in response to a claim against an entity as a result of intentional or unintentional failures of e-commerce transactions. Forensic audits can also be employed for an insurer to evaluate the liability of a claim (e.g. a disability claim through a work-related accident; a system failure claim through a computer crash; and so on).

It is not uncommon for professional accountants to be engaged as forensic auditors. The accountant is experienced in identifying evidence and is able to evaluate losses such as loss of earnings. Typical materials reviewed in a forensic audit concerning e-commerce include all system documentation, log trailers, authorisation signatories, transaction reports and registers.

The forensic auditor should be capable of understanding the network systems and should seek symptoms using specially designed programs (e.g. a data analysis program). A forensic audit involving the e-commerce environment may feature:

- comparing employee e-mails and addresses, log-on times and messages;
- searching for duplicate numbers on payments or receipts;
- scanning lists of suppliers, customers and inventory movements;
- analysing the sequence of transactions to identify the intervention by unauthorised personnel; and
- finding users of the same addresses and signalling phantom users.

A proactive, critical approach to controlling e-commerce transactions is necessary to minimise risks. The forensic auditor may be able to identify suspicious matters in the process, but the skilful evaluation of the results will demand professional judgement, competence and experience.

◁ LEARNING **CHECK**

16.5 Auditors must understand the implications of the e-commerce transaction cycle, which includes information sharing, on-line submission, fulfilment of orders, service and support systems.

16.6 Different types of audit and assurance service available for e-commerce include those relating to risk analysis, system selection, customer service, security reviews, on-line audits on information quality, review of the maintenance and monitoring of e-commerce systems, internal control audits and continuous audits.

16.7 IAPS 1013 provides guidance on auditing in an e-commerce environment and in the areas of the required skills and knowledge, knowledge of the business, risk identification, internal control considerations, and the effect of electronic records on audit evidence.

16.8 With the increasing concerns to combat cyber crimes, forensic auditing has been developed to investigate the causes and effects of electronic crimes, including cyber crimes. The auditor is experienced in identifying evidences to evaluate losses attributable to an identifiable occurrence of e-commerce.

SUMMARY

This chapter discussed the development of the information economy and the emerging significance of e-commerce. It presented a conceptual model of the information economy (with infrastructure, applications, intermediation and e-commerce layers), and identified the emergence of e-commerce as the highest level of an information economy, using all aspects of the economy in an integrated manner. The nature and development of e-commerce was described, highlighting the wide-ranging implications for business managers and accountants in terms of the changes in business processes and strategies, technological and organisational infrastructures, and the role of professional accountants in performing audit and other assurance services.

The latter part of the chapter described the audit risk and control considerations to be evaluated by auditors in an e-commerce environment. The latest auditing guideline issued by the profession – IAPS 1013, Electronic Commerce – Effect on the Audit of Financial Statements – was discussed. The considerations include planning matters, risk assessment, control issues such as security of data, transaction integrity, process alignment and electronic record maintenance. Furthermore, an overview of audit and assurance issues in relation to e-commerce highlighted the impact on the approach adopted by auditors in providing an audit and assurance engagement service. The final part of the chapter looked at an inherent risk in e-commerce – cyber crimes. The nature and development of e-crimes was described, and the scope of forensic auditing was explored.

NOTES

[1] Fisher, L. 'E-commerce – A Threat or a Challenge?', *Accounting & Business* (March 2000), pp. 20–21.

[2] Austin Center for Research in Electronic Commerce, *Report of the Internet Economy Indicators*, University of Texas, 1999.

[3] Porter, M. *Competitive Advantage*, The Free Press, New York, 1985.

[4] Merrill Lynch, *E-commerce Virtually Here*, Global Securities Research and Economic Working Group, 1999.

[5] See Note 3.

[6] American Institute of Certified Public Accountants (AICPA) and the Canadian Institute of Chartered Accountants (CICA), *Continuous Auditing*, 2000. The CICA's Auditing Standards Board commissioned a research report on the viability of 'continuous assurance services' and the significant issues that auditors may likely encounter when performing them. The AICPA supported the initiative and appointed members to the study group.

FURTHER READING

Attaway Sr, M. C. 'What Every Auditor Needs to Know about E-commerce', *The Internal Auditor* (June 2000), pp. 56–60.

Bierstaker, J. L., Burnaby, P. & Thibodeau, J. 'The Impact of Information Technology on the Audit Process: An Assessment of the State of the Art and Implications for the Future', *Managerial Auditing Journal* (Vol. 16, No. 3, 2001), pp. 159–164.

Ceniceros, R. 'Understanding the Risks of E-commerce', *Business Insurance* (16 October 2000), p. 38.

Coderre, D. G. 'Computer-assisted Fraud Detection', *The Internal Auditor* (August 2000), pp. 25–27.

Conley, J. 'Outwitting Cybercriminals', *Risk Management* (July 2000), pp. 18–26.

Gatti, J. 'Integrating Hotdata into CRM and E-business Systems', *Direct Marketing* (June 2000).

Groomer, S. M. 'Continuous Audits: The Wave of the Future', *Infotech Update* (July–August 1999), pp. 1 and 5.

Helms, G. L. & Lilly, F. L. 'Case Study on Auditing in an Electronic Environment', *CPA Journal* (April 2000), pp. 52–54.

Huss, H. F., Jacobs, F. A., Patterson, D. A. & Park, M. 'An Integrative Model of Risk Management in Auditing', *American Business Review* (June 2000), pp. 113–122.

Kosiur, D. *Understanding Electronic Commerce*. Strategic Technology Series, Microsoft Press, Washington DC, 1997.

KPMG Forensic and Litigation Services. *E-commerce and Cyber Crime: New Strategies for Managing the Risks of Exploitation*. 2000.

Pathak, J. 'Assurance and E-auctions: Are the Existing Business Models Still Relevant?', *Managerial Auditing Journal* (Vol. 18, No. 4, 2003), pp. 292–296.

PricewaterhouseCoopers. *Retail Industry's First E-Commerce Roadmap*, Retail Systems 2000, Chicago, 2000.

PricewaterhouseCoopers. *Business Information for Corporate General Counsel*, February 2000. Web site: www.pwcglobal.com

Rezaee, Z., Elam, R. & Sharbatoghlie, A. 'Continuous Auditing: The Audit of the Future', *Managerial Auditing Journal* (Vol. 16, No. 3, 2001), pp. 150–158.

Rezaee, Z. & Reinstein, A. 'The Impact of Emerging Information Technology on Auditing', *Managerial Auditing Journal* (Vol. 13, No. 8, 1998), pp. 465–471.

Ros, L. 'New Economy, New Accounting, New Assurance', *Accountancy* (February 2001), pp. 116–117.

Turner, C. *The Information Economy, Business Strategies for Competing in the Digital Age*, Kogan Page, United Kingdom, 2000.

Williams, K. 'Preparing Your Business for Secure E-commerce', *Strategic Finance* (September 2000), p. 21.

MULTIPLE-CHOICE QUESTIONS

(Answers are on page 606)

16.1 IAPS 1013 on e-commerce provides guidance for the auditor on:
   (a)   all types of e-commerce transactions.
   (b)   specific business-to-consumer transactions.
   (c)   authorised government-to-business transactions.
   (d)   financial statements which are affected by e-commerce.

16.2 The infrastructure layer of the information economy includes:
   (a)   multimedia applications.
   (b)   informediaries.
   (c)   the Internet.
   (d)   security systems.

16.3 The key aspects of a risk analysis on e-commerce are:
   (a)   inventory access.
   (b)   authenticity of buyers.
   (c)   security and operational risks.
   (d)   system selection and implementation.

16.4 An on-line audit is:
   (a)   carried out to evaluate the likely acceptance of on-line sites or services.

(b)   a typical audit of internal controls within e-commerce environment.

(c)   appropriate only after a web site for on-line service is built.

(d)   a continuous audit of client security systems and information.

16.5 Which of the following is not an internal control consideration in an e-commerce environment?

(a)   Ensuring client's staff possess Internet skills and knowledge.

(b)   Evaluating security controls of transactions through the Internet.

(c)   Identifying transaction integrity by considering the information shared and monitored.

(d)   Examining alignment processes between the on-line shopfront and the reporting systems.

16.6 To assess the acceptance of electronic records as audit evidence, the auditor should consider:

(a)   detailed reconciliation between electronic records and manual entries.

(b)   the authenticity and accuracy of the customer database.

(c)   examining the internal and external security measures of the e-commerce environment.

(d)   performing verification procedures for information policies and proper implementation of controls.

16.7 Cyber crimes can be attributable to intrusion by:

(a)   international hacker groups.

(b)   existing and former employees.

(c)   competitors and fictitious customers.

(d)   all of the above.

16.8 In performing forensic auditing, the auditor should:

(a)   understand the network systems and seek symptoms of irregularities.

(b)   evaluate the person who identifies the fraud in the first instance.

(c)   destroy system log trails which are deemed unreliable.

(d)   disable the network in order to protect the systems.

16.9 Which of the following business risks is identified in IAPS 1013?

(a)   Loss of transaction integrity.

(b)   Non-compliance of regulatory matters relating to the Internet.

(c)   Security risks such as virus attacks or e-frauds.

(d)   All of the above.

DISCUSSION QUESTIONS

16.1 Identify examples of business-to-consumer e-commerce from your own experience and identify risk and security issues associated with your use of such web sites.

16.2 Identify and explain the key controls that are necessary in an e-commerce environment.

16.3 What is the potential impact of e-commerce on the public accounting profession (in addition to its role in financial statement audits)?

16.4 Given the total absence of a paper trail, is it possible for auditors to achieve as low a level of audit risk in reporting on an e-commerce business as for a conventional business?

16.5 Continuous auditing puts forward the premise that control over processes for capturing and recording data can be sufficiently reliable that all data recorded by the information system may be deemed reliable without the need for any substantive audit on that data. Discuss.

16.6 Explain the purpose of forensic auditing.

PROFESSIONAL APPLICATION QUESTIONS

(Suggested answers are on pages 658–659)

16.1 Forensic audit

The Standard Publishing Insurance Company provides cover for professional publishers. Cyber Publications recently filed a claim for the loss it incurred following a breakdown of its computer network in which its customers' files were lost. Cyber Publications sells business publications (magazines and newsletters) to 1,000 business customers through the Internet. The payment and delivery systems are also linked with the customers' files, held by the master e-commerce system. You are called in to conduct a forensic audit to establish the validity of the claim and the extent to which it is appropriate.

Required

Explain the key considerations of the forensic audit you will conduct.

16.2 Controls for electronic payment

Traditional financial transactions contain characteristics to safeguard the parties' interests by incorporating certain controls. In an electronic payment system using the Internet, the expectations of confidentiality of identities, the integrity of transaction details and the assurance that the parties to the contract are competent and trustworthy are pertinent to the businesses.

Required

Using the following headings, identify the controls you would expect to find in an e-commerce system:

(a) confidentiality of information;
(b) transaction integrity;
(c) authorisation of payments; and
(d) assurance of business credibility.

CONTEMPORARY ISSUES IN AUDITING

OVERVIEW

THE ROLE OF AUDITORS IN CORPORATE GOVERNANCE
Internal control and risk management
Earnings management
Audit independence
Audit quality
Ethical standards and the code of professional conduct
Auditing Standards and the internationalisation process
Reducing the expectation gap

INFORMATION TECHNOLOGY
Advances in financial software
The mobile Internet
Extensible Business Reporting Language (XBRL)

OTHER EMERGING ISSUES FACING THE AUDITING PROFESSION
Auditors' role on fraud and error
Forensic accounting and auditing
Changing landscape of accounting firms

QUALITY BENCHMARKING AND THE AUDITOR
The ISO 9000 series
Total quality management and the auditor

VALUE REPORTING AND ENVIRONMENTAL AUDITING
Value reporting
Developments in environmental auditing

SUMMARY

NOTES

FURTHER READING

PROFESSIONAL APPLICATION QUESTIONS

LEARNING **OBJECTIVES**

After studying this chapter, you should be able to:

1   discuss the role of the independent auditor in corporate governance

2   appreciate the latest developments in financial software, the mobile Internet and extensible business reporting language

3   describe emerging issues regarding fraud, forensic auditing and changes relating to the recent restructuring of audit firms

4   review some of the quality benchmarks applicable to independent auditors

5   define value reporting and describe its usage

6   describe the meaning of and standards for environmental auditing.

PROFESSIONAL STATEMENTS

ISA 315	Understanding the Entity and Its Environment and Assessing the Risks of Material Misstatement
ISA 220	Quality Control for Audit Engagements (Exposure draft)
ISA 240	The Auditors' Responsibility to Consider Fraud in an Audit of Financial Statements (Exposure draft)
ISQC 1	Quality Control for Audit, Assurance and Related Services Practices (Exposure draft)
IAPS 1010	The Consideration of Environmental Matters in the Audit of Financial Statements

Because of its importance in maintaining public confidence in the corporate sector and in ensuring appropriate resource usage and investment in maintaining a healthy economy, any lapse in audit quality is rightly viewed as a matter of concern. Efforts to maintain the quality of auditing in the light of changes in technology, financial markets and identified shortcomings are ongoing, and it is these efforts that are the subject of this chapter. Many recent developments have already been referred to in earlier chapters. This chapter consolidates some of the key aspects of these current developments in auditing. First of all, in light of recent initiatives in the interrelationships of financial reporting, auditing and corporate governance this chapter discusses the role of the auditor in the current development of corporate governance as considered by an International Federation of Accountants' (IFAC) Task Force and published in their report *Rebuilding Public Confidence in Financial Reporting*.[1] Issues covered include audit independence, audit quality, international auditing standards and the ethical behaviour of auditors. Other emerging issues to be examined are: information technology, forensic auditing, fraud and earnings management, value reporting and education and training of future auditors.

THE ROLE OF AUDITORS IN CORPORATE GOVERNANCE

Corporate governance refers to the structure, the systems and the relationships among parties such as the board of directors, management (including key officers), auditors and regulators on the one hand, and shareholders, employees, suppliers, customers and the broader community, often referred to collectively as stakeholders, on the other. The principles of corporate governance were introduced in Chapter 3 in the context of auditor independence. Recent corporate governance debates have raised concerns with respect to auditors' contribution to misrepresentation of financial statements relating to their ethical standards in general and independence in particular.

The existence of a credibility gap between the expected behaviour of auditors and the actual perceived behaviour of auditors has resulted in debates and reforms in corporate governance and the financial reporting regime. The recent report *Rebuilding Public Confidence in Financial Reporting* by the IFAC lists the following 10 main findings to address the current credibility crisis:

1. Effective corporate ethics codes need to be in place and actively monitored.
2. Corporate management must place greater emphasis on the effectiveness of financial management and controls.
3. Incentives to misstate financial information need to be reduced.
4. Boards of directors need to improve their oversight of management.
5. The threats to auditor independence need to receive greater attention in corporate governance processes and by auditors themselves.
6. Audit effectiveness needs to be raised primarily through greater attention to audit quality control processes.
7. Codes of conduct need to be put in place for other participants in the financial reporting process, and their compliance should be monitored.
8. Audit standards and regulation need to be strengthened.
9. Accounting and reporting practices need to be strengthened.
10. The standard of regulation of issuers needs to be raised.

It can be seen that accountants and auditors, the traditional gatekeepers of the financial reporting regime, play a significant role in strengthening corporate governance. From the above findings of the IFAC, in order to address the credibility crisis in corporate governance, the auditors' role can be summarised into the following categories:

- providing assurance of the integrity and reliability of the 'internal control and risk management' systems of clients;
- ensuring an awareness of, and performing relevant measures to detect, possible financial misstatements, such as 'earnings management' practices;
- ensuring 'audit independence' through safeguards and professional development programmes;
- enhancing 'audit quality control' processes;
- actively practising the 'code of conduct';
- monitoring the development of and adherence to 'Auditing Standards' nationally and internationally; and

- reducing the 'expectation gap' through communication, education and professional development.

These key roles are briefly discussed below.

Internal control and risk management

With respect to internal control and risk management systems, entities are now more vigilant in engaging and relying on the active involvement of internal auditors. With particular reference to the requirements of the Turnbull Report[2] and the *Sarbanes-Oxley Act*, chief executive and financial officers are expected to be able to 'certify' the adequacy of the internal control and risk management systems. The CEOs and CFOs are, therefore, more inclined to seek the expertise of internal auditors, especially as the Turnbull Report requires companies without such a function to assess, annually, the need for such a function. Management of large organisations and other companies, including the public sector, have developed different processes to identify and manage risk across the entity. While there are considerable amounts of information about risk management, no common terminology exists. The Audit Faculty of the ICAE&W defines risk management as being:

> about identifying and assessing key risks, and then designing and implementing processes by which those risks can be managed to, and be maintained at, a level acceptable to the board. To ensure the effective direction and use of the organisations' resources to manage these risks, the board should:
>
> - Have a clear understanding and assessment of the risks;
> - Ensure that the organisation has effective risk management and control processes; and
> - Be provided with assurance that the processes and the key business risks are being effectively managed.[3]

Internationally, in July 2003, the COSO Enterprise Risk Management (ERM) framework was introduced by the Committee of Sponsoring Organisations of the Treadway Commission (COSO) to integrate the principles of internal control and risk management. The framework details the essential components of enterprise risk management and the context in which they are effectively implemented. Key concepts that relate to the effective application of the principles and components are outlined.[4] Further, the framework identifies the interrelationships between risk and enterprise risk management, and with COSO's Internal Control – Integrated Framework, published in 1992.

It is increasingly recognised by company management and auditors that entities face uncertainty, and the challenge for them is to determine how much uncertainty the entity is prepared to accept. Value is created, or added, while decisions are made with an appropriate degree of recognition of risk and opportunity, requiring the management and auditors to consider the nature and extent of information to be used, and of the structure and processes to be put in place. Enterprise Risk Management is defined as:

> A process, effected by an entity's board of directors, management and other personnel, applied in strategy setting and across the enterprise, designed to identify

potential events that may affect the entity, and manage risks to be within its risk appetite, to provide reasonable assurance regarding the achievement of entity objectives. (page 3)

The ERM consists of eight interrelated components. These processes are derived from the way management runs a business:

- Internal environment where management establishes a risk management philosophy, the risk-taking approach (i.e. appetite for risk), in order to form a risk culture while integrating risk management with related initiatives.
- Risk objectives are set in four categories: strategic, operations, reporting and compliance. Some organisations include the objective of safeguarding of resources. These objectives allow management and the board to focus on separate aspects of risk management.
- Event identification is a process where both external and internal factors that might affect event occurrence are considered. The identification methodology may comprise a combination of techniques and tools, looking at both past and the future.
- Risk assessment then allows an entity to consider how potential events might affect the achievement of objectives. Two perspectives are determined: likelihood and impact.
- Risk response options are identified by management which considers the event impact in relation to risk tolerances, evaluates costs and benefits, and designs and implements response options.
- Control activities are the policies and procedures that ensure risk responses are properly executed throughout the organisation, at all levels and in all functions. Control activities are closely aligned with general and application controls discussed in Chapter 7.
- Pertinent information and effective communication are required to ensure enterprise risk management responses to changing conditions in real time. Information can be quantitative, qualitative, internal and external. Communication channels should also ensure personnel can communicate risk-based information across business units, processes or functions.
- Monitoring, a process that assesses both the presence and functioning of the ERM components and the quality of their performance over time. Monitoring can be done either as an ongoing exercise or a separate evaluation process.

As there is a direct relationship between objectives, components and units, the ERM matrix in Figure 17.1 provides an overview.

ISA 315, Understanding the Entity and Its Environment and Assessing the Risks of Material Misstatement, requires auditors to perform risk assessment procedures to obtain an understanding of the components of internal control. Auditors use professional judgement to assess audit risk and to design audit procedures to ensure it is reduced to an acceptably low level. It can be appreciated that in assessing the internal control components, auditors should gain an understanding whether the internal controls can ensure that the conduct of the business is orderly, including the ability to prevent and detect fraud, error and non-compliance, and the misappropriation of assets. The assessment of inherent and control risks by the auditor can be informed by the ERM

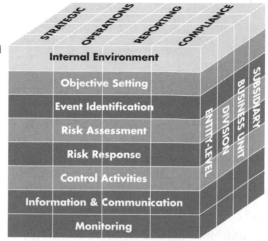

- The four objectives categories – strategic, operations, reporting and compliance – are represented by the vertical columns.

- The eight components are represented by horizontal rows.

- The entity and its organizational units are depicted by the third dimension of the matrix.

Source: Committee of Sponsoring Organizations of the Treadway Commission, 2003, Enterprise Risk Management Framework (draft version) Exhibit 1, p. 16.

Figure 17.1 *Relationship of objectives and components of ERM*

Table 17.1 Possible relationships between audit risk components (inherent and control risks) and the ERM components

COMPONENTS	STRATEGIC	OPERATIONS	REPORTING	COMPLIANCE	RESOURCES
Internal environment	I	C	C	I, C	I
Risk objectives	I	I	I	I	I
Event identification	I	I, C	C	I, C	I, C
Risk assessment	I	I	I	I	I, C
Response options	I	C	C	C	C
Control activities	N/A	C	C	C	I
Information and communication	I	C	C	I, C	I
ERM monitoring	I	C	C	C	I

Key:
I – Inherent risks
C – Control risks

framework, where objectives such as strategic, operations, reporting, compliance and resources can be categorised, as suggested in Table 17.1. Table 17.1 lists, in the left-hand column, the eight components of ERM. The auditors' assessment of inherent risk and control risk can link with each of the eight components, where each component is then viewed according to the risk objectives at strategic, operations, reporting, compliance and resource management levels. The table suggests that some of the components can form the basis of the auditors' determination of inherent risks (I), while others can be used to identify control risks (C).

Earnings management

The concept of earnings management has been around for some time. Earnings management occurs when judgement in selecting accounting policies and estimation techniques and in structuring transactions is used to alter financial statements in order to influence the impression about the underlying economic substance of the transactions or the economic performance of the entity. Such practice may affect the transparency and objectivity in the preparation of the financial reports. An extreme case of aggressive behaviour in relation to earnings management can amount to fraud.

Due to the subsequent disclosure of many earnings management practices by failed companies like Enron and WorldCom, there is now a heightened attention to the ability of auditors in detecting earnings management practices. The APB issued a consultation paper in 2001, highlighting some management incentives of which the auditors should be aware.[5]

Inherent to the management structure are incentives for earnings management. These incentives can be behavioural, such as political considerations, executive remuneration, or the ambiguity and inability of Financial Reporting Standards in dealing with complex transactions, or situations including financial distress, related party transactions, etc. The capital market may also present incentives where pressure comes from market expectations, analysts' forecasts, management transition, etc.

As indicated in the consultation paper, many of the earnings management techniques involve accruals, revenue recognition, restructuring charges, estimation of liabilities, delaying sales, manipulating research and development write-offs, etc. Auditors should attend to relevant guidelines as listed in the consultation paper, and maintain professional scepticism in management judgement. ISA 240, The Auditors' Responsibility to Consider Fraud in an Audit of Financial Statements (Exposure draft), also identifies earnings management as an area of concern.

Audit independence

Chapter 3 discussed in detail the independence debate and reforms. There are two schools of thought; a prescriptive rule-based model and a 'comply or explain' principle-based model. Under a rule-based model, the appointment, the scope of non-audit services, the independence and the discussion of audit issues are brought within a legal/third party regime, in which statutory processes replace the autonomy and the self-regulatory aspects of the profession. The 'comply or explain' principle-based model allows auditors to strive for best practice in the areas of independence safeguards. The reform of audit independence is still undergoing debate and the outcome will undoubtedly change the landscape of the professional firms. The USA has chosen the former approach with its passage of the *Sarbanes-Oxley Act*. The UK has moved responsibility for providing guidelines on independence away from bodies controlled directly by the profession, but the ultimate sanctions for non-compliance remain with the profession.

Audit quality

While audit quality is an overcrowning concept representing the adherence to independence, ensuring auditor competence, due diligence and quality control processes, audit quality continues to be a key issue. Following the corporate collapses, firms are seen to be reverting to basic audit techniques such as substantive auditing, in order to minimise audit risks. At the same time, Auditing Standards are placing greater emphasis on risk assessment, whatever audit technique is subsequently employed.

As part of the follow-up to the recent corporate collapses, the IAASB undertook a project to review its standards and guidance on quality control, as a response to the public demands in strengthening the quality of audits and firms' quality control practices. The project was to produce two separate quality control standards, namely ISQC 1: International Quality Control Standards No. 1 at firm level, and revised ISA 220 at engagement level.

Firms are required to comply with ISQC1 for all professional work undertaken by the practice whereas revised ISA 220 only applies to audit engagements. Some significant changes for ISA 220 include guidelines concerning:

- leadership and responsibilities of the engagement partner;
- ethics and expanded requirements with regards to independence on audit engagements;
- engagement performance of the engagement partner and the support team;
- engagement quality control review; and
- monitoring, including communication with the responsible parties within the firm regarding formal complaints and allegations of performance failure.

While there is no one factor contributing to audit quality, the support culture and the integrity of the firm and its audit staff are paramount. 'A firm which typically provides professional opinions to its non-audit clients which push the envelope to the edge of acceptable practice, is less likely to make a stand on an audit issue. Such an auditor probably lacks integrity, not independence', says Sean Van Gorp, Head of Audit and Assurance Services, Ernst & Young (2002). The abstract that follows provides an insight.

Ethical standards and the code of professional conduct

The IFAC issued an exposure draft *Proposed Revised Code of Ethics for Professional Accountants* in July 2003. The exposure draft adopts a framework approach, where risks and safeguards for ethical conduct are identified. The IFAC Ethics Committee believes that such a framework approach is preferable to a rules-based approach to ethics which cannot provide for all circumstances, and may lead to unquestioning obedience to the letter of a rule while setting definitive lines in legislation that some will try to circumnavigate.

The Revised Code offers guidelines on maintaining 'the public interest' and identifies threats and conflicts which accountants and auditors may encounter. It is divided into three parts: Part A applies to all professional accountants; Part B to professional accountants in public practice; and Part C to professional accountants in business. Part A sets out the fundamental principles and explains the framework approach. It also sets out the categories into which many threats to compliance with the fundamental principles may fall, with examples of safeguards created by the profession, legislation or regulation. Public interest has become the overriding key to the remaining principles of: integrity, objectivity, professional competence and due care, confidentiality and professional behaviour.[6]

Aside from compliance with and monitoring of the Code of Ethics, there is also a general concern about means to enhance ethical standards. Ethics can be said to be a matter of judgement and choice, not rules. The professional bodies, together with accounting educators and researchers, are actively looking into ways in which accountants and auditors are more sensitised with potential conflicts and ethical issues. Furthermore, in order to provide sufficient professional support, the professional bodies are committed to strengthen facilities such as ethical training, continual professional education and the monitoring of disciplinary measures.

Auditing Standards and the internationalisation process

As from 2005, auditors in the European Union and many other countries such as Australia will conduct their audits in accordance with International Standards on Auditing (ISAs). Auditors should report, in the Scope section of their report, that their audit has been conducted in accordance with ISAs.

The IFAC has also set up a Transnational Auditors Committee. Transnational audits are those on financial statements that are relied upon outside of the entity's home jurisdiction for significant investment, lending or regulatory decisions. The IFAC has invited firms engaged in transnational audits to join its Forum of Firms and to submit to having their compliance with quality control standards monitored. At a minimum, these firms are required to have policies and procedures for ensuring that transnational audits will be conducted in accordance with International Standards on Auditing, and that the firm complies with the IFAC Code of Ethics. Member firms must also maintain training programmes to ensure that partners and staff engaged on transnational audits are up to date with international standards.

The US *Sarbanes-Oxley Act* requires that all auditing firms engaged in the audit of entities listed on US stock markets register with the Professional Oversight Board and submit to monitoring of their compliance with the relevant terms of the Act. This applies not only to principal auditors of groups whose shares are listed in the USA but also to the auditors of US controlled subsidiary entities. There has been some concern that this represents unwarranted interference by the US in the domestic affairs of those countries in which the audit firms are based. However, this reflects the transnational nature of much audit activity. Moreover, concern has been muted by recognition that the effect will be to improve the quality of auditing generally without the need for introducing domestic legislation.

Reducing the expectation gap

Following the recent corporate governance and audit reforms, there has been an increasing demand for changes to the wording of the independent auditors' report in order to better explain what an audit is and what an audit report means. In particular there is renewed interest in separating the opinions on truth and fairness and on compliance with a financial reporting framework.

 ## LEARNING **CHECK**

17.1 The role of auditors in corporate governance includes providing assurance on internal control and the risk management system and ensuring awareness of earnings management practices.

17.2 Corporate governance also requires ensuring auditor independence, enhancing audit quality, ensuring compliance with the code of conduct, monitoring the standards and reducing the expectation gap.

INFORMATION TECHNOLOGY

Information technology is rapidly changing the global business market. It is altering not only the way in which business is conducted, but also the way in which information is accessed. These developments present auditors and accountants with a major challenge. Fundamental to the ability to deal with the pace of change in professional practice is an ability to manage change itself – to capitalise on the opportunities presented, and to recognise real and potential threats.

Key considerations of information technology and e-commerce have been dealt with in Chapter 16 and elsewhere. This chapter focuses on the advances being made in financial software, the mobile Internet and extensible business reporting language.

Advances in financial software

An organisation's financial systems are the most important software it operates. However, although technological advancements are typically widely reported, developments in financial software are often less publicised. This possibly is fuelled by the traditional perception that financial software – affording a means to record transactions, finalise annual accounts and perhaps to write management reports – is understood only by accountants. The reality is, however, that reliable financial software is crucially important to anyone concerned with managing finances efficiently and effectively, whether they are accountants, financial controllers, managers, business advisers or auditors. It is a prerequisite not only for business success but also for survival, because every organisation now does business by computer. Financial software is needed to keep track of business performance, access significant business data, identify problems, evaluate plans and formulate strategies.

A survey conducted of more than 600 chief financial officers of large and small government and private enterprises in Australia and New Zealand over a period of three years (1995–97) identified a continuing high degree of volatility in financial systems.[7] It found that an abnormally high number of organisations were changing their financial software and that many had lowered their expectations as to how long their software would last. The survey results showed, for example, that one third of the market had recently changed its financial system software, and about another third was doing so. Only about one third of the market had remained stable, uncertain about what to do in this regard. The average life span of an organisation's core financial systems was found to be 5.6 years, compared with 7.7 years for previous systems. This abnormal degree of volatility means that, to be effective, auditors must not only understand the rationale for changes in entities' financial systems (and the factors that influence such changes) but also appreciate the technological differences they may confront and be able to adjust their approach accordingly. Contemporary organisations need to be able to react sooner, access information more quickly and report it faster.

Information technology has been both a cause and effect of changes that have occurred in the business world over the past 10 years or so. There are three major developments, each a consequence of the previous one. First, desktop computers have proliferated to the point that they are now an indispensable business tool. Second, these computers have been networked to each other and to larger computers. Third, the focus of larger computers has changed from providing information to a few individuals to providing information across the organisation. As these changes have accelerated, they have demanded more from the technology that spawned them. The whole 'client–server' revolution – the key trend in information technology in the 1990s – was driven by the need for information systems to reflect more closely changed business imperatives. It is simply not possible to use the modern business model with old technology. Businesses and governments need access to timely business information, which can be delivered only by systems that integrate corporate data with end-user systems. It is therefore not surprising that businesses continue to look for new software to satisfy their needs.

The three primary reasons for changes in financial software are:

1. poor support by the software supplier (e.g. in providing expert advice, in supporting the implementation process, and in providing maintenance and upgrading services);
2. outmoded technology (e.g. where the supplier has not kept up to date with technological advances); and
3. the supplier going out of business.

An investigation conducted into a range of accounting software (such as ACCPAC and Visual Accounting), including the respective audit trails, controls and reporting functions, revealed some shortcomings.[8] For example, some packages retained journal data only until they were posted. However, such shortcomings have now been rectified and most systems retain journals for a year or longer. In addition, they now all assign sequential transaction numbers for identification, and print journals in transaction number order. Notwithstanding these recent improvements, some concerns about audit trails and controls still exist.

To provide adequate financial services and audits to clients, professional accountants must be aware of the business needs of their clients (and, therefore, of the limitations and strengths of financial software being used or being considered to meet those needs). Matters that accountants and auditors need to consider can be classified into the following categories:

- clients' business needs in terms of financial software;
- considerations when implementing financial software;
- audit trails in financial software; and
- necessary internal control features of financial software.

CLIENTS' BUSINESS NEEDS IN TERMS OF FINANCIAL SOFTWARE

It is imperative that any financial system be reliable. Auditors must, therefore, be aware when an entity's financial software presents problems (such as errors occurring due to functional limitations, a failure to detect errors or, simply, inadequate information being produced from clumsy data processing mechanisms). Quite often, accountants and auditors become involved in providing essential advice for the selection and implementation of financial software.

Experience has shown that many organisations make mistakes by opting to use complicated spreadsheet models rather than common-sense. Failure to prioritise their system requirements has meant that some businesses have not focused on the major feature (or limitations) of a financial package. One chief financial officer, for example, chose a complex spreadsheet model with complicated weightings only to discover that the selected package could not import files from various company databases, and that it was very weak in its ability to support multiple operating sites.

What one company considers a key feature may not necessarily be of crucial importance for others. Desirable features include flexible reporting, a single point of data entry, reliability and accessibility by spreadsheet, end-user access, flexibility in structure, on-line analysis, and the ability to work on different scales or levels of operation.

CONSIDERATIONS WHEN IMPLEMENTING FINANCIAL SOFTWARE

Once financial software is chosen as a prospective purchase (or identified as being preferable), the management of the business should develop a full list of the key issues to be addressed, so all parties concerned can consider them in detail. These parties include the vendor, the accountants, the auditors and other system analysts. The list of issues should be ranked in terms of importance. As has already been stressed in this chapter, flexible and timely financial management information systems are no longer a luxury – they are a necessity

Factors to consider include those detailed below:

- *Reporting capabilities*: The most important issue for accountants and auditors in their use of financial software is the ability to extract information. This entails consideration of the system's report writing capabilities and, often, the entity's executive information system requirements. Another issue is the ability to download data into spreadsheets.
- *Integration with other systems*: It is important that data from entity financial systems are able to interface with audit software and other expert analysis systems. Integration facilities may also mean that the financial software can interface with (or extract information from) other operating systems such as stock control, production management and credit control management files.
- *Flexibility and adaptability*: A financial system must be capable of flexible reporting, conversion or automatic adaptation to new environments such as those that involve different versions of a software, different currencies or multiple applications.

- *User friendly*: Ease of use is crucial to ensure that new software can be taught to and applied by staff (including non-financial personnel) as quickly and easily as possible. End-user requirements should be explained.
- *Timeliness and time pressure*: The new software needs to be able to respond quickly to changing demands and regular reporting requirements such as the end-of-month reporting. It needs also to be able to identify discrepancies quickly and to cope with a high volume of transactions.
- *Accessibility of data*: Different levels of data access must be specified and controlled. There must be ease of interrogation.
- *Expandability and upgradability*: Information technology is continuing to develop rapidly, so all financial software must be capable of future expansion. Its facilities must be able to be upgraded to meet both increasing technological demands and an increasing volume of data processing.
- *Data integrity and security*: The auditor must be satisfied with the physical security and data integrity within the system. They must be built into every phase of the operation and every function. This is the part of the system where audit trails exist and where internal controls are established to maintain the integrity and reliability of the information.
- *Reliability*: The system must be reliable in terms of its hierarchical security options, support mechanisms, information loads, etc.
- *Cost*: The issue of cost involves value for money, ensuring that the software does what is needed and that it provides assurance for future support and maintenance. Other issues that need to be considered are the limitations on existing resources, the implementation cost and budgetary constraints.

AUDIT TRAILS IN FINANCIAL SOFTWARE

The audit trail is an essential element in ensuring the reliability of financial software. Apart from the considerations raised earlier in this text, the auditor needs to be aware of the following issues:

- An audit trail should provide a means of tracing a transaction from its origin to the financial statements, and vice versa. Establishing a source document field (which accepts the identity of any source document, enabling an authorised user to look up the transaction by referring to that identity) is an additional useful feature. A look-up screen is also helpful for auditors.
- While most accounting software provides a listing of ledgers, some modules still do not have ledgers, preventing the accounting package from transferring all the transactions in debtors, creditors and stock to the general ledger. A continuing audit trail deficiency is the inability to trace entries easily from the ledger accounts to their original journal source.
- An audit trail that shows the flow of data among the various modules in an accounting package enables the auditor to examine either summary data or subsidiary modules. This depends on the availability of ledger modules and proper referencing or identification. An additional advantage is the possibility of using several modules at the same time, using Windows technology.

NECESSARY INTERNAL CONTROL FEATURES OF FINANCIAL SOFTWARE
In terms of internal control, the following are some essential features of which auditors must be aware:

- The Windows environment supports only passwords for access controls. The assignment of different passwords to individual users is a better control than a shared task password system. Password systems should require users to select hard-to-guess passwords, preferably with a minimum length of six characters (made up of a combination of alphabetic and numeric characters and other keyboard symbols).
- An ineffective program control exists when accounting software is not written in a compiler-based language. Those failing to use the compiled programming code rely on the programming ignorance of users, which is a risky security method.
- An effective way of protecting data files from exposure to unauthorised entry is to use encryption. However, while it may be an effective safeguard, encryption has drawbacks: first, storing encrypted data requires additional space and more processing time, and second, the higher the level of encryption, the more costly its implementation.
- Proper input controls ensure data input errors can be detected. Some data filters for account identifiers are code checks and check digits. However, a wrong but valid identification code depends on a visual check of the accuracy of code checks. Therefore, a screen confirmation must be in place to ensure its effectiveness. Check digits should also use audible checks.
- Processing controls can be established with electronic checklists that guide users in the proper sequence of operations. Interim print-outs can be made for checking purposes. Electronic archiving, however, is superior to hard copy, not only because access is easier, cheaper and can be controlled, but also because it is easier to store duplicates in alternative locations for security. A warning should be provided where the sequential checks are violated.
- Other controls – such as output controls, controls over changes to accounts without transactions, and reporting capabilities – are essential concerns for auditors. Commonly found controls include date–time stamps on output, access logs, authorisation for master file changes, and so on. A reporting capability now being used is the 'drill-down' method. This entails viewing an account balance, 'drilling down' to the details and, after selecting an item in the account, 'drilling down' even further to the underlying journal entry, and then to an on-line image of a transaction document.

Technology continues to change. It is essential, therefore, that auditors possess a general awareness of the contemporary developments in financial software if they are to provide effective advice on the selection and implementation of accounting programs. Financial software suppliers have completely rewritten their systems in recent years to take advantage of new technologies. A few years ago, for example, most practising accountants who used accounting software switched from DOS to the Windows environment. While some DOS accounting products continue to sell at a very modest price, most developers are either no longer updating their DOS products (choosing to continue them for as long as they keep selling) or abandoning them. Development efforts now focus on the Windows platform and some are written in Visual Basic. Demonstrating how fast Windows technology is moving, Microsoft NT is becoming the platform of choice for accounting programs. Developers have recognised that NT has the reliability and robustness needed for applications as mission critical as accounting processes. At the time of writing, financial software has been developed for enterprise solutions and small business accounting. Other integrated software for customer relationship management (CRM), human resources, manufacturing and e-business has also become mainstream.

The mobile Internet

The Internet is transforming traditional financial practices and services into a range of cheap commercial enterprising activities that are delivered quickly and easily accessed. The Internet provides an information-on-demand medium for electronic trading, the transmission of reports and documents, advanced software access, and virtual designs of goods and services.

Companies can deliver and use knowledge to produce relevant outcomes to suit immediate needs. On-line shopping and trading are already becoming a threat to many traditional market leaders. Chapter 16 provided an account of electronic commercial activity and the role of professional accountants, outlining the risks and issues such as security and certification. This chapter discusses the latest development in the Internet and communication technology – the mobile Internet and the emergence of mobile commerce (m-commerce).

The world's two fastest growing sectors – mobile technology and the Internet with broadband services – have converged into an opportunity that no organisation can afford to ignore. The revolution is called the mobile Internet, and it will have an immense impact on telecommunication systems, internet service providers and any organisation wishing to transact in the new information economy. The mobile phone has moved away from being solely a telephony service towards being a unique personal identifier and assistant. A wireless portal will be the norm for telecommunication systems and, soon, everyone and everything will become 'connected'. Some predict that within three years there will be more wireless connections to the Internet than fixed connections, and that the majority of e-commerce transactions will terminate or originate on a wireless device. A recent KPMG study on the mobile Internet listed examples of the global market trends[9]:

- Of current mobile traffic volume, 3% of second-generation mobile phones already offer basic data services. By 2003, more consumers will access the Internet via mobile phones than by personal computers.
- The market for m-commerce in Europe alone is estimated to be worth €23 million by 2003, compared with a mere €300,000 in 1998.
- The popularity of wireless devices for voice communications and the subsequent substitution of fixed telephones will accelerate the adoption of broadband mobile services.
- Mobile Internet-enabled laptops will free people from their desks, creating mobile offices, mobile application hosting and m-commerce.

Mobile Internet applications already exist in countries such as Japan and the US. Table 17.2 provides a summary of mobile Internet applications.

Table 17.2 Mobile Internet applications

SERVICES	DEVICE	AVAILABLE IN:
Lifestyle applications		
Remote access	E-mail, web browsers, televisions	Europe, Australia, Japan, the US
Information services	News, weather, stock prices, horoscopes, lottery, sports, train timetables, horse racing, public emergency	Europe, Australia, Japan, the US
Directory services	Restaurants, film sessions, television programmes, hotels, telephone directories, town listings, dictionaries, recipes	Europe, Australia, Japan, the US
Location-based services	Automatic teller machines, navigators	Europe, Australia, Japan, the US
Entertainment	Network games, karaoke, gambling, chat, jokes	Europe, Japan, Australia, the US
Interactive services	Banking, stock trading, ticket booking, on-line shopping, insurance, car rental, billing	Europe, Australia, Japan, the US
Telematics	Remote automative diagnostics	Europe
Telemetry	Vending machines, ticket machines, car parking	Japan
Mobile professional and business applications		
Videoconferencing	Videoconferencing	Japan
Remote access	E-mail, calendaring, shared scheduling, job postings, procedures manuals, corporate directories, bulletins, document sharing	Europe, Australia, Japan the US
Sales force and field automation	Customer account records, contact management, order entry/status, call scheduling, tracking, product/stock availability, delivery scheduling, on-site claims, loan/credit applications, interest rate information	–
Operations and maintenance	Remote machinery diagnostics, fleet tracking	–
E-tailing	Credit card authorisation, debit acceptance, smart cards, electronic funds transfer, identity verification	–

Survival of businesses in the mobile Internet economy will require a redevelopment of vision and a reorientation by businesspeople and managers with respect to the new technology. Speed, critical resource management, a solid customer base, and marketing and personalised services are key ingredients for survival. It is difficult to predict the ultimate impact on the functions of accountants and auditors, but professional accountants need to grasp the ongoing evolution in the role of operating systems such as financial management, customer support, reporting, risks and security measures for m-commercial transactions. Accountants may be required, for example, to provide assurance services in terms of:

- information risk management for clients in their management of technology and the security implications of mobile Internet-enhanced transactions;
- taxation advice on telecommunication operations on a global basis;
- the design, testing and implementation of customer support and billing systems; and
- financing decisions in the telecommunication industry, and in any likely mergers and acquisitions.

Extensible Business Reporting Language (XBRL)

The Extensible Business Reporting Language (XBRL) was developed by Charlie Hoffman, a USA Certified Public Accountant, who was looking for ways to transfer product pricing information from an accounting system to a web site. Hoffman used XML technology and had a vision to extend the usage of XML to provide a better way of reporting current financial accounting and other information to interested external and internal users of information. XBRL does not change accounting but provides a vehicle for better harmonisation of accounting.

The aim of XBRL is to enhance the reporting of existing financial accounting information in all countries and adapting to changes in standards. It enables the information, once created, to be presented in many ways without having to be re-entered. The XBRL information can be adapted to suit a particular format of presentation, analysis and search. It is regarded as a global effort to build a digital language of business. It allows businesses to communicate financial information without the need to rekey data.

Based on an analysis of the participants in the business reporting supply chain, XBRL separates information, defines a structure of the data, and presents it in several different ways by the use of XML and its related technology (the XML style sheets). The schema in Figure 17.2 suggests the process.

How does XBRL affect the accounting profession? XBRL not only streamlines the financial information supply chain in order to enhance the accountants' efficiency, knowledge of XBRL by organisations can generate value added activities and improves relationships between the accountants, the auditors and the client. With the global convergence into international accounting and auditing standards, XBRL provides a fast and economic means to simplify the process, and to allow for ongoing improvements.

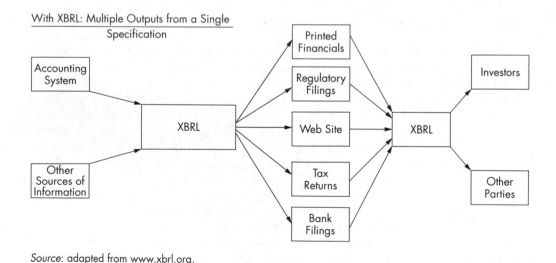

Source: adapted from www.xbrl.org.

Figure 17.2 *XBRL*

◁ LEARNING **CHECK**

17.3 Advances in financial software and use of the Internet are key information technology matters which have a direct impact on the approaches of audits and assurance services.

17.4 Auditors must be able to evaluate the needs of their clients' systems and their implementation of suitable financial software with particular emphasis on minimising risks and ensuring the availability of audit trails and internal controls.

17.5 The mobile Internet combines two fast growing technologies, those of information and telecommunication, and has become an important business application tool.

OTHER EMERGING ISSUES FACING THE AUDITING PROFESSION

This section will discuss other issues facing the professional firms and the professional bodies. In light of the credibility crisis and the continuing expectation gap, the auditing profession is actively seeking ways to re-examine its role. Three emerging issues are discussed here. First of all, the changing role of auditors in the detection of fraud and errors will be considered, with an understanding that there are increasing demands of investigation or forensic audit services. Readers will recall that this is an evolving issue of the shifting paradigm, discussed in Chapter 1. Then, following the demise of Andersens, the changing landscape of the accounting firms will be identified.

Auditors' role on fraud and error

In its exposure draft for the revision of ISA 240, The Auditor's Responsibility to Consider Fraud in an Audit of Financial Statements, to clarify the auditor's role in detecting and preventing fraud, the IAASB follows the US Public Oversight Board's Panel on Audit Effectiveness' recommendations that auditing and quality control standards be made more specific and definitive. It also recommends that auditors should carry out a greater number of procedures to enhance the prospects of detecting material financial statement fraud. This represents Phase I of an international project on fraud. In Phase II, proposals such as requiring the auditor to perform forensic style procedures in every audit will be examined.

ISA 240 (Exposure draft) emphasises the distinction between management and employee fraud and expands the discussion on fraudulent financial reporting. When planning the audit, the auditor is required to discuss with other audit team members the susceptibility of the entity to material misstatements resulting from fraud. The auditor is required to consider, as part of the planning process, the accounting and internal control systems that management has put in place in order to address the risk of material misstatements in the financial report arising from fraud. When the auditor discovers a material misstatement as a result of fraud and/or error, the auditor is required to communicate fraud-related matters to the appropriate level of management and those charged with governance of the entity, usually the Board or Audit Committee.

Forensic accounting and auditing

The new auditing standard is a contributing factor to the growth of firms turning their attention to forensic services. KPMG lists the common e-commerce frauds encountered by businesses. The most common frauds in on-line businesses involve false or stolen credit card numbers. The factors which contributed to the rise of e-frauds, as identified by KPMG, are:

- poor security of access devices and passwords;
- the ease with respect to the electronic transfers of funds and product globally;
- internal control breakdowns possibly with the poorly understood reliance of systems controls; and
- the growing tolerance level of fraud in businesses.

An adapted/summarised version of KPMG's e-fraud types and strategies is depicted in Table 17.3.

The KPMG survey showed that although members of internal management account for 28% of frauds by number, they account for 67% of the loss by value. The fraud survey of 361 companies found that 50% of respondents believed fraud was a big problem for business. A total of 44,654 fraud instances was reported between October 1999 and September 2001, with 55% of respondents experiencing at least one fraud.[10]

Changing landscape of accounting firms

In the last decade or so, there has been a significant battle between professionals providing business advisory services and those focused on compliance services. While the large international firms provide a suite of advisory services, the smaller firms mainly concentrate on compliance work such as compilations and financial reporting. One of the key changes is the development of consolidators. The consolidator model aims to bring together a large number of disassociated firms, often in various locations, and who have never worked together, and attempts to integrate them into a family, with an objective to increase efficiency.

While the consolidators look on, 2002 also marked the demise of one of the Big Five, the defunct accounting firm Arthur Andersen. In June 2002, the US firm was found guilty of obstruction of justice and was banned from conducting audits of companies in the US.

Auditing firms are also undergoing internal changes, with new audit independence guidelines and the looming legal changes on professional indemnity and liability cap. Furthermore, many auditing teams are compelled to perform critical reviews of their audit quality control and disclosure policies such as non-audit services, and to put in place additional safeguards to prevent audit and independence failures.

◿ LEARNING **CHECK**

17.6 The effectiveness of the independent audit in detecting and reporting fraud is being re-evaluated.

Table 17.3 E-fraud types and strategies

E-FRAUD TYPE	DESCRIPTION	PREVALENCE	MITIGATION STRATEGY
False Internet shopfront	A fake website offering goods on orders with a valid credit card number; website closed down as soon as credit card claims are processed	Rare but becoming more common	Consumers to verify supplier; avoid purchase of products offshore where verification is difficult
False Internet gambling	False website for players to establish opening balances which are to be topped up as required. After sometime, the site locks out the player denying access	Rare but increasing	Should deal only with known and trusted gambling service; avoid service providers based outside Australia
Trafficking credit card numbers	Trading in credit card numbers had increased	Very common and increasing	Anti-fraud systems by the bank
Fictitious purchase order	False orders are placed with stolen or fabricated credit card number; or goods delivered to a false address	Very common and increasing	Verification of identity of customers, customer analyses, and other security controls
Piracy	Downloadable products are copied and offered for resale	Very common and increasing	Electronic security and hardware solutions
Fraudulent online	Employee gaining access to online banking system	Rare	Online banking funds transfer compliance with password and ID security, bank reconciliations, regular audit
Internet banking fraud	Fraudsters gaining access to personal Internet banking facility	Rare	Strict security over password and access details

Source: KPMG Fraud Survey Sept. 2001.

17.7 Audit firms are developing new skills in the emerging area of forensic auditing in which they assist clients in identifying fraud, obtaining evidence as to the perpetrators and measuring the consequences.

17.8 Professional firms are undergoing restructuring in response to market conditions and regulatory pressures. Changes include the 'consolidation' of smaller practices into multi-firm groupings and the implications of the demise of Andersens.

QUALITY BENCHMARKING AND THE AUDITOR

There is a strong view that regulations that ensure the quality of the professional services prevail in the profession. These regulatory controls include:

- high education entry requirements;
- rigorous induction programmes;
- character checking upon entry to the profession;
- compulsory public practice induction;
- compulsory continuing professional development;
- extensive ethical rulings and codes of conduct;
- separate public practice registration;
- compulsory quality review programmes;
- compulsory professional indemnity insurance; and
- adherence to detailed and mandatory Auditing Standards.

These controls set a minimal list of mechanisms and standards with which professional accountants and auditors must comply. However, as auditors expand their services and as their roles become more complicated, it is expected that they must not only keep abreast of current demands in quality delivery applicable to businesses, but also have the ability to assess the impact of such standards on their own work. This section focuses on some of the benchmarks of which auditors and professional accountants must be aware.

The ISO 9000 series

The ISO 9000 series comprises a collection of standards for quality management published by the International Organisation for Standardisation (ISO). They define a framework of minimum requirements for the implementation of quality systems to be used in contractual situations. The standards in the ISO 9000 series have been adopted worldwide as suitable criteria for the assessment and registration of companies by independent accredited third party organisations. In brief, the ISO 9000 series comprises quality systems models for quality assurance and management standards. (Much information is available on the ISO 9000 home page.)

The advantage of the ISO 9000 series is evident when selecting, implementing and monitoring a new management system. The series uses tracking features such as internal quality audits, corrective action and management review processes. Companies that operate in accordance with ISO standards are better able to satisfy expectations and clearly identify the resulting advantages of their operations. A certified quality management system can:

- optimise organisational structure and operational integration;
- improve awareness of organisational objectives;
- improve communications and quality of information;
- better define responsibilities and authorities;
- improve traceability to the causes of quality problems;
- improve the use of time and other resources;

- formalise systems to ensure consistent quality and punctual delivery;
- enhance documented systems to provide useful reference and training;
- improve relationships with customers and suppliers;
- enhance the ability to bid for ISO 9000 contracts;
- provide for continual quality assessment by experienced professionals; and
- ensure improved records are available in the case of litigation.

A number of publications explain ISO 9000 quality systems, including those that provide a compliance guide and explain operational procedures. Accounting firms are well placed to capitalise on their understanding of and familiarity with quality system requirements. They have the opportunity to build on their audit skills to become a practice that provides ISO registration services. Many larger international audit firms are attempting to become accredited ISO 9000 registrars, because this represents a significant financial investment. (KPMG, for example, has obtained accreditation by the ISO and its authorised agents to provide accreditation service to its clients.) The accreditation process involves setting up focus groups to determine what clients want, hiring the necessary staff, advertising and undertaking the cost of the accreditation. The issue, however, raises 'conflict of interest' considerations. Accounting firms need to decide whether to provide consulting services related to ISO 9000 or whether to offer the registration service. Providing both services would put a firm in a conflict of interest.

If a company decides to go through the ISO registration process, the compliance audit may be quite exhaustive. A distinctive feature of ISO 9000 registration is that a third party conducts the registration process. These quality system registrars use common evaluation parameters and work under strict guidelines established by the ISO although there are some differences in how registrars interpret the standards and use the measurement techniques. For auditors who are involved in ISO audits, the following issues are relevant:

- There must be a quality manual which documents the organisation's structure, responsibilities, procedures, processes, resources and reporting framework. The auditor will look for objective evidence of an effective quality system such as effective communication of organisational philosophies, proper controls over processes, a management monitoring system, etc.
- The inspection and testing method must be designed in a way that is suitable for the organisational structure and its operations. The auditor should be made aware of the issues relating to the operations and industry standards.
- The criteria used by auditors to assess the effectiveness of a quality system are (1) proper documentation and communication mechanisms that enable the system to be well understood by the workforce, (2) proper implementation of the system and (3) an objective evaluation of the effectiveness of the system.

Total quality management and the auditor

With auditors becoming increasingly involved in auditing an entire business, ISO 9000 can be very useful in helping auditors to identify and review issues that have an impact on quality management in an organisation. Arguably, the primary consideration in total quality management is sustainability. Recent research into this issue (and the applicability of ISO 9000) has led to the design of a tool to audit issues that impact negatively on this sustainability. Based on work carried out in different manufacturing organisations, the sustainability of total quality management was found, for example, to rely on factors such as continual improvement, organisational behaviour, human resources management, industrial relations and the labour process. These factors reflect a variety of perspectives within business operations. The issues found to have an impact on such factors were analysis of strengths, weaknesses, opportunities and threats (SWOT), competitors, quality and performance standards, new technologies, industrial relations, management–worker relationship, policies design, the positioning of quality functions and resources, functional boundaries, communication, job flexibility, the supervisory structure, the improvement infrastructure, and education and training.

In providing various types of assurance review, auditors are generally able to assist management in pinpointing the matters that have a negative impact on the total quality management of an organisation. Furthermore, they may be able to use the standards specified in ISO 9000 as audit tool benchmarks to provide the necessary level of assurance for effectiveness.

An understanding of the total business process is one of the strengths that financial accountants and auditors can build on as they add value for their employers and clients. Most accountants and auditors are good at analysing situations in organisations, constructing detailed work plans, explaining complex situations to clients from a variety of backgrounds and keeping confidences. Auditors can also perform ISO audits or assist clients in achieving ISO registration/performance.

According to Barthelemy and Zairi,[11] quality auditing has progressed from a practice solely concerned with tools used to detect non-conformance (non-compliance) to one concerned with using instruments geared towards continual improvement. They postulate that it now encapsulates a much more dynamic approach, being more focused on innovation and best practice than on minimum levels of performance.

Undoubtedly, auditing is an important function for the effective deployment of quality systems such as ISO 9000. Not only is it conducted to ensure total compliance with set procedures and agreed standards at all times and at all stages during the productive and organisational process, but it also helps to develop the organisation by providing mechanisms for continual improvement, innovation and the fostering of a problem-solving culture. The steps involved in quality auditing are shown in Figure 17.3.

Although the scenario presented in Figure 17.3 may be well outside the scope of the traditional independent auditor, the current diversification of services provided by auditors and the growing prominence of the concept of adding value to client services indicate that such a trend (or similar developments) may be an issue in the future.

◿ LEARNING **CHECK**

17.9 Audit of quality management refers to the audit activities that help management to design, implement, monitor and improve quality within their organisations. Under the concept of total quality management, auditors are required to understand the entire business, in order to be able to add value to management in terms of continual improvements.

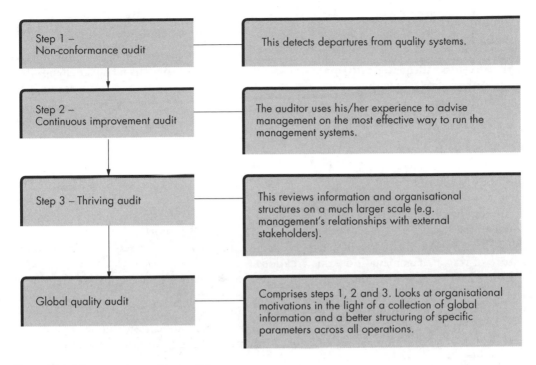

Figure 17.3 *The steps in quality auditing*

17.10 Certification under ISO 9000 requires registered auditors to carry out appropriate quality audits and, for certified organisations, to provide a quality assurance to general users.

17.11 ISO 9000 standards are universally accepted as the benchmark for quality assurance. An ISO 9000 audit requires the examination of a framework of audit procedures and the verification of adherence to certain standards in documentation, operation controls and communication.

VALUE REPORTING AND ENVIRONMENTAL AUDITING

Although, with their training as professional accountants, auditors are primarily involved with auditing financial information. The investigative skills acquired through auditing and their professional integrity that necessarily accompanies their audit role equip them to offer assurance in non-financial fields. Value reporting refers to non-financial aspects of business performance while environmental auditing refers to the attestation of reports as to the impact of a business on the environment.

Value reporting

The profession is keen to emphasise the role of independent auditing in ensuring capital market efficiency. However, value can only be realised if financial reports are effectively communicated to the markets. Methods of corporate valuation and reporting are evolving rapidly, but traditional accounting models are insufficient to be relied on to provide a full picture of corporate health. It is also vital for corporate management to communicate with investors adequately, to maximise total shareholder returns. The challenge for corporations is to enable the capital market to move its focus from short-term earnings to long-term value creation.

The concept of using shareholder value, which is underpinned by information on key value-creating activities, is not new. The Centre of Innovation in Corporate Responsibility (CICR) looks at maximising sources of value by integrating corporate social responsibility with strategic management.[12] The Blue Ribbon Committee report *Improving the Effectiveness of Corporate Audit Committees* – produced in response to concerns expressed by the US Securities and Exchange Commission about the quality of financial reports – refers to 'quality financial report' through integrity and transparency, effective interrelationships between the boards and the shareholders.[13] The Turnbull Report, which is endorsed by the UK Listing Authority for all listed companies in the UK, also refers to the inseparable nature of risk management and value creation.

Books have been written about the value reporting revolution and value-added reporting and research.[14] Many investors use shareholder values to support their investment decisions, build valuation models and assess future cash flows. Shareholder values are also used at corporate level to drive strategy and resource allocation. Value reporting is expected to receive an increasing amount of attention in the future of financial reporting and audits.

PricewaterhouseCoopers has devised a value reporting model, which will facilitate a top-down process of reporting and enable companies to communicate the internal workings of the company to investors in a language they use and understand. The key aspects of the proposed value reporting framework are:

- a comprehensive set of company specific financial and non-financial measures;
- both historical and predictive indicators; and
- shareholder value-creation activities.

The model comprises a shareholder value metric and a value scorecard, which does not focus on operational matters but on key value-creating activities of the business as a whole, as long-term measures. The model is underpinned by four key elements:

1. the use of prospective indicators;
2. cash flow-oriented information instead of traditional earnings;
3. non-financial indicators such as customer retention, employee satisfaction and community support; and
4. greater transparency to satisfy investors' demand for more information.

The concept of value reporting is supported by research. The Swedish Stock Exchange carried out research to determine the views of global investors and analysts on their information needs. The results of that survey show some key insights into best practice reporting, which includes:

- the extent of free cash flow;
- earnings per share;
- market leadership (or ranking in market);
- industry information (gross growth in comparison);
- corporate strategy and visions;
- objectives versus results;
- segmental analysis by business;
- quality management;
- key business activities;
- management activities;
- bad news; and
- challenges, risks and uncertainties.

To develop a value reporting best practice model, PricewaterhouseCoopers advises the following summary features:

- a market overview – the competitive, regulatory and macro-economic environments;
- a value strategy – goals, objectives, governance and organisation;
- managing for value – financial performance, financial position, risk management and segmental information; and
- a value platform – innovation, branding, customer relationships, supply chain management, people management and reputation (social, environmental and ethical).

Value reporting, together with concepts such as shareholder (or stakeholder) value and the development of the triple bottom line concept, can be said to become significant aspects of the role of professional accountants in the future.

Developments in environmental auditing

While auditing has gradually evolved into a much broader concept of performance review, the recent development in environmental auditing is a response to a growing concern by businesses with controlling their environmental performance more effectively and complying with environmental regulations. A single and universally accepted definition of environmental auditing does not exist, possibly as a result of the evolving nature of the function.[15]

Notwithstanding the differing views, a definition of environmental auditing that is widely accepted by businesses comes from the 1989 International Chamber of Commerce (ICC) position paper on environmental auditing[16]:

> [Environmental auditing is] a management tool comprising a systematic, documented, periodic and objective evaluation of how well environmental organisation, management and equipment are performing with the aim of helping to safeguard the environment by:
>
> (1) facilitating management control of environmental practices;
> (2) assessing compliance with company policies, which would include meeting regulatory requirements.

It is significant that environmental auditing, as described above, holds a fundamental contradiction. The ICC states that it is an internal management tool for company use only – that is, that it is not for publication or public disclosure/scrutiny. Yet, the ICC also states that it wishes to establish environmental auditing as a credible and trustworthy instrument in the mind of the public. Convincing the public of the credibility of company environmental audits requires transparency of purpose and information. This can be achieved by publication of audit reports. On the other hand, obtaining a full and frank appraisal of a company's environmental performance raises privacy considerations during the audit process, to the exclusion of external company stakeholders.

It has recently been suggested by Hillary[17] that the use of self-regulatory environmental/management tools such as environmental auditing could become a more powerful force for environmental improvement – that is, people could use such tools to bargain to secure better environmental protection. Environmental auditing is certainly beginning to establish a higher global profile. In its 1986 position paper requiring compulsory auditing, the US Environmental Protection Agency stated that it may request, under certain conditions, internal and potentially incriminating environmental audit reports. The European Union adopted a more holistic approach to environmental protection, with the Commission of European Communities releasing its consultation paper on an environmental auditing scheme in 1990.[18] The scheme entailed the operation of an environmental management accounting system (EMAS), which requires mandatory verification by independent accredited verifiers for sites registering with the scheme. This process gives some credibility to environmental performance efforts made by companies.

Hillary suggested that environmental auditing should be an umbrella term under which different audit scopes exist. The following types of environmental audit were identified:

- an activity audit;
- an issues audit;
- an associate audit;
- an occupational health and safety audit;
- a compliance audit;
- a process safety audit;
- an environmental management systems (EMS) audit;
- a site audit;
- a supplier/customer/contractor audit;
- an energy audit;
- a waste audit.

While the above list is not exhaustive, it indicates the broad range of environmental aspects that may be subject to the audit process. (In due diligence assessments, for example, the auditor may also be concerned with insurance liability audits, pre-acquisition and merger audits, and divestiture and pre-sale audits – all of which have a direct relationship with environmental matters.) The types of audit are not exclusive of one another

STANDARDS FOR ENVIRONMENTAL AUDITING
Recent initiatives have sought to structure and formalise environmental auditing. The British Standard Institution developed in 1992 and reissued in 1994 a British Standard

specifying an environmental management system – BS 7750, which includes environmental auditing for the environmental management system and the environmental performance of an organisation. Both BS 7750 and, more generally, any environmental management accounting systems outline environmental auditing as part of wider management systems, and provide guidelines on how to conduct an environmental audit. The broad principles are similar to those outlined in ISO 10011, Quality Systems Auditing Standards.

The ISO 14000 series
At the international level, the ISO developed a suite of 20 standards in the field of environmental management (the ISO 14000 series). This series was published in 1994. In terms of environmental auditing, the following three standards are applicable:

1. ISO 14011-1, Guidelines for Environmental Auditing – Audit Procedures. Part 1: Auditing of Environmental Management Systems;
2. ISO 14011-2, Guidelines for Environmental Auditing – Audit Procedures. Part 2: Compliance Audits; and
3. ISO 14011-3, Guidelines for Environmental Auditing – Audit Procedures. Part 3: Audit of an Environmental Statement.

In addition, ISO 14001 contains a requirement for organisations to maintain programmes and procedures for periodic environmental management system audits. The purpose of an environmental management system audit is to determine whether an organisation's environmental management system conforms to the ISO 14001 specification, and whether it has been properly implemented and maintained.

IAPS 1010, The Consideration of Environmental Matters in the Audit of Financial Statements, also provides some practical assistance concerning the impact of such factors as pollution, hazardous waste, compliance with environmental laws and regulations on financial statement accruals, the impairment of assets, disclosures and so on.

International codes of environmental conduct
A number of international codes of environmental conduct set out essential environmental management elements. These include:

- the Valdez Principles, developed by the Coalition for Environmentally Responsible Economics (CERES), in 1990;
- the ICC Charter for Sustainable Development; and
- the UK Chemical Industries Association Responsible Care Programmes.

The Valdez Principles were launched after the Exxon Valdez oil tanker disaster in Alaska. The CERES requires signatory companies to undertake annual environmental audits and make public the findings of these audits. The ICC Charter for Sustainable Development comprises 16 principles for environmental management in achieving sustainable economic development. The Responsible Care Programmes have been developed by many national chemical industry associations in the US, Canada and the UK. All are voluntary in nature.

Voluntary business environmental codes may include environmental auditing components, which could be either the Valdez Principles, the ICC Charter for Sustainable Development or the Responsible Care principles. In practice, however, these have not been as widely supported by industry as might have been intended. Nonetheless, there are many different approaches to environmental auditing that can be taken. For environmental management systems and auditing programmes to be effective, some of the characteristics of a corporate culture are required:

- top management commitment and board-level support;
- communication of relevant information to all levels of management and line management;
- agreement at all levels that the programme is valuable;
- leadership, with direct access to the company's board and a competent audit team; and
- environmental audit programmes that fit comfortably into existing management systems.

Furthermore, the International Auditing Practice Committee (IAPC is the predecessor body of the IAASB) suggested that conduct of environmental management system audits requires the following[19]:

- knowledge of the industry;
- knowledge of environmental issues, including environmental science and technologies;
- established auditing and verification philosophies and techniques;
- management systems and practices, including internal controls; and
- environmental laws and regulations.

The IAPC suggests that environmental management system auditing probably presents a wider range of unique issues for the auditor than does financial statement auditing. To respond to these effectively, auditors who are and may be involved in certain environmental operations need to be knowledgeable about the environmental systems standards of environmental management accounting systems and ISO 14001, especially when the environmental audit is part of the audit scope.

Such an environmental audit may result in the recruitment of on-site personnel in an audit team, although an inability to be objective may sometimes mitigate the advantages offered by having inside site knowledge and workforce credibility. Nonetheless, leading environmental auditing programmes nowadays also include a person with detailed knowledge of the facility to be audited.

The occurrence of environmental auditing will increase in businesses in response to the increasing adoption of ISO standards, the greater demands by stakeholders in business for accountability on environmental issues, and a growing sophistication in society's understanding of environmental threats and opportunities. The auditors of the twenty-first century must be aware of this development and equip themselves with the necessary skills to establish the relevance and value of their services. As a first step, they must be familiar with the legislative requirements in this area.

The latest developments in auditing and assurance (as discussed above) reflect the broadening role of accountants in value creation, as well as their social role.

◢ LEARNING **CHECK**

17.12 Value reporting refers to reporting by organisations on non-financial matters that are key value drivers. These value drivers are based on added shareholder value.

17.13 Communication of non-financial matters to investors involves reporting on value creation activities and other performance indicators.

17.14 Environmental auditing does not have a standard definition. It is generally considered to be a management tool comprising a systematic, documented, periodic and objective evaluation of how well an organisation (including its management and equipment) is performing with respect to environmental issues.

17.15 The aim of the environmental audit is to help to safeguard the environment by facilitating effective management control and environmental practices, and by assessing compliance with company and regulatory requirements.

17.16 The development of environmental auditing has given rise to a range of potential audit and assurance services, covering different environmentally related operations related to such issues as energy, occupational health and safety, waste, contaminated sites, and other activities such as production of environmental products (e.g. chemicals).

17.17 The ISO 14000 series has been published as a set of guidelines for environmental auditing procedures. Voluntary environmental practices are also adopted by organisations. Examples are (1) adhoring to environmental codes, (2) developing an environmentally friendly culture, and (3) implementing an environmental management accounting system to identify, control and monitor risk areas.

SUMMARY

This chapter aimed to provide an overview of some of the current issues that may affect the role of professional accountants and auditors in the foreseeable future. Issues such as corporate governance, information technology, the changing role of the profession, benchmarking, value reporting and environmental auditing continue to shape the work of professional accountants. Developments in information technology were reviewed with specific emphasis on the significance of financial software, the mobile Internet and XBRL. Auditors and professional accountants must be familiar with the characteristics and technical features of financial software to ensure their suitability for clients and employers. The convergence of the Internet and telecommunication technologies also provides an insight into possible future business applications. Readers should appreciate the changing nature of the work of professional accountants, but some external factors must not be ignored. The role of the profession, with the latest development of the independence framework, was examined, as was the trend of restructuring by accounting firms in the face of changing market conditions.

Audit quality benchmarking was discussed – elaborating on the issues of non-audit standards such as the ISO 9000 series – and the concept of the total quality management audit was introduced. This approach focuses on auditing the business as a whole, with the inclusion of value-added services such as certification. While highlighting the impact of quality auditing, this chapter also recognised the increasing attention given to value reporting – a form of business reporting that goes beyond the financial statements. Value reporting has formed the basis for the development of environmental auditing. The future of business reporting and auditing may well be underpinned by a demand of shareholder (or stakeholder) values, sustainability and long-term accountability.

NOTES

1 Task Force on Rebuilding Public Confidence in Financial Reporting, *Rebuilding Public Confidence in Financial Reporting, an International Perspective*, International Federation of Accountants, NY, July 2003.

2 Institute of Chartered Accountants in England & Wales, *Internal Control – Guidance for Directors on the Combined Code*, London, 1999.

3 Audit Faculty, Risk Management and the Value Added by Internal Audit, Institute of Chartered Accountants in England & Wales, London, 2000.

4 COSO, *Enterprise Risk Management Framework, Exposure Draft*, Committee of Sponsoring Organisations of the Treadway Commission, July, 2003.

5 Auditing Practices Board, *Aggressive Earnings Management*, CCAB, London, 2001.

6 International Federation of Accountants (IFAC), *Revised Code of Ethics for Professional Accountants, exposure draft*, July 2003.

7 The publication Accounting Software in Australia was published by the *CFO Magazine*, with the ASCPA in 1997. The publication reported on the findings of Strategic Research, the research arm of the company Strategic Publishing Group, following its recent survey of more than 600 chief financial officers in Australia and New Zealand on the use of accounting software.

8 Courtney, H. M., Prachyl, C. L. & Glandon, T. 'Guide to Accounting Software', *Journal of Accountancy* (March 1998), pp. 44–61.

9 KPMG, *Mobile Internet – Any Place, Any Time, Everything*, www.kpmg.co.uk/kpmg/uk/image/mobileint.pdf

10 KPMG, Fighting Fraud – Forensic Accounting, E-Commerce Fraud Uncovered, September 2001.

11 Barthelemy, J. L. & Zairi, M. 'Making ISO 9000 Work: The Role of Auditing', *Total Quality Management Magazine* (Vol. 6, No. 3, 1994), pp. 44–47. This article refers to quality audits which progress from non-conformance auditing into global auditing.

12 This is referred to in the President's message in the Centre for Innovation in Corporate Responsibility, *Triple Bottom Line Reporting*, Vol. 1, Washington, DC, 1999.

13 The Blue Ribbon Committee was charged by the New York Stock Exchange and the National Association of Securities Dealers in 1998 to review the effectiveness of corporate audit committees. Its report contained three conclusions: (1) quality financial reporting can only result from effective interrelationships among corporate boards, audit committees, financial management, the internal auditor and the external auditors; (2) integrity and transparency of financial reporting drives investor confidence; and (3) strengthening oversight in the financial reporting process of public companies will reduce incidences of outright fraud.

14 Eccles, R., Herz, R. H. & Phillips, D. *The Value Reporting Revolution: Moving beyond the Earnings Game*, John Wiley & Sons, New York, 2001. Also Riahi-Belkaoui, A. *Value Added Reporting and Research – The State of the Art*, Quorum Books, Westport Connecticut, 1999.

[15] The fact that a universally accepted definition does not exist was reported by the International Auditing Practice Committee in its 1995 publication *The Audit Profession and the Environment*. Cahill, L. B., in *Environmental Audits*, 6th edn, Government Institutes, Rockville, Maryland, 1992, suggested that the lack of definition may be due to the evolving nature of environmental auditing.

[16] International Chamber of Commerce, *Environmental Auditing*, Publication No. 468. ICC Publishing SA, Paris, 1989.

[17] Hillary, R., 'Environmental Auditing: Concept, Methods and Developments', *International Journal of Auditing* (Vol. 2, March 1998), pp. 71–85.

[18] Commission of European Communities, Council Regulation EEC No. 1836/93 of 29 June 1993. This regulation allowed voluntary participation by companies in the industrial section in EMAs.

[19] International Auditing Practices Committee, *The Audit Profession and the Environment*, Discussion Paper, July 1995.

FURTHER READING

British Standards Institution. *Specification for Environmental Management Systems*, British Standard 7750. London, 1992, 1994.

Business International. *Managing the Environment: The Greening of European Business*, London, 1990.

Carmichael, D. R. 'Hocus-Pocus Accounting', *Journal of Accountancy* (October 1999).

Chemical Industries Association. *Responsible Care*, London, 1989.

Clements, K. 'Environmental Auditing for Industry: A European Perspective', *European Environment* (Vol. 1, No. 3, 1991), pp. 1–4.

Coalition for Environmentally Responsible Economics. *The 1990 CERES Guide to the Valdez Principles*, Boston, 1990.

Collison, D. J. 'The Response of Statutory Financial Auditors in the UK to Environmental Issues: A Descriptive and Exploratory Case Study', *British Accounting Review* (December 1996), pp. 325–335.

Confederation of British Industry. *Narrowing the Gap: Environmental Auditing Guidelines for Business*, London 1990.

Dale, B. G. 'Total Quality Management Sustaining Audit Tool: Description and Use', *Total Quality Management* (December 1997).

Dowson, J. 'Environmental Management Systems Certification – An Assessor's View', in R. Hillary (ed.), *Environmental Management Systems and Cleaner Production*, John Wiley & Sons, Chichester, 1997.

Elkington, J., Knight, P. & Hailes, J. *The Green Business Guide*, Victor Gollancz, London, 1991.

Environment Business. 'Industrial Environmental Auditing – Environmental Performance Evaluation', Supplement to *Environment Business*, London, September 1990.

Environmental Protection Agency. 'Environmental Auditing Policy Statement', *Federal Register* (Vol. 51, No. 131, 1986), pp. 25.04–25.10.

Harrington, C. 'Socially Responsible Investing', *Journal of Accountancy* (January 2003).

International Standards Organisation. 'Environmental Management: TC 207 Steer a Course Resolutely Forward', *ISO Bulletin* (Vol. 25, No. 12, December 1994).

Lewis, R. & Moriyama, H. 'Environmental Audits: Don't Pay for Pollution', *Acquisitions Monthly* (March 1990), pp. 26–27.

Miller, R. I. & Pashkoff, P. H. 'Regulations Under the Sarbanes-Oxley Act', *Journal of Accountancy* (October 2002).

Myers, R. 'Ensuring Ethical Effectiveness', *Journal of Accountancy* (February 2003).

Rezaee, Z. 'Help Keep the World Green', *Journal of Accountancy* (November 2000).

PROFESSIONAL APPLICATION QUESTIONS

(Suggested answers are on pages 660–661)

17.1 Audit trails in financial software

An experienced (albeit elderly) audit partner was heard to make the following statement:

> I do not know why all this fuss is being made about audit trails when clients are implementing a new system. If advances in technology mean that there is less documentation, surely that must be a good thing. I think that there is a problem if auditors cannot audit a set of financial statements produced by a computer system without needing reams of paper. Especially with such auditing tools as analytical review now available to assist in auditing balances.

Required

Comment on the partner's statement. In particular, address some of the problems with a lack of an audit trail that can be caused by advances in technology.

17.2 Environmental auditing

Environmental auditing is becoming a more important issue in financial reporting and also in relation to auditing requirements. The British Standard Institution developed a standard (BS 7750) that included some guidance on environmental auditing.

> BS 7750 is a specification for an environmental management system. The system is used to describe the company's environmental management system, evaluate its performance and to define policy, practices, objectives and targets; and provides a catalyst for continuous improvement. The concept is similar to the use of ISO 9000 for quality systems, with the methods to be used open to definition by the company. The standard provides the framework for development and assessment of the resultant environmental management system.
>
> BS 7750 was developed as a response to concern about environmental risks and damage (both real and potential). Compliance with the standard is voluntary for companies, and complements required compliance with statutory legislation.

Source: www.quality.co.uk

Required

(a) What does environmental auditing mean?

(b) What are some other standards that have been issued in relation to environmental auditing?

(c) What sort of tasks might be involved in environmental auditing?

ANSWERS TO MULTIPLE-CHOICE QUESTIONS

1.1 What was the predominant objective of an 'audit' before 1900?
(b) To detect fraud.
1.2 What would *not* be described as part of the conformance role of auditing?
(a) Evaluate reasonableness of business plans.
1.3 What is the main concern of the accounting profession in relation to an increase in the level of assurance required for audits?
(b) It will increase their exposure to liability.
1.4 What provides the highest level of assurance?
(a) Audit.
1.5 What has been the primary growth area in recent years for the public accounting profession?
(b) Consulting services.
1.6 The primary objective of a financial statement audit is to:
(c) express an opinion on the truth and fairness of the accounts.
1.7 When hiring a new auditor, what should the firm consider to comply with quality control standards?
(b) The person should have adequate qualifications.

2.1 Which of the following relates to the auditing function in the financial reporting process?
(c) Obtain and evaluate evidence concerning the financial statements.
2.2 Even if there were no statutory requirement for an audit, some people suggest that self-interest would still impel management to engage auditors to audit the financial statements. What theory of auditing is this predominantly based on?
(b) Agency theory.
2.3 An independent audit provides a number of benefits to the company because it:
(d) lends credibility to the financial statements.
2.4 Who is responsible for the appointment of the auditors to a company?
(b) The members of the company.
2.5 What would be a valid reason for the company to remove its auditors?
(a) Evidence that the auditors did not perform a proper review of the company's fixed assets.

2.6 What is the meaning of the principle that requires the auditors to be independent?
   (a) The auditors must be without bias with respect to the client under audit.
2.7 Which of the below is a prime objective of Auditing Standards?
   (d) To detail mandatory procedures and principles with which the auditors must comply.
2.8 Independent auditors' primary reporting responsibility is to the:
   (d) members of the entity.

3.1 What *should* differentiate a 'professional' from a 'non-professional' culture?
   (b) Non-professionals do not have community sanction or ethical codes.
3.2 Which of the following best describes why the accounting profession issued a Code of Professional Conduct and established means for ensuring its observance?
   (b) A distinguishing mark of a profession is its acceptance of responsibility to the public.
3.3 Which of the following is most likely to be ethically unacceptable?
   (c) Receiving a bonus for performing the annual audit of a client within a prescribed time period.
3.4 Which of the following would be deemed acceptable by the accounting profession in evaluating whether a firm was maintaining independence?
   (d) The audit firm having a number of clients within the same industry.
3.5 An audit independence issue might be raised by auditors' participation in management advisory services engagements. Which of the following statements is most consistent with the profession's attitude towards this issue?
   (c) The auditor should not make management decisions for an audit client.
3.6 How are auditors normally appointed to audit a public company?
   (a) By directors on behalf of the shareholders.
3.7 What does a signed audit report mean with respect to the 'possibility' of fraud within a company?
   (a) There is a reasonable expectation that material irregularities due to fraud have been detected.

4.1 What most appropriately describes the implications of the Kingston Cotton Mill (1896) and London and General Bank (1895) cases?
   (b) The auditor has a responsibility to exercise the skill and care of a reasonably competent and well-informed member of the profession.
4.2 In which of the following situations is it least likely that the auditors would have been negligent in failing to detect a material misstatement of stock?
   (a) The auditors relied on a certificate provided by an independent expert.
4.3 In which of the following situations would failure to detect a fraud constitute grounds for a claim of negligence?
   (c) The auditor accepted local management representations as to discrepancies as the potential impact of the fraud was not material to the accounts as a whole.
4.4 In which of the following situations might a claim arise under privity of contract?
   (a) A bank makes a loan to a company on the strength of a report commissioned by the bank.

4.5 The decision in the Caparo case (1990) reduced the duty of care of auditors to:
(c) The shareholders as a group.
4.6 Would an investor who requests a copy of the audited financial statements of the company from company management before the audit is completed be able to rely on the work of the auditors?
(c) No.
4.7 What type of reform is being implemented by the government of the UK to alleviate audit liability?
(d) None of the above.

5.1 Which of the following can be controlled by the auditor?
(b) Detection risk.
5.2 If the auditor assesses control and inherent risks as low, what would you expect the auditor to do?
(c) Perform a relatively small number of substantive procedures.
5.3 Inherent risk would be considered to be high where:
(c) the newly appointed finance director was previously the marketing manager.
5.4 Which of the following statements best describes the audit approach to materiality?
(a) Materiality is a matter for the professional judgement.
5.5 In determining the level of planning materiality for an audit, what should not be considered?
(c) The cost of the audit.
5.6 Which of the following audit procedures is primarily intended to provide evidence as to completeness?
(b) Searching for unmatched goods received notes.
5.7 The auditor will check balances from suppliers' statements to the bought ledger in order to:
(d) ascertain the completeness of recorded creditors.
5.8 Which of the following audit procedures is primarily intended to provide evidence as to existence?
(c) confirming recorded debtors with the customers.
5.9 What does 'sufficient appropriate' audit evidence mean?
(b) Adequate evidence has been obtained in the auditor's professional judgement.
5.10 In verifying the valuation of work completed by a construction company on a long-term building contract, which source of evidence would you consider as most reliable?
(a) An independent architect called in to supply a valuation but who has not otherwise been involved with the contract.

6.1 Which of the following considerations on accepting a new client does not involve quality control?
(b) Previous auditor's advice as to whether audit fees are paid promptly.
6.2 Engagement letters are widely used in practice for professional engagements of all types. The primary purpose of the audit engagement letter is to:
(d) provide a written record of the agreement with the client as to the services to be provided.

6.3   When planning an audit an auditor would not normally be concerned with:

     (c)   the collection of the fee for the previous year's audit.

6.4   In the tour of the client's operations, the auditor noted two machines were not operating in the client's factory. This meant that production was 25% lower than normal. The factory manager informed the auditor that this was because the machine was being serviced; however, the auditor saw no evidence of this. How would this affect the audit plan?

     (d)   It would be necessary to perform more work on stock to check for obsolescence.

6.5   Which of the following is not one of the uses of a time budget?

     (a)   Determining the extent of reliance on internal control.

6.6   Analytical procedures used in planning an audit should focus on identifying:

     (d)   areas that may represent specific risks relevant to the audit.

6.7   When preparing audit working papers it is important that:

     (d)   they indicate the name of the staff members responsible for preparing and reviewing them and any conclusions that may be drawn from the evidence.

6.8   Which of the following is not a function of the preparation of working papers?

     (c)   For use by the auditor on other engagements such as advising another client on the desirability of making a takeover bid for the audit client.

6.9   Standardised working papers are useful because they:

     (b)   facilitate the review of the audit since the reviewer will be accustomed to the layout, contents and purpose of such working papers.

6.10   The auditor's permanent working paper file should not normally include:

     (b)   extracts from the client's bank statements.

7.1   The primary objective of obtaining an understanding of the information system is to provide the auditor with:

     (b)   enough understanding to design procedures to gather sufficient audit evidence.

7.2   Which of the following is not a method of documenting the understanding of the accounting system?

     (b)   Internal control evaluation checklist.

7.3   An auditor's flow chart of an entity's information system is a diagrammatic representation that depicts the auditor's:

     (b)   understanding of the system.

7.4   Which of the following would not be relevant in obtaining an understanding of the control environment?

     (d)   Adoption of accounting policies in conformance with accounting standards.

7.5   Where the preliminary assessment of control risk is low for any particular audit objective:

     (c)   the auditor may consider performing tests of controls to confirm the preliminary assessment if it would result in a reduction of the extent of audit effort.

7.6   Segregation of duties is a means of ensuring that:

     (d)   employees cannot perpetrate and conceal errors or irregularities in the normal course of their duties.

7.7   The maximum reliance an auditor may place on control procedures in reducing the extent of substantive procedures is determined by:

      (c)   their design effectiveness subject to sufficient evidence from tests of control that they are operating effectively.

7.8   What would be an appropriate sample of invoices to gain reasonable assurance that all payments are properly authorised as part of the annual audit?
      (b)   Randomly select a sample of 100 invoices from throughout the financial year.

8.1   Which of the following does not constitute sampling?
      (a)   Select all payments made during the year greater than £10,000 and ensure they have supporting documentation.

8.2   An advantage of using statistical sampling techniques is that such techniques:
      (a)   mathematically measure risk.

8.3   What would most effectively describe the risk of incorrect rejection in terms of substantive audit testing?
      (c)   The auditor concludes that the balance is materially misstated when in actual fact it is not.

8.4   An advantage in using statistical sampling over non-statistical sampling methods in tests of control is that statistical methods:
      (c)   provide an objective basis for quantitatively evaluating sample risks.

8.5   If all other factors remained constant, changing the tolerable deviation rate from 10% to 12% would mean:
      (c)   that the sample size would decrease.

8.6   An underlying feature of random-based selection of items is that each:
      (c)   item in the accounting population should have an opportunity to be selected.

8.7   Which of the following methods of sample selection is the least desirable in terms of extrapolating results to the population?
      (c)   Block selection.

8.8   What audit tests do you think would be most appropriate for monetary unit sampling?
      (a)   To select a sample of debtors to confirm their balances.

9.1   Which of the following is the only risk that can be manipulated by the auditors?
      (b)   Detection risk.

9.2   If the acceptable level of detection risk decreases, the assurance directly provided from:
      (a)   substantive procedures should increase.

9.3   The auditor assesses control risk because it:
      (c)   affects the level of detection risk the auditors may accept.

9.4   The auditor is more likely to use analytical review as a substantive test when:
      (a)   planned detection risk is high.

9.5   Which of the following analytical procedures should be applied to the profit and loss statement?
      (d)   Compare the actual revenues and expenses with the corresponding figures of the previous year, and investigate significant differences.

9.6   As the acceptable level of detection risk decreases, an auditor may change the:
      (c)   nature of substantive procedures, from a less effective to a more effective procedure.

9.7 The procedures specifically outlined in an audit programme are primarily designed to:
(d) gather evidence.

9.8 When would tests of details of profit and loss statement accounts be more likely to be required?
(c) When the auditor decides not to test the company's internal controls.

10.1 Which of the following controls would most likely ensure that all deliveries are invoiced?
(a) The invoicing department supervisor matches pre-numbered shipping documents with entries in the sales journal.

10.2 Which of the following internal control procedures would most likely assure that all receipts from cash sales are recorded?
(c) Sales are rung up on a cash register which displays the sale amount and issues a printed receipt.

10.3 For which of the following reasons might inherent risk over the occurrence of sales transactions be assessed as high?
(b) Sales department staff earn a bonus if they achieve annual sales targets.

10.4 Sales revenue is usually a material balance within the financial statements of a company. Why would an auditor mainly focus his or her work on sales transactions occurring at the end of the year rather than throughout the year?
(b) The auditor is concerned that the company may attempt to bring forward sales into the current year.

10.5 Which of the following tests of control would provide audit evidence for the financial statement assertion of the completeness of sales transactions?
(a) Check to ensure that all dispatch orders have been properly matched to a sales invoice.

10.6 If the auditor assesses control risk over the completeness of cash receipts transactions to be high, the control risk assessment would be high for the debtors' balance assertion of:
(b) existence.

10.7 After completing the testing of controls over cash receipts and sales adjustments, the auditor assesses the level of control risk to be higher than expected. How would this affect the auditor's substantive audit work on debtors?
(c) The auditor may consider changing the date of the debtors' circularisation from one month before the year-end to the actual year-end date.

10.8 Which of the following would give the most assurance concerning the existence assertion of debtors?
(b) Sending a debtor's confirmation letter.

11.1 Which of the following controls would be most effective in assuring that only purchases that properly occurred are recorded for payment?
(a) Suppliers' invoices are independently matched with purchase orders and goods received notes.

11.2 On receipt of a supplier's invoices the purchases clerk should:

(b)   match the invoice with the goods received note and purchase order.

11.3   Internal control is not strengthened when the following functions are segregated:
(c)   approving suppliers' invoices and recording the liability.

11.4   An auditor wants to perform tests of control on an entity's computerised cash disbursement procedures. If the control procedures leave no audit trail of documentary evidence, the auditor most likely will test the procedures by:
(d)   the use of test data.

11.5   Which of the following is a test of control over payroll transactions?
(d)   Observing procedures performed at a payroll distribution.

11.6   The sampling unit in an audit procedure providing evidence as to the occurrence of payroll transactions ordinarily is:
(a)   a clock card.

11.7   To ensure the completeness of recorded liabilities at the balance sheet date the auditor should:
(a)   select a sample of transactions from the bought ledger immediately after the year-end and vouch them to goods received notes.

11.8   The principal reason for the auditor to examine suppliers' statements at balance sheet date is to obtain evidence that:
(c)   there are no unrecorded liabilities.

12.1   If an entity maintains perpetual stock records the appropriate audit strategy for determining stock at balance sheet date would be to:
(c)   rely on book stock if its reliability had been confirmed by cyclical counts throughout the year confirmed by both tests of controls and substantive procedures.

12.2   The primary objective of an auditor's observation of an entity's stock-take is to:
(c)   obtain direct knowledge that the stock exists, and has been properly counted.

12.3   An entity maintains perpetual stock records in both quantities and value. If the preliminary assessed level of control risk is high, an auditor would probably:
(d)   request the entity to schedule the stock-take at the end of the year.

12.4   Which of the following procedures would not be appropriate for an auditor in discharging his or her responsibilities concerning the existence of the entity's stock?
(c)   Supervising the annual stock-take.

12.5   If the client maintains perpetual stock records and performs cyclical counts of stock rather than one major stock-take at the end of the year, what should the auditor do?
(b)   Review one or two of the cyclical counts – and not request a full stock-take if there is evidence of adequate procedures.

12.6   What should an auditor do to ensure that stock is stated at the lower of cost and net realisable value?
(b)   Select a sample of stock items held at year-end and compare their value with that for subsequent sales of similar items.

12.7   In auditing fixed assets, why might the auditor decide to assess control risk at the maximum and perform predominantly substantive testing?
(d)   It is more economical to audit fixed assets using substantive testing because of the relatively few associated transactions compared with other balances.

12.8 What audit procedure would most likely detect the incorrect capitalisation of an expense to property, plant and equipment?
(c) Selecting a sample of additions to fixed assets, and ensuring that they have adequate supporting documentation.

13.1 The balance of cash is often only 1% of total assets.
(a) Cash is always qualitatively material no matter how small the balance and should always be audited.

13.2 When counting cash on hand the auditor should:
(c) note the details of cash and cheques making up the balance.

13.3 In reviewing the bank reconciliation prepared by the cashier, the auditor finds a 'miscellaneous reconciling item'. From discussion with the cashier, the auditor is told that this relates to correction of a bank error. What should the auditor do?
(d) Note the details for checking against the subsequent period's bank statement.

13.4 Which of the following would be the best protection for an entity that wishes to prevent the 'teeming and lading' of trade debtors?
(b) Have customers send payments directly to the entity's bank.

13.5 Consider which of the following statements, with respect to the bank confirmation, is least appropriate.
(c) The confirmation is reliable because its accuracy is guaranteed by the bank.

13.6 The auditor usually adopts a predominantly substantive approach to the audit of investments because:
(a) with few transactions there would be no saving in audit effort from testing controls in order to reduce the level of substantive procedures.

13.7 Which of the following controls would be the most effective in assuring that the proper custody of investment assets is maintained?
(b) The recorded balances in the investment subsidiary ledger are periodically compared with the contents of the safety deposit box by independent personnel.

13.8 The following investment ratio is most likely to be of audit relevance.
(c) Interest income to investments in debentures and other interest-bearing securities.

13.9 Which of the following is least likely to require special attention when auditing consolidated financial statements?
(c) 100% owned subsidiaries.

14.1 In the auditor's completion of the audit, which of the following is not a subsequent event procedure?
(b) Make enquiries with respect to the previously audited financial statements to establish whether new information has become available that might affect those statements.

14.2 Which of the following would an auditor ordinarily perform during his or her review of after balance date events?
(c) Inquire of the entity's solicitor concerning litigation.

14.3 The auditors are concerned with completing various phases of the examination after the balance sheet date. This period extends to:
(b)   the date of the auditors' report.

14.4 The following matters came to the attention of the auditors before the audit fieldwork was completed. Which one would require an adjustment to be made to the financial statements?
(c)   The bankruptcy of a major customer of the client.

14.5 Auditors should send a letter of inquiry to those solicitors who have been consulted concerning litigation or claims. The primary reason for this request is to provide:
(a)   corroborative evidential matter.

14.6 Which of the following is ordinarily included among the written management representations obtained by the auditors?
(b)   All books of account and supporting documentation have been made available.

14.7 Six months after issuing an unqualified opinion on a set of financial statements, the audit partner discovered that the engagement personnel on the audit failed to confirm several of the client's material debtor's balances. The audit partner should first:
(b)   assess the importance of the omitted procedures to the auditor's ability to support the previously expressed opinion.

14.8 Subsequent to the issuance of the auditors' report, the auditors became aware of facts existing at the report date that would have affected the report had the auditors then been aware of them. After determining that the information is reliable, the auditors should next:
(c)   request that management discloses the effects of the newly discovered information by adding a note to subsequently issued financial statements.

15.1 What is an auditor required to state on completion of the audit?
(d)   A statement of opinion about the truth and fairness of the financial statements.

15.2 If the auditor believes that management should disclose further information about directors' remuneration but management does not agree to do this, what should the auditor do?
(c)   Disclose the information within the auditors' report.

15.3 Consider the following scenario. Restrictions imposed by the client prohibit the observation of stock-take, which accounts for about 40% of all assets. Alternative audit procedures cannot be applied, although the auditor was able to obtain satisfactory evidence for all other items in the financial statement. The auditor should issue:
(c)   a disclaimer of opinion.

15.4 In reviewing subsequent events, the auditor reviewed a number of sales transactions that raised serious concerns in relation to the recorded value of stock. The auditor believes that stock should be written down by 15% in the financial statements but management is satisfied that stock is stated fairly. The auditor should issue:
(d)   an 'except for' opinion.

15.5 The auditor has serious concerns about the going concern of the company. The company's going concern is dependent on obtaining a large sales contract that is still under negotiation at the time of signing the auditors' report. The management of the company has made full disclosure of this situation in the notes to the accounts. The auditor is satisfied with the level of disclosure. The auditor should issue:

(b)   an unqualified opinion with a reference to the notes to the accounts.

15.6   The auditor concludes that there is a material inconsistency in the other information in an annual report to shareholders containing audited financial statements. If the auditor concludes that the financial statements do not require revision, but the directors refuse to revise or eliminate the material inconsistency in the other information. The auditor should issue:

(b)   an unqualified opinion with an explanatory paragraph.

15.7   You have accepted the appointment to audit the financial statements of Hippo Ltd for the year ended 31 December 20X1. The financial statements of the company for the year ended 31 December 20X0 were unaudited. In relation to the opening balances in the 31 December 20X1 financial statements, you need to issue:

(a)   a disclaimer of opinion where you cannot obtain sufficient appropriate audit evidence on the opening balances.

16.1   IAPS 1013 on e-commerce provides guidance for the auditor on:

(d)   financial statements which are affected by e-commerce.

16.2   The infrastructure layer of the information economy includes:

(c)   the Internet.

16.3   The key aspects of a risk analysis on e-commerce are:

(c)   security and operational risks.

16.4   An on-line audit is:

(a)   carried out to evaluate the likely acceptance of on-line sites or services.

16.5   Which of the following is not an internal control consideration in an e-commerce environment?

(a)   Ensuring client's staff possess Internet skills and knowledge.

16.6   To assess the acceptance of electronic records as audit evidence, the auditor should consider:

(d)   performing verification procedures for information policies and proper implementation of controls.

16.7   Cyber crimes can be attributable to intrusion by:

(d)   all of the above.

16.8   In performing forensic auditing, the auditor should:

(a)   understand the network systems and seek symptoms of irregularities.

16.9   Which of the following business risks is not identified in IAPS 1013?

(d)   All of the above.

SUGGESTED ANSWERS TO PROFESSIONAL APPLICATION QUESTIONS

1.1 AUDIT OBJECTIVES

Required

Write a brief memo to the audit partner, Mr Dickens, discussing major changes that have occurred in the objectives of auditing since the publication of Dicksee's book in 1900.

Mcmo
Date: 23/3/X1
To: Mr Dickens
From: The Audit Assistant
Re: The Objective of an Audit

The traditional audit role was a 'conformance role'. Audits focused on finding errors in balance sheet accounts and on stemming the growth of fraud. The detection of fraud had a very important emphasis. As companies began to grow and become more complex during the nineteenth century the detection of fraud became an unrealistic objective – although it was still generally perceived as one of the main objectives of a financial statement audit.

The difference in perception of responsibilities and reality were addressed in the case of Kingston Cotton Mill Co. (1896) 2 Ch. D279. Lopes LJ said of auditors:

> ... He is a watchdog, but not a bloodhound ... If there is anything calculated to excite suspicion, he should probe it to the bottom but, in the absence of anything of that kind, he is only bound to be reasonably cautious and careful ...

This effectively stated that it is impossible to detect all fraud as part of the audit. The Auditing Standard SAS 110, Fraud and Error, places the following requirements on auditors:

Para. 18: Auditors plan, perform and evaluate their audit work in order to have a reasonable expectation of detecting material misstatements in the financial statements arising from fraud or error. However, an audit cannot be expected to detect all errors or instances of fraudulent or dishonest conduct.

Para. 41: The auditors should as soon as practicable communicate their findings to the appropriate level of management, the board of directors or the audit committee if they suspect, or discover fraud, even if the potential effect on the financial statements is immaterial.

[SAS 240 is due to be replaced by ISA 240, The Auditor's Responsibility to Consider Fraud in a Financial Statement Audit. Its requirements are more explicit but follow the same basis as SAS 240.]

In conclusion, the primary objective of an audit is to express an opinion as to whether the financial statements are prepared, in all material respects, so as to give a true and fair view. The objective to detect fraud is in the context of the auditor's opinion.

Regards
Audit Assistant

1.2 TYPES OF AUDITS AND AUDITORS

Required

1. *Indicate the type of audit that is involved: (1) financial, (2) compliance, (3) value for money, (4) environmental, or (5) internal.*
2. *Identify the type of auditor most likely to be involved: (1) independent, (2) internal, or (3) government.*

NUMBER	(1) TYPE OF AUDIT	(2) TYPE OF AUDITOR
1	Compliance	Government
2	Internal	Internal
3	Internal	Internal
4	Value for money/Internal	Internal/Independent
5	Financial	Independent
6	Environmental	Independent
7	Compliance/Value for money/Internal	Internal/Independent
8	Compliance/Internal	Internal/Independent
9	Compliance/Financial	Government

2.1 RELATIONSHIP BETWEEN ACCOUNTING AND AUDITING

Required

(a) *Prepare a diagram of the relationship between accounting and auditing in the preparation and audit of financial statements. Show each of the steps in the proper sequence.*

ACCOUNTING	AUDITING
Analyse events and transactions	Obtain and evaluate evidence concerning the financial
Measure and record transaction data	statements
Classify and summarise recorded data	Verify that financial information gives a true and fair view
Prepare financial statements per identified financial	Express opinion in auditors' report
reporting framework	Deliver auditors' report to entity
Distribute financial statements and auditors' report to	
shareholders in annual report	

(b) *'Management and the external auditors share the responsibility for the assertions contained in the financial statements.' Evaluate and discuss the accuracy of this statement.*

This contention is incorrect. Management has the responsibility for the preparation of the financial statements. The auditors' responsibility is limited to performing an audit of the financial statements and reporting the findings in the auditors' report. In the course of the audit, the auditors may suggest adjustments to the financial statements. However, management is responsible for all decisions concerning the form and content of the financial statements.

2.2 MANAGEMENT AND AUDITOR RESPONSIBILITIES

Required

Evaluate the above statements and indicate:

(a) *those (or, in the case of the first statement, which auditor) you agree with, if any; and*

(b) *those whose reasoning is misconceived, incomplete or misleading, if any.*

(a)
1. Auditor D is correct: it is the client's responsibility.
2. The first sentence of this statement is partially true. It is important to read the footnotes to financial statements because they provide important supplementary information.

   Footnotes often pertain to complex matters and are presented in technical language.

   Certainly it must be acknowledged that sometimes they could be presented in clearer form.

To the extent the footnotes supplement disclosures in the body of the financial statements. They could reduce the auditor's exposure to third party liability.

(b)

- The statement is clearly wrong in ascertaining that the footnotes can be used to correct or contradict financial statement presentation. Footnotes are an integral part of the financial statements. If there is contradiction or if the presentation is incomprehensible, this constitutes inadequate reporting and requires comment in the auditors' report.
- The statement fails to recognise that the need for accuracy and completeness sometimes overrides the desire for clarity.
- The statement incorrectly assigns the primary responsibility for the financial statements and footnotes to the auditors instead of the management.
- Because management prepares footnotes, the auditors cannot control their content.

3.1 PROFESSIONALISM

Required

Explain how you would try to convince the cynical accounts department employee that the accounting profession could make a valid claim to being professional.

The claims made by the accounts department are to a certain extent true. In recent years there have been a number of cases where it has been shown that professional accountants have acted in unprofessional ways. In theory a profession should have the following attributes: (1) a systematic body of theory, (2) authority, (3) community sanction, (4) ethical codes and (5) culture. It is acknowledged that non-professionals to a lesser degree also possess these attributes. Professional organisations differentiate themselves by emphasising the community sanction that they strive so hard to achieve. Professionals would also claim that they benefit society by their superior performance in fulfilling a highly competent and sophisticated role. (This may sound elitist and it may be difficult to use this argument to convince the accounts department employee.)

The main criticism that the accounts department employee has made is that members will still act in their own best interests anyway. This is quite valid as discussed above; however, the accounting professional bodies have recognised this potential problem and have implemented a built-in regulatory code to compel ethical behaviour on the part of its members. The profession would see this regulatory code as a key way of differentiating itself from other organisations. Through its ethical code, the profession's commitment to social welfare becomes a matter of public interest, thereby helping to ensure the continued confidence of society. Self-regulatory codes are characteristic of all occupations. However, a professional code is more explicit, systematic, and binding: it possesses altruistic overtones and is more public service oriented.

Whether this will convince the accounts department employee is a moot point!

3.2 ETHICAL ISSUES

Required

For each situation (a) identify the ethical issues involved, and (b) discuss whether there has or has not been any violation of ethical conduct. Support your answers by reference to the relevant professional statements.

1. (a) The ethical issues are those of independence and professional competence.
   (b) The guidelines permit the provision of write-up services to private company audit clients and, in exceptional circumstances only, which would appear to be the case here, to public company audit clients. However, it is important that the service does not require any member of the practice to make executive decisions on behalf of the client. A fundamental ethical requirement is that, if Sarah is to be assigned to the job, she must be competent to provide the required service.
2. (a) The ethical issue is that of the confidentiality of information acquired in the course of providing professional services to a client.
   (b) In this situation there is no direct action that Fobel & Hirst could take and Sarah's action certainly represents a breach of client confidence. The appropriate course of action would have been for Sarah to draw the matter to the attention of the partners who should attempt to persuade management to take corrective action. Pressure could be applied by way of requiring that an appropriate contingent liability for unpaid taxes be disclosed in the interim accounts. As a last resort the firm should consider the desirability of continued association with a client in the light of doubts as to the integrity of management.
3. (a) The ethical issue here is that of whether the acceptance of a gift prejudices the appearance of independence.
   (b) The gift would seem to fall outside the level of normal social courtesies acceptable under the rules. Acceptance of the gift by Sarah could give the impression that Sarah had not been impartial in performing her duties or that, in future, her objectivity would be impaired.
4. (a) The ethical issue here relates to the duty of care that accountants have with respect to handling clients' trust funds.
   (b) The partner's behaviour in this situation appears to be unethical. The client's trust fund should not be used for unauthorised purposes.

4.1 DUE CARE

Required

(a) *Has your accounting firm acted with 'due care'? What do you think will be the court's decision if the case goes to trial?*

The key issue in determining whether an auditor has acted with 'due care' or not is by looking at decided cases and the relevant professional standards. Cases such as Kingston Cotton Mill and London and General Bank have suggested that the auditor will have exercised due care if he or she exercises the skill and care of a reasonably competent member of the profession. Later cases state that the courts would consider whether the auditor had followed the appropriate professional standards in determining whether he or she had acted with due care.

In this case it appears as though the audit firm has acted with due care. They have followed all the appropriate work steps and have ensured that the audit was performed in accordance with Auditing Standards. There has even been a subsequent review by another audit partner in an associated firm who cleared the audit file.

The key auditing standard in this case, that the audit firm should be concerned about, is compliance with SAS 110. This standard requires that the auditor should plan the audit with an awareness of the possibility of fraud. It also requires that further work should be performed when there is a suspicion of fraud.

The court's decision would probably be in favour of the auditor in this case. (*Note:* this would be unless the court decided to extend the duties of auditors with respect to the detection of fraud.)

(b) *Even if the partner is convinced he acted with 'due care', why would he possibly offer Speedy Spares a substantial settlement amount?*

A large number of cases are settled before their ultimate conclusion. The high rate of settlement before verdicts has encouraged a large number of frivolous claims to be made against auditors. The reasons for settling include the following:

- litigation tends to be a lengthy and expensive process;
- bad publicity and reputation damage that will arise out of a court decision that goes against the auditor; and
- bad publicity and reputation damage that will arise out of a lengthy legal dispute.

It may make more economic sense to settle with Speedy Spares.

4.2 NEGLIGENCE, LIABILITY TO THIRD PARTIES

Required

Will City Bank succeed in its action against Donaghue Partners? Explain.

For City Bank to establish a cause of action for negligence against Donaghue Partners, City Bank must prove that:

- Donaghue Partners owed a legal duty of care to City Bank.
- Donaghue Partners breached their legal duty by failing to perform the audit with the due care or competence expected of members.
- Donaghue Partner's failure to exercise due care proximately caused City Bank to suffer damages.
- City Bank suffered actual losses or damages.

The facts of this case establish that Donaghue Partners were negligent by not detecting the overstatement of debtors because of its inadvertent failure to follow its audit programme.

However, Donaghue Partners will not be liable to City Bank for negligence because Donaghue Partners owed no duty to City Bank. This is the case because Donaghue Partners was not in privity of contract with City Bank, and the financial statements were neither audited by Donaghue Partners for the primary benefit of City Bank, nor was City Bank within a known and intended class of third parties who were to receive the audited financial statements. The decision in the Caparo case confirms that the defendant did not owe the plaintiff a duty of care.

5.1 AUDIT EVIDENCE

Required

(a) *Identify and describe the procedures for obtaining audit evidence.*

Inspection of documents	The physical examination of documentary records which may include vouching or tracing to related documents in the audit trail.
Inspection of assets	The physical examination of tangible assets.
Observation	Looking at procedures being performed by others.
Inquiry and confirmation	The process of seeking information by asking questions of knowledgeable persons inside or outside the entity. The information may be new to the auditor or may corroborate evidence from other sources. Confirmation is the written response to an inquiry to corroborate information contained in the accounting records.
Computation	Checking the arithmetical accuracy of source documents and accounting records or performing independent calculations.
Analytical procedures	The analysis of relationships such as between items of financial data to identify consistencies and predicted patterns or significant fluctuations and unexpected relationships, and the results of investigations thereof.

(b) *For each of the procedures, describe an audit test using that procedure to obtain evidence as to the balance of plant and machinery including the related balances of accumulated depreciation and charges to profit and loss.*

(The tests in this answer are illustrative only. Other tests using each procedure would be equally satisfactory.)

Inspection of documents and assets	Physically inspect additions to plant and machinery agreeing details such as model number and serial number with the purchase invoice and fixed asset register.

Observation	Observe entity staff comparing the physical existence of plant and machinery with the items recorded in the fixed asset register.
Inquiry and confirmation	Obtain written confirmation of the existence of plant and machinery recorded as being leased to customers.
Computation	Check the computation of depreciation for the year.
Analytical procedures	Compare the total depreciation charge for plant and machinery with the comparable charge for the previous year and consider the reasonableness of any difference.

(c) *For each of the procedures, discuss considerations affecting your judgement as to the reliability of the evidence with particular reference to the test described in your answer to (b).*

Inspection of documents	With the inspection of documents the reliability of evidence depends on: • the nature and source of the documents with the least reliable being documents created by and obtained from the entity and the most reliable being documents created by and obtained directly from third parties; • whether documents are originals or photocopies or facsimiles.
Inspection of assets	The reliability depends on the ability of the auditor to be certain as to the identification of assets examined is the one recorded in the records. Obtaining the services of an expert in identifying the asset will increase the reliability of the evidence.
Observation	The reliability of the evidence depends on whether: • entity staff had no advance warning that their performance was to be observed by the auditors (i.e the observation was conducted on a surprise basis); • staff behaviour is likely to be affected by the knowledge that they are being observed. Where observation is of the nature of a sample test, as in observing comparison of fixed assets to the records for only a sample of the entity's plant and machinery, the reliability of the evidence depends on the auditor's judgement as to whether the performance of procedures by entity staff might differ when they are not being observed.
Inquiry and confirmation	The reliability of the evidence depends on: • the knowledge of the other party;

> - the independence of the other party;
> - whether the reply is written or oral.
>
> Confirmations from customers as to the existence of plant and machinery on hire to them are highly reliable. They would have knowledge as to the subject of the inquiry. As third parties, they would be independent. Their response is in writing.

Computation

> Being entirely auditor created, computational evidence, such as verifying the calculation of the depreciation charge, is highly reliable.

Analytical procedures

> As auditor created evidence, analytical procedures are reliable but limited by the ability of the auditor to assess its reasonableness. In comparing the total depreciation charge for the year, the effect of additions and disposals of assets with different depreciation rates can only be approximated unless a full computation is performed. Where the procedure involves non-financial data or data from outside the entity, reliability is limited by the reliability of the other data.

5.2 AUDIT OBJECTIVES AND EVIDENCE RELIABILITY

Required

For each procedure (2) to (7) inclusive;

(a)   *identify its principal objective;*
(b)   *explain its objective in terms of the account balance or transaction class involved and the financial statement assertion to which the evidence principally relates;*
(c)   *discuss the reliability of the evidence obtained.*

TEST	(a) OBJECTIVE	(b) ASSERTION	(c) RELIABILITY
2	Test of operation of control.	Occurrence of purchase transactions. It ensures that the goods receiving clerk properly inspects the contents of deliveries as being (a) undamaged and (b) in agreement with the delivery note and purchase order.	As evidence obtained directly by the auditor it provides very reliable evidence of the procedure observed. However, it provides less reliable evidence as to the performance of procedures relating to goods delivered generally as the clerk may behave differently when not being observed.
3	Substantive test of details of purchase transactions.	Completeness of recorded purchase transactions. It ensures that all goods delivered are recorded in the accounting records.	Reliable in that the evidence is obtained directly by the auditor. However, the reliability is subject to further evidence that all deliveries are recorded on goods received notes.

ANSWERS

TEST	(a) OBJECTIVE	(b) ASSERTION	(c) RELIABILITY
4	Test of operation of control.	Occurrence of recorded purchase transactions. It ensures that the control procedure of independently checking invoices with supporting documentation is evidenced as having been performed.	Documentary evidence of the procedure having been performed is less persuasive than observation of the performance itself. However, the employees responsible have acknowledged, by initialling the invoice, proper performance of the procedure and may thus be held accountable if they are found to have performed their task carelessly. To this extent the evidence is reliable.
5	Analytical procedure as a substantive procedure relating to the creditors' balance.	Existence, completeness and valuation of the creditors' balance. If the closing balance, relative to purchases, is higher than expected, the balance may include liabilities that did not exist at balance sheet date or that individual liabilities included in the balance are overstated. If the closing balance, relative to purchases, is lower than expected, the balance may be incomplete through the omission of liabilities that existed at balance sheet date, or individual liabilities included in the balance are understated.	As auditor created evidence, the computation of the relationship, such as a ratio, is reliable. However, the reliability of analytical evidence is subject to the ability to develop expectations. If the incidence of purchases during the year and the entity's payment policy are unchanged, last year's relationship provides a reliable basis for developing an expectation for the current year.
6	Substantive test of details of creditors' balance.	Valuation of the creditors' balance. By virtue of the double entry system, any errors: • in entering individual transactions in the purchase journal, cash payments journal or purchase ledger; • in adding journals and posting totals to the ledger; • in determining the closing account balances; are likely to be revealed by a failure of individual creditor balances to agree, in total, with the balance on the control account.	As auditor created evidence it is highly reliable. However, the auditor will also need to obtain evidence that the list of creditors' balances has been properly taken from the ledger.

TEST	(a) OBJECTIVE	(b) ASSERTION	(c) RELIABILITY
7	Test of design of control.	Completeness and existence of recorded purchases during the period. If cut-off procedures are reliable, then control risk of purchase transactions being recorded in the wrong accounting period is reduced.	In so far as the auditor evaluates the effectiveness of the design of cut-off procedures the evidence is reliable. There is always the risk that management may deliberately misinform the auditor. Nevertheless, if the auditor considers the procedures are effectively designed, further tests of control need to be performed to ensure the procedures are properly operated. Because of inherent limitations of control, assessment of control risk as less than high always involves an element of uncertainty.

6.1 CLIENT ACCEPTANCE DECISION

Required

(a) *State factors the partners should have considered for and against accepting nomination.*

Arguments against acceptance of nomination

- Rapid growth is often accompanied by inadequate accounting systems and weak internal controls. This will increase inherent risk and may affect the auditor's ability to undertake a satisfactory audit.
- Rapid growth through aggressive takeovers implies a management philosophy that is willing to accept risks. This has adverse implications on the control environment which will increase both inherent and control risk and will tend to require adoption of a more expensive predominantly substantive approach to the audit.
- Failure to take action against employee fraud brought to their notice by the auditors suggests a culture that tolerates unethical behaviour that is likely to permeate the company and to be shared by all employees. This will result in a weak control environment.
- Introduction of a new computer system must be undertaken very carefully. In addition, an unnecessarily complicated system is one of the warning signs of fraud. Such a computer system may be difficult to audit.
- There are many documented examples of audit failure where aggressive behaviour towards audit staff has discouraged them from asking probing questions.
- The impending public listing means that the company is under pressure to show an improving performance with attendant risks of creative accounting. It also means that the work of the auditor will come under increasing scrutiny. There are always significant risks in accepting an audit under such terms.

Arguments for accepting nomination

As a larger firm your firm is likely to have the capability of influencing the directors of Bondi and persuading them of the benefits of a more ethical style of business. This will benefit the company's shareholders. If your firm rejects the audit they are likely to appoint a less reputable firm. This will not be in the shareholders' interest and may discredit the profession.

(b) *Detail the matters you would be concerned about in obtaining the required knowledge of the business and in developing your audit plan.*

Employee frauds

- I would need to investigate the alleged employee frauds in order to identify the control weaknesses that were exploited.
- I would inquire as to whether any changes had been made to the accounting and internal control systems as a consequence of the fraud.
- I would want to know the current positions held by the guilty employees.

Computer system

- I would need to ensure the audit team included sufficient computer audit specialists.
- I would pay particular attention to the control environment relating to computer systems and to evaluation of general and application controls.
- My tests of controls would almost certainly include the use of computer-assisted audit techniques.

Contracts with manufacturers

- I would enquire closely into such contracts and the strategies adopted by the company for securing maximum benefit from the contracts. I would need assistance from an industry specialist as to problems encountered by manufacturers and dealers in confirming compliance with the contracts.

6.2 AUDIT WORKING PAPERS

Required

(a) *State four matters you would expect to find recorded in working papers in the permanent audit file and explain their purpose.*

MATTER	PURPOSE
Summary of accounting policies.	It is useful for the auditor to keep a record of major accounting policies adopted as a means of ensuring consistency of accounting treatment between successive audits.

MATTER	PURPOSE
Key ratios and other significant performance data over the past five years.	A record of key ratios and other data developed in prior years facilitates the use of analytical procedures and enables the auditor to identify trends in predicting expected ratios etc. in the current year.
Copies of long-term contracts such as leases and loan agreements.	Having a permanent record of such agreements provides the auditor with a check that the financial implications continue to be reflected in the financial statements. If the entity accidentally or deliberately failed to make provision for expenses and liabilities arising under the terms of such an agreement, the omission would be readily apparent to the auditor. It also saves time that would otherwise be incurred in obtaining access to the original documents kept by the entity and protects against the risk that the originals may be tampered with to conceal an irregularity.
Description of the entity's business including its products, markets, production facilities etc.	This information facilitates continuity of the audit process. It enables audit staff to remind themselves of such matters on commencing a new audit of an existing client to ensure they evaluate the reasonableness of transactions in the context of the nature of the business. It is particularly important as a means of safeguarding such knowledge against the risk that it may be overlooked through the ongoing process of staff turnover.

Other contents that may be mentioned include:

(i) Continuing analysis of accounts particularly those relating to shareholders' funds, long-term debt and fixed assets.
(ii) Extracts from minutes of continuing importance.
(iii) Matters relevant to audit planning such as the location of branches and subsidiaries and, particularly, procedures performed and locations visited on a rotational basis.
(iv) Copies of significant correspondence with the entity of continuing relevance such as the engagement letter and management letters.
(v) Chart of accounts, flow charts or narrative descriptions of the accounting system, organisational charts etc.
(vi) The legal and organisational structure of the entity such as its memorandum and articles of association

(b) *Explain the design and use of audit programmes and the respective merits of standard and tailored audit programmes.*

Design and use

Audit programmes are lists of tests of control and substantive audit procedures to be performed by audit staff in order to obtain sufficient appropriate audit evidence. The individual procedures are determined after assessing the risks of material misstatement and determining the audit strategy to be followed. The procedures reflect the understanding of the system and will incorporate the mix of tests of control and substantive procedures based on the planned audit approach for each material financial statement assertion.

The programme also serves as a means of monitoring and co-ordinating the progress of the audit. The programme should be designed with columns alongside each procedure for staff members to enter their initials and date on completing the performance of each procedure and to note the reference of the working paper detailing the results of the tests performed and the conclusions drawn.

Standardised or tailored

It used to be common for audit firms to pre-print standardised audit programmes; usually one set for larger entities and another set for smaller entities. The advantages were:

(i)   A consistent approach to all audits.
(ii)   Reduced risk of procedures being omitted.
(iii) Reviewers could quickly check the progress of the audit being familiar with the contents of the programme.

Although most firms continue to provide model audit programmes, these are designed to be tailored to the specific circumstances of each engagement. The benefits of this approach are:

(i)   The design of procedures and the names of the documents and records detailed in the programme match the actual accounting system of the entity.
(ii)   The balance between tests of control and substantive procedures can be varied to match the preliminary assessment of inherent and control risk separately for each major financial statement assertion.
(iii) It provides engagement staff with greater control over the audit based on their knowledge of the entity and of the specific audit risks. This, in turn, results in a better understanding of the purpose of each procedure since the staff member performing the procedure will have been involved in designing the programme being followed.

(c)   *Explain the importance of recording details of the actual evidence examined in the course of the audit on which the conclusions are drawn. Your explanation should include consideration of the details to be recorded in the working papers and of the audit trail to be left in the books and records of the entity being audited.*

Recording details of evidence examined and leaving a trail that could enable the evidence procedure to be replicated serves a number of purposes.

(i)   It facilitates the progress of the audit on a day by day basis where a procedure is performed over several days or by different staff members. By maintaining detailed records, procedures completed, partially completed and as yet unperformed can be readily identified. For example, a variety of tests may be carried out on a sample of purchase invoices. Each of the sample of invoices is listed, as a row, on a working paper with columns for the separate tests to be performed on each invoice. Progress is indicated by recording the results of the test in the appropriate cell.
(ii)   As in any control procedure, requiring staff to evidence the work performed provides assurance that the task is likely to be properly performed. If staff members know

that their work could be checked, they are likely to perform it more conscientiously. One of the risks of auditing, especially where staff are required to work to a time budget, is that of premature sign-off – claiming to have performed tests that were not properly completed. The temptation for audit staff to skimp the proper performance of each procedure is also reduced by requiring them to leave a visible trail on entity records. In the above example, the invoices selected for sampling would be initialled by the staff member and where procedures require it, other documents examined and entries in the records would also be 'ticked' by the staff member.

(iii)   Marking documents and records provides evidence, to management of the entity, that a thorough audit has been performed. It also serves to alert entity staff that their work is subject to audit and adds to the incentives to perform their work carefully.

(iv)   Not least is the need to demonstrate proper performance of the audit in the event of a claim for negligence. Reliance on sample evidence means that it may be necessary for the audit firm to prove that a properly designed and selected sample was examined and that failure to detect an error or misstatement was not due to negligence in the performance of the audit.

Although the level of detail recorded is a matter of judgement, it is usually desirable to include:

(i)   Results of all tests performed.
(ii)   Details of individual items selected for sampling including an indication of how the sample was selected.
(iii)   A tick or some other mark on entity records and documents vouched, traced or otherwise inspected during the course of specific tests of details of transactions or balances.

7.1 ACCOUNTING SYSTEMS AND INTERNAL CONTROLS

Required
(a)   *Identify five internal control strengths on which you would rely for your audit.*

Controls

1.   To obtain new assets a purchase requisition form is completed and approved by the manager at each college.
2.   The purchase officer checks each requisition for approval before preparing a purchase order.
3.   Assets over £5,000 require approval by the financial accountant and assets over £20,000 require board approval.
4.   The asset is received by the central store where the receiving clerk agrees all the asset details to the goods received note and to the copy of the purchase order. The receiving clerk will then issue the asset with its computer generated sequential bar code number. This bar code is fixed to the asset and written on the goods received note and supplier invoice.

5. The college manager inputs the new asset details into the asset register using a copy of the purchase order, the original requisition and the asset's bar code.
6. For disposal or write-off of an asset, an asset disposal write-off form is completed by the college manager, signed and sent to head office. The financial accountant approves disposals and write-offs. A copy of the form is filed at head office and the approved original returned to the college manager for action. The college manager will then update the fixed asset register for the subsequent disposal.

(b) *Design tests of control to evaluate the effectiveness of each of the controls identified.*

Select a sample of purchase requisition forms from each of the colleges, and for each requisition selected:

- Ensure the purchase requisition form is completed and approved by the manager at each college.
- Ensure there is evidence of a check by the purchase officer of each requisition for approval before preparing a purchase order.
- Ensure the financial accountant approves assets over £5,000 and the board approves assets over £20,000.
- Check for evidence of a check by the receiving clerk that all the asset details agree to the goods received note and to the copy of the purchase order. Check the asset to ensure that it has been issued with a computer generated sequential bar code number.
- Ensure that the college manager has input the new asset details into the asset register using a copy of the purchase order, the original requisition and the asset's bar code.

Select a sample of disposals or write-offs and ensure an asset disposal write-off form is completed by the college manager, signed and sent to head office and approved by the financial accountant.

7.2 RELIANCE ON INTERNAL AUDIT
Required
(a) *Describe the evaluation of the internal audit function that your firm would need to undertake.*

The external auditor must first carry out a preliminary assessment of internal audit. ISA 610, Considering the Work of Internal Auditing, suggests that this review cover the following areas.

(i) Organisational status
We would satisfy ourselves that the internal audit department is sufficiently independent of management whose work is being assessed and is free from operational responsibility. In practice this requires that internal audit report to the highest level of management, preferably the audit committee, and is free to communicate fully with the external auditors. The department should also have a reasonable degree of freedom in determining the scope of its work.

(ii) Scope of function

We would select a few recent reports and sight evidence that their recommendations were fully acted upon in order to be satisfied that the findings of internal audit carry an appropriate degree of weight.

(iii) Technical competence

We would review the personnel files of existing internal audit staff for evidence of their qualifications and experience in order to be satisfied that the department is staffed by appropriately qualified personnel. We would also need to inquire into company policy with regard to the employment, training and promotion of internal audit staff members.

(iv) Level of resources

We would need to obtain firm assurance that internal audit had a sufficient level of resources to carry out all the procedures on which we would be placing reliance, particularly visits to branches.

(iv) Due professional care

We would inspect documentary evidence such as manuals, work programmes and working papers to ensure that the work performed meets appropriate standards of planning, review and documentation.

(b) *Assuming the evaluation confirms the adequacy of the internal audit function, explain the extent to which the external auditors could place reliance on the work of internal audit in the following areas:*
   (i) *obtaining and documenting the understanding of the accounting and internal control systems;*
   (ii) *performing tests of controls;*
   (iii) *assessing inherent and control risk;*
   (iv) *performing procedures requiring the use of computer assisted audit techniques (CAATs);*
   (v) *performing substantive tests on cash and inventory at the stores.*

ISA 610 requires the external auditor to evaluate and test the specific work of internal auditing on which external audit reliance is placed, to confirm its adequacy for the external auditor's purpose. Procedures and other considerations applicable to each of the areas is detailed below.

(i) Accounting and internal control systems

If we are to place reliance on internal audit prepared documentation of the accounting and internal control systems we would need to:

- review procedures followed in obtaining the understanding and in documenting the results to ensure that they are sufficiently thorough, such as through confirmation by walk-through tests;
- see that the documentation is reasonably current and that there is evidence that staff members undertaking the documentation were properly supervised and that the work has been properly reviewed;

- take a sample of such documentation, consider the adequacy of the level of detail recorded and perform a walk-through test in order to satisfy ourselves as to its accuracy and relevance for our purposes.

(ii) Tests of control

We would probably be able to rely on tests of controls performed by internal audit staff at branches. In relying on the results of these tests we would need to:

- be satisfied as to the timing and extent of the tests;
- sight evidence that the tests were properly planned, performed, documented and reviewed;
- ensure that the conclusions were consistent with the results of the tests;
- compare the evidence obtained with the results of similar tests performed by us at head office and at the principal store.

(iii) Assessment of inherent and control risks

It is unlikely that we would be prepared to rely on the assessment of inherent risk by internal audit. Neither would we rely solely on the assessment control risk by internal audit as this is critical to the development of an appropriate audit strategy. However, in forming our assessment of control risk we would consider the role of internal audit and the results of tests of control undertaken by internal audit.

(iv) CAATs

The use of embedded audit facilities is much more efficient than test data. Embedded facilities, such as an integrated audit test facility, test live data as it is processed by the system. Although external auditors may be consulted, such facilities are usually installed for use by internal audit. Moreover, the use of such facilities is an ongoing activity and cannot always be conveniently performed during the limited period of external audit attendance at the premises. Furthermore, internal audit may have more expertise in operating the particular facilities available than our own computer audit specialists. For all of these reasons it makes sense to accept the co-operation of internal audit in performing CAATs. However, we would need to:

- perform tests to ensure that the facilities are properly installed and operating;
- evaluate general controls over computer operations to ensure that the audit facilities are secure and can only be accessed by internal audit staff;
- be involved in the design of the tests to be performed;
- review the working papers to ensure that the tests are properly conducted, supervised, documented and reviewed and that the conclusions are consistent with the evidence.

(v) Substantive procedures

It would be reasonable to place reliance on routine substantive procedures performed by internal audit at branch stores. Such procedures could include surprise cash counts, attendance at periodic inventory counts, year-end cash and inventory counts including follow up procedures such as cut-off tests and checking count sheets to final inventory listings. However, we would need to perform similar procedures at the main store and at least one other store so that we can compare our experience with the evidence obtained by internal audit. The locations that our firm and internal audit visit should be rotated annually. As in previous situations, we would need to review the work performed by internal audit. We would probably also perform additional procedures if the work of internal audit reveals material misstatements or other unusual matters.

8.1 EVALUATING RESULTS OF SAMPLE TESTING

Required

(a) *Discuss Sarah's method of selecting items to be confirmed. Your answer should:*

  (i) *identify any aspects of her approach that might be considered inconsistent with sampling;*

  (ii) *suggest alternative means of selecting a sample ensuring that the more material balances stand the greatest chance of selection;*

  (iii) *compare and contrast the haphazard method of selection with random selection and systematic selection.*

(i) Inconsistencies with sampling

Sarah's approach does not meet the requirement that each item must have an determinable chance of selection:

- all large accounts are selected;
- no accounts under £100 are selected;
- no government accounts are selected.

Selective testing of all large accounts for testing is common but is not sampling. The population being sampled is that of debtors' balances below the threshold for items selected as large and the results projected accordingly. In addition, the basis for defining 'large' needs explanation.

Ignoring very small balances is irregular but, in a test primarily concerned with testing for understatement and valuation, unlikely to affect the results. The working paper should provide a rationale for the cut-off point of £100.

Treating government accounts as a separate sub-population is stratification and the results of each set of sample testing must be projected to each stratum separately. This presumes that alternative verification is performed on government accounts. Merely excluding them as being too difficult is not acceptable.

(ii) Alternative approach to materiality

Methods of drawing a sample from variable populations to ensure a sufficient sample of more material balances are stratification and monetary unit sampling.

Stratification divides the population into strata by value and draws relatively larger samples from higher value strata than lower value strata. Sarah has actually done this but not in a formalised way. Statistics can enable auditors to determine the optimum stratification to obtain the required assurance from the smallest sample. In evaluating results, error rates need to be projected separately to each stratum.

Monetary unit sampling identifies individual £s as the sampling unit. By systematically selecting £s, the larger the account balance the larger its chance of containing a £ being selected and thus being tested. Each £ is regarded as being in error proportionately to the error in the account balance of which it forms part.

(iii) Haphazard selection

Haphazard selection is a method of drawing a sample but introduces the risk of unconscious bias such as neglecting the first or last items on a page.

Systematic sampling overcomes this by requiring the staff member to follow a prescribed order. Selection can be replicated and any instances of failure to select the required sample detected. It is not convenient for populations in which the sampling units are not sequentially ordered. It also presents the risk that there may be a particular pattern to the population, which recurs at the same interval as the sampling interval.

Random selection can be undertaken by use of random numbers generated by computer or random number tables. In both cases bias is avoided by requiring the staff member to justify reasons for not testing the sampling unit selected by computer or through use of random number tables. It is inconvenient for populations not held on a computer in that physical selection of documents in random order can be time consuming. It is also not appropriate for sampling units, which are not serially numbered, such as stock items.

(b) *Consider qualitative aspects of each of the five categories of error or other reported differences analysed by Sarah. Suggest which of them should be included in arriving at an estimate of population error.*

Address unknown

- These affect the valuation assertion since the amount is potentially uncollectable.
- The extent of the error depends on whether the company does have a forwarding address.
- Assuming there is no forwarding address the error is one that may be projected to the population.

Cut-off

Since these have been established as goods or cash in transit, they are not misstatements and do not constitute errors.

Invoicing errors

- These would appear to result from a weakness in control.
  - The cause of discovered errors must be investigated as to whether they are consistent with the assessed level of control risk for invoice pricing.
  - If they suggest a higher level of risk than that originally assessed the level of substantive procedures may need to be reconsidered.
  - It may be they occurred during a particular point in time such as when the invoicing clerk was on holiday in which case further testing may be required on the sub-population of invoices prepared at that time.

– Otherwise they are consistent with expected errors and must be projected to the population.

Posting errors

These would appear to result from control weaknesses. Although there is a slight risk of such errors resulting in accounts becoming uncollectable, the fact that the customer to whom they are wrongly charged is likely to complain means that the error is likely to be detected and corrected within a reasonable time. The auditor is not unduly concerned about controls or discovered errors in a situation where monthly statements are issued and customer queries independently investigated. Assuming that to be the case, the error would not be regarded as a misstatement.

Disputed items

Each dispute is likely to be unique. The auditor must investigate each one to see if it is part of a material sub-population. For example it could reveal problems with a particular product and may require a provision against all outstanding sales of that product and even against unsold stocks. If the individual issues are isolated but symptomatic of errors that could be present in the population the error must be projected to the entire population.

(c) *Calculate the projected error in debtors based on the results of the sample test consistent with the qualitative considerations in your answer to (b).*

In projecting the error material accounts selected for testing should be excluded from the population samples. In theory, balances below £100 and with government customers should be excluded. However, the former are likely to be immaterial in total and may be ignored and we have no information as to the latter.

It is assumed that our qualitative analysis has determined that all errors except for cut-off differences and mispostings should be projected to the population. It is also assumed that the ratio method is appropriate.

Recorded value of sample			£265,450
Errors			
Gone away		950	
Invoicing (£2,800 − £2,200)		600	
Disputes (£2,800 − £2,300)		1,500	3,050
Percentage error			1.15%
Total debtors	£2,350,000		
less material items selected	205,000		
Population sampled		£2,145,000	
Error rate		1.15%	
Projected error		24,668	
Errors in material items		0	
Total possible error		£24,668	

Sarah must consider, in the light of the total possible error, whether to conclude that debtors are not materially misstated.

8.2 DETERMINING SAMPLE SIZE

Required

(a) *For each pair of tests, discuss the effect of each of the factors referred to in the tables above.*

Tests of controls

Population size

Population size has no effect where populations are over 5,000 and little effect, even, on populations over 500. A larger sample size will not, therefore, be required for test 2 even though it involves a larger population of transactions.

Assessed level of control risk

More reliance, as to the effective operation of the control, would be required in test 1 than in test 2. By performing fewer substantive procedures the auditor would stand less chance of discovering errors if control procedures are not as effective as believed. It will, therefore, need to select a relatively larger sample in test 1 than in test 2.

Deviation rate

This refers to the proportion of transactions not processed in accordance with laid down procedures, whether or not the invoices are still correctly recorded. A deviation indicates that a control is not operating and increases the chance that an error could occur. In practice, tolerable deviation rates are determined by reference to the level of control risk to be confirmed. The effect on sample size, therefore, is the same as in the previous test with a larger sample being required in test 1 than in test 2. A larger sample enables the results to be projected to the population with greater precision.

Expected deviation rate

In test 1, even if the sample deviation rate is significantly greater than expected, it could still be within tolerable limits. For test 2, however, it is more important that sample deviation rate closely reflects actual deviation rate as there is less margin for sampling error. A relatively larger sample size will, therefore, be required for test 2 than for test 1.

Substantive procedures

Inherent and control risk

The higher the risk, the greater the likelihood that controls have failed to detect or prevent errors and, therefore, the greater the likelihood of errors in the data being tested. To achieve a consistent level of audit risk for both tests, a larger sample is required for test 1 on inventory than for test 2 on accounts receivable.

Tolerable error
Tolerable error relates to materiality. Although other factors enter into the determination of tolerable error, the balance on inventory is probably substantially larger than accounts receivable such that a much smaller percentage error will be material to the financial statements as a whole. In order that sample results may be interpreted with the required precision, a larger sample of inventory items must be selected for test 1 than of accounts receivable items in test 2.

Expected error
In test 2, even if the sample error rate is significantly greater than expected, it will still be within tolerable limits. For test 1, however, it is more important that sample error rate closely reflects actual error rate as there is less margin for sampling error. A relatively larger sample size will, therefore, be required for test 1 than for test 2.

(b) *When subsequently performed, the sample tests of control indicated a deviation rate of 2.1% for test (1) and a deviation rate of 0.5 for test (2). Comment on these results.*

Results of tests of controls

The results indicated a deviation rate for test 1 greater than the tolerable rate. The intended reliance on controls is, therefore, not supported. It is possible, however, that I could still place some reliance on controls. I would need to re-evaluate the results of the sample and, possibly, extend the extent of testing to determine the actual deviation rate and revise my assessment of control risk accordingly.

Sample deviation rate in test 2 is much better than is necessary to support the assessed level of control risk. However, it does not enable me to assess control risk as less than moderate. Assessment of control risk is principally determined by the design effectiveness of controls, not operating effectiveness as tested by this procedure.

9.1 AUDIT PROGRAMME FRAMEWORK FOR SUBSTANTIVE PROCEDURES

Required

(a) *Using only your general knowledge of accounting for property, plant and equipment assets and the general framework for developing an audit programme for substantive procedures described in the chapter, develop an audit programme for your first audit of the property, plant and equipment asset accounts of Buildwell Manufacturing Company.*

(b) *Following each procedure in your audit programme, indicate the assertion (or assertions) to which it applies by using the letters EO, C, RO, VM, and D for the existence or occurrence, completeness, rights and obligations, valuation or measurement, and disclosure assertions, respectively.*

Note: Since inherent and control risk have been assessed as high for all plant asset assertions, substantive procedures must be designed to achieve a low level of detection risk for all assertions. In addition, because the entity has never been audited before, the beginning of the year plant asset balances must be audited as well as the current year's additions and disposals. Because this will likely be the student's first effort at developing an audit programme of substantive procedures, solutions are likely to vary considerably in content and detail. The following is generic in that it does not separately identify the several specific accounts mentioned in the background material.

(a) SUBSTANTIVE PROCEDURE	(b) ASSERTION
1. Perform initial procedures on plant asset balances and records that will be subjected to further testing.	V
(a) Review activity in general ledger plant assets and related accumulated depreciation accounts and investigate entries that appear unusual in amount or source.	
(b) Obtain entity prepared schedules of plant assets and determine that they accurately represent the underlying accounting records from which prepared by:	
• Footing and cross-adding the schedules and reconciling the totals with the related general ledger accounts.	
• Testing agreement of items on schedules with entries in related general ledger accounts.	
2. Perform analytical procedures.	E, C, V, D
(a) Calculate ratios:	
• Plant asset turnover.	
• Rate of return on plant assets.	
• Plant assets to shareholders' equity.	
• Repairs expense to net sales.	
(b) Analyse ratio results relative to expectations based on prior years, industry data, budgeted amounts, or other data.	
3. Vouch plant asset additions to supporting documentation.	E, RO, V
4. Vouch plant asset disposals to supporting documentation.	E, C, RO, V
5. Review entries to repairs and maintenance expense for misclassifications.	C, V, D
6. Inspect plant assets, being alert to evidence of additions or disposals not included on the entity's schedules and to conditions that bear on the proper valuation and classification of the plant assets.	E, C, V, D
7. Examine title documents, leases, and contracts.	EO, C, RO, VM, D
8. Review provisions for depreciation.	EO, C, VM, D
9. Compare report presentation with applicable Accounting Standards.	D
(a) Determine that plant assets and related expenses, gains, and losses are properly identified and classified in the financial report.	
(b) Determine the appropriateness of disclosures pertaining to the cost, book value, depreciation methods, and useful lives of major classes of plant assets, the pledging of plant assets as collateral, the terms of lease contracts, and the particulars of the construction-in-progress.	

9.2 AUDIT OF ACCOUNTING ESTIMATES

Required

(a) *Explain the approaches adopted by auditors in obtaining sufficient appropriate audit evidence regarding accounting estimates.*

Paragraph 11 to ISA 540 'Audit of Accounting Estimates' lists the following approaches in the audit of an accounting estimate:

- review and test the process used by management or the directors to develop the estimate;
- use an independent estimate for comparison with that prepared by management or the directors; or
- review subsequent events.

(b) *Describe the procedures you would apply in verifying the general provision for bad and doubtful debts.*

Identify and evaluate the company's procedures

- Consider the existence and likely effectiveness of controls over these procedures. Consider the benefits of testing controls over the procedures in order to reduce the extent of substantive procedures. For Coogee the appropriate audit strategy is almost certainly one of proceeding directly to substantive procedures.
- The company's procedures probably include:
  - ageing debtors at balance sheet date;
  - applying a percentage to debtors within each age banding (excluding those for which a specific provision is made) such as 5% of debtors 60 to 90 days overdue, 20% of debtors 90 to 120 days overdue and 50% of debtors over 120 days overdue.

Test the company's estimate

- Test the aged analysis of debtors by:
  - reviewing the results of tests of sales transactions to check the accuracy of the process of matching cash receipts against outstanding invoices such that the age of outstanding transaction could be readily ascertained. If necessary, trace a sample of customer payments back to remittance advices to establish the age of outstanding invoices;
  - testing the ageing of a sample from the aged analysis to outstanding invoices shown in the sales ledger;
  - considering the appropriateness of the ageing of balances where payments could not be matched with specific invoices;
  - adding the aged analysis;
  - agreeing the total of the aged analysis to the sales ledger balance.
- Check the calculation of the provision in accordance with the formula, cross checking with the list of debtors against which a specific provision had been made to ensure they are properly excluded.
- Examine bad and doubtful debts written off during the current financial year and consider the extent to which the formula predicts actual experience.
- If the formula has been changed from that previously used, consider management's explanation and test the effect on the provision.
- Consider the possibility the provision might be overstated in order to manage earnings in a poor year.
- Perform analytical procedures to ascertain the reasonableness of the provision. If the basis of provision were unchanged from the previous year the day's sales in debtors at

[£2.3 million/(£23 million/365)] 36 days and the provision as a percentage of debtors at [(£40,000/£2.3 million) × 100] 1.7% should be comparable with the previous year.
- Inquire whether the provision had been properly considered and approved by the directors.

(c) *Describe the procedures you would apply in verifying the specific provision for bad and doubtful debts.*

- Obtain the list of debtors against which a specific provision had been made.
  - Verify the reason for the provision against documentary evidence such as correspondence with the debtors or with their appointed receivers.
  - Check the amount of the provision, such as the receiver's expected payment to creditors on liquidation.
- Review the results of the debtors' circularisation.
  - For material debtors, consider whether the response indicated the need for a provision.
  - For non-material debtors, consider whether responses reveal problems that could require a provision against a number of debtors such as complaints over a particular faulty product.
- Review correspondence with debtors for evidence of problems that might require a provision.
- Review the aged analysis prepared in connection with the general provision for particularly unusual items for which a specific provision would be appropriate, such as individual unpaid invoices where subsequent invoices had been paid. This could indicate a disputed item.
- Review subsequent events. In particular:
  - Review cash receipts from customers against whom a specific provision had been made. If the debt is paid before the financial statements are approved, no specific provision is required.
  - Scrutinise lists of companies going into receivership up to the date the financial statements are approved to see if any are debtors to the company.
  - Read directors' minutes and review correspondence with debtors after balance sheet date in order to identify any subsequent event that might require a provision against specific debtors.
  - Review credit notes issued after balance sheet date pertaining to amounts outstanding at that date and consider whether the reason for the credit requires a specific provision to be made as at balance sheet date.
- Inquire whether the provision had been properly considered and approved by the directors.

10.1 ACCOUNTS RECEIVABLE CIRCULARISATION
Required
(a) *Consider the relative reliability and independence of the following types of evidence from third parties:*
   (i) *replies to a debtors' circularisation to confirm trade debtors;*
   (ii) *suppliers' statements to confirm purchase ledger balances.*

Debtors' circularisation

- Debtors are independent third parties and, providing there are suitable controls over the preparation and mailing of the confirmation requests and the replies are received directly by the auditor, the responses are likely to be free of bias.
- Replies are based on the customers accounts payable records and many customers maintain reliable records of purchases which they agree to the supplier's statement and may keep less reliable records of cumulative payables. In particular they are unlikely to admit to owing an amount greater than is disclosed on the confirmation request. Replies are, therefore, more likely to provide evidence as to existence and measurement than as to completeness.
- Responses are sometimes entrusted to junior staff who may not be adequately aware of the need to verify the request carefully before responding. Alternatively, more senior staff may regard the request as a waste of time and confirm the balance without checking or fail to respond at all. It may be difficult to support statistically valid conclusions.

Suppliers' statements

- These are supplied by independent third parties but are usually obtained from the audit client. There is a risk that the statements could have been altered before being given to the auditor. This applies particularly if the auditors are supplied with a photocopied or faxed version.
- Suppliers generally maintain reliable accounts payable records since failure to claim moneys from customers is likely to result in it remaining unpaid. Controls over completeness are likely to be particularly strong. Evidence as to the existence of the liability, however, is likely to be less persuasive.
- The proportion of suppliers providing statements is likely to be quite high enabling statistically valid sampling to be undertaken.

(b)   *In relation to selecting debtors for circularisation:*
   (i)   *explain how you would use monetary unit sampling to select the debtors to circularise;*
   (ii)   *consider the criteria you would use to select individual debtors for circularisation using judgement;*
   (iii) *discuss the advantages and disadvantages of using monetary unit sampling (in (i) above) as compared with judgement (in (ii) above) to select the debtors to circularise. Your answer should consider the reasons why it is undesirable only to use judgement to select the debtors for circularisation.*

Monetary (dollar) unit sampling

- I would first determine the tolerable error based on materiality considerations and reliability factor based on detection risk considerations. When applied to the population value, these would determine the sampling interval.

- I would then determine the progressive totals of the listing of accounts receivable balances and select each account that caused the cumulative total to exceed the sampling interval.
- This method increases the probability of larger balances being selected for circularisation and is sometimes referred to as 'probability proportionate to size sampling'.

Judgement sampling – criteria affecting selection

- Size – I would select all balances over tolerable error.
- Age – I would select all balances overdue for a certain period of time such as three months.
- Unusual – I would select balances that appeared unusual in any other respect such as with related parties.
- Other – I would make a haphazard selection of other balances.

Advantages and disadvantages of MUS

Monetary unit sampling eliminates the risk of subjective bias influencing the selection, whether consciously or otherwise that may affect judgement sampling.

Monetary unit sampling enables statistically valid conclusions to be drawn as to the population as a whole.

Judgement sampling enables the auditor to introduce prior knowledge as to the risks affecting the population that may enable a more efficient audit by targeting accounts more likely to be misstated.

It may be impracticable to determine a cumulative totalling of the population to permit a monetary unit sample to be drawn.

It may be preferable to use judgement to remove specific balances from the population for selective testing but then to apply monetary unit sampling to the remaining balances.

(c) *Describe the audit work you would carry out in following up the responses to a debtors' circularisation where:*
   (i) *the debtor disagrees the balance and provides a different balance;*
   (ii) *no reply to the circularisation has been received from the debtor and all attempts at obtaining a reply have failed.*

Disagreement

- My first consideration would be to determine whether the difference was due to cut-off. This would be straightforward if the debtor identified the specific item as being a payment made or an invoice issued immediately prior to the cut-off date. Alternatively, the difference may correspond to such an amount in which case it would be appropriate to conclude that it was due to cash or goods in transit over the cut-off date.
- Otherwise I would need to identify the specific item and the cause of the difference.
  - If it appeared to be an error in the customer's records I would verify the amount by the procedures described below and take no further action.
  - If it was due to a dispute, I would identify the cause, such as faulty goods, and consider whether there might be similar disputes with other customers and

review the provision for bad debts accordingly and other implications, such as net realisable value of similar goods in inventory.

- If it was an error in the audit client's records I would identify the cause. If it was due to a control weakness, I would consider whether my assessment of control risk was appropriate. If I considered it necessary to revise my assessment I would need to increase the level of substantive testing. If the error was isolated, such as while a temporary employee was covering for a regular employee, I might consider it necessary to extend substantive testing over that time period.

No reply

- I would first check after balance sheet date receipts. If the balance appeared to have been paid I would confirm details with the remittance advice to ensue that it was the balance outstanding at the year-end.
- If the balance, or some of it, has not subsequently been paid, I would verify the specific transactions. Ideally I would be looking for reliable evidence, such as a dispatch note signed by the customer or a purchase order signed by the customer.
- As a last resort I would rely on internal documentation such as internal sales orders, dispatch note and invoice copies and ensure that all documentation appeared to be complete and consistent and to have been properly processed.

10.2 CONTROL PROCEDURES – CASH RECEIPTS AND DEBTORS

Required

(a) *Explain in what way the functions assigned to the receptionist result in an inadequate segregation of duties. Your explanation should identify misstatements that could occur and indicate how those duties could be reassigned to other staff members.*

A basic principle of segregation of duties is that an individual employee should not be able to makes errors and be in a position to conceal the fact. A general rule of segregation is that the functions of processing transactions, recording transactions and maintaining records over the subsequent assets or liabilities, should be performed by different individuals. In this way, if an error or misstatement is made by an employee, it will be detected by another employee in the ordinary course of his or her duties.

The receptionist's duties should be restricted to processing cash receipts transactions. All other functions should be assigned to other staff members.

FUNCTION TO BE REASSIGNED	POSSIBLE MISSTATEMENT	REASSIGNMENT
Checking numerical continuity of invoices, determining the total cash sales and entering the cash receipts journal.	The receptionist could deliberately understate the total in order to misappropriate the cash or conceal a shortage of cash.	This should be assigned to clerk 1. (See additional procedure 1.)

ANSWERS

FUNCTION TO BE REASSIGNED	POSSIBLE MISSTATEMENT	REASSIGNMENT
Posting the sales ledger.	If done by the same person that has access to cash receipts, an invoice could be deliberately omitted and the subsequent cash receipt misappropriated. Errors, such as transposition errors, made in entering the sales journal are likely to be repeated in entering the sales ledger. Cash receipts could be temporarily misappropriated and the shortage concealed by delaying recording the receipt. (See the answer to part (b).)	Clerk 1 should post the sales ledger from credit sales invoices whose numerical sequence is checked.
Sending out monthly statements and chasing overdue accounts.	If there are errors in the sales ledger the monthly statements could be altered or suppressed. If payments by customers have been misappropriated and not credited to the customer account, customers' suspicions would not be aroused by chasing apparent overdue balances.	This function should be assigned to clerk 2 since clerk 1 could also falsify statements to conceal errors in recording sales in the sales ledger. (See additional procedure 2.)
Reconciling debtors with the control account in the general ledger.	This procedure detects errors, deliberate or accidental, in the maintenance of debtors' records. If the receptionist has made errors in processing sales and cash receipts transactions to debtors then he would have an incentive to conceal their discovery by falsifying the reconciliation.	Clerk 2 should perform the reconciliation as having no responsibility for recording either cash or sales transactions or maintaining the sales ledger. (See additional procedure 3.)
Writing off uncollectible balances.	If errors have been made resulting in an understatement of cash received from credit customers, their accounts will appear to be overdue. The error can be concealed by writing off the balance. Such an error could arise from the deliberate misappropriation of cash from credit customers.	Clerk 2 should advise the manager of overdue balances that may need to be written off. (See additional procedure 4.)

(b) *Identify other control procedures you would consider necessary to ensure the completeness of the recorded cash receipts and debtors.*

1. A bank reconciliation should be performed at least monthly by clerk 1 to ensure that cash deposited is in agreement with amounts recorded in the cash receipts book. The bank reconciliation should be scrutinised and signed by the manager.

2. The garage manager should review the list of customer account balances (which should, if practicable, be aged), enquire into steps being taken to collect overdue balances and consider whether further credit may be allowed.
3. The reconciliation of debtors' balances with the control account in the general ledger should be scrutinised by the garage manager to ensure that it appears to be properly drawn up.
4. Final decisions on bad debt write-offs must be approved in writing by the garage manager.

The opening of mail should be done in the presence of a second clerk who should confirm the total amount of cash receipts enclosed therein to minimise the likelihood of such receipts being misappropriated.

11.1 CREDITORS' SUBSTANTIVE PROCEDURES

Required

(a) *In your audit of creditors in the 30 September 20x2 financial statements explain which of the financial statement assertions you would regard as presenting the greatest inherent risk.*

Completeness is usually regarded as presenting the greatest level of inherent risk for the following reasons.

- Line managers who may be close to budgetary limits are under pressure to withhold recording of suppliers' invoices until after the year-end.
- If the company were seeking to raise additional finance or to renew existing borrowing agreements, senior management (the directors) would be under pressure to understate creditors in order to improve the company's apparent liquidity. The more liquid the balance sheet shows the company to be the more favourable the terms are likely to be.
- Control procedures placed in operation by the most entities relate to the perceived risk of improper purchasing by employees or overpayments to suppliers. These reduce risks relating to the occurrence assertion but leave the entity exposed to risks associated with completeness.
- The primary source of information initiating recognition of a liability is the supplier's invoice. During the year the company has no incentive to accelerate the receipt of suppliers' invoices. This means that, as at balance sheet date, there could be outstanding claims not yet invoiced by suppliers which the entity has no formalised procedures for identifying promptly.
- Valuation is rarely a problem except in complex contractual situations where the amount due is contingent upon some future event such as a volume discount dependent on total purchases at some future date exceeding some agreed amount.

(b) *Discuss the reasons for undertaking or not undertaking a creditors' circularisation.*

A creditors' circularisation is not normally undertaken for the following reasons.

- Examination of documentary evidence is usually a cheaper form of substantive evidence than confirmation.
- For creditors, much of the documentary evidence available is in the form of third party sourced suppliers' invoices and statements, in contrast to debtors for whom most of the available documentation is entity prepared.
- Although examination of third party sourced documentary evidence is less reliable than confirmations received directly by the auditor, it usually provides sufficient evidence.

A creditors' circularisation would be considered where:

- a substantial proportion of the company's suppliers does not issue monthly statements;
- statements from suppliers with whom the company does substantial business are unexpectedly unavailable for the last month of the year;
- only fax or photocopies of statements are available whose authenticity is doubtful;
- there are suspicions that the company, or a member of the company's staff, may be deliberately understating liabilities and there is a possibility that some of the suppliers' statements may be forgeries given the ease of replicating documents with modern scanning and desk top publishing technology.

(c) *Outline substantive procedures you would apply in your audit of creditors relating to production department purchases.*

Initial procedures

- Obtain and test the accuracy of a list of such creditors by testing it to and from the computer records and adding it and agreeing it to the control account. (If production creditors are not segregated from other creditors this procedure will apply to all creditors.)

Analytical procedures

- Develop expectations and analyse creditor balances to test actual with expectations on the following:
    - current year's balance compared with previous years;
    - average age of creditors compared with previous years;
    - gross profit compared with previous year and industry average.

Tests of details of transactions

- Ascertain cut-off data for goods inward notes (GINs) probably obtained during stock-take attendance.
- Check cut-off by obtaining GINs for two weeks prior to the year end and:

- checking their numerical continuity;
- tracing GINs to the purchases recorded before 31 December or the accrual journal entry.
- For a smaller sample, verify the existence or recorded purchases prior to the year-end by vouching a sample of purchases and purchase accruals to GINs in the sequence issued prior to the year-end.
- For a sample of the closing accruals, would verify the amount of the accrual by vouching the amount to a subsequently received supplier's invoice.

Tests of details of balances

- Select a sample of creditors using criteria such as:
  - all creditors from whom the entity bought more than 1% of its purchases during the year;
  - a random sample of all other creditors including nil and credit balances.
- For each creditor in the sample, compare the balance with the creditor's statement and investigate differences.
- If any creditor statements were unavailable, confirm the balance directly with the creditor.

(d) *Explain additional procedures you would perform in verifying the completeness of non-production department creditors.*

Completeness of non-production creditors

Planned detection risk for the completeness assertion must be low because of the assessment of control risk as only just less than high and from problems identified in obtaining the understanding of the accounting system in that:

- there are no goods inward notes to determine the date of receipt of the goods;
- invoices are not recorded until after approval by the department manager which could cause considerable delay and even a failure to record liability for invoices mislaid or even lost before being recorded;
- suppliers' statements are not reconciled which would otherwise detect most delayed or missing invoices.

Audit procedures would be centred on cut-off and the search for unrecorded liabilities.

- Vouch purchases entered in the purchase journal as at 31 December (including those entered while the journal was held open after the year-end) to invoices to verify that they are properly recorded as creditors at balance sheet date.
- Vouch larger purchases recorded in the first two weeks of the subsequent year to invoices to ensure that they are properly recorded after the year-end.
- Obtain suppliers' statements from major suppliers and reconcile them with the balance on the creditors' records for evidence of invoices missing or mislaid.

- Review outstanding purchase orders for evidence of goods or services received prior to the year-end not yet invoiced by the supplier.
- Similarly vouch cash payments for the first two weeks after balance sheet date for payments for goods and services received before the year-end not processed as creditors.
- Review both purchases and cash payments for items that may relate to goods or services received prior to balance sheet date. This review should be continued up to the date of signing the auditors' report.
- Compare prepayments and accruals with the previous year for items such as rent or utility bills normally paid in advance or arrears of receipt of goods and services and investigate differences.
- Analyse expense accounts for significant differences either in absolute amounts or relative to sales. Any unexpected difference could be due to unrecorded purchases at balance sheet date.

11.2 PAYROLL CONTROLS

Required

(a) *State the principal controls you would expect to exist in the above payroll system and explain their purpose.*

In discussing the potential controls for this system, the focus will be on ensuring that fictitious employees cannot be created and that wages cannot be misappropriated.

Hiring and changes

- The personnel department hires employees. All hiring should be documented on a personnel authorisation form. One copy of this form should be placed in the employee's personnel file in the personnel department. Another copy is sent to the payroll department.
- All changes should be authorised in writing by the personnel department before being entered in the personnel data master file.

Payment

- On receipt of the clock cards in the payroll department, they are batched and a batch total is prepared of hours worked.
- Payroll transactions should be subject to an edit check that checks for a valid employee number, and a limit or reasonableness check on the hours worked.
- Once the payroll run has been performed a number of printed reports are produced, including: exceptions and control report, payroll register, payroll register and pre-numbered payroll cheques, a general ledger summary. These outputs should be subject to proper review by appropriate personnel.

Paying the payroll and protecting unclaimed wages

- It would be a better control for wages to be paid by cheque or EFT transfer rather than cash.

- Cash payments should be signed by treasurer's office personnel not involved in preparing or recording the payroll.
- Unclaimed cash should be stored in a safe or vault in the treasurer's office.
- A check should be made to ensure that the cashier is always separate from the wages department.

If the misappropriation has been achieved by collusion it would be more difficult to implement controls to prevent it happening again.

(b) *How might you test to ensure that all employees exist?*

- Witness the distribution of payroll.
- Examine authorisation forms for new hires.
- Examine termination notices in the payroll department.
- Follow up all unclaimed cheques after payroll distribution.
- Select a sample of employees and check them to the phone listing.

(c) *Describe three analytical review techniques you might use to audit payroll.*

1. Calculate the average yearly wage expense per employee for the company and compare with prior years.
2. Compare monthly payroll expense for the year and explain any significant variations.
3. Calculate average liability for annual leave per employee and compare to prior year.
4. Calculate wages expense as a percentage of total revenue and compare to prior years.

(*Note*: Only three required.)

12.1 PERPETUAL STOCK RECORDS AND THE AUDIT OF STOCK

Required

(a) (i) *Describe the control procedures you would need to identify in order to accept book stock as the basis for determining the quantity of stock on hand at the year end.*

In evaluating control risk relating to the accuracy of stock records I would need to obtain an understanding of the stock record information system and evaluate the design effectiveness of control procedures relating to:

- transactions processed to the records; and
- comparison of stocks with the records.

Transactions processed to the records

Prior year audits have identified the existence of controls relating to the occurrence and completeness of purchase and sale transactions. It will be necessary to plan tests of control to confirm that these controls continue to exist and to be operated effectively. It will also be necessary to extend my understanding with respect to procedures relating to entries in the stock records, to evaluate the design effectiveness of controls over these procedures and to plan and perform tests of control over their operating effectiveness if the preliminary assessment of control risk is less than high.

Since the system is computerised the tests will largely be of the form of computer-assisted audit tests (CAATs) such as the use of test data. These will ensure that data scanned from tags both on delivery and on sale is correctly and completely recorded in the stock records.

The most important controls I will need to identify will be those relating to the stock records including comparison of physical stock with the records.

Comparison of stocks with the records

I will be enquiring into the procedures for

- making test counts;
- comparing counts with the records; and
- correcting the records.

Making test counts

My enquiries will, in particular, be directed towards the following matters in order to assess design effectiveness:

- who performs the counts and are they sufficiently independent from responsibility for maintaining the records and for custody of stock;
- how frequently test counts are performed, what proportion of stock is tested on each occasion and how stock to be tested is selected. At a minimum I would expect to see all stock counted over the course of a year;
- how test counts are performed. I would expect to find proper instructions issued with the counters properly briefed:
  - housekeeping should be such that all stock to be counted can be properly identified;
  - accuracy of counting should be checked and reliable records maintained of the count;
  - the count should be performed at a time when there is no stock movement, such as outside of shop opening hours.

Comparing test counts with the records

I would be interested in:

- procedures for ensuring the cut-off of the records to ensure that all movement in stock up to the time of the count is fully recorded;
- independence of the person performing the comparison from processing stock transactions or custody of stock;

- investigation of differences such as recounting and recording an explanation of reasons for discrepancies where determined;
- scrutiny of the count and of differences by a responsible person who enquires into control weaknesses detected as a result of the investigation and who authorises changes to be made to the stock records.

Correcting the records

I would enquire into procedures for correcting stock records to ensure that the adjustments are properly made and that access controls are sufficiently strong to prevent this procedure being used to improperly adjust stock records to conceal shortages.

(a) (ii) *Describe how you would test those controls.*

Tests of controls would include:

- inspecting stock-take instructions and considering their adequacy;
- observing the performance of a sample of periodic stock counts ensuring that it is conducted in accordance with the instructions;
- inspecting the records of counts to determine:
  - the extent of such counts;
  - the extent of errors detected and corrected;
- testing access controls over alterations to stock records to ensure that only properly authorised corrections can be made.

I would then assess the controls, my assessment being strongly influenced by the extent of differences detected and the causes of differences.

(b) *Describe the substantive procedures you would perform, both during the year and as at the year-end, in order to verify the completeness and existence of stocks.*

During the year I would need to:

- inspect physical stock by attending a number of periodic stock-takes;
- make test counts of stocks during attendance at periodic stock-takes. The extent of such counts and of the number of locations at which stock-takes are observed need careful consideration, particularly whether it is necessary to observe and test count stocks at each shop during the year. In following up test counts I would:
  - ensure that they agreed with the entity's count;
  - compare quantities with stock records at the date of the count;
  - investigate the cause of differences;
  - see that the records are properly corrected;
- check agreement of counts made by entity personnel with stock records and see that all differences are noted and investigated;
- verify the explanation of differences identified as a result of comparison of book to physical;

- see that the schedule of differences is properly approved and that stock records are properly adjusted;
- trace entries to stock records from sales and purchase transactions;*
- vouch entries in stock records to sales and purchase records and properly approved corrections arising from differences on counting;*
- test the arithmetical accuracy of the stock records;*
- review the records of test counts and differences detected, and:
  - ensure that all stocks are counted at least once during the year;
  - consider the accuracy of the stock records as determined by the extent of discrepancies discovered;
- discuss with management evidence as to the reliability of stock records and whether it might be necessary to carry out a full stock-take at or close to the year-end.

At the year-end I will need to:

- test check the stock listing to and from the stock records;
- check that the balance of stock per the stock records agrees with the control account on the nominal ledger;
- verify sales and purchases cut-off including entries to stock records;
- perform analytical procedures to confirm the reasonableness of the amounts recorded as stock.

(c) *State the systems development controls you would expect to find applied to the rewriting of the stock control system.*

I would expect to find development of the stock costing system to include:

- performance of a feasibility study to identify the requirements of the new system;
- clearly specified system requirements approved by the accounting department;
- proper testing of the new system with the results of tests recorded and approved by the accounting department;
- written approval for the new system from the accounting department;
- appropriate file conversion procedures including the initial determination of cost at FIFO;
- documentation of the new system including test results and approvals maintained in the company's files.

12.2 TANGIBLE FIXED ASSETS

Required

(a) *State, with reasons, the first audit procedures you would perform on the schedules provided by the company's accountant.*

*These tests will probably be performed using computer audit software.

Clerical accuracy

Because this schedule has been prepared by the company's accountant I must first make certain that it is correct in accordance with the company's books and records if I am to use the schedule as the basis for planning and performing my audit.

I would verify the schedule by:

- testing it to and from amounts recorded in the nominal ledger and with the draft financial statements;
- checking the correctness of additions and other calculations on the schedule.

The basis for this procedure is that of professional scepticism which requires making no presumption as to the accuracy of information provided by management.

Opening balances

I would check that the opening balances are in agreement with the balances in the previous year's audit file:

- to ensure that any amendments to the previous year's closing balance agreed at audit had been properly recorded in the company's books and records;
- to provide a starting point for verifying the closing balances. With tangible fixed assets most audit procedures are applied to changes in the balance. Reliance is placed on audit procedures performed in previous years in verifying assets brought forward at the beginning of the year.

(b) *Outline the substantive audit procedures you would apply in verifying plant and machinery additions. Your answer should identify procedures applicable to each of the financial statement assertions.*

Occurrence

- Vouch additions to suppliers' invoices.
- Inspect goods inward notes or other evidence confirming delivery of the items prior to the year-end.
- Inspect purchase orders, requisitions and other evidence, such as board approval, that the purchase had been properly authorised.
- Physically inspect some of the items confirming description and serial numbers to the invoice.

Completeness

- Analyse repairs and maintenance to ensure that items charged to this account should not have been capitalised.
- Scrutinise the company's capital budget and capital commitments recorded in the previous year's financial statements for details of proposed additions and enquire as to why any such items are not recorded as additions.

Rights

- Inspect the purchase documentation to ensure that ownership or equivalent rights are assigned to the company.

Accuracy

- I would ensure that the amount recorded as additions is in accordance with the cost on the purchase invoice including all matters properly included, such as delivery, but excluding amounts that should not be capitalised, such as the cost of removal of plant being replaced. Where other costs are capitalised, such as own labour for assembly and testing, I would verify the amounts as appropriate.

Classification

- I would ensure that the items properly meet the definition of plant and machinery and are properly recorded as such.

(c) *Describe the audit procedures applicable to verifying the revaluation of property.*

Competence and objectivity of the valuer

Although the valuer is an employee of the entity I may be prepared to accept the valuation if I am satisfied that the valuation has been performed with sufficient objectivity that it represents sufficient, appropriate audit evidence. This depends on factors such as the materiality of the amounts involved and the availability of corroboratory evidence. The revaluation is certainly substantial representing a gain of £144,000 on tangible fixed assets having a written down value of £603,000.

It is a common practice for interim valuations to be undertaken by valuers employed by the entity providing they are confirmed by less frequent independent valuations, such as every five years. If this is the practice I would examine the record of past valuations to see if the employee's valuations tended to be confirmed by the independent valuations.

I would also enquire into the professional qualifications and experience of the valuer to ensure that he or she is both suitably qualified to perform valuations and sufficiently experienced in valuations of the type undertaken.

Scope of work

I would obtain a copy of the valuer's report, and:

- check that the valuation given in the report is consistent with the valuation recorded in the financial statements;
- check that the basis of valuation is consistent with an acceptable basis of financial statement valuations, such as open market value and, in particular, that it relates to the property as it is and does not anticipate future uncertain events such as rezoning for planning, new roads etc.;
- form a view as to how thoroughly the valuer has undertaken his or her work.

Although the valuer was an employee of the company I would need to ensure that no undue restriction was placed on the valuer's access to relevant information having a bearing on the valuation.

Assessing the work of the valuer

When reviewing the work of the valuer I would expect to see the basis of the valuation explained and justified in the report. Where practicable I could confirm any data used such as recent transactions involving similar property. I could also consider the reasonableness of any assumptions made concerning which I have some knowledge, such as the effect of recent changes in legislation or in the economic climate.

Conclusion

If I find:

- that the valuer is professionally qualified, and sufficiently experienced;
- that the scope of the work is adequate;
- other evidence corroborates the reliability of the valuation;

I would probably be prepared to accept the work of the valuer as an expert providing sufficient appropriate evidence as to the valuation of the property. My confidence in the valuation would be enhanced if it were an interim valuation subject to periodic confirmation by independent valuers.

(d) *With respect to the correction to accumulated depreciation, and assuming the amount to be material, discuss the accountant's proposed treatment. If you disagree with the accountant's proposal, state, with reasons, the correct accounting treatment.*

According to IAS 8 the correction of errors which are the natural result of estimates inherent in the accounting process is normally dealt with in the P&L in the period in which they are identified. This would appear to be the accountant's argument.

An alternative view is that this is a fundamental error and the cumulative adjustments applicable to prior periods have no bearing on the results of the current period. In this case, as a prior period adjustment, it should be highlighted in the reconciliation of movement in shareholders' funds and noted at the foot of the statement of recognised gains and losses.

This latter treatment would appear to be correct providing its effect on P&L is sufficiently material to warrant such special treatment. Since we are told the amount is material, if the accountant refuses to amend its treatment we would need to consider whether to qualify our opinion on the basis of disagreement.

13.1 SUBSTANTIVE PROCEDURES FOR CASH BALANCES

Required

(a) (i)   *List the audit procedures to be followed by your assistant in verifying the bank reconciliation in sufficient detail for an inexperienced staff member to follow.*

    (ii)   *Explain the purpose of each procedure in terms of audit objectives.*

ANSWERS

PROCEDURE	PURPOSE
1. Agree the balance per bank with the bank statement and with the bank confirmation.	To agree the correctness of the amount.
2. Agree the balance per books with the trial balance and draft financial statements.	To agree the correctness of the amount recorded in the reconciliation.
3. Add the bank reconciliation.	To agree the correctness of the amount arrived at.
4. From the December bank statement trace deposits to the list of cash receipts in December or to the November bank reconciliation and:	
a. trace outstanding deposits on the November bank reconciliation (if any) and the December list of cash receipts not appearing on the December bank statement to the December bank reconciliation;	To verify that all outstanding deposits are recorded in the reconciliation and at the correct amount.
b. ensure that there are no other outstanding deposits on the December bank reconciliation.	To verify that all deposits recorded as outstanding are in agreement with the books.
5. From the December bank statement trace cheques to the list of cash payments in December or to the November bank reconciliation and:	
a. carry forward outstanding cheques on the November bank reconciliation and the December list of cash payments not appearing on the December bank statement to the December bank reconciliation;	To verify that all outstanding cheques are recorded in the reconciliation and at the correct amount.
b. ensure that there are no other outstanding cheques or other payments on the December bank reconciliation.	To verify that all cheques recorded as outstanding are in agreement with the books.
6. Obtain the January 1999 bank statement and:	
a. trace outstanding deposits and cheques from the December 31 bank reconciliation to the bank statement;	
b. list outstanding items appearing on the December bank reconciliation not traced to a subsequent bank statement for follow up before the end of the audit.	To verify the existence and correctness as to amounts listed as outstanding on the December bank reconciliation.
7. For returned cheques recorded on the bank statement:	
a. agree the amount with the original entry recording the receipt;	To verify the existence and correctness of the amount of the returned cheque.
b. examine reversing entry for correctness.	To verify that the returned item has been correctly credited to cash and debited to accounts receivable.
8. For bank charges recorded on the bank statement trace to the entry debiting cash at bank in the company's books.	To ensure that cash at bank per the books is reduced by the amount of the charges.
9. Enquire into other items appearing on the bank reconciliation as appropriate.	To ensure that there are no fictitious items that might be concealing an error or misstatement.
10. List, for partner's attention, outstanding items (in 6b) not cleared through the bank by the completion of the audit.	

(b) *Discuss the reliability of bank statements as audit evidence. What steps can be taken if it is considered desirable to increase their reliability?*

Bank statements are moderately reliable as they are provided by a third party from a source known to maintain reliable records.

The limitation is that they are obtained from the entity being audited. There is a possibility of the bank statement being altered or that it could even be a forgery. The auditor should be particularly suspicious if the entity provides a fax or photocopy for the auditor's use and not the original.

Where necessary their reliability can be improved by asking the audit entity to request their bank to send a copy statement directly to the auditor or, better still, for the auditor to collect a copy directly from the bank.

(c) (i) *Distinguish between 'auditing around the computer' and 'auditing through the computer'.*

(ii) *Explain the circumstances when it would be inappropriate for the auditor to rely on auditing around the computer.*

(c) (i)

Auditing around the computer is where the auditor traces transactions recorded on documents to the point of entry into the computer and picks up those transactions as part of the output and continues from that point to the entry in the ledger. (Or vouches transactions from the records to the output from the computer and picks them up at the point of entry to the computer back to the source documents.) Any processing performed by the computer is verified by reference to input or output documents.

Auditing through the computer is where the audit verifies the processing of the transaction by the computer using computer-assisted audit techniques (CAATs).

(ii)

Auditing around the computer is inappropriate where:

1. Auditing around the computer is impractical.
    - Source documents are not available in hard copy form.
    - It is not possible to follow the audit trail from input to output or vice versa because:
      - there is no hard copy of the output;
      - the output summarises input date in such a way that reconciliation is impractical such as where sales and cash receipts data are input into the system but the output is in the form of unpaid invoices listed by customer.
    - Control risk assessment is based on computerised application controls which cannot be verified by comparison of input with output, such as credit approval of sales orders evidenced electronically by the credit manager's password.
2. Auditing around the computer is inefficient.
    - Substantive procedures around the computer are practicable but computerised application controls which can only be verified by the use of CAATs could reduce control risk and the level of substantive procedures significantly. For example

invoice pricing could be verified against the hard copy of the price list but it would be much easier to verify the reliability of pricing information held by the computer.

- Substantive procedures could be performed more efficiently through the use of CAATs. For example, we can verify completeness by testing the numerical continuity of input documents, but the use of audit software enables us to program the computer to perform this test.

13.2 AUDIT OF CONSOLIDATED FINANCIAL STATEMENTS

Required

(a) *Explain how you would verify the intercompany balances.*

If the balances on intercompany accounts do not agree then group assets and profits will be incorrect. If company A pays its account with company B of £100,000 on 31 December and the cheque is not received by company B until 3 January, at the year-end A will have a zero balance on its intercompany payables account but B will have a balance of £100,000 on its intercompany receivables. If no correction is made and the £100,000 included in group receivables, cash will be understated by £100,000 and receivables overstated by the same amount. Even worse, if A charges B £100,000 for services rendered on 31 December and includes that amount in revenue and B does not receive the invoice until January and makes no accrual for it, then B's expenses will not be reduced by the charge. Group receivables and profits will then both be overstated by £100,000 if no adjustment is made on consolidation.

- I would ascertain the group's procedures for accounting for and reconciling such balances.
- I would ascertain the procedure for reconciling and eliminating such balances on consolidation. If the procedures are satisfactory and the amounts involved not material, it would be sufficient to check that:
  - the balances on the consolidation worksheets are in agreement with the audited financial reports of each group company; and
  - intercompany balances are in agreement with each other, or the consolidation worksheets provide a reconciliation showing causes of differences, that the correct adjustments have been made on consolidation, and the amounts involved are small.
- If the amounts involved are material either in terms of the balances outstanding or value of transactions or there are significant differences on reconciliation, then I would:
  - obtain a detailed statement of the outstanding items on each company's account;
  - consider the need to request other auditors to verify their client's statements (if this was a regular problem I would probably request other auditors to obtain, verify and supply such statements in my instructions issued at the time of planning);
  - verify the company's reconciliation against these statements (reconciling items will be those on one company's account with another but not appearing on that other company's account and may be due to such matters as goods or cash in transit, errors, disputes etc.);
  - check that the adjustment on the consolidation worksheet is consistent with the reconciliation and correctly eliminates such balances.

(b) *Describe other audit adjustments you would expect to find and explain how you would verify each of them:*

    (i) *where the subsidiary had been acquired prior to the financial year being audited;*

    (ii) *where the subsidiary had been acquired during the financial year under audit.*

Subsidiaries acquired prior to the current year

The principal adjustments necessary to consolidate the financial statements of subsidiaries with those of the parent company are as follows:

- adjustments necessary to ensure the consistency of accounting policies within the group;
- adjustment of the financial statements of subsidiaries to their fair value as at the date of acquisition;
- elimination of group balances, transactions and profits;
- elimination of minority interests;
- translation of foreign subsidiaries' financial reports into sterling.

Consistency of accounting policies
Evidence as to subsidiaries' accounting policies which may differ from those of the parent company will be obtained from the summary of accounting policies in the subsidiaries' audited accounts, from the working papers of subsidiaries audited by the same firm, and by direct inquiry of the auditors of the foreign subsidiary.

With the overseas subsidiary, it is probable that the audited financial report has been prepared to conform to local requirements and will not be consistent with applicable Financial Reporting Standards. As part of the planning process the auditor of the foreign subsidiary should have been advised of the parent company's accounting policies and to ask them to provide supplementary audited accounts consistent with those policies. Alternatively, the UK auditor can review adjustments made by the parent company in preparing the consolidated accounts and, where necessary, seek the assistance of the auditor of the foreign subsidiary in verifying adjustments.

Fair value
Determining the fair value of acquired net assets is considered in (b)(ii). The differences between book and fair value for each subsidiary should be recorded in the permanent audit file together with a schedule of the continuing effect of such differences, such as on group depreciation, in each subsequent year. The auditor must ensure that such ongoing adjustments are properly made by the group in the preparation of its consolidated financial statements in subsequent years.

Inter-group transactions
In addition to the elimination of inter-group balances on the balance sheet as described in (a), the auditor must also verify the elimination of inter-group transactions from the profit and loss statement and of any inter-company profit included in assets. For this reason it is important for group entities to be able to identify inventories and other assets arising out of such transactions and the original cost to the supplying company or the profit margin earned on sale. The auditor will need to verify the accuracy of such records in all

group undertakings as part of the audit of the UK subsidiaries. The auditor of the foreign subsidiary should be requested to verify that the amounts of such inventories are correctly determined and reported to the parent company, and to verify the profit margin on sales of such inventories to other group entities. Using this information the auditor must verify the elimination of inter-group profit from the group financial statements.

Minority interests
The adjustment for minority interests is relatively straightforward and the auditor can verify the adjustments by reference to the proportion of the parent company's interest in each subsidiary. Relevant details should be recorded in the permanent audit file.

Foreign currency translation
The auditor should ensure that the basis adopted for translating the accounts of the foreign subsidiary into Sterling for the purposes of consolidation is in accordance with the requirements of Financial Reporting Standards. In most cases, the net investment approach will be appropriate and the exchange rate at balance sheet date should be used for translating the balance sheet, and the same rate or the average rate for the year, for translating the profit and loss statement. Any exchange difference arising should be taken to reserves. The actual exchange rates should be verified with a bank. Where the affairs of the subsidiary are closely interlinked with those of the parent, the temporal method of translation should be used.

Subsidiaries acquired during the current year

Where the purchase of a subsidiary is to be treated as an acquisition, it is necessary for the parent company to determine the fair value of the net assets at the date of acquisition, and the amount of purchased goodwill. Purchased goodwill is the difference between the fair value of the purchase consideration and the fair value of the proportion of net assets acquired. The auditor will need to verify the amounts assigned, by the company, to the fair value of the net assets, and to the purchase consideration.

Purchase consideration, other than cash, is likely to take the form of shares of the parent company. The auditor should verify the reasonableness of the value assigned to these shares. For a quoted company, this would normally be the market value at the date of acquisition.

There are many technical problems involved in determining fair values of net assets. The auditor will need to consider the reasonableness of the bases adopted, check that the values assigned are consistent with those bases, and verify the values placed on the assets. The major changes are likely to be in the valuation of tangible and intangible fixed assets. On the acquisition of a major interest in a subsidiary undertaking, the auditor should approach management to discuss the procedures to be adopted in determining the fair values of the subsidiary's net assets. The auditor would be particularly concerned as to the availability of audit evidence pertaining to intended valuations and should offer suggestions as to procedures which might be more cost-effective from an auditing point of view, or, in extreme cases, would avoid the necessity of a scope qualification where the auditor is unable to obtain sufficient appropriate audit evidence as to the valuations. Where the company seeks the services of experts, the auditor will have to determine the reliance he can place on their work. It may be possible to obtain reasonable assurance as to changes, to fair value from book value, of other assets and liabilities, through evidence obtained at the time of performing the final audit. For example, additional provisions for slow moving inventories or bad debts, and provisions for liabilities and charges, can be considered in relation to the provisions considered necessary at the date of the balance sheet.

Since audited accounts are unlikely to be available as at the date of acquisition, the auditor will also need to be satisfied as to the completeness, existence and ownership of the assets recorded in the subsidiary's books at that date. The effect of errors will largely be reflected in the allocation of profits as between pre- and post-acquisition. During the course of the audit on the year-end accounts of a newly acquired subsidiary the auditor may need to undertake additional procedures so as to obtain reasonable assurance as to the amounts recorded in the books at the date of acquisition. If, however, the audit reveals that the accounting records cannot be relied upon, the auditor may need to consider issuing a scope qualification as to the determination of post-acquisition profits taken up in the consolidated profit and loss statement for the year.

(c) *Describe the procedures necessary to determine the level of reliance to be placed on the audited financial statements of the foreign subsidiary.*

- Inquire into the other auditor's reputation and professional standing. This would also include inquiry as to the comparability of the other auditor's professional body's entrance requirements and ethical rules with those in the UK.
- Write to the other auditor (with due clearance from management) explaining reliance on his or her work.
- Ask him or her to complete a questionnaire to provide information as to the other firm's quality control procedures.
- Evaluate the results of my inquiries and the replies to my questionnaire and consider the extent to which it might be necessary to perform additional procedures each year such as requesting permission to review the other auditor's working papers.
- During the planning stage of the audit, issue the other auditor with a questionnaire identifying the major audit procedures I would expect to be carried out to comply with UK Auditing Standards, such as attendance at physical inventory and review of subsequent events, and asking them to confirm that the procedures had been complied with. In drawing up the questionnaire it would be useful to obtain advice as to differences between auditing standards in the two countries.
- Ask management to let me have copies of all management letters sent by the other auditors and all letters of representation issued to them.
- Review working papers of the other auditor where:
  - there were doubts as to their reputation or quality control procedures;
  - returned questionnaire indicated that not all auditing procedures had been completed;
  - management letters or letters of representation indicated serious control weaknesses or other problems;
  - the other auditor's report was modified.
- If there remained any doubts as to the satisfactory nature of the work performed by the other auditor I would request them to perform additional procedures. If doubts remain

I would consider the need for a qualification in my report on the group accounts on the grounds of a scope limitation.

14.1 LETTER OF REPRESENTATION AND MANAGEMENT REPORT
Required
(a) *Letter of representation*
   (i) *Explain the purpose of the letter of representation and the extent to which it constitutes sufficient appropriate audit evidence.*

Purpose

Many representations are made by management to the auditors during the course of the audit. Some of these are implicit in the preparation of financial statements that are fairly presented, others are in response to direct enquiries by the auditors. During the course of the audit most of these representations will be confirmed by more reliable evidence such that reliance no longer need be placed on management representations. However, for other representations, there will be no independent corroboratory evidence available. The letter of representation, therefore, provides formal confirmation as to the representations made. In so doing, management may be encouraged to reflect more fully on the completeness of the representations made and provide further information that may earlier have been overlooked.

Reliability

It is important that auditors do not place reliance on representations where more reliable evidence would be expected. However, failure to confirm other representations in writing would constitute negligence by the auditors. The absence of corroboratory evidence would, in itself, be suspicious and should lead to further audit enquiry. Moreover, written representations do not necessarily constitute sufficient evidence. The auditor must consider all available evidence and its reliability in forming an opinion. For example, in a small business where significant audit reliance must be placed on management representations, auditors may occasionally form the view that, even with written representation by management, there is insufficient evidence on which to form an opinion.

(a) (ii) *Describe three matters you might find in a letter of representation (other than the acknowledgement by management of its responsibility for the financial statements).*

Matters that may be included in the letter of representation include representations that:

- all subsequent events have been properly reflected or disclosed in the financial statements;
- the entity is not in breach of any contractual or regulatory requirements that could have a material effect on the financial statements;

- all books of account and supporting documentation, registers, minutes of members' and directors' meetings, have been made available;
- there are no plans that may significantly alter the carrying value of any of the entity's assets;
- all related parties have been identified;
- the entity has title to all of its assets and none are pledged or otherwise assigned other than disclosed in the financial statements;
- all liabilities and provisions have been reported or disclosed whether actual or contingent.

(*Note*: Only three are required. Other matters may also be considered relevant.)

(a) (iii) *Explain the effect, on the audit, if management refuse to make one or more of the representations requested.*

Refusal by management to provide written representation as requested would need to be enquired into as to the effect on the overall sufficiency of evidence considered. A failure to obtain written representation would normally constitute a scope limitation since, if a matter is sufficiently important as to require written representation, it would be material to the expression of the audit opinion. This would result in the issue of a modified audit opinion which is either qualified or for which a disclaimer of opinion is issued.

(b) *Management letter*
   (i) *Describe the procedures associated with the communication of control weaknesses to management relating to:*
- *timing of the communication;*
- *method of communication;*
- *level of management to which communication should be made.*

Timeliness

Control weaknesses should be communicated shortly after completion of the audit. Where control risk was assessed during an interim visit, such as on larger engagements, a letter would normally be sent after that visit as well as on completion of the audit.

    Where the exposure to risk is great or where there is reason to suspect that fraud or failure to comply with laws or regulations may already have occurred as a result of the weakness the matter warrants more timely communication.

Method

The communication is normally made in the form of a letter. Often, however, a preliminary meeting is held with management directly responsible in order to confirm the understanding and to discuss the most appropriate form of changes to the system. The letter is, therefore, more likely to be accepted and its recommendations acted upon.

    Oral communication may also be appropriate for weaknesses that are in urgent need of correction followed up by a written communication.

Level of management

The letter would normally be addressed to the chief financial officer. However, it is common to discuss the detailed recommendations with line management before issuing the letter. The letter may refer to minor matters in brief with more detailed recommendations being sent to financial officers of divisions or subsidiaries. More serious matters may be communicated directly to the board of directors or, if the entity has one, the audit committee. These would include such matters as previous recommendations that have not been implemented where the auditors believe the risks to the entity are material.

(b) (ii) *Discuss the extent of the auditors' responsibility for detecting and reporting internal control weaknesses.*

The purpose of an audit is to obtain sufficient appropriate evidence for the expression of an opinion as to the truth and fairness of the financial statements. In the course of the audit the auditors may discover other matters that need to be communicated to management. Therefore, auditors are not primarily responsible for evaluating the effectiveness of all internal controls and reporting all weaknesses. In the letter of weakness and in the engagement letter the auditor should make it clear that the assessment of control effectiveness is restricted to those controls on which reliance is intended to be placed for audit purposes. If auditors intend to place reliance for particular financial statement assertions wholly on substantive procedures, they have no responsibility for controls over those assertions.

Where the auditors do become aware of internal control weaknesses, however, there is an expectation that they will warn management where the risk of loss or misstatement is considered material. Awareness of control weaknesses may come about from procedures other than those directed specifically at testing controls. For example, in obtaining an understanding of the system the auditor may become aware of major control weaknesses. Also, in performing substantive procedures, investigation of errors may alert the auditor to the presence of control weaknesses.

The auditors' duty to report, under auditing standards, is confined to the management of the entity. They have no responsibility to report on the effectiveness of internal controls to other parties. The letter of weaknesses normally carries a disclaimer of responsibility to any other persons to whom the letter might be shown.

Auditors may accept engagement to report on control weaknesses, either to managers, to regulators or to third parties. However, such engagements are not part of the audit of the financial statements.

14.2 AFTER BALANCE SHEET DATE EVENTS

Required
Consider what further action Reddy and Co. should take with respect to each of the matters listed.

(a) Subsequent event
Since it clearly relates to a prior period, the agreement to pay a backdated pay rise is an adjusting event even though the extent of the pay rise was unknown as at the year-end (IAS

10 *Events After the Balance Sheet Date*). The pay rise should be confirmed by sighting the agreement. The computation of the amount outstanding as at the balance sheet date should be checked and the materiality of the effect on profit should be assessed. Reddy & Co. should recommend the financial statements as at 31 March be amended to include a provision for the backdated pay for the period from 1 January to 31 March with an appropriate adjustment to profit and loss. If the directors do not do so then it represents a disagreement. The auditors' report will need to be modified by way of a qualified opinion due to disagreement or, exceptionally, an adverse opinion.

(b) Other information
The chairman's statement would appear to suggest that operating profit represents the true level of performance. This represents a material inconsistency with the audited financial statements in accordance with ISA 720 *Other Information in Documents Containing Audited Financial Information*. Reddy and Co. should advise the chairman to amend the information in his statement to avoid the apparent inconsistency since IAS 1 *Presentation of Financial Statements* requires items such as reorganisation costs and profits or losses on disposal of property, plant and equipment to be included in arriving at a measure of profit from ordinary activities for the period unless they are properly classified as extraordinary. If the chairman refuses Reddy and Co. should consider taking appropriate action. One possibility is the inclusion of an emphasis of matter paragraph immediately after the unqualified opinion paragraph in the auditor's report. If the matter were considered to be more serious Reddy and Co. could refuse to issue the auditor's report or withdraw from the engagement subject to receiving appropriate legal advice.

(c) Internal control
Advising audit clients of weaknesses discovered in internal controls is not the primary objective of an audit. However, various jurisdictions have held the auditor to be negligent if failure to make proper communication of such information results in losses being incurred by the company (*AWA v. Daniels t/s Deloitte Haskins & Sells & Ors*, Australia, 1995). It is generally known that potential losses from unauthorised trading of this kind can be very large (Barings Bank). Since the chief financial officer appears not to have taken appropriate action Reddy and Co. must, as a matter of urgency, raise the matter with the board of directors or, if the company has one, the Audit Committee.

(d) Subsequent event
On the basis of the preliminary information it would appear that this is a non-adjusting after balance date event (IAS 10) of a magnitude sufficient to require disclosure. The disclosure should describe the nature of the event and an estimate of its financial effect (i.e. the cost of cleaning up operations and of liability to pay compensation) or a statement that such an estimate cannot be made. If the company is unwilling to disclose the event in the notes to its financial statements then Reddy and Co. are in disagreement with management and must issue a qualified opinion in their auditor's report.

15.1 EFFECT OF CIRCUMSTANCES ON AUDIT OPINION
Required
Indicate the effect of these circumstances on the auditors' report.

ANSWERS

1. This is a material scope limitation. The auditors' report would have an explanatory paragraph in the Basis of opinion section with a disclaimer of opinion.
2. This is a departure from Accounting Standards. The auditors' report would probably have an 'except for – disagreement' or adverse opinion with the nature of the disagreement explained and quantified if practicable.
3. This is a scope limitation. The auditors' report would have an explanatory paragraph in the Basis of opinion section with an 'except for – scope limitation' opinion.
4. This is an inherent uncertainty and may result in one of the following audit opinions.
   (i) If the matter of litigation is not adequately disclosed then this constitutes a disagreement with management, and the appropriate form of qualification is 'except for – disagreement' or adverse with the nature of the disagreement explained and quantified if practicable.
   (ii) If the matter of litigation is adequately disclosed, an explanatory paragraph in the Basis of opinion section is added but the opinion is unqualified.
5. This is a departure from Accounting Standards. The auditors' report would probably issue an 'except for – disagreement' or adverse opinion with the nature of the disagreement explained and quantified if practicable.
6. This is a going-concern uncertainty and may result in one of the following audit opinions.
   (i) If there is adequate disclosure of the going-concern uncertainty express an unqualified opinion, and add a fundamental uncertainty paragraph within the Basis of opinion section.
   (ii) If there is inadequate disclosure, express a qualified opinion 'except for – disagreement' with the nature of the disagreement explained and quantified if practicable.
   (iii) If it is highly probable that the entity will not continue as a going concern express an adverse opinion if the financial statements are prepared on a going-concern basis.
7. This is reliance on other auditors. The auditors should not refer to this matter since they must accept full responsibility for the opinion given.
8. This is an inconsistency with an accounting policy from last year. There is no effect on the audit report as long as it is properly disclosed, the effect properly accounted for as a prior-year adjustment and the auditors concur with the reasons for the change.

15.2 GOING-CONCERN ISSUES, AUDIT OPINION

Required

(a) *What does the going-concern concept mean? Discuss the reporting options open to an auditor when going-concern issues arise.*

The going-concern concept means that it is assumed that the entity will realise its assets and extinguish its liabilities in the normal course of business.

The auditors reporting options are (ISA 570):

Going-concern basis considered appropriate

- Auditors should issue an unqualified auditors' report.

Significant uncertainty about going concern

- If the uncertainty is adequately disclosed in the financial statements, the auditors' report should include an explanatory paragraph when setting out their basis of opinion in accordance with ISA 570.
- If the financial statements do not adequately disclose the significant uncertainty, an 'except for – disagreement' opinion or an adverse opinion should be expressed explaining their reasons.

Going-concern basis considered inappropriate

- If the auditor is satisfied that it is highly improbable that the entity will continue as a going concern for the relevant period, an adverse opinion should be expressed in accordance with ISA 570.

(b) *Discuss the potential auditors' report options in relation to Fly-By-Night Ltd.*

There are a number of matters that indicate potential going-concern reporting issues for Fly-By-Night Ltd (FBN). These include:

- FBN operates in the defence industry and there have been significant cuts to defence expenditure.
- There is evidence that the cuts will directly impact one of FBN's contracts.
- FBN has been experiencing cash flow difficulties.
- FBN's borrowing facility is already fully drawn.

The auditors would need to perform a number of procedures to evaluate the appropriateness of the going-concern basis (as discussed in Chapter 14).

In this case all of the above should be disclosed in a note to the financial statements. If the auditors are satisfied with the disclosure they may issue an unqualified auditors' report with an explanatory paragraph within their basis of opinion.

However, if the auditors are unsatisfied as to the ability of the entity to continue as a going concern (which is difficult to tell from the information given in this case) they should issue an adverse opinion.

16.1 FORENSIC AUDIT

Required

Explain the key considerations of the forensic audit you will conduct.

Key considerations could include:

- Determination if there was a system failure, and if so, why.
- Analysis of the sequence of transactions to identify any intervention by unauthorised personnel.
- Checking of the adequacy of the backup procedures.
- Review of the security procedures including the adequacy of the firewalls.
- Review for evidence of corruption caused by hackers and/or viruses.

16.2 CONTROLS FOR ELECTRONIC PAYMENT

Required

Using the following headings, identify the controls you would expect to find in an e-commerce system:

(a) *Confidentiality of information.*
(b) *Transaction integrity.*
(c) *Authorisation of payments.*
(d) *Assurance of business credibility.*

Confidentiality of information

Controls could include:

- Logical and physical security measures.
- Information protection to safeguard the integrity of the files.
- Privacy issues relating to customer information.

Transaction integrity

Controls could include:

- Identity controls for authorised personnel.
- Processing controls to ensure accuracy and completeness.
- Authenticity, accuracy and reasonableness controls.

Authorisation of payments

Controls could include:

- Established levels of approval for expenditure.
- Reconciliations of payments with creditor records.

Assurance of business credibility

Controls could include:

- Review processes to ensure changes to the business system accommodate all aspects of e-commerce activities.
- Management's awareness of the risks involved in the management of data and associated security issues.
- Monitoring of the performance of the e-commerce system through parameters agreed by management

17.1 AUDIT TRAILS IN FINANCIAL SOFTWARE

Required

Comment on the partner's statement. In particular address some of the problems with a lack of audit trail that can be caused by advances in technology.

The partner is right to the extent that fewer audit trails will mean that there *should* be less documentation. This has not always been the case when new software has been implemented. Companies have often still printed lengthy audit trails and various reports from the new system. The reason for this is often simply because people (including the auditors) have felt more comfortable with hard copies of transactions.

However, it is crucial that the system does have an audit trail, which does not need to be on paper but may be as a backup file. This is because the audit trail should provide a means of tracing a transaction from its origin to the financial statements, and vice versa.

The lack of an audit trail can be a significant problem. It may mean that it is difficult or impossible to find evidence to verify a transaction. It will also make it very difficult or impossible to audit the financial statements of a company. Without a trail to vouch transactions back to source documents the auditor will find it impossible to perform substantive procedures.

The partner's comment suggesting analytical review as an alternative is also flawed. This is because analytical review will not generally provide an adequate level of assurance to form an opinion on the financial statements. Some balances within the financial statements do not lend themselves to the use of analytical review as an audit technique. Sometimes analytical review will highlight problems that need further investigation such as looking to the original transactions; this would not be possible without an audit trail.

Conclusion

An audit trail is an essential consideration in a new computer system for the use of management and auditors. However, it should be noted that this trail does not need to be paper.

17.2 ENVIRONMENTAL AUDITING

Required

(a) *What does environmental auditing mean?*

Environmental auditing is 'a management tool comprising a systematic, documented, periodic and objective evaluation of how well environmental organisation, management and equipment are performing with the aim of helping to safeguard the environment by:

(i)   facilitating management control of environmental practices; and
(ii) assessing compliance with company policies, which would include meeting regulatory requirements.'

(b) *What are some other standards that have been issued in relation to environmental auditing?*

In terms of environmental auditing, the following three standards are applicable:

- ISO 14011-1 Guidelines for Environmental Auditing – Audit Procedures – Part 1: Auditing of Environmental Management Systems;
- ISO 14011-2 Guidelines for Environmental Auditing – Audit Procedures – Part 2: Compliance Audits;
- ISO 14011-3 Guidelines for Environmental Auditing – Audit Procedures – Part 3: Audit of an Environmental Statement.

In addition, ISO 14001 contains a requirement for organisations to maintain programmes and procedures for periodic EMS audits.

A number of international codes of environmental conduct have been developed which set out essential environmental management elements such as the Valdez Principles (Coalition for Environmentally Responsible Economics (CERES), 1990), the ICC Charter, and the UK Chemical Industries Association Responsible Care (RC) Programmes. The Valdez Principles were launched after the Exxon Valdez oil tanker disaster in Alaska. The ICC Charter for Sustainable Development comprises 16 principles for environmental management in achieving sustainable economic development. The RC programmes have been developed by many national chemical industry associations in the US, Canada and the UK. All are voluntary in nature. The CERES requires signatory companies to undertake annual environmental audits and make public the findings of these audits.

(c) *What sort of tasks might be involved in environmental auditing?*

There are a number of different audit types of environmental audits. There are three main basic tacks that might be performed.

1. *Auditing of Environmental Management Systems* – A review of the effectiveness of these systems. The review is to ensure that the systems are operating effectively and may include a detailed analysis of controls in place within the environmental management system.
2. *Compliance Audits* – To ensure that the organisation is complying with the relevant government environmental legislation. This may involve detailed reviews of the internal reports used to monitor environmental impact within the organisation. It may also involve the use of specialists to measure the environmental impact from the organisation.
3. *Audit of an Environmental Statement* – This involves forming an opinion of the assertions of management as outlined in the environmental statement. It may involve the substantive testing of balances for environmental rehabilitation costs or the compliance testing of controls referred to in the statement.

STATEMENT OF AUDITING STANDARDS: GLOSSARY OF TERMS

Accounting estimate An approximation of the amount of an item in the absence of a precise means of measurement.

Accounting system The series of tasks and records of an entity by which transactions are processed as a means of maintaining financial records. Such systems identify, assemble, analyse, calculate, classify, record, summarise and report transactions and other events.

Analytical procedures The analysis of relationships:

    (a)   between items of financial data, or between items of financial and non-financial data, deriving from the same period; or

    (b)   between comparable financial information deriving from different periods, to identify consistencies and predicted patterns or significant fluctuations and unexpected relationships, and the results of investigations thereof.

Annual report A document which an entity usually issues on an annual basis which includes its financial statements together with the auditors' report.

Assistants Personnel involved in an individual audit, including experts employed by the auditors, other than the audit engagement partner.

Audit engagement partner The person who assumes ultimate responsibility for the conduct of the audit and for issuing an opinion on the financial statements.

Audit evidence The information auditors obtain in arriving at the conclusions on which their report is based. Audit evidence comprises source documents and accounting records underlying the financial statement assertions and corroborative information from other sources.

Audit of financial statements An exercise whose objective is to enable auditors to express an opinion on whether the financial statements give a true and fair view (or equivalent) of the entity's affairs at the period end and of its profit or loss (or income and expenditure) for the period then ended and whether they have been properly prepared in accordance with the applicable reporting framework (for example, relevant legislation and applicable accounting standards) or, where statutory or other specific requirements prescribe the term, whether the financial statements 'present fairly'.

Audit firm, auditors The partners of a firm or a sole practitioner or a company or organisation providing audit services.

Audit plan A formulation of the general strategy for the audit, which sets the direction for the audit, describes the expected scope and conduct of the audit and provides guidance for the development of the audit programme.

Audit programme A set of instructions to the audit team that sets out the audit procedures the auditors intend to adopt and may include reference to other matters such as the audit objectives, timing, sample size and basis of selection for each area. It also serves as a means to control and record the proper execution of the work.

Audit risk The risk that auditors may give an inappropriate audit opinion on financial statements. Audit risk has three components: inherent risk, control risk and detection risk.

Audit sampling The application of audit procedures to less than 100% of the items within an account balance or class of transactions to enable auditors to obtain and evaluate audit evidence about some characteristic of the items selected in order to form or assist in forming a conclusion concerning the population which makes up the account balance or class of transactions.

Comparatives The corresponding amounts and other related disclosures from the preceding period which are part of the current period's financial statements as required by relevant legislation and applicable accounting standards. Such comparatives are intended to be read in relation to the amounts and other disclosures related to the current period.

Component A division, branch, subsidiary undertaking, joint venture, associated undertaking or other entity whose financial information is included in financial statements audited by the principal auditors.

Computation Checking the arithmetical accuracy of source documents and accounting records or performing independent calculations.

Confirmation The response to an enquiry to corroborate information contained in the accounting records.

Continuing auditors The auditors who audited and reported on the preceding period's financial statements and continue as auditors for the current period.

Control environment The overall attitude, awareness and actions of directors and management regarding internal controls and their importance in the entity. The control environment encompasses the management style, corporate culture and values shared by all employees. It provides the background against which the various other controls are operated.

Control activities Those policies and procedures which are established in addition to the control environment to achieve the entity's specific objectives.

Control risk The risk that a misstatement that could occur in an account balance or class of transactions and that could be material, either individually or when aggregated with misstatements in other balances or classes, would not be prevented, or detected and corrected on a timely basis, by the accounting and internal control systems.

Detection risk The risk that auditors' substantive procedures do not detect a misstatement that exists in an account balance or class of transactions that could be material, either individually or when aggregated with misstatements in other balances or classes.

Directors The directors of a company or other body, the partners, proprietors, committee of management or trustees of other forms of entity, or equivalent persons responsible for directing the entity's affairs and preparing its financial statements.

Engagement letter A letter which provides a written record of the agreement of the terms of engagement both by the auditors and their client.

Enquiry The seeking of information of knowledgeable persons inside or outside the entity.

Error An unintentional mistake in financial statements.

Expert A person or firm possessing special skill, knowledge and experience in a particular field other than auditing.

Financial statements The balance sheet, profit and loss account (or other form of income statement), statements of cash flows and total recognised gains and losses, notes and other statements and explanatory material, all of which are identified in the auditors' report as being the financial statements.

Financial statement assertions The representations of the directors that are embodied in the financial statements. By approving the financial statements, the directors are making representations about the information therein. These representations or assertions may be described in general terms in a number of ways, as follows:

Existence An asset or liability exists at a given date.

Rights and obligations An asset or liability pertains to the entity at a given date.

Occurrence A transaction or event took place which pertains to the entity during the relevant period.

Completeness There are no unrecorded assets, liabilities, transactions or events, or undisclosed items.

Valuation An asset or liability is recorded at an appropriate carrying value.

Measurement A transaction or event is recorded at the proper amount and revenue, or expense is allocated to the proper period.

Presentation and disclosure An item is disclosed, classified and described in accordance with the applicable reporting framework (for example, relevant legislation and applicable accounting standards).

For example, applying these financial statement assertions to the figure for stocks included in an entity's financial statements gives the following:

Existence: the stocks existed at the balance sheet date;

Rights: the stocks pertained to the entity at the balance sheet date;

Completeness: there is no unrecorded stock;

Valuation: stocks are recorded at an appropriate carrying value; and

Presentation and disclosure: the stocks are disclosed, classified and described in accordance with the applicable reporting framework.

Fraud No precise definition of fraud exists; it is for the court to determine in a particular instance whether fraud has occurred. For the purpose of SASs, fraud comprises both the use of deception to obtain an unjust or illegal financial advantage and intentional misrepresentations affecting the financial statements by one or more individuals among management, employees or third parties.

Fundamental uncertainty An inherent uncertainty is fundamental when the magnitude of its potential impact is so great that, without clear disclosure of the nature and implications of the uncertainty, the view given by the financial statements would be seriously misleading.

Going-concern basis Financial statements prepared under the presumption that the entity is carrying on business as a going concern are described as being prepared on the going-concern basis.

Incoming auditors The auditors who are auditing and reporting on the current period's financial statements not having audited and reported on those for the preceding period.

Inherent risk The susceptibility of an account balance or class of transactions to material misstatement, either individually or when aggregated with misstatements in other balances or classes, irrespective of related internal controls.

Inherent uncertainty An uncertainty whose resolution is dependent upon uncertain future events outside the control of the reporting entity's directors at the date the financial statements are approved.

Inspection The examining of records, documents or tangible assets.

Internal audit An appraisal or monitoring activity established by management and the directors for the review of the accounting and internal control systems as a service to the entity. It functions by, among other things, examining, evaluating and reporting to management and the directors on the adequacy and effectiveness of components of the accounting and internal control systems.

Internal control system This comprises the control environment and control procedures. It includes all the policies and procedures (internal controls) adopted by the directors and management of an entity to assist in achieving their objective of ensuring, as far as practicable, the orderly and efficient conduct of its business, including adherence to internal policies, the safeguarding of assets, the prevention and detection of fraud and error, the accuracy and completeness of the accounting records, and the timely preparation of reliable financial information. Internal controls may be incorporated within computerised accounting systems. However, the internal control system extends beyond those matters which relate directly to the accounting system.

Management Those persons who have executive responsibility for the conduct of the entity's operations and the preparation of its financial statements.

Material weakness A condition in accounting and internal control systems which may result in a material misstatement in the financial statements.

Materiality An expression of the relative significance or importance of a particular matter in the context of financial statements as a whole. A matter is material if its omission or misstatement would reasonably influence the decisions of an addressee of the auditors' report. Materiality may also be considered in the context of any individual primary statement within the financial statements or of individual items included in them. Materiality is not capable of general mathematical definition as it has both qualitative and quantitative aspects.

Non-sampling risk The risk that auditors might use inappropriate procedures or might misinterpret evidence and thus fail to recognise an error.

Observation Looking at a process or procedure being performed by others.

Opening balances Those account balances which exist at the beginning of the period. Opening balances are based upon the closing balances of the preceding period and reflect the effect of transactions of preceding periods and accounting policies applied in the preceding period.

Other auditors Auditors, other than the principal auditors, with responsibility for reporting on the financial information of a component which is included in the financial statements audited by the principal auditors. Other auditors include affiliated firms, whether using the same name or not, and correspondent firms, as well as unrelated auditors.

Planning Developing a general strategy and a detailed approach for the expected nature, timing and extent of the audit.

Population The entire set of data from which the auditors wish to sample in order to reach a conclusion.

Predecessor auditors The auditors who previously audited and reported on the financial statements of an entity and who have been replaced by the incoming auditors.

Principal auditors The auditors with responsibility for reporting on the audit of financial statements of an entity when those financial statements include financial information of one or more components audited by other auditors.

Reasonable assurance When reporting on financial statements, auditors provide a level of assurance which is reasonable in that context but, equally, cannot be absolute, that the financial statements taken as a whole are free from material misstatement.

Sampling risk The risk that the auditors' conclusion, based on a sample, may be different from the conclusion that would be reached if the entire population were subjected to the same audit procedure.

Sampling units The individual items that make up a population.

Stratification The process of dividing a population into subpopulations, each of which is a group of sampling units, which have similar characteristics (often monetary value).

Subsequent events Those relevant events (favourable or unfavourable) which occur and those facts which are discovered between the period end and the laying of the financial statements before the members, or equivalent. 'Relevant events' are those which:
- provide additional evidence relating to conditions existing at the balance sheet date; or
- concern conditions which did not exist at the balance sheet date, but which may be of such materiality that their disclosure is required to ensure that the financial statements are not misleading.

Discovery of facts is relevant in this context if the discovery reveals material misstatements in the financial statements.

Substantive procedures Tests to obtain audit evidence to detect material misstatements in the financial statements. They are generally of two types:
(a) analytical procedures; and
(b) other substantive procedures, such as tests of details of transactions and balances, review of minutes of directors' meetings and enquiry.

Tests of control Tests to obtain audit evidence about the effective operation of the accounting and internal control systems – that is, that properly designed controls identified in the preliminary assessment of control risk exist in fact and have operated effectively throughout the relevant period.

Tolerable error The maximum error in the population that auditors are willing to accept and still conclude that the audit objective has been achieved.

Walk-through test A walk-through test involves tracing one or more transactions through the accounting system and observing the application of relevant aspects of the internal control system.

Working papers The material auditors prepare or obtain, and retain in connection with the performance of the audit. Working papers may be in the form of data stored on paper, film, electronic media or other media. Working papers support, among other things, the statement in the auditors' report as to the auditors' compliance or otherwise with Auditing Standards to the extent that this is important in supporting their report. Working papers are a record of the planning and performance of the audit, the supervision and review of the audit work, and the audit evidence resulting from the audit work performed which the auditors consider necessary and on which they have relied to support their report.

Source: Auditing Standards Board

INDEX

INDEX